God, the Flesh, and the Other

God, the Flesh, and the Other

From Irenaeus to Duns Scotus

✦

Emmanuel Falque

Translated from the French by William Christian Hackett

NORTHWESTERN UNIVERSITY PRESS
EVANSTON, ILLINOIS

Northwestern University Press
www.nupress.northwestern.edu

Printed in the United States of America

ISBN 978-0-8101-3441-6

The Library of Congress has cataloged the original, hardcover edition as follows:

Falque, Emmanuel, 1963– author.
[Dieu, la chair et l'autre. English]
God, the flesh, and the other : from Irenaeus to Duns Scotus / Emmanuel Falque ; translated from the French by William Christian Hackett.
pages cm
"Originally published in French in 2008 under the title Dieu, la chair et l'autre: D'Irenee a Duns Scot. Copyright (c) 2008 by Presses Universitaires de France."
Includes bibliographical references.
ISBN 978-0-8101-3023-4 (cloth : alk. paper)—ISBN 978-0-8101-6816-9 (ebook)
1. Fathers of the church—History and criticism. 2. Christian literature, Early—History and criticism. 3. Philosophy and religion—History. I. Hackett, William Christian. II. Title.
BR67.F3513 2015
189.2—dc23

2014037055

To my parents

CONTENTS

TRANSLATOR'S FOREWORD

Emmanuel Falque, dean of the Faculty of Philosophy at the Institut Catholique de Paris, is both a philosopher and a theologian by training. He passed his *agrégation* for philosophy in 1988, and then proceeded to receive his canonical licentiate in theology in 1993. His philosophical *Doctorat* was only subsequently conferred in 1998 (the habilitation in 2006). This dual specialization, effectively unique in France, stands out even to English-speaking readers today as at least worthy of comment and probably seems a little suspect to some: is the philosophical "specificity" (I do not say "purity") of the following work compromised in some way by the theological proficiency, or worse, *religious convictions*, of the author? This question is of course a microcosm of a historically important and controversial question regarding the relationship of philosophy to theology and religion. The way we answer this question, or, more importantly, our assumptions about it, determine our understanding of philosophy itself in its task(s) and scope, and perhaps also even our understanding of religion as well. As often is the case in intellectual matters, and particularly matters with such far-reaching implications as this one, it helps at least to try to avail ourselves of a broader frame of reference, in relation to which our most "contemporary" discussions and debates may suddenly appear all too narrow if not insular. For it could be the case that the most compelling answer to the question may very well be the opposite of what it implies (at least in the way I so pedagogically phrased it), even if, or especially because, the theological always seems to press itself into every nook and cranny of our thinking (concerning this, one only needs to think of Heidegger himself, in relation to whom it is no longer all that controversial to say that the Christian universe of ideas fundamentally shaped some of his most basic concepts).[1] It is in relation to this important lesson regarding our philosophical and/or theological insularities, whether potential or actual, that the present text has much to teach us, whether or not we share the "religious," "theological," or "philosophical" convictions of the author.

A historical observation, and then a biographical one, will suffice in order to begin. First, the historical: we know that in an age long past, but which nevertheless remains at the root of all of our thinking today, even if it was not theologians who inhabited the faculty of arts where philosophy was taught, it was nevertheless the case, even then, that theologians were philosophers (I do not say necessarily "good" philosophers), at least in a rudimentary way—and this not merely because they were all required to finish the course in philosophy before entering theological studies itself. Theologians were philosophers, and there was no contradiction whatsoever with the fact that they were also theologians. Should it not give us pause that the best theologians of the past were almost always the best philosophers (let us only mention Aquinas and Scotus from the period with which we are dealing)? Even today, the Jesuit "scholastic," for example, pursuing his studies in what is no doubt the most complete curriculum imaginable, begins with (at least) two years in philosophy before proceeding to four in theology. Now the biographical observation: what stands out in Falque's case (a Catholic layperson) is that he proceeded in a different manner altogether, from philosophy to theology and then back again, from theology to philosophy. For good or ill, neither of these disciplines can remain the same, once their insularity is shattered. Arguably, this biographical detail (dismantling, from the beginning, a Hegelian approach to the relation: the passage is not a "one-way street" and especially not a matter of elevating the *Vorstellungen*, representations of religion into the higher region of the *Begriffe*, of comprehension by the concept) can be seen as an important symbol of Falque's unique style of thought and even, as it were, a cipher for the interpretation of his writings. I place it here at the beginning of these brief orienting comments and which perhaps you can keep in mind as you allow him to become your teacher by reading this book.

In any case, Falque's specialization lies in this very medieval period to which I have just alluded, particularly, though certainly not delimited to (if the following pages are any indication) Saint Bonaventure.[2] On top of that, or rather, in some relation to it that you would perhaps like to understand more clearly, he is a philosopher in the school of phenomenology. There is, for him, *no contradiction* between these two or three fundamental orientations of his thought: the historical, philosophical, and theological. I say "two or three" because for evident reasons the "historical" dimension of his specializations can just as easily be seen as the unique condition for his approach to his central methodological question, of perpetual concern: the relation of philosophy and theology in today's context. From the historical vantage, his dual specialization in medieval and modern thought means that their juxtaposition sheds special light on the question, which, as the following pages show again and again, is a light that shines in both directions: we understand the medieval (or patristic) period(s) more clearly when we recognize that the questions we pose today were very much theirs also (though, of course, uniquely so), and we understand ourselves more clearly when we find that our most radical ways of questioning already find anticipations in that era, anticipations that from time to time advance beyond our own thinking, often reinvigorate it, and even critique it (if, of course, we are willing to listen). Such is the argument of the present book in relation to three themes, as the title suggests: "God," the "flesh," and the "other."[3] This is a book, then, about the relevance of the past for the present, about the "contemporaneity" of patristic and medieval thought to our own most pressing philosophical questions—even if, or especially because, their thinking is theological and religious and hence philosophical in a unique manner. There is no need to elaborate on the contents of the book in this introduction. Let me simply note for you that the three grand themes shared by the past and present compose the three parts of the book, and the three parts have three chapters each, and each chapter focuses on a specific thinker, either from the patristic period (in the order of their appearance: Augustine, chap. 1; Irenaeus, chap. 4; Tertullian, chap. 5; Origen, chap. 7) or from the Middle Ages (Erigena, chap. 2; Eckhart, chap. 3; Bonaventure, chap. 6; Aquinas, chap. 8; Scotus, chap. 9).

The point that I would like to express for the sake of this introduction is minimal: that it is probably not misleading at all to assert that the whole of Falque's thought can be fruitfully conceived as taken up with demonstrating the very exclusive non-contradiction that I just mentioned: theology and philosophy, though irreducible, are not necessarily opposed, but can work together, reciprocally becoming the means toward advancing each other's proper inquiry. How does this demonstration work? First, it is clearly not merely a matter of some minimalist argument for the possibility of a working arrangement between estranged partners. Instead, it is first a matter of "doing" the relation for which he argues, "showing" that it works by its fruit. As they still like to say in classrooms and dissertations everywhere, the argument is "performative," though in the second place there are significant pauses in the text that reflect on the progress made in the performance (see especially the introductory sections of each part, as well as the conclusion).

Let us step back from this question of demonstration toward two complementary vantage points that together will afford as broad a survey of the terrain as possible. (1) From the phenomenological point of view, first, the mutual reciprocity of philosophy and theology is derived from the straightforwardly philosophical conviction that there is no domain forbidden to phenomenological description, since every appearing has the right to be described. Second, and as a direct consequence of this conviction, the observation arises that the theological kind of phenomena are often (if not paradigmatically) the most important, or at least most challenging, precisely by the "radicality" of their appearing, that is, their appearing in such a manner as always to break apart and refigure our anticipative grasp of them, dissolving the conditions by which we can conceive ourselves as grasping them—in short, their "nothing greater" (to allude to Anselm) or "ever greater" (to allude to the Fourth Lateran Council's critique of Joachim of Fiore) character. This general perspective, which marks, on my reading, the two fundamental emphases of what was denominated about two decades ago as the "theological turn," should not be new to any of us now. Falque works wholly from within the "renaissance" of phenomenology in France of which the "theological turn," or more adequately (though less attractively) described, the philosophical turn to theological phenomena, is a central trajectory but in no way the sole course taken.[4] This is not to say that Falque is a carbon copy of his teachers and forebears in the—forgive me—philosophical turn to theological phenomena of French phenomenology (Levinas, Ricoeur, Lacoste, Marion, Henry, Chrétien, et al.). His particular "position," like all of theirs, stands on its own two legs and is marked by its own unique emphases. I will only mention here his most striking distinction: the rejection of his teachers' Heideggerian malaise toward "metaphysics." For Falque, keeping metaphysics in play is actually a requisite, the very difficulty and danger of which is a virtue, *for* theological (and philosophical) thinking, as the first chapter of the present work, on the "tension of metaphysics and theology" in Saint Augustine, powerfully elaborates. (2) From the theological point of view, second (here), it means, simply, that the theological is open to the theological import of non-theological domains: if we better understand what the philosophers say about our finitude or our flesh, might we then be able to understand perhaps a little better the theological conception of the human being as destined for the resurrection *of the flesh*? The answer of course is crystal clear. To take an example developed partially in the present text (part II, chaps. 4–6) and elsewhere in Falque's oeuvre (e.g., *Métamorphose de la finitude*),[5] belief in the resurrection of the flesh can be illuminated (and, often fruitfully, challenged) by, for example, Husserl's distinction between objective "body" and subjective "flesh" (and its developments in Merleau-Ponty, Henry, etc.). As Falque says apothegmatically in the preface to the English edition of the text just mentioned: "The more we do philosophy, the better the theology."[6]

More difficult to swallow for many would be the reciprocal, and, if we are honest, perfectly compelling assertion that the data of belief, here, the resurrection of the flesh (a dogma no less) is itself illuminative for—and yes, fruitfully challenging to—philosophical reflection on human finitude. Sticking with this example, the fact remains, as Michel Henry wrote decades ago, that whatever the "radicality" of philosophical finitude, say, in Nietzsche or Heidegger, the dogma itself appears as a radical affirmation of the finitude of the flesh, and one that proposes itself as more radical than a non-dogmatic, or rather, non-theological (for it is perhaps, at this level, always a matter of some dogma or another) conception.[7] Theology, philosophy, and even historical studies (inasmuch as it contains living philosophies and theologies, often presupposing them for its very intelligibility) are together engaged in a mutual investigation, which, by virtue of the (seemingly) incongruous collaborators involved, may both expand and even renovate each of their self-understandings. This expansion and renovation is a result of the phenomena studied. Such is the risk—fidelity to the phenomena, no matter the consequences for our certainties—that Falque requires these disciplines to take. And it is through undertaking this risk that we come to find that the medieval period is then much like our own, at least insofar as our thinking occurs after the advent of phenomenology and in its wake: here where the philosophical and theological marshal their forces for the sake of an adequate approach to the "object(s)" they are asked to study and are mutually refigured.

It is this very tension and risk, then, that marks the drama of Falque's work, and especially the pages of *God, the Flesh, and the Other*. Its driving conviction is in the first place that this tension between the philosophical and theological, where all is risked for the sake of fidelity to the phenomena investigated, is the source of the greatest theological and philosophical fruit. What we are dealing with here, then, is a philosophy of which its very (if I can say it) *philosophicity* is defined by its openness to and hence irreducible tension with the theological and hence a theology, the very *theologicity* of which is measured by its willingness to expose itself to the trial of the philosophical.

The final hermeneutic of Falque's methodology, to which I would like to draw your attention here, concerns what I see as an eschatological undercurrent to his work, an undercurrent that, I suggest, creates the conditions for the theological intensification of the philosophical, in particular, the historical conditions of human finitude, including our materiality. This undercurrent is made explicit as a fundamental argument of his recent work *Les noces de l'Agneau* (2011), according to which the Christian notion of body, particularly in its destiny (as we proleptically taste it in the Eucharist and in the marriage bed), is a radical embrace of our material and animal conditions with which philosophy is currently concerned.[8] Let me develop this here, however, in relation to the Augustinian recognition of the necessity of metaphysics for theology broached above, since it serves as the first doorway of the present book: an important result of Augustine's "Trinitarian" transformation of Aristotle's categories is that the accusation, for Falque, of "onto-theo-logy" becomes "impossible," not only because of its historical "inaccessibility" (that is, to an approach by way of the "history of ideas," since the sources are themselves much more complicated than the "Heideggerian" philosophical narrative told and retold today) but also because it is refused precisely by the very "insoluble tension" between the metaphysical and the theological that God's "entrance" into the horizon of human reflection demands. Metaphysics is here much less "overcome" than it is transfigured from within. It seems for Falque, therefore, that every attempt to be done once and for all with metaphysics is, as it were, an "over-realized" eschatology (that is, insofar as it attempts, by its own power, to resolve the native "tension" of the encounter between metaphysics and the theological within the limits of our historical conditions, which makes it impossible). Such an "over-realized" thinking (1) seeks to think, in the theological domain, God in himself without reference to his acts *ad extra*, and therefore without the categories that "metaphysics" provides, and in the philosophical domain, seeks to think the radical finitude of creaturely being apart from revelation, although the thought of revelation, in actuality, by means of an irreducible tension, only pushes historicity, finitude, and the philosophical further than they can go on their own. It is therefore, finally, (2) ultimately an a priori refusal of the innate capacity of created being to receive and even anticipate (however paradoxically) the grace of divine Being in the entrance of God into history and therefore human thought. The tension is upheld therefore by an appropriate eschatological conception of the human, which draws the lines and limits of human finitude—including historicity and materiality—all the more concretely.

This undercurrent, however, remains for the most part unarticulated in the present work. For the sake of understanding more clearly its setting within the scope of Falque's aims and fundamental "project," a brief juxtaposition with another oeuvre of another thinker, Hans Urs von Balthasar, may be illuminative. In the conclusion to the fifth volume of his seven-volume *Theological Aesthetics* (III/2 in the original German edition), Balthasar reflects on the work accomplished in the two-part study of "The Realm of Metaphysics in Antiquity (vol. 4) and the Modern Age (vol. 5)" (III/1–2). Here Balthasar famously suggests, with the last words of his text, and at the end of a long, critical conversation with Heidegger, that, after all, the Christian is "the guardian of metaphysics for our time."[9] According to Balthasar, religious faith does not constrict philosophical questioning by posing "ready-made answers from revelation" in advance, but rather itself actually creates the possibility for a more "open" questioning precisely because the believer "believes in the absolute love of God" and is therefore "obliged to understand Being in its ontological difference as pointing to love" as its source, a love that increases the perception of the mystery of Being since it has no ground but itself in its absolute freedom.[10] It is at least an analogous advancement on Heidegger which drives the texts of Emmanuel Falque.[11] Faith (and its content) is no inhibition to philosophical inquiry, but is rather an "attitude" that serves as a powerful condition for it. If Falque is, to be sure, less concerned directly with "the question of the meaning of Being" than Balthasar and Heidegger, he is all the more concerned with the paths in which such questioning has opened up in today's context, for example, with the themes of "materiality" or "alterity" (pts. II and III of the present text), or of finitude and mortality found elsewhere in his oeuvre.

Now allow me briefly to introduce a fuller picture of this elsewhere. Falque is the author of what he calls a "philosophical *triduum*," which itself is a case in point for what I put forward here. Like the present work it brings into conversation the theological and philosophical domains, exposing their "point(s) of contact," particularly the place(s) where philosophical and theological data mutually inform one another, precisely because of their irreducibility and tension between them. The volumes of this "triduum" follow, thematically, the central mysteries of the Christian faith, and which themselves grow out of the critical moments at the historical dénouement of Christ's ministry on earth: his institution of the Eucharist on Holy Thursday, his passion (from his anguish in the garden on the eve of his death to his crucifixion) on Good Friday, and his resurrection on Easter Sunday. These books are, in the order of their appearing, *Passeur de Gethsémani, Angoisse, souffrance et mort: Lecture existentielle et phénoménologique* (1999), *Métamorphose de la finitude: Essai philosophique sur la naissance et la résurrection* (2004), and *Les noces de l'Agneau: Essai philosophique sur le corps et l'eucharistie* (2011). As their titles make plain, these books assume Falque's familiar manner of proceeding: taking up a thematic dear to contemporary Continental philosophy (death, finitude, and flesh) and setting them beside corresponding, perennial themes in theology (the suffering of Jesus, the resurrection, and the Eucharist) in order to bring about both a dilation or widening of the philosophical questioning and a new illumination of the theological. The work of Falque's text is accomplished out of a *determined inhabitation* of the juxtaposition, which often exposes the fact that philosophical inquiry is concluded too hastily (see, in the following pages, Falque's judicious critiques of Heidegger, as well as Marion, Henry, and others). The determined inhabitation shows theology's own tendency to close the inquiry too quickly as well (Falque does not spare criticisms from this vantage of many of the major figures studied in this book).

Manifest most clearly (and perhaps controversially) in the philosophical *triduum* is what we can only call a "Christological concentration" of philosophy. From this perspective, the philosophy at the dawn of the new millennium is only catching up to theology of the twentieth century, which was marked if not defined by such a concentration. But is this reading of the situation really the case? The introduction of the name of Xavier Tilliette, the great French specialist in Schelling, would at least give us pause. He is the notorious author of a number of books that seek to explicate a "philosophical Christology" (and if there is, indeed, such a discipline as "philosophical theology," then why not?). Among these texts of his are the following titles: *La Christologie idéaliste* (1986), *La semaine sainte des philosophes* (1992), *Le Christ des philosophes* (1993), *Les philosophes lisent la Bible* (2001), *L'eglise des philosophes* (2006), and *Philosophies eucharistiques* (2006). The significance of Tilliette's work for our present concern is that he shows almost encyclopedically how modern philosophy, from Descartes to Marcel to Marion (and in some precursors, for example, Nicholas of Cusa), has been perpetually, if not maniacally, concerned with theological themes. In Hegel and Schelling, in Kierkegaard and Rosenzweig, to mention some of the most profound figures, the philosophical is not *merely* philosophical, but also, at the same time, quite comfortably doing what in other cases we are all happy to call theology (if it is still right to talk of "theology" in the case of Rosenzweig's Jewish thought): rather, in all these cases—and well before the "theological turn"—it is revelation that sets before philosophy its highest and most demanding task.[12] Questions about the orthodoxy of, say, Hegel's "speculative Good Friday," and even about the nature of the theology itself that is employed (is it philosophy *and* theology at once?) are secondary. The point is that revelation has specifically philosophical import in his case (and, it turns out, in many others).

The work of Tilliette, though less influenced by phenomenology than German idealism, may be seen as an approximate precursor to Falque's own work.[13] What is distinct, perhaps, in Falque's work vis-à-vis Tilliette is that, like others today in France, for him it is phenomenology in particular that is seen as the best means toward, on the one hand, illuminating the native intelligibility of theological phenomena (unlike Tilliette, Falque is neither developing a "philosophical Christology" nor a "philosophy of revelation"). And on the other hand, such a phenomenology open to the theological also carries the conviction that theological phenomena, as a constitutive element within their own luminosity, propose themselves as paradigm cases of intelligibility in general. The theological is then necessary for any (relatively) complete or coherent philosophy.[14] Yet Falque's distinction from his fellow *phénoménologues* is found particularly in what I have called above his manner of "determined inhabitation" of the juxtaposition of philosophy and theology regardless of the degrees of pressure sustained at their "point of contact." His particular incarnation of the phenomenological task opens up, perhaps, a new domain, or at least inhabits the dual domains of philosophy and theology in a new way, an inhabitation which cannot be simply reduced, as I mentioned above, to a "theological turn" shared by a set of French thinkers. Though the latter nomination can be helpful as a first approach—and let us pause to thank Dominique Janicaud—it nevertheless quickly becomes inadequate and with Falque we can see perhaps most clearly why: the theological domain becomes necessary for the integrity of philosophy itself (the reverse, again, is less controversial, and has almost always been: theologians seem to have a tradition of being more open in this regard . . .).

If we had to confer on Falque a motto (at the risk of being a little misleading, unless we keep in mind that it is a motto) it would be irreducibly double: if in Falque there is "faith seeking understanding," at the same time there is "understanding seeking faith." If theological phenomena can be approached philosophically, then philosophical phenomena can be approached theologically. It is the former that Falque emphasizes for the sake of our contemporary context. The fact that these two modes of approach, on the one hand, occur through a rhythm of reciprocal exchange, or, to borrow from Merleau-Ponty, as an "interlacement," but also, on the other hand, that at moments they occur, however strangely, *at the same time*, and in a way that precludes a final determination in their regard, is precisely the point Falque wants us to understand: it is a determining element of our finitude (radicalized by what I named above the underlying eschatology of Falque's thinking) that we cannot make a final judgment between them. Fidelity to "the things themselves" of phenomenology demands this forfeiture of a final judgment regarding their ultimate provenance, or, more reservedly, at least regarding their relation to what we differentiate as the philosophical and theological domains—for the time being, that is, in the midst of what we understand as our (present) human condition. The fact is that we do not know if we know the whole meaning of our humanity, and this un-knowledge becomes the condition for a special kind of inquiry that joins the philosophical with the theological, and which is marked by, to borrow an appropriate term from Jean-Luc Marion, "certitudes négatives," where the impossibility of a complete and final judgment regarding some phenomena (such as God, or the flesh or alterity) itself bears a unique epistemic force that draws philosophy into its profundity.[15] Falque's "determined inhabitation" has perhaps been sufficiently enough explained to orient your reading of this masterful text, which will illustrate further, or better, "perform," what I mean to say here.

Finally, a note on the current English-language literature related to Falque before the necessary comments on the translation itself. Besides the present work and *Metamorphosis of Finitude*, other representative works of Falque's in English are a few articles[16] and a far-ranging interview in a book entitled *Quiet Powers of the Possible*.[17] Finally, Crina Gschwandtner has dedicated a chapter of her *Postmodern Apologetics?* (2013) to Falque's oeuvre;[18] she has also penned an article on his philosophy of corporeality (2012).[19] Gschwandtner's reflections fill out some important aspects of what I only gloss over here; they would serve any reader well as supplementary reading to the following text.

Regarding the translation: like any translation, great or small, this one presented some of its own difficulties that the translator had to decide how best to navigate. Translator's notes are set off from Falque's own by brackets: these most often explain the methodology of citation that I used when converting Falque's French into my English rendering. Perhaps it is worth stating the general rule here. Falque again and again quotes and modifies standard French translations of the primary authors who are the focus of each chapter. Therefore, in consultation with the French or original-language text to which he refers as well as with the standard English-language translations, I was typically compelled to translate Falque's French rendering itself into English. In the case, therefore, of his quotation and modification (slight or major) of the French translations of Greek or Latin sources, I provide reference to the original source (often, but not always, the celebrated *Sources chrétiennes* series) and retain his acknowledgment of modification in parentheses. However, I retained this methodology only for the primary author who serves as the focus of each chapter. Regarding all other sources quoted and cited, which are mainly modern sources, I found the English-language equivalent—if there was one—and used it instead of proffering my own translation of the French (or German) text. *Dieu, la chair et l'autre* is, to say the least, a lively text in French, marked by a certain characteristic breathlessness natural to a unique style of thinking that is as rich as it is freely unencumbered by anything but its very task. This style of thinking is always ambitiously unfolding a little more before stopping suddenly, looking up, surveying the field in order then to look back down, and then abruptly starting again from a fresh angle of attack. The reader is required to embrace this style or risk getting seasick, thereby trusting that their guide—philosopher-theologian-medievalist—busier than a bee, is hard at his work producing something as unique, idiosyncratic, even sui generis as honey. The translation strives, simply, to be faithful to this style and its results.

I would like to thank the author himself for entrusting me with this massive project, as well as for his indefatigable generosity, especially during my original sojourn in Paris while still a doctoral student, under the pretext of *pensionnaire étranger* at the École Normale Supérieure. It was then, in 2010, that I began this project, which has been a constant companion since, not only while writing my dissertation in Paris and Charlottesville, but also during the inaugural year, and now a little more, at my first academic post in Melbourne. For the translation of the first chapter, I consulted, and benefited from, Joeri Schrijvers's translation of a slightly different version of a considerable portion of it.[20] Heartfelt thanks also are due to Genevieve Fahey for her expert proofreading services. I would finally like to thank Marianne for so often pushing me out of bed while it was still dark in order to make this translation a reality. If the translator may be granted the space to dedicate his labors here, then may they be to her honor. This is only right since we have her most of all to thank for the completion of this text, but also, as you can surmise, for any mistakes it contains . . .

William Christian Hackett

ACKNOWLEDGMENTS

The present work was first written for a postdoctoral degree (*Habilitation à diriger des recherches* [HDR]) undertaken at the University of Paris IV (Sorbonne), on Saturday, June 10, 2006, with the result of the awarding of the title of professor. I would like to thank the members of the committee, who were, in order of priority: R. Imbach (University of Paris IV, Sorbonne, director), J.-L. Marion (University of Paris IV, Sorbonne), J. Greisch (Catholic Institute of Paris), P. Capelle (Catholic Institute of Paris), O. Boulnois (École Pratique des Hautes Études), G. Ferretti (University of Macerata, Italy). The completion of this work would not have been possible without the constant support of my associates, colleagues, and students at the Catholic Institute of Paris. May you all be here gratified for having made implicit contributions to this work. Let me offer my profound gratitude to J. Alexandre and J. de Gramont for having read over the entire volume—without omitting, of course, J.-L. Marion who, besides welcoming this book into his prestigious collection, has never belied either his friendship or his confidence toward me.

PREFACE (2008)

The audacious claim with which this book opens and the wager on which it is based is this: it is possible today to read the church fathers and the medievals *philosophically*—up to and including the corpus of theology. Certainly, we have not been waiting on phenomenology in order to interrogate the corpus of theology with renewed effort, nor, for that matter, patristic and medieval texts in order to discover in them new bearings for phenomenology. It remains, however, that from patristic and medieval philosophy to phenomenology the relation is decisive and even exemplary. We could surely point out that the Thomism of Franz Brentano was at the root of Husserlian intentionality, that the young Martin Heidegger began his career with a habilitation on *The Treatise on the Categories and Signification in Duns Scotus* (or rather Thomas d'Erfurt) (1915) before planning a course never given on *The Philosophical Foundations of Medieval Mysticism* (1918–1919), that Max Scheler was not indifferent to the *Nature and the Form of Sympathy* in the "Canticle of Creatures" of friar Francis (1923), that Edith Stein attempted an "essay of confrontation" between *The Phenomenology of Husserl and the Philosophy of St. Thomas Aquinas* (1929), and that Hannah Arendt's project would remain totally incomprehensible without *The Concept of Love in Augustine* (1929) and her analyses of medieval philosophy in *The Life of the Spirit* (published posthumously).

But within the "way" that we want to initiate here, there exist more and better options, or rather, as it were, another way. We will not be content, in this work, with sounding out the patristic and medieval roots of phenomenology—a work today largely accomplished (A. de Muralt, D. Perler, J.-L. Solère, J. D. Caputo, etc.)—but we will practice phenomenology from within the corpus of theology, in order to show what neither of them, perhaps, have yet been able to see: the ultimate possibility of phenomenologically describing the modes of manifestation of theology, up to and including the *lived experience internal to the texts of the tradition* in order to (re)discover it again today. Independently of their efficacy, *theologoumena* are translated into a number of *philosophemes* that phenomenology could and ought legitimately to interrogate: relation and substance in the Trinity and onto-theology (Augustine), theophany and appearance of the phenomenon (John Scotus Erigena), detachment and reduction (Meister Eckhart), creation of Adam and visibility of the flesh (Irenaeus), Christological incarnation and density of the body (Tertullian), conversion of the senses and incorporeity

(Bonaventure), communion of saints and genesis of the community (Origen), treatise on angels and intersubjectivity (Thomas Aquinas), call of the name and singularity of the other (Duns Scotus).

In both cases, as in every case, it is not at all a question either of juxtaposing the terms without showing the possibility of co-engendering them (reduction to God, constitution of the flesh, genesis of alterity), or of requiring belief in the revealed in order to give free rein to its act of manifestation (imperative of the *epochê*). The method or the way (*meta è hodos*) is always worth more than the result, if indeed we allow ourselves to carry it out. This is how we would want to attain our "phenomenological practice of medieval philosophy," here justified only through its practice. The concepts of *God, the flesh, and the other* belong, in a certain and exemplary fashion, to the field of contemporary phenomenology, but in the corpus of patristic and medieval philosophy they find that which not only grounds them but also renews them.

Profunda fluviorum scrutatus est, et abscondita produxit in lucem: "He has *scrutinized* the depth of the waters and has *brought to light* that which was hidden" (Job 28:11). What is true here of theology (Bonaventure) is even more so of philosophy, and in particular of phenomenology, for which the *perscrutatio*—the act of "sounding out" or of "descending into the depths"—defines the gesture, as well as the risk, of setting out from there. This work desires to chronicle the attempt of this setting out, entrusting to others the task of returning to its results and developing them.

PREFACE TO THE ENGLISH-LANGUAGE EDITION

I consider it both a tall order and a personal challenge to release this work of medieval philosophy, of phenomenology (and of philosophy period) into the hands of the Anglo-Saxon and American public. It is a tall order because it wants to open up a new way of practicing medieval philosophy in our day. And it is a personal challenge because this mode of philosophizing aspires to revive for us a past that one would be forgiven for believing long dead. *God, the Flesh, and the Other* steers a course across the disciplines and through very distinct ways of writing, studying, and thinking. What matters here is not knowing from where one speaks, nor even "who" is doing the speaking. For the text, navigating a course with numerous "crossings" is as surprising in its detours as it is unexpected in its discoveries. This holds I think for each chapter, which stands on its own. Yet together they form a unified whole.

It has been thought that everything has been said that could be said about Saint Augustine, yet there is revealed a tension of metaphysics and theology that is no longer content (once the blind habit is broken) with the much too famous and insufficient "overcoming of metaphysics." It also seemed that the question of the phenomenon was a discovery of the twentieth century, or at least the eighteenth, yet its hidden roots are found in the Carolingian era, in the ninth century, in John Scotus Erigena's notion of theophany. It was also thought that Mary was superior to Martha in the episode at Bethany, yet the surprising thing is, following Meister Eckhart, that only Martha lives "in the mode of reduction" with God within, whereas Mary her sister always remains in the "natural attitude," in a presence so objectifying of the divine that she only stands there over and against it.

It could even appear that the question of the body is today something new. But the fathers prove the contrary. Because philosophy forgot it in the first place it failed to return to it. The "visibility" of the flesh in Irenaeus and its "solidity" in Tertullian reveal in fact the density of the body, prohibiting thereby every form of gnosis, certainly in philosophy and theology, but also, specifically, in phenomenology (through the encounter with Michel Henry in particular). Even better, only a serious consideration of the incarnation of man as well as God expects of us a true "conversion of the senses" so that (following Bonaventure) we finally cease fleeing from our humanity in order to take refuge in the divine. Because we all experience the death of our loved ones, suffering the pain of that separation, Origen via Saint Bernard teaches us that the space of the communion of saints does not signify another world, but another way of living in the same world. Our beloved dead have not simply disappeared, but are held in the Word and experience our feelings, our joys and pains.

The interrogation of alterity is not so new either. Thomas Aquinas allows us to demonstrate this in his analysis of the relation of one angel to another. And following his indications we discover today a way of thinking human interrelationality. This is why we will not be satisfied any longer with a characterization of alterity that is too universalized, admittedly characteristic of Judaism (Levinas for example) but not Christianity. Duns Scotus is not interested in this sense, nor first, in the singular character of the rock or blade of grass, simply for philosophical or dialectical reasons, as is often so wrongly suggested. The vocation of the singular man, in the call made to each (and in particular to the disciples), provides the highest justification for returning to singularity in the problem of alterity. Once again, it is by forgetting a theological motive behind a philosophical thesis that the root of the problem was forgotten yesterday, and today, even its meaning.

God, the Flesh, and the Other therefore makes the decision to return to a patristic and medieval tradition often wholly uninterrogated or studied in such a historical fashion that it becomes far too distant from us. The fruitful and necessary work of the historians of philosophy certainly delivers precious material which feeds the work of thought. In order to reflect on this material today the fact remains that it must be given meaning in our contemporary situation without at the same time reducing it to a mirror image of ourselves. There is a virtue to progressing slowly in relation to that which we have only too often forgotten by dint of traveling intellectual routes too often frequented (including within the practice of reading). The "phenomenological practice of medieval philosophy" undertaken here designates neither a method nor an intellectual fashion. Rather, it wants to attain to a new way of seeing and of living in the world—certainly of today, but also of yesterday, for the sake of learning how to think otherwise, and to make us the worthy successors of those who have preceded us.

This book, translated into English and thereby handed over to the Anglo-American public, is certainly inscribed within the famous "theological turn of French phenomenology" (Levinas, Ricoeur, Marion, Henry, etc.). But actually it by and large surpasses it. What matters is neither to stand one's ground among a distribution of disciplines nor to brandish interdictions. I have demonstrated this elsewhere. The time has come to "cross the Rubicon" and to discover new boundaries between philosophy and theology. Where it has previously been wrongly thought sufficient to interpret theology phenomenologically, today I call for a "return shock" of theology back onto philosophy itself. *The Metamorphosis of Finitude* (now published in English) is not simply the title of my book on birth and resurrection, but properly speaking a "method" through which no apprenticeship to the tradition can be undertaken without becoming completely transformed in one's convictions in the process.[1]

I am grateful to the translator, Chris Hackett, for taking on this task and to Northwestern University Press for making it possible. One does not climb up the hills and into the mountains in order to reach the heights without a lot of hard work. This certainly involved a high level of skill. But only a real empathy with what is expressed and an unfailing fidelity made possible by a common bond of friendship is the justification of such labors: to cause to pass truly from one language into another what is otherwise hidden behind undecipherable hieroglyphs. Chris—and his wife, who also carried the burden—have my profound gratitude, now leaving the reader with the leisure to accomplish the crossing for him- or herself. Arriving at the summit one can contemplate the plain and see there the place that everyone has taken during the trip: Irenaeus, Tertullian, Origen, Erigena, Bonaventure, Thomas Aquinas, Duns Scotus, Meister Eckhart become . . . *as though* our contemporaries.

Emmanuel Falque
Mettray, September 2013

God, the Flesh, and the Other

Fons Signatus: The Sealed Source

Is phenomenology a jack-of-all-trades [*bonne à tout faire*]—or better, *the* jack-of-all-trades? The question is not new, even though a certain phenomenon of "modality" makes a case for its absolute novelty, however outdated it may seem. Max Scheler, in the preface of the second edition of *Vom Ewigen im Menschen*, already calculated the danger in 1922: "Phenomenology, as method of a descriptive theory of views of the world, is a jack-of-all-trades [*ein Mädchen für alles*]." [1] But "to be a jack-of-all-trades," even "the" jack-of-all-trades, the "all-purpose" do-it-all, was not, in the eyes of the philosopher, an unworthy role for phenomenology. Nor, as we will see, is it indecent, in the words of Saint Thomas, for philosophy nobly "to serve" theology. Max Scheler adds that it is even "the fact that phenomenology is a jack-of-all-trades [*dass sie ein Mädchen fur alles*] which rightly constitutes its *positive* and *remarkable* value [*ihr ausgezeichneter positiver Wert*]."[2] We could therefore positively use phenomenology without losing phenomenology. Better, phenomenology would perhaps never itself be as "good" [*bonne*] as when it is left "used," that is, borrowed for a purpose (*usage*) that pertains to its essence as such: "Phenomenology can be practiced and identified as a manner or style of thinking," emphasizes Maurice Merleau-Ponty in the preface to the *Phenomenology of Perception* (1945), adding also that it is not just a question of "myth" or of "fashion," and that it refuses to be circumscribed as a "movement" or as a collection of "doctrines."[3] Briefly, and this can now be understood, it is a question here of seeking "the handyman phenomenology [*la bonne de la phénoménologie*]"—less in order to draw up an invoice for his work accomplished, or even to set up shop in the household amidst all other approaches, than to assess, in a methodological way, his capacity to renew the practice of medieval philosophy itself.

The Contradictions of a Practice

Yet it is necessary to recognize that the hypothesis of a "phenomenological practice of medieval philosophy" does not come naturally and appears, from the vantage of phenomenologists as much as medievalists, if not exceeded, at least displaced.

(a) Let us begin with the phenomenologists first, because "to use" phenomenology in this way is unworthy of its aims and limits. Firstly, in its aims, phenomenology is not allowed to be annexed by any other discipline, for this would court the opposite risk of reducing it to the simple role of ancillary method unworthy of the "things themselves" (Husserl, *Ideas I*, § 19). Tied too much in its essence to theology, medieval philosophy will offer itself therefore to phenomenological interpretation only in an illegitimate way, at least insofar as it ignores the "methodological atheism" which always remains the rule. In its limits, then, the originary donating intuition of the phenomenon would not "exceed the limits in which it is thus given," without immediately going against the "principle of principles" (*Ideas* I, § 24). There again, the constant return to transcendence condemns medieval philosophy to a phenomenological inadequacy, in that it makes every *epochê* of God impossible and exceeds the bounds of the immanence to consciousness assigned to every phenomenon in order for them to appear. "Methodological atheism" and "absence of every presupposition" are thus the two principles transgressed from the beginning by medieval philosophy, and which make impossible every attempt at a "phenomenological practice" of medieval philosophy—unless we were to use it only as a procedure to translate, as a sort of "flavor of the month," the language of yesterday (albeit falsely accused of obsolescence).

(b) From the medievalist point of view, this divorce, or this impossible marriage, of medieval philosophy and phenomenology thus appears to be definitively consummated. Those well versed in medieval philosophy, all too aware of the complexity of its sources and the historical strata of its texts, would never allow the medieval corpus to be so disfigured by those who would approach it. Could we not argue for the tension of metaphysics and theology in Augustine's *De Trinitate* (primacy of relation over substance) without forcing ourselves to look through the lens [*prisme*] of the overcoming of onto-theology, which itself is rather hard to find in the actual history of philosophy? Or still, is not connecting Heidegger's definition of phenomenality with Erigena's conception of theophany only to miss the point of the disclosure of things themselves in Heidegger and God's manifestation in Erigena? Further, is it legitimate to see a mode of Husserlian "reduction" in the impossible reification of God at the heart of Meister Eckhart's sermons on Martha and Mary (*Serms.* 2 and 86), without simultaneously losing the radicality of the phenomenological *epochê* and the meaning of theological conversion itself? Is it not completely inadequate to attempt to elucidate the "glory of the flesh" in Irenaeus and/or the "density of the body" in Tertullian with the help of the phenomenological duality of body (*Körper*) and flesh (*Leib*)—all the more so as the "becoming flesh" of phenomenology (*Leiblichung*) does not at all resemble the "becoming man" of theology (*Menschwerdung*)? And is it possible for the "conversion of the senses" in Bonaventure and the "experience of the stigmata" in Saint Francis to bring to light something of the meaning of the "phenomenalization of the flesh" and the "silent experience that accompanies it" without betraying both the pure immanence of what gives itself in phenomenology and the ordinary nature of experience that it is supposed to describe? Finally, what should be said about the search for a "community of monads" in Origen's description of the communion of saints (*Homilies on Leviticus*), the new and revolutionary meaning of alterity in Aquinas's question in the *Summa* about the knowledge of one angel by another (Ia, qq. 50–64), and the discovery of the haecceity of the other in Duns Scotus, which lies in contrast to all the contemporary tendencies to posit some kind of neutrality in the discourse on alterity (*Ordinatio* II, d. 3)? These questions and interpretations all fall under the three headings of "God," "the flesh," and "the other," which happen to be the three great questions of contemporary philosophy and which are therefore a way of testing medieval philosophy as a possible phenomenological practice—with, of course, an awareness of the ever-present danger of anachronism.

What is the profit of such a transgression of boundaries? Is it for phenomenology, which would only suffer by being annexed by theology here? Or is it for medieval philosophy, which would not withstand very well being the "flavor of the month" without clearly measuring the distance that separates it from our times? Is it for those who practice both disciplines together, and who would thus be suspected of trying to reheat stale dishes and present them as fresh and in this way ignoring their historicity? The objections are too clear here to spend time multiplying them, which would only be willful obfuscation rather than a concern with not taking them seriously.

The Programmatic Relevance of the Middle Ages

And yet it is true that only those who take the risk can succeed, and "to think is to decide," as Heidegger said so well. Critique is too easy for those who make a profession of it, but the task of conceptualization borders on impossibility for those who bear the burden of its realization. I suggest that today medieval philosophy ought to find, or rediscover, its relevance (*actualité*)—not simply in the sense of becoming the current fashion (*l'actualité*), but more deeply in its etymological sense as deploying its potentialities not yet actualized (*actualitas*). Few fields are so replete with texts, gestures and attitudes than medieval philosophy, which phenomenology would associate with ways of being in the world. Whether these are Christian or not—this is not the question. The point is that these ways of being in the world are there to be rediscovered for our time. And numerous medievalists today endorse medieval philosophy's contemporary relevance. Alain de Libera asks in the preface to his *Penser au Moyen Âge*: "why should we work on the Middle Ages if we do not let the Middle Ages work in us?"[4] Pierre Alferi, at the beginning of his book *Guillame d'Ockham, Le singulier*, quite rightly notes: "there is nothing so untimely as medieval philosophy. Despite scholarly literature that has improved over the course of several decades, it is more absent and distant from contemporary culture and thought than the philosophy of the Ancient Greeks."[5] Better yet, phenomenology itself has had the pretense of renewing medieval philosophy, although the philosophers who have drawn on it have never risked pushing the hypothesis to its end: "The logic of mysticism is simultaneously a logic of the overcoming of metaphysics," suggests Olivier Boulnois in relation to Bonaventure's *Six Days of Creation*,[6] and Jean-François Courtine, in quest of the sources of *Suárez and the System of Metaphysics*, again asks whether "there are not also other, even more radical, exits, which go so far as decidedly altering the language of metaphysics. Generally speaking," he continues, "let me mention spirituality, mystical theology and without a doubt apophaticism."[7] Referring to the "anthropology of humility" in Saint Bernard, Rémi Brague supposes that "St. Bernard's attempt will possibly continue to enable us to rethink the essence of philosophy; it will especially aid phenomenology in realizing its native possibilities."[8] Finally, Emmanuel Martineau writes in his book *Malevitch et la philosophie* that "we profess the need and possibility of a 'phenomenological mysticology,' the validity of which does not depend on the primary alternative between belief and unbelief."[9]

The number and strength of these kinds of discourse, which are always only programmatic, ought to leave us stunned since the declarations of principle are almost never followed through in practice. Indeed, all occurs as if the task was to liberate medieval studies from its purely historical shackles—as has been the case for Aristotle (Pierre Aubenque), Descartes (Jean-Luc Marion), Kant (Martin Heidegger), and many others. But at the same time no one dared to enact the "liberation." This is certainly not because of weakness or ignorance but rather fear—sometimes, let it be said, legitimate and probably specific to medieval philosophy—of a confusion of genres: philosophy and theology, on the one hand, and phenomenology and the historiography of texts, on the other. However deep the polemic, there is no denying that medieval philosophy still awaits its *aggiorniamento*, which I already called for at the beginning of my *Saint Bonaventure et l'entrée de Dieu en théologie* (2000).[10] This is not to say that what others have accomplished and continue to do should no longer be done, for the phenomenological interrogation of medieval philosophy is impossible apart from an updating of its sources, not to mention the translation of texts, which ensures their accessibility. Yet the rediscovery of texts quarried by our pioneers ought now to help us explore the depths of the mine. The era of translation and transmission of texts certainly ought to continue, but it will not serve anything if it is not passed on to those who try to "see the thing itself." For such is required by phenomenology—as Heidegger once confided that Husserl "had implanted eyes" in him (*GA* 63: 5).

The one who *practices* medieval texts *in phenomenology* "will see" what has not yet been seen—not in seeing that which was never there, but rather because the *self* of the phenomenologist and/or the medievalist has not yet reached the place of "the thing itself," *there* where the "withdrawal" occurs of that manifestation that still remains anticipated. *Profunda fluviorum scrutatus est, et abscondita produxit in lucem*—"he has *scrutinized* the depths of the waters and has *brought to light* what was hidden" (Job 28:11). The task that Bonaventure assigned to the "theologian *perscrutator*" in his prologue to the *Commentary on the Sentences*—"to scrutinize" the depths (*scrutare profunda*) and "to bring to light" the hidden or not yet revealed (*producere in lucem*)—correlates precisely with the task of the phenomenologist who rediscovers here the original and, as it were, anterior, attitude: first to "sound and attain the ground by *sounding*" (*ergründen*) rather than "to ground in reason and provide a foundation for" (*begründen*), and second to make clear the "*illumination* of being [*Aufweisung von Seiendem*] as it is shown in itself [*so wie es sich an ihm selbst zeigt*]," rather than presupposing a doubling in its appearance which is never shown.[11] Descending the river, or scrutinizing its depths in order to discover there its "hidden treasures" (*abscondita*), the medievalist who *at the same time* practices phenomenology will become a "diviner" or "perscrutator," thereby becoming a contemporary with the corpus of his ancestors the medievals in the same way that Heidegger traversed so many philosophers. As his disciple and friend, Hans-Georg Gadamer, put it: "His path through the history of philosophy resembled that of a diviner. Suddenly his stick comes to a halt: he found it."[12]

The Stages of a Journey

A single question orients us here, and then the entirety of our research: "How and in what way is God given to be seen ("he who has seen me has seen the Father," Jn. 14:9) and touched today ("the Word of life that our hands have touched," 1 Jn. 1:1)"? What yesterday, in the fathers and medievals was in the order of sensible evidence (the presence of God as "relation," his "manifestation" in the world, his "visibility" to others, his "taste" in the Eucharist, etc.), has in our day become much more distant and ethereal. To rediscover the *meaning of the incarnation in general*, whether of man or God, is thus to interrogate the tradition anew and to avoid sinking into a purely "abstract" mode of thought that contemporary philosophy especially wants to disavow. The course is not primarily confessional, nor even theological. It is above all philosophical inasmuch as the "carnal mode of the human" is what we must rediscover today.

Discoveries are rare, but the search is priceless. And we hope that we have also made some discoveries. Let us offer some examples that bear witness to our searching: the discovery of "relation" where "substance" was expected in Saint Augustine's *De Trinitate V–VII* (chap. 1); "theophany" as a mode of "phenomenality" in John Scotus Erigena's *Periphyseon* (chap. 2); "conversion" as mode of "reduction" in Meister Eckhart's *Sermons* 2 and 71, including the reduction "to nothing" and "to the nothing" (chap. 3); the determination of Adam as the "ark of flesh" who "works" and "opens" the world of the incarnate in Irenaeus's *Adversus Haereses* IV–V (chap. 4); the "flesh of death" which is first a "flesh for birth" in Tertullian's *De Carne Christi* VI, 6 (chap. 5); the "conversion of the senses" as the location of an "intercorporeality" of man and God in Bonaventure's *Breviloquium* V, 6 (chap. 6); the communion of saints as interaction of monads in the divine sphere in Origen's *Homilies on Leviticus* VII, 2 (chap. 7); alter-angelic knowledge as the first prohibition of solipsism in Aquinas's *Summa theologiae* Ia, q. 50 (chap. 8); and the singularity of the other as an exemplary mode of all forms of haecceity in Duns Scotus's *Ordinatio* II, d. 3 (chap. 9).[13] In short, the "*phenomenological practice of medieval philosophy*" is hardly content to acknowledge *negatively* a prism of onto-theology which barely existed in the medievals if at all. Everyone now knows that Heidegger found it in a certain Avicennian interpretation of Duns Scotus (really Thomas of Erfurt).[14] On the contrary, we ought to seek positively in medieval philosophy gestures, concepts, and attitudes that properly manifest modes of being common to the man of yesterday as much as today: his relation to God (part I: Augustine, Erigena, Eckhart), the flesh (part II: Irenaeus, Tertullian, Bonaventure), and the other (part III: Origen, Thomas Aquinas, and Duns Scotus)—in other words the three great themes of contemporary philosophy rediscovered at the heart of medieval philosophy.

Let us be clear: to *practice* phenomenology or *live* as a phenomenologist while reading the fathers and medievals is not simply to apply a method to them or force them into the straitjacket of some new current of thought, or even to impose questions on them that are not their own. In this work, much like the novels of Faulkner for Claude Romano (*Le chant de la vie*), the texts of medieval philosophy "in no way constitute a general, neutral and universal method which would hold good for any text whatsoever. It is precisely the opposite. This book would have never been written if the *phenomenological* character of these [texts] had not, in some way, 'leaped into view,' if it had not imposed on us its authority and evidence. In the phenomenological context, it is not the phenomenologist who applies a method to the object from the exterior, but rather the object which ought to prescribe its own method to us, that is to say, etymologically, *meta e hodos* in Greek, signifying the 'path that leads beyond the obstacle,' the mode of access which is appropriate for it . . . Thus the thing which the text opens is less the object than the subject of the phenomenological method . . . A truly phenomenological reading ought to yield the word to the author *as* phenomenologist."[15]

In this study we will not be content, therefore, to find "the medieval origins . . . of phenomenological thought," which was moreover perfectly executed regarding intentionality in particular by A. de Muralt and D. Perler.[16] We will attempt instead *to think* medieval philosophy in a *phenomenological* way, to *see*, or better *to read in seeing*, what the fathers or medievals themselves have "seen" or "wanted to see." What matters, according to the attitude of true thinkers, is less what they say (*quid*) then the way they say it (*quomodo*)—the elucidation of "meaning" through the exposition of "acts," or even to find the "asked" (*Erfragtes*) behind the "questioned" (*Gefragtes*) and the "interrogated" (*Befragtes*): in §7 of *Being and Time*, Heidegger famously declares that "the expression 'phenomenology' primarily signifies a *concept of method*. It does not characterize the 'what' of the objects of philosophical research in terms of their content, but the 'how' of such research."[17] This is also true, for example, and it will be our goal to demonstrate it below, for John Scotus Erigena and his definition of God as "He who runs and sees" in his *Periphysion* (I, 452 B). To derive the name of God from the etymology *thêo* (I run) and not only from *theôrô* (I see) is to show precisely that the divine is not first manifest in "what he is" (*quid*) but in the "mode" or "way" that he appears and is manifest to man (*quomodo*): "His word runs swiftly" (Ps. 147:15).[18] Similarly, the affirmation of Tertullian in his *De Resurrectione carnis* (IX, 2–3) that "the flesh is sister to Christ [*Christi sororem*]" because "Christ loves the flesh [*diliget carnem*] which is so close to him in many ways [*tot modis sibi proximam*]," is only possible because the flesh appears as the most proper *modality* of his incarnate, christic being—that to which he is attached as that which is "closest to him," as opposed to a simple corporeal substance in a potentially reified sense.[19] Likewise Thomas Aquinas's treatment of alterity is phenomenologically decrypted from the starting point of his angelology. In light of the question "whether an angel knows another angel" (*utrum unus angelus alium cognoscat*) in the *Summa* (Ia, q. 56, a. 2), Thomas draws a distinction between the knowledge of one angel by another "according to its natural being [*secundum esse naturale*]," and its knowledge "according to its intentional being [*secundum esse intentionale*]." Here he reveals, in a virtually phenomenological way, that the second (intentionality) is fitting for alter-angelology. Not "being" a body, but only assuming a body "in order to appear," the phenomality of the angel manifests its mode of true being as "being-for-another"—through his intentional consciousness in his relation to another angel, and through the flesh appearing in relation to man: "It is not for themselves [*propter seipsos*] that the angels need to assume a body, but for us [*propter nobis*]."[20]

We could multiply the examples infinitely, so rich is the medieval corpus and so unsuspected its hidden treasures. How often the diviner's rod comes to a halt: "he found it!"—the diviner knows how to read and to disclose the *acts* or *lived modalities* of consciousness where one ordinarily searches for *things* or *regions* within being. The return "to the things themselves" has never sought to find anything else than the ascent of beings of the world (*Ding*) toward the acts which constitute them and insofar as they concern us (*Sache*): "We want to return to the things themselves [*auf die Sachen selbst zurückgehen*]," said Husserl in the first formulation of this imperative at the beginning of the *Logical Investigations* (1901). "By means of *fully-fledged intuitions*," he continues, "we desire to render self-evident that what is here given in actually performed abstractions is what the word meanings in our expression of the law really and truly stands for."[21] Thus phenomenology is "at the same time and above all a *method* and an *attitude of thought*: the *specifically philosophical* attitude, the *specifically philosophical* method"—always "implanted" in the eyes of Husserl, as in our own.[22] Therefore neither a myth nor fashion, nor even less a movement or point of view, phenomenology is first a *way of being*, a sort of *relation*—to oneself and to God of course, but also to the world and its diverse expressions, to others and to texts that interpret them, often intimately: "The one who philosophizes . . . *understands* the others in whose company, in critical friendship and enmity, he philosophizes. And in philosophizing he is also in company with himself, as he earlier understood and did philosophy, and he knows that, in the process, *historical tradition*, as he understood it and used it, entered into him in a motivating way and as a *spiritual* sediment."[23]

The Tree and Its Fruits

Nothing is totally new, even less in medieval philosophy, for pure novelty only exists as it is rooted in and drawn from the past that precedes us, and moves through us from end to end. The past never gets as much "authority" as in the corpus of the Middle Ages, for here more than elsewhere *authoritas* is first asserted by its author (*auctor*), in a "saying" that he thoroughly assumes, whether in a soliloquy or sermon, and even more in a "respondeo," in the sense that *yesterday's* decision ought to make an echo *today* in our own declaration: "Whether the answer is 'novel,'" says Heidegger in §2 of *Being and Time*, "is of no importance and remains extrensic. What is positive about the answer must lie in the fact that it is *old* enough to enable us to learn to comprehend the possibilities prepared by the 'ancients.'"[24]

"The tree is recognized by its fruits": a famous expression, but it is not the appanage of the Gospel alone (Lk. 6:44). For it is also the leitmotiv of every philosophical quest, and in particular of the *medievalist*, who, far from measuring his success by the yardstick of his own a priori *principles* (for example: can I treat theological thematics while being a licensed philosopher? Do I have the right to think from my contemporaneity while I study a historical body of work?), ought on the contrary to understand it by extending it to his a posteriori *practice*. This is only because downstream, the experience of "the phenomenological practice of medieval philosophy" is sufficiently verified that it becomes, upstream, finally possible to proclaim some rules or baselines. Such is a required condition in order not to devolve into some kind of new formalism.

The gain of the enterprise, if I understand it correctly, will thus be double: for medieval philosophy texts can be read as they have never been read before, not in order to see *something else* there, but to see the *same things in a new way*; for phenomenology, gestures, attitudes and postures will be discovered that are capable of opening its horizon to *kinds of experience* that it has itself not yet described or even suspected. Rémi Brague, concerning the rapprochement between "nothingness" [*nihilité*] in St. Bernard and "nothingness" [*néant*] in Heidegger notes: "I suspect that it is not a question here of thinking of these theses as if they were identical. Each occupies a determinate place in a determinate context determined in each thinker—which I am not able to outline here. We can, however, suggest *a convergence* toward a thesis of which it would be necessary *to await phenomenology*, that 'secret nostalgia of the history of philosophy' (Husserl), in order to see it formulated fully. Regarding St. Bernard, it is not a question any longer of pretending to leap over the centuries, of demeaning the status of anything. To the contrary, it is a matter of seeing how he could help our present to go beyond itself . . . to allow phenomenology to give birth to possibilities with which it still remains pregnant."[25]

Let me say it once and for all in order not to sink into gross anachronism: *to practice medieval philosophy phenomenologically* is not to require authors to respond to our questions—they already have enough to do with their own, and we ours. Rather it is to see *how* and *with what* they have responded to their own, in order to learn from them how to respond to ours. At this price (alone), philosophical anachronism reveals its prophetic vocation: not in being content to reread the old in light of the new, but in interrogating the ancient itself so that it can teach us to work in the region of the new. If yesterday's concepts (God, the flesh, and the other) are not the same as today's, we can nevertheless learn from yesterday how to resolve the questions that are ours today—less in imposing a lens or prism onto them than to propose a new filter: that of our own life which necessarily lends itself to them in order to extract, for us as well, an absolute novelty.

The "jack-of-all-trades" [*bonne à toute faire*] of phenomenology will in this sense "do it all," according to Max Scheler, for only phenomenology can do it: not, however, providing answers to everything, but rather giving "eyes with which to see" to the one who, lacking a real *habitus* and a true *hexis*, always remains blind to the "thing itself" that is, however, expressed and seen at the heart of the text. The "phenomenological practice of medieval philosophy" therefore ennobles *both* the corpus of the Middle Ages *and* phenomenology itself: the first because by it one finds what it contains but has not yet been seen; the second because it verifies yet again its efficaciousness, less in order to let itself be absorbed than to progress in the "descriptive exercise" where it finds its true fecundity: "The *descriptive method*," says Scheler again, "consists in reducing any metaphysical and religious system to the *content of its original experiences*, that is, *renewing its intuitions* in order to articulate its *original sense* in *reconstructing* it and, by that very fact, to make it *live again* in all of its *intuitive* force."[26] "To look for experience at its source": the leitmotif fixed by Henri Bergson in his vitalist philosophy, and largely explored by Maurice Merleau-Ponty in the context of his phenomenology, will thus serve as the rationality and guiding thread for this new foundation of a "phenomenological practice of medieval philosophy."[27]

The Sealed Source

"Today we are reading from the book of experience (*hodie legimus in libro experientiae*) . . . It is a sealed source (*fons signatus*) to which the stranger has no access. Only he who drinks from it will still thirst for it."[28] With these words, at the beginning of Sermon 3 on the Song of Songs, Bernard of Clairvaux sets out a program which will lay down some rules which still need formulation for the sake of the phenomenological practice of medieval philosophy: certainly a return to the sources (in our case, patristic and medieval), but beyond that it is particularly the unconcealment or liberation from its flux by the "reaching back to *experience*" which alone gives access to it. Said otherwise, neither the text with its mediation (hermeneutics), nor the disciplines and their disassociation (hypothesis of a separated theology), nor religion and its study (philosophy of religion rather than religious philosophy), can nor ought to distance us from the "mode of lived being" of which they are carriers.

In his study of medieval philosophy, Martin Heidegger grasped, as early as 1919, the meaning of Bernard of Clairvaux's lines on the "sealed source," copying them "by hand and in small letters" for his course on "The Philosophical Foundations of Medieval Mysticism" (*GA* 60).[29] Heidegger refers to it again in 1927 in §6 of *Being and Time*, where, keeping with the metaphor of the river, he defines the task of the "deconstruction of the history of ontology" as "the need to re-animate the dried up tradition and to dissolve its *alluvial deposits*."[30] Already in his thesis of habilitation (*Treatise on the Categories and Signification in John Duns Scotus*, 1915), he indicated and insisted that medieval thought more than any other contains "with the most intensity latent points of phenomenological consideration." He adds: "I consider, as particularly pressing, a philosophical study, more accurately a phenomenological study, of the mystical, moral and ascetic writings of medieval scholasticism. It is only by these paths that it is possible to reach the heart of medieval life [*zum lebendigen Leben*], as it grounded, animated and fortified in a decisive way an entire cultural era."[31] Moreover, all of Husserl's disciples who, as we know, questioned his idealist turn, turned to medieval philosophy, as if this corpus was best placed to unveil this *mode of experience* with the goal of renewing our own thought: this goes for Max Scheler in his *Nature and Form of Sympathy* (1923) and his reference to Saint Francis as the type of "cosmic love," for Edith Stein and her comparison of "the phenomenology of Husserl and the philosophy of St. Thomas Aquinas" in the *Jahrbuch Festschrift* for Husserl's seventieth birthday (1929), and for Hanna Arendt in *Love and St. Augustine* (1929).[32]

What was this *kairos*, so brusquely deployed in the 1920s, which marked the lineage of origin between medieval philosophy and phenomenology, a filiation either progressively forgotten, on account of the "system of Catholicism" (Heidegger, Scheler, and Arendt), or reinforced by others in the name of a conversion that also provoked a certain return to tradition (Stein)? Has not the common source of Franz Brentano (Dominican, scholar of Thomas Aquinas, teacher of Husserl, and in some sense father of intentionality) definitively sealed together phenomenology and medieval philosophy, such that the earliest disciples all but followed the first love of their forgotten master? Without tracing its genesis here, it is at least necessary to recognize as a historical fact and a problem for thinking that the relation of phenomenology to medieval philosophy, and probably logic and psychology as well, constitutes both ground and source. Returning there is to betray neither phenomenology nor medieval philosophy. On the contrary, it is to liberate what still awaits its actuality in the sealed source: a new deciphering of the "book of experience" (*liber experientiae*), and thus to modify the entirety of the *status quaestionis*—(a) first of hermeneutics, (b) then theology, (c) and finally the philosophy of religion.

Phenomenology and Hermeneutics. (a) Firstly, it is certainly clear that phenomenology does not have the same meaning in philosophy and in theology (or in the philosophy of religion in general). Theologians and the philosophers of religion make phenomenology a descriptive approach to the real, independent of any method, as if it were sufficient to deploy a given in its pure objectivity in order to expose its truth. This is true for pioneers such as Rudolf Otto in his *Idea of the Holy* (1918) and Mircea Eliade in *The Sacred and the Profane* (1956) as well as of Hans Urs von Balthasar in his book *Truth* (1952). Husserl, on the contrary, at the very same time that such a reading of the philosophy of religion was emerging, defines phenomenology in his *Ideas I* (1913) as a "purely descriptive discipline exploring the *field of* transcendentally pure *consciousness* in light of pure intuition." Rather than, like the philosophy of religion, describing an objectivity, phenomenology as such turns away from objectivity by means of the method of the reduction and returns to the *lived acts of consciousness*, toward "the originary presentive intuition" as "legitimizing source of cognition."[33]

The distinction of the two disciplines—philosophy of religion as the description of an objectivity and phenomenology as an enaction of the reduction—would matter little if one were studying here a corpus independent from theology, and therefore in some way indifferent to its phenomenological use. But this is not the case, precisely in medieval philosophy, which is too attached to God to subject him to the least *epochê*. Independent from the so-called "system of Catholicism," we will only recover "the *values* latent in the Catholic Middle Ages"—to follow Heidegger's "Letter to Krebs"—to the degree that we know how *to appreciate it*.[34] The "heart of medieval life" is certainly discovered within the structure of Scholasticism, erected for all of history starting from the medieval era—this is well known. But this "system of knowledge," according to Kant's expression (the Scholastic concept of philosophy), far from being opposed to the "general ends of humanity" (cosmic concept of philosophy), on the contrary returns there. There are not two concepts of philosophy, one to be rejected as pure "architectonic," and the other posed in its "teleological" function. The concept of medieval philosophy is first and foremost a "regulative" concept. The fathers examined in this book (Irenaeus, Tertullian, Origen, Augustine) relate to the medievals (Erigena, Bonaventure, Aquinas, Scotus, Eckhart) in that what makes their "period" is less their history than it is a certain way of conceiving a text and its interpretation as a kind of relation to the other (*respondeo*) or to God (*confessio*).[35]

To think philosophy with the medievals, including the Scholastics (see Aquinas or Scotus) is to be made capable of deciphering, at the very heart of systematization, both the "mystical" and the "experiential." The Middle Ages, with its commentaries, disputations, and summas, certainly brings about a new mode of exposition. But the *spiritual aim* is always the source of its texts, writings, and dictations, written by fathers, monks, and clerics. Reading is here a "mode of living" or "mode of spiritual life" of the Middle Ages—and in this way, precisely, medieval philosophy can renew the aim of contemporary hermeneutics. The *art of reading the world* of the medieval epoch requires that we take a new look at the relation of phenomenology to hermeneutics. It is all a matter of "grafting." A *conflict of interpretations* where, as in Paul Ricoeur's famous phrase, the "grafting of hermeneutics onto phenomenology" is enacted, makes possible the diversity of meanings in a text, it is true. But I suggest this *textual struggle* finds its first source in a *conflict of lived experiences*—and in the Middle Ages more than anywhere else. For during this period, however little explored by Paul Ricoeur (excepting Augustine), the text is not only *mediation*, but also, I suggest, *exposition* that brings about a certain meaning, but also and above all the exposition of a self in the entirety of a life which makes it hard to read apart from its author, reader, and its referent.[36]

Jean Decorte has emphasized that medieval culture is a "culture of reading" except that "people do not read books [as most people were illiterate] but reality itself."[37] In other words, if there is hermeneutics, it pertains not to texts but to the world, not to words but to life: "Books [*libri*] are the hearts of men [*corda hominum*]," says Hugh of Saint Victor, "and the book of life [*liber vitae*] is the wisdom of God [*sapientia Dei*]."[38] Indeed, signs matter little, and we are prohibited from reducing mysticism to pure logic in medieval philosophy. "Symbols" matter more, understood here in a descriptive manner as *aisthêsis* or "the good use of the sensible" (*recte utamur sensibilibus*).[39] Language certainly carries a meaning which is appropriate to it, and both hermeneutics and analytic philosophy have demonstrated this in the diverse modes of contemporary interpretation of the medievals. But as a collection of signs (logic) or vehicle of meaning (hermeneutics), the act of speech is no less revelatory of a lived experience that fully overflows it, including "the pure—and, so to speak, still dumb— . . . experience, which now must be made to utter its own sense with no adulteration" (phenomenology).[40] Otherwise put, and in order to pass in a new way from phenomenology to medieval philosophy, the experience of the world, in both cases, has primacy over the reading of texts, and the experience of the self has primacy over the conjunction of signs. The proof is the originarity of the "book of the world" (*liber mundi*) over the "book of Scripture" (*liber Scripturae*) which Bonaventure establishes following Hugh of Saint Victor, and in relation to which only sin justifies a new order of priority: "It is certain that in the state of innocence man had knowledge of created things and by way of representations he praised, honored and loved God . . . But when man fell and lost this knowledge, there was no one to lead him back to God. This book, the world [*scilicet mundus*], was dead and effaced. Thus another book [*alius liber*] was necessary by which man was enlightened in order to interpret the metaphors of things. This book is Scripture [*liber Scripturae*]."[41]

Avoiding any facile shortcut, and because such linkages often suffer many dangers of anachronism in order to bear meaning for today, the originarity of the "book of the world" (*liber mundi*) makes man into a "being in the world" before being a "being in relation to the text" in Bonaventure (*liber Scripturae*). And the "book of life" (*liber vitae*) makes man into a "being to oneself" or to his own heart before being a "being of language" (*zoon logikon*) in Hugh of Saint Victor. Here is found the "heart of medieval life" (*lebendigen Leben*) so avidly sought by the young Heidegger, only later to abandon it. And this is also what justifies today—in contrast to Paul Ricoeur—the choice of the *short path* rather than the *long path*, of "the ontology of understanding as a mode of being of *Dasein*" rather than "degrees which pass from semantics to reflection."[42] The cost is high and seems to ignore the mediations that necessarily abound in the Middle Ages. But this is to forget that one does not pass to the world except through the self, albeit in and through a *community of lived experiences* out of which is born a *conflict of interpretations*, and never the inverse. The "grafting" of hermeneutics and analytic philosophy, occurs only on the "living body" of phenomenology, not in the sense that the latter wields supreme power over the others, but rather in the sense that the unspeakable aspect of the carnal dimension of man (descriptive phenomenology) always has primacy over the verbal interpretation of its meaning (hermeneutics) and over the grammatical formulation of its propositions (logic).

Philosophy and Theology. (b) The problem of the relation between philosophy and theology is not independent of the "phenomenological practice of medieval philosophy" and the "sealed source of the book of experience." As I have already emphasized, a methodological atheism is appropriate to the phenomenological method, and there is nothing more unfitting than always wanting to baptize those who, deliberately and sometimes justifiably, refuse to be. At the very time when Heidegger embarks on his quest for "factical life" (*Phenomenological Interpretations of Aristotle*, 1922) that some years earlier he thought he found in the "heart of medieval life" (*Treatise on the Categories and Signification in John Duns Scotus*, 1915), he makes a definitive break with every form of transcendence which wrongly consecrates facticity as a product of a humanity derived from God: "If philosophy is fundamentally atheist [*grundzätlich atheistisch*] and understands this, it has made a decisive choice and retained for itself and as its object factical life [*das faktische Leben*] with regard to its facticity."[43]

Does this mean that a phenomenological approach to medieval philosophy is impossible, since in its transcendence and dependence on God it definitively exceeds the mode of being of immanence and the separation of *Dasein* proper to modern man? The question is certainly worth being asked but cannot be fully treated in this short introduction. It is perhaps enough to say that the very idea of a weight of existence constituting the anxiety of mankind is derived primarily from Heidegger's interpration of Saint Augustine—*oneri mihi sum* ("I am a burden to myself," *Confessions* X, 28). This marks the fact that in philosophy there is no bracketing of history. Scripture (Saint Paul), the fathers, and medievals (Augustine and Duns Scotus), as much as the moderns (Luther), serve as the source of Heideggerian facticity, even though their interpretation was necessarily truncated by virtue of their placement outside of every form of transcendence.[44]

What remains is the examination of the conditions for a relation between philosophy and theology—not only for today, but also to liberate in the past, along with the medievals, the source which lies hidden there. But the paradox is that the more we theologize, the better we philosophize, even though the thesis of a "Christian philosophy" as such can no longer be maintained.[45] The proportionality of the relation between philosophy and theology in the medieval corpus in fact outweighs the opposition in principle. "It is to misinterpret history," argues Etienne Gilson in his trenchant article, "Les recherches historico-critiques et l'avenir de la scolastique" (1951), to believe that the theologians of the 13th century first got a foothold in philosophy in order then to pass to theology: "they did not begin on the basis of the philosophical sciences of their time in order to adapt theology; they began with faith in order to assume the philosophy of their time and metamorphise it in the light of faith."[46] This capital formula deserves comment. Indeed, we would be wrong to look for a pure philosophy where first it is a matter of theology. Thomas Aquinas, at the beginning of the *Summa theologiae* (Ia, q. 1, a. 5), says that sacred doctrine makes use of the philosophical sciences "as inferior and ancillary sciences [*tanquam inferioribus et ancillis*]" not as "servants" or slaves, as later dialectical readings have asserted, but as "its servants [*ancillas suas*] which Wisdom has called upon in the highest places of the city [*vocare ad arcem*]" (Prov. 9:3). In other words, in the Middle Ages it was an *honor* for the servant to be exhorted to serve and to work in the house of the master, just as it is appropriate for philosophy, after having first attended to its own tasks (the cosmos and humanity), to receive the invitation from theology to *remain* within it as well (at the heart of the *theos* or the divine).

Let us be careful: to plead for philosophy the *honor of theology* is not to destroy the philosophical as such; indeed, far from it: "Neither Duns Scotus nor Thomas Aquinas founded their theology on any philosophy, not even that of Aristotle," notes Étienne Gilson, "rather, as theologians, they have used philosophy in the light of faith and there philosophy came forth transformed."[47] This does not mean that there is no philosophy in the Middle Ages or that every philosophy is necessarily annexed by theology, but rather only that the light of faith (*lumen fidei*) always remains, at least for the medievals, the source and root of *their own* thought. We could, and perhaps we should, study the medievals apart from a personal conviction of faith—because no one is obliged to believe and the fact remains that such a prism could distort thought or objectivity. But we cannot, and we ought not, act *as if* the medievals themselves did not think, read, and write in and by the light of faith. Said otherwise, it matters little whether the medieval authors themselves embraced the methodological atheism that is the rule for phenomenology. What matters is the recognition of the impossibility of the idea of atheism for the medievals themselves, out of which, however, a new form of humanism or philosophy can emerge for our time. Gilson himself remarked that "experience reveals that the more we re-integrate historical studies with their theological syntheses, the more the *philosophies* of the Middle Ages appear original."[48] Gilson's final Amen in this same text—so astonishing in the French context past and present—is not a plea *for* theology as the supreme science, but a call for a return *to* theology as source out of which the "heart" of medieval life is expressed: "To return Scholasticism to itself, let us listen to the counsel of history: *return to theology* . . . To exercise the intellect in the transcendent light of the virtue of faith is something other than pretending to derive an article of faith from philosophically demonstrable conclusions . . . The true *Scholastic philosophers* will always be theologians."[49] Gilson still awaits his faithful disciples on this point.

Philosophy of Religion and Religious Philosophy. (c) Let us ask then: where do we place the mystical élan when it is translated into the most abstract rationality, and what role to give to conceptual logicization when it is rooted in a hidden and lived mode of one's self-existence? Said otherwise, if it is clear that the study of the Middle Ages requires no faith-conviction, how is such conviction, when shared with the medievals themselves, actually able to clarify the approach that I adumbrate here? If the unsealing of the source amounts to the removal of the stone that obstructs the entrance, we should not prohibit the believer from reading the medievals in the horizon of his own faith just as we do not refuse the non-believer the right to study them independently of any conviction, even though, again, it is always necessary to recognize that the medievals themselves experienced nothing outside the horizon of faith.

Beyond his famous essay on *Le problème de Dieu en philosophie de la religion* (1957), Henry Duméry was also the translator of the *Itinerarium* of

Bonaventure. This all too often overlooked fact is not insignificant, because of how much it nourished his entire project and in what ways it could open onto a potentially new approach to medieval philosophy. Beyond the sometimes justified reticence so characteristic of philosophers in the face of the distinction between the "philosophy of religion" and "religious philosophy," Duméry contends that it is nevertheless the case that "we can only recognize the blessing of the application of personal religious experience; though not required, such an application is often of *great help* in the critique of the religious object."[50] In other words, in Dumery's time (1957) when modernity was probably less open to religion than today, he states that the kerygmatic enunciation is no longer an obstacle to the exegesis of patristic and medieval texts, but instead, its most important adjuvant. Medieval philosophy can be studied either in the domain of the "philosophy of religion" or "religious philosophy"—the first consists in objectively describing the phenomena as such, and the second proposing "*another philosophical approach to religious experience* in which the parameters of belief are explicitly taken into account" (it is enough to think here of the medievals themselves and even of Pascal or Kierkegaard, for example).[51] Neither position ought to envy the other. However, to "unseal the source" and to reach "the heart of medieval life" depends primarily on each approach adopting the position that is most appropriate for them, eschewing any false appearances or deceptions according to an imposed dogmatism that necessarily kills thinking. Where exactly the "there" (*Da*) of man's "being-there" is in phenomenology (*Da-sein*) does not matter, so long as he makes of his own "topos" the most approprate starting point by which the body of texts and the lived experiences internal to them are given to thought.

In this sense mysticism is not opposed to rationality, but nourishes it and is nourished by it in a criss-crossing of intuition and concept which alone furnishes the key: I call "mystical theology" (*theologiam mysticam*) states Bonaventure, "that which leads us to raptures and transports of spirit [*ad supermentales excessus*]."[52] The excess here not only indicates the negation of the concept, but also the entrance into a new type of rationality—that by which man, elevated beyond himself in being penetrated by God, enters into what Jean Baruzi calls a "theopathy": "a mystical intuition" which reveals "that which, *interior to metaphysical systems*, evades scientific verification and yet exists for us in the world of thought in the form of a *vivifying element*."[53] Thus in phenomenology no more than in Baruzi—and no more than in medieval philosophy itself—there is no so-called "overcoming of metaphysics," nor even a "renunciation" of its formalization. The prism of onto-theology—its time is over, as I will argue in part I. And if it is necessary to see, though only in a first step, where the tension between theology and metaphysics plays out in the re-covering [*recouvrement*] of "relation" by "substance" in books 5 and 7 of Saint Augustine's *De Trinitate*, then we will not rest for long in such a methodological preamble. No one learns how to swim without diving in the water, and no one tastes a fruit without picking it from a tree. *To consent to the Middle Ages* means for author and reader alike the acceptance of the break by *consenting* to its history [*assentire*], though also to note the proximity by means of a certain *community of experience* [*communauté de sentir*] that is possible with it [*cum-sentire*]. Every "world-view" [*Weltanschauung*] discloses a "certain *way of seeing the world*" at the same time as it determines the "*spirit of an age*." The wager is that what was true yesterday will still be true tomorrow, so long as we do not lock away into history the "hidden treasures" (*abscondita*) which still await their time of "manifestation" (*produxit in lucem*): "He has *scrutinized* the depths of the waters and has *brought to light* what was hidden" (Job 28:11).[54]

Part One

God

The Onto-Theology in Question

"The fundamental trait of metaphysics is called the *onto-theo-logical*. We are from now on, it seems, engaged in explaining *how God enters into philosophy*."[1] The way in which the question of God is posed today is found in this well-known formula of Martin Heidegger—certainly in phenomenology, but also in the discipline of medieval philosophy. That *God enters into philosophy*—or rather, *into theology*—I have shown elsewhere with Bonaventure as a guide.[2] But is a linkage necessary, and furthermore, should we connect this account to the constitution of the metaphysics called "onto-theo-logical"?

And here is precisely the rub. Onto-theo-logy is like the quest for a soul mate: the more one searches for it, the harder it is to find. It is true that the term originates in Kant's *Critique of Pure Reason* (this is textually indisputable), and comes to term in the severe critique of Martin Heidegger ("The Onto-theo-logical Constitution of Metaphysics").[3] But what of its efficacy? Could it be that what remains "unobtainable" is at this point nonsensical? "Onto-theo-logy" is the idea of a leading back of the whole of being (*ontos*) to God as to its principle (*theos*) in a self-contained [*enfermant*] and all-engulfing [*engloutissant*] (*logos*) discourse—it has indeed no rights of citizenship in the history of philosophy. There is not an author who today does not escape from this seemingly acute humiliation [*fourches caudines que l'on croyait pourtant si affutés*]. From Aristotle (P. Aubenque) to Hegel (C. Bruiare), by way of Thomas Aquinas (E. Gilson), Duns Scotus (O. Boulnois), Descartes (J.-L. Marion), Pascal (V. Carraud), and even Malebranche (J.-Ch. Bardout)—all the interpreters agree in not recognizing its validity, at least in a historically founded sense. Does this mean that the notion itself means nothing and its tradition of research means nothing? Is it enough to take the "exact contre pied" [precisely opposite position] of the hypothesis of the overcoming of metaphysics in order to restore or rediscover metaphysics as such—beyond the "vulgate du dépassement" [common or crude view of an overcoming] (F. Nef)?[4]

In the perspective of patristic and medieval philosophy which matters to us here, it is fitting to highlight again (see the "Introduction"): "For a medievalist, this characterization (onto-theo-logy) of the essence of Aristotelian metaphysics is valuable, in fact principally as *one of the Latin interpretations of Avicenna* which is imposed in the School" (A. de Libera).[5] And this Avicennian interpretation of Duns Scotus finds its source precisely in Thomas d'Erfurt, the sort of pseudo-Duns Scotus to whom Martin Heidegger unwittingly consecrated his dissertation of habilitation defended in Fribourg in 1915 (under the title *Treatise on the Categories and Signification in Duns Scotus*).[6] It is only one step further to conclude from there that onto-theology belongs only to this first theological model encountered by Martin Heidegger at the age of twenty-six.

However, one should guard against hastily made simplifications, which is rather like handing over our own weapons to those who always critique without ever doing anything constructive. That the structure of onto-theology does not exist in the texts, apart from a particular form of medieval tradition, does not invalidate it as an attitude, or as a manner of thought that is proper to avoid. The philosophers have done their best to castigate the inanity of the model, as have the theologians also in foiling its thrust. Both of them, however, do not remain any less dupes of the systematization to which they are themselves also subject. Those who reject the model rarely challenge the idea of a unificatory and transcendent principle. Likewise, the restoration of ancient categories (essence, substance, properties, or accidents) will not suffice to make us believe in a revival of "metaphysics itself" beyond phenomenology.[7] The "metaphysical restoration" faults phenomenology for having wanted to cut ties with every form of transcendence, while its "overcoming" has never in reality signified a de-valorization of the divine, but only another manner of approaching it and of speaking about it. Briefly, if onto-theo-logy can now consider itself dead as a concept, it has however not yet admitted its end as "prism"—that is, as "filter" which enlightens by a "new light" the "spectrum" [*spectre*] of the scheme of thought.[8]

But better options exist, I suggest, as far as the "overcoming of metaphysics" is concerned, particularly as it regards the question of God. For the "negative" side of onto-theo-logy as a nearly inaccessible model ought not to make us forget its "positive" side: the quest for an "other language" which is capable of saying the divine otherwise. One could always, as much as possible, accuse phenomenology of selling off the heritage of classical metaphysics. But one will not remove from it, however, the right and the prerogative of the opening of new realms of philosophy until now unexplored—we think here only of all the modes of the everyday described by Martin Heidegger and his followers: anguish, gossip, boredom, fatigue, lassitude, or even birth, joy, exaltation, jubilation, praise, and so on. If there is therefore something to conserve from the phenomenological attempt today, independent of its simplifications of the history of philosophy, it is indeed this opening toward unexplored possibilities. Following the example of a Picasso (cubism), a Monet (impressionism) or a Cezanne (post-impressionism), it opens up into new fields of research of which the very existence has been until now ignored—at least as being reachable from the starting point of philosophy.

God, the flesh, and the other: It goes without saying that we certainly have here three themes present from the beginning of the history of thought. But by starting from the suspension of the *quid* of the thing, and placing it in the perspective that starts from its "how" (*quomodo*), the "descriptive" treatment of these themes nevertheless allows to appear some unsuspected vantages on beings themselves: the primacy of relation over substance in Augustine, God as phenomenon in John Scotus Erigena, conversion as a mode of reduction in Meister Eckhart, flesh as a mode of visibility in Irenaeus, body as substance of the incarnation in Tertullian, and so on [see the "Introduction"]. In each case, what is seen is no longer the simple definition of things, but rather their mode of appearance, by which these phenomena, so essential to philosophy itself (God, the flesh, the other) have become today all the more recognizable in their own proper *ways of being*. The list of things "disclosed" is certainly important here, but not exhaustive. For the joys of patristic and medieval philosophy are so numerous, though not so easily discovered, and even less brought to light. In order to handle the question of God [part I], it will be fitting therefore *first* to follow—but only for a while—the "negative" side of the *overcoming of metaphysics in its tension with theology* (chap. 1: Augustine). Once the field opens, or rather the moving frontiers are established, then the "positive" side will come, as well as the dazzling *phenomenality of God in his theophany* (chap. 2: John Scotus Erigena) and its *reduction to an impossible reification* (chap. 3: Meister Eckhart).

The question of God [1st part], as that by which it is necessary to begin so as to define his mode of "entry" (into theology or philosophy), also determines our proper relation to our body [2nd part: the flesh] as also to those who surround us [3rd part: the other]. Once again, the "overcoming of metaphysics" will not be overcome or forgotten, finally, if one supposes that phenomenology still has to struggle only with a "structure" that is impossible to find anyway (onto-theo-logy). Rather, philosophy's task is to illuminate some "existentials" which compose our everyday (God, the flesh, the other). In its phenomenological and mystical mode in particular, patristic and medieval philosophy reveals some *habitus* or ways of being that we will reach in order to interrogate. With Augustine as a guide, we will therefore first show how metaphysics and theology remain always in tension when "God enters into philosophy," so that "all the categories *undergo a transformation* [*mutantur*] when they are applied to God" according to the beautiful adage of Boethius.[9]

Chapter 1

✦

Metaphysics and Theology in Tension (Augustine)

Transformation of the Categories

With Saint Augustine, something paradoxically "begins" in philosophy, or rather in theology. Of course, it goes without saying that Christian thought does not begin with the bishop of Hippo. All patristic thought which has preceded him (and we will see what this was in Irenaeus, Tertullian, and Origen) possesses its own proper greatness. But in this nascent and stormy fifth century—with the sack of Rome and the beginning of the redaction of *City of God* in 410—something new, or nearly new, begins to be forged within theology: namely its dialogue with Greek philosophy and thus metaphysics. The endeavor of Justin, where "philosophy passes over to Christ," maintains of course its proper value, as does the remarkable metaphysical translation of the theological in the famous "that is" of the Council of Nicaea.[1] But proper to the bishop of Hippo is the attempt to measure its scope, certainly not in order to regulate it, but rather to demonstrate its ambiguity. We cannot resolve the tension *between metaphysics and the theological* so easily. There are numerous contemporary attempts that desire to rediscover completely certain theological schemes independently of their historical and dogmatic deployment, the Trinity or the Incarnation for example. Such are the pretended virtues of a "de-hellenization of dogma" to which these attempts return, sometimes in an artless way (H. Küng). No one today can truly doubt the principle that "the hellenization of the faith is the counterpart to the de-hellenization of its content" (A. Grillmeier).[2] The question is therefore not, or at least not only about indicting the "indigence of language" and the "indigence of history" in order thus to speak the "truth of Christianity" (M. Henry). On the contrary, it is about measuring, more humbly but perhaps more faithfully, the capacity of men themselves to speak and to translate the "truth of God" into their own "language" as into their own "history."[3]

Theological categories do not overcome the concepts of metaphysics to the point of denying or abrogating them. On the contrary, *theologoumena* dialogue with *philosophemes* in order to compel a "transformation" within them (*mutantur* [Boethius]) since they cannot anticipate precisely when "God enters into philosophy." In this sense, God comes "into philosophy" only when he enters *also and at the same time* "into theology." Here the hypothesis of onto-theo-logy collapses on itself: not only in the sense that it is historically inaccessible, but because it remains principally impossible within the insoluble *tension of metaphysics and theology*. We are forced to recognize, then, that the old wineskins do not break so easily under the pressure of new wine, even though the good taste of the new would want to do without the bitter difficulties of the older. The new attempt of Saint Augustine in book V of *De Trinitate* of thinking God as "relation" is original in the way that it refers tirelessly to the older idea of "substance" in book VII, which shows precisely that the prime tension is always only moving toward resolution, and that every attempt at "overcoming" remains no less a profound "nagging conflict."

The Augustinian discovery of "relation" (book V) is abandoned in fact immediately upon its retrieval, by turning it toward its own transgression (book VII). Speaking hypothetically, if the particular relation to the tradition that we desire to preserve is primarily one of just fecundity, a relation of both "critique and dependence," and not of a simple rejection or arbitrary denial, then it would obviously be simple pretentiousness or an inordinate gamble to speak of a "missed turn" in Saint Augustine.[4] Turning back to the source does not mean "thinking against metaphysics" but "excavating the foundation and tilling the soil"[5]—"to sound" (*ergründen*) and no longer "to found" (*begründen*).[6] To dare to speak and to think a "missed turn" requires the implementation of a "long way to travel" from the source down the river, inasmuch as it was diverted in its trajectory by the alluvium of a falsely metaphysical "onto-theo-logical." Only that which is before and after the bend determines the turn as taken or missed—as if it were a country path (*Holzweg*) meandering just as much as it clears out an unknown way and opens toward a new future.[7] If in Saint Augustine there emerges an "official report of a violation," as if one were witnessing an accident, a true policing of concepts will attempt then to see there, instead of so much misconduct, an opening of a new way even in the failure at the bend. In this sense, the turn will not be termed a failure to the degree that there is found a way opening toward a certain "modification" [*deport*] outside of metaphysics (relation as first category), and will rather be termed a bare sketch, closed and diverted by the force of a tradition and a more potent straight path (the transfer [*report*] of relation in a scheme of substance). Like Galileo, the "discovering and concealing genius" [*dé-couvrant et re-couvrant*] according to Husserl (*Krisis*),[8] Augustine first "uncovered" in his *De Trinitate* "relation" as the first category of a Trinitarian God (book V), and then "covered over" his discovery in linking it continually—if not in its nature, at least in its activity—to substance, which is thus understood as a philosophical "reading" of the theological (book VII). The conversion of Augustine, conceptual at this point and no longer merely existential, is made thus the index of a true discovery and of a turn taken on the path of faith in search of understanding.

The Genius of the Discovery

Toward a Scheme of Non-Substantial Unity

Metaphysics in Theology. Like Irenaeus and Tertullian who both directly oppose Valentinian Docetism [see chaps. 4 and 5], book V of Saint Augustine's *De Trinitate* opens with the polemical prerogatives fixed by the Arian opposition.[9] Instead of denouncing their theses, the bishop of Hippo first denounces their strategy. Consider the direct application in Christian theology of a Greek metaphysical scheme (substance/accidents) to the Trinitarian God revealed in Jesus Christ (Father—Son—Holy Spirit): "Among all the arguments that the Arians usually oppose to the Catholic faith," insists Augustine, "there is one that they seem to consider the most ingenious of all traps [*maxime callidissimum machinamentum*]: When they say that all the qualifications or concepts applied to God are said not according to accident [*non secundum accidens*] but according to substance [*sed secundum substatiam*]."[10] This passage does not show us that Saint Augustine refuses to attempt a transcription of philosophy into theology—on the contrary, his task will be precisely to accomplish such a transcription in the framework of Christian orthodoxy. Rather it shows us only that the Doctor rejects an application that is too immediate and univocal. If God enters into *theo*-logy, how could it be that a dualizing Greek scheme would be able to articulate in a direct translation the total novelty of a God simultaneously one and triune?

As a mediated translation, the stakes of the Augustinian refutation of Arianism are thus doubled: first, a translation, with the risk, inversely, of never giving faith the means of transmitting its content (Grillmeier); second, one that risks losing the originality of the Trinitarian mystery revealed as such (contra Arianism). Here arises, then, a challenge that is double: how to come to terms with [*assumer*] the inheritance of the Aristotelian categories in order to speak the Trinity (theology), without falling into the double aporia either of pure substantiality or of simple accidentality (metaphysics)? I will now show that such aporias lead, theologically, to the impasses of tritheism and divine mutability.

Substance or the Danger of Tritheism. Apart from two inversions, in book V of *De Trinitate* Augustine explicitly rearticulates the Aristotelian list of categories. This is a confirmation, if there is one, of the necessity for the bishop of Hippo to place himself on the terrain designated by his adversaries: namely, Aristotelian metaphysics.[11] However, and here begins the decisive turn, the necessity of a non-immediate translation of the Trinity into conceptual language requires the abandonment of the too-costly (because too exclusive) alternative between substance and accidents: "Nothing in God has an accidental signification [*nihil in eo secundum accidens dicitur*], because there is no accident in him. Nevertheless [*tamen*], everything that one attributes to him does not have a substantial sense [*nec omne quod dicitur secundum substantiam dicitur*]."[12] Once again, this does not imply for the bishop of Hippo that substance and accidents are incapable of speaking God, but only that the primacy of the one (substance as logically and ontologically first) does not authorize one to conceive it independently of its relation with the others (nine secondary categories subject to change and related to substance as their necessary substrate). The Trinitarian God translated *immediately* as substance effectively leads to a tritheistic scheme unacceptable for the Christian faith: to understand God "in the non-accidental but substantial sense"—as "the Arians teach [*cum Ariani dicunt*]"[13]—is ineluctably to affix three substances (tritheism) wherever there are three "persons" (Father, Son and Holy Spirit).

Hence the following explication of the thesis of Arius, starting from his immediate transcription of the Trinitarian scheme into a philosophical model: "The Father who is the cause of all beings is absolutely the sole being without beginning [*anarchos*]. The Son, begotten by the Father, created and founded before the ages, was not before his generation . . . he has only been brought into being by the Father. He is not eternal, nor co-eternal, nor co-engendered with the Father."[14] Moreover, because every substance is spoken such that "by relation to itself [*ad se ipsum*]," neither the Father nor the Son remain then "for" the other, but only "apart" from the other.[15] "An immediate utilization of the schemes of Greek thought," says theologian Bernard Sesboüé, "leads to the placing of the Son on the side of the creature. But the Christian faith has always considered him on the side of God."[16]

The Accident or the Immutability in Question. The profit from rejecting pure substantiality is balanced by a loss no less considerable, namely, divine immutability. With its autarchic fate inadequate for speaking the reality of a God at once one and triune, this first and separated substance leaves no flexibility at all in its implacable incorruptibility as this single determination whose permanence guarantees only the eternity and immutability of God.[17] This is why, inversely, simple accidentality would not resolve the aporia either. To confer on God some "accidental" attributes (quantity, quality, place, time, etc.) actually renders unintelligible the very essence of God, at least from the vantage of classical theology, for which he "remains absolutely immutable" (*omnino incommutabilis manet*).[18] For the massive objection of the divine mutability that results from accidental attribution to God itself contains some unexpected difficulties, much like the no less evident objection of tritheism resulting from the determination of God as pure substance. Not that it would be necessary here to interrogate the immutability or impassibility of God (see Origen [chap. 8, below]), but only that substance is spoken of indifferently in temporality and in eternity, at least from within the theological repetition of Aristotelian metaphysical categories.[19] It is true that the immediate translation from Hellenism to Christianity of the determination of substance to the Father and the Son dangerously confers upon the one an immutable eternity (the Father as immutable and incorruptible substance) and to the other temporal becoming (the Son as human and temporal). Accidental attribution to God signifies in this sense not that the Trinity is no longer a substance—a very naive objection—but that the Son, as substance, in being incarnate, is given to thought by means of having the determinations of accidental categories (generation/corruption, increase/decrease, change, movement, etc.). "God against God": such is the dualism, not in the sense of a tension in the Moltmannian manner,[20] but of exclusion, by virtue of the opposition of contradiction between the Son as corruptible substance and the Father as incorruptible substance. This does not reach, as it were, the reality either of man, or of God, and even less the God-man. A single proposition suffices to condemn the "Son having begun to be [*coepit esse Filius*]" of the Arians in order to let appear the "Son ever-begotten" of the true Trinity:[21] "Father and Son are no longer qualifications of an accidental order [*non secundum accidens*], since the one called Father and the one called Son are eternal and immutable [*aeternam atque incommutabile*]."[22]

Tritheism and divine mutability are the two prohibitions imposed in order to exclude at once pure substantiality and simple accidentality and thus to be able to say, in one Greek conceptual scheme, the reality of a Trinitarian God. Is it sufficient then to renounce all properly philosophical argumentation such as the entire Greek scheme itself? Reborn here with force is the warning of A. Grillmeier—of which Michel Henry could also have been one of its addressees—of a necessary "hellenization of the faith as a counterpart to the dehellenization of its content" (supra). Saint Augustine, in a liberating gesture but not one of unbridled liberty, actually works an act of internal transformation of the elder (metaphysics), starting from which is also expressed the formulation of the totally new (revealed theology). Such is the condition for the "uncovering" of relation as the first category in book V of *De Trinitate*, the middle term between the complete substantialization of trinitary tritheism and the pure accidentality of a total modalism.

The Turn of Discovery

The Impasse: Quid Tres? "Therefore, there is no accidental signification in God [*nihil in eo secundum accidens dicitur*], because in him there is no change [*quia nihil ei accidit*]. Nevertheless, everything that is said about God is not said in a substantial way [*nec tamen omne quod dicitur secundum substantiam dicitur*]."[23] If the determination is neither merely accidental nor purely substantial, then what is it? The impasse stands there before us, an unavoidable obstacle without a detour. The bishop of Hippo asks, at the end of his research, in an extremely halting manner: "Since the Father and the Son and the Spirit are three, we seek to understand, therefore: three what [*quid tres sint*]?"[24] We have shown, moreover, that the Augustinian question "*quid tres?*" certainly remains in the sphere of ontology (the empire of *ti esti*, "what is"), which Richard of Saint Victor will later draw to the side of "*quis* (what)" and Bonaventure toward the "*quomodo*" (how).[25] What remains, and to this we shall return, is that this question extracted from book VII of *De Trinitate* resonates in a different way when read in light of book V. The question "three what?" is not here a quest for substance, since "everything is not predicated of God in a substantial sense," nor an assertion of accident, since in God "there is no accidental signification." It appears to be the case that only a third term, neither of the order of substance nor of accident, can pull theology out of the ruts of metaphysics—without, however, totally renouncing their usefulness. From out of this tension (between metaphysics and theology) a new way of seeing and thinking God is born, or rather, reborn—now within the context of Christian Trinitarian theology: namely, as "relation" and "person."

Relation: Ad Aliquid. When the turn is laid down, the discovery is laid bare [*Quand le tournant s'impose, la découverte s'expose*]. A something (*quid?*)—a concept or tool for thought—clears a new path and delivers us from the disastrous alternative. The passage is central here and discloses the turn: "But in God nothing is said according to accident, because in him there is nothing changing. It does not follow that all attribution has a substantial sense, however. There is also *relation*—literally 'movement toward something' [*ad aliquid*]—*for example* the Father toward the Son [*sicut Pater ad Filium*] and the Son toward the Father [*et Filius ad Patrem*] . . ."[26] Something (*quid?*) is therefore "relation to another thing" (*ad aliquid*): "movement toward," from one to the other (*esse ad*) and not the "to be in" of the same substance (*esse in*).[27] The example (*sicut*) serves here as a paradigm and not the reverse. Relation is not first discovered in order then to be applied to the Father, Son, and Spirit, but rather the necessary connection of the three (Father, Son, and Holy Spirit) requires the concept of relation, first applied to itself and only later to man. "Person" (*persona* or *hypostasis*) makes of God "someone" and not by way of transferring what is first a human category to the divine. It is actually the inverse because God is completely "relational" by nature, and it is within the context of Trinitarian Christianity, precisely, that the "movement toward" (*ad aliquid*) first takes on meaning. The movement of analogy so fully developed by Thomas Aquinas actually begins with Saint Augustine, for whom however the movement does not yet concern being but only relation itself.

The simple expression "*ad aliquid*," in its narrow formulation and apparent insignificance, ought not therefore to mask the grandeur of the discovery (not yet covered over) and the decision to turn (not yet missed because it was not yet taken). It is in the *prepositions* where a new *proposition* is often articulated. The nuggets often remain invisible to the inexperienced seeker (see the "Introduction"), as does the indomitable turn to the clumsy guide. It is by "extraction and transfer," as two subsequent operations, that there appears then the discovery where the turn arises.

Extraction and Transfer: A Double Operation. Precisely as a discovery, the "*ad aliquid*" is not left here to be only the translation into Latin of Greek philosophy's "*pros ti*," whch is ordinarily called "relation" and is fourth among the well-known enumeration of the ten Aristotelian categories, at least as received from the tradition: "substance [*ousia*], quantity, quality, relation (*pros ti*), place, time, position, possession, action, passion."[28] In a theological context, on the contrary, the fourth term (relation) becomes the first (taking the place of substance)—at least in book V of *De Trinitate*. Metaphysics seems not to be able to withstand the weight of the theological, and the tension always seems to be reaching its breaking point. But the operation is not so simple, at least from the vantage of *De Trinitate*, because the bishop of Hippo is not satisfied simply with "de-hellenization" in order to think otherwise. All the while retaining the Greek (the categories), Augustine sees its limits in expressing the Trinity (the primacy of substance and/or some other categories when one needs to resort to the realm of the accident), but is not satisfied with a facile rejection. Instead of jettisoning Hellenism altogether—a temptation which we have seen is ever-present even in theology today (Küng) as also in philosophy (Henry)—Augustine dares to transform it from within.

The first operation is "extraction." The category of relation (*secundum relativum*) is alone among all the Aristotelian categories capable of supporting—contra the "Son who has begun to be [*coepit esse*]" of the Arians—the sempiternal "Son ever begotten [*semper natus*]" of the "true" Trinity: "Relation is not an accident [*non est accidens*] because it is foreign to change [*quia non est mutabile*]."[29] Against the notion of divine mutability tied to the attribution of accidents, the category of relation (*pros ti*) is strangely extracted from the list of categories in order to be divorced from the modes of accidentality and change. Its rank is changed (from the fourth to the first) as well as its nature (no longer simply accidental or connected to substance). Such is the first condition of speaking the novelty of the God who is simultaneously one and triune.

Yet a second operation actually accomplishes the transformation—and brings to light the tension of metaphysics and theology: the "transfer" of this "extracted" category (relation) to another order or another kind of discourse which wants to proceed without reference to substantiality. Neither substance nor accident, suspended between these two orders, the "movement toward" (*ad aliquid*) seeks then another model, even a new "order" that would be adequate to the uniqueness of the object (*quid*?) that it seeks: God as Father, Son, and Holy Spirit. The quest for a conceptual adequation out of a metaphysical discourse (substance and/or accidental categories) capable of articulating the novelty of the mystery (relation) explodes metaphysics itself. In this way metaphysics is less negated or overcome than it is preserved and pushed toward its final limits by theology. The capacity to work and transform ("*mutantur*" [Boethius]) from within the categories of metaphysics measures the very power of God to speak to men in another and new form.

The Quest for Another Model

The Weight of Substance. The sliding of the concept of relation from its prepositional formulation as "movement toward" or "relation to" (*ad aliquid*) to its substantive form as that which is called "according to relation" (*secundum relativum*) appears only at the conclusion of this passage.[30] Everything appears as if practiced at this turning point is a resistance to substantification of relation (*secundum relativum*) to the profit of the single "*pros ti*" ("*ad aliquid*") as "movement toward"—and thus forcing the discovery to be concealed. By virtue of this search, perhaps all the more mystical as it is speculative, the quest for another model of attribution is again made explicit in book VII of *De Trinitate*: "But it is not at all that it is necessary to represent the Father [*ullo modo ita putandum est Patrem non dici*] by this model [of relative essence (*essentia relative*)]."[31] One will find therefore as many models and as many manners in which God enters into philosophy as there are "reluctances" of theology to install itself directly into the long sojourn that philosophy has prepared for it. The tension between metaphysics and theology is not reabsorbed here, but to the contrary, in this specific example of the formation of Trinitarian concepts in particular, it discloses both the force of its resistance and the weight under which it succumbs. The discourse of substance seems to be all the heavier as the attempt to pass it by seems impossible. From here the attempts to transform previous models are manifestly doomed to failure if they attempt to initiate a novelty that is absolute.

Attempts and Failures to Transform Previous Models. Three inherited models—attempts or temptations—test a total reformulation (in book VII): (a) the scheme of logical attribution (substance/accident); (b) the theology of the Word (signifier/signified); and (c) exemplarism (image/paradigm). The respective failures of each of these attempts at transformation will first invite silence (the impossibility of directly speaking God in a Greek scheme), before proffering a new word, however minimal and for Saint Augustine a word that is always still only stuttering (the necessity, that is, of saying something in order not to remain saying nothing).

(a) The classical scheme of logical attribution, in its own way, rehearses the model of substance and accident. Because their relation of strict opposition has sufficiently shown its aporias, this duality that is all-too sterile seeks to be overcome by means of establishing as fundamental rule of attribution the relation of attributes to their substance "as to their subject [*hypokeimenon*]."[32] Hence the complete revisiting by Saint Augustine at this point of the example in Aristotle of "color" related to a "colored body" as accident to substance, out of which he makes a paradigm in order to confirm the repetition of the former scheme of classical logic.[33] Yet the Doctor objects: "It is not certain that by this model it is necessary to represent the Father," because in God substance and attributes are one.[34] In order to return to Augustine's anti-Arian interpretation of "Christ the power and wisdom of God" (1 Cor. 1:24), in man "being" and "being wise" are distinguished since being man (substance) does not cease if a man ceases to be wise (accident). In God, by contrast, being and wisdom are united since "to be is to be wise." In God's case, the only means of attributing wisdom is in an "essential" manner, not only for Christ but also the Father and the Spirit (*Christum Dei sapientiam*).[35] But what remains in such a scheme, at least on a cursory reading, that pertains properly to the Father, Son, and Spirit?[36] Against the tendency, or rather Arian temptation, to substantialize the divine attributes in order to predicate them properly to each person of the Trinity, the scheme of logical attribution (substance/accident) fails by the fact that it cannot separate substance and attributes in God.

(b) However famous is the scheme of the theology of the Word, particularly in relation to the contemporary retrieval of the signifier/signified relation, it would no longer be able to resolve the aporia of a triune God who is neither purely substantial nor merely accidental. Its operation is double: first, bringing to light the relation of auto-dependence and of manifestation (*ostensio*) between human words and the realities to which they refer; second, reading into the figure of the Son, the "Word made flesh," the supreme dignity of the One who sends him, the Father: "If this temporal and ephemeral word that we express manifests itself [*se ipsum ostendit*] and manifests that of which we speak [*et illud de quo loquimur*], how much more the Word of God by whom all things were made? He manifests the Father exactly how the Father is [*quod ita ostendit Patrem sicut est Pater*]."[37] The advantage of this new scheme over the former consists in that it no longer thinks of the relation of the Father and the Son in terms of pure exteriority, logically articulated in the form of substance and accident, but according to a structure of return deciphered at the very heart of language and attempts to hold together the divine persons in identity and difference: the Word, even if it "manifests the Father exactly as the Father is," is "not what the Father is."[38] However, the bishop of Hippo can no longer retain this theological scheme of the Word, but here for the opposite reasons to those related to the first scheme. Whereas the substantialist model (metaphysics), reacting against all division in God, tends necessarily to substantialize the divine attributes, the verbal model (theology) makes the identity in nature of the Father and Son hard to see: the Son, as the signifying of a signified, "exactly manifests the Father" precisely by the fact that "he is not himself the Father." But how is it possible to continue to say that they are "of the same nature" or "consubstantial" (*homoousios*)?[39] In the verbal scheme there remains a certain amount of lingustic extrensicism and logic of expression, which is probably carefully avoided today by means of the aesthetic model of the Trinity, in its taking account of the sensible (Balthasar).[40]

(c) The last scheme, more Platonic then Aristotelian, is exemplarism, or the relation of image to paradigm. Would the Son relate to the Father as the "image" (*imago*) to its "model" (*exemplum*)? The usual deficiency seen in the relation of image to model would be enough to reject the proposal as null and void. The necessary equality of Father and Son would thus be superseded until we fell again into the aporias of Arianism. Yet if we kept in the background the Alexandrian distinction between "image" (*imago*) and "resemblance" (*similitudo*) as "image of the image" (*eikôn eikonos*),[41] the most proper characteristic of the image, when it refers to Christ, consists in rendering the model perfectly and without deficiency: "If the image [*imago*] truly and perfectly renders the object of which it is the reproduction [*perfecte implet illud cujus imago est*], then it is the image which is equal to the object and not the latter to its own image."[42] The previous aporia of the theology of the Word, consisting in an impossible identity of persons by virtue of an extrinsicism of the signifying/signified relation appears here to be resolved: as the river flows from its source without changing its nature, "the Word is able to be called the image of God since it is the Father who engenders him."[43] The ancient Platonic (or rather Plotinian) dichotomy of the image (*eikos*) and idea (*eidos*) appears reworked from within as God enters into philosophy. "The image without model [*imago sine exemplo*]": such is the necessary and no less surprising paradox of a God at once one and triune. "The Son is an image without its own model [*sine exemplo*] . . . He does not model himself on a guide that would precede him in relation to the Father from whom he is absolutely inseparable, since he is identical [*idipsum est*] to him who is his source."[44]

But what could be the rigorous meaning of an image without a model?

The bishop of Hippo responds: "Without a model for itself, it is a model for us [*illa sine exemplo nobis exemplum est*]."[45] The argument here moves from a solution to the Trinitarian aporia to an *imitatio Christi*, as if to speak first negatively about the failure of former schemes to signify God, and then positively about the ineluctable necessity of silencing philosophy, at least for a time, in order to allow God to enter *theo*-logically into *theo*-logy: "Therefore, when it is asked: what are these three things?, or, Who are these three subjects?," the author of *De Trinitate* humbly admits, "we try to find a specific or general name by which we can embrace these three; but no such name is presented to the mind because the transcendence of divinity surpasses the resources of ordinary speech."[46] Before the grandeur of the mystery, the philosopher is interrupted,[47] and the theologian is silenced as well.[48] Metaphysics, if not rendered destitute,[49] is at least *put in tension* with theology.

From the Entry into Silence to the Emergence of Word. When silence is imposed, God is exposed. The opening and closing of *De Trinitate* responds to this paradoxical and double exigence of silence and speech. The imperative of silence before the ineffable mystery is the first thing to say: "Now I will be trying to speak of things of which no one, especially me, is able to say as they are thought by God . . . , it is first to this Lord our God, about whom we ought always to think without being able to think him worthily, to whom, with praise, is due blessing at all times" (book V).[50] However, there emerges a necessary word—this is the last thing to say: "In order to speak of the ineffable, it is necessary to speak, as one is able, those things which one is not able to understand" (book VII).[51] The bishop of Hippo, more than any other, is wary of hemming theology in by the silence of a deviant mysticism of fusion. For him the absence of discourse is even graver than its exuberant presence. Only God himself can guarantee its legitimacy: "To the Lord our God . . . I pray that he will help me to understand and to explain this that I design as well as indulge my eventual offenses."[52] To speak about what "the three of the Trinity" are (*quid tres?*) while not losing sight, as a theologian, of "either his desire [*non solum voluntatis*] or his weakness of means [*verum etiam infirmatatis meae*]"[53] thus depends on the welcome one gives to a word, since it is necessary to speak about that which one cannot explain, and always on the foundation of silence because every human word will remain irremediably inadequate at expressing the profundity of the mystery.

As complex as philosophy and its models are, mere contradiction of its models does not suffice for theology. It is necessary to live in and to transform the tension between the disciplines. Certainly, when God enters into theology, it is fitting to speak otherwise and to speak about another: "If the god *enters into philosophy*, if therefore philosophy, or more precisely metaphysics assigns to him a determined place, a particular site," emphasizes Jean-François Courtine, "it is perhaps because God *has left philosophy*, in order to be spoken no more in a discipline that is characterized as special by relation to a more general quest pertaining to being as such, but in an 'other' doctrine, perhaps also in an 'other' language, with an 'other' syntax and according to 'other' principles."[54] And yet, at the very instant of the uncovering (of relation as first category in book V of *De Trinitate*), the covering over (of the transfer of relation to substance decidedly always posed as originary in book VII) also comes to birth. Would it be in this sense that the irresolvable *tension of the metaphysical and the theological* is made manifest, and that to yank theology to a place outside of philosophy is to leave theology to theologians in order better to delineate the proper field of philosophy? The question at the very least is posed, and the constant attempt (or temptation) to break them into distinct orders is not done without interrogating the history of concepts, which is never satisfied with such a neat distinction for the sake of a rapid solution. Augustine struggles more than he resolves the problematic—all to his honor. To accept the resistance or the pressure is not to renounce every position. On the contrary, it is simply to acknowledge a *theological language* always caught up in the movement of the *terms of metaphysics*: "Why do we call the three persons 'the three' (*tres personas*) . . . ?," as I have already asked following Saint Augustine, "except in order to say something [*aliquod vocabulum servire*] and not to remain with absolutely nothing to say [*ne omnino taceremus*], when we are questioned about these three [*interrogati quid tres*]?"[55]

The Act of Covering

Bearing in mind the previous failures at the transformation of ancient models, it is necessary to begin a new quest, from the starting point of silence, for this other model of theological attribution that we desperately seek. And yet, as I will now demonstrate, the theological explication of revelation is always held in tension with the metaphysics of relation—which is probably a signal that a rupture of orders is not reached in such a facile manner as is usually sought, at least when we carve things up precisely where the discourse appears all the more undividable—always, as we must, attempting to catch the divine in human language.

The Moment of a Crucial Decision

The Decision and Its Destiny. It is well known that the history of thought is first the telling of the story of its "decisions." If it is mainly about "turns" of thought, then it is here that the course thought takes is more important than its objects, its "way" more important than its terms themselves. The failure of previous models (logical attribution, theology of the Word, and exemplarism) remains too pregnant with possibility for Augustine not to call for another and new order. Everything occurs, from the beginning of book VII of *De Trinitate*, as if the *tension* in the passage from metaphysics to the theological was such that it seems better to reduce the tension by eliminating it rather than resolving it—"to cut the knot instead of untying it," as Kant said.[56] Is a crossing into this "other order" possible, and more importantly, is it a path which ought to be taken, both as means of classification and as a command: a non-metaphysical order on the one hand and a demand for another discourse on the other? The question certainly ought to be posed inasmuch as it haunts contemporary philosophical discourse, as well as theology itself. Reread, nevertheless, in light of Saint Augustine as well as from the paradigmatic example of the Trinity as "transformation" of the metaphysical categories when applied to God (Boethius), the response is not self-evident. The moment of crucial decision is at the same time the decision of a particular moment: a "decision of a particular moment" if the act of discovery of relation as first category (book V) always remains covered over by an ontology ever still substantial (book VII); and a "moment of crucial decision" to the degree that the destiny of Trinitarian theology itself (as understood by Thomas Aquinas) corresponds to the closing of the "discovery" or the "missing of the turn" (Augustine).

The Hypothesis of Another Order. When God enters into theology, is there a "distance infinitely more infinite" or the necessary passage to another order—from God as substance to the Trinitarian God of theology? The eminently Pascalian trait of the hypothesis cannot and ought not to hide the serious nature of the formulation in the bishop of Hippo.[57] According to Irénée Chevalier, the famous exegete of Saint Augustine's thought, the Augustinian request for a new mode of thinking possesses a certain legitimacy, since "relation in God comes neither from substance nor accident but rather constitutes *a separate order*."[58] The "relative qualification" of God for certain predicates called "according to relation" (*secundum relativum*)[59] is in fact opposed explicitly to its "absolute qualification" for other predicates called "according to substance" (*secundum substantiam*):[60] "Above all," indicates the Doctor of Hippo, "let us hold that every absolute qualification [*quidquid ad se dicitur*] of this sovereign and divine sublimity has a substantial signification [*substantialiter dici*]; and that a relative qualification [*quidquid ad aliquid dicitur*] pertains not to the order of substance but to the order of relation [*relative*]."[61] On the one hand, therefore, the predicates called "absolute" are proportionate to substance when they are "without relation to something" (*ad se dicuntur, non ad aliud*), designating God in his totality: for example, "wisdom" or "power." On the other hand, predicates called "relative" are related to relation, when "in mutual relation" with each other (*uterque ad invicem*), specifying what is appropriate to each of the divine persons: as "Son," "image," or "Word" specifically designate Christ.[62] To the two distinguishable orders (substance/relation) correspond thus two types of attribution (absolute/relative) and two fields of attributive categories (wisdom, power . . . /Son, Father, image, Word . . .). It is only a small step to conclude from here that the order of relation escapes the order of substance and renders it destitute. The *separate order* of relation (*ad aliquid*) seems prima facie to be established in that it apparently has a certain autonomy in its field of application (neither substance nor accident, but appropriate for each person in his relation to the others, etc.).

However, and it is here that the discovery begins to be covered over, or rather that the tension is measured: the scheme of substance, despite the request for a "separated order," does not cease to exercise its power on the bishop of Hippo, as if metaphysics ought never to innervate theology, and impose itself as co-inhabitant with it. Taking into account the whole of his work, at least the Trinitarian block from books V to VII in *De Trinitate*, requires us not to be satisfied only with the discovery of relation as first and new category that is neither substantial nor accidental (book V), but rather with how it opens in a new way onto substance that is impossible to erase completely from Trinitarian theology (book VII).

The Meaning of a Tension. Again, the hypothesis of a "separate order," however expressed here, appears to me all the more hopeless as it wants to ignore the metaphysical categories in which theology has been articulated from the beginning. The suspicion of dogma is in reality a mistrust of metaphysics and its categories (Küng). It is not an act therefore of the dogmatic alone, but also of philosophy. The principle of a necessary "hellenization of faith as counterpart to the de-hellenization of its content" (Grillmeier) does not indicate absolute submission to dogma without reflection, but tries on the contrary to recognize the metaphysical truth there (substance/accident) where it attempts to articulate the categories of theology (Trinity), thereby being transformed by theology (relation leaping out of the pair substance/accident). In this sense, it would be totally illegitimate to want to renounce all translation or hellenization. The *tension of metaphysics and theology* constitutes the dignity of theology more than it marks some supposed failure. The simplism of onto-theo-logy and the necessity of taking leave of it does not signify its ineptitude, as we have seen (see the "Introduction"), but instead, forgets to disclose the tension because it believes too quickly in some other resolution. It is not a choice between the exiting of metaphysics, on the one hand (to be without it, as Augustine understood, is an impossibility) and a simple transcription into theology on the other (the double aporia of the "tritheism of substance" and the "mutability of accident"). "Relation" (*ad aliquid*) in the Doctor of Hippo becomes the first category in place of substance (the former first category), but not like substance or any other category (being designated as neither substantial nor accidental). The gesture certainly makes a first break with metaphyics and effectively seeks a new order (book V). But substance, as we will see, remains afterward the support and substrate of relation itself (book VII). What is read here as a failure in reality indicates the way toward a greater success. Not in the sense that Augustine finds a way to resolve the tension, but rather that he brings it to light and maintains it there in the impossibility of its reabsorption. Theology is never more philosophical as when it imposes the obligation to pass through philosophy, all the more so when it would desire to surpass it. Likewise, philosophy is never more entangled with theology as when it raises itself to the level of a necessity, albeit in order to be transformed. The act of the recovering of relation (book V) by substance (book VII) therefore indicates the "resistance of substantialist ontology," not in the sense that it would be necessary either to be discarded or submitted to. Certainly a turn is deciphered in the recovering, but it is found in the tension more than in a resolution. The true interest of the metaphysical is found precisely here in its confrontation with the theological—and vice versa.

The Resistance of Substantialist Ontology

The Decision to Close. "Relation" (*secundum relativum*) or "relative qualification" (*quidquid ad aliquid dicitur*) does not suffice to constitute a "separate order" (Irénée Chevalier). However, such was the initial project of the bishop of Hippo. To consider merely the relentless energy with which Augustine tried to evade both pure substantialism and simple accidentality—no one can reasonably deny at least the validity of the attempt (book V). But to follow this hypothesis to its end, that is, to exclude completely substance from theology, would only, according to Saint Augustine, lead the [doctrine of the] Trinity toward the final point of failure: "Let the Son be qualified as essence [*ut essentia*] in a relative sense to the Father [*relative ad Patrem*]" (book VII).[63] The ultimate consequence would be to return to a total reversal of the Aristotelian scheme of the categories that would render "essence" or "substance" itself relative to relation, which in the Stagirite is actually the support of relation. It would then receive being and permanence only in and by such a mode of attribution: "But in order to return to the question," concludes the bishop of Hippo, thus achieving a definitive closing of the way that was opened, "if essence itself is taken in a relative sense [*si ipsa essentia relative dicitur*], then essence is no longer essence [*essentia ipsa non est essentia*]."[64] That "essence would no longer be essence" (*essentia non est essentia*)—not distinguished here from "substance" by Saint Augustine ["in our language (in Latin) essence and substance are commonly synonyms"][65]—is completely impossible for the Doctor of Hippo. Such a liberation of the category of relation from the scheme of substance—in the Aristotelian sense of *ousia* rather than the Thomist sense of *existentia* (we will return to this shortly)—will be realized only later in modern philosophy and will define its very task. Thus Descartes, who by the "inversion of categories" in the *Regulae*, holds that "absolute and relative are themselves relative terms" in their "relation to us." Then Husserl, who, in completing the hypothesis, also reduced the passage of the cogito to the *res cogitans*, and renders relation itself relative to a simple act of consciousness. In this sense and this sense alone, the *ad aliquid* will be act rather than thing—a deliverance which is already played out, as I will demonstrate, in the interpretation of "conversion" as mode of "reduction" in Meister Eckhart (see chap. 3).[66]

The Unexpected and the Absurd. The hypothesis of an *exit from the categories*, or the notion of an "*essence itself relative*," which therefore "*would no longer be essence*," remains, for Augustine at least, just as unexpected in its decisiveness (*inopinatissimus*) as it is absurd in its reasoning (*absurdum*).

First, the unexpected decision is like the warrior who, in Latin terms, attacks by surprise the one who has not kept on his guard (*inopinatum*). To say that "essence is not essence" (*ut ipsa essentia no sit essentia*) assumes a meaning all the more "unforeseen or unexpected" (*inopinatissimus sensus*) as such a possibility always remains, at least as understood in a pre-Cartesian tradition, unthought and unthinkable.[67] The decision to close the hypothesis of an absolute primacy of relation over substance does not uniquely consist here merely in not tolerating the possibility that an essence is able to be taken in a "relative" sense: this goes for "all essences" (*omnis essentia*), for example when one designates the attribution of the relative "master" to the substance "man" (the master), while master itself can also designate a substance.[68] The closure of the hypothesis finds its key, furthermore, in the definitive refusal of a designation of "essence itself" (*ipsa essentia*), in its nature, as "relative"—which would be a suppression of "nature" itself. According to Saint Augustine—and this should be understood in the "realist" mode of the Aristotelian categories—if there is not some "thing" (*quid*) to which relation is (as it were) related, then "relation" itself is suppressed.

The absurd or the non-sense, for the bishop of Hippo as for all Greek metaphysics, leads to the point of thinking for example "man" or "horse," said to "exist by themselves," as terms themselves relative. For, "if there was no man, that is, a substance, then there would be no person to call 'master' in the relative sense (and) if the horse was not an essence, there would be no occasion for speaking of a 'draft horse' in a relative sense."[69] The refusal to speak of the "essence itself" (*ipsa essentia*) in a relative sense, thus putting to the test the very categories of the discourse from which it derives, finds its source therefore in the resistance of an ontology that is completely Aristotelian, according to which, as the Stagirite expresses it: "it is evidently necessary that, if one knows a relative in a definite way, then one knows also in a definite way *that to which* it is relative."[70] Because to render "essence itself relative" is immediately to suppress the very support of all relation and at the same time to invalidate all predication, the resistance of an ontology of substance is forced into condemning as non-sense, or even as absurd (*absurdum*), the hypothesis of an absolute primacy and of an autarchy of relation over substance: "To give to substance a relative sense would be an absurdity [*absurdum*]," asserts Saint Augustine, "because everything subsists by relation to itself [*omnis res ad se ipsam subsistit*]. How much more so with God [*quanto magis Deus*]?"[71]

Our concern now appears fully evident. The tension of the metaphysical and the theological is held within the "force of resistance" of metaphysics itself. Would it be necessary to win the combat, and even to enter into the battle—as if the philosopher in his autonomy would always accuse theology of attempting its so-called annexation? In a new way here the position of the Doctor of Hippo has something to teach us. Because, far from demanding either an "exit from metaphysics" or a "de-theologization of philosophy," the study of medieval philosophy today finds in reality its meaning in the act of the "theologization of metaphysics itself." Of course, this is not to take leave of philosophy, as is sometimes wrongly believed, but rather on the contrary to remain and attempt the transformation of philosophy from within. Certainly, and I have emphasized, the "other language" of philosophy, and of phenomenology in particular, retains its meaning—especially in the sense that it brings to light new concepts (infra). But the dependence of metaphysics itself on theology—not to be confused with the innovation of phenomenology relative to the corpus of metaphysics and theology—is probably, in the first place at least, that which renders the "exit" all the more awkward as it remains always impregnated by that on which it depends, namely, metaphysics itself. The "other language" of that which is to come in the present work—the phenomenon (Erigena), the reduction (Meister Eckhart), the visibility of the flesh (Irenaeus), its consistency (Tertullian), and its conversion (Bonaventure), intersubjectivity (Origen), its angelic model (Thomas Aquinas), and its singularity (Duns Scotus)—on the contrary stems from this very tension of metaphysics and theology.

In the context of philosophy, "absolute and relative" would never have in this sense been called "relative themselves in their relation to us," as in Descartes (supra), if for example Augustine had not first attempted, in a mainly theological way, to think the "*ad aliquid*" as pure relation in the Trinity in book V of *De Trinitate*. As often happens in the history of philosophy, the modification of concepts pass by God first in order then to be applied to man (we will see the exemplary way in which the status of alterity in contemporary accounts derives from the status of angels in the Middle Ages [chap. 8]). In this sense one does not have to regret that the bishop of Hippo in his *De Trinitate* had related "relation" (book V) to "substance" as its only possible support (book VII) since this covering over makes patently clear, if not the exit of theology from metaphysics, at least their necessary and insoluble tension.

The Categorical Function of Relation. The question imposes itself with insistence. Faced with the prohibition of an essence itself relative, and as much "unexpected" as "absurd," is there still a way to bring the gesture to its term and to liberate definitively relation (*secundum relativum*) as a separate order? Otherwise said, could the bishop of Hippo not have broken under the weight of an ontology of substance and be delivered from the force of its resistance? Even though not envisagable according to an Aristotelian scheme, the only operation which had perhaps allowed, if not the liberation, at least the untying of "relation" enchained to "substance," had been that which does not accord (as book V does) "absolute qualification" to substance, and therefore implicitly does not accord "relative qualification" to a categorical function. Two reasons, however, prohibit such an emancipation: a dogmatic and a polemical one. First, the dogmatic reason: the father-son "relation" introduces an asymmetry of correlation (the impossible inversion of terms)[72] not suggested by the Aristotelian model of "*pros ti*" which is based on the reciprocal relation among friends or neighbors.[73] Because it would be necessary to respect the equality of the divine persons, and that this asymmetry puts it in danger for Saint Augustine, the equality takes the step beyond asymmetry and therefore asserts substance over relation.[74] The polemical reason: the question precisely of the equality of the divine persons, largely presented in the polemic of book VI of *De Trinitate*[75] against the Arian inequality,[76] confers a certain occasional character and a primarily heuristic origin to the conceptualization of relation in Saint Augustine. As Irénée Chevalier has rightly emphasized, this explains, perhaps, why "relation is never presented for itself, as a prolonging of the reflection for the sake of satisfying the legitimate avidity of the spirit (but) rather gives the impression of being unilateral and incomplete."[77]

Where is the significance of the discovering of "relation" (*ad aliquid*) but in the very incompleteness of the thought, at least in its quasi-immediate recovering? "Above all let us maintain," states the bishop of Hippo, "that every absolute qualification of this sovereign and divine sublimity has a substantial signification; however [*autem*], a relative qualification pertains not to the order of substance but to relation."[78] How, indeed, by a simple juxtaposition of two types of attribution (*autem*) and in the enigmatic conciseness of the formula, no more or no longer to connect from then on relation to substance as its necessary substrate, even though it would happen, moreover, by extraction and transfer, which as we have seen, is neither categorical nor accidental? The tension remains here insoluble as it stands between, on the one side, the introduction of the term of relation—against the aporias of Arianism (tritheism and divine mutability)—that is neither substance nor accident, and, on the other side, the retro-application of relation to substance as its support and necessary foundation (distinction between absolute and relative qualification). Non-categorical as far as *name* (book V)—"in God nothing is said to be according to accident . . . it does not follow, however, that every attribution has a substantial sense . . . , there is also relation"[79]—the "*ad aliquid*" does not remain less as an ordinary category as to *its function* (book VII): "if there was no . . . substance, there would no longer be one who could be named in the relative sense."[80] The discovery of the theological in book V for the sake of properly speaking of the Trinity (the *ad aliquid*) gives way under the weight of metaphysics in book VII in always connecting it to a "*quid*" capable of justifying the question of "*quid tres sunt?*"[81] In *Saint Bonaventure et l'entrée de Dieu en théologie*, I have shown that Augustine's avowal of a quasi-failure to say what there is to the notion of person—"one indeed answers three persons [*tres personae*], not that it might be spoken, but that we might not remain with nothing to say [*non ut illud diceretur sed ne taceretur*]"[82]—comes not from the impossibility of giving an intelligible account of *persona* in order to articulate the *Trinitas*, but from the question which is posed (*quid?*) from the beginning. One will probably have to wait until the interrogation of "*quid tres sunt?*" of Augustine passes progressively to that of the "*quis tres sunt?*" in Richard of Saint Victor and the "*quomodo tres sunt?*" of Bonaventure in order for the "empire of the *ti esti*" which governs metaphysics and theology even now to be finally and definitively developed.[83]

Relation in Becoming

Subsistent Relation. By means of an overly rapid reading, one would wrongly accuse Aquinas's notion of "subsistent relation" (*relatio subsistens*) of simply achieving the work of substantial recovering begun by Augustine—the first term distinguishing the persons ("relation") and the second unifying them in a single essence ("subsistent"). Certainly, to define with Thomas Aquinas in the *Summa Theologiae* the "divine person" (*persona divina*) as a "relation as subsisting" (*relationem ut subsistentem*) is to pose the relation as "mode of subsisting" or as "way of substance" (*modum substantiae*) (1a q. 29).[84] But for Aquinas substance is not only "mode of subsistence" or "dwelling," despite the etymology of the term (*sub-sistens*) and Heidegger's error in interpreting it.[85] The *Summa* in reality states the inverse, at least when it understands the definition of the being of God as "act of existence" (Aquinas) and not "mode of subsistence" (the false accusation of Heidegger): "Being [*esse*] is said in two ways," insists the author of the *Summa*, "in a first sense in order to designate the act of existence [*actum essendi*], in a second sense it indicates the composition of a proposition [*compositionem propositionis*] . . . If one takes Being in the first sense, we can neither understand God's being [*esse Dei*] nor God's essence [*nec eius essentiam*]" (1a q. 3).[86] The debate concerning being—"with" or "without" being—is well-known and there is no need to revisit it here, except perhaps to insert into the debate the specificities of "relation" in the Trinity. This much, moreover, is accomplished by its author, Jean-Luc Marion, who, in a famous retraction, made the point. *God without* being, most fully understood in Thomas Aquinas, is not understood as a God without "acts of being" but only of a God whose being would be falsely extended to the "community of entities" of all beings. Said otherwise, Thomistic being itself paradoxically escapes "the prism of onto-theology," however sought and hardly ever found (see the "Introduction").[87]

Far from being relieved or resolved, the *tension* of metaphysics and theology therefore remains understood in Thomas Aquinas. Or rather, it is reinforced all the more as it is stated in the language of being (*esse*). And thus the transformation penetrates into its mold: it is no longer only *ousia* as "substance" or "mode of subsisting" which pertains to theology when God enters into philosophy (Aristotle perhaps), but *existence* as "act of being," that is to say, as gift *before* being, or better as gift *for* being (Thomas Aquinas). Aristotelian "substance" is distinguished from the Thomist "act of being," for that which is hypothetically true of *ousia* according to Martin Heidegger—"being receives the imprint of the presence and the consistence in the sense of *subsistence* (*ousia*)"[88]—will never be the *esse essendi* of Thomas Aquinas. Aristotle's "*being in act*" is never identified with the "act of being" of Thomas Aquinas, precisely because the second *gives* in order to be while the first *is* in order to give.[89]

The exit from metaphysics—the detachment and then reattachment of the category of "relation" to the substance/accident pair—paradoxically operates *within* metaphysics itself, at least when it passes through the filter of medieval philosophy. Similar to the ruse of the hedgehog (in Grimm's fairy tale) placing his hedgehog wife at the finish and passing himself off as "already there" wherever the hare runs, metaphysics is therefore "always there" when theology is tried within it—but the difference is that the second totally modifies the first (primacy of relation over substance in Saint Augustine), all the while serving it (modification of the concept of substance of "being" in Aristotle to the "act of being" in Aquinas).[90] The metaphysical categories "are transformed [*mutantur*] when applied to God" (Boethius).[91] Theology does not destroy them in order to pass to another order, but only works from within them in order to attempt to render them adequate, as far as possible, to the novelty of the object studied: the Triune, and therefore relational (*ad aliquid*) God.

Extension of Relation. One cannot reproach in this sense Thomas Aquinas, as some do, for having falsely separated God *and* the world, the immanent Trinity *and* economic Trinity, God *ad intra* (Ia, q. 2–43) *and* God *ad extra* (Ia q. 44–119). A unified reading of the *Prima Pars* of the *Summa*, starting from the concept of relation, shows on the contrary, in the *ad aliquid*, the community of relation of God to himself (*ad intra*) as also to the world (*ad extra*). The personal God defined as "subsistent relation" (*relatio subsistens*) in the treatise on the Trinity (Ia. Q. 29) is also the God who is author of the world thought as "relation" (*relatio*) in the treatise on creation: "creation posits something in created beings, but only *according to relation* [*secundum relationem*]" (Ia q. 45).[92] The homonymy of "relation" here, in the double relation of God to himself (Trinity) *and* to the world (creation) posits a "dependence [*dependentia*] of created being to the principle that has established it" such that the category of "relation" (*relatio*) designates what is proper to the "creation" (*creatio*): "*creatio est de genere relationis*" (*Contra Gentiles*, II, 18).[93] Far from the false accusations of Heidegger concerning a creation thought as "production," to which we will have occasion to return,[94] in Aquinas the extension of "relational" relation that defines the Trinitarian structure of God himself (the person) to his relation to the world (creation) holds together in unity the *Deus ad intra* and *Deus ad extra*, immanent and economic Trinity, God in himself (*per se*) and God for us (*pro nobis*). The tension of the metaphysical and the theological does not appear here to be resolved but rather extended. Relation and substance: the connection between them applies not only to the Trinity (Saint Augustine), but also to the creation (Thomas Aquinas).

Negation of Relation. However, a question remains, which could allow contemporary philosophy to interrogate medieval philosophy, and its modification of the Aristotelian scheme in the name of God's entry into theology (Trinity). The category of "relation," as is well known, is now largely utilized by every history of philosophy, to such a degree that its primacy over substance, at least at the opening of book V of Augustine's *De Trinitate* (and covered again in book VII), seems today to have become the common currency of phenomenology—for example, in Emmanuel Levinas: "Being before the existent, ontology before metaphysics . . . The *terms must be reversed*," one reads in *Totality and Infinity*. "This 'saying to the Other'—this *relationship with the Other* as interlocutor, this *relation* with an existent—precedes all ontology; it is the ultimate *relation* in being. Ontology presupposes metaphysics."[95] In short, and the issue is clear at least since the Levinasian reversal of Heidegger's comprehension of being where the other is subsumed as one among other categories: relation definitively outweighs substance (agreement with Heidegger on the refusal of reification) and metaphysics as relation over ontology as much as being (the difference between Heidegger and Levinas). The tension of the categories of classical metaphysics (substance/accident) with Augustinian Trinitarian theology (discovery of relation as first category), does not therefore seem resolved (with no solution found or sought), but does at least seem surpassed (in a definitive exit from substantialism). The deliverance of relation from the prism of ontology, commencing with Saint Augustine, is certainly accomplished with Levinas, but pays the price of a strong secularization of relation, where, now, it "would be false to qualify this metaphysical relation [in the Levinasian meaning of the term] as *theological*" (Levinas).[96]

One reaches then the questioning that now must be raised, albeit for the renewal of the concept of the Trinity: "The relation [*rapport*] to the Other [in Levinas] is thematized on several occasions as a relation [*relation*]. By what right does one use here a category eminently *ordained for ontology* in order to attain that which, par excellence, is supposed to escape ontology?" (Marion).[97] The quest at least has the merit of "pushing" the hypothesis "to its end": that is, of extricating it from its last entrenchments and exhausting its possibilities. If it is a matter here of unraveling the relation of substance, or better of ordering ontology to an alterology, would it not be fitting to eliminate the usage of "relation" completely, since its term always supposes some external poles that it does not intend, and a sort of "overhanging attitude" [*attitude de surplomb*] which is not fitting for the veritable "Conciliation" (*Austrag*) of being and the existent? The interrogation is certainly radical, but is at least worth being raised. Otherwise said, and in our own proper terms: would not the "metaphysical relation" in the Levinasian sense of the term (alterology) actually be "metaphysical" in the classical sense of the term (relation between poles)? Whether by inverting the categories (primacy of relation over substance) or exiting from them (alterology without ontology), is it not true that one still remains a slave to metaphysical categories themselves by dint of always using them?

It is clear that the tension between the metaphysical (substance) and the theological (relation) in Saint Augustine, or of Levinasian metaphysics (alterology) and Heideggerian ontology (conciliation), is far from being weakened and even less dissolved. The exercise of philosophy always remains precisely to be said in a language which is hardly sufficient for it, as if words are never able to suffice, particularly when it is a matter of speaking of God. To pass to the "other language" (as I have emphasized) that negates neither the tension nor accepts onto-theology except as a "prism" for thought (see the "Introduction"), one comes perhaps to accept the displacement (*metaphorein*) while at the same time believing oneself still capable of predication concerning God, particularly relation itself: "It would be necessary for us to understand that this category of relation [*hanc categoriam relationis*]," indicates Erigena, whose radical apophaticism will now be our focus (chap. 2), "following the other categories [*sicut et ceteras*], is also predicable of God only in a metaphorical sense [*translative*]." Indeed, the Carolingian continues, displaying an insightful understanding of the aporia of Saint Augustine's *De Trinitate*, "the category of relation will no longer be counted among the ten kinds of category, if it becomes predicable in the sense proper to God [*si proprie de Deo dicitur*]."[98]

✦

Thought is radicalized when it attempts to say something new. The price to pay is certainly a tendency to reject everything else. Such is, however, not the gesture of phenomenology nor of medieval philosophy itself—in which case it would be necessary for us to continue the interrogation of tradition and to dialogue with our own modernity. It would be a matter therefore of speaking "God" (1st part) before describing the "flesh" (2nd part) and of clarifying the structures of the "other" (3rd part). The *tension of the metaphysical and theological* in Saint Augustine (chap. 1) passes then to the *phenomenological* in John Scotus Erigena (chap. 2), in order finally to be found in the *reduction* at work in the concept of conversion in Meister Eckhart (chap. 3). After the attempt of an exit from metaphysics as complex as it is difficult to carry out (Augustine), the God of Christianity is revealed now as a "*phenomenon*" in the double meaning of the term: phenomenologically, on the one hand, and in its everyday sense on the other (Erigena). The God of Christianity is "*God phenomenon*" in the sense that, phenomenologically speaking, he "appears [*apparuit*]" and "is manifest" (*phaînô*) according to a strange correspondence between theophany in Erigena (*Periphyseon*) and the definition of phenomenology in Martin Heidegger (*Sein und Zeit*). And the God of the Christians is also a "phenomenon" in the current sense of the term, in the measure that he sometimes shows, I suggest, an individuality such that we are dazzled at the humility in the mystery of the incarnate Word: "Do not be surprised that the flesh, that is, mortal man, is capable by grace to become a child of God, when it is even more miraculous [*maioris miraculi*] that the Word is made flesh" (Erigena).[99]

Chapter 2

God Phenomenon (John Scotus Erigena)

The transition through the displacement and overcoming (chap. 2) of the category of "relation" (chap. 1) simply does not work. For if it is necessary "to say something in order not to be left saying nothing at all" (Augustine), then what we have just said ("relation," as specific to the Trinity, was always referring to substance) could be rendered mute if we were content to speak "metaphorically" about God, without ever ascribing anything to him "literally" (Erigena). The tension of metaphysics and theology certainly appears indissoluble, but its resolution will not come through its denial, which bears the opposite risk of destroying what we had yet to build: this progressive measuring of the force of resistance of substance, which is impossible, or at least very difficult, to surpass (chap. 1). The other way remains (chap. 2): not a way that forgets the dialogue with metaphysics, but one which maintains it, so much so that it opens onto "another phenomenality," or even better, onto a new mode of speech. Interesting indeed. John Scotus Erigena is not the kind of thinker who claims absolute novelty. His deep knowledge of Greek, so rare in the Carolingian epoch, on the contrary, makes him particularly suitable for our discussion, if also rather controversial. In this sense, and this sense alone, if there is a necessary exit from ontology toward phenomenology—speaking from within the framework of a contemporary rereading of the Erigenian corpus—then it is precisely in this sense that the debate about the divine is all the more "ontologized" (metaphysics) as it causes another figure to appear, that of a "phenomenalized" God (theophany): "It is not only the divine essence [*essentia divina*] that connotes the word God," emphasizes Erigena, gesturing toward a radical break, "but also this mode [*sed modus ille*] under which God is shown [*ostendit*] to the intellectual and rational creature . . . which is frequently also called God by Holy Scripture. The Greeks are accustomed to calling this mode a theophany [*theophania*], that is, an appearance of God [*hoc est Dei apparitio*]."[1]

Theophany and Phenomenology

We must nevertheless be careful here. In proposing the mediation of essence (*essentia*) by theophany (*theophania*), or of the ontic (*quid*) by this mode (*modus ille*) of the appearance of God, the exiting from metaphysics is not simplified. Far from it. On the contrary, it is now further in question. What is new in Erigena (chap. 2) relative to Saint Augustine (chap. 1) is not the pursuit of a convolution of the Aristotelian model of the categories, at the risk of totally transforming it in order to adapt it to the Trinity (see Thomas Aquinas, above). It is an act, rather, of a "paradigm shift," as in the celebrated distinction of "ordinary science" and "science in crisis" of Thomas Kuhn.[2] There where one (Thomas Aquinas) perfects the model of "relation" even to the extension of the Trinity to the entire creation, the other (Erigena) bursts the paradigm itself—preferring theophanies to categories, modes of being to being, and the phenomenal to the substantial: "Behold an example of this theophany," states the Carolingian, "'*I see the Lord sitting*' (Is. 6:1), and other analogous formulae, since it is not the essence of God [*non est essentia Dei*] that the prophet sees, but a theophany [*theophania*] created by Him."[3]

With Erigena therefore, a further step is somehow made. We do not remain in the sphere of the metaphysics of the categories (Augustine, Thomas Aquinas), nor do we require the notion of the ineffable in order somehow "to think the unthinkable" (Denys the Areopagite).[4] The *Erigenian theophany* is distinguished from *Dionysian apophaticism* (to which we will return), on the one hand, insofar as it argues with metaphysics in order to be divested of it rather than setting it aside by ignoring it, and, on the other hand, insofar as it orients all movement of divine kenosis toward its carnal incarnation, and further, that it withdraws into the dazzlement of its unthinkable distance (see part II, "The Flesh"). With John Scotus Erigena one certainly exits from the tension of metaphysics and theology, since theophany, in the guise of the Christian mode of phenomenology, somehow mediates by *thirds* in order to transgress duality. But the exit is not accomplished by virtue of a "jump," no more than it makes use of biblical categories in order to play against the Hellenic. Inheriting in a unique way the *logica vetus* (old logic) of Boethius (evidently ignored by Denys), Erigena struggles anew with Aristotelian categories. As I will demonstrate, it is better to say that he "destroys" or rather "deconstructs" them, not by rejecting them according to this or that position, but by repudiating any "position itself" as still a mode of reification and seeking to think somehow "beyond all affirmation and negation." In short, apophaticism is not the only discourse coming out of theology to be able to "play" with phenomenology.[5] "Theophany" proposes another partner, more worthy and even more fit for a radical engagement. Hence, the etymological work on the Greek term "*theoyphania*" by the pen of John Scotus Erigena is probably capable of rivaling, or at least of foreshadowing, certain later phenomenological works which could even implicitly depend on it (Heidegger): "And it is fitting to notice," emphasizes the Erigenian in a paradoxical preface to his translation of Denys, "that *theophany* is virtually able to be interpreted as *THEOYPHANIA*, that is, as *appearance of God* or *illumination of God*;

if it is true that *everything that appears* shines and is derived from the word *PHAINÔ*, that is, *I shine* or *I appear*."[6]

"Everything that appears shines [*omne quod apparet lucet*] and comes from the verb *phainô* [*et a verbo phainô derivatur*], that is, I shine or I appear [*id est luceo vel appareo*]" (Erigena). The informed reader, of course, would see here Heidegger's definition of the "phenomenon" as recorded in paragraph 7 of *Sein und Zeit*: "that which shows itself, manifests itself." For Heidegger likewise derives the definition of the phenomenon from the Greek "*phainesthai*" (to show itself) and from its root "*phainô*" ("to disclose," "bring to light"). Perhaps it is the case after all that *theology* has something to say to *phenomenology* concerning visibility or manifestation (theophany as mode of phenomenality), if not also the inverse.[7]

"The astonishment of Erigena's contemporaries before this *immense metaphysical epic*, manifestly unbelievable," according to Etienne Gilson,[8] only intensifies for us moderns who, on the one hand, often see in the Carolingian era a simple step of transition or "middle age" between the church fathers and the Scholastics, and on the other hand, find in Erigena that which we have been looking for elsewhere: the sense of a phenomenality freed from an essentialist metaphysic. We will not explore the relation of Erigena to Heidegger any further here, in order not to fall into a crude anachronism, nor will we pass directly from Denys to Erigena, at least in order no longer to make one (Erigena) the simple servant of the other's thought (Denys), as is often thought. We are thus compelled to return to Erigena himself precisely in his distance from the Areopagite, and to shed light on some of the most contemporary phenomenological applications. Sometimes an unfaithful translator despite his declaration of principles, Erigena was in this sense rather preoccupied with "justifying his own teaching" or of "understanding Denys better" rather than simply "making Denys intelligible to the Latins" as in the formula of Albert the Great devoted to Aristotle.[9]

From the Apophatic to the Meta-Ontological

The Apophatic: The Deviation from Denys

Distance and Proximity. John Scotus Erigena is too often reduced to performing the simple role of "translator" or "introducer" of negative theology into the Latin world. Of course, it is the case that he explicitly claims this for himself at the beginning of his commentary on the *Celestial Hierarchies* of Denys. Fearful of being castigated as an "unfaithful translator" (*ne forte culpam infidi interpretis incurram*), he puts on the hat of *literal translator* of the Dionysian corpus (called *interpres* in Latin) and not of commentator or exegete who would be introducing his own personal touch to the works: "If you judge my text to be obscure and less evident than the aforementioned interpretation," he confesses with circumspection, "then you see me as the *translator* of this work [*interpretem huius operis*] and not its commentator [*non expositorem*]."[10] But in spite of such declarations, the Irishman does not remain any less an *interpreter* (*expositor*) of the Dionysian corpus in the English sense of the word—insofar as his attempt at transcription far outstrips and goes beyond the preceding translation of Hilduin: "John Scotus presents a translation such that nothing appears to contradict his essential theses."[11] Out of his (own) theses, that of an exit from affirmation and negation, no longer by means of the ineffable transcendence of eminence (Denys) but rather by the carnal immanence of a shining theophany, is probably his most original contribution: "This notion of theophany controls perhaps the entire economy of Erigenism."[12] In Erigena, a *proximity* of man to God establishes itself, therefore, somehow by means of the theophanic modes of divine manifestation, precisely where Denys always maintains a *distance* in his apophasis. In Erigena, negative theology is not (only) a *hermeneutical* question about the status of discourse and its possible overcoming, but first a *phenomenological* affair about visibility and its possible transcription in terms of its capacity to be described. The point of difference between Erigena and Denys is that Erigena neither "liberates Christian theological concepts from their Greek horizon," nor maintains God in "the unthinkable distance of his dazzlement."[13]

It is well known that Denys was the first to distinguish the *apophatic* from the *cataphatic*, the way of negation from the way of affirmation (thus making here negation not the inverse of affirmation but beyond any position whether affirmative or negative).[14] Erigena, however, "emphasized the distinction with more insistence and vigor than Denys"[15]—to the point of consecrating for the first time in history these two ways no longer as two modes of thought in general (Denys), but as two unique branches, if not of, theology itself, at least of a constituted "discipline": "Mystical theology [*mystica theologia*] is divided into two general branches of a *logical discipline* [*in duas maximas logicae disciplinae dividitur partes*], that is to say, into *cataphatic* on the one hand and *apophatic* on the other [*cataphicam plane et apophaticam*], which correspond respectively to Being and non-Being [*id est, in esse et non esse*]. In this context, one should utilize the rules of *analysis* [*analyticae artis*], and Denys very clearly warns us that we can only reach the truth through the practice of the privation [*per privationem omnium*] of everything that comes back into the field of discourse or thought in order better to reach the super-eminence of his Essence."[16]

The Ontologization of the Debate. The terms of the division already no longer correspond to those in force in Denys. The transfer of the cataphatic onto "Being [*in esse*]" and of the apophatic onto "non-Being [*et non esse*]" produces an *ontologization of the debate* proper to the Erigenian, insofar as *Being* and *non-Being* no longer appear exclusively as categories to overcome (in the same capacity, for example, as the knowable and non-knowable in

Denys) but are identified here explicitly with the *affirmative* and *negative* ways.[17] Besides the influence of Boethius and his celebrated Latin introduction of the term "nature" (*natura*) to mean "being" (*esse*),[18] the principle reason for this ontologization of negative theology in Erigena from the beginning of his *Periphyseon* is to fully establish this "metaphysical epic" as a treatise of theology engaged with and in tune with the "things which are" (*ea quae sunt*) and "those which are not" (*ea quae non sunt*): "The principle and fundamental division of all things into either that which can be perceived by the intellect or that which surpasses its scope, occurs between that which is [*ea quae sunt*] and that which is not [*ea quae non sunt*]. I have chosen to designate all things [*omnium*] by this generic term that is translated by *phusis* in Greek [*graece phusis*] and by *natura* in Latin [*latine vero natura*]."[19]

The allegation of "pantheism" to the philosophy of the Irishman is customarily insisted on and probably overdone. Besides the mistaken character of such a judgment, which confuses *identification* and *expression* in the relation between God and the world (to which we will return), this reading of Erigenian exegesis from the single side of *natura* masks and obscures the debate which it maintains with what philosophy will later name *ontologia*. In the Erigenian, the *ontological formulation* of the way of affirmation in terms of "being" and of the way of negation in terms of "non-being," even if the super-eminence of Non-Being would not be identified with the simple negation of affirmation, originally marks (despite the anachronism here) a will "to construct an agathology or a henology and not at all an ontotheology."[20] Where today's exegetes of philosophy still strive to determine the non-onto-theological aspects of this or that author, whom I measure by the yardstick of this first part [God], we can properly bring John Scotus Erigena to bear on a debate now neither overestimated nor arbitrary in the sense, at the very least, of an "ontologization of the debate," either on the side of being (way of affirmation), or on the side of non-being (way of negation). To define a mode of discourse (*logos*) which is not reduced to a simple metaphysics of presence and which would yet be in dialogue with it—such is the originality of the Irishman here (chap. 2). In this way he definitely takes leave of the categories of substance always left in operation by the bishop of Hippo (chap. 1).[21]

The Nihilation of Eminence. Besides the *ontologizaton* of negative theology, a second operation that is only its ultimate consequence also marks Erigenian apophaticism in an exemplary way: the *nihilation* [*néantisation*] of the Dionysian way of eminence. It is very well known that the way of eminence defining "negative" theology in Denys does not remain within affirmation and negation, but on the contrary, provides, properly speaking, a third way. Briefly, the originality of the Areopagite beyond all his predecessors, including the tenets of the Platonic *epekeina tês ousias* (*Republic*, VI, 509 b), is that he not only posits a beyond to essence, but draws it outside of the ruts that its position (or non-position) presupposes: "In itself the supreme Cause remains perfectly transcendent to all privation since it is situated *beyond every position* either negative or affirmative."[22] But a great danger (already understood by Denys) remains, specifically of positing "the beyond of all negative or positive position" (*uper pasan kai aphairesin kai thesin*) in the very mode of position which was surpassed: "To say that God is totally other," asks Jean-Claude Foussard in a judicious reading of Erigena, "is it not still to determine him as *another of the same?*"[23] In this sense, God appears here less beyond being (Denys) than (as he is in reality) *otherwise* than being (Erigena)—meaning that in relation to "being" God does not uniquely transcend all position, but adopts *another mode* according to which he *is not* now qualified by a determination of the positional type, as remains the case in the mere overcoming of being.

The reduction to nothing of eminence (or of the beyond) leads eminence thus to drop itself into the nothing (or non-being), as God is no longer counted among the collection of "things which are" (*ea quae sunt*) but reveals on the contrary "those which (precisely) are not" (*ea quae non sunt*) in the mode of being. God "is *not*," not in the sense that he *is* not being, but in the sense alone that he is *not* in the ordinary mode of being: "When we say that *God is* [*unde Deum esse dicentes*], we do not mean that God is *according to a determined modality* [*non aliquo modo esse dicimus*] . . . Because God escapes the comprehension of every reason and intellect, and when we predicate Being of him [*praedicantes ipsius esse*], we do not want to say that God *would himself be Being* [*non dicimus ipsum esse*], because Being proceeds from God [*ex ipso enim esse*], but *God in himself* is not Being [*sed nom ipsum esse*]."[24]

The God who "is not being" (*non ipsum esse*) is uniquely "not," precisely as a "God who does not have to Be, but loves," in a surpassing that at its summit is very Dionysian.[25] The "overhang" [*surplomb*] (Merleau-Ponty) of ontology by agathology does not have the same sense in Erigena as in the Areopagite. For Denys the Good explicitly marks the passage to another properly divine order—charity; for Erigena it designates God as "Non being," that is, as "nothingness." God should be understood to be "eminent" here in the sense that his superiority is of *not* being according to the current modality of beings: "The divine Goodness [*bonitas divinae*], when one considers that it subsists in itself, is *non-being* [*neque est*], has always been *non-being* [*neque erat*], and will always *not be* [*neque erit*]. Because the divine Goodness is still left unknowable by the intelligence of every existing being, it still exceeds everything that exists . . . Since the divine Goodness remains unknowable by every intelligence, we have not erred in giving him the name of *Nothingness by eminence* [*per excellentiam nihilum non immerito vocitatur*]."[26]

Beyond Denys (who, in not explicitly dialoguing with ontology, has not as such thought Non-being) and beyond Boethius (who never extended the concept of nature from the affirmation of being to its negation), the Erigenian *Non-being* therefore originally designates neither a default nor a privation of being, but the excellence or eminence of the One who is *not* according to the ordinary mode of being—albeit in his eminence itself. Where Denys still thinks a *beyond* being by charity in the way of eminence, Erigena radicalizes it by making the Good itself the eminence of unsurpassable Nothingness ("Nothingness by eminence"). God is "without being" in the sense of the being of "Without," that is to say, as pure Non-being or "Nothingness by eminence" (*per excellentiam nihilum*) to the degree that nothing remains in the formulation of his divinity except the Nothing of everything that pertains to the ordinary mode of simple entities. Eminence itself, or that which is ordinarily named the third way in Denys (*via eminentiae*), will therefore paradoxically not conserve its eminence in Erigena, except as its very *negation* as eminence, at least in the sense of a "super-position" beyond every position and negation. Since to posit a "Beyond essence" is not immediately to exit from the mode of essentiality that it seems to surpass, "the prefixes *super* or *more than* in Erigena do not at all imply a way of eminence which would surreptitiously reintroduce affirmation at the heart of negation itself."[27] In a different way than the Areopagite, therefore, however affirmative in its formulation, every turn or every proposition, whether that of eminence or of the superlative, will thus be understood by the Irishman to signify in a negative manner: "All the names which are predicated of God by the addition of prefixes 'super-' or 'more than' [*super vel plusquam*] such as Super-essential [*superessentialis*], more-than-Truth [*plusquam veritas*], more-than-Wisdom [*plusquam sapientia*] and other similar names, form in themselves the full synthesis of the two aforementioned branches of theology (cataphatic and apophatic); so that, if *in their formulation* itself these names adopt the expression of *affirmative theology* [*ita ut in pronuniatione formam affirmativae*], *in their meaning* these names remain within the meaning inherent to *negative theology* [*in intellectu vero virtutem abdicativae obtineant*]."[28]

It is not too little to say, therefore, that Erigena, the intentionally unfaithful translator of a Denys whom he makes iridescent out of his own genius, appears resolutely more *negative* or *apophatic* than the Areopagite himself in his persistent usage of the superlative. Erigena attempts a radicalization of Denys, not against him, but beyond him—"there where Denys had left some 'room to play' or, if you prefer, some indetermination, thanks to which some interpreters of diverse tendencies have been able to attribute to the Dionysian doctrine of weaker or stronger doses of negativity."[29] The significance of the *Erigenian nihilation of eminence* is not that it is no longer only a matter of reaching a realm beyond being and non-being by means of the surpassing of all position in the simple Dionysian hierarchy, but of radicalizing the effort that Denys had been able to carry out while lacking a true dialogue with ontology: to think the "*otherwise than being*" as the unique and veritable manner of designating the "beyond essence."[30]

To affirm that God is the author of a creation ex nihilo, as in Christian doctrine, allows us to recognize that the *nihil* or the nothing from which the world itself is drawn is nothing other than God himself as "Nothing," or "Nothingness" in the sense that he is precisely the *nothing*, not only of beings, but also of "things," which makes up the ordinary *mode* of beings: "We believe that God has created everything that exists from nothingness [*de nihilo omnia fecisse*]; but what is this nothingness if not that of the One who . . . is not without reason called a Nothingness by eminence [*nihil per excellentiam*] since it is completely impossible *to number him among the collection of all things that exist* [*in numero omnium quae sunt*]."[31] Related to this ontological nihilation in Erigena (chap. 2)—radicalized again by the reduction from "to nothing" to "to the nothing" ["à rien" *au* "au rien"] in Meister Eckhart (chap. 3)—the possibility of another discourse will arise: not against ontology but beyond it (meta-ontological), in the impossible reification of God as well as of man.

The Meta-Ontological: The Impossible Reification

In his debate with ontology and by virtue of the principle of the nihilation of eminence, Erigena is led by the apophatic toward a sort of "meta-ontology," at least in the sense of an overflow of the definition of God as Being in the direction of his own non-Being: "Negative theology doubles as a meta-ontology or a meta-ousiology no less negative."[32] However, let us make no mistake: the metaphysical formulation of the questioning in terms of ontology—or better of the negation of all ontology—remains properly theological in its aim. God defined as "Being" or as "Non-Being" truly exits from the *ordinary mode of the existence of things* only if he appears as himself starting from himself in his *auto-manifestation*. Said otherwise, if "the objective of phenomenology does not coincide with objectivity,"[33] then Erigena has accomplished his goal, in no other way than by means of his concern to protect God from reification.

God Is Not (Some)Thing. Among the great leitmotifs of medieval philosophy—from the "*aliquid quo nihil majus cogitari possit*" (that than which nothing greater can be conceived) of Anselm to the "*cum gratia non tollat naturam sed perficiat*" (grace does not destroy but perfects nature) of Aquinas[34]—there is surely one so striking in Erigena that it would also merit similar notoriety, at least insofar as it accomplishes the program of making utterly impossible the reification of the divine: *Deus nescit se quid est, quia non est quid*—"God does not know *what* he is because he is *not some thing*."[35] There again a gap widens between Erigena and Denys, so that the originality of one (Erigena) is always achieved through the ontologization of the other (Denys). Yet two traits of the non-knowledge of God always remain common between them: that *man is not able to know God* because of his Super-essentiality on the one hand, and that *even God is not able to know himself anymore* at least according to the ordinary mode of knowledge, on the other. Yet the reasons for this double unknowing are not identical in both thinkers. The nescience *of* God—of man concerning God (objective genitive) and of God concerning himself (subjective genitive)—no longer only emphasizes the surpassing of the concept which produces the way of eminence, but now expresses the radically thing-less status of the divine being: "Because God is *not some-thing* [*quia non est quid*]," he "does not know *any-thing* about himself [*nescit se quid est*]." Otherwise said, the non-reification of the divine precedes and founds his unknowing. It matters little to Erigena that God is only "known as unknown" according to the scriptural imperative of Acts 17 of which the one who calls himself the Areopagite claims to be the hearer, but instead, for him, its non-determination as (some) thing, that is, as *quid*, renders it unknowable because non-reifiable. Erigena attempts to perform a quasi-phenomenological reduction of God who "suspends" or "puts in brackets" his existence itself in the form of *quid* (*non est quid*)—a concept already so pregnant in Augustine (chap. 1)—and opens thus in the direction [*sens*] of a new way of being for the divine: as phenomenon, namely, as manifestation or theophany (chap. 2). Whereas the non-knowledge of God, posited for *epistemological* reasons in Denys, continually maintains negative theology in the realm of discourse or of concept (logos), its nescience draws it to the side of manifestation, precisely for *ontological* reasons in Erigena, who consecrates it first as a mode of de-ontologization: "To posit the question 'what is it?' [*quid*]," emphasizes Jean-Claude Foussard with regard to Erigena, "is to inquire about a definition of the object. But to define is to determine a being, that is, to posit it immediately in a multiplicity which encompasses it, making it a being *among other beings* among which it can be numbered . . . It is not therefore a failure of some kind that God does not know what he is, rather, it is more simply because he is *nothing definite*."[36]

Conforming to my original hypothesis and without exceeding the decent limits of anachronism, a true "reduction" of God paradoxically makes Erigena one of the first phenomenologists in the context of theology. Like Heidegger's "the term 'Dasein' which we use to designate this being does not express its what," God ignores the (some-)thing that he is or could be (*nescit se quid est*) in the sense that he is not or is no longer spoken of according to the mode of things which are (*quia non est quid*). Neither "ready to hand" (*zuhanden*) nor "present at hand" (*vorhanden*), God is therefore at least negatively defined as a mode of opening whose openness [*apérité*] first negates the ordinary guise of beingness.[37] *Negative theology* ("God's not knowing what he is") doubles as a *negative ontology*, or better, as a sort of *meta-ontology*, which forsakes being, inasmuch as it is always only said according to the mode of things—that is, according to the pure and simple *presence of its quiddity* ("he is not some thing"). In phenomenology (Heidegger) as in theology (Erigena), the being of a being "does not appear"—whether of God or man—not because *it is not tout court*, but because "*it is not itself a being*," at least in the sense of a being present.[38]

The non-entitiness [*néantité*] of God achieved through hard struggle by the nihilization of the way of eminence in dialogue with ontology, now comes to signify the reverse, or rather the impossibility, of inquiring into any "quiddity" in the etymological sense of the term (being a *quid*). Nothing remains of being except of being nothing—of a being.[39] For Erigena, the "reduction to the Nothing," as a singular possible escape from the ordinary mode of presence, is in this way decrypted, although in another sense than in Heidegger (since it is not here a question of anguish or of any other affective tonality): "How can the divine nature therefore know itself *for what it is* [*quid sit*], since it is *Nothingness* [*cum nihil sit*]? For the divine nature exceeds every being [*superat enim omne quod est*], as it is not itself Being [*quando nec ipse est*], but as every being proceeds from it [*sed ab ipsa est omne esse*]."[40]

Such a divine nothing (*cum nihil sit*) is not here the simple bottomless well of a definitively unfathomable deity (*das Nichts*). This would be closer to Eckhart later and in this sense more Dionysian than properly Erigenian.[41] Rather it marks the impossibility of God himself being conceived and known as Being, that is, explicitly, as "subsistent." It is not man who seeks to deliver God from "substance"—an enterprise that can only be terribly promethean in light of the insoluble tension between metaphysics and theology—but God himself who *makes an escape*. Such an initiative does not consist in breaking free from metaphysics, at least partially (as for Augustine), but more simply in resisting all forms of reification which would make of his "person" a "thing" as if he had to answer to "something [*quid*]": "God, who is not an objective *quid* [*qui non est quid*], does not know completely the *subsistence* in him of everything that is not himself [*omnino ignorare in se ipso quod ipse non est*]. But God does not know himself as an objective *quid* [*seipsum autem non cognoscit aliquid esse*]."[42] Nothing subsists in God which could define his "substance," his permanence. God is not ignorant of his own nature simply because it would make him inaccessible to himself, as by a failure of power or knowledge, but only in that he *is not* himself *nature*, albeit in an eminent or Super-essential way: "God does not know what he himself is [*nescit itgitur quid ipse est*]; God does not know his being [as] an objective *quid* [*hoc est nescit se quid esse*] because God knows that he is absolutely none of the existent beings which become knowable as *subsisting* in a subject [*quoniam cognoscit se nullum eorum quae in aliquo cognoscuntur*] about which the *quiddity* could be put into words or known."[43]

But the Erigenian radicalization of the Dionysian corpus, in the twofold sense of negativity and the ontologization of the debate, does not stop there. Under the influence of Maximus the Confessor, whom he also translated, Erigena extends the negativity of God to man himself, in the sense that the hyper-*distance* established between man and God in Dionysian apophaticism is now understood to be rectified by the closest *proximity* in their likeness in Maximian exemplarism. "Negative theology" is paradoxically and brilliantly doubled by a "negative anthropology" in Erigena who makes what seems to be the *most remote* for man (God's unknowing of God) now that which appears as the *closest*: the unknowing of man through man.

Man Is Not (Some)Thing. It is well known that John Scotus Erigena has not only transmitted (and interpreted) the works of Denys the Areopagite for the Latin world, but also the works of Maximus the Confessor and Gregory of Nyssa. From Maximus, vis-à-vis his principle of the extension of the attributes from God to man, Erigena retained this lesson: "Cataphatic theology does not at all affirm the negations of apophatic theology [*et kataphatikê non confirmet quod apophatikê abnegat*], and the apophatic does not at all negate the affirmations of cataphatic theology [*neque apophatikê abneget quod kataphatikê affirmat*]. These two general parts of theology apply not only to God [*non solum in Deum*], but *even to every creature* [*sed etiam in omni creatura*] as is shown by eloquent examples."[44]

Extending the Christological principle of the communication of idioms to all of humanity, what pertains to God, according to Erigena, also pertains therefore to all of humanity, to the degree, at least, that humanity is rendered capable of receiving it. Such is the meaning of the apophatic mode of self-knowledge which now will not be reserved to God alone (Denys), but will be extended also to the entire collection of created beings (*sed etiam in omni creaturae*)—and thus to the human creature in an exemplary way. In other words, if "God does not know what he is because he is not something [*Deus nescit se quid est, quia non est quid*]" (supra), then humanity will also remain totally ignorant of its own quiddity) in order not to remain also locked in its solitary "subsistence" as a thing or being (*quid*). Erigena states: "Similarly to that which concerns his Creator, man knows only that God exists [*tantum cognoscit quia est*] but does not know *that which* God is [*non autem percipit quid sit*]; similarly also to that which concerns his own nature, man knows only that he has been created [*solummodo definit quia creatus est*] but is not able to know at all *how or in which substance* he has been created [*quomodo vero vel in qua substantia substitutus est intelligere non potest*]. If man knew in any way whatsoever *what* he is [*si enim quid sit aliquo modo intelligeret*], he would necessarily deviate from the resemblance to his Creator [*necessario a similitudine Creatoris deviaret*]."[45]

The Principle of Resemblance. The principle of *resemblance* (*similitudo*) or the image of God in man—about which we will demonstrate how it models our carnal invisibility according to Irenaeus (chap. 4)—is found therefore pushed to the extreme through Erigena's rereading of Maximus the Confessor. Nothing is prohibited to man in his participation in the divine, including his impossible consideration of himself through himself as thing or "kind of *quid*." In phenomenological terms, the non-reduction of the self to the mode of being of the *thing*, always "subsistent" (*vorhanden*) and "available" (*zuhanden*), sanctions a *Dasein* or a way of being human which there again does not have *to be* inasmuch as "the being of the being is not itself a being."[46] But in Erigena the theologian, contrary to Heidegger the phenomenologist, man does not achieve *by himself* some sort of *authenticity* to conquer this non-being-ness of his own humanity. On the contrary, he has received it from God alone, the unique *Being-there* capable of not considering *himself* as *quid*, as well as of receiving the totality of beings and of conferring the same power to humanity. "Negative anthropology" here becomes the necessary equivalent of "negative theology." God progressively travels the *distance* which separates him from humanity in order now to hold him in *proximity* as that which he has forged in his image. The *horizontal* phenomenology of the existentials (Heidegger) is now enriched in an exclusively Christian perspective (Maximus and Erigena) of a *vertical* theology of the *imago Dei* that legitimates access to humanity and confers upon it its proper status.[47]

The work of the negative (the apophatic) is accomplished through the observation of a necessary *proximity* of the divine capable of abolishing distance. Humanity, as the image of God, understood precisely as the impossibility of knowing oneself, thus partakes of the sharing without measure that is God's learned ignorance. John Scotus Erigena "*negates the 'distance'* between God and primordial humanity, a distance filled by the theophanic process," emphasizes Francis Bertin (thus marking the difference with Denys), "all the way until the divine essence theophanically descends into the rational and intellectual creature and causes him to merit the name of 'God' by derivation."[48] Therefore God now somehow exits from the inner reaches of his Essence and is given to *visibility* no longer negatively in the *philosophical* field of the "apophatic" (and of the meta-ontological), but positively in the *scriptural* logos of the "apophantic" which manifests him while at the same time making a setting for it: "It is *not only the divine essence* [*non enim essentia divina*] which connotes the *word* God," as we have already emphasized following Erigena, "but also this *mode* [*sed modus ille*] under which God *is shown* [*ostendit*] to the intellectual and rational creature . . . which is frequently called God as well by *Holy Scripture* [*Deus saepe a sacra Scriptura vocitatur*]."[49]

The Apophantic or the Setting of *Logos*

Manifestation thus legitimately abides with the logos, in phenomenology (the manifest) as in theology (the theophany), deploying a type of discourse which is made the *setting* [*écrin*] without being made a *screen* [*écran*]. The exiting from being by the nihilation of eminence and the struggle against every form of reification of the divine leads Erigena, like Aristotle before him and Heidegger after him, toward a new mode, properly called the "apophantic" that is *revelatory* of the thing itself (*apo-phaines-thai*): "*Logos* as speech really means *dêloun*, to make manifest 'what is being talked about' in speech. Aristotle explicates this function of speech more precisely as *apophainesthai* [to be manifested]."[50] The Dionysian *apophatic* (that which lies beyond speech (*apo-phanein*) is found in fact radically modified and transformed by the

Erigenian *apophantic* (the crossing of the manifest [*apo-phainesthai*]). One is not allowed to remain either taking refuge in an apophaticism or on the quest for a meta-ontology, at least insofar as John Scotus Erigena is taken into consideration and not Denys the Areopagite alone. For Erigena, the act of speech, if it truly traces an image like the sculptor who "strips" the block of marble in order to liberate the form (Denys),[51] nevertheless ought to remain "like a kind of vestment" (*veluti quibusdam vestimentis*) which "reveals" or "manifests" (*manifestare*) a body already constituted all the while hiding it.[52] Otherwise said, whereas the Dionysian model of the "opening" of the sculpture liberates a figure of God only by abstracting from that which he is not, the Erigenian paradigm of "unveiling" by clothing over shows on the contrary that which it leaves to see of itself only by hiding it. Whereas for one nothing is shown except precisely that there is nothing to show (the Dionysian stripping), the other on the contrary shows that everything remains to be shown, or rather to be manifested, since the One who is manifest may very well wish to remove the veils himself (the Erigenian unveiling). The destruction of categories, in the Heideggerian sense of the term, will be in this sense all the more radical in Erigena as it progressively assists the manifestation of a phenomenon—God—which possesses no other requirement, by way of the paradigm of all phenomenality, than to "show starting from itself that which is shown such that it is shown starting from itself."[53]

The Destruction of the Categories

The work of the apophantic as "manifestation through the discourse about that which it speaks" ought therefore to pass first through the "task of a destruction [*Desktruktion*] of the history of ontology."[54] "To destroy" overly used categories or rather to "deconstruct" or "dis-obstruct"—but not to "annihilate" them: such is precisely, if also paradoxically, the task fixed for Erigena from the very beginning of his *Periphyseon* (book 1).[55] (a) "Without being"; (b) "without relation"; (c) even "without love," the Irishman radicalizes the Dionysian reduction for which *nothing* remains of God outside of his negation—except, in an original fashion in Erigena, the "veridical and metaphorical" meaning of his proper manifestations in his auto-affirmation: "If the *negation* proves to be truly in God [*si vera est negatio in divinis rebus*], then the *affirmation* proves truly not to remain in Him, but it proves to be only metaphorical [*non autem ver sed metaphorica affirmatio*]."[56]

God "without" Being. (a) "Without being": here we return to the debate with Thomas Aquinas (chap. 1). God is here considered "without being" not simply insofar as he "is not a thing" (supra), but for the reason that "the divine nature is not *ousia* because it is *more than ousia* [*non est igitur ousia, quia plus est quam ousia*]."[57] The question no longer concerns the status of *ousia*—substance as "being" or "act of being" (see the debate between

Aristotle and Thomas Aquinas)—but is a matter instead of a surpassing of substance itself in the meta-ontology of a discourse which does not overflow the categories as much as it destroys them, or better, deconstructs them. Contra Augustine for whom no category is predicable to God in the sense proper to God except that of essence or substance ([see chap. 1], *De Trinitate*, V, II, 3), Erigena maintains the inverse position, namely that no mode of "subsistence" could be legitimately predicated of God, if the term "being"—as I have indicated already—is understood as a certain determined mode of the divine in the same way as the collection of beings: "When we predicate Being of him [*ideo praedicantes ipsius esse*], we do not want to say that *God ought to be himself Being* [*non dicimus ipsum esse*]: because being proceeds from God, but God in himself *is not Being* [*ex ipso enim esse, sed non ipsum esse*]."[58]

God "without" Relation. (b) "Without relation": definitively surpassing the question of the link between relation and substance (chap. 1), God is thought here in Erigena in an even more radical manner than in Denys. Everything happens, in fact, as if, as René Roques has said, Erigena "denied relation to God . . . , which Denys had not expressly done even if the logic of apophasis ought to have led him there."[59] Without necessarily exiting from the tension of metaphysics and theology or wrongly believing in the end of a dialogue with Hellenism (chap. 1), the author of the *Periphyseon* is however plagued by some limitations. Contra Augustine, according to whom "relation" (*ad aliquid*) of the Father and Son does not constitute an accident in God but rather designates what is proper to God [*De Trinitate*, V, V, 6], Erigena holds to the contrary an impossible adaptation of it in the field of Trinitarian theology. He knows the cost of such a move, but it remains here the condition sine qua non of his double discourse, which is all the more *apophatic* as it is *apophantic*, that is to say all the more a "negator" of the ordinary mode of beings as it is a "revelator" of the proper way that God gives himself to humanity: "If this category of connection or relation [*relatio sive habitudo*] is predicable in the proper sense to God [*proprie de Deo*], then almost all of our preceding reasoning would be obsolete [*omnis ferme praedicta nostra ratiocinatio evacuabitur*]. I have previously asserted as a general rule that *nothing can be formulated or conceived in the proper sense concerning God* [*nihil proprie de Deo aut dici aut intelligi posse*]. And above all the category of relation [*praesertim categoria relationis*] will no longer be counted among the ten kinds of categories, if it becomes predicable in the proper sense to God . . . It would be necessary for us to understand therefore that this category of relation, like the other categories, is also only predicable of God in a metaphorical sense [*translative de Deo praedicare*]."[60]

God "without" Love. (c) "Without love": in a drastic way, God is finally without *agapê*, at least from the point of view of eros. The acting out and the lived suffering of love (*amor*) are in fact for Erigena categories that are all the more appropriate to becoming as they are unable to designate in themselves the stillness of the Non-Being that is God: "These two categories are therefore without a doubt predicable of Him (God) only in a *metaphorical* (*translative*) sense."[61] What are the verbs "to love" and "to be loved" but respectively the active and passive reception of a certain movement? The conclusion, which places love outside of the divine realm, imposes itself: "It will necessarily follow that everything that I have conceded in the case of acting and suffering, I ought also to concede in the case of other active and passive verbs, whatever category of verb to which they pertain. That is, *God neither loves nor is loved*, he neither moves nor is moved, and a thousand analogous examples [*neque Deus amare, neque amari, neque movere, neque moveri, similiaque mille*]."[62]

It goes without saying that the God "without being," "without relation," and "without love" is not a God who *neither is* nor *has* being, relation, or love: no more than God "is not" (*tout court*) in the *God without Being* of Jean-Luc Marion, but "is only because he gives." Further still, God neither lives nor is nourished by being, relation, and love in John Scotus Erigena—who risks the inverse of making "without" only the negation of that which yet belongs appropriately to God.[63] The danger of the characteristics that we qualify as "categorical" according to the very precise note of Heidegger, is that "they belong to beings *whose kind of being is unlike Dasein*," and "all have the same kind of being—that of being *objectively present* (*vorhanden*)—as things occurring 'within' the world."[64] Otherwise said, the "without" of being, relation, and love indicates less here the *privation* of a quality inherent to God, as it does the *deconstruction* of all categorical predication to its subject, of which the closure in this type of predicative logos necessarily entangles and restricts without ever being able to contain it. In the same way that the "phenomenological reduction" requires a kind of philosophical *ascesis* in order to suspend the categorical and to reach the existential, there is also a *radicalization* in the "putting between parentheses" of all the divine categories that appears to be necessary in order for negative theology to exhibit that which is manifest at the heart of every manifestation in a fashion that is more demonstrative (*phainesthai*) than predicative (*categorein*): "The validity of the categories becomes entirely *void* when it comes to *theology*," Erigena patently emphasizes, "[*ad theologiam pervenitur . . . , categoriarum virtus omnino extinguitur*]; and I in nowise designate by the word *nothingness* [*nihilo*] this negation which denies that God is some existing being [*negationem qua negatur Deus esse quid eorum quae sunt*], but rather that which negates *God and the creature simultaneously* [*sed illam quae negat Deum et creaturam*]."[65]

Therefore God comes to us precisely because we are no longer on our own able to go to him—because of the inadequacy of our language as well as the limits of our capacity to receive him. This coming, like phenomenological consciousness, precisely makes of him first, and then of us, an *act* and no longer a thing.[66] His proper mode of existing will in fact for him not be of being or subsisting, but of *going* and *coming*, in the sense of the indefatigable way of the One who travels theophanically, and no longer only negatively or superlatively, the distance which separates him from humanity. *Y aller* ("To go there")– that is to say in French as for the Erigenian theophanic God, not only "to come and see [*venir pour voir*]" (to take a look [*y jeter un oeil*]), but even "to be fully involved in this coming [*s'engager pleinement dans ce venir*]" (speeding along while running [*foncer en courant*]) to the degree that He is also known in this coming of man. Not only (a) as "*the One who sees*," he comes also to us (b) as "*the One who runs*."

The One Who Sees and the One Who Runs

Supporting Etymology. The characteristic that distinguishes Erigenian "apophantic discourse" from the simple Dionysian "apophatic way" is that it manifests (*apophainesthai*) that which alone remains beyond speech (*apophansis*). It is therefore understood as a type of logos that escapes from categorical norms, not only in order to transcend them but also in order to show that which is being spoken about (phenomenology and theophany). We are compelled then to recognize that God first *communicates himself to humanity by his modes of manifestation*—a speech that is not uniquely tied to the power of words.

A surprising text in Erigena distinguishes God in terms of celerity or rather haste [*l'empressement*]. For Erigena God is all the more anxious to join man by showing him that he is not left closed or isolated in a *distance* from the One about whom nothing can be said—except, precisely, that he is not able to be spoken about. The Greek etymology once again discloses something significant much like the second meaning of theophany drawn from the verb *phainô* (supra). Here we are concerned with God—*ô theos*: "The Greeks have drawn an etymology from the name God [*theos*] according to which the name derives from the verb *theôrô* [*aut a verbo quod est theôrô derivatur*], that is to say, 'I see' [*hoc est video*], or even that it derives from the verb *theô* [*aut ex verbo theô*], that is to say, 'I run' [*hoc est curro*], or yet again—and this is the more likely because their meanings converge on a single and same meaning—it could be rightly argued that this one word derives from two verbs."[67]

God as the One Who Sees. (a) God as "the one who sees" (*theôrô*)—an etymology inherited from Denys, Basil, and Gregory of Nyssa, but which here receives its most important theological treatment before Nicholas of Cusa. In good negative theological manner, God sees first, and he sees precisely because he does not see, or rather because there is nothing to see except Himself in whom everything "visible" always remains contained. Otherwise said, it matters little to Erigena that God is able to see *this* or *that* among the number of created beings if it is the case that the mode by which he sees is nothing other than *Himself* as he carries within the collection of possibilities of the visible—that is, the totality of phenomena, the visible as well as the invisible yet to be seen: "Where *theos* comes from the verb *theôrô*, it is interpreted as signifying *the One who sees* [*videns interpretatur*] because God sees *in himself* everything that exists [*ipse enim omnia quae sunt in seipso videt*], where he contemplates nothing outside of himself [*dum nihil extra seipsum aspiciat*] because nothing subsists outside of God [*quia nihil extra seipsum est*]."[68]

Only the passage from the second to the third division of Nature—from the primordial causes of all existing things containing the Word (the *Created creator*) to the manifestation of the collection of beings including man (the *Created non-creator*)—renders intelligible the conception of the reserve of possibles of phenomenality that God carries quasi-maternally in himself without having brought them all forth into the light.[69] With the majority of the entire creation still awaiting its birth, the Word holds hidden in itself the totality of existing beings in "the most secret recesses of nature [*ex secretis naturae*]," which are called to come out in order to bear forth, now in the mode of visibility, that which, for the time, remains obscure in the realm of invisibility or the non-manifest. The invisible phenomena contained in God (as in Nature as well) progressively ascend toward their own visibility before the *One who sees* (*videns*), who is thereby phenomenologically manifest (*phainesthai*) or rendered visible: "Every day God calls men from the hidden recesses of nature [*ex secretis naturae sinibus vocat*] in which they are judged as 'non-being' in order to appear in a visible mode [*ut appareant visibiliter*] in form and matter and through all the other properties by which the hidden existing beings are able to make their appearance [*in quibus occulta apparere possunt*]."[70]

God, understood as "the One who sees" (*theôrô*), has nothing to do with a voyeuristic onlooker whose eye oppresses the collection of creatures embarrassed by their very visibility because they are held under such a surveillance. On the contrary, it is precisely in order to remove vision from such an oppressive, tawdry Stare that the visible, that is, the creature, unites—or more precisely constitutes "a single and same reality [*unum et idipsum*]"—with the Invisible, that is, God himself. This is the point where a number of interpreters falsely read some kind of pantheism into Erigena. Yet it is more fitting to understand the inverse, especially here, which means substituting the model of an auto-manifestation about which the terms of "auto-creation" say nothing except that, for God himself and in himself, *the act of creation is never anything other than a self-showing*: "Therefore we ought to understand that God and the creature do not constitute two distinct realities [*non duo a seipsis distantia*], but constitute a single and same reality [*sed unum et id ipsum* (*sic*)]. Because it is by a mutual concurrence that the creature subsists in God and that God *is created* [*se faciens*] under an extraordinary and inexpressible mode in the creature, *manifesting* Himself there [*seipsum manifestans*]."[71]

A "pantheistic conception of theophany renders theophany just as inconceivable as an abstract apophaticism."[72] Erigena himself already makes this clear: according to him, the belonging of all creatures "to a single and same thing" which is God (*unum et id ipsum*) does not signify that the creatures are themselves God or the Creator. The totality of God as essence (a monadological conception inserting all creatures into God) and the essence of God as totality (a pantheistic conception which leaves nothing subsisting at all, neither of the Creator nor of the creature) are hardly confused here. The double rapport of *participation* and *expression* in the relation of beings to God justifies the auto-manifestation of the Creator in his creature, but it does not justify in any way their pure substantial identity. There would have been nothing to say about participation or expression if God had been identified *stricto sensu* with the world: "The Divine Nature *is created* [*creatur*] in the sense that no other essence than it exists because it is itself the Essence of all existing beings . . . , in the same way that everything that is said to exist does not exist in itself, but exists only *by participation* [*participatione*] in the sole truly existing Nature . . . It is because this divine Nature which in itself is invisible, *becomes visible* [*apparet*] in everything that exists, that it is not incongruous to say that it *is created* in everything that exists [*non incongrue dicitur facta*]."[73]

It is therefore only by extension and "in an extraordinary mode" (*mirabili modo*) that it can be said of this Nature (God) that it "creates everything that exists" (*omnia creat*) and "is nevertheless created in all the existing beings which proceed from it" (*et ab ullo creari in omnibus*).[74] Thus to be created, as far as God is concerned, means "to be manifested in something [*in aliquo*]" and this manifestation is the substantial foundation of everything that exists more than it is some facile refuge in a transcendence as unsayable as it is remote. "When the divine Nature is said to create itself [*seipsam creare*], it should be understood in no other way than that it creates the nature of existing beings, because the auto-creation of the divine Nature [*ipsius namque creatio*], that is, its manifestation in something [*hoc est in aliquo manifestatio*], is tantamount to the act of the creation of all existing beings."[75]

"The One who sees," the seeing or self-manifesting God (*theos* drawn from *theôrô*) is therefore paradoxically "the one who works," that is the creating or self-becoming God: "In God, seeing and working do not constitute distinct properties," emphasizes Erigena, "but his vision coincides with his operation [*sed ipsius visio ipsius est operatio*]. God sees in his operations and operates in his seeing [*videt enim operando, et videndo operatur*]."[76] For God, to see is therefore *to be seen* in creatures and to create is *to be created* or *manifested* by them. To speak in Bergsonian terms, the "being made" of a God who works *interiorly* and is made visible in his creatures is opposed to and distinguished from the "ready-made" of *external* subsisting beings.[77]

With Erigena, a new and perhaps first mode of being of a *monadology* is born into the history of philosophy: God as "the One who sees" does not first see things external to him, but *sees himself* as in a mirror, carrying in Himself all existing beings in their primordial causes.[78] Far from being a *distant* spectacle to which the Dionysian negative theology leads (Eminence, Super-essentiality, etc.) and not at all like the great mass of all the possibles waiting to be manifested (passage of primordial causes to existing beings), the divine seeing is so *close* to the creature that it is identified in reality with it only in order better to signify and to show how it carries the creature within itself. The schema is here theophanic (and Erigenian) and hardly demiurgic and Platonic. God does not see (the primordial causes or exemplary ideas) in order to create or then to produce existing beings (created beings subject to space and time). But he creates as soon as he sees the primordial causes and sees as soon as he creates existing beings. God is no longer content "to say that this is" as in an Old Testament conception of the word (Gen. 1:3–31) but "sees" and is "made seen" in the New Testament vision of the auto-manifestation of God: "Whoever has seen me has seen the Father" (Jn. 14:9). What God sees is therefore identical to what God creates since in creating and in becoming incarnate the Word *makes himself seen* in his creatures as unique exemplary things: "Theology teaches that the existing beings that God has seen within himself before they were created are not distinct from the existing beings that God has then created in themselves, but these are *the same existing beings* [*sed eadem*] who have been both seen and created from all eternity; their vision and creation have taken place in God [*in Deo*], since nothing is able to take place outside of God [*extra Deum*]."[79]

One could object that to define God as "the One who sees" (*theôrô*), even when for him to see would be to see Himself in seeing the collection of beings in him by whom he is auto-manifested, is still to think theophany in the mode of seeing that is so properly human that it would be for God like being struck by blindness. Erigena would thus lose in his concept of theophany precisely what the Areopagite contributes in his negative theology. The contributions of Dionysian apophaticism to Erigenian theophany result in the refusal to make the act of seeing—since it pertains properly to God as to be capable of creating through auto-manifestation—the simple aim of a subject either suffering the imperfection of blindness or removed from the visibility of certain beings. God is called "all-seeing" because of the omnipresence of his seeing, such that he even creates through seeing, and is, in this sense, "more than seeing" (*plusquam videns*), since his seeing is reduced neither to the possible blindness of a subject, nor to the eventual invisibility of an object: "It is also called God [*theos*] but it is not properly speaking God at all [in the sense of 'I see' (*theôrô*)]: because the vision is opposed to blindness and to the one who sees is opposed the one who does not see; God will be therefore *upertheos* [*sic*]—more than seeing [*plus quam videns*]—if one interprets *theos* as the One who sees."[80]

Nevertheless, make no mistake: I have already emphasized that "all the *uper-* superlatives to which Denys makes recourse" ought to be understood in a negative manner within Erigena's thought, since what is apparently affirmative in the very formulation (*super* or *plus quam*) should be understood as negative in meaning and in reality.[81] The principle of the nihilation of eminence thus makes God, as "the One who sees," not a pure seeing withdrawn into the invisibility of an unseen, but an arch-Visible beyond every modality of ordinary seeing—in particular of that which would accidentally make him unable to see. Therefore, God as "more than seeing" (*plus quam videns*) does not indicate in Erigena that God does not see or takes refuge alone in the bottomless mystery of his luminous obscurity (exit from the *via affirmationis* and the *via negationis* by the *via eminentiae*); but first and only that his seeing is such that it sees all, and even "more" (than all), since the all that he sees is *Himself* who contains all things and manifests them (exit from the *via affirmationis* and the *via negationis* by what can be called *via theophaniae*).

The "seeing" of God in his auto-manifestation and in his auto-creation by the creature, each being only the inverse of the other, therefore holds back nothing for itself in some kind of self-invisibility. In order that the apophantic logos manifests and realizes the theophanic movement that it carries, the spectral dimension of seeing abides with the Word as it crosses the *ford* that separates it from the visible, which is insurmountable for man and crossed by God alone. "The One who sees" is thus the same as "the One who runs [*court*]"—or better who "runs through [*par-court*]" the distance that separates all Seeing from the visible according to the ordinary scheme of visibility: "But when *theos* is drawn from the verb *theô*, it is rightly interpreted as signifying *the One who runs* [*currens recte intelligitur*]. Because God runs across everything that exists and is never impeded, he fills all in his course, conforming to this verse of Scripture: 'his word runs with haste' (Ps. 147:15)."[82]

God as the One Who Runs. (b) "Courir" [to run]—from the verb *theô* (I run), the second etymological root of the word God (*theos*)—designates in reality the proper way to describe God as creator in Erigena. The divine Verb "runs" in his creation in the sense that he alone effects the distance which separates him from creatures and unfurls himself in them, so that nothing may exist outside of him except sin: "The Word is unfurled from one end of the world to the other, and he runs with haste across all existing beings [*et voliciter currit per omnia*], that is to say that the Word creates them all instantaneously, and that the Word becomes all in all. And then even as the Word continues to subsist in himself . . . , he is unfurled across all existing beings and this extension itself is constitutive of all things."[83]

The "unfurling" or "extension" of the Word in his creatures is such that it assumes precisely as its own the role of *logos apophantikos* as we found above, that is, of the Word who manifests what comes to him from another and which is reduced neither to apophatic speech (saying nothing except that there is nothing to say) nor to metaphysical judgment (massively opposing "the things which are" to "those which are not"). "Running" (*currens*) even more than "Seeing" (*videns*), the Word not only works to bring existing beings from the status of "primordial causes" to that of "beings manifest by their generation in time and space" (passage from the second to the third division),[84] but he makes them subsist and maintains existing beings in their creation as a word continually uttered from the Father (*verbum Patris*): "'His word runs with swiftness' (Ps. 147:15)—under the term of Word [*sermo*] the prophet has designated the Word of the Father [*verbum Patris*], who runs with swiftness through all existing beings in order that they may exist [*quod velociter currit per omnia ut omnia sint*], because it is the multiple and infinite course of the Word through all existing beings which makes them subsist."[85]

The reason for a pretended pantheism in Erigena has thus sometimes been (wrongly) sought in his conception of the Trinity insufficiently differentiated from the creation. Even though such a judgment would not be meaningless with regard to the prevalence of the "creative Trinity" in Bonaventure, for example,[86] it nevertheless remains no less incomplete as it is one-sided here since the scheme of running speaks precisely about the auto-subsistence of the Word in his creatures as the unique speech of the Father. No more than that the unveiling of beings by the Father in the Son (creation) is opposed to the manifestation of the Father in the Son (incarnation), is God's "act of running" in maintaining the subsistence of creatures opposed to his "act of seeing" which brings them to light: "In God the act of running through everything that exists is no different from his act of seeing everything that exists, but everything that exists is produced concurrently by his running and by his vision [*sed sicut videndo, ita et currendo fiunt omnia*]."[87]

In the dialogue of the *Periphyseon*, the Alumnus (student) rightly objects to the Nutritor (teacher): But where does this Word run who "is unfurled from one end of the world to the other" in order that he subsist through all subsistent beings? "I do not understand very well," he says, "where the One who resides everywhere could be moved, apart from whom everything would cease to exist and outside of whom nothing subsists." Matching the pertinence of this question, the response is only more clear and incisive: "I have mentioned that God does not move outside of himself [*non extra se*], but rather starting from himself, within himself and toward himself [*sed a seipso, in seipso, ad seipsum*]."[88] If God "runs" after his creatures—in the double implication of the word as haste and intentional aim—it is first "in himself" that he runs in order to "cause to run" the creatures who are in him. The "running in God" is also the path taken by beings in him in view of their own manifestation: "If God is therefore called the One who runs [*currens dicitur*], it is not because God—who always remains at rest in himself in an immutable way, who fills everything that exists—could run outside of himself, but because he causes everything that exists [*sed qui amnia currere facit*] to run from a state of nonexistence to that of existence."[89]

The power of such a monadology as Erigena's, since everything except sin happens and is produced first only in God, appears with even more force in this instance of the race. The swiftness of the One who runs has in fact no other end than of crossing the impassable distance that the prism of vision always imposes—in the irreducible gap between the One who sees and the very one who is seen. For God, to run signifies to cross himself and "to join the two ends" in himself of a course that is always accomplished beforehand by remaining contained in itself. Man, however, makes the inverse choice of "intentionally leaving the race" through sin. The theophanic vision is clearly announced here in the Word as *logos apophantikos*, the revealing Speech in whom every creature finds its course and tends toward its own manifestation.

The Word "*causes to run* [*currere facit*] every existing being from a state of nonexistence to that of existence" in order to give them the capacity to move to a state of visibility which they do not on their own possess (passage from the second to the third division of Nature). God (*theos*) "more than runs [*plusquam currens*]"—a notion that differs from slowness to no greater degree than the God who "more than sees" is opposed to blindness.[90] In this way, room opens for a true *manifestation of God* by which the truth of divine movement is no longer uniquely given by his *Essence* in a Neoplatonic or Dionysian apophaticism, but through his *Appearance* (*apparitio*) in a scriptural and Erigenian theophany.

The Theophanic, or the God Phenomenon

Without doubt, one could define the general trend of all of Latin theology from Erigena to Marcilio Ficino as a perpetual attempt to "vanquish dissimilarity" by means of a certain deviation from Denys. Thus Thomas Aquinas vanquishes dissimilarity "by analogy," Ficino "by love," and Jean Scotus Erigena "by theophany."[91] God is no longer only *manifest* here in the sense that he *manifests himself* in the Word of the Father as his apophantic discourse (supra), but as he *attests* and *witnesses* to himself in the present of his own "appearance" (*apparitio Dei*). It is fitting, since the Greeks, to call this appearance a "theophany" (*theophania*), which is also written in the Latin manuscripts of Erigena as the Hellenic "*theoyophania*."[92] The "reduction" or "putting in parentheses" of every declaration of the *quid* of God, which would always qualify Augustinian discourse (chap. 1), in Erigena opens onto a true "phenomenology of the inapparent" which has absolutely no reason to be envious of the Heideggerian determination of the phenomenon.[93]

Theophany and Anthropophany

Non Apparentis Apparitio. To speak of the "phenomenology of the inapparent" in Heidegger is to announce that "the possibility even exists that they can show themselves as they are *not* in themselves"; and "precisely because phenomena are initially and for the most part *not* given phenomenology is needed."[94] Otherwise said, for phenomenology as for theology, neither the phenomenon nor God pertain to the crude concept of the phenomenon where being shown suffices in order to be. The "word God" for example is quite capable of "connoting the divine essence" (*essentia divina dicitur*) as Erigena emphasized, without yet indicating "*this mode* under which it is shown" (*modus ille quo se ostendit*): "theophany" is an "appearance of God" (*theophania, hoc est apparitio Dei*).[95] Erigena, much like Heidegger after him, nicely traces therefore the frontier between "what appears" (*quid*) and "the thing as it appears," that is to say its "mode" of appearing: *modus* or *quomodo*. To see "the Lord seated" (Is. 6:1), the prophet Isaiah does not first see the Lord as he *is*, but only as he shows himself under the *modality of sitting*. The seat of God, as his most appropriate modality according to scripture, is probably more important than his definition by essence from the point of view of metaphysics. His kinestheses or "movements of his appearance" give more being to him than his essence as a determination of his *quiddity*. Thus God, for Erigena, is discovered to be defined in an exemplary way, almost phenomenologically, as "the appearance of what is non-apparent"—*non apparentis apparitio*: "Everything that can be conceived by the intelligence or perceived by the senses is nothing other than the *appearance* of the one who is *non-apparent* [*nihil aliud est nisi non apparentis apparitio*], the *manifestation* of the one who is *hidden* [*occulti manifestatio*] . . . , the *corporealization* of the *incorporeal* . . . , the *visibility* of the *invisible*, the *localization* of the one who is *without a place*, the *temporalization* of the *non-temporal*, the *finitization* of the *infinite*, the *circumscription* of the *uncircumscribable*."[96]

The critical problem of Erigenian theophany, like Heideggerian phenomenology, concerns the difficulty of not separating the *apparent* (*apparens*) from its *appearance* (*apparitio*). Or, to say it another way, and in phenomenological terms, it concerns not reducing the divine appearance in its "automanifestation" (*Offenbarung*) either to a simple "illusion" (*Schein*) or to an "appearance" which only shows what it is not (*Erscheinung*). Not as "semblance" or as "appearance" is it able to show something of the revelation of God as he is in himself, but only as both show God only as not showing himself, as not truly received by man, although man alone is capable of welcoming him and of himself participating in his own formation in God—today in his state of wandering as tomorrow in the fatherland: "Every theophany [*omnis theophania*] . . . , both in the present life where it begins to be re-formed inchoately in men who are becoming worthy of it, as well as in the future life in men who will obtain the perfection of divine beatitude, is therefore produced not outside of them [*non extra se*] but in them [*sed in se*], simultaneously *by God* and *by themselves* [*et ex Deo et ex seipsis*]."[97]

Theophanic Man. Against a number of normally Greek mystics who hold to a radical passivity and the subjection of the believer to the *weight* of the glory of God (*kabôd*), Erigena professes that men possess in themselves the *capacity* to phenomenalize in themselves (*in se*), through themselves (*ex seipsis*) and starting from Him (*ex Deo*), a figure of the divine that is never given outside of such a human reserve—requiring such a mode of constitution in order to be able precisely to be phenomenalized. The absorption of the subject (man) in the object (God) kills the act of reception as it annihilates the substantiality of both. The "appearance of the one who does not appear" (*apparitio non apparentis apparitio*) thus progressively rises toward the appearance by searching for a place to appear in man or in any rational creature. Angels and human souls are like "household receivers" for theophanies (F. Bertin); they "*are*" even "theophanies" themselves (*thephaniae sunt*). Phenomenologically speaking, they manifest that God is never anything other than the One who manifests *himself* in such theophanies, and therefore uniquely *through them* and not immediately in himself. Erigena asks, therefore, in his commentary on the verse "No one has ever seen God" (Jn. 1:18) from the prologue of John's Gospel: "What do the souls of holy men and the intelligences of holy angels see when they see God, if they do not see God himself [*si ipsum Deum*] whom they are allegedly seeing? What will they see, since Ambrose and Denys the Areopagite both very clearly and without hesitation affirm that God, the supreme Trinity, *has never appeared in himself* to anyone [*nulli per seipsam umquam apparuisse*], and does not appear today, nor will he ever appear? God will appear by means of his *theophanies* [*apparebit in theophanis suis*], that is, in his divine appearances in which he will appear according to the degree of purity and virtue in each one. But *the theophanies are all visible or invisible creatures* [*theophaniae autem sunt omnes creaturae visibiles et invisibiles*] by which and in which God has often appeared, appears and will appear."[98]

In Erigena theophany is therefore not a simple *means* of passing over to God, as if the mirror is a "prism" that one moves through [*du miroir comme prisme à dépasser*]. It designates the very *structure* of God (immanent Trinity)—at least insofar as it is given to man (economic Trinity). God is nothing for us outside of his divine manifestation (*theophania*), for man and the angels.[99] Therefore God gives himself "theophanically" provided that man is at the same time "anthropophanic." Or, said otherwise and in a new way, following our phenomenological theme according to which all truth (*alêtheia*) is also "the simple sense perception of something [*aistheisis*],"[100] man, in order to receive theophanies, and possessing within the structure of encounter or the capacity for reception, consecrates himself as a theophany manifesting nothing but himself as "anthropophany." Desiring to manifest God as phenomenon, man exhibits *himself as phenomenon* insofar as he is the condition of the possibility of all phenomenality, "in whom all creatures have been *constituted* [*in ipsa omnis creatura constituta est*], and shows himself first as such."[101] Anthropophanic man, as the uniting point [*trait d'union*] between the intelligible and sensible worlds, and in his capacity to manifest God, ought thus to be considered as a "third world" (*tertius mundus*), precisely because he possesses, along with the divine, this unique phenomenological capacity to constitute a world—the very same as God in his own appearing: "The third world [*tertius mundus*], as a middle term, enacts in itself the junction of the superior world of spiritual realities and of the inferior world of corporeal realities, making them one. This third world is only discovered in man [*et in homine solo intelligitur*], in whom all creation is organized into unity [*in quo omnis creatura adunatur*]."[102]

The Operation of a Synthesis. The famous Erigenian theme of man as "mediating and unifying agent of all creatures [*medietas atque adunatio omnium creaturarum*], since there exists no creature that one could consider as subsistent apart from man" ought thus to be understood not from a dialectical point of view (union of contraries), but first phenomenologically and anthropophanically (the manifestation of God in man).[103] "Man is the crucible of all creatures [*creaturarum omnium officina*] since all creatures subsist in him in a synthetic mode [*quoniam in ipso universalis creatura continetur*]."[104] Man, as the *enactment of synthesis*, supports and displays the manifestation of God himself in creatures. Because man alone among all the creatures somehow lives in this state of "remaining" (F. Bertin) by his capacity to welcome the totality of created things, God intends that he would be the one *in whom* creatures would also be manifested. The cooperation of the divine and human is thus such that in the act of auto-manifestation of God in his creatures the *theophany* of one never subsists apart from the *anthropophany* of the other.[105] At the end of the road, anthropophanic man, traversed by the theophanic God, will leave nothing to appear in celestial beatitude except the One who is the Manifestation himself (*apparitio*)—phenomenologically from whom everything appears and toward whom every appearance is directed. In this way the *Periphyseon* closes, definitively marked with the seal of phenomenality, even to God's complete opening or appearing: "Nothing appears except God alone [*ita ut in nullo appareat nisi solus Deus*], as in the air so pure that nothing flows except the light of the sun [*quemadmodum in aëre purissimo nihil arridet nisi sola lux*]."[106]

Beatitude as Theophany in Act

But does the "self manifestation," actualized absolutely in celestial beatitude, lead then to the pure and simple suppression of all theophany, that is to say, of all phenomenality? Said otherwise, does Erigenian phenomenality not exhaust itself in its phenomenalization since the theophanic appearance is never anything but a stage toward the vision God "as he is" (Jn. 3:2) and "face to face" (1 Cor. 13:12)?

Theophanies of Theophanies. Erigena remains substantially phenomenological even to the *ultimate manifestation* of the One who is manifestation itself. Even as the phenomenological concept of the phenomenon is never manifest outside of the Being which gives being,[107] so also there is no theophany in Erigena apart from its sensible or intelligible manifestation. Nor is there any theophany apart from the appearance of *something* that appears—even up to and including the final encounter: "It is therefore *by means of* the body and *in* the body that God will be seen [*per corpora ergo in corporibus videbitur*], and *not through Himself* [*non per seipsum*]. In a parallel way, it is *by means of* the intellect and *in* the intellect, *by means of* reason and *in* reason, and *not through itself* [*non per seipsam*], that the divine essence will become *visible* [*divina essentia apparebit*]."[108]

The Word who alone will transgress his proper phenomenality in order to contemplate himself in his nature and creatures in him. Man, on the contrary—saints and blessed included—will never see God but *through* theophanies, even some "theophanies of theophanies" (*theophaniarum theophaniae*) not reducible to some divine being supposedly overtaking or suppressing them. The incompressibility of the theophanic prism makes of the theophanic God a God who has another mode of being than the one appropriate to his manifestations—at least for man: "God will impart and fix a degree of beatitude to each of these natures as is fitting with their proper mode of analogy . . . If we use such language, this does not mean that any creature, *except for the humanity of the Word* [*praeter Verbi humanitatem*], could be elevated beyond all theophany . . . This means only that the elect will succeed in acquiring such transcendent theophanies . . . that they will obtain a contemplation of God that is *almost* direct [*proxima Deo contemplatione intelligantur*], and which will constitute in some way some *theophanies of theophanies* [*ac veluti theophaniarum theophaniae*]."[109] The act of theophany in Erigena, at least for man, is not accomplished in an invisibility all the more ineffable as it is forgotten in the vertigo of its mystifying cloud that is its own visibility (Denys). God does not require the invisible in some Neoplatonic way, but on the contrary descends into visibility itself—up to and including the encounter of transfigured flesh.

The Call to the Visible. A rereading of Saint Paul's Epistle to the Romans is sufficiently convincing: "God *calls* the things which are not as if they are" (Rom. 4:17). According to Erigena, this kind of "call" is not simply another denomination made in order to say what God *is*. Rather, it introduces the creatures into a *structure of the call* until, like God himself, they respond to their ultimate vocation of emerging into the visible. The hidden mystery is always waiting to be unveiled like the sea, which ever only withdraws to uncover each time a new shore.[110] Man, held deep within the "secret folds of nature" (*ex secretis naturae*), is sought by the theophanic God of Erigena, who conquers man by the seductive "call" of his voice in order that he may be raised as his most perfect "respondent." The act of "hearing" certainly defines Judaism ("*Hear* O Israel," Deut. 6:4), but is also, in Christianity, folded into the service of "seeing" ("he who has *seen* me has *seen* the Father," Jn. 14:9) and of "touching" ("the Word of life whom our hands have *touched*," 1 Jn. 1:1). Here we climb back up to *the* basic guiding question of this work. There is no Word on one side and flesh on the other—like a sort of false opposition between the first and second Testament. On the contrary, the Word "was made flesh in order that *flesh might become word*," as Mark the Ascetic said.[111] The structure of the call according to Erigena is not only a *concord or harmony* between God and man. It is a *seeing* and a *touching*, much as the "yes" spoken by spouses is transmuted in the visible flesh and the intimate union of interlaced bodies: "God the Father *calls men to exist* [*vocat ut sint*] by faith in his Son . . . Each day God *calls* men from the secret folds of nature [*vocat homines ex secretis naturae sinibus*] where they are judged as 'non-being,' in order that they may *appear in a visible mode* [*ut appareant visibiliter*] in form and matter and through all the other properties by which the *hidden existents* are able *to make their appearance* [*in quibus occulta apparere possunt*]."[112]

The brilliance or irruption of *what is seen*—man or God, and the manifestation of God in man—only relays the word provided that the flesh more adequately speaks, and speaks otherwise, the One who in his incarnation has deliberately chosen this other language in order to speak to man (part II: "The Flesh"). The Word does not stop speaking in order to enter into a complete silence, but he proclaims by his body what his speech no longer has to say. The profundity of the mystery of the flesh remains unfathomable—above all when it is a matter of God: "Do not be surprised that the flesh, mortal man, is able by grace to become a child of God [as we have already indicated following Erigena's comments on the Prologue of John], while it is even more miraculous that the Word was made flesh [*cum maioris miraculi sit verbum caro factum*]. Because if the superior has descended to the inferior, is it a surprise that by the action of grace of the superior, the inferior is elevated up to the superior? And all the more so as the Word was made flesh precisely in order that man might become a child of God. The Word descended to humanity in order that, by Him, man would be elevated to God [*descendit enim verbum in hominem ut, per ipsum, ascenderet homo in Deum*]."[113]

The Incarnation is therefore not (as is sometimes wrongly thought) absent from the concept of theophany in Erigena. On the contrary, the author of the *Periphyseon* brings it to a fuller realization. More miraculous than the resurrection (*maioris miraculi*), it accomplishes the descent ("from the superior to the inferior") without which there is no ascent ("from the inferior to the superior"). The *birth of God in the flesh* at the nativity already says everything about the *final glorification* of the "children of God," while itself disclosing the figure of a God made in order *to show himself*—or rather in order to be phenomenalized: "It is the unique Son of God *in the flesh* [*in carne*]—*man entirely assumed* [*hoc est in toto homine quem accepit*]—who not only has himself appeared [*non solum seipsum aperuit*], but has even *manifested to men* God the Father [*sed dum patrem hominibus manifestavit*] who up to then has remained unknown."[114]

From the "Face to Face" to the Conjoint Clamor. The final face to face with God (1 Cor. 13:12) does not reduce or suppress its visibility when it pierces the mystery. Even into final beatitude "the blessed will see God face to face [*facies ad faciem*], but calling *face* [*faciem appelans*] a comprehensible *appearance* of the divine power for the human intellect [*comprehensibilem quandam humano intellectui divinae virtutis apparitionem*]."[115] The "face of God" (*facies Dei*), understood here as a *visage* that appears instead of a (now) translucent vision in a mirror, always remains visible at the same time as irreducible. For Erigena, the final "face to face" (*facies ad faciem*) designates a sort of "encounter" or "direct confrontation," where the brilliance of the one (the face of God) never absorbs the visibility of the other (the face of man)—since every "figure" or "*facies*" always makes visible an "*appearance* of the divine power [*apparitio divinae virtutis*]"—even within the beatific vision. For Erigena, the visible never flees into invisibility, for the theophanic comprehensively maintains the total meaning of the economy of salvation.

There is a sort of "phenomenology of the call" in the creation and incarnation that responds, like an echo, to this final "face to face" of man and God in the resurrection. For the Father, *the act of creation*, and for the Son, *the act of incarnation*, both witness to a common ambition toward visibility, the one by his works and the other by his flesh. The condition sine qua non of their no less common will to save, the divine appearance or the "God phenomenon" indefatigably "races" toward humanity who sometimes nestles so far into the depths of its obscurity that only a "conjoint clamor" of the Father and Son (*clamor*) yet succeeds to draw it out: "In this way the Word of God *cries out* [*clamat*] into the very distant solitude of the divine goodness . . . He it is who *calls* [*vocat*] the things which are as though they were not; it is by him that God the Father *has cried out* [*clamavit*], or created all that he has desired to create. He has *cried out in an invisible way* [*clamavit invisibiliter*], before the creation of the world, in order that the world would come into being; he has *cried out in a visible way* [*clamavit visibiliter*] in coming into the world, in order that the world would be *saved*. He has first *cried out in eternity* [*prius clamavit aeternaliter*] before the incarnation, by his unique divinity; he *has cried out*, then, *by his flesh* [*clamavit postea per suam carnem*]."[116]

✦

By means of this "cry of the flesh" (*clamavit per suam carnem*), and with salvation in view, Erigena opens Christianity to "another language": first, of the body (part II) and then the relation to the other (part III). Certainly, the tension discovered in the Augustinian corpus between metaphysics and theology remains (chapter 1). Erigena destroys or "deconstructs" the categories, as we have seen, instead of settling there and attempting to resolve their conflict from within. The Irish theologian differs from the Bishop of Hippo by the way he uses the negative theology of Denys (unknown, of course, by Augustine), as well as in the attempt to overcome it that he puts in operation. The "category of relation" (*categoria relationis*), so dear to Saint Augustine, is here "predicable of God only in a metaphorical sense [*translative de Deo praedicare*]," not in the sense that Erigena refuses substance or pleads for some kind of self-sufficiency of the divine essence. To say that God is *neither* "relational" *nor* "being" *nor* "love" does not signify, as we have seen, that these categories are not fitting for his nature. Here one would fall back into the double aporia of the "separation of orders" and the "de-hellenization of dogma" that we have already denounced. Such a radical account of negation in Erigena relative to Denys the Areopagite contrarily indicates only that the language for speaking the "appearance of God" (*apparitio Dei*) exceeds that which adheres to the "divine essence" (*essentia divina*), just as the ways of being of God (as in "I see the Lord seated" of Is. 6:1 and other analogous formulae) speak his being further or otherwise than all the categories inherited from metaphysics, including "relation" (Augustine), and substance determined as "act of being" (Thomas Aquinas). The Dionysian *apophaticism*, under the goad of Erigenism, endures a triple transformation which causes it to leave definitively the sphere of invisibility (the cloud): (A) from the *apophatic*, the designation of the divine first passes to the *meta-ontological* in the impossible reduction of God to the modality of a thing; (B) from the *meta-ontological*, the discourse on God is then announced in the context of an *apophantic logos*, which negatively destroys the categories and positively constructs the figure of God as "the One who runs and the One who sees"; (C) and from the *apophantic*, God himself is finally unveiled as *theophanic*, since man is never so anthropophanic as when he manifests God and himself in the final "face to face" which constitutes their true encounter. In the "God phenomenon" (Erigena), the call to the visible takes the place of the categorical (Augustine) and the Neoplatonic requisite of the invisible (Denys).

A question nevertheless remains, and for now remains completely insoluble: is such an "appearance of God" not reduced, at least for man, to a simple mode of its "reification"? For, starting from scripture, one could seek to define a God first who "reveals himself" (*ostendit*) in his ways of being rather than in his being. And it would again be necessary for the individual believer to be rendered capable of receiving him *in this way* and not otherwise. Speaking in the categories of the theologian Hans Urs von Balthasar, the "objective evidence" of the form of revelation simultaneously requires "subjective evidence," not in order to reduce the "form" to itself, but on the contrary to render us capable of receiving it as we are in ourselves, as living subjects, receivers of such an Appearance (*Gestalt*): "Not only intellectual but *existential prerequisites* must be fulfilled in order that the form that makes its claim on one's total existence may also find a hearing in this total existence."[117]

The "God phenomenon" in John Scotus Erigena (chap. 2) therefore thoroughly overflows the "categorical God" as it was reworked in Saint Augustine (chap. 1). But now we will focus on the *act of faith* that does not reduce God to the status of a "thing," if indeed neither God nor man meet the requirements of a "something" (*non est quid*). Personal conversion thus becomes the condition of the non-reification of the One in whom we believe. It would be necessary, in this case, to turn to Meister Eckhart and his notion of "detachment" (*Abgeschiedenheit*) interpreted as a mode of the phenomenological reduction that allows the "epochal conversion" of the receiving subject (chap. 3) in order to respond to the "phenomenality" of the appearing God (chap. 2).

Chapter 3

✦

Reduction and Conversion (Meister Eckhart)

Phenomenology admits no "phenomena" apart from the method called the reduction (*epochê*)—which, moreover, clearly distinguishes the theological usage of the term (simple description of objective phenomena) from the specifically philosophical usage (suspension of the world and attention to acts of consciousness).[1] The tension between metaphysics and theology (chap. 1), relayed by the "other discourse" of the God phenomenon (chap. 2), now waits to be explored vis-à-vis the receiving subject who does not reify God (chap. 3). For, if "God does not know what he is, it is because he is not something [*Deus nescit se quid est quia non est quid*]," then it is appropriate for the believer or retreatant himself to take leave of all things, including the conception of himself as a thing, in order to welcome God as no-thing: "Man ought to be *so poor* that he would be and have *no place* where God is able to act," emphasizes Eckhart in his brilliant manner. He continues: "There where man *guards a place*, he guards a *difference*."[2] The possible relation between Eckhart and phenomenology is a familiar theme: in his course on *The Foundations of Medieval Mysticism* (1918–1919), the young Heidegger returned to the Thuringian as one who developed a "specific concept of knowledge"; and Michel Henry continues the theme in his *Essence of Manifestation* (1963), quasi-inverting it, seeing in the figure of the Dominican master the one who enacts "the true critique of knowledge" understood as "exteriority" or "putting at a distance." Henry quotes Eckhart: "The Jews stood at a distance, and it is precisely for this reason that they could not understand God."[3]

If Heidegger or Henry's debt to Eckhart is famous, then the father of phenomenology himself, Edmund Husserl's filiation from the Dominican master, specifically concerning the passage from Eckhart's conversion as "detachment" (*Abgeschiedenheit*) to Husserl's reduction as "bracketing" (*epochê*), remains much less known. Noting this is not exactly catching an error in the history of philosophy, especially since recent works have shown that it had never really been forgotten.[4] Rather, it is above all to demonstrate, at least from the vantage of a reduction from God outside of his substantiality from the outset (chaps. 1–3), that the subject itself ought also to submit to this mode of *epochê*, at least in order not to reify the phenomenality of the One that it is supposed to display. It is because an adequate logos is necessary in order to "gather" (*legein*) the *phaïnesthai* of the *apparitio Dei*, as I have emphasized, that John Scotus Erigena defines the conditions of the apophantic in order to receive the apophatic (chap. 2). But it is Meister Eckhart who will establish such a *disposition* in the believer that he will, as it were, convert himself from within his natural attitude in order to be rendered capable of receiving God phenomenologically (chap. 3). If Eckhartian detachment (*Abgeschiedenheit*) is able to appear as a harbinger of Heideggerian "serenity" (*Gelassenheit*), and if the "rose without why" of Angelus Silesius demonstrates the premonitory meaning of Henry's "auto-affection," then the Husserlian "reduction" also finds one of its possible origins explicitly in Eckhart. To climb toward the mystical source of the phenomenological *epochê* is not simply to open onto a phenomenological path, but onto a medievalist one at the same time. The detour by Husserl—who, according to his private correspondences, had read Eckhart's *Sermons* (infra), appears in fact as the indispensable starting point for a renewed interpretation of Meister Eckhart today, beyond Heidegger's filiation with which we are all so familiar. The necessity of a *phenomenological practice* measured by the mode of being of the medievals will find in Eckhart its fruit—yet a fruit that, if not the safest to grasp, is at least the ripest: that which is "essentially new about the phenomenological reduction" (Husserl) is measured in fact by the "always new" of religious conversion (Eckhart).[5]

✦

From the Confession to a Twofold Secret

From Husserl's confession in § 35 of the *Crisis* (1936), "reduction" and "conversion" have always been tied together. The relation between them that lies at the heart of medieval mysticism is therefore hardly arbitrary. To research "religious conversion" as a mode of "phenomenological *epochê*" is on the contrary a concern of the first phenomenologist himself: "Perhaps it will even become manifest that the *total phenomenological attitude* and the *epochê* belonging to it are destined in essence to effect, at first, a complete personal transformation, comparable in the beginning to a *religious conversion*."[6]

At least twice Husserl refers "personally" to the religious attitude as foundational and explicative of phenomenology itself. He does this first in relation to Meister Eckhart and then in conversation with Edith Stein. On June 27, 1932, Husserl confided to Dorion Cairns that Eckhart was one of phenomenology's principle initiators: "I would be able to take over *whole pages* of Meister Eckhart *unchanged*."[7] A private conversation with Edith Stein in 1935 attests that "the life of man is nothing else than a path toward God": "I have attempted to get through to the end without the help of theology, its proofs and its methods; in other words, I have wanted *to attain God without God*."[8] However the goal is reached (the approach toward God), whatever the final status of the "*atheist* way toward an authentic humanity,"[9] it is therefore possible, and even probable, that Meister Eckhart was one of the earliest vanguards of phenomenology because of his attempt to reduce all exteriority to interiority, all objective realism to transcendental subjectivism and all divine transcendence to the pure immanence of the ego: "However remarkable the exit toward itself [*extase*)] is, remaining *in itself* [*instase*] is something even higher," Eckhart insists in his *Treatise on Detachment*. Similarly, Husserl emphasizes in the *Crisis*: "The spirit, and indeed only the spirit, exists in itself and for itself, is self-sufficient."[10] Husserl's confiding to Dorian Cairns and to Edith Stein, some years apart (1932 and 1935) therefore leaves open the possibility that the influence of Meister Eckhart on the father of phenomenology was more than merely occasional or secondary.

A Double Transcendence

The terms used by Husserl concerning the "phenomenological reduction" recall in fact terms used currently to express "religious conversion": thus the "reduction" (*epochê*) is required to be understood as an experience "of a totally other order" than the natural order, understood as the place of a "new experience," marked as a "radical modification of attitude."[11] A question is nevertheless posed at the heart of this parallelism between Husserl and Eckhart. An interdict is in fact thrown up by the master of phenomenology as concerns all theological practice of the reduction, insofar as God himself ought to be "put out of play" (*Ideas I*, § 58), by contrast to the "pure I" which alone is maintained in this massive operation of suspension (*Ideas I*, § 57). The transcendence of the ego is distinguished from the transcendence of God insofar as the second is reduced, but not the first: "Because of the immediately essential role played by this transcendency [of the *pure I*] in the case of any cogitation, *we must not undertake its exclusion* [§ 57]," whereas "we *extend the phenomenological reduction* to include [God as] this 'absolute' and 'transcendent' being. It shall *remain excluded* from the new field of research which is to be provided, since this shall be a field of *pure consciousness* [§ 58]."[12] Certainly the ultimate God suspended here [§ 58] seems rather distant from the truly religious consideration of a God that can be believed in and who is the operator of conversion—indeed so much so that Emmanuel Levinas himself will attest to having struggled "to take seriously" these instructions of Husserl on God in the *Ideas*.[13] There is no evidence that the reduction of a "real transcendence" implies the suspension of "intentional transcendence," no more than the putting between parentheses of "real immanence" leads us outside the circuit of "intentional immanence."[14] Briefly, the way of "transcendency within immanency"[15] does not prohibit thinking God himself as a *phenomenological type of transcendence*, that is to say, as a *mode of opening* to the very heart of the *intentional immanence* of the ego.[16]

Egocentrism and Theocentrism

Edith Stein, however, despite the sanctifying panegyrics offered justly in her honor (as religious sister and saint, Benedicta of the Cross), is precisely the one who, in my opinion, will forbid such a return to the ego in relation to speaking of God. It is certainly appropriate to recognize the merit of the future Carmelite in tracing the path that moves from phenomenology to Thomism in the context of her conversion to Christianity. It is nevertheless the case that the former assistant to Husserl will follow less the way of the reduction of transcendence to immanence, than she will accentuate her own way of conversion to God who is both absolute and objectively transcendent. A text from 1929, offered in honor of Husserl's seventieth birthday, testifies to this, and, as far as the thought of Husserl goes, it is even doubtful that what she offers is really a "gift" (as much as a critique). She states: "So, here we may well have the sharpest contrast between transcendental phenomenology and Catholic philosophy: the latter has a *theocentric* and the former an *egocentric* orientation."[17] Phenomenological egocentrism is opposed therefore at every point to theological theocentrism, in an impassable distance gaping between two boundary lines. Methodological atheism on one side (Husserl) and objectivist theocentrism on the other (Stein), phenomenology is definitively separated from theology to the point that no confrontation between them would be foreseeable, nor any longer possible: We "can start with nothing but the *ego cogito*," insists Husserl in his *Cartesian Meditations*,[18] and as Alexander Löwith comments in a definitive fashion, "Husserl therefore is *not* able to search for the solution of his problem in theology but rather in egology."[19]

The Choice of Eckhart

Does this mean that one cannot today return to the ego in order to constitute a new mode of theology—not opposed to Thomism, of course, but rather more apt to articulate the doctrine "in such a way as to correspond to the particular demands of our time"?[20] The choice of Eckhart, which could seem to some a passing fad, is in fact particularly judicious for taking advantage of the sermons of the "brother preacher" to the Beguines for the sake of renewing an egocentric philosophy which is revealed to be theocentric *as well*, and capable of illuminating theology's own ambition toward renewal. If the professor of Göttingen and Fribourg im Breisgau certainly read the master from Thuringia (as the discussion with Cairns of 1932 discloses) and also perhaps underwent an experience of conversion (as the discussion with Stein in 1935 insinuates), it is not certain that he has reduced or "put out of play" God himself in the same way at the end of his career (in the *Krisis*, Fribourg period) as at the beginning (in *Ideas I*, Göttingen period). Let us make no mistake, however. It is not a question here of a hijacking, of which the phenomenologists are sometimes so poorly accused when they also write theology, but only the testimony of an encounter between a mystical path on the one hand (Eckhart) and a phenomenological way of thought on the other (Husserl). There is always something insidious about "forced baptisms," which are disrespectful of modes of thought that are never avowedly Christian. It is still the case that a return to an interiority which is also capable of engendering and even constituting a world (be it God's), finds in Eckhart its first roots inasmuch as it is first investigated there. Eckhart confides in "Sermon 4": "I once said that I am not properly capable of putting into speech that which moves from the interior to the exterior . . . : that ought not to come from the exterior, on the contrary, it must *exit from the interior*."[21] That word which is like speech coming from the mouth is also, and eminently, the Son as Word who comes out of the mouth of God. If it is fitting for us also to "engender God the very God" (infra), it would not in this sense be a theocentrism outside of a certain form of egocentrism, which should not be confused of course with all the forms of egoism of the subject which do not have anything to do with its return to itself.[22]

We will follow the counsel of Eckhart in the *Talks of Instruction* (*Rede der Unterweisung*) since he confirms all the recommendations of Husserl, as well as Heidegger later, concerning the conditions of access to the things themselves as moments of lived experience of consciousness: "Begin therefore *first of all by yourself*, and let yourself [be]."[23] It no longer suffices to speak of God as "relation" covered over by substance (chap. 1), nor of extracting the conditions of his theophany in order to disclose in it the possibility of a certain phenomenality (chap. 2), but only principally to center the discourse on the mode of being of the *subject* that receives, even produces, the phenomenon "God" (chap. 3). Will such an engendering of the divine starting from the ego be reduced to a simple "ontological monism" or a "pure immanence" in a quasi-identification of man and God (Henry)?[24] Will the hypothesis of an "articulated monism" of exteriority and interiority have anything further to say within a more dialectical perspective (P.-J. Labarrière)?[25] These questions, which are today at the heart of many, often extreme conflicts, should in reality return us to the texts: is the phenomenological *epochê*, as Husserl thinks it, capable of illuminating the Eckhartian movement of religious conversion and its proper detachment (*Abgeschiedenheit*)? And does this Eckhartian abandonment allow a return, as if by an automatic recoil, to the pretended exclusion of the theological by the egological (*Ideas I*, § 58)? These are the true questions that it would be necessary for us to reinvestigate independently of every polemic, most of which are usually as sterile as they are trivial.

Rereading Eckhart in light of phenomenology, we come to see biblical figures as models of theological "conversion" that illustrate this path of a "progressive reduction," the *philosophical* resiliency of which will not be without consequences for theology itself: (A) the reduction to the I, or the apprenticeship of Mary of Bethany; (B) the constitution of God, or the fecundity of Martha; (C) egoity as nihilation, or the figure of Paul. In each biblical figure, reread phenomenologically (Mary, Martha, Paul), as in each posture (reduction, constitution, nihilation), something is articulated of the suspension of a self gradually rendered capable of receiving the God phenomenon as such. On this progressive and radical return toward an egoity in love with the divinity (1st part), will depend then our own capacity to receive God in his flesh as in ours (2nd part), as well as the urgency of constituting together a common world which no longer forgets the other as condition of all singularity (3rd part).

The Reduction to the I: The Apprenticeship of Mary (of Bethany)

It seems that the originality of Meister Eckhart is found in his prioritization of the exegesis of Holy Scripture in order to aid philosophical problems.[26] But such a process, in Eckhartian discourse as in the context of a "phenomenological praxis," is not reduced to the simple usage of the natural light (philosophy) in order then to clarify the supernatural (theology). On the contrary, by using another light (that of God, being, art, etc.) the believer, like the phenomenologist, will uncover the light of another intentionally dwelling within (the Trinity, other people, aesthetic dazzlement, etc.). The figures of Martha and Mary of Bethany, so dear to Eckhart (*serm.* 2 and *serm.* 86) will serve as the Ariadne's thread to follow the path that leads, step by step, from the "reduction to the I" to the "constitution of God in the I"—and thus makes *religious conversion* a possible mode of the *phenomenological reduction.*

Natural Attitude and Phenomenological Reduction

"As they (the disciples) continued on their way, Jesus entered into a village and a woman named Martha received him into her house" (Lk. 10:38). This famous episode of Martha and Mary, particularly in its *introductory section* just quoted, serves as the fulcrum of a rare philosophical exegesis in Meister Eckhart ("Sermon 2" and "Sermon 86").[27] Indeed, Martha, ordinarily accused of dishonestly dealing with her sister who on the contrary chose "the better part," actually does a work of kindness according to Eckhart and hence outclasses even Mary of Bethany by her true sense of obedience in a "detached" hearing of God. Here everything is inverted. The one who is most often reprimanded for her jealousy (Martha) is in reality the one who is recognized for her quality of empathy toward her sister (Mary)—seeing that which her sister has not yet understood, the "reduction" itself: "Lord, command her to help me (Lk. 10:40)." "This," emphasizes Eckhart, "Martha says *not by contrariety*, rather: she speaks from a *benevolence* which compels her."[28]

The "reductive" reading of the conversion alone explains this strange reversal of a traditional malice and a surprising benevolence. Where Martha stunningly practices the phenomenological *epochê* and opens a path to it for her sister (hence her benevolence), Mary remains in the "natural attitude," taking God in a worldly or "thetic" manner, as a "reality" always at once existing and objective (*Wirklichkeit*).[29]

Mary, or the Natural Attitude. By contrast to a hasty reading of this passage from the Gospel, the natural attitude, or in other terms that which entertains the most ordinary relation to things and to beings, is signified by Mary of Bethany rather than Martha—especially as Mary herself would with all her heart "remain sitting at the Lord's feet listening to his word" (Lk. 10:39). Indeed there is nothing here that excludes the fact that Martha, taken up with "the multiple cares of serving her guests" (Lk. 10:40) is actually not listening, as it were, to that which listening signifies, that is, obedience: "In true obedience," Eckhart emphasizes, "she has completely *exited from herself into God*."[30] To hear or to obey, since they share the same root (*akouô*), is primarily understood by Eckhart as *to climb out of* or *to undo* the self—or better, as a certain *mode of self* in its relation to the world. Who is the one who truly hears and obeys in this passage from the Gospel? That is, who discards more of the conception of God as "thing" and understands him as act of a "life in itself"? Not Mary, who sits, far from quotidian occupations, absorbed in God as "thing," but rather Martha—who stands "*with or close to* things" without being "*in* things."[31] The true concern of Martha is less in finding help for serving her guests (Lk. 10:40) than of fearing for her sister insofar as she remains in a simple posture of hearing from God: "She feared that her sister *remained stuck in the feeling of well-being* and failed to be elevated to *a higher state*."[32]

Martha does not have the *concern of self* in a busy relation with the world, but *concern for the other* who remains in a relation of absorption *in God*. Fearing for her sister, Martha accuses Mary not for her failure to engage in material tasks, but rather for her non-detachment from a purely sensible and reifying listening. Translated into the phenomenological language of Husserl, Mary remains in some sense beholden to the *natural attitude* and therefore "perceives the world, and lives there, in a completely natural way being *interested* in it"—that is, here, in the world of God.[33] Mary, if she is attached and absorbed in listening to the Lord, is progressively *lost* in him in a "sensible delight"—"*lost* in the world," Eckhart says "*lost* in things, *lost* in ideas, *lost* in the plants and the beasts . . . : *outside, diverted*."[34] In being forgotten out in the world the sister of Martha is so to speak "already ready to be treated *as a thing in the world*" as Ricoeur said in commenting on Husserl.[35] The apprenticeship of Mary led by Martha becomes in a sense the phenomenological *epochê*: "Martha says 'Lord order her to help me' (Lk. 10:40), as if she had said: my sister believes that she can do what she wants as long as she is *sitting close to you* in consolation. Let her see if all is well and order her to *rise up* and *leave you*."[36]

Martha therefore does not require that Mary be *attached* to things in being preoccupied with quotidian aspects of the world, as a much too rapid reading of her own business as a form of natural attitude. On the contrary, she desires that her sister be *detached* from the Lord as "thing" (*Abgeschiedenheit*), a sort of phenomenological reduction. In Husserl's terms, yet remaining aware of too abrupt a rapprochement, Martha requires that Mary should not lack, like Descartes much later, "the transcendental orientation," letting the cogito slide down into the *res cogitans*, to the point of a surreptitious affirmation of a new "realism" of the subject, which definitively annihilates it as a pure I or ego constitutive of the world.[37] If, as we have seen (chap. 2), Erigena in some sense liberates the "God phenomenon" in order to allow it to appear in its modes of appearing rather than in its essence ("I see the Lord, seated on a throne" and other formulae), Eckhart, in producing the necessary detachment that makes it impossible for God to be identified within the mode of being of "substance," portrays man as a receptor of a non-reified divine (chap. 3). It is not sufficient simply to confirm that God is not "some thing" (*non est quid*); again it would be necessary that this non-reification attains the *practical modality* of man himself in his apprehension of God—that is, in his "detachment" from things in general and particularly from God as thing (Eckhart). It is Martha's task to teach her sister this "conversion of self" as a mode of phenomenological *epochê*, operating already from herself and on herself, that is, according to Eckhart's remarkable formula, teaching her "no longer to take God as if you would wrap his head in a coat and stuff it under a bench."[38]

Martha, or the Phenomenological Epochê. The Lord's response to Martha—"Martha, Martha, you concern yourself with many things, and only one thing is necessary" (Lk. 10:41–42)—cannot nor should not be interpreted as a reproach of Martha by Jesus, no more than what Martha said to Mary was a tirade, since it advocated that she leave the Lord and detach herself from being buried in the world of things—or rather, the world of God considered as a thing. For Eckhart, "you concern yourself" (Lk 10:41) means, "You stand *along with* things and the things are not *in you*"; or again, "You stand *near* things and not *in* things."[39]

Eckhart's *positive* conception of "care"—contrary to the *Sorge* of Heidegger,[40] is the condition of a proper understanding of this passage. When the Lord says, "you concern yourself," normally understood in a negative way, it is necessary actually to read: "You are *watchful*, Martha."[41] This signifies not that Martha is busy with all the needs of service and attempts to lead her sister into them, but only that she worries with Jesus about seeing Mary so objectively seated "at the feet of the Lord" that she is rendered incapable of breaking from him and living according to the mode of reduction, and thus that she remains in some sense "along with" him instead of being "in" him. The relation of *inherence* indicated by the second formula ("being in" or "being within") takes precedence over the relation of *proximity* indicated by the first ("being near" or "being with"). Martha holds the Lord "in her," or rather is taken "in him," that is, "in the kitchen" (inherence), so she does not necessarily have to be *there* like Mary, seated "before" him, in the locality of encounter or of attentive hearing (proximity). The "reduced" presence of the Lord in Martha or of Martha in the Lord withdraws in some sense from the *objective* mode of their relation, which constitutes the greatest *objection* to the resurrection. "I am *with you* [*vobiscum*] always even until the end of the age" declares Christ at the end of Matthew (Mt. 28:20)—not because the Resurrection One is *there* present "before us" or "with us" (proximity), but in the sense alone that he is "in us" or that we are "in him" (inherence). "If someone says to you 'the Messiah is *here* [*hic*] or that he is *there* [*illic*],' do not believe them . . ."; he is *not here* [*non est hic*] because he has been raised as he has said (Mt. 24:23; 28:6). Translated into phenomenological terms, "detachment" (*Abgeschiedenheit*), reread as a mode of "reduction" (*epochê*), operates principally in the resurrection, and even accomplishes God's "apperceptive transposition of the other," that man, in himself, is incapable of realizing.[42]

The shared concern (of Jesus and Martha for Mary) has in this sense a *positive* meaning in Eckhart as it keeps man "in the middle of things" and things "in the middle of man" without however leaving him "consumed by them." Contrary to Heidegger, Eckhart's "care" protects man from being thrown into the world and consumed by it. Retroactively returning to the second Heidegger, the just "care" of Eckhart remains more on the side of "dwelling" or the being "at home" of man with the world (*bauen*) than of "care" or being "outside of self" and projected into the world (*besorgen*). Such care is "vigilance" in an authentic relation with the world and not "being-in-and-before-oneself," always escaping oneself, lost and forgotten in a worldly preoccupation.[43]

The "at Home" of Egoity. The reduction of Martha in her positive relation of care to the world is therefore accomplished in a manner that is all the more remarkable insofar as it does not negate care but realizes through it a sort of "suspension" or "bracketing" of the world, which does not destroy the world but is uniquely attached to a proper lived experience of the world: "Martha, and all the friends of God along with her, stand *with care*, not *in care* . . . ; she stood *among* things, not *in* things."[44] Like the phenomenological *epochê* (*Ideas I*, § 31), indeed, like a counter to Cartesian doubt or Hegelian dialectic in advance, the Eckhartian detachment accomplished by Martha (*Abgeschiedenheit*) neither destroys nor annihilates the world. Instead, it consecrates the world as a place of relation, of the unveiling of an interiority that constitutes it as such: "The little phrase that I have cited earlier says: God has sent his only Son into the world (1 Jn. 4:9). You ought not to relate to him in the *exterior world* where Christ ate and drank with us; you ought to understand it from the *interior world*."[45]

The "little city" or "small fortress" into which Jesus enters in Bethany is thus Martha's and not Mary's—who is not mentioned by the Evangelist: "Jesus entered into a *village*, and a woman, named *Martha*, received him into her home" (Lk. 10:38). The place where God resides has nothing to do with Mary's comfortable residing "at the feet of the Lord" (Lk. 10:39) in the mode of a thing among things. In the world of beings God remains "without home" or "without place," "u-topic" (*u-topos*). He does not "subsist" in the house of Martha in the mode of being made present ("presentification"), as he would be under the reifying regard of Mary in the "natural attitude." Rather, he penetrates into the "small fortress" of Martha as into her "depths." Suspending or bracketing the world of things (*epochê*), Martha moves from her sister to the *middle* of the world of quotidian tasks without reducing God to a thing. Precisely because God remains *within* her, she is able to be elsewhere (in the kitchen) and to conserve God within (in her fortress). In contrast to Mary who in leaving God would lose the one whom she had reified, Martha lives with the fullness of the Spirit, which only theology allows one to recognize. The discovery of egoity in Eckhart, like the subject in Augustine, finds its reasons in mysticism—in which theology precedes and founds the philosophical approach: "It is no longer I who live, but Christ lives in me" (Gal. 2:20). One would therefore be very wrong in wanting to "de-theologize" medieval philosophy, and Eckhart in particular. The mystical and Augustinian movement of introspection finds its culmination in medieval theology and especially in Eckhart. The "at home" of Martha in her egoity, rather than remaining to be defined, stands as a figurehead of all egological philosophy, in order to reach God within: "*At home*," insists Eckhart, "that is, seeing God without intermediary, *in his own being*."[46]

The emphasis on Eckhart in the *Essence of Manifestation* (the focus of the only section uniquely centered on an author) was able to lead Michel Henry to interpret the "world" as interior world (*I Am the Truth*) and the flesh as the experience of pure auto-affection (*Incarnation*). In both cases it is actually Eckhart who speaks: "interior world" without exteriority, on the one hand, and "auto-affected flesh" without body on the other hand. We have shown that it is appropriate to interrogate these decisions anew—less in order to reject them than to understand the type of phenomenality that they have engendered. The subject in whom God comes to dwell is not first given in the empirical I that can always be decomposed, but in the transcendental I all the more interiorized as it obtains the One who comes to be manifested in it.[47]

Empirical I and Transcendental I

To Say "I": Neither This nor That. Indeed, some have interpreted this identity of the "at home" or the "being one's own" in Eckhart either as a dialectical unity of differences (a "gathering together"),[48] or as the place of a suppression of all intentionality (auto-affectivity).[49] It is hardly necessary to overtake Hegel (P.-J. Labarrière) or to take leave of Husserl (Henry) in order to carry out a *phenomenological practice* of the reduction like that of Meister Eckhart. The "little town of Bethany" or "little fortress" where Jesus was received (*castellum*), such that it no longer designates only a geographic place but the very *person* of Martha, confers on her ego an inviolable role: that of a "pure ego," an original transcendence that could never be "put out of play."[50] What Eckhart calls the "I" is not an empirical or countable collection of *powers of the soul* that we see in all the "psychical" classifications inherited from Aristotle: imagination, volition, intellection, and so on. Nor does the "little fortress" signify merely a "power in the spirit," a "rampart of spirit," a "light of the spirit," or even a "little spark," even though Eckhart himself uses these expressions (and one ought to attend to their specific use in "Sermon 2"). "Powers of the soul" and "inner light" remain too reifying to signify the truth of the manifestation of God as such. Rather, Martha seeks to teach her sister the phenomenological discovery of bracketing the empirical nature of experience and returning to the transcendental ego as lived experience or the collection of the acts of consciousness. Eckhart says: "Our little inner fortress is *neither here nor there*; yet it is something elevated beyond *here or there*."[51]

Husserl emphasizes that the transcendental ego itself as reduced "is not a piece of the world" and the objects of the world "are not real pieces [of my ego]."[52] It is therefore not appropriate to define the ego according to *the mode of the world*—power, rampart, light, sparks, and so on. Like Husserl's transcendental ego "carrying the unity of the world's meaning" without itself being in the world,[53] the "*soul in its ground* [*Seelengrund*] is," according to Eckhart, "as inexpressible as God."[54] Because it is necessary—and here Eckhart advances beyond all failures of Cartesianism—not to confound the pure ego (as seat of meaning or the ego in its ground) and the empirical ego (properties of the ego as properties of the soul), Eckhart will progressively renounce the word "soul" which "does not signify the ground [*Grund*] and has not reached human nature"[55]—which Descartes in his time precisely does not do by folding the cogito into the *res cogitans*.[56]

The One Thing Necessary: Detachment. By realizing, on the one hand, the phenomenological *epochê* by means of the suspension of God as thing, without failing, at the same time, to move to the heart of the world, and, on the other hand, by constituting the root of the soul as pure me or seat of meaning [*foyer du sens*], Martha exhibits—according to the *Treatise on Detachment*—the exemplary figure of the *Abgeschiedenheit*: "Our Lord says to Martha: 'The one who wants to be without trouble and clear, she ought to have one thing—*detachment*.' "[57]

The only "necessary thing" granted to Mary by the Lord (Lk. 10:42) is therefore not such that "the better part" would be either possessed by Mary (absorption of self in listening to the Lord) or prohibited to Martha (by virtue of her busyness in the world). On the contrary, and against the unworthiness of such a comparison in the eyes of God, this "better [part]" paradoxically indicates to Eckhart that it is a matter of Mary *taking part in the better* already possessed by Martha—of "happening" herself upon the one thing necessary, that is, onto detachment, which alone renders blessed. It is as if Christ said: "Be *reassured* and not indignant, Martha, your sister Mary has chosen the better part [Lk. 10:42]; she *must pass through this*. The greatest thing which can happen to the creature must *happen* to it: she must *become blessed as you are*."[58] It has often been emphasized that it is wrong to oppose the two sisters—the active life on the one hand (Martha) and the contemplative life on the other (Mary). For Meister Eckhart's Dominican predecessor, Thomas Aquinas, the well-ordered Christian life is "mixed" (active and contemplative). We will have a chance to see the endorsement given to this position by Saint Bonaventure (chap. 6).[59] Eckhart of course radicalizes the concept, and sees contemplation at the heart of action. Or better: he makes action, as concerned immersion in things, the condition of contemplation, as presence of God in himself as non-thing. The "detachment" from God as thing (by virtue of action) makes possible the reception and manifestation of God in himself as non-thing (contemplation). In Eckhart there is not a separation between a purely active life and a purely contemplative life—yet neither is there a Dominican "mixed life," well ordered by active and contemplative faith. On the contrary, contemplation is lived at the heart of action—not in the sense that one sees or prays to God through action, but rather insofar as action achieves the necessary "detachment" from God as thing, producing thereby a new "attachment" to God for his own sake and as the "nothing" of all things.

The Fullness of God: Attachment. Detachment, simultaneously from things and from their modality as thing (being absorbed in listening to the Lord), is not operative outside of a *new attachment* to God and to his proper mode of being: "Detachment makes me *receptive to nothing but God*."[60] The *emptiness* of *Abgeschiedenheit* in the relation of man to creatures ought not to obscure the *plenitude* of his attachment to God, in a listening which is no longer a mere sensible delight (Mary of Bethany), but is elevated, on the contrary, beyond into a "letting go" of oneself and the world (Martha).[61] "Listening" is here "obedience" insofar as it reveals the dependence of the listening to the one who is listened to, a dependence that is all the more stringent as it abolishes the distance between the emitter and the receiver, ordinarily established in the relation to the other and to God, understood as things or "being there" (like Mary "seated at the feet of the Lord"). The emptiness of the self liberates in this way a space for the fullness of God or rather makes space itself the place of the fullness of God. The numerous Buddhist or Zen interpretations of Eckhart have not adequately grappled with its properly Christian intention. Better—and we will return to this below in relation to Bernard of Clairvaux's correction of the "mysticism of *pathos* [*mystique pathetique*]" of Origen (chap. 7)—"detachment" does not have meaning in and for itself, any more than "nothing" should be sought in pure vacuity. On the one hand, one is only "detached" from God as *thing* in which one delights in an exterior manner, because one is "attached" to a God as *life* interiorly: "'Lord, command her to get up!' says Martha to Jesus about her sister, as if she said: 'Lord, I would love that she not be seated there in *delight*; I would love for her to learn *to live*, that she would possess it essentially.'"[62] On the other hand, one is only "empty" and understood as a subject before God because we let ourselves be fully filled by the whole of our source as a fontal plenitude. As Eckhart says in his *Treatise on Detachment*: "*To be empty of every creature* is to be *full of God*, and to be *full of every creature* is to be *empty of God*."[63] The life of God in himself gives way to or replaces the relation of the thing to the self's exterior; and the whole of the divine takes the place of the whole of the human, including the very idea of a place, which alone justifies the *nothing* of all creatures in relation to the Creator.

True "poverty," the central focus of the commentary on the first beatitude ("Blessed are the poor in spirit"), is not simply the index of a humble man "drawn from the earth" (*Adamâ*) and returning to the "earth" (*humus*).[64] Instead, in the Eckhartian and metaphysical reading of the "poor man," it stems from the absence of distance and of place in which to receive God, which again would be for him a sign of wealth. Eckhart certainly abolishes differences, which gives rise to perhaps an appropriate suspicion that he has not fully respected the necessary difference between Creator and creature. But it is not the case that in this ontological suppression there hides a mystical position more than a philosophical thesis. *In order to give his entire place to God man no longer has a place*: not as if he wanted to leave his place (deification), or even to fill all place (pride), but rather that the action of having a place is for him some sort of "de-place" (detachment)—whereas it is for God alone to take the place that he will have determined in constituting our egoity (attachment): "man ought to be so *poor* that he has *no place* where God would be able to operate [as I have already indicated, following Eckhart]. There where man *guards a place*, he guards a *difference*."[65]

Far from the Augustinian tension of "relation" and "substance" which always conserves a certain exteriority between the poles (chap. 1), like distance in Dionysian apophaticism and even like proximity in Erigenian theophany (chap. 2), the poverty of Eckhartian detachment creates such a *coincidence* of man and God that the subject itself loses its being in the nothing of its egoity (chap. 3). In the experience of *Abgeschiedenheit*, I am never more "me" than when I am not or no longer "me"—not in fusion with God but detached from myself in order to receive God. We empty ourselves only in order to be full of God. The detachment from self, which includes the detachment from a reified God, thus marks the attachment to the deity by a suspension or a reduction from the world and myself, which finally "leaves" God to be God (*Gelassenheit*—a concept to which we will return). It would be necessary to insist: the Christian plenitude of an *attachment* to an identified Other (deity as Trinity) remains much more present in Eckhart than does the vacuity of the Buddhist type, a simple annihilation of the creature to the point of a total lack of differentiation with God himself. The second (the annihilation of the creature) is an expression of the first (the identified affirmation of the Trinity); the first (attachment to the Trinity) is not an expression of the second (detachment in nothing). Hence Alain de Libera: "If Eckhart sometimes seems to flirt with *Trinitarian heresy*, that is because we *do not understand* and *do not recognize* what he is saying, transmitted and transposed into the coarse idiom of his predication." Lefert confirms: "The theology of Eckhart *always remains Trinitarian*: because the world is created *in the Word*, the divinized soul participates in the creation of the world." Such is the meaning of the famous affirmation in "Sermon 29," which follows the Trinitarian monadology initiated by Bonaventure: "Insofar as God perceives *in me*, I perceive myself *in him*."[66]

The suspension of the world and the discovery of the *pure I* therefore does not suffice, in phenomenology as much as theology, to engender a new world—now generated starting from a subject detached from itself and attached to God. Poor in his detachment and believing in his attachment, the believer himself ought to be rendered capable of constituting a new world—the world of God precisely, where the concept of "birth" unlocks the meaning of the Word even today, starting from a self mediated by another (reverse intentionality) and no longer locked within the *solus ipse* of being closed in on itself (solipsism).

The Constitution of God: The Fecundity of Martha

Having been accused of reifying God in relation to "Mary seated at the feet of the Lord," should egology [*Ideas* I, § 57] banish theology [*Ideas* I, § 58] in an intensified reverse opposition, from a supposed theocentrism that suppresses egocentrism? The objection would be valid, but only to the degree that its conception of theology is objective and not relative to the object (*objectale*) within the insurmountable relation of God and the ego. It is precisely this, however, that Eckhart refuses, discovering the inverse: namely the strange possibility for man of engendering the first (God) starting from the second (the ego) and thus giving birth to God starting from that which is human. After having *negatively* reduced or bracketed God as thing (the "reduction to the I" or the apprenticeship of Mary), Eckhart *positively* shows the astonishing possibility for man of giving birth to the divine starting from this reduced I (the "constitution of God" or the fecundity of Martha). The argument passes from "reduction" to "constitution," or from Mary to Martha insofar as they exemplify this transfer. Explicitly naming the apprenticeship of Mary, Eckhart emphasizes: "That the human being *receives God into himself*, it is well, and in this receptivity he is intact." Eckhart continues, this time designating the work of Martha: "But that God would become *fruitful in him*, it is better; because the fecundity of the gift is only the gratitude for the gift."[67]

Martha, pregnant with God, under the form of the "little fortress into which Jesus has entered" (*intravit Jesus in quoddam castellum*), ought now to generate the one who has in some way made her fruitful. It is no longer sufficient merely to find God within, which was the condition for remaining at once tied to the things (in the kitchen) and present to God (in a more intimate way). It is necessary now to engender God as "no-thing," that is, as "no one" [*personne*] or "flux" for which the very act of birth depends at least as much on the human soul which comes to generate it, as on its existence in its avowed objectivity. Hence Angelus Silesius said (at least in this respect a perfect disciple of Eckhart): "If Christ is born a thousand times in Bethlehem and not *in you*, then you remain forever lost."[68] Otherwise said, God is "act" and not "being" for Eckhart. Neither relation still bound to substance (Augustine), nor simple appearing phenomenon (Erigena), nor even "act of being" formulated in the terms of a revised metaphysics (Aquinas), the divine is here pure "deity"—in Eckhart's language: "generativity" and not "substantiality," "flux," "flow," or "effusion" and not "substance," which is definitively abandoned in the name of a mysticism "detached" from all objectivity. Jesus responds to Martha: "'There is one thing necessary' [Lk. 10:42] and not two." This no longer means here simply that Mary is seated at the feet of the Lord, one the one hand, and Martha is busy in the kitchen, on the other. On the contrary, it signifies that "you and I (Martha and Jesus) make *one*, once enveloped in eternal light."[69] Eckhart always says in relation to Martha: "It is still a *power* which is equally incorporeal: it *flows* out of the spirit and remains in the spirit and is in every way spiritual."[70] The *divine cogitatum* imprinted onto the *human cogitatio* thus transforms the meaning of all thought (intentionality), in the same way that the engendering of the divine starting from the human makes of the believer himself a being capable finally of giving birth (generativity).

Intentionality

Work and Activity. Martha, by way of the "phenomenological I"—or the "disinterested spectator" in relation to the world into which she refuses to be absorbed (Husserl)—neither leaves nor negates the world, since "care" understood as "vigilance" at the very least maintains it in the lived modality of things without itself being a thing.[71] Articulated in Eckhart's terms, Martha is detached from "work" in no longer being in things but remains nevertheless in the "activity" by remaining with things: "work [*Werk*] is when one is exercised *exteriorly* in works of virtue; but 'activity' [*Gewerk*] is when one is exercised *interiorly* with reasonable discretion."[72] An identical and first step is accomplished therefore in the phenomenological *epochê* as in religious conversion. It is in the *inner* transformation of the self (activity [*Gewerk*]) that the world is suspended or one is converted to God, and not in the simple obedience to external rules (work [*Werk*]). Such a return above the self does not imply that God or the world are not able to exist independently of the I. It indicates only that the *lived experience of the world* like the *lived experience of God* designate for me the "thing itself"—the act of my consciousness by which the world and God are seen at once.

A kind of work on the self is therefore necessary for the method of the reduction" as for the "act of conversion," since it rejects the temptation to make of God an objective reality (existing in himself independently of me) in order to show his objectal data (constituted by the meaning that he gives and that I give to myself). Work and activity (*Werk* and *Gewerk*) are in this sense for Martha among the modes of her intentionality, that is, manners of looking at things rather than of living among them: in no longer being only "in" things as work external to the self (*Werk*), Martha remains "with" things as an "activity" internal to the self (*Gewerk*).[73] Jesus names Martha twice: "*Martha, Martha*, you are concerned with many things" (Lk. 10:41). Why, Eckhart asks, "does Christ name Martha twice?"[74] The first appellation "attests her perfection in temporal *works*" (*Werk*) whereas the second "attests to everything that is required for eternal beatitude": activity or internal exercise (*Gewerk*). There are not two Marthas, one busy in the kitchen and the other attentive to the self within as well as to God, but rather two different manners of intentionally aiming at God and things, even, for a time at least, of recognizing God in things: "You worry yourself" (Lk. 10:41) is not the *negative* formulation of a reproach of a person wholly absorbed in the quotidian, but the *positive* recognition of this religious and phenomenological capacity of remaining "with," "near," or even "very near" things without being "in" things: "I say very near because every creature performs the *duty of intermediary*."[75]

Neither the things themselves nor the world are denounced in Eckhart (which is why a purely auto-affective reading, as in Henry, is not fully justified), but rather the *relation* to things and to the world. If true "activity" (*Gewerk*)—as we will shortly see—is being "free and stripped of all intermediary," understood particularly as the very idea of an intermediary, creatures nevertheless perform at least at first the "duty of intermediary." By them we experience our own power of remaining concerned *along with* things (in oneself in the kitchen, for example) without being *in* things (that is, absorbed in the things of the world, or in God as thing). With the Dominican master's rereading of the episode of Mary and Martha—much like Husserlian intentionality—the relation to things is changed, though not the things themselves, which are in no way annihilated. Said otherwise, the world does not disappear in Eckhart, as it does for the Cartesian *dubitatio*, but it is in some way "bracketed" or "reduced" in order to leave the mode of objectivity behind. *Abgeschiedenheit* is a mode of the *epochê* as "detachment" diverting consciousness from its relation to things in order to show its lived experience of things—of all things the only thing necessary: "Detachment [*Abgeschiedenheit*] is *free* from all creatures. This is why the Lord says to Martha that only one thing is *necessary*."[76] God is not *objectively given exteriorly* but is *intentionally engendered interiorly*. Such is the message of Eckhart who shows his originality—inasmuch as he is reread in light of the concept of intentionality.

The Ground of the Soul and of God

But Eckhart is not content with these intermediaries of work and of activity—exercise from the exterior and from the interior—in order to rediscover God in the depths of the self. As I have emphasized, Eckhart demonstrates his radicality in his assertion of the "other intermediary" which does not pass by way of creatures at all, but rather is "to be denuded from the all" that is, from all intermediary: "The one who works in the light, he is elevated toward God, *free and denuded of every intermediary*; his light is his activity, and his activity is his light."[77] One should certainly be surprised at seeing a Dominican rejecting every intermediary or mediation, while another Dominican, only a few decades earlier (Aquinas) had on the contrary made the relation of primary and secondary causes the heart of all his teaching.[78] Their aim is not the same: Thomas's is ontological and Eckhart's is mystical. The weight that Thomas loans to the world is totally granted to the subject in Eckhart. The "one thing necessary" that Christ requires of Martha is their divine-human unity in the interpenetration of their consciousnesses, and not the reifying relation with the other exemplified by Mary: "She is *doubled* who does not see God without intermediary."[79] This teaching is the origin of Eckhart's famous identification of the ground of the soul and the ground of God, in which not only is the human called to the divine, but also in itself engenders God the very God: "Here *the ground of God* is *my ground*, and *my ground* the *ground of God*."[80]

There is no lack of astonishment here from both the philosophical and theological perspectives. (a) First, on the philosophical side, phenomenologists in particular have relied on this quasi-total identification of the divine and the human in order to interpret Eckhart's thought as a total immanentism: "The ontological identity of the soul and God expresses and likewise signifies the identity in being of its reality and phenomenality on the metaphysical level" (Henry).[81] In this sense to affirm, following Eckhart, that God is made man "in order that *I give birth to God*, the *very* God" ("Sermon 29"), is to identify man and God completely and therefore definitively loses any meaning for transcendence.[82] In 1969 Brunner had foreseen this only a few years after the publication of the *Essence of Manifestation* (1963): "It is absurd to assert that the unity of the soul and God puts divine transcendence in peril because the soul which is one with God has left itself and is nothing other than God in it and it in God . . . In order to understand the thought of Eckhart and *to avoid the facile accusation of immanentism*, it is necessary to get rid of every *static* representation of the relation of the creature to God . . . Man is *not the Image of God*, he is *according to the image of God*; he is *not the Son* of God, but rather his *adopted son*, and so on."[83] Pure auto-affection was skillfully transferred from the relation of man to himself (*Essence of Manifestation*) to the relation of man to God (*I am the Truth* and *Incarnation*), and therefore suggests in some sense that one enters, without explicitly saying so, within the scope of the Eckhartian formulations condemned by Pope John XXII in the bull of March 27, 1329, where 28 articles of Eckhart are stigmatized: "God made me one with his being and not simply his likeness" (*ipse operatur me suum esse unum non simile*) and "The Father engenders me like his Son, with no distinction" (*generat me ipse suum filium sine omni distinctione*).[84] Identification instead of resemblance (to be according to the image of God and not God), and generation instead of creation (engendered, not created—a formula which applies to the Son and not to creatures in the Creed), are two pitfalls on which Eckhartian thought could run aground if it is not correctly interpreted. The absence of distinction leads to confusion, as does the refusal of transcendence for the sake of pure immanence, if the necessary *distance* between man and God, as required by Trinitarian theology, does not remain (which is assured by the conception of the Father as origin (*archê*).[85]

(b) Hence the second objection, now purely theological: Does not the identification of the "ground of the soul" and the "ground of God" lead to the suppression of all distance between man and God and therefore the suppression of the idea of creation itself? As has already been seen above with Erigena (chap. 2, and which we will see below with Saint Bonaventure, chap. 6), when man "runs in God" within a Trinitarian monadology, he "runs" within the collection of created things, as contained within the Word. Eckhart's thought is radicalized here. For him we no longer run only within the Word, but rather we "are" somehow the Word itself: "Starting from the *very same ground* as the one in which the Father births his Speech, Martha becomes fruitfully co-engendering."[86] There again, the co-engendering of God by Martha in the encounter with Mary her sister, following therefore the Lord himself, ought to be well understood. If "all that which is proper to the divine nature is also *completely* proper to the just and divine man" (*quidquid proprium est divinae naturae, hoc totum proprium iusto et divino*) (condemnation 13), one should wonder what is appropriate to man and to God and what is the responsibility of Martha and what pertains specifically to the Lord.[87] It is hardly a matter here of condemning Eckhart again, but, on the contrary, only of discerning in his thought what is in danger of being poorly interpreted. For it is certainly the case that Eckhart's thought should be rehabilitated today. But some total "absolution," made in a backlash against a much too totalizing condemnation, ought not be itself hastily made either. It would be just as false to want to anathematize Eckhart as it would be to denounce his accusers. Each case requires careful discernment—not in order to oppose the parties involved, but in order to avoid a dogmatism that seems to appeal to theology in its lucubration but in reality is secretly fed by the stream of a dubious philosophy.[88]

Appropriation. The appropriation of man *to* God thus responds to the accusation of the identification of man *and* God. For what is appropriate to the fecundity of Martha is rightly understood less in the identification of properties—which would lead to a total fusion of man and God—than in the *exchange of one's own.* It is precisely here that the collusion of Husserlian phenomenology and Eckhartian mysticism is broken. The meeting points and rapprochements of Husserl and Eckhart are indeed often less acknowledged than the distinctions and oppositions by which they differ. The "rejection of every intermediary," even the capacity to engender God starting from a self which itself is only able to be received from God, is the measure of the distance which separates a phenomenology that is "egological" such as Husserl's, and a theology that is "alterological" such as Eckhart's. It is not a matter of opposing egocentrism and theocentrism, as if the return to the self was always paid in return for a purported objectivity about God. From a Christian perspective the engendering God is only understood starting from God himself. The radicality of the phenomenological *epochê*, which in Husserl supposes that God himself ought to be suspended (*Ideas* I, § 58) in order to leave to the subject alone the care of engendering all things including God (*Ideas* I, § 57), is thus rejoined by another yet more original radicality for which the engendering of God starting from the self returns, as if after the fact, to an engendering of the self starting from God: "The Latin word *ego*, which signifies 'I' pertains to no one for it is *appropriate to God alone* in his unity."[89]

Otherwise said, in the identification of the "ground of the soul" and the "ground of God" I do not see *myself* starting from my own proper ground [*fond*]—the ground [*le fond*] understood here as both that which makes the abyss of my being as well as the riches on which it draws (as in the expression "transfer of funds" [*transfert de fonds*]): "In the soul there is something that is *so visible to God* that it is *one* and *not united* [*un et non uni*]. It is one in that it has nothing in common with anything and holds nothing any longer in common with anything created."[90] We constitute *with* God *in ourselves* as we are *in him* a single and same ground insofar as the intentional aim by which I see *myself* is or becomes the intentional aim by which *he* sees me: "My eye and the eye of God are a single and same eye, a single and same vision, a single and same knowledge, a single and same love."[91] In this way Martha becomes "fruitfully co-engendering" as we have seen ("Sermon 2"),[92] not in that she draws God only from herself, but on the contrary in that God is somehow born in her when she is born of him in faith: "God engenders *me* as *Himself* and He engenders *himself* as *me*."[93]

The "transfer of what is one's own"—the identification of the "ground of the soul" and the "ground of God"—leads, mystically and phenomenologically speaking, to an "exchange of properties": "Here I live from that which is properly *mine* as God lives from that which is properly *His*."[94] The essential for Eckhart as for every Christian is not that I live my life but that I live *his* life in living mine, or better, that I enact in *mine* the best way of living *his*: "It is no longer I who live but Christ lives within me" (Gal. 2:20). The appropriation of the self by the self is, in Christianity, all the more paradoxical as it never acts by itself but is always won over "by another." Because I do not accede to myself (ego) without another than me within me (*ego alter*), I articulate myself as another self (alter ego). Here also do I detach myself from my I, or reduce my ego itself, as I discover myself constituted as an ego that I would have never engendered: "Without *her own attachment*, Martha is always equally *near* God and herself."[95] Such impropriety paradoxically makes for the most proximity and the most appropriate self, just as the incapacity to articulate the self paradoxically leads to the affirmation of the self constituted by another. In seeing myself I do not see only me but I see God seeing me and giving me the vision of myself. Somehow engendering God intentionally in me, I observe myself in hindsight as engendered by him, seen before being seen, constituted before being constituted. God somehow gives man *his* own vision of the world—making the vision of man the vision of God: "If you want God to be your own, make yourself his own and think of nothing but him."[96]

"Oneself *as* another"—the rupture of Eckhart or Ricoeur with the first Husserl (apperceptive transposition), though not the second (generativity), is therefore consummated: "To the '*as*' I should like to attach a strong meaning, not only that of a *comparison* (oneself *similar to* another) but indeed that of an *implication* (oneself *inasmuch as* being other)."[97] No more than phenomenology, Christianity today gains from the movement of inverse intentionality, therefore neither reducing nor suspending "God" or the "other" (*Ideas I* § 58) in order to constitute the "self" starting from the "I" alone (*Ideas I*, § 57). To the contrary, in Christianity, community precedes identity (chap. 7: Origen), knowledge of the other justifies knowledge of the self (chap. 8: Thomas Aquinas), and my *haecceitas* is received from the singularity of God (chap. 9: Duns Scotus). We will return to this with the conception of "alterity" as the spearhead of a new phenomenological interrogation of medieval philosophy in the third part of this work. The generativity of God in me, and starting from me *insofar* as I dwell in God, maintains thus "in me" the possibility of an awareness of God in the world and of creation in general. The experience of detachment (*Abgeschiedenheit*), the abandonment or suspension of creatures (*epochê*), thus constitutes the starting point from which I liberate myself from creatures in order to give every place to the Creator, and by which a new vision of the world resurfaces—now through his own vision of it over me: "The eye in which *I* see God is the *same eye* in which God sees *me*."[98]

Generativity

The movement of radicalization which we have chronicled from "relation" in Augustine (chap. 1) to "phenomenality" in Erigena (chap. 2) thus leads to the consideration of a kind of birth and genesis of God within the I. Similar to the movement of the *Cartesian Meditations* of Husserl, a simple "static phenomenology" of the welcoming of the phenomenon—or of God inasmuch as he appears to me—does not suffice for Eckhart. To say it again in phenomenological terms, it would be necessary to pass to the "questions of *universal genesis* and the *genetic structure* of the ego."[99] In the passage from intention (the reduction of every intermediary according to a mode of the lived experience of things [work and activity]) to constitution (the generation of the other starting from my ego which is also constituted by him), the effect is profound—and, in Eckhart, exemplary. Carrying to term the work of reduction (and conversion), two traits make the mystical ego in Eckhart the source of the generativity of God in man: (a) in the *active genesis* of the "birth of God in the self"; (b) in the *passive genesis* of the "recognition of a pathos of the self in God."

Active Genesis: The Birth of God in the Self. (a) According to Husserl, *active genesis* designates the case when "the Ego functions as productively constitutive, by means of subjective processes that are specifically acts of the Ego."[100] But generating and constituting (God) starting from one's own self as if to confirm here the *secrets* of the phenomenologist in relation to Rhineland mysticism (supra) was, according to Eckhart (modifying, only a little, the Gospel text), precisely the task assigned to Martha: "Jesus ascended to a small fortress and was received by a *virgin* who was a *woman*."[101] The transformation of the text, introducing the virginity of Martha where it is not noted, has no other purpose than accenting *a contrario* fecundity as a feminine trait. Not only symbolically "virgin," that is, capable of detaching herself from all sensible delight (the opposite of Mary totally absorbed in listening to the Lord),[102] Martha was in fact first termed a *woman* according to the letter of the text: "He entered into a village and a *woman* named Martha received him into her house" (Lk. 10:38). Against an entire tradition which sings the praises of virginity at the expense of femininity, Eckhart, teacher of the Beguines, finds in femininity something greater than virginity: "*Woman* is the noblest title of the soul, and is even nobler than *virgin*. That the human being receives God *into himself* is good, and in this receptivity humanity remains intact. But it is better that God becomes *fruitful in him* [in the constitution of God by Martha], because the fecundity of the gift is the sole way of being grateful for it."[103]

Therefore it is not sufficient for Martha to receive God in an ego that resembles God, especially as it abolishes the distance between them. It is also fitting for her to give birth or engender God starting from the self, to save the world through the self. The task of the feminine is thus nicely defined in the analogy of the carnal and spiritual. As woman, or as what it is insofar as it is essentially feminine, "the soul *gives birth* to God starting from itself starting from God in God; it truly gives birth starting from itself; it does this in order to give birth to God starting from itself."[104] The Socratic method (*maïutiké*) discovers here its properly Christian meaning: "This *fruit* and *birth of God himself* is specifically that this virgin who is a woman *gives birth*, and she bears fruit a hundred times, a thousand times, or even countless times a day, *generating* and *bearing fruit* from the most noble ground . . . ; starting from there she becomes *co-engendering and fruitful*."[105] Eckhart responds to Socrates's boast in the *Theaetetus* of a birth "from man and not from woman" and a giving birth to "souls and not to bodies" by way of the figure of Martha who gives birth to *God himself* and not to human beings and gives birth in herself to a divine flux rather than a soul or a body always separated from the self in their objectivity.[106] The complete identification of egos human and divine no longer permits saying whether the mother or the child is the true birth-giver. Martha gives birth to God in herself insofar as God *gives birth to himself* there, as the way in which man participates in God's action of "entering the world [*mise au monde*]." In an unjustly condemned proposition (if properly understood), Eckhart dares to affirm: "Man is the generator of the eternal Word of God [*generator Verbi aeterni*] and God cannot do anything [*nescuret quidquam facere*] without such a man."[107] The genesis appears here all the more "active" as the generated (God himself) contributes fully to the activity of the generator (Martha, at once virgin and woman)—who becomes progressively *one* with him. Such is the "*one* thing necessary" required by the Lord in the story of Martha and Mary: "*God* absolute must become *me* and *I* must become *God*."[108]

Passive Genesis: The Pathos of the Self in God. (b) But the active genesis of the human ego that engenders God does not yet bring to full term the work of reduction. In the same way that, for Husserl "anything built by activity [active genesis] necessarily presupposes, as the lowest level, a passivity that gives something beforehand [passive genesis],"[109] so also for Eckhart, all "theogenesis" is necessarily rooted in a "theopathy": "I affirm that there was never anything nobler than *to suffer* God."[110] Not only in fact (and in order to return to the figure of Martha in a new way), Jesus enters into this "little fortress" of the soul by going to Bethany (the reduction to the pure I); not only was he welcomed by one who was not just a "virgin" but also a "woman" in order to engender her (active genesis); but still he "was received" by her to the degree that he was discovered, in Martha and by Martha, as already there or as given within her, *suffering* God (passive genesis).[111] The novitiate of Mary—to which her sister invited her to enter quasi-phenomenologically, in the mode of the reduction (being absorbed, then, neither into things nor into God considered in the mode of a thing), does not exempt Martha from a certain work of conversion herself. The all too beautiful share given to Martha in her "reduction" that was already effected (*Abgeschiedenheit*) would prevent her from seeing how a work of "constitution" is now also to be accomplished in the act of the birth of God within the self (the co-engendering woman).

Martha still retains indeed a suffering or a *pathos* as well as the prohibition of being free from herself in order to be free *only* to suffer God: this comes precisely from *seeing her sister* rest in the "sensible delight" of hearing the Lord without passing beyond or being detached from him. Affected too much by her benevolence, Martha fails to be separated from this affection for her sister and to let God alone take care of her. This "suffering" in fact remains for Martha a suffering of man—not of God. Here comes the force of her invective aimed at Jesus to correct her sister: "Tell her to help me!" (Lk. 10:40)—a formula, as I have already said, which does not indicate that she suffers from her own labor in her concerned relation to the world (in the many tasks of service), but only that she suffers the non-detachment of her sister to the Lord as thing, and now even from her own preoccupied relation to her sister from which she cannot liberate herself. *Detached from the Lord, Martha is not yet detached from Mary*. The natural attitude of her sister—to speak phenomenologically again—punches its weight, as it were, even if this is yet the affair of God and not of men. Eckhart thus asks in his sermon on Martha and Mary ("Sermon 2"): "Do you truly want to know if your suffering is your own or God's? You ought to find out in this way: you suffer *as a result of your own will*, in whatever way, when your suffering causes evil for you and is heavy to bear. But you suffer *for God's sake* and *God alone*, when your suffering does not cause evil and is not heavy to bear, because *God bears the burden*."[112] The *pathein* of the suffering that Martha experienced concerning her sister is here, according to Eckhart, neither heroism nor masochism, nor even expiation. It simply and completely consists in being *detached from suffering itself*, to give it to another in order that this suffering of mine, to which I so often cling and which sticks to me, would thus become his suffering—the suffering of God and of God alone who tears me from it and delivers me. The suffering of Martha, undergone in a passivity that she could not control (in relation to Mary), is thus doubled in a second passivity (in relation to the Lord). This suffering is more radical in accepting, precisely, the loss of control, or in other words recognizing that God alone suffers her suffering more than she could ever suffer and ever will suffer: "God suffers *with man*, indeed, he suffers in his fashion before, and far more than that man who suffers for his sake."[113]

Far from all moralizing considerations and far from renewing all my adherences to myself, the act of suffering reveals the very truth of my being in the authenticity of its relation to God: first exhibiting "my resistance to letting God be born in me"; then signifying "my consent to mourn the former man in order to assume the new man"; and finally facilitating "the work of God within me to detach me from the inessential adherences of my existence."[114]

Well before Emmanuel Levinas, and in a language at once surprisingly modern and going against all the expiatory theologies already so developed in the fourteenth century, "suffering" (like "mourning") in Eckhart is therefore interpreted as an "experience of the passivity of the subject who until then has been active"; perhaps as the "impossibility of retreat" which renders man "forced into life and being."[115] From here comes the ultimate teaching of Eckhart concerning Martha, in whom precisely Jesus "was received": "What man *suffers by God and for God alone*, God renders it for him light and sweet."[116]

To Give Birth to God Himself. "Why did God become man?" Eckhart asks by way of a conclusion. The response, for only the time being, is lapidary: neither for the satisfaction of the Father (Anselm) nor for the reparation of our faults by the Son (Aquinas), nor even for the manifestation of the Word (Scotus), but rather, "in order that I may give birth to God himself."[117] The Christian's dying to the world or his detachment leads to the birth of God within him, that is, his appropriate attachment: "O my soul, go out! God enters!"[118] Such is the distinct thing from the song "Granum Sinapis" ("The Mustard Seed") that this route—from the reduction to the I to the constitution of God in me—has thus wanted to effect by means of the figure of Martha of Bethany. But for Eckhart the exit of God identically designated his entrance into the self, in such a way that in me and of me (in an ultimate fashion) nothing remains, except God: "Absolutely nothing [*nihtes niht* (high German)] is able to divert the saint from God."[119] Martha is not the end, then, in the radicalization of the experience of conversion as a mode of reduction: there is Paul on the road to Damascus. "When Paul rose from the ground, he opened his eyes, and *saw nothing* [Acts 9:8], and *this nothing was God*, because *when he saw God*, he called him *nothing* [*niht/Nichts*]."[120] The experience of the nihilization of Saul as a paradoxical vision of nothing ("he saw nothing"; see Sermons 71 and 52) legitimately carries forward the lived experience of the reduction rendered visible by Martha (Sermons 86 and 2). Eckhart makes reference to this precisely in the midst of commenting on the story of Martha and Mary: "Saint Paul saw God without intermediary when he was caught up to the third heaven, and the language of the angels was for him far too great."[121]

Partly reducing to the reduction itself, Eckhart almost abolishes egoity, confounding the reduction with the most complete nihilation. A new debate is opened here, no longer with the father of phenomenology and the proper mode of reduction (Husserl), but with the collection of his followers who—from Heidegger, Fink, and Patocka, to Levinas, Henry, and Marion—deny the primacy of the ego and begin starting from the question of nihilation. Could we go all the way with "reducing the reduction" and "converting the converted"? Such is the question that the radicalization of the experience of God in himself, running from Saint Augustine (chap. 1) to Erigena (chap. 2) and Eckhart (chap. 3), must carry to full term—in a movement to bring closure on the question of "God" (part I), but which his own opening to the "flesh" (part 2) and to the "other" (part 3) would never shut down.

The Reduction to Nothing: The Vision of Paul. With Meister Eckhart a "new nobility" or "honor of emptiness" is born.[122] This is undeniable. In order to examine the question of nihilation after what we have seen in Eckhart, we must take a passing look at the debate maintained with Eckhart in the works of Heidegger. In the beginning of this chapter I noted that the second much more famous debate between the philosopher from Fribourg and the Dominican from Thuringia will spare us from retracing it here in too much detail. It suffices to bring to light its main contours in order to indicate the point(s) where interpretations differ. In his long career, there are five key places where Heidegger refers to Eckhart: (1) in his *Habilitationsschrift*, the *Treatise on the Categories and Signification in Duns Scotus* (1915), (2) in the epigraph of his *The Concept of Time in the Science of History* (1915), (3) in his course on the *Philosophical Foundations of Medieval Mysticism* (1918–19), (4) in the *Letter on Humanism*, at least implicitly under the lemma of the Deity (1946), and (5) in the famous discourse given in honor of Conradin Kreuser ("Memorial Address for Conradin Kreuser"), published in the collection *Gelassenheit* (1955). The point is clear: Meister Eckhart was *the* critical companion of Heidegger throughout his career.[123]

A question imposes itself here, which has not ceased to hold the attention of phenomenological commentators, and which should be of concern to medievalists as well. A key passage from the text which "can *serve as a commentary on Gelassenheit*" (interview from 1944–45) in fact challenges the claim of a pure filiation of *Gelassenheit* or "Heideggerian serenity" from the *gelâzenheit* or "letting be" of Eckhart: "Even *serenity* can be thought of still *within the domain of the will*, as happens with the old masters of thought such as Meister Eckhart," whereas "*what we are calling serenity* evidently does not mean the casting-off of sinful selfishness and the letting-go of self-will in favor of the divine will."[124] It could not be clearer: Eckhart's *gelâzenheit* remains a prisoner, according to Heidegger (and probably a result of a pietistic interpretation of Eckhart à la Fenelon, Madame Guyon, Oetinger, etc.), to a voluntarist mysticism of abandonment where everything can and ought to be abandoned except the act of abandonment itself, which always remains "*interior to the will*." But as Jean Greisch has rightly emphasized in relation to this passage, "the recognized debt to speculative mysticism [Eckhart in particular] is accompanied in Heidegger by a strange misreading."[125] It is more likely the case that Eckhart goes farther than Heidegger himself in this movement of complete "abandonment": not only in that he is detached from the will, even to the point of his integration into God—contrary to what Heidegger suggests, but also because he "undoes" the *gelâzenheit* as such from every "attitude in regard to things," which Heidegger's "serenity" or "*Gelassenheit*" does not "accomplish" inasmuch as it is always bound up with the *Geviert* or the four dimensions of the sacred (earth, sky, divinities, and mortals).[126] If, in order to "let be" it is necessary not only to leave things and oneself, but even to let go of the very act of letting go, it seems Eckhart has radicalized what Heidegger always retains. Heidegger, in short, remains too attached to the thing-dimension in the category of the sacred, thereby failing truly to liberate the self in a complete nihilation. To disclose—now speaking as a medievalist—how the "nothing" of Eckhart is therefore "nothing," not even the "nothing of something," nor of the "self as thing," is thus to show that in terms of the reduction proposed to Mary and of the constitution enacted by Martha (Sermons 2 and 86) there is deciphered also a complete radicalization operated by Paul (Sermons 52 and 71) whereby precisely "he who speaks of God *through nothing*, speaks of God in the appropriate way."[127]

The Reduction to Nothing

Radicalized Nothing. Surrexit autem Paulus de terra apertisque oculis nihil videbat: "Paul rose from the ground and although his eyes were opened *he saw nothing*" (Acts 9:8). In a similar way to his reversal of the interpretation of the episode of Martha and Mary (Sermons 2 and 86), Eckhart ingeniously reveals anew here what neither reader nor hearer could anticipate ("Sermon 71"). Seeing nothing is ordinarily "absence of vision," and the blindness with which man is affected is either by lack of light (obscurity) or by its excess (dazzling brightness). But Eckhart understands the *absence of vision* in the figure of Paul as the *vision of the Absent*: "He saw *nothing, which is God*."[128] The "nothing" no longer designates the impossibility of seeing things, but rather the possibility of seeing otherwise: whoever embraces the nothing that is God himself sees through God the nothing of God. Here Eckhart *radicalizes* even further the nihilation discovered by Erigena in his break from the apophaticism of Denys (chap. 2). Here, where Erigena posed negation not only as beyond all position, whether affirmative or negative (as in Denys), but as the non-position of position itself, Eckhart penetrates into the heart of this very non-position: to be "open-eyed" and at the same time to "see the nothing" that is God himself.

Not seeing anything is not the same as seeing nothing. To be "open-eyed" in the radiance of a light is meant to indicate a "that" which is to be seen by negation of all things seen, or better, of all that is seen only in the modality of the thing: "When he sees all things as *nothing*, then Paul sees *God*."[129] The vision of the whole of God presupposes therefore the vision of the nothing of being. But nothing ensures that the anything is not some inverse of nothing, as if it would do to overcome a simple dialectical opposition. In the same way that the "nothing" of Heideggerian anxiety (*das Nichts*) is at once "the integral negation of the totality of being" and "brings *Dasein* for the first time before beings as such,"[130] so does the vision of things as nothing in Eckhart manifest God as the unique place of the reception of being in general, without, however, being reduced to some sort of entity (the term "black-entity" [*neg-entité*] is derived here, which is sometimes attributed to Eckhart).[131]

The "small word nothing" (*Nichts*) used by Luke in the vision of Saul (Acts 9:8), contains four meanings according to Eckhart, of which the explication reveals the definitive way the "reduction" is a pure operation—from God and by God alone. The explicit exposition of these four steps unfolds the different moments of the reduction to nothing in Eckhart that are not present in the angst of Heidegger. (a) The first is synthesized already in Eckhart: when he rose up from the ground, he opened his eyes and saw nothing and *this nothing was God*, because when he saw God, he called it nothing. (b) The other meaning: when he rose up he saw *nothing but God*. (c) The third: in all things he *only saw God*. (d) The fourth: when he saw God, he saw *all things as nothing*.[132] We will now see that these steps unfold the process that moves from having "*nothing to do*" [*rien à voir*] with things (the two first negative steps relative to creatures) to "*seeing the nothing*" [*voir le rien*] of God (the two last positive steps in regard to the Creator).

Seeing God and Only God. (a) The first meaning: "Paul saw nothing, and *this was God*."[133] This first milestone is sufficient in itself to indicate a radicality that Heidegger did not seem to notice. Certainly Eckhart makes God *being's nothingness* [*néant d'étant*] and probably reaches here a mode of being of *Dasein* which is neither "ready-to-hand" nor "present-at-hand," neither "available" nor "subsistent": "If you see something or if something falls into your knowledge," says Eckhart in "Sermon 71," "*it is not God*, for the main reason that he is *neither this nor that*."[134] But regarding this *nothingness of being* ("neither this nor that") the Dominican originally extends the concept to a *planar negation* [*néant de plan*] as well ("neither here nor there"): "The one who says that God is *here or there*, do not believe him."[135] Saint Paul on the way to Damascus, like the fiancée in the Song of Songs, designates God, not only as a determined object, but also according to a fixed place—in order better to persecute him: "The fiancée [or St. Paul] seeks for him *on her couch*; she means by that, for the one who is attached to or suspended from a thing that is below God, *her couch is too small*. Everything that God can create is too small."[136] In his soul, Saint Paul "sees nothing" because he lacks the power of vision capable of seeing. Totally oriented within a space *where* God is not—as something or some being "to persecute"—the "nothing" of vision first designates the space of a "presence" of a being of which the absence risks not being supported, and the objectivity or presentification constitutes it precisely as an idol. It is no longer sufficient, according to Eckhart, to say, "God is not something because he does not know what he is" (Erigena). Eckhart takes away from God himself every *place* where he could yet be a thing, knowing that the very thought of a space for a non-thing is still something: "God is a nothingness and God is a *something*. What is *something* is also a *nothing*."[137]

(b) Second meaning: the moment of recognizing that "seeing nothing" for Saint Paul is not only "seeing God as the nothing of things and the place of things" but seeing "*nothing but God*." Paradoxically, seeing "nothing but God" for Eckhart does not exclude creatures outside of the Creator, but instead reveals that it is "*in* God" *where* all creatures are nothing.[138] The difficulty is not about incorporating creatures into God or into the Word, as in Bonaventure's monadology (chap. 6), but rather about showing that it is precisely as they are *in* God that they are nothing. It is evident here that creatures are not something more by being held outside of God—which, properly speaking, defines sin—but it means that the totality of God brings to nothing any remainder of creatureliness outside of God. One can give both a dialectical and phenomenological interpretation here. It could be held, certainly, for Paul, that seeing "any particular thing is to place oneself outside of the whole" and that it would be necessary to reach a state of apprehending God "as all in all." The nothing of creatures will thus be identical to the "all of God," in a dialectical assumption supposedly sufficient to assume them (P.-J. Labarrière).[139] But there is also a phenomenological way to envision this relation of nothing to the whole. Creatures are "nothing in God" not merely because they are assumed in him. Rather, the exteriority reconciled into a new divine interiority leaves God and creatures in a process of opposition and then unity which already supposes a thought shaped by exteriority, the poles overtaken and assumed into a new totality. In Eckhart this works for the *meaning* rather than the structure. Creatures are "nothing in God" because in him they are struck by vanity. Like Heidegger's "profound boredom, drifting here and there in the abysses of our existence like a muffling fog, removing all things and men and oneself along with it into a remarkable indifference," the "*nothing but God*" that Paul perceives here signifies, as he later writes in Romans, that "the entire creation has been subject to vanity" (Rom. 8:20).[140] Said otherwise, the "nothing but God," like the "nothing in God" of creatures in the Creator is not only able to be read in terms of interpenetration but discloses what it is in the sense of revelation. If, according to a natural attitude, creatures are something in themselves, as we have seen in Mary of Bethany, they are "nothing" not only according to the mode of reduction operated by Martha who sees with God deep down, but even in Paul's eyes, which consist precisely in "seeing nothing" apart from the vanity of all things, which would be a seeing everything relative to Him who is visibility itself in his shining forth: God as "nothing but God."

The two first determinations of "nothing" in Eckhart (*nichts*) are thus *negative* in the sense that they are always related either to creatures or to created space in order then to be detached from them: the first ("seeing God") rightly refuses to reduce God to a thing ("neither this nor that") and even to extension or the very idea of a reified space ("neither here nor there"). The second ("seeing nothing but God") strikes the totality of creatures with vanity (a phenomenological reading), rather than reconciling in its totality the separated parts of creation (dialectical interpretation). But God was not satisfied with this "nothing at all"—that is, the act of being differentiated from things. This is self-evident. Eckhart goes farther by pulling out its *positivity*. By seeing "nothing but God in all things" and "all things as a nothing," God himself is *positively* seen in his nothingness.

Nothing Appropriated. (c) "The nothing was God": the formula rises up for us in all its clarity, independently of creatures since it is now a matter of penetrating into the nothingness of the Creator.[141] We will not see, or rather we will see the nothing of that which is above the mode of beings (creatures) in seeing God as non-being, but we will reach to the Nothingness as the name that is now the *most appropriate* for the divine itself: "If God is neither goodness, nor being, nor truth, nor One," Eckhart asks in "Sermon 23," "then what is he? He *is Nothingness*, neither this nor that."[142] Being nothingness for God means "being the *nothing of nothing*"[143]—in other words not only the nothing of the totality of being and its modes, but also the nothing of being which would designate it even as "being" a nothingness ("he *is* Nothingness"). Seemingly commenting on Eckhart, Heidegger states: "Because beings as a whole slip away, so that just the nothing crowds round, in the face of anxiety *all utterance of the 'is' falls silent*."[144] In this third step God is given in action rather than by speaking, by the articulations of language that necessarily predicates God in terms of *being* or *non-being*. The image of light alone properly characterizes God here, in which Paul, on his way to Damascus, is "enveloped" as the light "falls from heaven" (Acts 9:3). We cannot say that God "*is* the light," as I have already emphasized, because of the opposite risk of defining him still "as a being or as a good," for by that "we still know nothing of him." But we will nevertheless simply indicate that "the light which is God *flows* from beyond." If the light *is not* but makes visible all things by not being among the things that it illumines, then Paul sees "God in this light and nothing else."[145] Everything occurs in this third level as if it were given to the Apostle to the Gentiles to see the light that we never see, since we only see the things illumined by it. Such a reading is justified by the following: "His traveling companions were struck dumb: they *heard* the voice but *saw no one*" (Acts. 9:7). This implies that they certainly heard something but were nevertheless not struck by that which struck Saul alone—that exceptional gift to men of "seeing God," seeing "God as nothing." Passing from *not seeing anything* to *seeing the nothing*, Paul has reached the state of supreme detachment (*Abgeschiedenheit*), which sometimes appears "at the point closest to nothing that anything *that is not God alone* would be able to dwell in detachment."[146]

(d) The last stage: "When Paul saw God, he saw everything as nothing." It is necessary to go a little further here—like the fiancée in the Song of Songs: "going *a little further* she finally found the one whom her soul loves."[147] In this stretching of creaturely being is found the greatest proximity to the Creator. Here "detachment" is truly radical. One must return to the source and belong to the source itself. Here the paradigm of climbing from the creature to the Creator is manifest in the discussion of "color." The eye ought not "to contain any color" in order to see "every color," much like the luminous prism which, being without color, confers all the colors of the spectrum. Turning one's gaze from "things" to the "nothing of nothing" that is, God himself, Saint Paul reaches the focal point "where the light first breaks in."[148] But regarding this "even further" of the Song of Songs, already very far indeed, it is still necessary for Paul to go "yet even further," according to Eckhart, proof, as it were, that "conversion" in the theological sense does not happen without a radical "reduction" in the phenomenological sense. The Dominican adds with an unattainable radicalism: "When even I would reach the light at the very point of its irruption, it would be necessary for me to be completely laid bare by this irruption itself."[149] In Eckhart one does not simply return to the source, as in the *exitus-reditus* schematic that informs all the theological summas since Erigena's *Periphyseon*, for in Eckhart one is unmade by the source itself. The God who is reached here is a God "without mode," a "mode without a mode," or a "being without being," because "he possesses no modality."[150] Certainly, Bernard of Clairvaux, explicitly mentioned here, has defined the "measure of the love of God as a love without measure." But the exact formula of *De diligendo Deo* should be understood, in my opinion, according to a qualitative mode despite the customary quantitative interpretation. *Modus diligendi Deum, sine modo diligere*—"the *mode* of loving God is to love him without a *mode*." This must be interpreted and translated, yet not in the following typical way: "The *measure* of the love of the love of God is to love him without *measure*." With respect to the manner of the reception of God, the quantitative excess should give way here to a new qualitative modality. Seeing, with Saint Paul, "the divine nothingness" as seeing nothing is no longer being with nothing to see, but rather with seeing everything, not according to a dialectical power of "over-sumption" [*sur-somption*], but according to a phenomenological capacity of "manifestation." Eckhart concludes: "We must approach God in a *way without a way* and as *being without being* because he possesses *no modality*. This is why St. Bernard says that the one who wants to know you, God, must measure you without measure."[151]

At this point we could consider the broader path to be traveled and therefore conclude that from the discovery of relation (chap. 1: Augustine) to theophany as negation of every objective *quid* (chap. 2: Erigena), and then to nihilation as suspension of all modality (chap. 3: Eckhart), it would be impossible to attain any greater degree of radicality. Yet such would be a misunderstanding of Eckhart. We should not yet entertain the suspicion of having finished the work begun. The reduction *to nothing* does not work, in fact, without reduction *to the nothing*, and therefore from an I itself capable of posing it. It does not yet suffice to define God as a "mode of love without mode" for such still requires that the subject itself be deprived of all its modalities or faculties by which it would still be able to pose God as a mode. As I said above, Eckhart completed the step that Husserl always refused to make, thus anticipating here all the philosophies that turn on the deconstruction of the ego (Levinas, Marion, Merleau-Ponty, Deleuze, Derrida . . .). We do "not have the right to bracket the residue of the pure I" (*Ideas I*, §57), said Husserl. But this is precisely what Eckhart negates, according to a mode of "mystical conversion" that is even more radical than all the "phenomenological reductions"—which means that contemporary philosophers will learn what truly concerns philosophy by reading theology.

Reduction of the I

In the act of "bracketing" (*epochê*), nothing remains in Eckhart but the brackets themselves: "Everything that ever came from God is ordered to a *pure operation* . . . Thus it is dispossessed to the point of not knowing anything but God working within it."[152] Passing here from "Sermon 71" ("When Paul rose from the ground, he opened his eyes, and saw nothing.") to "Sermon 52" ("Blessed are the poor in spirit for theirs is the kingdom of heaven."), the question is no longer merely about God himself appearing in his light (Saint Paul), but concerns instead the capacity of man to become detached from this light in order to enter into "true poverty" ("Commentary on the First Beatitude"). Here arises the ontological meaning of the poverty internal to the subject: "A poor man is the one who *wants nothing* and *knows nothing* and *has nothing*." Not "wanting," not "knowing," and not "having": such are the traits that in an ultimate way reduce the *I itself* in its pretended capacity to receive the light of God.

To Want Nothing. We would wrongly interpret Eckhart's "not-wanting" of the I if we considered it some kind of asthenia or apathy. This would be a result of not understanding the properly ontological perspective (as opposed to an ethical one) in Eckhart's thought. The phrase "blessed are the poor in spirit" (Mt. 5:3) in fact first designates the poverty of the "heart" or rather, of the will itself in its desire "to accomplish the very precious will of God."[153] Certainly, the desire to offer oneself to God, and God alone, always remains laudable. One can "see nothing" in order to "see nothing but God," and like Saint Paul to seem to have already arrived. Eckhart, however, insists that there is more. For, "as long as a man retains *his will* in wanting to accomplish the very precious will of God, he does not yet have the poverty of which I want to speak."[154] Said otherwise, *I* do not want to unite myself to God—even with the best possible intentions. Further, even God himself does not incorporate *me* with himself by virtue of any desire that is his own. In both cases—the human desire for union with God and the divine desire for the same—it is a matter of two wills standing over-against each other: the human "will that desires," on the one side, and the divine "desire to receive," on the other. Those who talk this way, says Eckhart, preaching to some Beguines who would certainly be hard of hearing, "they are *jackasses*": they think that "man should live in such a way that he never accomplishes his will in anything" or even that "man ought to attempt to accomplish the very precious will of God."[155] Again, in both cases, renouncing oneself and union with God, it is always a matter of *the self*, either refusing its desire for things or being absorbed into the desire of God. There is no question however in Eckhart of wanting to adhere to the will of God and not being tied to one's own will. The yes and the no of the will do not yet suspend the will itself. On the contrary, and steadfastly against all the Nietzschean forms of nihilism to come, it is the "desire for desire" that is in question here. One is "poor" who "wants nothing" and "desires nothing" in the sense that this "nothing" is that of the will itself, the desire to be attached necessarily to that which it desires: "As long as you have the will to accomplish the will of God and desire the eternity of God, you are not poor."[156] Therefore the will itself in its desire to be united with God is here reduced—for it is by this very desire itself that it always remains something, at the very least the wish to be someone or something in its union with God.

Let us recall here what I mentioned above. In his *Commentary on Serenity*, Heidegger did not hold back from castigating the *Galâzenheit* of Eckhart "conceived as *interior to the will*" in opposition to his own *Gelassenheit* which is clearly "*something other* than the rejection of the culpable egoism or the abandonment of one's own will to the divine will." The "misreading," already indicated by reference to Jean Greisch above borders on a "misinterpretation." A detailed reading of "Sermon 52" shows the opposite, namely, that true poverty, in the ontological sense, *is not* "interior to the will" and it ought to be *detached from* this "abandonment of one's own will to the will of God": "Man ought to have true poverty, he ought *also to be deprived of his created will*."[157] Dare I suggest, despite its provocativeness, that on this point there are not, among phenomenologists, even some "*jackasses* who understand nothing of the divine truth," if the role of the jackass is not to understand the necessity of "*being detached from oneself*"?[158] Whatever the diagnosis, and to say it in a less severe way, we should recognize that such a truth is not easy to understand, for theology as much as philosophy. Meister Eckhart has warned us twice in this sermon, for those who want to hear: "If you don't want to measure up to this truth about which I now want to speak, you cannot understand me."[159]

To Know Nothing. In such a radical excess, it is not sufficient to desire nothing, at least in order to realize "conversion" as an act achieved by "reduction." The reduction of the pure I requires in fact that the "I itself" ignore its own suspension, bearing the opposite risk of putting everything in parentheses, except itself in the very act of imposing them. As I have already mentioned, Eckhart the Christian is never so separated from Husserl the phenomenologist and a whole region of contemporary philosophy as when he critiques and rejects every position of egoity overlooking the divinity. If an "irreducible residue" would still remain after the "elimination" [*mise hors circuit*], it is on the side of the "transcendence of God" (*Ideas I*, §58) rather than on the "pure I" (*Ideas I*, §57) that resistance to the hegemony of the suspension should be sought. For any "abiding" for man, in the Christian regime at least, has no meaning outside of God himself in whom one is held, no more than "action" is able to be understood independently of the proper action of God. Let us only recall the formula relayed above: "The Latin word '*ego*,' which means 'I,' pertains to no one, it is *appropriate for God alone* in his unity."[160]

Well before Nicholas of Cusa, the "unknowing" of the self already reaches its height in Eckhart. (i) The first point on this way of "learned ignorance": we do not definitively depart, here, from all primacy of the intellect over the affect, just like, inversely, that of desire over knowledge: "The beatitude of poverty consists neither in knowledge nor in love."[161] Dominicans (emphasizing the primacy of the intellect) and Franciscans (emphasizing the primacy of the affect) seem, in fact, to be reconciled in Eckhart, while they are surpassed. The divergence—concerning which I will show the importance relative to the word and the flesh [chap. 6: Bonaventure]—is rooted in a radical *poverty* of which the mendicancy creates the mode of being of their community (mendicant brothers). (ii) Second point: "to know that we live," for Eckhart, is not life, in the same way that "experiencing that one experiences" is not experience, or "knowing that one knows" is not truly the "springing forth of knowledge" [*co-(n)naître*]. What is envisaged here is not knowledge itself, but the act of "reflection" by means of which all knowledge of the self is immediately put at a distance and thereby objectified. Sin alone *reflects* man as in a mirror, where necessarily, he is deformed. This primal origin in pure immediacy, named auto-affection by Michel Henry (rooting it precisely in Eckhart), is that which man today must rediscover in order to constitute a new unity with God: "When man is held in the eternal disposition of God, another does not live there; what lives there is himself."[162] (iii) Third point: The *blessed poverty of the self* in its "learned ignorance" does not know anything, either of the destiny of life (its own or God's) or of that which makes it live (God himself), or even of the very mode by which it lives (knowledge): "The poor man *knows nothing* . . . He ought to live in such a way that he does not know anything about what he lives for, neither for himself, nor for the truth, nor for God; *further*, he ought to be so deprived of all knowledge that he knows neither by knowledge nor experience that God lives in him; *further*, he ought to be deprived of all knowledge that lives within him."[163] One cannot be any more radical. In this triple reduction—of the aim, the object, and the mode of knowledge itself—is found the most complete suspension. Knowledge itself ought to free itself from its act of knowledge just as the will, as mentioned above, ought to be freed from its act of will. The *Abgeschiedenheit* here attains its apogee, the nihilation of the faculties, which, already before Eckhart in Hadewijch Antwerp, makes the "nothing of the soul" the transcendental condition of any access to the all of God: "When the soul has *nothing else but God*," says the woman troubadour of God, unveiling the beginnings of the *Gêlazenheit* of Eckhart, "it is engulfed in him, and is *brought to naught*—then [Christ] is exalted above the earth, and then he draws all to him."[164]

What remains, then, if we truly penetrate into this radical "nothing of nothing," not of God alone (Saint Paul on the Damascus road) but also of the soul itself (Blessed are the poor . . .)? Precisely *nothing*—except the *operation* or *act of reduction* which ignores itself: "All that ever comes from God is ordained to a *pure operation* . . . Further, we say that man ought to remain aloof and detached in such a way that he neither knows nor comprehends that God works in him."[165] "Detachment" is not in Eckhart a pure abstraction at all. It is not a matter of getting rid of all in order to enter into a pure indifference regarding creatures or the world. One "remains detached" when and only when he is attached to the operation and not to that which receives the operation nor to the operator. As I already indicated, God is a flux and not a thing. The poor in spirit *know nothing*, to the degree, as Eckhart says, that "there is something in the soul out of which *flows* knowledge and love," but which is neither knowledge nor love itself.[166] Knowledge arrests the flux and stops the operation, only in that it knows it in the moment of its original flowing forth and stands to immobilize it, whereas the divine flow itself has not ceased flowing. The only learned ignorance is that of an "unknowing knowledge"—of God himself in his activity, of the creature in its reception, and of the subject in its subsistence: "It is necessary that the one who wants to be poor in spirit be poor in relation to all his own knowing, in such a way that he knows nothing, neither God, nor the creature, nor himself."[167] Only "conversion" or "reduction" paradoxically remains as an act of pure suspension, independently of God conceived as "final" (*Ideas I* §58), certainly, but also of the "pure I" (*Ideas I* §57). Eckhart's path *toward God* advocates in advance, as it were, Husserl's *conception of time*, albeit in a more direct way—perhaps because better inspired. This way reduces every way to the point of the irreducibility of the I itself (*Ideas I*) in order to enter into a flux which constitutes it in a more original way (Husserl's *Lectures on Internal Time Consciousness*). "[Time] has the absolute properties of something to be metaphorically designated as a '*flow*,'" emphasizes Husserl in a way strangely close to Eckhart, "of something that *originates in a point of actuality*, in a *source-point*, 'the now,' and so on. In the actuality-experience we have the *primal source-point* and a continuity of moments of reverberation. For all of this, we lack names."[168]

To Have Nothing. In order to bring to term the detachment of the self, Eckhart adds the "third poverty," which is "the last poverty . . . that man *has nothing*."[169] Here we reach the height of radicality. Yet we would have thought the opposite, that the "poverty of having" would be only the first degree of poverty, following the temptations which climb progressively from having to power and from power to honor (Mt. 4:1–11). But here detachment is located in the interior renunciation of having all given and even of a space for giving because "having nothing" is here not even having "a proper place where God would be able to operate."[170] Said otherwise, if God is "ordained to pure action" (supra), then I am not even myself a place of his operation, for this would be to attribute to me too much, namely, that of being a place for welcoming him. Does this mean that God operates "nowhere," in the *no man's land*[171] of an activity that no longer knows to which saint it turns? Far from it, at least in Eckhart. For if God does not operate in man at the risk of new attachments, he introduces man into himself in order for man to be left totally affected by him: "God is *himself the place* in which he wants to operate . . . and man is thus the one in whom God *suffers* and God is *the place of his own work* such that God is the one who works *in himself*."[172] For Eckhart, all false riches contrary to true poverty come from difference, which is always a manner of existing by the self where one does not want to be totally auto-affected by the other. To guard difference is to keep existence. But true abandonment is to be detached from everything, including God as the one who ought to be received and the self as the way by which one exists: "We say therefore that man ought to be so poor that he is and has no place where God would be able to operate. Where man guards a place, he maintains a difference."[173]

Let us repeat the question anew: what is left in this act of "conversion" as radical operation of the "reduction"? Nothing—but nothing as God himself who *is*, or rather, *flows* as the act of reduction or conversion itself. Our prayer becomes here that "God himself detach us from God," in the conviction that the "operation" itself—what I have termed elsewhere a "*metamorphosis*"—is his better attribution.[174] The "flux" here becomes the "breakthrough," more "noble" in the opening and the irruption of man in God (breakthrough) than the flowing of God himself to the final ground of the soul of man (flux). Indeed, the language of flow must be exceeded here because it is still a manner of marking a difference and therefore of exteriorizing. The "breakthrough" is the true operation of God and through God for the man who is held in him and therefore acts at one with him. The spark of the soul is the upsurge of God himself in man acting at One with him, in whom the phenomenological *epochê* translated into the terms of Christian conversion reveals the remarkable possibility of reducing the pure I, which will renounce all its own egoity and every autarchy of the subject. Hence Eckhart concludes his great sermon on poverty: "A great master says that *his breakthrough is nobler than his flowing*, and it is true. When I *flow* in God all things speak: God is. But this would not render me blessed because in this I recognize that I am a creature. Further, then: in the *breakthrough* where I am deprived of my own will and the will of God and all his works and even God himself, I am above all creatures and am neither God nor creature any more.

I am what I was and what I ought now to remain forever . . . because *in this breakthrough* I see that I and God are *One*."[175]

We would be right to wonder about this absence of difference from the perspective of philosophy as much as theology. Does not the unity of creature and Creator destroy the act of creation itself, reduced to a single engendering? Better, does the position of the Deity beyond the Trinity not render Christianity anonymous, relegated to a "divine energy" that cannot be truly, that is, Christianly, avowed? The questions posed here to Eckhart are those we have elsewhere wanted to pose to Michel Henry. Let us not revisit this any further, insomuch as the negative critique moves us away from the positive forward motion of "description"—the method elected for the present work (see the "Introduction").[176] Let us simply restate, then, the path we have taken: from Mary of Bethany to Martha we have learned the reduction as interiorization of God in the self (Sermons 2 and 86); from Martha to Saint Paul we have been taught the suspension as entrance into the "nothing of the nothing of God" ("Sermon 71"); and with the "poor in spirit" ("Sermon 52") we have entered into detachment from all, and understood ourselves as the place for the reception of God, revealing him to be, in an ultimate fashion, "pure operation" in the act of his primal "breakthrough," which was in the last analysis beyond his simple "flowing."

✦

What could appear here as a simple affair of words for Eckhart is actually a matter of an attitude, even a manner of being properly human, and therefore also divine by virtue of the incarnation of God. Is who we are in the first place found in the articulation of the "relation" of the One who gives himself as Trinity (chap. I: Augustine)? To what degree is the theophany of the One who comes to reveal himself to us made worthy then of bearing such a phenomenality (chap. 2: Erigena)? And finally, how is the reduction of all (including the self) capable of opening onto the paradoxical demand of a God who teaches us "to depend on him" (chap. 3: Eckhart)? These questions, following a process of growing radicalization in history and the relationships among concepts (relation [Augustine], phenomenalization [Erigena], reduction [Eckhart]), paradoxically find in the most concrete context of Christianity itself the site of their highest realization, that is, in the Christological incarnation itself as the exemplification and transformation of phenomenological incarnation. The "flesh" (part 2) thus takes the place of "God" (part 1), not in order to be substituted for him, but rather in order better to incarnate him, in the same way that the "other" (part 3) comes to manifest him: "It would be *of little value for me that 'the Word was made flesh' for man in Christ*," Eckhart indicated in the conclusion of his *Commentary on the Gospel of John*, "unless he was also *made flesh in me personally* so that I too might be God's son."[177]

Part Two

The Flesh

The Other Beginning: The Flesh

After "God" (part I) comes the "flesh" (part II). As I have already mentioned, the relation here is not one of simple juxtaposition or even of substitution. Instead, the relation is a matter of radical implication. Indeed, for Christianity, one must pass by way of the flesh in order to speak of God properly, *and then*, even pass by way of his flesh in order to speak of the human properly. The notion of a "God-man" or the "transubstantiation of the Creator in the creature" (Levinas) *is not* confined to the order of the impossible, at least for Christianity. On the contrary, it is precisely because God became man that it is necessary to go through man to get to God. Said otherwise, neither the "flesh" nor the "face" are only "traces of an invisible and un-seeable God, who was seen only "from behind" when Moses renewed his covenant with Yahweh (Ex. 33:23). Yet because of the incarnation of the Word, on the contrary, it should be emphasized—with the help of Merleau-Ponty in a non-confessional way—that in Christianity "transcendence no longer looms over man: he strangely becomes the privileged bearer of it."[1] Therefore we have come to understand in a new way at this beginning of the second part that when it is a question of theology (Christological incarnation), we will inevitably deal with philosophy as well (phenomenological incarnation). In the same way that the relationship of substance to relation has made us see the tension between metaphysics and theology (chap. 1: Augustine), and that theophany has led us to rethink phenomenality (chap. 2: Erigena), and that, finally, the progressive conversion from Martha to Saint Paul has radicalized the reduction itself (chap. 3: Eckhart), so also in part II we will see that the figure of Adam exhibits the visibility of the flesh (chap. 4: Irenaeus), that Christ confers on it all of its profundity (chap. 5: Tertullian), and that brother Francis reveals to man the possibility of its phenomenalization (chap. 6: Bonaventure). It is not at all here a question of juxtaposition but rather of rigor in formulation: the logic of theology (moving from the uncreated God to the incarnate Word) is also a philosophical logic (from the manifestation of the absolute [God] to the phenomenon of his bodily life [the flesh]). Thus the famous philosophical question of Nietzsche, posed in light of the corpus of medieval theology: "Has not philosophy in general, even until today, been simply an *explication of the flesh* and a *misunderstanding of the flesh*?"[2]

This formulation, extracted from the foreword to the second edition of the *Gay Science* (1886), sufficiently indicates on the one hand that we have in no way finished "letting ourselves be explicated or unfurled" by this flesh that we are, and on the other hand, that we must always remain subject to a profound "misunderstanding" regarding what is probably the root of our own nature: our existence in the flesh. Since the dawn of thought, and in its opening consecrated by Parmenides, "what thinks in man is the development of the flesh [*meleôn phusis*] in all and in each one."[3] Thus the thought of the flesh invites us to return to the beginning before the beginning, to the pre-Socratics before Plato. And here we observe the "failure of the flesh" in the very one who made such a return the first axis of his thought: Heidegger.[4] But beyond this attempt at a pure "return" a more justified and probably more smoothly conducted *other beginning* of Western thought can be found attested to in patristic and medieval sources. Philosophy sometimes delays needlessly the reinterrogation of the sources that the most cutting-edge investigations on the status of the "flesh" would do well to reappropriate.

We should certainly be cautious about accusing the tradition of a massive "forgetting of the flesh." A number of analyses have suggested to the contrary, that even up to Platonic thought there was present the "terror of the beautiful" [*l'effroi du beau*] that considered the body as the original place of access to divinity.[5] It is nevertheless the case that what pretends to be a novelty of Platonic thought, or at least such in Plotinus—the attainment of the divine by the progressive beauty of bodies (*Phaedrus*)—does not serve as the norm. It is better to say that, insofar as it is a question of the body, the turn taken by Neoplatonism marks a breaking point, though not to say a final point, in the assumption of the carnal for the sake of a single quest for the spiritual. To nuance rightly this lapidary judgment is not sufficient to contradict it, at least in its basic thrust.[6] For, by dint of undervaluing or of discriminating against it in the history of philosophy that is anything if not plural, we forget that *another* history of thought was given birth in Smyrna (Irenaeus), Carthage (Tertullian), and even later in Paris (Bonaventure). This narrative of the flesh, in three steps made by three authors, will disclose to us what is *philosophically* at stake as regards embodied existence, namely for Adam's "visibility," the Word's "solidity," and the believer's "conversion." The confession of faith will not be the object of attention, or rather it will only be appealed to insofar as it exhibits, in those who confess it, *a certain experience of the flesh* extendable to all: first for man (Irenaeus), then for God (Tertullian), and finally for man in his relation to God (Bonaventure). The question of the body has today become essential for philosophy in its quest for an exit from Platonism, and the means now given to us are of *phenomenologically* describing our embodiment, which we can do without making it merely the inverse of spirituality.[7] Without necessarily having to partake of the *light of faith* shared by the church fathers and the medievals together—although certainly not imagined otherwise by them—the reader is invited to encounter along with the author the new conceptuality of the body to be gained by philosophy in the triple experience of "the simple flesh" (Adam), of "the Word made flesh" (Christ), and of man "transformed in his flesh" (the believer). Far from being closed, the debate between phenomenology and Christianity is in reality just opening, if we dare to venture to the place where the *phenomenological experience* of God is most clear as well as most potently described—in patristic and medieval philosophy more than anywhere else.

Chapter 4

The Visibility of the Flesh (Irenaeus)

Adam: Return to the Origin

Omne corpus fugiendum esse—"It is necessary to flee from everything bodily."[1] This famous formula of Porphyry, near contemporary of Irenaeus and Tertullian, marks the summit in Western thought of the forgetfulness of corporeity. Not that the hypothesis of the flight from the body (*corpus fugiendum*) properly pertains to Neoplatonism, especially to Christian Neoplatonism—indeed, far from it. Together, and the one from the other, they receive it on the contrary from a certain ancient tradition that should be interrogated rather than simply denounced.[2] Nevertheless, in the second century, a new beginning in the history of thought opened a space to *corporeity* which will not be occupied again until the dawn of modern times. Thus Balthasar trenchantly writes: "With Irenaeus [and Tertullian] . . . even for the spiritual man the experience of existence is close to the *earth* and the world of the *senses* . . . It is not until Claudel [and Péguy] that a similar language appears in Christianity . . . Not only does Spirit speak to spirit, but *Flesh which speaks to flesh*. 'Our flesh has ceased being an obstacle; it has become a means and a mediation; it has ceased being a veil to become perception.' "[3]

Where then can we locate the forgetting of such a beginning, since the "forgetfulness of origins" occurs most often in the "origin of forgetfulness"? What is the point of origin starting from which thought ceased to interrogate its decisions most often un-thought? It always comes, according to theology and then philosophy, from the "preliminary fatal option," or the "decision" which, "since the time of the Fathers (as a reaction against Montanism), and in particularly since Augustine, everything having to do with the senses and the imagination in mystical experience is held to be fundamentally questionable in the extreme."[4] Whatever the validity of such a diagnosis and suspicion which raised the derision of Balthasar, something happened at the dawn of the third century to this inheritor of Neoplatonism (Augustine) that the second, in its Greek (Irenaeus) and Latin (Tertullian) modes, neither knew nor was affected by, inasmuch as it remained caught up in the novelty of a Christianity still infatuated with corporeity. The philosopher Michel Henry, for example, though seemingly ignorant of every theologian (such as Balthasar, for example), has seen this with clarity when he rests his text, *Incarnation*, on these two authors (Irenaeus and Tertullian). As debatable as the patristic exegesis practiced here is, the general diagnosis remains nevertheless just: "Thus by way of *Greek concepts* is sought the intelligence of truth the most *anti-Greek*. Such is the *contradiction* in which the Fathers and Councils are taken up more than once."[5]

The figure of Adam in Irenaeus confirms in an exemplary way the necessity of returning to the ancients in order to rediscover what they have to say anew. For, if the incarnation leads us first to the *profundity* of the "Word made flesh" (Tertullian), it is however no less rooted in the *visibility* of the one who was *first* "made flesh"—Adam, or the earthly man (*adâmah* [earth], Irenaeus). Not only in fact does man *see God* according to the bishop of Lyon, as in his celebrated formula that "the life of man is the *vision* of God,"[6] but God himself also *sees man* in the flesh of Adam, the flesh he would assume by his Word in the mode of prefiguration: "The Word, artisan of the universe had, in Adam, *sketched in advance* [*praeformauerat*] the future economy of the humanity that the Son of God assumes."[7]

For *living* man, God is therefore certainly "*revealed* by the creation" in Adam: "The Glory of God is a living man." Yet for him the *seeing God* is developed further in a text so well known that it is often only partially quoted. The Word (new Adam) "has *manifested* the Father [*ostendebat Patrem*]." Hence: "And the life of man is the vision of God." Said otherwise, in the very terms of the bishop of Lyon, "the invisible in the Son is the Father [*invisibile et enim Filii Pater*], and the visible in the Father is the Son [*visibile autem Patris Filius*]" (manifestation by incarnation). This leads to the unique condition that "the Father was revealed *to all* in rendering his Word visible to all." To say "to all" (*omnibus*) includes the "work modeled at the origin that he has recapitulated in himself," namely, Adam, the revelation of God by creation.[8] The chiasm of the revealed and the manifested is such that we will understand nothing of the salvation borne by the *second Adam* in the incarnation (new Adam/Christ) until we have first examined the *first Adam* in creation (first Adam/man)—not in some logical or chronological anteriority, but according to an ontological figuration according to which the latter (the Word made flesh) who is paradoxically revealed as the one who already dwells in the first (Adam, drawn from the earth): "That which has been tied [*colligatur*] cannot be untied [*solueretur*] unless the loops of the knot are done again *in reverse* [*retrorsus*]."[9] Irenaeus therefore insists, and here we see that he is a philosopher as well as a theologian, that "to speak truth [*verum dicere*] is precisely what concerns *Adam* . . . because we ourselves are all issued from him. If man is therefore to be saved, it is necessary that he be saved who is fashioned after the first."[10]

If there is an originality in the Irenean corpus, especially concerning its contemporary relevance, it is not, paradoxically, in the direction of the deification of man, so often invoked, but in the *hominization of God*—neither going without the other. And along with the emphasis too often put on the *glory of God* in the "living man" by theology's rediscovery of the church fathers since Vatican II as well as by philosophy, in Chrétien, Marion, and Henry, for example, it is sometimes forgotten what grounds it: the life of man in the "vision *of* God" understood not only as the vision of God by man (objective genitive) but as the vision of man (Adam) by God (subjective genitive).[11] It was in fact necessary that God *be seen* in Adam drawn from the earth in order for him to become flesh. The focus on the life of man achieved in the "vision of God" is therefore legitimate, if it is first accepted as being *seen by him*, in other words surprisingly serving if not as its model, at least as the "place of visibility" for his human and carnal incarnation: "God took on from *his own features* the work thus formed, in order that even that which *appears visibly* [the flesh] was made in a divine form."[12]

I emphasize *seeing man* and *beginning with man* (Adam) because from the origins the Word is "foreseen" in the flesh of man (the new Adam). Such is paradoxically what Irenaeus envisaged—contra a current reading which, by emphasizing the theological realm and especially divinization (the "theomorphosis of man"), has forgotten the philosophical and humanizing character (the "anthropomorphosis of God") that is also present.[13] The flight from the sensible or some medieval angelism does not taint the bishop of Lyon, and it is wrong to interpret the "Irenean vision of God" in the sense of a pure beatific vision, as if seeing God by the soul implied renouncing all sensation of the body in a Platonic dualism that is entirely foreign to the very first point of anchorage of Christianity: "He has given his soul for our soul [*dante animam suam pro nostra anima*] and his flesh for our flesh [*et carnem suam pro nostris carnibus*]."[14]

The Ark of Flesh

The *Ark of Speech* is well known. It is all to Jean-Louis Chrétien's credit for having formulated the name and articulated its efficacy. When God brought the animals to Adam "in order to *see what* he would name them" (Gen. 2:19), he established the first man, by means of his earliest vocalization, as the locus of the first welcome of creatures in words, which is also an abode in which to dwell. This triple primacy (of the first man, his word, and the animals' abode in him) therefore makes the ark of Adam (the "ark of speech") the guarantor of the most original *safeguard* for creatures before the ark of Noah ("the ark of the flood"). In the word uttered by Adam, the appellation, falsely understood as the dominion of the concept (Hegel), signifies instead the act of naming by which God tests man and establishes the measure of his creature in its proper capacity to receive, in the *first ark* (language), the collection of living beings that he leads to him: "The animals have been gathered for human speech and brought together in this speech, which names them long before they are brought together, according to the same story, in Noah's ark to be saved from the flood and the destruction it brings."[15]

But before the *ark of speech* there is the *ark of flesh*, that holds a primacy even more original, that is, the formation of Adam "drawn from the dust of the earth" (Gen. 2:7), and that of Eve manifest in his astonished acclamation: "bone of my bone and flesh of my flesh" (Gen. 2:23). In support of this more original ark in Adam, it is fitting to rediscover "its beginning," as Husserl says, "the pure—and so to speak *still dumb*—psychological experience which now must be made to utter its own sense with no adulteration."[16] Such will be our leitmotif for the following. "Doing" comes before "speaking;" or even better, before "saying" is discovered the "pre-saying," in the sense of a pre-predicative *formation* by which God gives man the existence and activity of his flesh itself as the original place of his first dwelling. Such is in fact the teaching of Irenaeus, which we are today strongly encouraged to reappropriate. God *first* "gets his hands dirty" [*la main à la pâte*], as it were, in order that Adam, drawn from the earth, exhibits by way of anticipation the "visibility of the flesh" of his Word manifested by this image. Only *then* is it consecrated "flesh" as the place of a "common speech" where the animals, along with him, find their main habitation. "The Word was made flesh so that the flesh could become Word," says Mark the Ascetic, as we have seen above. For us here this means precisely that the Word speaks even better in his flesh than in his speech, and it is by the flesh that his speech speaks.[17]

Getting His Hands Dirty

Very far indeed from the Augustinian perspectives further centered on *Acts of Speech*,[18] Irenaeus asserts the formation of Adam from the earth as the essential: "The Lord God formed man from the dust of the earth and breathed into his nostrils the breath of life, and man became a living being" (Gen. 2:7). For the bishop of Lyon, God appears as a sort of "artist" or "potter" (*artifex*), even as a plastic surgeon (*cheriourgia*), as it were, who has formed us by a quasi-*amorous plasmatio* out of the womb of our mother (*plasma*) as Adam is drawn from the earth (*adâmâ*). Our carnal conception corresponds to the divine formation of the Adamic body, thus extending to the height of our flesh what was first given in the bosom of the earth: "Jeremiah affirms that the Word of God *forms* us in the maternal bosom [*plasmat in ventre*]: 'Before forming you in the womb of your mother, I knew you' [Jer. 1:5]. In this way therefore are we formed [*plasmemur*] in the maternal bosom by the Word."[19]

A question is nevertheless posed here about Adam himself and also then about the Word to come in the flesh: "Where did the substance of the first man come from [*unde ergo est protoplasti substantia*]? For according to Scripture God had not yet made rain until the man was created and there was not yet a man to work the earth" (Gen. 2:5).[20] The most naive questions are often the most essential, and here more than elsewhere. Not yet having "one beside him" of his kind (Eve), Adam in fact had no father, except for God himself, nor a mother, except the earth. Therefore it is from the "*virgin soil*" that Yahweh God, in a *divine quasi-fecundation*, takes from the dust of the earth and forms the first man, "in order that he would be the point of departure for humanity." His "will" and his "wisdom" were therefore joined to the "virginity of the earth" in order to make it fecund or at least to inform it.[21] The literality of such an exegesis of the narrative of creation, where the virginity of the earth is almost chronologically deduced from the double absence of man and of rain in order to cultivate it (Gen. 2:5), together with the fecundation by God of that which is still "virgin" (Gen. 2:7), is almost enough to make the modern reader smile—if it did not articulate the profound symbolic relation that unites man to God from the vantage of corporeity. The act of the creation of Adam, the union of the mother earth with father God (setting aside the question of the mythological reprise of this reading of Genesis), teaches us anew what "dwelling" means: to dwell on "the earth" to be sure, but also to dwell in the "flesh," or even to dwell in the "flesh" because it is our own "earth" and vice versa. In other words, to retrieve a strikingly Irenaean passage from Pèguy, it means "the incarnation as a *history*, a history arrived *in the flesh* and *on the earth*."[22]

Earth and the Flesh. The earth, or the work formed by God (*plasma*), and thus the flesh (*caro*), becomes that which the Son suffers and joins himself to in his incarnation. Irenaeus reveals to us a long-forgotten perspective that, in a new way, reveals that the "incarnation" of the Son is prefigured by the "formation" of the flesh of Adam: "The only Son, who was always present to humanity, was united and mingled with his own work that was formed by him [*unitus et consparsus suo plasmati*] according to the good pleasure of the Father, and so he was made flesh."[23] The work of the Father makes a unified whole, between the generation of the Son and the anticipation of his incarnation in the figure of the first man. Similarly, the "plasmation" of the Word, his "taking on flesh,"[24] depends on the formation or taking on flesh of Adam as if it were itself a return to the origin. If the first Adam (of Genesis) *prefigures* the second (the Word made flesh), it is because the second (Christ) *manifests* the full humanity of the first in his original formation (Adam drawn from the earth). This is evidenced by the strong parallel consistently established between "the virginity of the earth" in the creation of Adam and the "virginity of the Virgin" in the incarnation of the Son. In the first material earth of Adam is also revealed the human womb of the Son of God—and together they are related to the one act of "formation" and "creative power" of the Father. Far, then, from removing the Son from his true humanity, his virginal birth actually reinforces it insofar as it symbolically borrows from the original virgin birth of Adam himself (i.e., of the earth and flesh): "In being born of a Virgin by the will and wisdom of God, the Lord received a flesh formed according to the same economy [*eandem dispositionem* (*oikonomia*)] as Adam, for the sake of showing that *he also* was formed in a flesh *like that* of [*similitudinem*] Adam and was being made the *same man* as him."[25]

By forming Adam in the act of *creation*, the Father in some sense "gets his hands dirty," drawing Adam out of "the dust of the earth" and breathing into his nostrils the "breath of life" (Gen. 2:6). And in the same way, in the *incarnation*, he remains the very same artisan in drawing his Son from the "womb" of Mary his mother by the Holy Spirit who "overshadowed" her (Luke 1:35). The second Adam, by espousing himself to the dust drawn from the *earth*, therefore assumes the first Adam by virtue of the *materiality* of his own mother, receiving from her the *breath of life* in the Spirit welcomed by Mary. This relation of the first and second Adam, of the breath of life and the Spirit, and of the virgin earth and Mary the Virgin, is not a matter of a simple correspondence, but rather that of a profound marriage or covenant. Adam is not initially a sinner (Gen. 3:6) but rather a "living man" (Gen. 2:6), and Christ (the new Adam), "by the righteousness of one," does not merely heal "the fault of one" (see Rom. 5:20). Instead, the "form of the one to come" ought to be recognized already in this first man (see Rom. 5:14)—especially in his flesh.[26] The first work of God in Adam discloses the second act of work performed by God, in the *hand* of the potter by which the clay is fashioned.

To say that God "gets his hands dirty" is to recognize that he *possesses hands* and that in the precise case of the sixth day of creation (that of man), the Father is not content with *speaking*, even words that perform absolutely what they signify ("he spoke and it was"—*the ark of speech*) but also requires a sort of divine-human "hand to hand" [*corps à corps*] by which he *works* the clay out of which comes his creature (*Adama—the ark of flesh*): "As for man, God forms him *with his own hands*."[27] God's hands, in a similar way to man, which are a tool (Bergson) and an "extension of the body,"[28] or in other words organs which are of the same nature as he is. Having no need—contra every conception of Gnostic demiurges (esp. Valentin)—of angels or "any other power" in order to create, we ought not to think that the "Father has *hands of a different nature* [*quasi ipse suas non haberet manus*], since he has always had with him his *Word* and *Wisdom*, the *Son* and *Spirit*."[29]

The Hands of God. The famous thesis of the "two hands of God"[30] in Irenaeus's account of the formation of Adam ought to be taken here in the strictest literality, and as such will be shown below definitively to deliver Christianity from Heidegger's false accusation concerning the equivalence of "creation" and "production." Not only is the Father engaged in the formation of Adam for the sake of his own self-manifestation, but also engaged are those with whom he eternally works: the Son (Word) and Spirit (Wisdom). The Word is the one "through whom all things have been made by the Father," and the Spirit "cries 'Abba, Father' and forms man in the likeness of God." The *Word* "governs the Spirit [*articulat Spiritum*]" inasmuch as he executes the creation decided by his Father, and the *Spirit* "reveals the Word [*ostendit Verbum*]" inasmuch as he ordains his action according to the model foreseen by the Father.[31] Without the doctrine of the Trinity, which is not yet fixed (Nicaea) and the idea of the appropriation of definitive attributes (Augustine), Irenaeus, against the Gnostics who separate the persons and lose the unity of God, nevertheless conceives of the creation from the beginning in the terms of a "common work" of the Father, Son, and Spirit.[32]

It is thus not too much for the "two hands of God" to create man, since the "hand of God [*manus Dei*] by which Adam was made" is also "the one according to which *we* have been modeled in our turn [*plasmati autem autem sumus et nos*]."[33] Far from any extrinsic "flick into existence [*chiquenaude*]," not only does God "preserve" his creation according to a thoroughly metaphysical model of the permanence of substances, but he works and works in *us* as he did in Adam himself who "never escaped [*non enim effugit aliquando*] the hands of God."[34] The *continuity* between the formation of Adam and our own image is for Irenaeus such that it is necessary for us to conceive of ourselves in a quasi-Adamic fashion, as the psalmist states, "coming forth from the hands of God": "Your hands have knit me together, fashioned me and affirmed me" (Ps. 118 [119]: 73). Where Augustine, for example, envisioned a hereditary transmission of sin, Irenaeus, by contrast, understood the descent to be in the act of the formation of the flesh as mud drawn from the earth: "Go down to the *potter's house* and there I will make you understand my words" (Jer. 18:2). The "act of conforming" to the image is deeper, therefore, than all fault, and the "clay" of the creatures will come alive all the more as the splendor of the "King" will be manifest to it and thereby seduce it. Never have the *theological aesthetics* attained such a height as they did here in Irenaeus at the beginning: "It is not you who have made God [*non enim tu Deum facis*], but God who made you [*se Deus te facit*]. If you are therefore the work of God [*opera Dei*], wait patiently for the Hand of your Artist [*manum artificis*] who does all things at the opportune time [*opportune*]. I say 'opportune' by relation to you who are made. Present to him a supple and docile heart and protect the form [*custodi figuram*] that this Artist has given you, bearing within you the Water which comes from him along with the sin which hardened you and caused you to reject the imprint of his fingers [*vestigia digitorum eius*]. By guarding this conformation [*custodiens compaginationem*], you will climb to perfection, for by the art of God the clay that is in you is going to be covered over [*absconditur quod est in te lutum*]. His hand has created your substance and it will cover you with pure gold within and without so that you will be so well adorned that the King himself will be smitten by your beauty [*concupiscat speciem tuam*]."[35]

Creation and Fabrication. We ought to realize that Irenaeus's conception of God's "hands"—that by which the Father created Adam from the dust of the earth, prefiguring there his Son, and shaping the pattern for ourselves in the very same work—stands at a far remove from Heidegger's false accusations of the creation as "production" where one immediately conceives, "on the basis of a religious faith, namely, the biblical faith" that "the totality of all beings is represented in advance as something *created*, which here means made."[36] The accusation is aimed of course at Thomas Aquinas more than Irenaeus, and intends to suggest that one should attribute to the "Thomist philosophy"—wrongly—the paternity of a thought of *ens creatum* which immediately transforms the creative activity of God to that of an "artisan": the "philosophy of this faith" does not represent the creation in any other way than as "that of a craftsman" (*Handwerker*).[37] Suffice to say that the concept of *Architectus* in Thomas Aquinas and *Artifex* in Irenaeus is both poorly and confusedly understood. Neither Irenaeus's "hands of God" (*manus Dei*) nor Thomas's "first principle" (*primum principium*) has anything to do with an *artisanal fabrication* understood as a *technê* producing a work exterior to it. Since, as we have shown above in the context of the Thomist extension of the "Augustinian relation" (*ad aliquid*) of the Trinity to the world,[38] "creation pertains to the genre of relation" (*creatio est de genere relationis*) in Aquinas. The creation understood theologically is not only a "poetics" of the Hellenistic type, but also a sort of "praxis" at least from the point of view of God and his proper engagement in the world. Thus Thomas says that God "recognizes himself in the work that he has produced," in an immanent and not merely transitive action.[39]

The aesthetic model of creation, as deployed by Irenaeus (retrieved to a certain degree in Thomas Aquinas), therefore establishes Adam as the continual work [*oeuvre*] of God, in other words, his true "work" [*ouvrage*]: "you are the work [*ouvrage*] of God" (*opera Dei es*). "To be made" (*te facit*) rather than "to make oneself" (*tu facis*), awaiting the "opportune time" of creation [*oportune*], presenting itself as material ready for the formation of a "form" (*figura*), conserving this "conformation" (*compaginatio*) until the "imprint of his fingers" (*vestigia digitorum eius*), revealing "the clay hidden within" as the work lies already *in nuce* in the clay (*absconditur quod est in te lutum*), and rendering the Creator himself "struck with the beauty" of his created work [*oeuvre*] (*concupiscat speciem tuam*): such are the traits of an aesthetic creation, rather than a technical production, of a work [*oeuvre*] which "opens" [*ouvre*] or "installs a world," rather than one that "rules" the assemblage of some kind of "framework" (*Gestell*). Measured by Irenaeus's description of the creation of Adam as the "flesh of man," it is rather the case that the critique applies to the "work" in Heidegger, and not to creation. The falsity of the accusation of creation as production is extendable to the conception of the act of the Creator in other fathers of the church as well: "When the work of art emerges, then a world is opened, of which it maintains the reign. To be a work means *to set up a world* . . . The world is not the mere collection of the countable or uncountable, familiar and unfamiliar things that are at hand. But neither is it a merely imagined framework added by our representation to the sum of such given things. The *world worlds* [*Welt weltet*], and is more fully in being than the tangible and perceptible realm in which we believe ourselves to be at home . . . The work as work *sets up a world.* The work holds open the open region *of the world* . . . In setting up a world, the work *sets forth the earth* [*stellt es die Erde her*] . . . The work moves the earth itself into the open region of a world and keeps it there. *The work lets the earth be an earth.*"[40]

We should not take the analogy any further: first in order to avoid the danger of any anachronism, and second in order not to identify the simple horizontal relation of man to the *sacred* of the earth (the numinous) with the vertical relation of God to the *saint* in creation (the economy of salvation). It nevertheless remains that God, "getting his hands dirty" *has* or *possesses* his own hands (*manus*). Bending the rules a bit, we could rightly observe that these hands do not pertain at all to the regime of "understanding" or "knowledge" as if the divine in Christianity had no other end than being reduced to that which is "present-at-hand" (*vorhanden*) in order then to be "ready-to-hand" (*zuhanden*). On the contrary, they have the responsibility of welcoming, or better, of "gathering" (*lesen*) into the *ark of flesh* that which is woven in the *plasmatio* of Adam. Since the Son "governs" (*articulat*) and the Holy Spirit "reveals" (*ostendit*)[41] as the two hands of the Father, God as artist *works* [*oeuvre*] *with his hands* in *opening* [*ouvrant*] the world that, in molding it, leaves the mark of the maker. If there is therefore one who is phenomenologically "there" (*Da-sein*) in order to make the world "world" when he reveals the earth, it is therefore the Father as "absolute artist" (*artifex*) who makes man at the same time the place of the habitation of his own flesh. The incarnation, prefigured in Adam, allows us to see, like every work of art, that in the constituted work [*oeuvre*] the one is recognized who has carried out the work [*ouvrage*]. Here no exteriority of the Creator to his creature is possible, nor even conceivable. The true "shepherd" is not the "shepherd of being" alone, but rather the One whose "voice" becomes the sign of his recognition and maintains his creature in existence: "The Voice of the Father is present, from beginning to end, in the work [*ouvrage*] shaped by it [*vox Patris ab initio usque ad finem adest plasmati suo*]."[42]

A question arises, however, which brings us back to the unique Irenaean perspective: what about the formation of Adam as such? Better, how is the Word made flesh, and how is it then that no longer only in the one who is "drawn from the earth" (*adâmâ*) is spoken very precisely this *carnal language* by which he has "given his flesh for our flesh" (*dante carnem suam pro nostris carnibus*)?[43] Now revealing itself is a new and "wise mixture" of "earth" and "breath" (Gen. 2:6) to be sure, but also that of "body" (*sôma*), soul (*psuchê*), and spirit (*pneuma*) (1 Thess. 5:23). The earth and breath of the first Adam is thus totally renewed by the second (body, soul spirit) insofar as the second (the Son visible in his flesh) comes to manifest everything of the first (man drawn from the earth). *Man as such* (body and soul) serves as the foundation in Irenaeus for the *insertion of God* into the human compound (by the Holy Spirit) which transforms it in each part. Thus the divinity is never given independently of the *fullness of humanity*, alone fit to receive the divine and to be converted by it.

Man as Such

In the New Testament, particularly in the Gospel story of the healing of the man blind from birth, the question of man as such is first an affair of "mud" and "earth" before there arises any consideration of whether he is bipartite or tripartite in structure. The passage is famous, of course, but rarely interpreted according to the chiasm of creation and re-creation: "It is clear that the earth [*terra*] with which the Lord reshaped the eyes of the man blind from birth (Jn. 9:6) is *also that with which* man was shaped in the beginning [*quoniam et ab initio plasmatus est homo*]."[44]

Mud and the Voice. Here again we find the same mud—if not also in some sense the same man. We are the descendants of Adam, more so by the constitution of our flesh, according to Irenaeus, than thereafter by the accident of our sins. We will see, therefore, in the healing of the man blind from birth, not the liberation from fault with some return to an Adamic state in view, but rather the place of visibility and manifestation of the original creative act. "After saying this, he spit on the earth and made mud with his saliva. He then applied this mud to the eyes of the blind man" (Jn. 9:6). To the *reshaping* of the man blind from birth by Christ the healer, there corresponds our own *maternal shaping*, itself corresponding to that *maternal shaping* of the Word made flesh (Lk. 1:31; Jn. 1:14), as well as the *original shaping* of Adam drawn from the earth (Gen. 2:7). Moving up the chain in reverse, the first (reshaping of the blind man) manifests the second (maternal shaping) and both make manifest the third (original shaping). A kind of *metonym of shapings* is therefore established, as Ireneaeus himself says: "The whole is disclosed by means of the part" (*ex parte totum ostendens*). Here the economy of salvation as "language of the flesh" always remains identical, from the creation (Adam) to the incarnation (Word made flesh), and from the incarnation to redemption (of the blind-born). In each case the same act (mixture or blending) in different modes (earth and breath/plasma and holy Spirit/mud and saliva) occurs, though always with the same aim: to make *seen* and *known* the (re-)creative act of the Father in his perpetual *shaping of the flesh*: "Thus, since we are shaped [*plasmemur*] in the maternal womb by the Word, this same Word reshapes [*formavit*] the eyes of the man blind from birth: in this way he makes to appear in the open [*in manifesto ostendens*] the One who shapes us in secret [*in abscondito Plasmator noster*], because it is the Word himself who was made visible [*manifestum*] to men; at the same time he made known the original formation of Adam [*antiquam plasmationem*

Adae], in other words how Adam was made and by what Hand [*manum*] he was shaped [*plasmatus est*]; and he made seen the whole by means of the part [*ex parte totum ostendens*], because the Lord who reshaped [*formavit*] the eyes was the one who had shaped [*plasmavit*] all men in executing the will of the Father."[45]

But the Father of his two Hands (Son and Spirit) is not content merely to touch Adam in his act of creation, and the Word is not satisfied simply to reshape the blind in the moment of his re-creation. The "*voice* of the Father" uttered "from the beginning [*ab initio*]" is also joined to the flesh in order that it be made the place of a "call": "As God formerly called to Adam in the evening in order to find him ["Where are you?" Gen. 3:9], so also in the latter days, *by the same voice* [*per eandem vocem*] he has visited the race of Adam (the blind) in order to find them ["in order that the works of God be manifest in him" (Jn. 9:3)]."[46] The *identity of the flesh* of Adam and the blind man is understood therefore to be found in the *singularity of "voices"* (the Father and Son's), which establishes the body as the locus of a "vocation." Theologically understood, the *call of the flesh* does not articulate the unbridled desire of a body in search of satisfaction, but rather the unity of a substantial whole (soul and body) completely turned toward God (Spirit): thus the passage of a *dichotomous* anthropology (earth/breath, body/soul [Gen. 2:7]) to a *trichotomous* anthropology (body/soul/spirit [1 Thess. 5:23]), the ultimate aim of which is not to differentiate the elements of a substantial compound, but rather to mark a new existential attitude of the entirety of the human person turned toward God (hence the supplementation of the [holy] Spirit).

Mixture. A close reading of Irenaeus's *Adversus Haereses* affirms that humanity is most simply understood as a mixture of body and soul or earth and breath. Against the line of interpretation that overemphasizes divinization, it should rather be seen that, as certain commentators have seen (A. Rousseau or J. Fantino), what matters first is the *density of humanity* as such in Irenaeus—and such not without God but as a living animal *tout court* (or "psychic being"). Body/soul or earth/breath suffice to define humanity in its proper being or nature: "All this is able to be said of men [*in hominibus*] because they are composite by nature [*cum sint compositi natura*], being constituted by a body [*et ex corpore*] and a soul [*et anima subsistentes*]." Likewise: "Man is a mixture of soul and flesh [*temperatio animae et carnis*] and a flesh formed in the likeness of God and formed by his hands." And again: "Spiritual men will never be spirits without bodies; but it is our substance [*substantia nostra*], composed of soul and flesh [*hoc est animae et carnis adunatio*], which, by receiving the Spirit of God, constitutes spiritual man."[47]

This can never be repeated enough, in order to avoid drawing Irenaeus's anthropology into an angelism that does not pertain to him: "Man and therefore Adam, considered in the common nature that makes him man, is constituted of two elements, a *body* and a *soul*."[48] Such is the formulation of "man as such" or even better "man *tout court*," and it certainly seems that the *finitude of existence* already characterized Christian theology from its earliest beginnings, and which has so often been only deeply forgotten since.[49] The distinction of terms is still fluid in Irenaeus, for man is composed of "body and soul" (*corpus et anima*) as much as of "flesh and life" (*sarx et psûchê*)—yet the point is that man evades all dualism here. Of course, we often need a third term, "spirit" (*pneuma*) in order to correct the Hellenistic body/soul "bipartition" by a Pauline body/soul/spirit "tripartition" (1 Thess. 5:23). Yet it would of course be hasty to designate the bishop of Lyon's composite humanity as some kind of dualism. It is simply man as *plasma* or the "initial mixture" upon which is established the possible but not de facto realized deification of man as *capax Dei*.

Animality. It is therefore in Irenaeus the fundamental recognition [*prise en compte*] and the assumption of responsibility [*prise en charge*] of *animality*—the psychic understood as "enlivened clay" or "animated body" (following Gen. 2:7)— that later theology massively obscured. For man to be "psychic" is not to be opposed to his animality, as if the soul (*psuchê*) would make us leave our animality, but rather on the contrary to receive it, assume it and to "recapitulate" it in Christ: "Sown an animal body [*sôma psuchikon*], it is raised a spiritual body [*sôma pneumatikon*]" (1 Cor. 15:44).[50] As later in Augustine's *Literal Commentary on Genesis*, neither "reason" (*ratio*) nor "spirit" (*mens*), nor "intelligence" (*intelligentia*) constitute the image of God in man and his "prerogative" over the other animals.[51] Man "in his totality" is made in the image and likeness of God as "flesh" united to the soul, and as we will see below, vivified by "the Spirit of God": "It is man (soul-flesh-Spirit) and not a part of man (soul without body or spirit without flesh or soul) that is the image and likeness of God."[52] The Gnostic, and particularly Valentinian Docetism in the earliest days of Christianity, giving the force of law to the quasi-*animal* or *psychic* appearance of man and Christ, matters at least as much or even more than the Christic angelism or his pneumatic character that some claim to have rediscovered today (the so-called *Christos angelos*). The readings of the Irenaean corpus that are too quickly divinizing ("the glory of God is the living man"), as we emphasized above, forget his entrance into matter from top to bottom humanizing. It is by his taking of a body, the "vivification" of man by God, precisely, that humanity is justified: "There are two dimensions to the living man [*vivens homo*]: he is living [*vivens*] thanks to participation in the Spirit, and man [*homo*] by the substance of the *flesh*."[53] The realism of the Word made flesh fights here against his mere semblance and the Adamization of Christ makes a stand against his too immediate glorification: "By virtue of his superabundant love he *became what we are* [*factus est quod sumus nos*] in order to make us that which he is [*uti nos perficeret esse quod est ipse*]."[54]

The Divine Interlacing

For Irenaeus man "as such" or man "*tout court*" bears an existence *through himself*. It is not that he does not depend on God or is not ordered toward him, but rather that he is discovered to be created capable of welcoming the novelty of the divine Event—according to a *metamorphosis* or *transformation*, though not by a pure restoration (of the Edenic state) or simple achievement. The ontological consistency of the composite (soul/body) ought thus to be maintained in order to serve as a support to the transforming action of God (by the Holy Spirit): "May the God of peace sanctify you, and may your being—spirit [*pneuma*], soul [*psuchê*] and body [*sôma*]—be guarded against reproach in anticipation of the coming of the Lord" (1 Thess. 5:23). Irenaeus is clearer here in his interpretion of Saint Paul than the later equivocations of the commentators. The mixture "soul/body" (*psuchê/sôma*) of the first Testament (Gen. 2:7) receives the "divine breath" (*pneuma*) in the second and is prefigured in the first, since the initial mixture forms a constituted whole capable of receiving the power of God. Here the spirit (*pneuma*) or, in other words, God or the divine Holy Spirit is neither totally inscribed in the interior of man in a purely intrinsicist way (de Lubac, Sesboüé), nor totally coming from the exterior in a unilaterally extrinsicist perspective (Fantino). Let us attempt to prove (a) the complete distinction, on the one hand, of the "mind" (*psuchê*) animating the body (*sôma*) and the Holy Spirit (*pneuma*) in-breathing them together and (b) the insertion, even the interlacing, on the other hand, of the Holy Spirit himself (*pneuma*) in relation to the spirit of man (*psuchê*) animating his body (*sôma*).[55]

Sôma, Psuchê, Pneuma. (a) The bishop of Lyon could not be clearer: "Our substance [*nostra substantia*], that is, the composite of soul and flesh [*hoc est animae et carnis adunatio*], constitutes spiritual man [*spiritalem hominem perfecit*] in receiving the Spirit of God [*assumens Spiritus Dei*]."[56] We can nicely distinguish here between the "spirit of man" (*psuchê* or *anima*) tied to his "flesh" (*sarx* or *caro*) or "body" (*soma* or *corpus*), and the "Spirit of God" (*pneuma* or *spiritus*), which by "in-breathing" or interlacing with him, renders him spiritual or pneumatic. The human spirit (*psuchê*), given to psychic men or living beings, is in fact in relation only with "the act of their creation," and is their "condition" (*secundum conditionem*). Thus the *psuchê* or *anima* is a "created thing" (*quod est factum*) since it remains constitutive of the human composite given at its very creation as an element of the mixture or composite of soul and body which makes man "as such" (*psuchê* and *soma*). The Spirit (*pneuma*), on the contrary, given to spiritual or pneumatic men only, is not an originarily given element of the human constitution. Man receives it by "adoptive filiation" (*secundum adoptionem*), which indicates, according to the motif of finitude, that it is first necessary to be man in order then to be called son of God. Thus the Holy Spirit does not indicate man "in his finished state" [*tout fait*] but man "in an unfinished state" [*se faisant*], which indicates that what is given by God (*quod est ex Deo*) can be refused. The ontologically neutral thickness of the creation that confers on man a membership in animality and life in general is also the condition of the reception of grace. The Father is given to "sons" who are capable of receiving him, and not to beings so oblivious of their creaturely ontological weightiness that they lose the originary pedestal that is theirs by virtue of their very being: "He gives to the psychics by relation to their creation [*secundum conditionem*], the mind [*anima*] fitting for creation, and which is a created thing [*quod est factum*]; he gives to the pneumatics by relation to their adoptive filiation [*secundum adoptionem*] the Spirit [*pneuma*] which comes from the Father and which is his 'Offspring.'"[57]

God and Man Interlaced. (b) Now comes the "Spirit of God" or the "Holy Spirit" (*pneuma*) himself to animate or vivify the "spirit of man" (*psuchê*) which animates or vivifies his body (*sôma*). This the bishop of Lyon indicates with similar clarity: "Everyone will agree that we are a body drawn from the earth [*corpus sumus de terra acceptum*] and a soul which receives the Spirit of God [*et anima accipiens a Deo Spiritum*]."[58] The soul (*psuchê*) serves here as "node" or "point of enfleshment" (Péguy) between the corporeal (*sôma*) and spiritual (*pneuma*)—even a sort of *medium* or middle term between the human and divine. It is the "soul" (*anima*) and not "the body drawn from the earth" which receives the "Spirit of God." This certainly does not signify that the body itself (*sôma*) makes the choice of passing by the mind [*l'esprit*] of man (*psuchê*) in order to be given to his spirit and his body (*psuchê* and *sôma*). Therein only what is animated by the most ordinary breath of life is able to receive or refuse God: "Man passes to the glory of the Father by being *interlaced* with the Spirit of God [*complexus Spiritum Dei*]."[59] Such an *interlacing* of the divine and human, as a spiritual chiasm relaying the carnal plasmation of Adam, accounts for what we name here a true *insertion of the divine in the human*, following Péguy: wherever the "very mystery of the carnal" is, there is the "insertion of the spiritual in the carnal," and wherever the "mystery of the temporal" is, there is the "insertion of the eternal in the temporal"—"in a word, there is the mystery of the incarnation."[60]

Thus the (Holy) Spirit is not added to the composite of soul and body in the manner of a third substance nor in order to tie them together as if they had no substantiality or unity in themselves. On the contrary, the *pneuma* requires or rather proposes a quasi-*divine* mode of being on the composite itself—inserting and in-breathing his Spirit (*pneuma*) on the mind or soul of man (*psuchê*) as it becomes one with his body (*sôma*) or flesh (*sarx*). The mention of the *perfection* of the pneumatic over the psychic marks precisely this mediation of the choice proper to the human soul that renders man perfectible: "The perfect man [*perfectus homo*] is the mixture and union of the soul [*commixtio et adunitio animae*] which has received the Spirit of the

Father [*assumentis Spiritum Patris*] and has been mixed with the flesh [*et admixtae ei carni*] modeled according to the image of God."[61]

What matters in Irenaeus is therefore the *perfection* in the union and interlacing of the Creator and his creature, and the *modality of being* rather than substance, by which the "soul" (*anima/psuchê*) receives the "Spirit" (*spiritus/pneuma*) in being itself combined with a "flesh" (*caro/sarx*) or a "body" (*corpus/soma*). Here lies the properly *philosophical* and *existential* thought of Irenaeus, who, instead of dividing man into discrete substances as much as into regions of being (soul, body, Spirit), makes on the contrary the dynamic of the encounter between man and God the place of their eternally sealed espousal. As Adeline Rousseau has emphasized: "One thing is a man considered from an *abstract* point of view, in the *nature* he holds common with all men; another thing is a man considered from the *concrete* point of view, in his *existential* comportment, in the drama of the decision in which, in opening (or closing) himself freely to the call of God, he receives (or refuses) the full realization of his being in view of which he has been created. From the first point of view, man is body and soul; from the second, he is—or at least is invited to be—infinitely more."[62] The spiritual man is therefore not distinguished from the psychic man, understood as a unity of soul and body only inasmuch as the first has something else that the second does not have. On the contrary, he is the *same* man, identically drawn from the earth and breath (body and soul), but realized in his divine vocation since he receives the Spirit of God. Neither does the "flesh" nor the "soul" nor even the "Spirit" constitute the perfected man for Irenaeus, but only the one who, having sufficiently measured and inhabited the depths of his properly human mixture, is able thus to receive the breath and insertion of God, as the *amorous plasmatio* most proper to his created state: "The formed flesh [*plasmatio carnis*] in itself is not perfect man: it is only the body of man and therefore a part of man. The soul [*anima*] in itself is not more of man [than the body]: it is only the soul of man and therefore a part of man. Neither is the Spirit [*Spiritus*] man: for we give to it the name of Spirit and not man. It is the union and mixture of all these things [*commixtio et unitio horum omnium*] which constitutes the perfect man."[63]

From the Invisible to the Visible. There remains then the image (*imago*) or likeness (*similitudo*) that man acquires, or loses, in his relation to God according to whether he receives or not the Spirit (*pneuma*) come to vivify divinely his composite as such.

The metaphor of the "icon" has certainly been appropriately developed close to the heart of Christian thought, established against all the idolatrous representations of God: "The Son is the image [*eikôn*] of the invisible God" (Col. 1:15). But the primacy of the "icon" (*eikôn*) over the idol (*eidolon*) masks at the same time the truly positive status of the "image" (*imago*) in Christianity.[64] Not only does the Son refer to the "invisible profundity" (*bathos*) of the Father, but even more he *renders visible* the Father himself and works his *manifestation* through himself. The *visibility* of God, or better, his act of *visibilization*, is what properly characterizes Christianity, especially in Irenaeus from the beginnings of the *tempora Christiana*: "The invisible reality [*invisibile*] seen in the Son is the Father," Irenaeus affirms, if only to add that "the visible reality [*visibile*] in which we *have seen the Father* is the Son."[65] This has been noted from the beginning of this text, in the guise of the guiding question of this entire work. That "no one is able to see the face of God, except his backside" (Ex. 33:23) is a fundamental trait of Judaism more than Christianity, which a number of Neoplatonic theologians, including Denys the Areopagite, resume in their own way. The originality of Christianity lies elsewhere—perhaps in the response of Jesus to Phillip seeking the "way" to get to God: "He who has *seen* me has *seen* the Father. Why do you say, 'show us the Father'?" (Jn. 14:9). Commenting on this, Irenaeus finds in "seeing" and "touching" the divine our own most pressing questions: "By the agency of the Word become visible [*visibilem*] and palpable [*palpabilem*] in person, the Father is shown [*Pater ostendebatur*] . . . The Father is revealed to all by rendering his Son visible to all [*omnibus visibilem faciens*], as the Word *has shown the Father and Son to all* [*ostendebat Patrem et Filium*], since he has been seen by all [*ab omnibus videretur*]."[66]

It could not be expressed any more clearly. Insisting rightly on the *visibility* of the Father in the Son, Irenaeus requires a sort of "revenge of the image over the icon" since the *visibility* and *carnal manifestation of God* are nothing other than the center and heart of the Christian message: "The motif of the incarnation is therefore in the *visibility* of the Son," even of the Father himself.[67] Far from being uniquely theological, the opening appears here at the same time philosophical. Is it sufficient to speak of an *aesthetic of invisibility* (Malevich, Kandinsky, Rothko) as far as the meaning of the Incarnation in Christianity is concerned, given that the *figuration* or even the "figural" returns in force at the heart of the most contemporary artistic research (Bacon, Lucian Freud, etc.)? The question certainly exceeds the scope of this little study on Irenaeus but it cannot nevertheless be avoided given that from *theology* to *aesthetics* there plays a relation for which a "theological aesthetics" (in distinction, of course, from "aesthetic theology") is able to teach us about philosophy as much as theology.[68]

The Revenge of the Image

We will not linger here on the purely contemporary perspectives which evoke a possible or even necessary "revenge of the image" over the icon. Some critics of contemporary art have attempted this, and justify the enterprise in this way: "With the new positioning of the artist proclaimed *image-maker*," as Wim Delvoye says, "it is perhaps *the revenge of the image over the icon* which is happening . . . By opting for the icon, modernity took advantage of a disincarnation of art . . . The reintroduction of figurative painting over the last few years, faithful to an avant-garde conception of art . . . restores the place of the image in the modern perspective . . . Here the human figure takes up a dominant position which is often manifest across the entire frame or by way of a close up of the body."[69] Against some "abstractive" derivatives of theology (separating man from God and keeping him in his unfathomable invisibility) and also of aesthetics (abstract art), Irenaeus serves as a counterpoint in order *theologically* to reveal the "figural" in the apparition of the incarnate Word and *aesthetically* to render visible, like Francis Bacon for example, flesh in motion: "It took the extraordinary work of abstract painting to tear modern art away from figuration." So said Gilles Deleuze. He continues: "But is there not another way, one that is more direct and more sensible . . . ? If painting is fond of the Figure, if it takes the second way, it will be in order to oppose the 'figural' to the figurative."[70]

The Figural

What then is the meaning of the "image" in Irenaeus (*imago*) and also of the flesh as "image of the Incarnate Word"? If the vocabulary of the "image" (*imago*) and "likeness" (*similitudo*) is not yet fixed in Irenaeus,[71] the reality that they designate is no less clear: the image takes the side of the *visibility of God* and therefore of the "flesh of Adam" as the prefiguration of the visibility of the incarnate Son (*sarx*); and the likeness, less commonly used in Irenaeus, leads to the *perfecting of the soul* (*psuchê*), which, receiving the Spirit of God (*pneuma*), freely passes, through a decision, to its own glorification, attracting to this end at the same time its own body to which it always remains attached.[72]

The Image and the Figure. In order to show precisely how the "revenge of the image" properly characterizes the Irenaean doctrine of the *imago Dei* relative to the later theologies that take refuge in invisibility, the *Adversus Haereses* yields a philosophical definition of the image, of which it properly belongs to the incarnate Word to initiate or rather to form a model for it: "The figure [*typus*] and the image [*imago*] are sometimes different from the reality by virtue of their material [*secundum materiam*]; but they ought to guard its likeness [*similitudinem*] by the form [*secundum habitum*], revealing by means of what is present [*per praesentia illa*] that which is not present [*quae non sunt praesentia*]."[73] What "makes the image" in the image, according to Irenaeus, is therefore less the *matter* as such (*secundum materiam*) (an image or statue of the emperor is commissioned precisely in order to reveal him who is absent) than it is the *manner* in which the one who is presented there is rendered present yet nevertheless remains absent (*secundum habitudinem*). The image in this sense does not represent [*figure*] the absent only in a negative way, as is normally believed in an ontological depreciation of the image by relation to the original [*modèle*], but it renders it on the contrary otherwise and positively *present*, according to its manner of being (*habitus*) rather than according to matter (*materia*). I even see the "same emperor" when I see the statue of the emperor and when I encounter him "in flesh and bone"—similarly it is the "same sheet of paper" as in the famous example of Sartre, that I "represent" to myself in my head and that which is set before me when I write. Both the emperor and the sheet of paper appear to me in two different modalities: either according to "matter" or according to "manner."[74] The philosophical perspective, which does not depreciate the image at all but rather lays bare its phenomenological character as a possible *mode of presence* in absence, precisely establishes the character of the image of the Son in his relation to the Father, on the one hand, and his relation to Adam, on the other.

The Image of the Father. Let us first look at the relation of the Son to the Father. Irenaeus is wholly faithful to the hymn from Colossians (1:15): "The image of God [*imago Dei*] is the Son [*Filius est*], in whose image man was made."[75] It is certainly to Irenaeus's merit to have seen that the imaging structure holds not only in the relation of God to man. It is first rooted in the Trinity itself in which it gains meaning. The Son is "image of the Father" insofar as he *reveals the Father*, certainly, but also in that this act of revealing *also reveals himself*. This "self manifestation" (*phainesthai*) characterizes the knowledge of the Father as such, *arch-phenomenon* of all phenomena: "The Son reveals the knowledge of the Father by his own manifestation [*per suam manifestationem*]: this manifestation of the Son is *the knowledge of the Father* [*agnitio enim Patris est Filii manifestatio*]."[76] This "self-showing" that is for Irenaeus prohibited to the Father held in invisibility is not negative in the sense that he is not able to do it, but positive in the sense that he chooses to use his Son as a sort of "prism" and "emissary" in order to *make himself seen*, just as a "good" son reveals and manifests his father as he resembles him trait for trait: "In the same way as a king who has himself traced the portrait of his son [*imaginem filii*] rightly says that this portrait is his own [*sui*] for this twofold reason that it is his son and he made it himself, thus it goes with the name of Jesus Christ."[77] This Son who so fully reveals the Father, what more does he bring forth? *Himself*: "He brings forth everything new [*omnem novitatem*] in bringing forth his own person [*semetipsum*] announced in advance." Understood always with his Father, the Son is not content to remain in the refuge of the kingdom of invisibility in order to manifest the one he resembles trait for trait—his Father. He is also himself as this King who, once he has "arrived in the court of his subjects," makes it so that the "judicious Gentiles no longer pose the question concerning what the King has brought forth anew [*quid novi*] by relation to those who announced his coming, for he has brought forth his own person [*semetipsum*]."[78] Such is the meaning of the *incarnation of the Word* considered dynamically in his original relation to the *creation of Adam*, where the image (*imago*) is no longer simply spatial resemblance (the "portrait") but a temporal dynamic (the "figure").

The Model of Adam. In the relation of the Son to Adam, the Word who was the image (of the Father) somehow becomes the model of the one who now becomes the image (Adam). Let us make no mistake, however. The theme of *expression* from the Father to the Son and of the Son to the figure of Adam in no way resembles the degrading movement of the copy to model as one finds famously in book 10 of Plato's *Republic.*[79] Expression is not *decline*, but rather an act of *visibilization*, even of *manifestation*. No ontological loss is produced from model to its image—on the contrary. It is precisely because and thanks to its expression in and by an image (*imago*) that the model enjoys the precedence of serving as model. As I have already noted above, Irenaeus states: "His hand has created your substance; it will cover you with pure gold within and without, and it will adorn you so well that the King himself will be struck by your beauty [*concupiscat speciem tuam*]."[80] Far indeed from any Neoplatonic derivation, here the visible overtakes the invisible, as the tangible overtakes the intangible, without falling into some kind of empiricism which would grossly substitute the physical reality of the thing itself for the phenomenological expressionism of its manifestation. The Son, *model of Adam* who is his own *model*, sees in the rough *sketch* of the first man drawn from the earth the first traits of the *work* that will render him fully visible by manifestation in his own flesh. There is an ambiguity to the notion of "modeling" here that should be highlighted. "Paul calls Adam himself the 'figure of the one who is to come' [*typus futuri* (Rom. 5:14)], because the Word, artisan of the universe, *had drafted* in advance of Adam [*praeformaverat in Adama*] the future economy which the Son of God would assume."[81]

*From a Rough Sketch (*Ébauche*) to Depravity (*Débauche*)*

Everyone knows the two famous sculptures of the "creation of Adam" at the north portal of the cathedral of Chartres, however well hidden they are in the arches—even so, they are incapable of hiding the absolute novelty that Chartrean humanism was in the process of rediscovering: on the one hand, there is Adam lying down with his head on the knees of the Word in order to be shaped by him; on the other hand, there is the same Adam standing up behind the figure of Christ as his most proper prefiguration. What we see here—standing many centuries apart from Irenaeus—shows precisely what must be thought through in his work, though of course a filiation of Chartrean humanism from Irenaean Greek patrology would not be able to be established.[82]

The Rough Sketch of the Word. Adam as a sketch of the Word made flesh is hardly a rough draft, but rather its "pre-formation" (*praeformaverit*).

Coming *before*, he paradoxically also came *after*, since it is only later or after the fact—that is, in the incarnation of the Word—that the one who came first (Adam) appears as the one formed later (as a simple sketch), and that the one who came later (Christ) is revealed as the one who was presented first (the model). Adam, as "prototype" of humanity or "figure of the one who was coming" (*typus futuri*), will never be the "antitype" as he will later be in Saint Augustine, who focuses on the other part of this same verse from Saint Paul's Epistle to the Romans: "Death reigned from Adam to Moses, even over those who did not sin by a *transgression* identical to that of Adam" (Rom. 5:14).[83] By a temporal reversal of the image, in which Irenaean anthropology has nothing of the static character of a number of later theologies, the "figure" (*figura*) announcing what has already been accomplished makes the *first Adam* the "reason for being" of the *second* in his project of salvation (Christ), less in order to exist than in order to be fully manifest: "Since the One who would save [*saluans*] already existed, it was necessary that the one who would be saved [*salvaretur*] came also into existence so that this Savior was hardly without a reason for being [*non vacuum sit*]."[84]

Neither a Thomist simple attribution of the motivations for the incarnation starting from redemption, nor a Scotist preeminence of the incarnation by glorification rather than redemption, the "justification" of salvation here envisaged (*non vacuum sit*) is concerned less with *motives* or *reasons* (as if it were necessary to abstract from the incarnation in order to justify it by some "necessary reasons") but rather depends on a simple observation of the fact established by "reason of its fittingness" according to which "God had no need of man [*indigens Deus hominis*]" in forming Adam except "in order to have someone on whom to dispose his benefaction [*ut haberet in quem collocaret sua beneficia*]."[85] In the beginning God formed Adam "with his gifts in view" (*propter suam munificentiam*). He thus consecrated man as "*l'adonné*," as the screen on which is revealed and projected the movement of the donation of the Father.[86] The "flesh" in this sense (*sarx*), this plasma of the earth vivified by the "soul" (*puchê*) and awaiting the "Spirit of God" (*pneuma*), is a place of *weakness* and *infirmity* (*infirmitas*) not only as a result of sin or fault (as in the Augustinian perspective), but also because its *fragility* makes it *vulnerable*, thus submitting to the excess of the donation of the Creator's power: "The flesh [*caro*] will be found capable of receiving and containing the power of God [*virtutis Dei*], since in the beginning it received the art of God . . . ; the power of God, which procures life, is deployed in weakness [*in infirmitate*], that is, in the flesh [*hoc est in carne*]."[87] As for the relation of the *flesh of Adam* to the *flesh of the Word* that comes to complete it, the first is not already lacking in humanity since his composite suffices to constitute it. For Irenaeus, to think of man always "lacking" is to demean him as well as to render indecent the figure of God by defining him only as a collection of benefits destined to satisfy our needs. A "salvation of our flesh" (*salutem carnis nostrae*) is properly speaking necessary, as ought to be well understood by now, not only to make reparation for our faults, but in order to manifest how, in the restricted framework of the visibility of the body, the invisibility of the excess of God can also be given there: "If the flesh should not be saved [*si non haberet caro salvari*], the Word of God would not have been made flesh [*nequaquam Verbum Dei caro factum esset*]."[88]

For Irenaeus of course, the carnal figuration of God remains counted among those things that are the most difficult and even impossible for man: "What is man that you think of him, human being that you care for him?" (Ps. 8:5). Where the "image" (*imago*) designates hitherto the double visibility of the Father in the Son and the Son in man inasmuch as the *rough-hewn form* in Adam only fully appears in the full realization of the *work* that is the incarnation itself, God leads or maintains the "likeness" [*similitude*] there, less in order to distinguish the one from the other, than to leave man the choice of being conformed to the likeness when he does not have the choice to receive the image. Transposing this into the framework of the "revenge of the image," what we discovered in the "ark of flesh," that is, the purely human constitution of man, makes the soul and body (*sôma* and *psuchê*) suffice to constitute the image: "Man is a mixture of soul and flesh, flesh formed according to the likeness of God [*secundum similitudinem Dei*]"—though here the "likeness" (*similitude*) is not distinguished in any way from the "image" (*imago*).[89] Said otherwise, we are already by means of our body the image of God, inasmuch at least that the "God-made body" in the incarnation will reveal that of which we were already the image—a divine body, or at least one called to be divinized.

Things are otherwise from the moment that the Word, "showing the image" (*imaginem ostendit*)—showing the Father as much as the flesh of Adam—"reestablishes the likeness" (*similitudinem restituit*). Therefore something has been *lost* of the likeness [*similitude*], which does not pertain to the image (*imago*), that is, liberty rather than the flesh, the power of "depravity" [*dé-bauche*] rather than the formation of a rough sketch [*é-bauche*]: "When the Word of God is made flesh [*caro Dei factum est*] he will confirm both: he makes the image appear [*imaginem ostendit*] in all of its truth, by himself becoming that which is his own image, and he reestablishes the likeness [*similitudinem restituit*] to stability by rendering man fully like the invisible Father [*invisibili Patri*] by means of the Word henceforth visible [*per visibile Verbum*]."[90]

The Depravity of Adam. Let us say of man that he was "de-bauched" [*dé-bauché*] or better "led astray" [*dé-baucha*], understood etymologically as the one who was not faithful to his "rough sketch" [*e-bauche*] (the carnal figuration of God) for which also he was, as it were, "recruited" [*embauché*] (in order to work to prepare the figure of the One who was to come). The vision here is far removed from the "ethical debauchery" which we see, for example, in Augustine's reading of his "conversion" in book 8 of his *Confessions*.[91] For

Irenaeus, the loss of the "likeness" (*similitude*) does not affect the "image," that is, the "flesh" (*sarx/caro*) and "soul" (*psuchê/anima*) as initial mixture, but only the power of man to receive the "Spirit of God" (*pneuma/spiritu*) in the act of a free choice: "To the contrary when the Spirit [*Spiritus*] lacks the soul [*animae*], such a man, truly remaining psychic [*animalis*] and carnal [*carnalis*], will be imperfect, possessing the image of God [*imaginem Dei*] in the work formed through him [*in plasmate*] though not having received the likeness [*similitudinem*] by means of the Spirit [*per Spiritum*]."[92]

It could hardly be clearer. The image (*imago*) remains ever unchanging in the initial soul-body composite (*anima* and *corpus*). Only the likeness (*similitudo*) can be earned or lost by virtue of its relation to the "Spirit of God" (*Spiritus*) in its insertion or interlacing with the soul of man tied to his proper body. The likeness is therefore only given to a freedom capable of accepting or refusing it, whereas the image simply accounts for an ontological consistency of humanity and serves as the ground for reception of the likeness. Man must first be the image of God in order to receive God (by means of the simple constitution of his natural being), or in other words to receive or refuse the likeness (which is a manner of living this constitution as radically animated [*insufflée*] by God). Thus the "likeness" properly characterizes "man free in his decision [*libera sententia*]," like God, also "free in his decision [*libera sententia*]," which is precisely the "likeness" (*similitudo*) according to which we have been created, since we have been revealed fit to receive it: "From the beginning man is free in his decision [*liberae sententiae ab initio est homo*] because God is also free in his [*et liberae sententiae est Deus*] in whose likeness [*cujus ad similitudinem*] man has precisely been made."[93]

Perfectible Man. Here we may note a striking coherence between the anthropology of Irenaeus and his ethics. Put more strongly, his ethics itself is "anthropological," even "metaphysical" in that it designates not so much a collection of rules which can be either obeyed or transgressed, but rather a manner of being of the one who lives by relation to the Other in general, and here, especially, to God—the one who *faces* me to whom I am in my being fundamentally *indebted*.[94] For Irenaeus it is hardly a sign of imperfection that Adam was not created "perfect from the beginning" (*perfectum ab initio*). In the same way that the possible "perversion" [*dé-bauche*] (not receiving the divine *pneuma*) presupposes a "recruitment" [*em-bauche*] or a work to be accomplished, so also is true perfection found in the "perfectibility" yet to come rather than in the pure and simple possession of that which, by rendering me perfect, forgets the very passage leading to perfection. "That which is offered automatically and that which is found only at great cost are not loved equally [*similiter*]." He continues later: "In the same way that a mother can give perfect nourishment to her newborn, who is yet incapable of receiving nourishment beyond his age [1 Cor. 3:2], thus God could give to man his perfection from the beginning [*ab initio perfectionem homini*], but man was incapable of receiving it [*impotens percipere illam*] because he was only a little infant."[95] Everything is inverted and justifies the work we have to do as the passage from the "ready-made" image to "being made" in the likeness. The model is pedagogical and not metaphysical, pertaining to the economy of salvation and not to theodicy: *the most imperfect will paradoxically be perfection itself*, the greatest perfection returning first to be recognized "imperfect," the Adamic rough sketch of the glory of God yet to be completed in the flesh.

It is death that truly puts an end to our perfectibility, that is, to our capacity to *become* better when we are far from yet *being* the best. Is this something to be distressed about for Irenaeus? Far from it. The benevolence of God is such that he will arrest by death the insupportable weight (at least for us) of not having attained perfection. If life in the Spirit (*pneuma*) is an *expansion*, the resurrection of the soul, carrying with it the flesh (*sarx* and *psuchê*), is *salvation*, in that it transforms or metamorphosizes all at once what we could have never reached by our own strength.

Mortality and Salvation

Following Saint Augustine, Catholic doctrine has often been thought to teach that biological death was a "consequence of sin"—an argument that some of the most recent research has shown to require nuance.[96] Such is not the view of Irenaeus, standing as he is at the beginning of Christianity, for whom death does not signify the lone end of life, but rather "a manner of being appropriate to the living" when the living experiences the loss of the breath of life by which he has received existence: "To die is to lose the manner of living proper to the living [*vitalem amittere habilitatem*], to become without breath, without life, without movement, and to dissolve into the elements of which one has received the principle."[97] One must be careful here in understanding this. Irenaeus does not make of death a "mode of life" as in Heidegger by his distinction between anguish of death and the fear of death.[98] Yet it is true that death designates the putrefaction of the body for Irenaeus, which is itself envisaged as a manner of living, not in anguish as in Heidegger (which would only be a result of the human composite cut off from God), but in the act of welcoming, even awaiting, that which arrives (from the time that God liberates, by means of this very destruction, a soul attached to itself and thereby not completely filled with the divine *pneuma*).

Death through Mercy. Far from being a punishment (Augustine), for Irenaeus death paradoxically marks an excellence—that by which "God, mercifully [*miserans*] puts an end to the transgression, interposing death and thereby causing sin to cease."[99] The perspective here is retrospectively original and merits being recalled today. Like many of our contemporaries, the totality of the Irenaean corpus at the beginning of Christianity witnesses to a view according to which to be born is to be ordered toward death. Far from being a response to the prohibition of a life misled by the fault, the "dissolution of the flesh" on the contrary saves from being further misled into sin. This is certainly a radical idea, particularly when seen from our vantage at the far end of a tradition many centuries old. Death as a result unfolding from sin, as its consequence and most appropriate punishment (Augustine), is given as if it were before the deed as salvation from what is otherwise a perpetual accusation (Irenaeus): "In order that man not remain always a transgressor . . . God assigned to him a limit by means of the dissolution of his flesh [*carnis resolutionem*] which would be done on the earth."[100] In short, the victory of the Resurrection over our mortal being does not ensure the protection or even a return to some kind of immortality from which we fell in sin. For Irenaeus, death is already the place of salvation, putting a physical end to our possibility of sinning, rather than designating the consequence of a sin already realized.

We can therefore ask: Why the Resurrection if the paradoxical salvation by death frees us already from the achievement of what is impossible for us? The answer: in order to achieve, precisely, the salvation *of the flesh by the flesh*, for nothing of the human remains in God if it is not "recapitulated" in Christ: "If God did not vivify [*si Deus non vivificat*] that which is mortal and if he did not elevate to incorruptibility that which is corruptible, God would cease being powerful [*jam non potens Deus*]."[101] The power of God in his Spirit justifies the very act of elevating Adam in the heart of his flesh, making of his *metamorphosis* or *transformation* the admission of his powerlessness to accomplish it by himself: "The *transfiguration* [*transfiguratio*] by which our mortal and corruptible flesh becomes immortal and incorruptible *does not come from out of his substance itself*; this transfiguration comes from the action of the Lord who has the power of procuring immortality for that which is mortal and incorruptibility for that which is corruptible."[102]

The Lectio Difficilior. In order to complete the carnal logic of the carnal salvation of Adam in the incarnate and resurrected Word, Irenaeus's thought continues with the idea that it was "otherwise more difficult" to create Adam "when nothing existed [*ex non exsistentibus*]" than to "reconstitute him afterward [*deinde*]," once he has already come into existence.[103] The act of creation is paradoxically more complicated than new creation or resurrection in that in the act of creation "everything" is made from "nothing" whereas the second transforms "something" (us in our terrestrial combination) from someone (the Son resurrected by the Father in the power of the Holy Spirit). The *lectio difficilior* for us today was the *lectio facilior* of yesterday (the meaning of resurrection), and the *lectio difficilior* of yesterday is the *lectio facilior* today (the awareness of the world as created). Perhaps philosophy, like theology, separating the extremes too much, has lost the sense of the unity and carnal integrity of salvation made visible in the flesh of the Resurrected.

Hence in a magisterial and almost carnal way, the bishop of Lyon writes: "In the *flesh* of our Lord [*in carnem Domini nostri*] the light of the Father has burst in [*occurat paterna lux*]; then, in shining *from his flesh* [*et a carne eius rutila*], this light came into us [*veniat in nos*]. In this way man has passed on to incorruptibility [*et sic homo deveniat in incorruptelam*], enveloped by the light of the Father [*circumdatus paterno lumine*]."[104]

A Near God. Moving from the creation in the flesh to the resurrection of the flesh by way of the node of carnal incarnation, Christianity definitively parts from some mere far off God, so effaced in his invisibility to be accused of remaining indifferent to our humanity, and conceives of him as one who is *as close to us as* our everyday nature: "He is also with each one of us [*cum unoquoque nostrum*]: 'Am I not also a God nearby [*appropinquans ego sum*], declares the LORD, and not a God far off [*et non Deus de longinquo*]? Who can hide in secret so that I cannot see them?' " (Jer. 23:23).[105] We therefore have nothing to envy of the angels—and surely it is to the merit of Irenaeus and Tertullian after him (chap. 6) that they teach this valuable insight. The true good of man is not found in becoming incorporeal, but rather in being and forever remaining "con-corporeal" with the Son who is "made" flesh (incarnation) all the way to its resplendence (and ours in his) in the light of the Father (resurrection). And so Irenaeus concludes the *Adversus Haereses* with these words: "The angels aspire to contemplate these mysteries, but they are not able to fathom the Wisdom of God, by the action of which the work modeled by him is rendered *conformed* and *con-corporeal* to the Son [*conformatum et concorporatum Filio*] . . . the creature thus surpasses the angels and develops into the image and likeness of God."[106]

✦

The Sign of Jonah and the Sign of Emmanuel. The *sign of Jonah*—where "God permitted him to be swallowed by a sea monster" (Jonah 2:1)—reaches its deepest meaning in and through the *sign of Emmanuel*—where "God is with us" (Is. 7:14) and descends into the depths of the earth in order to find his lost sheep. By means of the first sign we are drawn out of "sin," as Jonah provokes a strong repentance in the Ninevites (Jonah 3:1). By means of the second sign the Lord "effects in himself the resurrection from the dead" (1 Cor. 15:20) where his flesh joins ours to form a single body. With the incarnate and resurrected Word, "something greater than Jonah is here" (Matt. 12:41) not only because he overflows and even surpasses the necessity of the sign by his presence, but because salvation in his flesh, certainly leading to repentance (salvation by redemption), also reveals his brilliance (salvation by glorification).[107] If in the Augustinian tradition man sins by a "malice" without concomitant powerlessness or ignorance but by the simple pleasure of sin (as in the theft of the pears),[108] in the Irenaean tradition Adam falls or stumbles "by accident" in a pedagogical—as opposed to juridical—model of the Father: "He had pity on man who had welcomed disobedience by accident [*neglegenter*] and not by malice [*male*]."[109] Without opposing the two traditions too much, I would suggest that we ought to learn from Irenaeus and the entire Greek tradition not to hang it all on a single sin as the locus and cause of human salvation. At the dawn of the *tempora christiana* such was not in fact the case. Such is proof that Christianity says more than that. Yet the Latin tradition can teach us *something else* no less urgent for our context today, namely, the act by which man is always taken up there where he is (humanization of God), rather than called to become what he is not yet (divinization of man). Thus says Augustine, relating his mother Monica's guidance: "It was not told to me that 'where *he is*, there shall you be' [*ubi ille, ibi et tu*], but 'where *you are*, there will he be also' [*sed: ubi tu, ibi et ille*]."[110] This movement of the "anthropomorphism of God" is every bit as profound as the "theomorphosis of man"—as we will now see in Tertullian, who shows in the *solidity* [*consistance*] of the flesh what Irenaeus first showed in its *visibility*.

Chapter 5

✦

The Solidity of the Flesh (Tertullian)

Passing from Irenaeus to Tertullian, we see a striking continuity. Their contexts are certainly different (the Greek and Latin worlds), but their ambitions remain the same: to show that Christianity is essentially carnal, all the way from its starting point, in the "Word made flesh" of the incarnation, to its end, in the "flesh become Word" of the Resurrection. Even so, the emphasis is displaced in the passing. If Irenaeus strives to disclose in Adam the *visibility* of the flesh of humanity, Tertullian attempts to feel the weight of the flesh of the incarnate Word in all its *solidity* and makes of his weight the defense against all our attempts to angelize the Incarnation. If Irenaeus's is a theomorphosis of man, in Tertullian we pass to an anthropomorphis of God: "We have also published a volume on the Flesh of Christ, where we establish his *solidity* [*solidam*] against any view of the unreality of his appearance."[1] This commitment to the "solidity or density of the flesh" brings Tertullian so close to us in our understanding of our own flesh and indeed our very humanity "*tout court*." In passing from the Smyrna of Irenaeus to the Carthage of Tertullian, theology is burdened with a humanity become suffering and onerous and makes the struggle against Docetism not only the occasion of the manifestation of God in the flesh of man (Adam) but even more the locus of the involvement of man in the flesh of God (Christ): "Tertullian, more a philosopher in his approach, seeks to understand with the help of the Scriptures what man is in his *definitive constitution* or his *essential nature*. In Irenaeus, by contrast, the creation is accomplished only from the vantage of salvation. The Creator never ceases perfecting man promised incorruptibility."[2]

From here we can offer the necessary revision of the Greek adage from a Latin perspective. The "glory of God is a living man" indeed, inasmuch (as Irenaeus taught us) as the formation of Adam as soul and body welcomes the Holy Spirit into himself and thereby manifests the divine glory. But, let us say that (as Tertullian will teach us) "the life of man is the vision *of* God" not only means that to be man refers to the act of turning one's gaze toward God (objective genitive), but because to be God in view of man, in the mystery of the incarnation, is a divine act done completely in order to espouse our flesh in its grandeur as much as its misery (subjective genitive). The *translucent* quality of the flesh of Adam in Irenaeus gives way to the *density* of the flesh of the incarnate Word in Tertullian. These two hold different perspectives but share the same vision. The "mixture and union" (*commixtio* and *adunitio*) of the soul and body interlaced with the Holy Spirit in Irenaeus is what announces the flesh as "sister of Christ" (*caro Christi sororem*) in Tertullian. But the very same flesh, so glorified in Irenaeus that it sanctifies Adam by way of the "perfect man" (*perfectus homo*), becomes in Tertullian the place of a hyper-proximity and linking of Christ to our pure and simple humanity: because "he who is so close to it [*sibi proximam*] in so many ways loves the flesh [*diliget carnem*]."[3] The glorification of Adam in one thinker cedes to the humility of God in the next. Both are concerned with the same earth (*humus*), but one that, if already fertile in Irenaeus, is yet to be worked in Tertullian. From Smyrna to Carthage the task of making resplendent becomes laborious. Here is a Christianity chronologically farther from its source, but which nevertheless loses nothing ontologically by being developed in this way. After the manifestation of God in his theophany (part I) comes its progressive immersion in the flesh (part II). Here will come to birth a new mode of relation to the other, by means of which each one will be singularized and will respond to the call that is its own (part III).

From the Reduction of the Flesh to the Reduction to the Flesh

On the path of such an immersion in the flesh, Tertullian's *De carne Christi* is required reading. Far from any discussion about the soul of Christ, which will of course greatly occupy the medievals later (for example, the *quaestio disputata De anima* of Aquinas or the *quaestiones disputatae De scientia Christi* of Bonaventure), here the debate is centered on the body. Tertullian departs from Irenaeus inasmuch as everything unfolds as if the question of the *animation* of Christ was already settled, though like Irenaeus, the Holy Spirit (*pneuma*) is intertwined with mixture of soul and body. In other words, the animation of the body no longer poses the problem. The principal agreement in early Christianity that Christ is spiritual and in this close to the angels demands that his uniqueness be found elsewhere, namely, in his corporeity, even his quasi-organic "solidity." "Everyone," at least, that is, Tertullian and the Gnostics, seem to agree on one point: Christ possesses a soul, which is understood simply as a "spiritual reality" that constitutes his primary being. But "certain people"—that is, one of them, namely, Tertullian—contest the view that Christ's spirituality constitutes the meaning of Christ's revelation. Even Irenaeus's conception of the *visibility of the flesh* in Adam could still draw Christian discourse toward a certain Docetism or angelism—even though there is certainly no greater destroyer of the Gnostics than the author of the *Adversus Haereses*, which was, indeed, otherwise entitled: "Denunciation and Refutation of Gnostics as Liars." The *solidity of the flesh*, on the contrary, is in Tertullian, such that the very question of the psychic is "bracketed" in a kind of *epochê* of the spiritual that has the effect of focusing the debate on the physical or incarnate dimension. Here it is a question "*only* of his flesh." "We are examining the corporeal substance of the Lord [*corporalem substantiam domini*]": thus Tertullian describes the program of his *De carne Christi*. He continues, "Everyone agrees about the spiritual substance [*de spiritali*]. It is only a question of his flesh [*caro quaeritur*]. We will discuss its reality [*veritas*] and its quality [*qualitas*], whether it preexisted [*an fuerit*], its origin [*unde*] and its kind [*cuiusmodi*]."[4]

But there is more in the theologian from Carthage—and it is this that makes his inquiry both theological and phenomenological. Tertullian in fact does not remain satisfied with the sole reality (*veritas*) of the flesh of Christ. Once the reality is admitted, it is necessary to extract the quality (*qualitas*). In order to say it in other terms—and embarking here on a methodological rapprochement with phenomenology—Tertullian sees not only the "*quid real*" of Christ's flesh but its "*quomodo* or how character" (Heidegger), in the same way that the determination of meaning first orients the "object in its how" (*das Objekt im Wie*), that is, in the "how of its modes of givenness" (Husserl).[5] It seems that it is not too much to say that the rhetorical structure of existence (*an*), origin (*unde*), and mode (*cuiusmodi*) had already become classical in the epoch of Tertullian (traces of it can be found in Quintillian along with the numerous occurrences in Tertullian himself).[6] Yet this rhetorical structure will not be allowed to remain phenomenologically surrogate to a meaning whose operation of the "reduction" itself already gives sufficient witness to the impossibility of a substantializing reification of the flesh of Christ: not only to pose the existence of the "bodily substance of the Lord" (*an*), but even more to describe the genesis of its donation (*unde*) and the modes of its givenness (*cuiusmodi*). Such a progression of meaning in reality appears all the more decisive as it structures the *De carne Christi* and at the same time designates each of its Gnostic adversaries as steps toward the discovery of a reduced meaning of the incarnation of Christ (beyond mere reification, but not less, to its appearance in a phenomenological sense): "Those who attempt to undermine faith in the resurrection . . . divide into pieces the flesh of Christ and either desire that it does not exist [*aut nullam omnino*] or that it exists in a totally non-human mode [*aut quoquo modo aliam praeter humanam*]."[7]

From the question of the existence of the flesh (whether it exists or not) to its modality of appearing (whether a human or non-human mode) and passing through, as we will see, its genesis (whether from the earth or the stars), the path that the *De carne Christi* takes seems to be phenomenological, leading indeed from the *reduction of the flesh* (the existence of which is suspended only once accepted) to a *reduction to the flesh* (the donation of the flesh in its mode of appearing). That the *De resurrectione carnis* (circa 211) closely follows upon the *De carne Christi* (between 208 and 211) indicated well the steps of such an anabasis, and consecrates each of his Gnostic adversaries partners in the service of his thought: "The heretics have stumbled over his flesh, pretending either that it had no reality [*nullius veritas*], as in Marcion or Basilides, or that it had a proper quality [*proprie qualitatis*], as in the heirs of Valentinus and according to Apelles."[8] From reality to its own quality—these are the logical steps that authorize the renewal of the meaning from *quid* to *quomodo*, from the reified existing thing to its modes of donation in a specific appearance. Against such a regressive interpretation of being to the appearance of the flesh of Christ, a naive and often patent realism in theology sometimes wants to give a pretended primacy to the thing ("the material substance Christ incarnate") over the pure and simple appearance of his being in a flesh (*in-carne*)—as if by means of this contrast to prove that there was something there "in flesh and bone" (given a non-phenomenological interpretation this time!) called the Christ who had to prove his messianicity.[9] If it is true that Tertullian, against Marcion and Basilides, allows the existence of a something there (*quid*), necessarily in "flesh and bone" of the person of Christ, Tertullian nevertheless does not remain with this bare real and existing thing (*das Ding*), but he leads it back, now with Valentinus and Apelles as interlocutors, to the sense of its "appearance for us" or the "thing itself" (*die Sache selbst*). There is nothing to prohibit a reading something like a suspended existence or reduction of the flesh of Christ in Tertullian—once it is "naturally" established as such (a gesture which surely separates him from phenomenology)—in order then to think something like its genesis and modes of appearing in its donation to itself and to our own flesh.

In the justly polemical attempt of the "declension of the flesh," moving from the simple manifestation of its pure appearance (Valentinus) to the necessary position of its nonexistence or fabrication (Marcion), it will be fitting to let an "analytic of the incarnation" unfold, which, through a phenomenological recovery, will indicate how the mineness of my flesh (contra Marcion) also requires that a necessary description of the flesh [*chair*] be achieved in order for the body [*corps*] to be born in a non-identical way (contra Apelles), which also appears in the economy of salvation (contra the disciples of Valentinus) and dies in the assumption of human finitude (contra Valentinus himself). In this way alone the flesh of Christ is displayed for him as for us (and for us by him), as his "most proper" property (*proprietas generalis*) and the most connatural to ours.[10] The central question of the *De carne Christi*, as it reflects on the modality of the flesh of Christ insofar as it informs the modality of our own flesh, is forcefully articulated in the following unique formulation: "What sort of flesh [*carnis qualitatem*] can we and ought we recognize in the Christ [*debemus et possumus agnoscere in Christo*]?"[11]

The Attempt at a Declension of the Flesh

In light of such a typology fixed by his adversaries, Tertullian establishes that no human flesh received from man (*ex homine sumptae*) could be made, "either of spirit" (*non spiritalis*) "or of soul" (*nec animalis*), "or of astral matter" (*nec siderae*), "or as an illusion" (*nec imaginariae*).[12] Therefore, spiritual or pneumatic flesh (Valentinus), soul-flesh or flesh-soul (Occidental disciples of Valentinus), astral flesh (Apelles), and spectral or illusory flesh (Marcion) are the forces that make it necessary to compose a declension of its diverse modalities in order better to liberate, *a contrario*, the originality of Tertullian's own determination of the flesh. In the present enumeration Tertullian implicitly inverts the scheme of declension (Valentinus [spirit], Valentinians [soul], Apelles [astral matter], Marcion [mirage]) from the preceding order prescribed by the questions posed (Marcion [*quid*], Apelles [*unde*], Valentinus and the Valentinians [*quomodo*]) in order to unfold a hierarchy of Gnostic heresies. This hierarchy commences with the most complex (Valentinus), which gives free reign to a true appearance of the flesh, be it merely spiritual or pneumatic, and descends little by little to the most simple or least composite (Marcion), which purely and simply negates every appearance of the flesh, or at least designates it as illusory. In order therefore to carve a clear path into this *lectio difficilior* of the *De carne Christi*, it is best to follow its author stride for stride and (analytically) descend with him from the *quomodo* of the carnal appearance in its modality (Valentinus) to the *unde* of its origin (Apelles) and the *quid* of its existence (Marcion). At a second step, moving to the heart of a reading that will be all the "easier" as it follows the logical order of the reduction, (synthetically) climbing up the path from the existing thing (*quid*) to its modality (*quomodo*) in order to achieve, phenomenologically, the specificity of a flesh (of Christ), which is all the more human as it is confessed a priori to be real and necessarily marked in advance by the seal of life and death.

The Flesh in Its Modes of Appearance (Valentinus)

Spiritual or Pneumatic Flesh. As I have already emphasized, Valentinus, far from negating any carnal existence in Christ, on the contrary attributes to his corporeality a supreme dignity: his kind of flesh exists in "another mode than the human" (*quoquo modo aliam praeter humanam*) or has a "unique quality" (*proprie qualitatis*) and is consecrated thus both in its superiority and its specificity. Unfolding from here is the famous Valentinian distinction of the three degrees of carnal appearance inherited from a certain reading of Saint Paul's discourse on the resurrected body (1 Cor. 15:42–48), of which the tripartition of carnal man divides all men into so many classes, according to the levels of the divine pleroma: first, the "material or hylic" flesh (of the pagans); second, the "animal or psychic" flesh (of Jews or the general faithful of the Great Church); third, the "spiritual or pneumatic" flesh (of the initiates to the perfect gnosis, and by essence the sole immortality).[13] Tertullian comments, not without irony: because "he wants to be made a flesh of a quality not that of the human womb [*quae non erat uoluae*], Christ thus assumed a spiritual flesh [*caro spiritalis*]."[14] As we will see below, this "particular flesh" has no other end than that of escape from ordinary flesh, the flesh of the entire world, and, as Péguy says in his *Dialogue de l'histoire et de l'âme charnelle*, from the "death of all the world, the common death, the death of all men . . . that death of your father, my child, that which your mother will also suffer one day, and your wife, your children, the children of your children, your very self at the center."[15] The Son will thus only be born of the Virgin as he receives his flesh, exceptionally, not "from" the human womb (*non ex uolua*), but "in" the womb (*in uolua*), in the same way that God, for example, only breathed a soul into a flesh—which alone comes from man.[16] In being born the flesh of Christ remains outside of the conditions of birth for ordinary humans—inasmuch as the flesh only always draws forth a flesh of the same nature.

I therefore repeat the question: "What kind of flesh [*carnis qualitatem*] can we and ought we to recognize in Christ [*debemus et possumus agnoscere in Christo*]?"[17] Does it suffice to attribute to him a "particular quality" (*proprie qualitatis*) in order to render to his humanity, and ours through his, the dignity which properly pertains to it? It is such a question which, posed to the lived experience of Christ, will inform in return the specificities of our own birth and death in the flesh. Without negating angelism, but rather bearing it to full term, the Western Valentinians will emphasize so strongly the unity of the soul-flesh that it will become, at least for them, difficult if not impossible to distinguish the qualities that pertain to the soul, on the one hand, and the flesh on the other.

Soul-Flesh or Flesh-Soul (Western Valentinians). According to the "disciples of Valentinus," Christ has so thoroughly wed himself to our human condition that his flesh itself would become soul or "soul-flesh" (*animam carnem*) and his soul would become "flesh-soul" (*carnem animam*):[18] "The flesh of Christ is composed of soul because the soul became flesh [*quod anima caro sit facta*]. Consequently the flesh itself is soul [*caro anima*], and just as the flesh is made of soul [*caro animalis*], the soul is equally made of flesh [*anima carnalis*]."[19] A mode of manifestation of the soul by and in the flesh thus presides over the indissoluble unity of the soul-flesh at every possible point. Hence the Valentinians state: "In Christ the soul became body [*corpus in Christo*] so that it is possible for us to see [*quod sit uideremus*] it being born, die and, even more, resurrect."[20] Such a model, eminently phenomenological in its description since it comes under the horizon of the manifestation of the soul-flesh more than its existence, thus seems to bring to completion the hypothesis of a real interaction of the soul and flesh, such that their epiphanic community dominates over their simple ontic reality: "Because God desired to render the soul visible to men [*animam visibilem hominibus exhibere*] his soul became body [*faciendo eam corpus*]."[21] The visibility of Christ in his body witnesses then, not to the real or ontic existence of an incarnate body, but first to a mode of being of his soul rendered visible in order to be shown (*exhibere*) to men in the occurrence—that is, in being incarnate or in "adopting" a flesh. Setting aside for the moment any danger of anachronism, we would probably find realized, in the disciples of Valentinus and retrieved in Tertullian, at least in part, Merleau-Ponty's requisite of a "[thought of the] flesh [not] starting from substances, from body and spirit—for then it would be the union of contradictories—but we must think of it . . . as an element, as a concrete emblem of a general manner of being."[22] Because the soul, according to the Western Valentinians, has no other end but to be manifest by a body, and the body, likewise, to show forth the soul, the manner of being of the body manifests in reality the manner of its soul more than the nature of their respective substances. Even more, the use of the term "body" (*corpus*) by the Valentinian disciples, as in "the soul became body in Christ [*corpus in Christo*]," instead of the "flesh" (*caro*), in order to indicate the visibility of the invisible, could put us on the path toward finding a possible distinction between "flesh" and "body" in the Valentinian corpus. Yet, as we will see below, the non-employment of the flesh (*caro*), like Tertullian, only gives more clear appearance to its concept of the body (*corpus*), all the more melted into the soul (*anima*) as it hides a profound dualism under the cover of an apparent monism. If "soul-flesh" first refers, for the Valentinians, to the "soul-body," this is probably because the Greek dualism of *psuchê* and *sôma* is never inserted so well into theological language as when it negates the specific novelty of the biblical *sarx*—or *bâsâr* in Hebrew—as the primordial unity of human beings.

Uniting the soul and body in a theophanic model of appearance or manifestation thus leads to the recognition that these elements were, for a time at least, unduly separated. But a question nevertheless remains, one that Tertullian will never stop raising: What does the union of soul and flesh ("soul-flesh") mean for the "manifestation of the soul *by* the flesh" (*ostensa sit anima per carnem*)? Said otherwise, if man, taken as a whole, belongs to "life" (*vita*), is this a sufficient reason to reduce him to his soul, or to his flesh, or to their confusion without distinction (as "soul-flesh")? As *De carne Christi* emphasizes, the soul is "naturally endowed with senses" (*sensualis est animae natura*), in that it is expressed in and through the kinesthesis of the body, without, however, fully being identified with it.[23] As we will see below, such will be the phenomenological meaning of a "manifestation (without confusion or separation) of the flesh" attested by the theologian from Carthage in his confrontation with the Valentinians of the Occident. But first, let us stick to the program of an enumeration of the adversaries of Tertullian, now that the modes of appearance of the flesh (*cuiusmodi*) developed by Valentinus (spiritual soul) and his disciples (soul-flesh) have been manifest, and continue to move downstream—with the phenomenological interrogation always on the horizon—toward the *unde* of the carnal origin of Christ (Apelles) and the *quid* of his existence (Marcion).

The Flesh in Its Origin (Apelles)

Sidereal Flesh. Neither Valentinus nor his disciples have properly speaking crossed out the act of "birth" from Christ's flesh. If his flesh is in fact born of a woman, nothing prohibits him from appearing for us according to a particular mode of appearing which destroys nothing of his spiritual nature or divine filiation. If Apelles no longer objects to the reality of the flesh of Christ, he still definitively removes the "birth": "The flesh is admitted [*admissa carne*]," says Apelles, "but not its birth [*natiuitatem negare*]."[24] The flesh of Christ is not born of flesh, for Apelles, but "it takes its flesh from the stars and superior substances of the world" (*de sideribus et substantiis superioris*).[25] To look for such a genesis of the flesh of Christ—in its origin and formation—is to draw it out from among the other bodies and superior substances from whence it derives. That the flesh (*caro*) is considered born from a body (*corpus*) or from superior substances (*substantiae superiores*) requires a distinction (as we will see coming from an encounter with the ambient Stoicism of the second century) between what pertains to the "flesh" and what pertains to the "body." The question is announced by Tertullian in a magisterial fashion: "Where does his *body* come from [*unde corpus*] if his body is not *flesh* [*si non caro corpus*]?"[26]

The Body of Flesh. This key question of the *De carne Christi* indicates at the very least that the flesh is not identical to the body. Again, it is fitting at this point to avoid a hasty rapprochement with the well-known phenomenological distinction. Remaining aloof from a greatly anachronistic identification of *caro* and *Leib* or *corpus* and *Körper* (Tertullian-Husserl), some analogies nevertheless remain, as we will see below, since the being in flesh of Tertullian, contra Apelles, is a being capable of specifically human kinestheses (the "eating" of Christ before the tempter, his "drinking" before the Samaritan woman, his "lament" upon hearing of the death of Lazarus, etc.). Being in the flesh will no longer signify the state of "having" or "borrowing" a body. The borrowed body, be it celestial, spiritual or soul-flesh, will be substituted in Tertullian with a true "body of flesh," which, far from being reduced to the body, as we will soon see, on the contrary makes the theophanic appearance of the flesh the very place of the soteriological redemption of the body. The flesh is necessary. Such, according to Tertullian, his staunch adversary, is a view that Marcion radically negates by virtue of an intransigent Docetism.

The Flesh in Its Existence (Marcion)

Spectral Flesh or the Mirage of the Flesh. We have seen that Marcion objects to the reality (*ueritas*) of the flesh itself, thus retroceding the question of its modality (*cuiusmodi*) and origin (*unde*) to that of its pure and simple existence or nonexistence (*an fuerit*).[27] If Christ had in reality no flesh, for

Marcion, he had nevertheless the appearance of the flesh. Further, precisely because he only carried the appearance or likeness (*dokein*) of the flesh he can teach those who are truly in the flesh how to be liberated. It would be fitting to oppose to the crude Marcionite descriptions of the "phantasm" (*phantasma*) of the flesh of Christ, especially "after his resurrection" (*etiam post resurrectionem*) a certain mode of appearance, which, far from refusing to posit any existence to the flesh of Christ, refuses on the contrary only to confine it to this particular existentiality alone.[28] It is still the case that such an appearance of the flesh in Marcion thoroughly denies its reality (*ueritas*)—not only as such, but in such a way that Christ himself was subjected in his own body to it. Tertullian objects that the flesh assumed by Christ was first "his own" (*sua*): "It is not very likely that he portrayed a spirit which was his own [*de spiritu quidem suo*] and a flesh that was not [*de carne uero non sua*]."[29] This flesh that is his—let us hasten to add—is also immediately ours, so that it may be a word that speaks and is addressed to us: "If it is not ours [*non nostram*] that he has liberated . . . nothing in all this concerns us [*nihil ad nos*], since it is not ours that he has liberated."[30] Speaking phenomenologically, the mineness of Christ's flesh (*Jemeinigkeit*)[31] always leads us back to the mineness of our own flesh. Even as I am in fact always alone in living and dwelling in my flesh, the carnal Christ proposes in his resurrection nothing less than an "interlacing" or "intertwining" of flesh (Merleau-Ponty) so that what he says of his own flesh (mineness) is identified with what I say of mine (connaturality). Following Paul Claudel (in this sense the late progeny of Tertullian), we can hold that "spirit alone does not speak to spirit, but flesh which speaks to flesh,"[32] and which leads us first to accept, contra Marcion, that there was a true *quiddity* to the flesh of Christ—which seems to me at least irreducible to his existentiality alone and is first disclosed in his exemplary phenomenality.

From Appearance to Solidity. From the spiritual flesh of Valentinus or the soul-flesh of his disciples in its mode of appearing (*cuiusmodi*), to the sidereal flesh of Apelles in its origin or genesis (*unde*) and the phantom or illusory flesh of Marcion in its very inexistence (*quid*)—thus is *declined* Tertullian's Gnostic typology of the flesh which lacks "solidity" (*solidam*). On the contrary, and in complete connaturality with ours, the exemplary density of the flesh of the Word in theology poses, today even more than yesterday, the philosophical question of the meaning of an *analytic of the incarnation*: (a) the status of an ordinary flesh, which, being born, would no longer die (the spiritual flesh of Valentinus); (b) the mode of manifestation of the soul by the flesh, which, by dint of the expression of one by the other, forgets their distinction (the soul-flesh of the Valentinian disciples); (c) the distinction of flesh and body which prohibits deriving the flesh of Christ from a simple material and corporal substance (the sidereal flesh of Apelles); (d) finally the mineness of my own flesh, and the intertwining of my flesh with the flesh of the other, which alone authorizes a common world of the flesh in contrast to the illusory appearance of a Christ in a flesh even less "carnal" as it comes only to teach me how to depart from my own (the phantom flesh of Marcion). The task now is to climb back up the course of the river in order to rejoin the double movement of reduction *of* the flesh and *to* the flesh of Christ. Here we will see how astonishingly contemporary (via Moltmann) are the theological accents that appear in taking this course: namely, a community of that which is supported in the Son (*in filio*) and in his flesh (*in carne*) and that the Father also suffers, in a Trinitarian way, with him (*cum filio*)—though in a completely different, because not directly carnal, fashion. "The Spirit of God does not suffer in his own name [*suo nomine*], for if suffering was possible in the Son [*si qui passus in filio possibile*], it is necessary for the Father to suffer with the Son [*cum filio*] in the flesh [*in carne*]."[33]

Toward an Analytic of the Incarnation

Christ had no other purpose in becoming incarnate than to assume our ordinary flesh that exists wholly within the horizon of birth and death (contra Valentinus) and of manifesting through it a salvation of the flesh rather than of the soul alone (contra the Valentinians), but let us not forget to give to the flesh a "real solidity" in its appropriation (contra Marcion) and to confer on it its true genesis in its specificity relative to other bodies (contra Apelles).

Oneself as Another (contra Marcion)

Mineness of the Flesh. As we saw above, Marcion denies the existence of Christ's flesh, or at the very least objects to its true existence (*ueritas*) and considers it to be only illusory and phantasmic (*phantasma*). Far from depicting it in a trivial substantialism, the necessary affirmation of the reality of the flesh of Christ, justifies, I suggest, the necessity of making a detour through our own flesh in order to define the flesh of Christ himself. To say "the Word was made flesh" (*et uerbum caro factum est*) is to recognize in the first place that he became that which I am in my most originary and most proper being: a being of flesh. In light of this let us read Tertullian's harsh invective against Marcion: "Marcion, you misunderstand this natural object of veneration [the flesh and the path of childbirth]; yet how were you born [*et quomodo natus est*]? You hate the birth of man; and then how do you love anyone at all [*quomodo diligis aliquem*]? You, in any case, can hardly be said to love yourself [*plane non amasti*] when you withdraw yourself from the Church and faith in Christ."[34] The virulence of the attack aside, Tertullian makes the quasi-phenomenological insistence that Marcion pass by way of the experience of his own birth in order to go even as far as loving himself in his own generation, and then Christ also in this very act. The rejection of birth is equivalent to the hatred of oneself, since along with such a refusal is implicitly suggested either regret for having been flesh or the preference for never having been. In light of the failure of the Gnostics to love themselves and their own birth, Tertullian will himself pass by the love of Christ for his own birth, in order that, by him and with him, he can finally reach the point of loving himself: "At least Christ [by contrast with Marcion] loves this man [*dilexit hominem illum*], this clod formed in the womb among the refuse, this man coming into the world by the passageway of the shameful organs, this man nourished in the milieu of ridiculous caresses."[35]

Interlacing of Flesh. To love "oneself as another" means to accept that one must pass first by another in order to love oneself; his love for his own flesh implicitly teaches me to cherish mine. At the heart of such a "transcendence in immanence"—that is, the phenomenological and horizontal opening toward the absolute other and the possible appropriation of his flesh (Husserl)[36]—resides the truth of the love of the other's flesh as well as my own flesh, which requires first the recognition of their common genesis. Thus Tertullian says: "One is not able to love a being [*nihil amari potest*] without at the same time loving what causes it to be what it is [*eo per quod est id quod est*]."[37] To love myself in the flesh, and thus to assume it as specifically mine (*sua*) first requires the attestation that another, in his own flesh, constitutes it before I myself adopt it, or better, receive it. Only another, in his flesh and in an "interlacing of flesh," gives to me the world.[38] So, in an exemplary way, we can say that nothing is given to me apart from the recognition that it is by the flesh of Christ alone that true access to the love of my own flesh is opened for me. Against the later classical image of God in man conceived within the soul alone—be it in the intelligible (Augustine) or affective (Bernard) dimension—Tertullian designates the individual body as "loved of God" (*dilexit a Deo*), and as the locus and trace of the image and likeness of God within. The diversity of Christ's own and my origins, either from heaven or from earth, does not imply a "difference of material" (*materiae differentia*). The identity of our carnal texture on the contrary indicates our common membership in the same world created by God and received by men—the very one of whom my body in its very passivity and (as we will soon see) filiality, always carries the trace: "The first man was born of the dust of the earth, the second, of heaven (1 Cor. 15:47). Yet the text does not envisage a difference of material (*non tamen ad materiae differentiam spectat*): to the old, carnal substance of the first man, Adam, who was merely terrestrial, it opposes the celestial substance of the second man, Christ, who comes from the Spirit."[39]

Thus the analytic of the flesh, or better, of the flesh of Christ as it reveals my own flesh, shows how, against every expectation, this *caro*—however denigrated in certain regions of Latin Christianity (excepting of course Tertullian)—constitutes me precisely and paradoxically as the image and likeness of God. The Word was made flesh; it is in his flesh therefore that first resides the secret of the love of my own flesh. It would be necessary then to accept this genesis: in order to be distinguished from my own a flesh came not from the heavens (or rather the stars), but was rather drawn from the earth or soil (*adâmâ*)—at least inasmuch as it rightly links up with my own that remains in Adam, the first man, who was also drawn from the earth (Gen. 2:7).

My Sister the Flesh (contra Apelles). The flesh "accepted" [*admise*], and as suspended in its very admittance [*admission*] (even though it is not totally reduced in the necessary presupposition of its existence, contra Marcion): it is fitting to retrace its origin or mode of provenance (*unde*), which specifies it by relation to the body (or bodies). As we have already seen, Apelles draws the flesh of Christ (*caro*) from the celestial bodies (*corpus*). The Gnostic élan of Apelles borrows here from a well-known Stoicism. And in order precisely to exempt the flesh of Christ from ordinary corporeity he somehow folds back the human body over the totality of material corporeity from which the cosmos is received. To the key question, "Where did his body come from [*unde corpus*] if his body was not flesh [*si non caro corpus*]?"[40] Tertullian offers a vigorous response that turns on a near-phenomenological distinction between "flesh" and "body": namely, that the flesh is not body inasmuch as it always assumes attitudes or corporeal movements (kinestheses) that are proper to it and therefore does not yield itself to being characterized as a celestial substance, whether angelic or astral: "Why call it celestial flesh [*caelestem carnem*] if nothing about it lends itself to being interpreted as celestial? Why deny that it was terrestrial [*terrenam*] if you have good cause to recognize it as terrestrial? He was hungry [*esuriit*] in the presence of the devil, and thirsted [*sitiit*] in the presence of the Samaritan woman; he wept [*lacrimatus est*] over Lazarus and trembled [*trepidat*] before death, saying, 'The flesh is weak [*caro infirma*],' and, to boot, he pours out his blood [*sanguinem fundit*]. Behold all these indications of a celestial origin!"[41] The kinesthesis of the body and the esthesiology of the living are really the same thing: (a) the movements of his body make it appear to us as flesh, (b) and therefore as a living being experiencing itself.

Kinesthesia of the Body and Esthesiology of the Living. (a) Eating and drinking in the presence of another (be it the devil or a Samaritan woman), weeping over a deceased friend (Lazarus), trembling at the approach of his own death, experiencing the weakness of his flesh and pouring out his own blood: is there not there something much more than the simple substantialization of a body among other (celestial) bodies, joining together a certain number of kinestheses that are human and terrestrial, and which make of Christ in the flesh the premise and the model of the first man drawn from the earth (*adâmâ*)? Does not the "I can" of Christ's flesh described by the movements of his body according to the near-phenomenological interpretation of

De carne Christi actually precede the intentionality of his I think?[42] The sensory lived experiences of his body (*Erleibnisse*) noted above (refusing to eat in the presence of the devil, requesting a drink from the Samaritan woman, weeping for his deceased friend, etc.) incarnate his body in the flesh (*es wird Leib*), inasmuch as by means of them, he constitutes the world.[43] There is likely no spatiality for Christ beyond the progressive constitution of his flesh throughout his terrestrial pilgrimage and which could never testify to any "astral corporeity" (Apelles). Further, the world regenerated by his resurrection is properly speaking nothing but that which he reconstitutes in a new and strange way by his resurrected flesh in its diverse kinestheses of the body (for example, "appearing in their midst" even through locked doors; in giving himself to "be seen" and eventually "touched" by Thomas—even the marks of the nails and the wound of the lance; in desiring "something to eat" when he was with his disciples on the shore of the Tiberian sea, etc. [Jn. 20–21]). The "history come to earth" when God became man is also "a history come in the flesh"—to quote Péguy—precisely because there is no divine historicity at all, according to Christianity, outside of this "enfleshment" which constitutes him even to the point of a pure adequation of himself to the mode of being of his single corporeity: "This is my body" (*hoc est enim corpus meum*).[44]

(b) These sensorial lived experiences of his body, which are the means of his appearing in the flesh, are also revealed in an exemplary and unique way in Tertullian's analogy between the "composite of the flesh" and "life of the earth": "muscles [*musculos*] similar to mounds of dirt, bones [*ossa*] similar to rocks and even hillocks and gravel, the interlacing of nerves [*nervorum tenaces conexus*] like forking roots, the branching network of veins [*venarum ramosos*] like winding streams, the downy fuzz [*lanuguines*] like moss, hair [*comam*] like grass, and the hidden treasure of marrow [*medullarum in abdito thesauros*] like ores of the flesh [*ut metalla carnis*]."[45] One would be wrong to see in this "terrestrial origin" (*terrenae originis*) of all flesh—and therefore in Christ as well (*et in Christo fuerunt*)[46]—only the naive portrait of a simple reified metaphor of human corporeity. The composition of the body in muscles, bone, nerves, veins, and so on corresponds to the living and moving and gestating earth (mounds of dirt, rocks with gravel, forking roots, winding streams, etc.). Extending the phenomenological metaphor, the "life" of the body (*Leben*) constitutes Christ in the "flesh" (*Leib*). The lived body or body proper, the "flesh" (*caro* in Tertullian and *Leib* in Husserl)—ignoring, here, all danger of anachronism—far from designating merely the pure and simple material reality of something (*corpus* or *Körper*), be it even of celestial or astral origins, actually designates in Tertullian the very organicity of a specifically human body. And it does so in a double sense: on the one hand, it is disclosed capable of kinestheses proper to it and which constitute it in its original and specifically human "I can" (eating and drinking in the presence of another, weeping, etc.). On the other hand, the analogies of the body immediately point back to the metaphors of the life of the earth (mounds of dirt, rocks with gravel, forking roots, winding streams, etc.). As Husserl points out, "[Being related] 'through the living body' (*leiblich*) clearly does not mean [being related] 'as a physical body' (*körperlich*); rather, the expression refers to the kinesthetic, to functioning as an ego in this peculiar way, primarily through seeing, hearing, etc., and of course other modes of the ego belong to this (for example, lifting, carrying, pushing, and the like)."[47]

For Tertullian, being the flesh (*caro*), as in Husserl later, reveals the life of the body (*Leib*): the collection of these "signs" (*signa*) carnally constitutes Christ (muscle, bone, nerve, veins, etc.), "hiding the Son of God all the more in him [*dei filium celaverunt*] as he had no other reason for being taken simply for another man than to show [*extantem*] the human reality of a body."[48] The act of showing the "human substance of the body" (*humana substantia corporis*) is definitively what constitutes the "flesh" (*De carne Christi*). If the muscles, bones, nerves, and veins make up the body (*corpus*), just like other bodies or substances, these corporeal elements are given in Christ's flesh as well since by them he experiences in himself diverse kinestheses by virtue of which he constitutes the world (eating, drinking, weeping, etc.). The two raisons d'être of the flesh of Christ, according to the *De carne Christi*, namely, the kinesthesis and the esthesiology of the living, are therefore founded on one, since that which reveals his movement to us (kinesthesis) is at the same time that which attests to him as living (blood in his veins, the interlacing of nerves, etc.).

Flesh and Body. It is more than fitting, then—for Christ in an exemplary fashion and then for us through him—not only to be in the flesh through the experience of the body (objective), but even to love his body through experiencing it as flesh (subjective or phenomenological body). As we have already seen, contra Marcion, the love of the body, in an ultimate and probably uniquely Christian way, consecrates it as flesh. The flesh (*caro*) is now the "sister of Christ" (*Christi sororem*) as in the striking formula of *De resurrectione carnis*, inasmuch as "Christ loves the flesh [*diliget carnem*] which is so close to him in so many ways [*tot modis sibi proximam*]."[49] (i) The proximity of the body to oneself (*sibi proximam*), or in other words the impossibility of unstitching that which ties me to my skin, is precisely what makes it flesh. Paradoxically, from Tertullian to Husserl, the body, as "physical thing" (*Körper*) composed of bones, veins, nerves, and so on "becomes flesh" (*es wird Leib*) since it is aware—or better said—feels. Thus the same goes for the inevitable chiasm of the touching-touched (Husserl)[50] or from the experience of the Son auto-affecting himself in his body ("being hungry" [*esuriit*], "feeling thirst" [*sitiit*], "weeping" [*lacrimatus est*], etc.). (ii) Further, Christ's "love of the flesh" (*diliget carnem*)—and his own in the first place, which is "so close to him in many ways" (*tot modis sibi proximam*)—thus makes of his ordinary corporeity a unique mode of filiality. The flesh, as his "sister" (*soror*), *his* flesh, is passively recognized and received in a Trinitarian way from the same origin: his Father. In the same way as all flesh, the flesh as "sister of Christ" therefore never gives itself to itself but always receives itself from another. The auto-affection of the flesh is attested immediately and directly in Christ as an auto-affection desiring and loving what I am and what he is in himself.

The "charity of my flesh" makes of my own body the place of the most intimate fraternity. Here we are very far removed indeed from the Gnostic disgust at the heart of Marcion's illusory flesh or of Apelles's sidereal flesh as well toward that which constitutes my body in its most trivial of activities (childbirth, drinking and eating, weeping, etc.). We are also at the antipodes of the thinly veiled dualism hiding under the apparent monism of the disciples of Valentinus's soul-flesh. Here the flesh manifests my life (*vita*) more than my soul (*anima*), just as Christ did in giving himself. Thus it is necessary to look on the flesh of Christ not only as it is manifest in the mode of a theophany, but even as it recapitulates and saves by means of this very manifestation of life in it, which is, soteriologically speaking, within the competence of the flesh.

The Manifesto of the Flesh (Contra the Valentinians)

The soul is seen so much through the flesh, as I indicated above, in the context of Tertullian's exposition of the soul-flesh, that the Valentinian disciples failed to distinguish what belongs to the soul and what belongs to the flesh. In Tertullian the truth of the manifestation of the Christic flesh in its modality (*cuiusmodi*) is revealed in a completely different way. More than merely the soul (*anima*), Christ first shows life (*vita*) in his flesh, and by way of an excess, saves the soul in saving the flesh, for surely the Hellenizing dualism of *psuchê /sôma* is very far removed from the biblical conception of man as *sarx*: "The 'life was manifested' [*vita manifesta est*]" [Jn. 1:4; 2 Cor. 4:10] and not the soul [*non anima*]. Or again, "'I have come to save the soul' [*animam saluam facere*] [Lk. 9:56]. Christ did not say 'to show it' [*non dixit ostendere*]."[51] The purpose is clear: (a) in theophanic perspective: the flesh of Christ manifests his life more than his soul; (b) in soteriological perspective: more than merely showing it, this same flesh saves the soul.

Theophanic Flesh. (a) The "manifested life" (*vita manifesta est*) is cashed out first in Tertullian, likely in reaction to the absolute monism of the disciples of Valentinus with its (implicit) total separation of soul and flesh—itself close indeed to the Nestorianism that will later become such a great object of reproach (e.g., in the controversy between Leo the Great and the Greek fathers of the Council of Chalcedon).[52] "As far as Christ is concerned," emphasizes Tertullian, "we find his soul and his flesh designated by direct and clear-cut terms: his soul is designated as soul [*animam animam*] and his flesh as flesh [*et carnem carnem*]. There is no trace of a flesh-soul [*animam carnem*] or soul-flesh [*aut carnem animam*]."[53] Rather everything is purely tautological: "The soul is soul" (*animam animam*) and "the flesh is flesh" (*carnem carnem*). Does our hypothesis, then, of an analytic of the incarnation at the heart of *De carne Christi* find itself nearly ruined, at the precise point where no bridge or chiasm between the soul and the flesh seems any longer possible? It is it then appropriate to conclude, in regard to such formulas, that Tertullian holds to a pure, dualizing substantialism of the flesh and soul, which is, in a word, very far from the neat analyses of the "flesh-soul" and the "soul-flesh" of the Valentinians? To draw such a hasty conclusion seems to ignore precisely the soul and flesh themselves, since they are in themselves related to each other. Tertullian's apparent dualism (of flesh/soul or of soul/flesh) is in fact established only in relation to the complete monism of the Valentinians. In the midst of his polemic, Tertullian puts in operation a quasi-reduction (*epochê*) of the soul and flesh, which lets a third term appear: life (*vita*). "We are ready to admit now [*nunc*] that the soul has been manifested by the flesh [*ostensa sit anima per carnem*]."[54] "Now," that is, once the massive confusion has been forestalled between flesh and soul where the soul is lost in the soul-flesh and the flesh is lost in the flesh-soul.

Therefore for Tertullian the soul is what is "here manifested by the flesh" (*ostensa per carnem*) provided that it reveals what Christ carried in his life, even more than the flesh: "Behold why the Son descended and was imbued with a soul [*animam subiit*]."[55] Note here that Tertullian implicates the soul rather than the flesh, which he paradoxically passes over. Like the first Adam, Christ from all eternity bore, at least in a precursory way, in himself the body or earth. This is a strange but apposite reversal. Of course, what also must be seen here in such a "prototype" is that it be animated or "imbued with a soul" in a flesh, precisely in order to be joined by the movements of its body (life of the muscles, tension of the nerves, etc.) with that which man experiences in his flesh, such as the diverse sensory and incarnate lived experiences that are proper to it and by which it constitutes the world (eating and drinking in the presence of another, lamenting the absence of a friend, etc.). There is in other words no veritable incarnation without a complete animation or "experience" [*épreuve*] of the body, which transmutes it into flesh by means of its diverse kinestheses. We are very far removed from the numerous Platonizing conceptions of the incarnation as "putting on flesh" of a soul (*in carne*) or even its "putting on the death" of the body (*sôma-semâ*). In Tertullian by contrast the soul animates a body and takes on flesh. Here we suggest that the phenomenological conception of incarnation is discovered, which, far from finding itself anchored in the Valentinian monism of soul-flesh, on the contrary makes of the "manifestation of the soul by the flesh" (*ostensa anima per carnem*) a specifically human way of inhabiting the body in order to finally "become flesh" or be incarnate (*es wird Leib*).[56] And if in being "manifested by the flesh" the soul is discovered animating a body, it is also the case that what is revealed in Christ's life is also revealed in my own to the end that he is known in me rather than it is that I am known in him: "The Son descended and was imbued with a soul in order to teach the soul not to know itself in Christ [*non ut ipsa se anima cognosceret in Christo*] but to know Christ within it [*se ut Christum in semetipsa*]."[57]

In advance of and in contrast to all Hellenizing theologies that replace man's self-knowledge for the image and likeness of God in man (from Augustine to Aquinas, for example), Tertullian requires that we pass—in the double sense of the word, as a passage and as a surpassing—from the knowledge of the self in God to the knowledge of God in the self. Thus the famous Pauline formula—"It is not I who live but Christ lives within me" (Gal. 2:20)—ordinarily interpreted egologically, should, in light of *De carne Christi*, be first understood Christologically. This recommendation of the Apostle, not only indicating the place of the passive constitution of the subject and one's access to the self by the mediation of another in me (me/Christ), also above all indicates the complete auto-manifestation of another "life" in me, from the moment that I accept its initial act of decentering me from myself: "He is imbued with a soul in order to teach the soul to know Christ within it [*ut Christum cognosceret in semetipsa*]."[58]

While I know myself in God through the mediation of Christ (according to the egological interpretation), it is no less the case that I *first* know God in me in knowing Christ as my very life (according to the Christological interpretation).[59] It is no longer simply the soul that "is manifested by the flesh of Christ" (*ostensa per carnem*)—may the contemporary disciples of Valentinus and the numerous Hellenizing theologians please pardon my offense—but the very life of God, inasmuch as it constitutes his being, woven from his glorious flesh, and that which I encounter in my mortal flesh: "*vita manifesta est, non anima*."[60] The theophany of the flesh of Christ ecstatically gives the life of God in man more than it lets the soul appear to the self in an egologically focused way. What is the nature of this "manifested life"? Simply put, it is that which reveals the theophanic flesh of Christ—and it is manifested first in a soteriological manner. As we have already quoted above: "'I have come in order to save the soul' [*animam saluam facere*] [Lk. 9:56], Christ did not say, 'in order to show it' [*non dixit ostendere*]."[61]

Soteriological Flesh. (b) In what sense does the soul need saving, if Christ "bore the burden" (*animam subiit*) in his flesh through experiencing it in a body? It needs saving because, simply, along with the flesh (*cum carne*), it composes the whole human being: "We surely do not know the soul resurrected with the flesh [*cum carne*]. Behold what Christ has manifested [*manifestauit*]."[62] The theophany of the soul by the flesh—that which Christ has manifested—is a deliberate expression of soteriology—that which Christ has saved, namely, the flesh with the soul. This chiasm of flesh and soul (the manifestation of the soul by the flesh and the salvation of the flesh with the soul), very far indeed from the unilateral monism of the Valentinians, means that nothing happens to the soul which is not also in some way produced in the flesh, be it in a completely other mode. Tertullian discovers here, in a striking way, the implacable analogy between the senses of the soul and the experience of the flesh and thus anticipates the very famous and fecund doctrine of the spiritual senses (which we will seek to understand in chap. 6 with Bonaventure): "I consider the soul to be naturally endowed with senses [*sensualis est anima natura*]. This is so true that no part of the soul is lacking in sensation [*nihil animale sine sensu*] and thus nothing that is endowed with sensation at all lacks soul [*nihil sensuale sine anima*]."[63] Because the soul immediately experiences its organic flesh or its own body in that it is naturally endowed with senses (*sensualis est anima natura*), it is thus known, or better, is recognized, and suffers or is aware of itself [*se re(s)-sent elle-même*] in its body. Whoever is fond of going into ecstasies or distancing themselves from the "knowledge [*cognosceret*] of the self that pertains to the soul"[64] (as for the Valentinian disciples and Hellenizing theologies), is negligent since "from the beginning the soul has received the feeling of itself [*ipsa sensum sui ab initio*]."[65] The soul "feels" (*ipsa sensum*) or experiences itself, without distance, precisely in its own flesh. It "auto-affects," to speak in Michel Henry's terms, who uses it in direct reference to the author of *De carne Christi*.[66]

However, the experience of the self loses nothing of its "density" or "solidity." Here Tertullian makes an a posteriori break with Henry the phenomenologist and the reading that he proposes. For Tertullian it is not enough to experience oneself "in life and through life" in order to be in the flesh. Through the encounter with all the Gnostic schools, Tertullian asserts that life itself is only given if a "body," made of "muscles," "bones," "nerves," and "veins," constitutes and supports it in its exteriority as well as in its very materiality. There is no "flesh without body" (and here he paradoxically courts the inverse risk of falling into an ethereal angelism that he works to condemn). Yet it is true that the definition of "Life" as "auto-revelation of the self" (Henry) is already discovered in Tertullian. It is necessary, however, to unite such a conception directly with the "density" and "solidity" of the flesh (*solidam carnem*). For in the general project of salvation there is not only life to be manifested (*uita manifesta est non anima)*, but there is also the soul to be redeemed (*ueni animam saluam facere, non dixit ostendere*).[67] Theophany and soteriology are ultimately tied together in the resurrected flesh. The manifestation of the flesh is at the service of the salvation of the soul (and the flesh along with it). Tertullian's perspective is here soteriological and it assumes the whole of humanity that the lone phenomenological auto-affection wrongly forgets: "The flesh is washed in order for the soul to be purified; the flesh receives the unction in order for the soul to be consecrated; the flesh is marked with a sign in order for the soul to be protected; the flesh is covered by the imposition of hands in order for the soul to be illuminated by the spirit; the flesh is nourished with the body and blood of Christ in order for the soul to feed on the power of God."[68]

My flesh interlaced with the flesh of another (contra Marcion), an organic flesh in the experience of the kinestheses of its own body (contra Apelles), a theophanic flesh in the soteriological goal of its resurrection (contra the Valentinians): it is this flesh that is a flesh for the sake of being born (as we have already said) and, as we will now see, is a flesh for the sake of dying (contra Valentinus himself). In this way will a new path for a metaphysics of finitude open before us, all the more hidden in the kenosis of the cross as it is anchored first in the "kenosis of the flesh."

The Hypothesis of a Flesh for the Sake of Death (contra Valentinus)

A Flesh Made to Be Born, a Flesh Made to Die. Valentinus does not reject the possibility of a birth for flesh. Nevertheless, he objects to its properly carnal composition, in the sense that whatever is born in the flesh or "in the womb" (*in uolua*) is not identically born of the flesh or "from the womb" (*non ex uolua*).[69] One must surrender to the evidence: a body "agglutinated" (*adglutinatur*) to another body, either from the exterior (*extraneo*) or in the womb (*in uolua*), produces along with it a veritable "community of flesh and entrails [*concarnatur et conuisceratur*]."[70] One could return to Psalm 22:10 ("you have knit me together in my mother's womb," *ex utero matris meae*) and find there certain aspects of the Irenaean *plasma*, yet it would still be necessary to suppose that what has been knit together "attached to the womb" (*adhaesit utero*).[71] Beyond the literality of the argument (less glorious if also more realist than the Irenaean line), it is fitting to note the specifically phenomenological pertinence of the doctrine. The weaving together of flesh in childbirth is such that not only love of another for the sake of his own flesh and for mine leads also to value it in my own birth. But, even more, the act of birth marks for both of us such a great tear within our carnal community that it signals at the same time for both of us a community of nature (the flesh)—even a community of world (in the perception of space constituted by the flesh). More than a simple substance or some material, the interweaving or chiasm of the flesh of the other with my own (Merleau-Ponty) from birth ratifies a common human belonging to the world: "hence the Word was made flesh" (*uerbum caro ex uolua factum est*).[72] The hypothesis of a birth carnal in origin (recognized by Valentinus) necessarily implies a community of flesh in texture and in end (as Tertullian suggests). Thus goes the rustic formula of Boehme commented on by Heidegger: "As soon as a human being is born, he is old enough to die right away."[73] The triviality of the proposition aside, it is enough to note that it recalls something that Tertullian even applied to the Word himself: "Christ, sent to die [*mori missus*], had to be born in order to die [*nasci quoque necessario habuit ut mori posset*]. In fact, nothing dies except that which is born [*non enim mori solet nisi quod nascitur*]."[74]

The ordinary insistence of Western theology on death as the means of the Son's act of redemption (death for our sins) often makes us forget his death by communion (death of being born—that is, through having espoused our corruptible flesh and submitted to the ordinary law of the self's destruction). In being born his flesh is immediately a dying flesh. We can therefore hold this with the highest degree of certitude (*sum moribundus*): "The rule of death was the reason for his birth [*forma moriendi causa nascendi est*] . . . Christ became death for the sake of that which is submitted to death by reason of its birth [*quia nascitur, moritur*]."[75] Further, this flesh that dies renders him truly carnal (*acceperit carnem*) as he espouses it through the path of birth (*nascendo*). This position therefore cedes nothing to a pure angelic or Gnostic appearance: "Both Christ and the angels appeared in the flesh [*in carne processerint*]. Yet no angel ever descended in order to be crucified [*ut crucifigeretur*], to know death [*ut mortem experiretur*], and to be resurrected [*ut a morte suscitaretur*]. Never has an angel had such reasons to take a body [*angelorum corporandorum*] and such is the reason why they were never incarnate [*non acceperit carnem*] by the path of birth [*nascendo*]: not coming in order to die [*non venerant mori*], they did not come through being born [*ideo nec nasci*]."[76]

As we will later see in Thomas Aquinas (chap. 8), the angelic incorporation (*angelorum corporandorum*) is distinguished from the incarnation of Christ (*acceperit carnem)* in that the carnal angelic appearance—which it shares with Christ (*in carne processerint*)—neither submits to the law of the genesis of the flesh "by birth" (*nascendo*) nor to its disappearance by being subject to "the experience of death" (*ut morteum experiretur*). The truth of the incarnation of Christ is therefore first, not merely the carnal appearance (*Leiblichkeit*), which it shares with the angels, but first its paradoxical corporeity (*Körperlichkeit*) as an "object of the world," subject to the ordinary law of birth and death, which is precisely that which the angel has never attained in its purely apparent flesh. The complexity of a phenomenological reading of the incarnation of Christ therefore no longer merely concerns the appearance of the angel more than the being of man, as Christ become flesh (*caro*) by the diverse kinestheses of his body (*corpus*). Rather the complexity lies now in that he could remain body (*corpus*) as an object in the world subject to life and death even though he pursued no other end than of showing his flesh (*caro*) as the place of the shining forth of the divine glory. In this he is like the angels without being reduced to one. Rather than merely extolling his becoming the flesh of man (*Verleiblichung*) through a simple series of phenomenological reductions, let us also attempt, still following Husserl, to think through the enigma of his becoming body (*Verkörperung*), that is, his being in the world as a simple object of the world: "Elucidating how the flesh [*Leib*] is constituted as a physical flesh [*Leibkörper*] is therefore a fundamental problem that needs to be thought through starting from the foundation."[77] Christ's flesh becomes or becomes again his body as soon as he comes in the flesh "in order (there) to die" (*ut mori posset*) as much as "in order (there) to be born" (*nasci quoque necessario*).[78] His "flesh toward birth" is at the same time a "flesh toward death." The implied Heideggerian interpretation here no longer lacks the necessary incarnation of anguish in the flesh.[79] If the soul is manifested in a flesh provided that it implements the kinestheses of its body and finds there along with it its salvation, then it experiences in its flesh precisely the double sentiment of the emptiness of its own existence as well as the call from the divine or its own self-entrusting to the divine. Thus Tertullian, with a surprisingly modern outlook, states: "Before learning anything about God the soul names God. Without knowing the outcome, it says that it commends its cause to God [*deo commandare se dicit*]. It understands only these words: 'There is no hope after death' [*spem nullam esse post mortem*], and yet it still makes vows for and imprecations upon those who are no more [*et bene et male defuncto cuique imprecatur*]."[80]

The Cadaver. The flesh toward death (*ut mori*) is marked as the place of a vocation toward God, even of a call of God. Said otherwise, the knowledge that I am going to die and therefore lose, at least in a terrestrial fashion, the ensemble of kinestheses which constitute my flesh (eating, drinking, weeping, etc.), establishes the lived experience of my body as the site of a claim to my entire being: experiencing to the end the feeling of a total "absence of hope after death" (*spem nulam esse post mortem*), the soul, manifested in its flesh and saved along with it (*cum carne*), has not ceased "to commend its cause to God" and "to make vows for and imprecations upon those who are no more." In an expected synonymy established in *De resurrectione carnis* (which could also be named *De resurrectione mortuorum* here) the "word flesh (*id est carnis*) thus designates the same word as death" [*eadem erit et in nomine mortui*]. The flesh does not only die here in order to deliver the soul (as in a Platonic perspective) but reveals at once that by which I fall into the emptiness of death (*cadere*) and that in which I rise in the hope of the resurrection (*resurrectio carnis*): "Truly the flesh [*adeo caro est*] is wearied by death, for it is from this word fall, *cadere*, that it is called cadaver [*cadaver*] . . . Even as the resurrection truly concerns a transitory [*caduc*] element [*caducae rei est*], namely the flesh [*id est carnis*], that very word designates the word death [*eadem erit et in nomine mortui*] since what we call the resurrection of the dead is the resurrection of a transitory [*caduc*] being [*quia caducae rei est resurrectio quae dicitur mortuorum*]."[81]

It is needless to say that we know not to hold with the Gnostics and Marcion in particular that Christ has not endured the agony of his passion by virtue of being "a phantasm too empty to feel [*quia ut phantasma uacabat a sensu earum*]."[82] On the contrary, his flesh that adhered to the womb from whence it came in birth (*ex uolua*) is now "glued" to itself and even to its own death. Like all men, the Son of Man "falls" in some sense into his own demise (*cadere*) and, in his "transitory" [*caduque*] flesh or "cadaver," disappears. Let it suffice here to see how the mineness of his flesh in its suffering (*Jemeinigkeit*) joins up with the mineness of my own flesh: "A flesh like ours, supplied by blood, structured by bones, interlaced with nerves, crisscrossed by veins . . . this flesh was born to die [*nasci et mori*] and was human beyond any doubt [*humana sine dubio*] since it came from man [*ut nata de homine*] and was mortal for this reason [*ideoque mortalis*]. This flesh in Christ will be man and Son of Man."[83] To say of the "death of the Son of God" (*et mortuus est dei filius*) that it ought to be believed because it is absurd (*credibile est quia ineptum est*),[84]— the most famous if also most misunderstood phrase of Tertullian—does nothing to respond either to the false accusations of irrationalism of the *credo quia absurdum* so denigrated in the Middle Ages or to the relishing of the death of God theologies in the exemplary nonsense of the so-called death of God that saturates contemporary consciousness's awareness of the absurdity of the world.[85] To elevate the absurd or foolish character of the death of the Son properly on the contrary consists in recognizing that dying *for us* he no less dies *as one of us*—that is, with us in the texture of our own flesh, subject to the natural law of corruptibility and death. If there is an anguish of the Son before his own death, it will not be an anguish "of sin," but rather one "of finitude," for he died not only from taking on himself our sins, but first, in an exemplary and quotidian way, from espousing himself to our very flesh.[86]

✦

The Kenosis of the Flesh. It is not enough, according to Tertullian, that Christ "carry the cross" (*crucem gestare*). It is first necessary that he "carry the flesh" (*carnem gestare*). "What is more unworthy of God that he should blush: birth [*nasci*] or death [*an mori*]? Carrying the flesh (*carnem gestare*) or the cross (*an crucem*)? Being circumcised or nailed? Being fed or buried? Being tucked in a crib or deposed in a tomb?"[87] The kenosis of Christ is therefore first anchored in the kenosis of his flesh: "The first meaning of 'the Word became flesh' is quite straightforward: word, this particular form of personal utterance, known to everyone, takes on a form of being which, as such, is foreign to the word, for flesh as such does not speak. Even if 'flesh' here stands for 'man,' speaking is only one of the forms of activity of the being 'man' " (Balthasar).[88]

Both the newborn in Bethlehem and the crucified man on Golgotha lack speech. Only the flesh speaks here. Put precisely, that which speaks has no knowledge. Or: "Its beginning is the pure—and, so to speak, still dumb—psychological experience, which now must be made to utter its own sense without adulteration" (Husserl).[89] The history "come to earth" when God became man is also, as we have already seen, a "history come to the flesh" (Péguy). If it thus seems to the phenomenologist (Heidegger) that "the essence of the divinity is closer to us than what is so alien in other living creatures," the theologian of the Christic incarnation teaches, following Tertullian, that the (Trinitarian) essence of God becomes even closer as soon as this same divine is made living and corporeal and manifests himself as such.[90] "*Caro salutis cordo est*"—"the flesh is the hinge of salvation":[91] in this movement of the hinge (of salvation) or around this joint, is found the key to opening up a fecund and non-polemical confrontation, ever renewed and never achieved, between phenomenology (the overcoming of metaphysics by the analytic of the flesh) and theology (the redemption and recapitulation of our own flesh by the flesh of Christ).

It is this "very flesh," rendered fully *visible* and glorious in Adam (Irenaeus) and finding all its *solidity* in the incarnate Word (Tertullian), that is necessary for us now ourselves to assume, or rather, *to convert*. Both the "ark of flesh" of the first Adam (Irenaeus) and the "kenosis of the flesh" of the second (Tertullian) matter little if I myself, as carnal being, do not also participate in this double movement that fashions salvation. The exteriority of the object to belief in theology and of the experience to description would be enough to ruin the entire enterprise if the examination of the "flesh" would not at the same time carry out my own self-transformation—as a believer, certainly, but also as a philosopher. The affair here is not apologetic, but first a matter of phenomenological conversion. To think as a phenomenologist, as we said at the beginning, requires that I "see otherwise" the "thing" as it "concerns me" (*Sache*), to "scrutinize the depths" (*scrutare profunda*) and to "bring to light" that which has not yet been laid bare (*producere in lucem*). The experience of the conversion of my own gaze through that which I see (Bonaventure) matters at least as much as, and probably more than, all the just directives and descriptions about that which is seen: Adam, on the one hand (Irenaeus), Christ on the other (Tertullian). Saint Bonaventure, as a disciple of Saint Francis, himself also earthbound (*Canticle of Creatures*) and engaged in the flesh (through the experience of the stigmata), establishes *today's experience of the senses* and their *conversion* as the site par excellence of man's encounter with God through a "hand to hand" [*corps à corps*], of which their interlacing goes all the way to the physical nourishment of man by the presence of the incarnate and resurrected Word: the Eucharist. The hypothesis of the *conversion of the senses*—another mode and name of the *conversion of the flesh*—draws us "out of our seats in the theatre" in order "to throw us onstage."[92] Called for by the flesh of both *Adam* (Irenaeus) and *Christ* (Tertullian), the time has come for the *believer* to offer his own flesh for the sake of its metamorphosis in God (Bonaventure). Where certain people will only see a Dolorism—in particular in Saint Francis's experience of the stigmata—it will be necessary to show instead that such an expressivity of the divine in the materiality of the human signifies—for the philosopher as well—a specific mode of the body as "concrete emblem of a manner of being in general"—that is, the flesh, or more specifically, my flesh (*Leib*).[93]

Chapter 6

✦

The Conversion of the Flesh (Bonaventure)

The Carnal Experiment

The leap that we are making here, from the church fathers (Irenaeus and Tertullian) to the medievals (Bonaventure), is not accidental. One could rightly object that Bonaventure knew nothing about Irenaeus and Tertullian, nor had any access to them at all. This is true for any medieval author. Yet, as numerous interpreters agree, Bonaventure's filiation from Irenaeus and the first fathers of the church is most evident on a conceptual plane, although not historically founded. This goes for Bonaventure's "monadological" vision according to which we are all bound together "in the Word" (Col. 1:16), as well as the aesthetic vision of creation as a work and not a product, and, finally, for the soteriological motif according to which sin is not the sole reason for the incarnation, but includes the unique desire to transfigure the world into the dwelling (*habitacle*) of God.[1] But there is more in the Seraphic Doctor. For if there is a point on which he differs from his predecessors it is that he finds a conceptuality for the nearly forgotten doctrine of the "conversion of the senses." Thus Balthasar states: "It was Origen, who, so to speak, 'invented' the doctrine of the 'five spiritual senses' . . . in St. Bonaventure this straitened water-course suddenly swells up again to become a mighty river."[2] Here more than elsewhere, the word of Claudel cited above applies: "Not only does spirit speak to spirit, but flesh speaks to flesh."[3]

The *visibility* of Adam's flesh (Irenaeus) and the *solidity* of Christ's (Tertullian) will therefore not return to God void, that is, "without having fecundated the earth" (Is. 55:10)—in other words, without having *converted and transformed* the flesh of the believer himself (Bonaventure). As we said at the end of the previous chapter, the exteriority of the object studied now awaits its intercorporeity, where the one who sees is implicated in what he beholds and offers himself for the sake of his own metamorphosis. There is no better guide than Bonaventure for this act, for the Franciscan experience is carnal through and through. From the staging of the nativity scene, to the *Canticle of Creatures* and the manifestation of the stigmata—everything speaks of the flesh and to the flesh: "The flesh is for the sake of flesh" (*caro propter carnem*), states the Seraphic Doctor, "in view of final salvation."[4] Stressing the spiritual experience of Saint Francis, Bonaventure translates the carnally lived experience of his founding father into a *philosophical key*. It is well known that "intuitions without concepts are blind." It is also safe to wager that the Franciscan inspiration would not have acquired such a posterity if it had not received its most adequate formulation from the Franciscan Doctor (Bonaventure) and the tools for thought transmitted by his master (Alexander of Hales). "Concepts without intuitions are empty" as well.[5] The originality of Bonaventure's thought does not come from the *theologoumena* that he developed, but also from the carnal experience that he indirectly shared with Francis, even though he did not, of course, show on his own body such a divine excess (the stigmata). To speak of a "conversion of the flesh" in Bonaventure is therefore to reveal how the *carnal experience* of the Poverello of Assisi can and should be transmitted, albeit in a conceptual mode, to anyone who claims also to express in his own body such an experience of God. It goes without saying that it is hardly a question here of delimiting the examination to believers alone. What mystical experience gives to be seen says something about our phenomenological mode of being in general. It certainly can be said that limit experiences, like the stigmata in religion or performances in art for that matter, draw discourse toward some spheres that it could never attain on its own and gives to the body new paths of living as soon as thought transforms it. We will proceed as follows: First, the life of Saint Francis's flesh in his break with Saint Dominic; second, its translation into a new doctrine of the symbol as well as the spiritual senses; third, the new language which is drawn out of the experience of receiving the stigmata. These will constitute the three moments of "carnal conversion," according to Bonaventure, and therefore lead to the fulfillment of our Adamic filiation (Irenaeus) and to our new engendering through adoption in Christ (Tertullian).

Language of the Flesh and Flesh of Language

I repeat what I have already mentioned in relation to Meister Eckhart above: the difference between the *affective* and the *intellectual* in the Franciscan and Dominican modes of being-in-the-world, respectively, finds its origin, for both, in the unique *mendicant* order where the veritable poverty of the first beatitude ("Blessed are the poor . . .") is rooted in the detachment and nonknowledge of poverty itself (chap. 3: Eckhart). After this community of nature (the mendicant order), the foundational experience of the flesh in Saint Francis becomes clarified in its difference with the original experience of the word in Saint Dominic (chap. 6: Bonaventure). Yet the *word of the flesh* in Francis and the *flesh of the word* in Dominic signifies more than two divergent options for radical discipleship. These two postures between the word and flesh indicate two distinct but complementary manners of envisaging the task of philosophy today: descriptive phenomenology, on the side of the carnal experience of the Friars Minor (book of the world), and hermeneutic on the side of the linguistic translation of the Order of Preachers (world of the book). This is a harsh distinction indeed—requiring significant nuance in order to avoid a hardened opposition between two perspectives (and two orders!). The word is not the exclusive right of hermeneutics or of the Dominicans, just as much as the body is not the exclusive property of descriptive phenomenology or of the Franciscans. The hermeneutics of the text is at the same time a hermeneutics of the body (see Ricoeur, *Oneself as Another*); the blackfriar is even close to the body (see the doctrine of transubstantiation in Aquinas); descriptive phenomenology does not leave the flesh without a voice (see Merleau-Ponty, *The Prose of the World*); and the carnal silence of the greyfriar is nothing if not in search of a voice (see the canticle of Francis).

But such a methodologically necessary prudence in our approach does not prohibit the recognition of a certain divergence or distinction. The way of the hermeneutic of the text (in Gadamer or Ricoeur) is not that of the phenomenology of the body (Husserl or Merleau-Ponty), and the intuition of the flesh of language or of the world of the book (Saint Dominic) does not come under the jurisdiction of the language of the flesh or of the book of the world (Saint Francis). The visions differ and yet complement one another, understood mystically as well as philosophically. The diverging paths only reveal all the more the richness of thought—and it hardly ought to end in an interminable quarrel (either ecclesiastical or philosophical). To take note of it is simply, once again, to reveal in a new way that recourse to the tradition is never merely traditional and that the reappropriation of past approaches opens the way to a new future that constantly reinvents it.

Saint Francis, or the Language of the Flesh

As is well known, with the appearance of the mendicant orders, the "regular clergy" come to take on the tasks once reserved for the "secular clergy" even as they institute a new kind of relation to the world. Against Rupert of Deutz, for whom "all the apostles were really monks" (*omnes apostoli vere fuerunt monachi*), marked by "the teaching, fraternal communion and the breaking of bread" (Acts 2:42),[6] Saints Francis and Dominic broke down the walls of the cloister and consecrated the world as the new space of the presence of God and his glorification. To Lady Poverty, who asked the new Franciscan community to show her its cloister, "the brothers themselves," says the letter on the *Sacrum commercium*, "led her up a hill and showed her a splendid panorama. 'Madam,' they said, 'behold our cloister.' "[7] What gives the world its density [*épaisseur*] through the evangelization of the mendicants also gives to the body its importance as the locus of the conversion of the believer. The Christian being-in-the-world, posed in a new way by the Franciscans, determines its "being-in-the-flesh." The "book of the world," as locus of the proclamation, does not go forth apart from a profound conversion of the "flesh of the believer" as the expression and visibility of God. The *imitatio Christi* (in the form of the evangelical rule of poverty) and the nudity of the flesh (manifested in Bernardone's lawsuit against his son Francis) are joined together in order to make the creation's praise (*Canticle of Creatures*) the locus of a conversion of the carnal relation of man to the world. The life of Francis, mystically shared and philosophically conceptualized through Saint Bonaventure's retelling (*Legenda maior*), thus serves as the head of the lance, which, when thrust, manifests Franciscan spirituality as a true language of the flesh.

The Imitatio Christi. The *imitatio Christi*, instituted in the twelfth and thirteenth centuries by the mendicants as a Christian mode of being in the world, is a precise answer to the Christian requirement to make God visible in the lived experience of the flesh of the believer. Although other great figures had espoused the ideal of evangelical poverty well before Francis and Dominic, this new birth of the thirteenth century made the Gospel itself a way of life (*ordo vivendi*): "Some new rule, I have not," exclaimed Francis to the papal curia, "my single rule is the Gospel." Here the Gospel, if it has ever ceased being such, becomes the rule (*regula evangelica*). Under this evangelical imperative there lies no longer simply the common life of the Apostles as model of the monastic life (Acts 2:42) but also the call of Jesus to the twelve: "Procure for yourselves neither gold nor money for your belts, neither purse for the road, nor two tunics, neither sandals, nor stick because the laborer is worthy of his pay" (Matt. 10:9). "Behold what I desire, all that my soul longs for!" exclaims Francis, enraptured by joy, who, out of the blue, "removes his shoes, lets his stick fall, and, throwing away his pouch and money as objects of horror, keeping only a single tunic, leaving behind his belt and replacing it with a cord . . ."[8] Here, the habit makes the monk, contrary to convention, not in the sense that the tunic or the cord properly identifies him, but rather because the "dispossession of goods" makes the saint into a "good man," the one to whom "an impulse communicated by God pushes him to the conquest of evangelical perfection and to a campaign of penitence."[9] Here the flesh is "a concrete emblem of a general manner of being" and not a simple "contradictory union" of bodily and spiritual substances (Merleau-Ponty). It reveals and is revealed, both mystically and phenomenologically, as the "visibility of a manner of being-in-the-world" and the appearance of a new "style" by which man is properly identified.[10] The others that soon follow—brother Leo, brother Rufin, brother Bernard, brother Gilles, or brother Sylvester—not only heard the words of the blissful father, but also followed his example, seeing his flesh imitate the flesh of Christ and following suit in *their* own bodies his manner of living in *his* own body. So Francis said to them after reading the Gospel: "if you want to be perfect, go and put into practice what you have come to hear."[11] The *imitatio Christi*, advocated anew in the thirteenth century, rediscovered the meaning of the body as a sort of practice of existence, but one that is here no longer deciphered in the figure of Adam (Irenaeus) or the incarnate Word (Tertullian), but in the posture of the saint transformed by strict obedience to the rule of the Gospel (Bonaventure). Following upon the flesh of Christ, the visibility of the believer's flesh embarks on the path of the fullest dispossession, even to the point of nudity as expressed by brother Francis when his father took him to court.

The Nudity of the Flesh. When, in 1206, Francis denuded himself before the incredulous inhabitants of Assisi, he indicated more than a simple familial rupture or the pure abandonment of material goods. By this act the saint substituted the spiritual adoption of living flesh [*corporalité*] (*Leiblichkeit*) for the genetic filiation of bodiliness [*corporéité*] (*Körperlichkeit*). Bernardone, notably called by Saint Bonaventure the "carnal father of a son of grace," sought to bring to justice the one whom he considered a biological part of his "body." What came to be exposed was that his son lived in his own proper "flesh," and that his mode of being in the world in no way partook of the material possession of goods that his father wanted to inculcate in him. Bonaventure comments, "Consumed by an admirable fervor and carried away by a spiritual intoxication, Francis stripped down and, *completely naked* [*totus denudatur*] before the audience, declared to his father, 'To this day I have called you father on this earth; however, I can say with assurance: "Our Father who art in heaven," since it is to him that I have entrusted my treasure and faith.' "[12] Francis's nudity does not lie completely under the sign of renunciation. It also bares, to borrow the words of Levinas, a body exposed to the other, the fragility of being "without defense," and "the absolute opening of the Transcendent."[13] In exegeting this passage, Saint Bonaventure himself attributes a symbolic meaning to this manifestation of the flesh, understanding it in the sense of the *sequela Christi* more than within the horizon of a simple anecdotal rupture with a familial body: "They gave him the poor homespun coat of a farmer in the service of the bishop. Francis received it with gratitude . . . the vestment signified well the crucified and this poor, half-naked one [*seminudi*]. In this way was the servant of the Great King left naked [*nudus relictus est*] in order to walk behind his Lord who was affixed naked [*nudum crucifixum*] to the cross."[14] There is thus a clear analogy between Christ "affixed naked" to the wood of the cross at Golgotha and Francis "half naked" in Assisi. Following the Crucified, the saint, against less authentic forms of spiritualizing Christianity, reveals that the "Lord is for the body," and that it is fitting within Christianity to "glorify the Lord by the body" (1 Cor. 6:13, 20). Far from any Dolorism, the nude (*nudus*) pertains to Christianity in an exemplary fashion. The artists, from the first Cluniac representations (Vézeley) to the altarpiece of Mathias Grünewald (Isenheim), were not wrong to make the representation of the *naked Christ* the heart of an "incarnate" spirituality that would only be interpreted falsely in later centuries as an apology for suffering.[15] According to the interpretation of Bonaventure, the flesh of Francis reveals the flesh of Christ. In his carnal "hand to hand" [*corps à corps*] is articulated the true espousal of man and God, extended, according to the Franciscan perspective, to the entirety of the relation of man to the world.

The Canticle of Creatures. After the *imitatio Christi* (rule of the Gospel) and the nudity of the flesh (trial), the third and last trait of the "language of the flesh" in Franciscan spirituality is the praise of creation (*Canticle of Creatures*). The *Canticle* has certainly been well examined, but most authors, lacking theological good sense, tend facilely to draw it toward a kind of paganism. We would be wrong to see it as a simple ode to creatures, as if it were sufficient to shine a little divine light on them to make them worthy of praise. It therefore does not suffice to reduce, as Max Scheler did in his phenomenological commentary on the *Canticle*, the predications of Francis to a "continued incarnation of God the Father in nature and its continued vivification by God" because of his "sympathy for the world." To argue that the saint "would have introduced into his account a good dose of pantheism" if he had himself to exegete the song, appears at the very least to contradict the first ambition of this praise itself.[16] This song is not a Canticle of Creatures as much as a Canticle to the Creator. And if it is a matter of understanding its title (*Il Cantico di Fratre Sole/Cantico delle Creature*), the canticle *of* creatures invites them, subjectively, to praise the Creator (subjective genitive) rather than objectively praising other creatures (objective genitive). This observation is important, for otherwise we would soon be interpreting the poem in a pantheistic or numinous sense which does not fit it: such exegeses are all too common and if sometimes more attractive they are also more superficial than the straightforward reading of the text.

The succession of praises suffices to indicate the purpose of the canticle: "Praised are you my Lord, *with* every creature, especially my lord *brother* sun . . . for *sister* moon and the stars . . . for *brother* wind and the air and clouds . . . for *sister* water, for *brother* fire . . . for *sister our mother* earth."[17] Let us retain three traits that make the Franciscan vision a mode of the "flesh of the world." (a) First: the exhortation invokes the Lord "with" his creatures. Its addressee is therefore clear. The *Canticle of Creatures* does not praise the creatures, but the Creator, on whom they depend. (b) Second: the appellation of the creatures always carries with it the patronymic of "brother" (*fratello*) or "sister" (*sorella*). Such is already the sign if not the proof that the song does not first concern the creatures but rather the Father from whom they come. Much like Francis becoming the "spiritual son" of the Father of heaven by breaking with his "carnal father," the creatures are called to recognize the paternity of God from whom they receive their filiality, and thanks to whom they receive a fraternity among themselves. We do not praise the sun for its own sake, even though it is the source of light and energy that enlightens and warms men—no more than we praise water because it fecundates the earth. Only *because* the Father is the origin of the light of the sun is it necessary to praise him *for it* (rather than her), and only *because* he is the source of the fecundity of the earth is it fitting to recognize *him* as the one who quenches our thirst (rather than her). Scheler's "sympathies of nature" are not able to be understood apart from Bonaventure's "creative Trinity" by whom all things are given to the world. Saint Bonaventure's exegesis of the intuition of Francis is not wrong in the interpretation it gives precisely to this dependence of creatures on the Creator as to their sole principle, that is, the Father in his fontal plenitude: "By means of *climbing up to the first Origin* of all things, Francis conceived for them all an overflowing friendship, and called even the smallest creatures *brother* and *sister*, for he knew that *they, along with himself, flow together from the same unique principle*."[18] (c) Third: the paradoxical formula of "sister our mother earth" accomplishes the conferral of a Trinitarian design, rather than one merely numinous, on the *Canticle of Creatures*. Irenaeus's interpretation of the Adamic narrative and the Greco-Latin tradition certainly teach us the "maternity" of the earth. The "dirt" of the second narrative of the creation of Adam in Genesis, like the "*chôra*" of the *Timaeus* of Plato, serves as a "matrix" for our engenderment. Thus Plato: "The mother and receptacle (*chôra*) . . . [is] an invisible and characterless sort of thing, one that receives all things and shares in a most perplexing way in what is intelligible, a thing extremely difficult to comprehend."[19] The Christian vision, however, is totally other, neither merely Jewish (Genesis) nor completely Greek (*Timaeus*). Our "mother earth" becomes "sister," as Saint Francis says so well, in that this earth from which we are formed also depends on another whose unique paternity we come to recognize. The Trinitarian filiation of all creatures from the Father includes even our mother earth. Cosmic fraternity springs up all the more for all creatures as they recognize together their common and unique origin, which is the Father of heaven (more than it is our mother the earth): "Seeing in nature a mother is to find only a stepmother. Nature is not our mother but our sister: such was in this regard the major affirmation of Christianity."[20] So says Chesterton, justly, concerning Saint Francis.

The necessity of a personalizing and sanctifying, that is, Trinitarian interpretation as opposed to an anonymous and sacralizing and therefore ontologically neutral interpretation of the *Canticle* is therefore proposed by the very letter of the text. Fraternity comes solely from a shared filiality, and thus "cosmic" and "sympathetic" nature cannot be understood independently of Trinitarian donation. It follows that an apophatic reading of the *Canticle* likewise has no place. Bonaventure, along with his inspiration, Saint Francis, is not Denys the Areopagite. The latter's negative theology can only be juxtaposed here with the cataphatic theology of the former. The Franciscan does not overcome creatures in order to reach God in his nudity, but rather recognizes, on the contrary, *in* creatures themselves, and their ways of being in the world, the best means of living and seeing the ways of God's being itself. Such is accomplished by "transfer of language" or "metaphors." Thus Bonaventure in his *Commentary on the Sentences*: "With the praise of God in view, it is necessary to make recourse to metaphor [*translatio*]. Since in fact God is well worthy of praise, and so that praise does not cease from lack of words, Holy Scripture has taught us to transfer the names of creatures toward God."[21] The beginning of Francis's *Canticle* affirms nothing else, but invokes the impossibility of the direct nomination of God, not in order to renounce speaking to him, but rather to make possible his decipherment through his creatures who reflect and reveal him: "To you alone are praise, honor and glory worthy, O Most High, and *no man is worthy to speak your name* . . . Be praised *my Lord with all your creatures*."[22]

By analogy with the phenomenology of Merleau-Ponty, here the flesh completely overflows the sole corporeal being of man to which philosophy had up to this point been restrained. In Bonaventure's sense, it is not contradictory to speak of the "flesh of the world" for which the "book of the world" precedes the "book of Scripture."[23] In Franciscan praise, the believer enjoys such a familiarity with the world that the latter seems to speak to him, even to see him. The legend of the "wolf of Gubbio," when Francis "addresses him" and the wolf "acquiesces by the movements of his body," or for that matter his counsels to "his brother birds" that they silence their loud songs during the recitation of the Psalms—all these are not mere fabulous accounts of Franciscan mysticism. They speak to us of something that our contemporaries have mostly lost, namely, a sort of friendship with "this sensible universe of bodily things" understood as a "house built for man" (*domus homini fabricata*), to use Bonaventure's language, or the "arch-originary-earth" which does not move, to use Husserl's.[24] Merleau-Ponty emphasizes in a similar way that "science renounces dwelling in things inasmuch as it manipulates them." In light of the Franciscan experience, yet without simply repeating it, the present task is therefore to discover *a mode of inhabiting the world*, in which the latter no longer appears as a stranger, and a *cosmic fraternity*, in which the relations among creatures articulates their common dependence on the Creator. Much like the painter who "takes his body into the world in order that the world would change into painting," the creature, in the Franciscan vision of the world, *expresses* his Creator. Such is the extraordinary inversion of the act of seeing and of the visible, already lived mystically by Saint Francis in the *Canticle*, and rediscovered by phenomenology in Merleau-Ponty's meditation on the experience of the painter in *L'œil et l'esprit*: "Between the painter and the visible," he says, citing Paul Klee and André Marchand, "the roles are inevitably *reversed*. This is why painters have said that *the things see them* . . . : in a forest I have felt numerous times that it was not me who was looking at the forest. Some days I have felt that it was the trees who were looking *at me*, speaking *to me* . . . I was there, listening . . . I believe that the painter ought to be *transpierced by the universe* instead of simply endeavoring to transpierce it . . . I expect to be interiorly submerged, *buried*. Perhaps I paint in order *to rise back up*."[25]

Saint Dominic, or The Flesh of Language

From the descriptive reading of the Franciscan experience of the body enlarged to the dimensions of the world it is necessary to distinguish the Dominican experience of language proper to the Order of Preachers. Here phenomenology becomes hermeneutics, where interpretation means "making a proposition about the world such that I can inhabit it in order to project within it one of my most proper possibilities" (Ricoeur).[26] The mute experience of the body now enacts its distanciation through spoken discourse where textual significations take the place of corporeal kinestheses. Jean-René Bouchet emphasizes this in his exegesis of the Dominican experience: "Preaching is not a work for St. Dominic. It is a matter of creating a *manner of being* in the Church: being before God, being together, being in the world . . . Through the encounter of preaching on the basis of the key theme of the *vita apostolica*, the elements of canonical and monastic life take on a new tonality. They are harmonized in a new kind of life, a new manner of being that they seek to structure and support."[27] The preacher of grace (*praedicator gratiae*) and the grace of preaching is in fact the new mode of Christian being in the world instituted by the founder of the preachers.[28]

By analogy to *the itinerancy of the body*, two by two on the roads, as in the Franciscan mode of life, *the grace of the word*, first the exclusive privilege of the secular clergy, is suddenly introduced into the rule of the Dominicans: "Let it be known to all, now and in the future, that I, Bishop Foulques, by the grace of God humble minister of the See of Toulouse, do institute as preachers [*praedicatores*] in my diocese brother Dominic and his companions . . . Their regular program is to live like a monk, to go on foot and in evangelical poverty to preach the evangelical word."[29] To confer "order" onto speech—setting aside the pun—is immediately to dictate the order of finding one's body and even inhabiting a flesh. In other words, in a similar way as the flesh was instituted in language in Saint Francis, language or speech finds a flesh to assume a body in Saint Dominic. The three moments of this "flesh of language" or hermeneutics, implemented in the Dominican way are the sharing of the word, its use as a weapon to convert the heretic, and the work of language [*langue*; or tongue] conceived as an organ.

Sharing the Word. The gift of all his goods to the poor was the first gesture of Dominic that cast him into the mode of being of the beggar, which thus allowed him to discover the density of the world. Like Francis, who exchanged his belt for a cord, discarded his shoes, stick, pouch, and money and even dispossessed himself of his tunic in the trial at Assisi, Dominic "sold the books that he possessed, however truly indispensable, and all his personal effects. Making alms of everything, he will disperse his goods, giving them to the poor."[30] For the visibility of the *imitatio Christi* in a denuded flesh in Saint Francis, corresponds the sharing of a book as a "truly indispensable" gift in Saint Dominic, following the example of the widow "giving from out of her poverty" (Mk. 12:44). When the book was given, or abandoned, the word is shared and already inscribed on flesh. In order not to stay a dead letter, the text is first offered to the most poor, to the suffering and to beggars, to those whose disincarnate flesh says nothing other than the expectation of a word which will again "incarnate" them into existence.

The *sequela Christi* here becomes "preaching": we are no longer in the realm of the monastic life, allegedly rooted in the apostolic life (monastic orders), nor the marriage of the fool to Lady Poverty in order to accompany those for whom nothing remains but tears with which to cry (Franciscan order), but rather the office of preaching (*officium praedicationis*) in order to bring speech to the one who has lost it. Thus Paul's exhortation to Timothy becomes a leitmotif for Saint Dominic: "Proclaim the word, be ready in season and out of season; reprove, rebuke, exhort, always with passion and the desire to instruct" (2 Tim. 4:2). Poor here does not merely designate the one for whom material misery conceals spiritual ambitions. Impoverished of sane doctrine, the heretic on the contrary, has unfortunately raised up false speech, a word warped by the absence of flesh to welcome it, the insupportable bursting open of the one who perverts the meaning of the Word from within. Such will be the ultimate signification of the preaching of the Saint Dominic against the so-called pure Cathari.

The Weapon of Speech. The one is called pure (*katharos*) or perfect whose word is not incarnated in a flesh any longer: "The flesh is the work of Satan: he imprisons within it the spiritual element perpetuated by carnal generation born from concupiscence and which is fundamentally impure."[31] Speech remains without a flesh because desire no longer exists in the flesh of the one who utters it (sexual abstinence, condemnation of eating animal flesh, etc.). Against this perversion of the Gospel, only the word of preaching founded on sane doctrine furnishes the antidote. Hence the affair of Saint Dominic and the Catharist innkeeper in Toulouse (1203): "During the very night that they lodged in the city, the sub-prior (Dominic) attacked with force and passion the heretical host of the house, multiplying discussions and arguments meant to persuade him. The heretic could not resist the wisdom and the Spirit who was speaking: through the intervention of the divine Spirit, Dominic reduced him to faith."[32] Suddenly, in the play of words is found the goad of conversion. For the blows of the lance of the chevalier on crusade is replaced the argumentative assaults of the preacher. One menaces and kills, the other converts. One reaches the body (*Körper*), the other penetrates the flesh (*Leib*), ripping open like a wound a proper mode of being at the heart of the being of the world.

No more than genetic filiation suffices to translate the being in the world of Francis at the trial of Assisi, no more than the material weapon fits to express the profundity of the spiritual breakthrough: when the soldier gives up his vainglory, relinquishing bloodshed, the speech of the preacher is inscribed on the flesh and transforms it. It is thus a "more refined work to defend the faithful by spiritual arms [*spiritualibus armis*] against the errors propagated by the heretics," says Thomas Aquinas, "than by means of material arms" (*quam corporalibus armis*).[33] That which cultivates the flesh and determines a concrete emblem of a manner of being in the world as the proper sphere of belonging, is thus discovered implicitly in this incompressible residue of the act of speech. Like the deployment of the "world of the text which," according to Paul Ricoeur, "forms and transforms the reader's being-a-self in accordance with his or her intention,"[34] language takes on flesh in this predicational hand-to-hand combat [*corps à corps*] of the preacher and the heretic: a battle of language of which the single end is to defeat, through the formation and information of speech, the future believer in his last stages of resistance.

The Work of the Tongue (Langue). Since speech, in the preachers, chooses a body to be inscribed in an order for which the essential first consists in action and the promise associated with preaching, the question becomes: which works—or better, what works—(are) within this body? Neither the hands, as in the Benedictine modality, nor even the feet, as in Franciscan itinerancy, but rather the tongue [*langue*] in the proper sense of the term (*lingua*): "It still needs to be known that by manual work," states Thomas Aquinas, "we ought to understand every human industry that honestly assures our subsistence, whether they utilize the hands [*sive manibus operari*], the feet [*sive pedibus*], or the tongue [*sive lingua*]."[35] However surprising, the *tongue* [*langue*] for Saint Thomas (on this point a hermeneut of Saint Dominic and the Order of Preachers) is paradigmatically the "organ" by which a word [*parole*] is given and transmitted. Words [*les mots*] of language find in this organ their flesh, not simply in the sense of a pure emission of phonemes (*bodiliness* [*corporéité*]) but in the sense that, by its very articulation is transmitted an original meaning from the speaking to the hearing subject (living flesh [*corporalité*]).

Here the focus is no longer on the single act of language put in operation by the speaker, nor on the content of the message, but rather on the hearer himself established, for himself and in himself, as the formal object of the discourse perceptible to the ear. Aquinas adds: "The second object of teaching is found on the side of the discourse perceptible to the ear. And this object is the hearer himself" (*ipse audiens*).[36] The originality of this unique formula, even for the history of subsequent philosophy, ought to be clear. For the first time perhaps in the history of thought, a theory of the acts of language is conceptualized for which the act of "speaking" (or better, of "preaching") brings explicitly into view the "hearer himself," and specifically conceived as the perception of the discourse through the organ of his ear, rather than the simple content of the teaching. We are very far indeed from the mere birth of pedagogy or even a repetition of ancient sophism (as if he were really talking about the necessity always to adapt the discourse to the addressee). What is discovered here in Thomas's consideration of the hearer as the formal object or category of discourse is the locus of a veritable reflection on intersubjectivity (as we will see below in chap. 8), namely, the consideration of a truth "to transmit" rather than merely "to contemplate" and "to communicate" rather than "to keep within oneself." Thus he famously emphasizes that "it is more fitting to illuminate than it is simply to shine [*maius est illuminare quam lucere solum*], in the same way that it is more fitting to transmit to others what one contemplates [*sicut enim ita maius est contemplata aliis tradere*] than it is simply to contemplate in itself [*quam solum contemplari*]."[37]

The discourse of the preacher, being thus addressed to the heretic with his conversion in view, therefore makes of the other (the heretic) the recipient of a discourse for which the category of the dumbfounded interlocutor [*interlocuteur interloqué*] dominates over the very object of the interlocution itself. To see this from the light of another context (and to avoid confusion), namely, Ricoeur's critique of Rudolf Bultmann's view that the evangelical kerygma is simply the occasion for an existential decision of the believer: in the same way the act of speech in Dominic is not merely the pretext for the transformation of the heretic. On the contrary—and to return to the Dominican mode of being as "preacher"—as soon as the organ of language articulates some words (*corps*) in order thus to give to them a meaning [*sens*] (*chair*) for which the hearer himself is the object (*ipse audiens*), the word [*parole*] itself and it alone produces its work in the interlocutor and converts the heretic. We can distinguish here two thresholds of comprehension, in contemporary hermeneutics (Ricoeur) as much as in Dominican preaching (Aquinas): "There is meaning (what the text says) and there is signification (what the text says to me) which is the moment of repetition of the meaning by the reader." In the same way that "the moment of exegesis is not that of an existential decision, but that of 'meaning,' "[38] the moment of preaching is not that of the consideration of a *statement* [*énoncé*] but rather the manifestation of a situation of the *act of stating* [*énonciation*] (relation of two interlocutors for which the transformation by the discourse takes precedence over the very object of the discourse).[39] Language finds its flesh in this conversion of the heart. This is a flesh for which the proper manner of being in the world consists in uttering a word [*parole*] through which the logos produces its "transforming effect" by means of the very One who is Logos and Word. When language takes on flesh, the flesh becomes language. Such is a strange return which always makes of the dumbfounded believer the receiver [*interloqué*] of this Interlocutor who as it were expresses nothing but himself, at once the flesh of language and the language of flesh: "In the beginning was the Word and the Word was with God and the Word was God. He was in the beginning with God . . . And the Word became flesh and dwelt among us" (Jn. 1:1, 14).

As *language of the flesh* or *flesh of language*, the world is thus a "book" to be deciphered (as we will shortly see) for both Franciscan and Dominican modes of spirituality, both of which inherited a Victorine thematic of the *liber scriptus intus et foris*: "There are two books," says Bonaventure, with reference to the Apocalypse (5:1) and citing Hugh of Saint Victor, "or better, there are two readings of the same book [*duplex est liber*], one writes interiorly [*intus*], which is the art and eternal wisdom of God, and the other writes exteriorly [*foris*], which is the sensible world." But in both cases, whether as the eternal wisdom delivered by the Scriptures (*liber scripturae*) or the sensible world unveiled by creatures (*liber mundi*), it is *one and the same book* that is read—neither only text (hermeneutics) nor merely flesh (phenomenology); rather the "Word made flesh" writes *within by his speech* (Word) and *without by his incarnation* (flesh): "Because the eternal wisdom and his work is found reunited in the one person Christ, he is called the *written book without and within* [*liber scriptus et foris*] for the salvation of the world."[40]

Responding to the vacuity of a word without flesh (hermeneutics without phenomenology) as to the blindness of a flesh without word (phenomenology without hermeneutics), the sudden appearance of the Word made flesh unites together and originally the two main lines of contemporary philosophy. *Flesh of language* and *language of flesh* (book of the world and world of the book), the two modes of being in the world, are thus held in an ultimate recapitulation about which theology teaches that the Word is never seen without a body, nor is the body expressed without speech. The incarnation of the Son is therefore not only an experience of the past, according to Bonaventure, even if the Ascension and the closure of the canon would mark the rupture. The doctrine of the spiritual senses and the philosophical interpretation of the stigmata of Saint Francis lead us to think otherwise—and phenomenologically—the carnal relation of man to God. "The Franciscan mystery is the center that crystallizes all" (Balthasar),[41] the spiritual experience of brother Francis leads back to the heart of Christianity in the mystery of the incarnation—an incarnation, not of the Word alone, but also of man "*tout court*," sanctified in his encounter [*corps à corps*] with the Word made flesh.

From Symbol to the Spiritual Senses

It is too little known that after Origen but before Ignatius of Loyola, Bonaventure, the exegete of Saint Francis, developed the doctrine of the "spiritual senses." Here we are not under the regime of concepts. The *spiritual senses* indicate the entirety of the human person that is summoned forth in order to manifest God. Rather than simply "understanding," they first have to do with "seeing"—in the precise sense of seeing "how" (*quomodo*) God is given and reflected through his love in human flesh. Saints and men of God in general reflect by their countenance the "mystery of charity." Saint Francis of Assisi himself bore the carnal marks in his body (holes in his feet and hands and a pierced heart). Here, by way of the carnal experience of the divine, is established a new relation to God, to the body and to the world in general—a relation to which the Christian seems to be called by the voice of the incarnate and resurrected Word. This Merleau-Ponty said in such a penetratingly astute way: "Christianity is, among other things, the recognition of a mystery . . . which rightly holds that the *Christian God does not want a vertical relation of subordination* . . . Christ attests that God would not fully be God without wedding himself to the *human condition* . . . Transcendence *no longer hangs ominously* over man: he becomes strangely the *privileged bearer* of it."[42] Something similar goes for the Franciscan mystery, for which the "symbolic vision of the world" and the doctrine of the "spiritual senses" (Bonaventure) provide a philosophical framework and serve as the theological content for the sake of a proper understanding of the "experience of the stigmata" of Saint Francis.

The Density of the Symbol

The Symbolic, or the Good Use of the Sensible. Inherited from Denys the Areopagite, the Bonaventurian definition of symbolic theology remains to this day forgotten, to say the least: "By the symbolic mode of theology [*per modum symbolicam theologiae*] we learn the good use of sensible things [*recte utamur sensibilibus*]."[43] Here distinguished from "speculative" theology (the good use of the intelligible) and from "mystical" theology (raptures and transports of the spirit), the "symbol" in Bonaventure (Greek: *sumbolon*) does not simply designate a "sign of recognition" or the "relation of a signifier to other signifiers" (E. Ortigues).[44] On the contrary, it marks a *certain manner of relating to the sensible world* "in a mirror" (*in speculum*), "through creatures" (*per creaturas*), and "in creatures" (*in creaturis*), so that they are "vestiges" (*vestigia*) by which God is seen dwelling and remaining with them: "Starting from the grandeur and beauty of creatures, the Creator can become known," says the Book of Wisdom (13:5), heavily commented on by Bonaventure.[45] The "vestige" here, in the Franciscan doctor in particular, is not merely a "trace" of an absent God toward whom one must climb (Augustinian perspective), but rather the "icon" of a God who is present and on whom it is necessary to alight (Bonaventurian perspective). The density of the sensible for Bonaventure is of such a kind that it expresses something of God himself, and the modes of being of the world are also the modes of being of God himself inasmuch as he espouses even our sensations in his incarnation: "To be a vestige," says Trophime Mouiren on Bonaventure, "is not an accidental feature of any creature, something added by the piety of our regard; it is the very being of the thing, its manner of being, of being tied and dependent and reflecting."[46] Despite the loss of the Dionysian manuscript, Bonaventure appears here as the true inheritor of the *Symbolic Theology* of the Areopagite—though let us recall that the conservation of this text alone would have probably changed our conception of the figure of Denys as much as, perhaps, the entire history of Western thought. And let us see this text less as the inheritor of Neoplatonism and more the operator of its transformation at the heart of Christianity. Thus the Areopagite indicates at the heart of his *Mystical Theology* that "in my *Symbolic Theology*, I have discussed analogies of God drawn from what we perceive. I have spoken of images we have of him, of the forms, figures, and instruments proper to him, of the places in which he lives and the ornaments he wears. I have spoken of his anger, grief, and rage, of how he is said to be drunk and hung over, of his oaths and curses, of his sleeping and waking, and indeed of all those images we have of him, images shaped by the workings of the symbolic representations of God."[47]

The interpretation of Denys often loses its way in the clouds of divine ineffability, to the point of leaving, as much as possible, human sensibility. Things are completely otherwise under the impetus of the "symbolic," which designates neither the flight into "speculation" nor the élan of the "mystical," but rather the act by which the "holiness" of God *takes shape*, namely, by forms (parts, organs), location (and adornments), affects (anger, sadness, enthusiasm, intoxication), even kinestheses (sleep, vigilance). As the inheritor of Denys's symbolic theology, Bonaventure's conception of the relation of the sensible and intelligible is not a simple "correspondence" or "recognition," as if it were a matter of the relation between some tesserae artificially disjoined and reunited with each other, but rather involves the covenant or carnal espousal as "metonymies of the sensible to the divine" which see in the smallest part of the lived experience of man something of the total presence of God himself. The "symbol" (*sum-bolon*) certainly reunites, contrary to the diabolical (*dia-bolon*), as we will shortly see. The act of union is not content with a simple formal "analogy" of worlds. The "conformity of worlds" (microcosmos/macrocosmos) occurs in such a way that one does not have to overcome the sensible in order to pass to the intelligible. Rather, one discovers "in" (*in*) and "through" (*per*) the sensible itself whereof to read and decipher the presence of the intelligible: "At each degree, one can discover God through his mirror [*per speculum*] or in his mirror [*in speculo*]."[48] Creatures here are not conceived as beings in an ontic gap inadequate to Bonaventurian symbolism, but rather as "modes of being" of God starting from the "condition of creatures" (*conditionem creaturum*), considered as a "testimony" (*testimonium*) of his grandeur in his abasement.[49] The sensible therefore "signifies" God himself, revealing his presence (icon) rather than returning to him in the mode of absence (trace). The "vestige" (*vestigium*) no longer witnesses simply to the "past" and "passage" of God in creation in a totally Platonic way, but in itself retains *for those who know how to see him there*, the One who today still passes through and remains. The always secondary attempt in Augustine of "detecting, if we are able [*si possumus*], in the exterior man some vestige of the Trinity [*qualecumque vestigium Trinitatis*]," becomes in Bonaventure the first ambition: "Being a vestige [*esse vestigium*] is not an accidental feature of any creature [*nulli accidit creaturae*]" (II *Sent.* 16).[50] If Augustine sees the necessary modification of Platonism in the framework of the Christian vision of creation (though without accomplishing it)—"I have read the books of the Platonists . . . but that *the Word was made flesh and dwelt among us*, I did not read there"[51]—then Bonaventure accomplishes it by annulling the separation of worlds by making the sensible the very symbolic support of the full Trinitarian manifestation of God. Hans Urs von Balthasar noted this break, which discloses the *carnal originality* of Bonaventure's thought: "The Trinity is not (as for Denys) the absolutely separated and unknowable, nor (as for Augustine) is everything in the world that speaks of the divine Persons mere appropriation. Rather, the Trinity is truly revealed in its overflow into the world (in creation and the Incarnation of Christ), and shows itself thereby to be the a priori ground of everything that exists in the world."[52]

With this rediscovery of the "symbolic" as "good use" (*recte utamur*) of the sensible in Bonaventure, contemporary sacramental theology would have much to gain from a reinterrogation of the patristic and medieval corpus—a way, to say the least, of giving flesh to the symbol. Recent sacramental theology has an all too worn-out concept of the "recognition" of the sign and thing through the metaphor of tesserae (as signs of recognition between two parties or tribes) that no longer offers an illuminative conceptualization. Despite the necessary structure of the return of the "sign" (*signum*) to "thing" (*res*) in the sacrament, the symbolic theology still remains locked in an escape from the sensible, as opposed to a real consideration of the body which it is prohibited to surpass. Witness Maurice Blanchot, who offers a definition of the symbol that still awaits a theological appropriation: "The symbol signifies nothing, expresses nothing. It simply renders *present*—in *rendering us present to it*. It is a reality that escapes any derequisition and seems to rise up, there, prodigiously close and prodigiously far, like a foreign presence . . . The symbol, so it is a *wall*; then it is a wall, which, far from being opened, becomes not only more opaque, but of a depth and density, of a reality so powerful and exorbitant that it modifies us ourselves . . . Every symbol is an *experience*, a radical changing that is necessary to be lived, a leap that is necessary to be accomplished. There is therefore no such thing as a symbol, but rather a *symbolic experience*."[53]

Reading the Book. But to affirm and to acknowledge [*reconnaître*] the iconic presence of God in creatures does not suffice to know [*reconnaître*] him there. It is in fact f*or those who know how to see him there*, as we mentioned above in a formula that must be taken at face value, that the Trinity comes to light through (*per*) and in (*in*) the "vestiges" set up as so many "mirrors" (*speculum*). Those who know how to see are not content with sensible things themselves, however admirable they truly are in their beauty and radiance. The believer will first strive *to convert the senses* in order to make of his "gaze" the place of transformation by the intentional aim of God, and not the simple organ of a seeing so overwhelming that it bypasses any junction with the visible. The intentional aim of the subject who sees matters as much as the eye by which things are seen—all the more so in the Seraphic Doctor. The modality of the gaze (*aspectus*) prevails over the organ of vision (*oculus*) as well as that which is seen (*res*): "In accord with this triple approach," insists Bonaventure, "our soul exercises three principal gazes [*aspectus*]: the first onto exterior bodies . . . , the second in itself and on itself . . . , the third on the transcendent." With this Bonaventurian triad (*sensualitas*, *spiritus*, *mens*), Henry Duméry comments, "we are *not dealing with faculties in the substantialist sense*, but rather with access, gazes, functions."[54] Here the symbolic depends on the interpreting subject, and not simply on the interpreted object—with this reservation: the density of the sensible is due to the depth of the "vestige," and it is not sufficient to see God mentally in the thing in order to recognize him there.

In order to admire truly the beauty of creatures it is fitting to decipher the beauty of God himself in them. The break between Erigenian theophany (chap. 2) and Bonaventurian conversion of the senses (chap. 6) comes about through the hermeneutics implemented by Bonaventure that is totally absent in Erigena. If Erigena looks at the world starting from the light that glows in its interior—at the risk of sinking out of a truly Trinitarian deployment into a faulty pantheism, then Bonaventure articulates [*decline*] an authentic discourse on method for the sole purpose of deciphering the book of creation—and the Trinity itself as the key to its decryption. As already established, in the Franciscan and Dominican spiritualities, the world is a *book* to be decoded: the language of the flesh on the Franciscan side (descriptive phenomenology), and the flesh of language on the Dominican side (hermeneutics). Yet a *literacy* is necessary so that the conversion of the senses is also, in the first place a transformation of the self: "The totality of this sensible world like a book [*quasi quidam liber*] written by the hand of God." So says Hugh of Saint Victor, repeated by Bonaventure. He continues, "If an illiterate [*illetaratus*] sees an open book, he sees the figures [*figures aspicit*] but does not recognize the letters [*litteras non cognoscit*] . . . Whereas the sot [*insipiens*] only admires the appearance, the sage [*sapiens*] is well down the path of the unfathomable thought of the divine wisdom. It is as if both had a single and same writing before their eyes [*una eademque Scriptura*] and one admired the color and formation of the figures [*colorem seu formationem figuram*] while the other appreciated the meaning and signification [*sensum et significationem*]."[55] From within the "heart of medieval life" (supra) something similar pertains to the admiration of God in the works of creation as for the difference between the lay brother and the educated brother. Whereas the first sees the works as letters on parchment but cannot manage to decipher the presence of God, the second traverses the materiality of the letter in order to discover the spirit and find its signification. God wrote this world with "his own finger" (*digito Dei*), but he demands that we learn the codes in order to discover him there, just as one passes through the act of reading the letter in order to find the meaning. Precisely because we have lost the sense while reading the "book of the world" (*liber mundi*) by virtue of sin, we were given the "book of Scripture" (*liber Scripturae*) as a kind of textual intermediary by which we discover life anew. Therefore, hermeneutics, for Bonaventure the successor of Hugh, is only an act of reading the text (Ricoeur) in a secondary sense. First it is a modality of factical life of the believer or of man *tout court* (Heidegger) in the sense that the lived experience of being in the world precedes the reading animal and founds it through and through. In Bonaventure as much as in Heidegger, the world is first read in order to find one's life there (and God's), and it is only then that one receives the scriptures in order to learn anew how to decipher it. Thus Bonaventure says in a famous passage from the *Hexaemeron*: "When man fell and had lost knowledge there was no one to take him back to God . . . This book [*iste liber*], that is, the world [*scilicet mundus*], was dead and erased. This is why another book [*alius liber*] was necessary by which man was illumined in order to interpret the metaphors of things [*metaphoras rerum*]. This book is the Scripture [*autem liber est Scripturae*]."[56]

Exterior Sense and Interior Sense. Without returning to the Bonaventurian use of metaphor, largely developed elsewhere,[57] we can note here that the conversion of the senses, like the reading of the text, merits an apprenticeship, or better, a kind of *metanoia*. What we read matters less than our "manner of living." The "art of reading" or the *Didascalion* does not, in this sense, properly belong to the Victorine school (Hugh), but rather passes into and is transformed by the Franciscan school (Bonaventure) which makes of the "art of reading" (*ordo legendi*) an "art of living" (*ordo vivendi*), and now expects even the possible conversion of the senses themselves. I maintained above that Christ, as a "book written within and without" (*liber scriptus intus et foris*), holds together descriptive phenomenology (flesh) and hermeneutics (word); now he is addressed in the "interior sense" in the contemplation of the divinity of the incarnate Word (*sensus interior*) as in the "exterior sense" in the consideration of his humanity (*sensus exterior*): "God was in fact made man in order to render the whole man blessed in him [*totum hominem*], so that, whether he goes in or comes out he finds pasture in his Creator: an external pasture in the flesh of the Savior [*pascua foris in carne salvatoris*], an internal pasture in the divinity of the Creator [*et pascua intus in divinitate creatoris*]."[58] The assumption of the responsibility of "humanity in its totality" certainly belongs to the theology of Irenaeus (chap. 4) and its assumption by Christ in his flesh to Tertullian (chap. 5), but the divine-human encounter [*corps à corps*] in the apprehension of the "sensible" of God marks the uniqueness of Bonaventure's approach (chap. 6). What was given in Adam (Irenaeus) and partaken of by

Christ (Tertullian) is now offered to the believer in order that he also share in the experience (Bonaventure) of a divine-human body of which the doctrine of the spiritual senses marks the most exemplary formulation.

The Spiritual Senses

A famous passage from Bonaventure's *Breviloquium* defines the "spiritual senses" (*sensus spirituales*) as "mental perceptions of contemplated truth" (*perceptiones mentales circa veritatem contemplandam*).[59] The only justification Bonaventure gives for this definition is its effectiveness starting from the experience of the prophets and other righteous people (Moses and the burning bush, Elijah and the chariot of fire, Jacob's ladder, etc.).[60] It is as if the aforementioned "doctrine of the spiritual senses," because it is disclosed through figures which bear its trace, paradoxically unfolds its true meaning beyond all "doctrine." Just as each sense in its own way sees, feels, understands, smells, and tastes—as we will see below—so also does the definition of the spiritual senses show that even that which lives physically is capable of being spiritually converted. The spiritual senses are "perceptions" and always remain such, yet in such a way that they are transformed in their own way of approaching the world, and rendered "mental" or converted into spirit, hence *perceptiones mentales*. The same goes for a number of "other righteous people," for example, brother Francis who "heard," in the call of the Crucifix of Saint Damien (1206), "with the ears of flesh [*ad eum corporeis audivit auribus*], a voice from the crucifix telling him three times: 'Francis go and repair my house which has fallen into ruin.' "[61] It goes without saying that this does not mean that Francis heard a voice, but rather that what is lived spiritually is received carnally at the same time, or "like" the mode of ordinary hearing but converted in God. The realism of the incarnation imposes the thought of an encounter [*corps à corps*] of man and God even today.

Let us not be mistaken, however. Whether one is a prophet or among the righteous, or even a founding brother of a new monastic order, even if by contemplation one is elevated by "degrees" (*gradibus*), as on "the ladder of Jacob the summit of which touches heaven or on the throne of Solomon,"[62] his feet never leave the firm earth. The erected scaffolding, otherwise, would risk becoming yet another tower of Babel: "The mental perception of contemplated truth," says Balthasar, "possesses *nothing of the intellectual*. It remains from beginning to end *perception*, even in its supreme elevation."[63] Does this mean that it is a matter here of a *bodily perception* of God? We can affirm this to the degree that God is given to perception in a body, even multiple bodies (word, Eucharist, brother . . .). Yet we must oppose it to the degree that these senses that perceive God are not, properly speaking, the bodily senses but the spiritual senses "after the manner" of the bodily senses. To understand their relation to one another we must approach them starting from the experience of the "bodily senses" themselves.

Analogy and Conformity. In his numerous "reductions" or "renewals" [*reconductions*] (*reductions*) of knowledge to God or to theology (*De reductione artium ad theologiam*), Bonaventure begins by *extending* [*reconduire*] "the illumination of sensible knowledge" (*illuminatio cognitionis sensitivae*) to the "senses of the heart" (*sensum cordis*): "Each sense avidly seeks the sensible domain proper to it; it finds it with joy and returns there without flagging . . . In the same way [*per hunc etiam modum*] the senses of our heart ought to be put in quest of that which is beautiful, harmonious, of good odor, sweet to the taste or soft to touch, discovering it with joy and searching for it without ceasing. Behold the way [*ecce quomodo*] that sensible knowledge contains the divine wisdom in a hidden form; see also the marvelous contemplation of the five spiritual senses [*quinque sensuum spiritualium*] in their conformity to the five bodily senses [*secundum conformitatem ad sensus corporales*]."[64] There is not only analogy between the bodily and spiritual senses (*analogia* as identity of relations), but also conformity (*conformitas*).

(a) First "analogy": in "the same way" (*per hunc etiam modum*) that the bodily senses are put in quest of their proper object (for example, vision desiring that which is pleasing to the eye), the sense of the heart desires what is fitting to its nature (for example, prudence or temperance): hearing and spiritual vision accord with the uncreated Word, smell to the inspired Word, taste and touch to the incarnate Word: "By faith does the soul believe in Christ as the uncreated Word, the Word and splendor of the Father, it recovers then spiritual hearing and sight [*spiritualem auditum et visum*]; hearing receives the teachings of Christ, sight contemplates the splendors of his light. By faith does it catch the scent of the coming of the inspired Word: desire and fervor give off the spiritual odor [*spiritualem olfactum*]. Finally, by love it embraces the incarnate Word, from whom it draws delights and which cause it to pass into him in an ecstasy of love: it finds spiritual touch and taste [*spiritualem gustum et tactum*]."[65] The *ordo vivendi* of the bodily senses serves as the normative regulative principle of the *ordo vivendi* of the spiritual senses. Said otherwise, by learning to direct our gaze onto the light which illumines the world or onto the uncreated Word who illumines our heart, our sight (*visum*), whether carnal or spiritual, will be refined in order to see God in all things. In practicing the taste of the perfume of honey (*gustum*) and touching the softness of things (*tactum*), that is, in a very Franciscan attitude, our taste and touch, both carnal and spiritual, will, as it were, come to their senses regarding the Word incarnate. "In the same way as each sense exercises its activity on its proper object, avoiding what is harmful to it, not annexing what is foreign to it, so also [*per hunc modum*] does the sense of the heart lead a well-regulated life when it acts in relation to its own object, combating negligence, etc."[66] The analogy between the bodily and spiritual senses is here brought to completion, so that "if we consider the activity of the senses, we will see a rule of life" (*intuebimur ibi ordinem vivendi*).[67]

(b) There is a "conformity" (*conformitas*) of the "bodily senses" to the "spiritual senses," which goes beyond an identity of relations (*analogia*) between them (*per hunc etiam modum*), and reaches a structure of resemblance, even of "interweaving," which largely overcomes the borders fixed by analogy. Since Aristotle it was common to think a relation of correspondence or "relational ratio" [*rapport de rapport*] (*ana-logia*) of the external senses to the internal senses.[68] However, in Bonaventure's terms, rooted in the perspective of a new ontology of creation of Christianity, the simple "correspondence of lived experiences" becomes "the conformity of worlds" inasmuch as the sensible world is structurally related to the soul or intellectual world, through a relation brought about by the transforming power of God himself to create the passage from the external senses to the internal: "The sensible world or macrocosm [*macrocosmus*] penetrates [*intrat*] into the soul or microcosm [*microcosmus*] by the gate of the five senses," which, as we will shortly see, is otherwise named the cross. We are thus rendered fit "to see God [*contemplandum Deum*] in any creature that enters into our spirit [*ad mentem nostram intrant*] by the bodily senses [*per corporales sensus*]."[69]

A Divine Sensorium. The identity of the form or structure (*con-formitas*) between the bodily and spiritual senses is absolute. Just as for the bodily senses certain objects or qualities correspond to their proper activity (color for sight, sound for hearing, flavor for taste, etc.), so also for the spiritual senses a certain manner of approach to the same object will be attributed to each. A true "divine sensorium" (Balthasar) is put in place,[70] not only to read the presence of the Trinity at the heart of things (*Canticle of Creatures*), but also to experience carnally the Word in the deepest depths of our sensations (doctrine of the spiritual senses). That which serves as the guiding question of this work, which was "from the beginning" (*ab initio*), according to Saint John—"that which we have heard [*audivimus*], which we have seen with our eyes [*vidimus oculis nostris*], which we have contemplated [*perspeximus*], and which our hands have touched [*manus nostrae contrectaverunt*] concerning the Word of life" (Jn. 1:1)—will not remain a dead letter in Bonaventure, nor will it be reserved to the exclusive apostolic succession. A sensible apprehension of God is also offered to the believer today, albeit in a distinct manner altogether rooted in a true *conversion of the senses*. Of course, a corporeal and tangible experience of the incarnate Word after the manner of the first disciples is absurd. But the absence in material body does not prohibit the presence of a phenomenal flesh, as we will see below. We can even say that precisely because the materiality of his body does not appear as such that his spiritual flesh is given today to be seen and apprehended. The resurrection is the condition for a new apprehension of the incarnation, so that what was "from the beginning" (*ab initio*) is given today in a continued fashion, if we are made capable of receiving it. The converted senses, the bodily senses transformed into spiritual ones, comprehend the incarnate and resurrected

Word in another mode than the apostles, though not without some likeness. Thus says Hans Urs von Balthasar, rightly: "In his plight and guilt, our fellow-man as we encounter him is in every case our neighbor, and this neighbor of man's is Christ. In his neighbor man encounters his Redeemer with all his bodily senses, in just as concrete, unprecedented and archetypal a manner as the Apostles when they 'found the Messiah'" (Jn. 1:41).[71] Seeing God in one's brother, tasting him in the Eucharist, hearing him in his Word, touching him in prayer, and smelling him in the aroma of incense, are all so many ways of putting the senses and thus the "entire man" (*totum hominem*) in the service of the sensible appearance of God. That which is no longer possible, namely, a material comprehension of the body of God, of which Tertullian worked to show the "solidity" (chap. 5), nevertheless remains for us today under another form: our "converted flesh" or our bodily senses transformed into spiritual ones.

After Origen and before Ignatius of Loyola, a capital text of the *Breviloquium* makes of the continued apprehension of the Word by the senses the very place of the lived experience of faith, for *fidelity to the flesh* is the unique identity proper to the Christian message: "When man possesses the spiritual senses [*sensus spirituales*], he sees [*videtur*] the supreme beauty of Christ under the aspect of his Splendor [*Splendoris*], he hears [*auditur*] the sovereign harmony under the aspect of the Word [*Verbi*], he tastes [*gustatur*] the sovereign sweetness under the aspect of Wisdom [*Sapientiae*] . . . , he smells [*odoratur*] the sovereign scent under the aspect of the Word inspired in the heart [*Verbi inspirati in corde*], and he embraces [*astringitur*] the sovereign sweetness under the aspect of the incarnate Word [*Verbi incarnati*]."[72] Seeing the splendor of Christ, hearing his Word, tasting his wisdom, smelling his inspiration and touching his incarnation are so many acts or modalities of apprehension of God which pertain to the ordinary Christian life. To say, with Karl Rahner, that "there is something artificial about wanting to discover for each sense a particular object, a special *ratio* by which it attains the Word," is to fail to recognize that the integration of the totality of the human senses to the apprehension of the uncreated, inspired and incarnate Word touches, as it were, on the essential.[73] The Pauline imperative of a plenitude of the divinity of Christ dwelling "bodily" (*sômatikos*) in us (Col. 2:9) ought here to be taken literally. In the sensible apprehension of God we do not flee earth for heaven, nor do we just classify different manners of human relation to the divine. On the contrary, we are here immersed all the more in the "sensual" in order there to read the presence of the "spiritual." In this "sinking-burying"[*enfoncement-emfouissement*] the truth of the incarnation in its kenosis is articulated, as well as of the Resurrection in its manifestation. Even today we can see and hear the uncreated Word (*videre et audire*), smell the inspired Word (*odorare*), taste and touch the incarnate Word (*gustare et astringere*), if we make a gift of our own senses to God so that he can form them together with our desire to know the one who first transformed or converted us: "The spiritual senses absolutely do not constitute a second and more elevated power beyond the physical senses . . . rather, by them the Christian definitively acquires his Christian senses which, of course, are *none 'other' than* the bodily senses, but *these senses insofar as* they have been formed according to the form of Christ."[74]

It is still necessary to be made fit for such a conversion or conformation. Otherwise said, it is not sufficient to be attached to terrestrial things in order to enter into the "sensation of the divine." The sensible sometimes lends itself to the sensational, which forgets its necessary metamorphosis. The conformation of the "bodily senses" to the "spiritual senses," however radical, does not lead to their fusion, and even less their confusion. Thus it is necessary to distinguish what we have considered up to this point in a unified structure apart from its content: the bodily senses on one side and the spiritual senses on the other. A poor use of the sensible—what we will call "diabolical"—corresponds to the good use of the sensible, or the "symbolical." It is possible that one could be incapable of reading God in creatures and of apprehending the Word according to a converted use of the senses. In this case, though in this case alone, sensation more than imagination becomes the "mistress of error and falsehood," only worthy of distrust.

The Diabolical, or the Bad Use of the Sensible. Let us be careful here. One's attachment to the senses does not work without a conversion of the senses—otherwise one courts the opposite risk of confounding the sensible apprehension of God with the sensory enjoyment [*jouissance*] of things. The spiritualism of the doctrine of the spiritual senses, without ever leaving sensation (as I have already indicated), is not equated with the hedonistic possession of beings. If the doctrine of the spiritual senses gives way to the "metaphysical Desire which tends toward the totally other thing, the absolute other," hedonism feeds on a "need" which can never be fulfilled.[75] It is hardly here a question of the possession of the world, in a relation all the more perverse as it lives on through the single mode of inveiglement [*captation*], though only of the carnal experience. In the face of such a mistake, Bonaventure warns of the danger in the *Soliloquium*, inviting the reader not to flee sensation but rather to protect it when it is not conformed to the "figure" of the incarnate Word: "Alas! Lord," he confesses in the midst of this interior dialogue, "I understand now but I blush as I confess it: the beauty, the form of creatures has deceived my eyes [*species et decor creaturarum decepit oculum meum*]; I could not conceive that you were sweeter than honey . . . O Jesus, source of universal piety and sweetness, forgive me if in the creature I did not recognize your inestimable sweetness equal to honey, if I did not taste it in the interior love of my soul . . . The perfume of the creature seduced my sense of smell [*decepit odor creaturae olfactum meum*], and I did not know your perfume . . . Forgive me if I have only so late cast myself into the pursuit of its traces. Finally the deceptive voice of creatures has charmed my ear [*decepit sonus fallax creaturarum auditum meum*] and I have hardly tasted how fresh are your words on the lips of your chosen ones, how sweet are your counsels to the ears of those who love you . . . And, to crown my condemnation, worldly weakness deceived my poor senses [*carnis mollities tactum meum nimis miserabiliter decipiebat*], and I have ignored all the sweetness of your embraces, O good Jesus, all the honesty of your attractions, all the delights of union with you."[76]

Despite the devotion, the danger he speaks of here is that of captivation (*captation*). One would wrongly confound the beauty of a landscape with the splendor of God, the tasting of honey with the taste of the Eucharist, the perfume of a flower with wafting incense, the siren songs of creatures with the chant of praise, and the lust of the flesh with the divine embrace. If the symbol requires that we rest with sensation without immediately surpassing it, the "good use" of the sensible ought nevertheless to prevent its "bad use," the *symbolical* protect against the *diabolical*, and the conversion of the senses ought not to be confounded with simple sensation. The kenotic burying of God in the sensible does not indicate an absorption of the believer in his sensations; yet neither does the condescension of the divine occur without a certain elevation of the human: "No man is worthy of acceding to this sovereign good which transcends all the limits of nature, unless God, in his condescension [*Deo condescendente sibi*] elevates man beyond himself [*elevetur ipse supra se*]."[77] Briefly, a sort of "reduction" or *epochê* of the sensible ought to be effected here, no longer after the manner of Eckhart's disobjectification of the world in the relation of the Creator to his creature (as in the sermon on Martha and Mary, chap. 3, supra), but rather in the properly Bonaventurian fashion of opening up sensation from its blind enjoyment [*jouissance*] and recognizing at the very heart of its bounty the true joy of the one who provides it for us. Balthasar says of Bonaventure: "The renunciation of an autonomous, acquisitive experiencing is the only preparation possible for the experiences which the Word of inspiration wishes to mediate itself."[78]

Dying with Christ, our senses themselves resurrect in some sense with him. The affair here is certainly theological, but is no less aesthetic and philosophical. Art is in fact nothing but another possible and derivative mode of the conversion of the senses, so that a Paul Klee, as we have seen, will sense himself, much like Saint Francis, "looked upon by things" more than he is actually seeing them. But Christianity makes of this "conversion" of our sensible apprehension of the world the locus of a true "metamorphosis" or "transformation." It is not sufficient, as far as Christianity is concerned, to change oneself in order to see things anew. It is rather necessary to be changed, or better, transformed by another who gives me the gift of sensing and experiencing even the very same way he experiences and thus in an exchange of consent and even of sensations for which the presence of the Son in me attains mystical and philosophical summits rarely reached: "Let this attitude [*ressenti*] be in you [*hoc enim sentite in vobis*] which is also the attitude [*ressenti*] of Jesus Christ [*quod et in Christo Jesu*]" (Phil. 2:25). It is not therefore that our body dies and our soul resurrects alone, according to an all too common conception of Christianity. But rather "our senses, together with images and thoughts, must die with Christ and descend to the underworld in order to rise unto the Father" (Balthasar).[79] The crossing of the ford, as it were, is necessary in order to bring about the passage from the purely human bodily senses to the spiritual senses converted in Christ. This passage, as I will now show, through "the gate of the five senses" (*per portas quinque sensuum*), marks the threshold where the Resurrected One transforms our apprehension of the world, even to the point of making us see in the stigmata of brother Francis the full carnal expression of the very thing that is impressed there.

The Limit Experience of the Stigmata

The limit experience of Francis's stigmata ought not to be restricted to pure devotion, nor be allowed to slide into some kind of mysticism or irrationalism. As we know, the event has surely been used to support the attribution of sanctity to the founder of the Franciscans. Yet the fervor attached to the event (an event which it is not my intent to judge) has sometimes a level of Dolorism that we ought to be on guard against. Bonaventure, the humble interpreter of Saint Francis's life (*Legenda major*), proposes a reading that is theological rather than Dolorist, and confessional more than devotional: "He came to be totally transformed [*totum transformandum*] into the likeness of Christ crucified, not through the martyrdom of his body [*non per martirium carnis*] but through the burning love of his soul [*sed per incidium mentis*]." The essential thing is clarified in the middle of the thirteenth century (1263) some forty years after the death of Francis in 1226: the meaning [*sens*] of the stigmata resides not in its Dolorism but in its exemplarism. What matters here is the "impression in the flesh" (*imprimere in carne*) and the "complete transformation" (*totum transformandum*), much more than acts of suffering and devotion: "Then the vision disappeared," continues the exegete Bonaventure, "leaving in the heart of brother Francis a marvelous ardor, but not without also impressing on his flesh some marks just as marvelous. At this moment in fact there appeared [*apparere*] in his hands and feet the traces of the nails such as he came to see them in this crucified man." Now we reach the object of the present study: the "conversion of the flesh" in Bonaventure ought to be seen as making visible, in *the bodily experience of the saint*, the very thing that was said and lived in the experience of *the conversion of the senses*. We cannot therefore reduce this conversion of the flesh to some simple "mental perceptions of contemplated truth," since this transformation of the bodily into the spiritual first had to constitute the primary experience even for that which is most commonly shared: the vision of

God in the neighbor, tasting him in the Eucharist, hearing him in the word, and so on. But the doctrine of the spiritual senses will now be extended to a kind of experience (the stigmata) which discloses, even in a wounded and transformed flesh, the action of the Resurrected One in a possible but rare divine-human encounter [*corps-à-corps*]. Though refraining, through a sort of *epochê* as we emphasized above, from judging here of the stigmata's effectiveness (*quid*), the manner in which Bonaventure describes it (*quomodo*) will show that the passage of God through the "gate of the five senses" opens and reveals a new space for which the body itself marks the horizon of its visibility as much as of its transformation.

The Gate of the Five Senses

The Transit. Metaphysics in Bonaventure is a "passage" (*meta-phusis*), and not a simple "break" or "leap." Like the later "mystics of excess" Jean-Joseph Surin and Meister Eckhart, the true residence of the itinerant monk is always a "transit," a "movement toward" rather than a "remaining there," and hence a "hodology" more than an "ontology."[80] Hence the *Itinerarium* says to the reader or the one following the retreat of the "three days walk into the desert": "Considering the universe as a mirror through which we pass to God [*per quod transeamus ad Deum*], we will thus become true Hebrews passing [*transeuntes*] from Egypt to the land of promise, and true Christians passing with Christ [*cum Christo transeuntes*] from this world to the Father."[81] The experience of the passage through the senses, in a truly Christian and therefore incarnate mysticism, thus marks *the traversal of the phusis* (*meta-phusis*) rather than the flight into another world (metaphysics).

The "gate of the five senses," as the threshold required at the heart of the intimacy through which God enters and reveals himself to man, is enough in fact to allow the divine to enter the depths of the human and to indwell that which we would have thought to have kept safely under guard: our senses themselves. "Man, or the microcosm, has five senses that are like five gates [*quasi quinque portas*], where the knowledge of all sensible beings penetrates [*intrat*] into the soul. Through the vision enter [*per visum intrant*] the celestial and luminous bodies and every colored object; through touch, the solid and terrestrial bodies. The three intermediaries: taste for liquids, hearing for impressions in the air, smell for vapors which result from a mixture of humidity, air, fire or heat, as we see in the perfume that emits its aromas."[82] Each sense pertains to a certain category of objects: celestial and luminous bodies for vision; solid and terrestrial bodies for touch; liquids for taste, and so on. These are less the things themselves than their impressions received by the senses that "penetrate into the soul" (*intrant in animam*). There is certainly nothing very original here, at least as far as Greek anthropology goes, whether Platonic or Aristotelian.[83] But the power and exemplarity of the doctrine of Bonaventure is found in the fact that beyond the normal working of our sensory organs, the Word himself, in being made flesh, becomes himself the "gate" (*per portas*) through which the bodily senses are converted into spiritual ones.

A True Heart to Heart (Coeur à Coeur). The experience of the contemplation of the cross as well as Eucharistic adoration rises up in the teaching of Bonaventure as the emblematic figure by which this "Christian alchemy" of the conversion of the senses is accomplished. *In it* our "divine sensorium" is properly speaking transformed for it is *through it* that our bondage to sensible things dies and there is resurrected in its place a converted and open mode of our senses. Bonaventure counsels some Franciscan sisters on spiritual retreat (*De perfectione vitae ad sorores*): "Consecrated souls: approach! Carried by your love approach Jesus covered in wounds, Jesus crowned with thorns . . . With the apostle Thomas, do not merely put your finger in the scars and your hand in his side, but by way of the gate opened at his side [*per ostium lateris*], penetrate all the way to his Heart [*ingredere usque ad cor ipsius Iesu*]. There, transformed in him by the ardor of your love for the crucified Divine [*ibique ardentissimo crucifixi amore in Christum transformata*] . . . await no other consolation than the capacity to die on the cross with Jesus Christ [*cum Christo in cruce mori*]. Along with the apostle, you will shout: 'I have been crucified with Christ. It is no longer I who live but Christ lives in me' " (Gal. 2:20).[84]

The "heart" of the crucified, "wounded and open," will lend itself in two ways to the "transformation in Christ" (*in Christum transformata*) of the bodily senses into the spiritual senses.

(a) As "heart": this organ, pierced by the thrust of the lance, is revealed in all flesh, for Christ as for man, to be the "center of the microcosm" just as the sun is the "center of the macrocosm": *medium maioris mundi est sol, medium minoris est cor.*[85] When the heart that is pierced is Christ's—who is the "center" of all creation and "in whom is hidden all the treasures of wisdom and the knowledge of God"[86]—it is the "heart of the heart" that is pierced, the heart of the Word who is the heart of the world and in whom the world subsists. The "gate opened at his side" (*per ostium lateris*), seen also by the disciples who beheld *the one whom they had pierced* (Jn. 19:37), confers a Christian meaning on the "gate of the five senses" so that they become the threshold of the "transformation" (*transformata*) of our love for the "crucified Divine." (b) As "wounded and open": the heart of Christ on the cross "spilling forth blood and water" is a sign and gift for the multitude (Jn. 19:34). Starting from the heart (the incarnate Word) and spreading to the entire creation contained in him is the gift of a transformed apprehension of the sensible by way of the "transfigured" senses themselves.

A true heart to heart is performed between God and man, precisely when he dies on the cross, inviting us to convert our senses. Although the carnal wound of the heart of Christ is no longer "bodily visible" today as it was for the witnesses on Golgotha, it is given, according to Bonaventure, to a "spiritual perception" found in the believer's ardor of love for the Resurrected ("by the open gate of his side, penetrate all the way to his heart. There, transformed in him by the ardor of your love for the crucified Divine . . ."). Thus this mysterious and no less real "conversion of the senses" bears value for the Christian of every age. Nothing on Golgotha would have been seen in this open heart but the "organ" (carnally wounded by the soldier's lance), if his authentically and definitively spiritual nature would not have manifested the ardor of a love, like that of the fiancé of the Song of Songs, the Spouse put on the cross, even that of the Father himself: "His heart was wounded so that, through the visible wound [*per vulnus visibile*], this invisible love would become visible to us [*vulnus amoris invisibile videamus*] . . . The carnal wound [*carnale vulnus*] therefore reveals a spiritual wound [*vulnus spirituale ostendit*] as it is said in the Song of Songs: 'You have wounded my heart, O my sister, my fiancée, you have wounded my heart . . .' It is as if the Spouse meant to say: because you wounded me in the ardor of your love [*quia zelo amoris tui vulnerasti*], I was also struck by the lance of the soldier [*lancea quoque militis vulneratus sum*]."[87]

In itself and starting from itself, the original and invisible vulnerability of the heart of God (*vulnus amor invisibilis*) is shown (*ostendit*) in the "heart of Jesus" pierced on the cross, by way of the visible wound on his side (*per vulnus visibile*). The body (the pierced heart) returns to the spiritual (the compassionate heart) without surpassing it. If there is indeed a prompt to the "conversion" of the believer's senses, or a passage from the bodily senses to the spiritual senses (*conformitas*) in an identical "mode of being" (*analogia*), this only indicates the opposite of a flight into some kind of disincarnate mysticism. This "conversion" in the mode of apprehension of the object, purified by the "bracketing" of the direct knowledge of the sensible, turns me to the "ardor of the Father's love" who desires a relationship with me as his creature. What I sense is not first myself sensing the suffering Christ (in a sort of Dolorism far removed from the true message of the cross), but rather the communion of love between the Father and Son, moving from the spiritual vulnerability of the heart of God to its sign and iconic presence in the wound of his side on the cross. The inversion-conversion of the senses produced here in the passage from the bodily senses to the spiritual senses across an identical mode of being thus consists no more in the vision of the bodily in order to pass over wholly to the spiritual (as if the simple vision of the crucifix ought to carry me into a mystical ecstasy). Instead, it consists in living from the spiritual in order to read it in the bodily. "Touched by God" in his carnal death to his own captivation by the senses, I come with him to "touch the world" with senses converted by dint of crossing the ford of the "gate of the five senses." The heart to heart [*coeur à coeur*] is accomplished here by touching bodies [*corps à corps*] even to the point of discovering a meaning [*sens*] of the flesh which is not related to either the substantial or accidental dimensions, in order to describe this mystical experience of the stigmata of brother Francis.

The Disciple Touching and Touched. Returning here to a practice of phenomenology justified by medieval philosophy, the "flesh" as "concrete emblem of a manner of being in general" appears here in the form of the contemplation of the cross as the very place of the conversion of the senses. Neither the body alone nor the soul alone, nor even the unique face of the "sensing body" (phenomenal body), nor the "sensed body" (objective body) constitutes the experience of the body as such. Only the intersection of the two marks the limit of sensing and the sensed, the "coiling over the visible and the seen body, and of the tangible and the touched body."[88] Reappropriating the famous Husserlian chiasm of the "touching-touched" (*Ideas II*, §36), we can observe that the believer contemplating the heart of Christ wounded "in his flesh" on the cross does not therefore only look at himself seeing in a pure phenomenal intentional aim (risking closing himself in the sadly famous solipsism from which phenomenology must endeavor to be extricated), nor does he uniquely see Christ suffering in a unilaterally objective intentional aim (remaining then only the powerless spectator of a "representation" that hardly concerns him). Thus commenting on the fifth of the *Cartesian Meditations*, Marc Richier emphasizes that "there is in the apperception of the other this immediate apprehension that 'I live my life' and not the other's, and yet I am not a *solus ipse* closed in on itself, but an *ipse* which is phenomenologically open in its life and time, to the life and time of the other."[89] By contrast to a subjectivist solipsism and a pure objectifying spectacle (one being only the inverse of the other), in the contemplation of Christ on the cross, the "flesh of Christ," at least as "flesh of the other," is seen as the limit of the visible and invisible, participating as a "texture" of my own flesh and the flesh of the world. A mysterious "chiastic" relation of "interlacing," according to which I do not suffer as he does although he does not suffer without me, happens here where the believer and suffering Christ are tied together in an intercorporeity that can neither be "explained" nor "analyzed," only "described": "For the first time, *through the other body*, I see that, in its coupling with the flesh of the world, the body contributes more than it receives, adding to the world that I see the treasure necessary for what the other body sees."[90] This statement by Merleau-Ponty would not at all be rejected by Bonaventure the Franciscan.

Thus it is not only "the same" of my own power to espouse things that I here experience through "touching," albeit spiritually, the Word on the cross (through my wounded brother, for example), but the enigma of this fourth term which means that, in the interlacing of our worlds, I touch him not only touching myself, nor only himself touched or the capacity to touch him, but also touching himself or touching me in a way I could not reach on my own.[91] To say it otherwise, and recognizing that it would require more ample development, "touching Christ on the cross" is less touching Christ himself or touching myself touching him, than it is touching *him* touching me and touching the world. I have already quoted Bonaventure's apperceptive transposition with the body of Christ: "Because you have wounded me with the ardor of your love [*quia zelo amoris tui vulnerasti*], I was also struck by the lance of the soldier [*lancea quoque militis vulneratus sum*]."[92] Touched objectively (objective body, the sensed Christ), Christ on the cross is revealed thus phenomenally touching (phenomenal body, the sensing Christ). This chiasm of the sensed and sensing in the very person of the Word incarnate reveals to me how touching him "spiritually" but "in a bodily manner" I am first myself also touched in the manner in which he touches me. What returns me to myself is thus not the blow of the lance which only leaves us in the pure spectacle of an invisibility both blind and ignorant to its own meaning [*sens*], but rather the ardor of my love rooted in the excess of the Father's. Every danger of anachronism aside, the phenomenological reading of the "touching-touched" at the very center of the relation of intercorporeity of man and God in Bonaventure recalls that the "primacy of touch" finds in the Franciscan tradition one of its most proper expressions: "Man embraces [*astringitur*] the sovereign sweetness under the aspect of the Word incarnate, dwelling in us bodily [*corporaliter*] and letting itself be touched, caressed, embraced by us [*reddentis se nobis palpabile, osculabile, amplexabile*] through the ardent charity which, by excess and transport, makes our spirit pass from this world to the Father."[93]

Against the Greek and even Augustinian tradition, the ordinary ladder of the senses is inverted: the inferior sense, touch, is understood here to be the most appropriate in Christian experience in the embrace of the Word, while the most elevated sense, vision, becomes again all the more common as it puts at a distance the world that it intends and sees. Because for the Seraphic master "the earth has been chosen as the center of the world and of the manifestations of divine grace" (Balthasar),[94] the passage from the macrocosm to the microcosm like that from the bodily senses to the spiritual senses is enacted starting from the sense of touch and without ever leaving the earth. The word of the Apostle Thomas, "If I do not see the marks of the nails in his hands, and if I do not place my finger in them, and if I do not place my hand in his side, I will not believe" (Jn. 20:25), no longer sees the heart open and wounded simply as the crucible for the transformation of the senses, but first sees the unsurpassable and irreducible experience of touching as that which "gives flesh" in phenomenology and theology to the world and to being. Such is the ultimate meaning [*sens*] of the cross, being at once, according to Bonaventure, "center" and "passage"—the pole starting from which the phenomena are seen and liberated. "Everything is manifested on the cross [*omnia in cruce manifestantur*] . . . Thus the cross is the key [*clavis*], gate [*porta*], way and splendor of the truth [*via et splendor veritatis*]."[95]

But is it necessary to remain at the cross, even as it is the center and heart of all phenomenality? According to the hypothesis of a flesh as "concrete emblem of a manner of being in general," does the "de-figured" Christ not call man to take on his form? And if "taking [his] form" means more than a simple act of representation, does that mean that this flesh of Christ—from crucified and open to resurrected and offered—is also able to give to man the "definitive obtainment of his Christian senses"?[96] The Franciscan experience of the stigmata precisely indicates its value and its possibility. The luminous rays of the stigmata of brother Francis on La Verna, the very place the winged Seraphim appeared in the form of the cross, indeed make visible in all the religious representations of the event (Giotto, Lorenzo, Gozzoli, etc.) this strange divine-human encounter [*corps à corps*]. The lines traced on the fresco or the canvas make visible this intercorporeity of the two wounded bodies of the Seraphim and brother Francis according to a representation which, in Giotto for example, directly refers to the *Legenda major* of Bonaventure. Feet and hands pierced and side opened, something happens or at the least is expressed in a carnal language so appropriately Christian that it remains even today as the type of word principally used by the incarnate Word to articulate our own flesh always formed by him.[97]

The Stigmata of Brother Francis

On La Verna. As I have already mentioned, short of the question of its effectivity (*quid*), the phenomenon of the stigmata describes the how (*quomodo*), or the modality of a God who is "impressed" and "expressed" in the flesh of man. The "interlacing" of the flesh of the crucified Seraph with the stigmatized Francis serves as the key to a new phenomenological elucidation of the human flesh (phenomenological incarnation) interwoven with the flesh of God (theological incarnation). Bonaventure, who from the beginning of the *Itinerarium* followed the steps of Francis on La Verna, is made the interpreter of the vision of the "winged seraph in the form of the cross" and of the "manifest" stigmatization of the saint: "There on La Verna, where I meditated on the elevations of the soul to God, I recall, among other things, the miracle that occurred to St. Francis himself: the vision [*de visione*] of the winged seraph in the form of the cross. But it seems to me as soon as this vision represented the rapture of the blessed father that it indicated the itinerary to follow in order to get there . . . This itinerary [*itinerarium*] to be followed is nothing but the ardent love of the crucified [*ardentissimum amorem Crucifixi*] . . . This love so impregnates the soul of St. Francis that it finishes by showing through his flesh [*in carne patuit*] when he carried about in his body [*in corpore suo deportavit*] the sacred stigmata of the Passion the two last years of his life."[98]

Impression and Expression. The opening of the *Itinerarium* explicitly teaches what I suggest concerning corporeity and the expression in it of the flesh of the Resurrected. The stigmatized "body" (*corpus*), like a simple, wounded substance lets the "flesh" (*caro*) appear in the figure of the saint, the transparency or "manifestation" of his love for the crucified. Flesh and body: the mystical duality here does not precisely correspond to the simple phenomenological bipartition of *Leib* and *Körper* (as we have already noted in regards to Tertullian above). Yet what is given here to see as "flesh" in Saint Francis marks the manifestation of his internal lived experience (impregnated love in his soul), while his "body" only refers to the trace of this physical pain [*douleur*] to which, in addition, it gives meaning [*sens*] (the sacred stigmata). Therefore his flesh expresses (*patuit*) what his body only bore (*deportavit*). Without pushing this analogy of the mystical and the phenomenological any further, Bonaventure's theological rereading of the experience of the stigmata reveals in the "flesh" of Francis the very expression of that which his "soul" sees, even rendering visible as a trace on his "body" "the very ardent love of the crucified" (*ardentissimum amorem Crucifixi*). Let me repeat then that his flesh expresses (*exprimit*) that which is impressed (*impressit*) on his body. Inheriting this from Bernard of Clairvaux, Bonaventure takes up and reworks his "positive optic on the flesh" (Brague). The "flesh," at once "resolution of continuity," "consciousness of finitude and mortality," and "affection of the self by the self," is certainly the body as sensible and mortal but precisely as it makes visible this fragility and mortality. One can therefore speak of the "resurrection of the body" in theology, even in phenomenology, inasmuch as it is made plain that our incorruptibility *in patria* (the body—*corpus*) fully inherits the lived experience of our mortality *in via* (the flesh—*caro*).[99]

The stigmata on the body of brother Francis finds its meaning [*sens*] only when it manifests the fragility and vulnerability of his flesh, and is thus sensible to the internal lived experience of his relation to the Crucified more than to the suffering that it makes visible. The flesh of the disciple first reveals his love for his master (and not some hypothetical dolor) in order to resemble him, just as certain people today let show through their flesh, facial expression, or look an affection which overflows them and then illumines them through and through. Thus Hans Urs von Balthasar: "The stigmata were branded on the body *precisely* while the soul was in *ecstatic* rapture: it is when the form of the divine beauty is seen that this divine beauty receives its form in the world. For Bonaventure, it is vital that ecstasy, even in its Dionysian aspects, is not a flight out of the world that leaves it behind, but rather the opening of the world for God, or more precisely the revelation of the fact that the world has already been grasped by God."[100] So there is no mysticism of flight from the world in Bonaventure—no more than in Christianity in general. On the contrary, the hidden becomes progressively manifest, by striking the gate of the five senses and the body in general in order to be revealed by the flesh.

First secretly "impressed" (*absorbuit*) in his heart by contemplation—Bonaventure thus tells the sisters of Lonchamp "put Jesus crucified as a stamp on your heart . . . just as a stamp is impressed on hot wax"[101]—love, impregnating the soul of the saint, becomes suddenly visible or "manifest" (*patuit*) to those who witness the scene of the reception of the stigmata. Such is the sense of the "expressive and impressive" appearance of the winged Seraph in the form of the cross to blessed Francis and which will later gain for Bonaventure the title of the Seraphic Doctor. Bonaventure said that "this expressive and impressive appearance [*expressa et impressa*] of the Seraph to blessed Francis showed that this order should correspond to brother Francis."[102] When love, "impressed" in the heart (transformation of the senses in the crucible of the contemplation of the cross), is "expressed" in the flesh (the miracle of the stigmata), the bodily senses are thus made simultaneously the most spiritual and the most sensible. They are made the most spiritual because contemplation requires a "good use of the sensible" by the conversion of the senses and the most sensible because the visibility of the stigmata is given to be read in the "interlacing" of two fleshes, the unsurpassable intercorporeity of the flesh of the resurrected Christ and the flesh of the transformed Francis.

A Union Neither Accidental nor Shameful. Apart from the metaphysical quarrel of hylomorphism, which has no bearing on the mystical experience of stigmatization, Bonaventure's surprisingly unified and integral anthropology founds this relation of "impression-expression" of the soul to the body in the figure of Francis. Far from a simple bipolarity of bodily and animated substances, or of a purely accidental composition of the spiritual and bodily, the soul and body in this experience of the stigmata disclose their interaction more than their superposition, their chiasm rather than their substance: "The action whereby the soul unites itself with the human body and gives it life," says Bonaventure in an important passage from his *Commentary on the Sentences*, "is neither accidental nor shameful. It is not accidental [*non accidentalem*] because the soul is the substantial form in the body. It is not shameful [*et non ignobilem*] because in the body the soul becomes the noblest of all the forms, and all the longing struggle of nature finds its goal in this soul. For the human body possesses the noblest constitution and organization that exist in nature [*nobilissima complexione et organizatione quae sit in natura*], and therefore it finds its fulfillment only in the noblest form or nature. The character of the soul through which she is able to be united [*unibilis*] to a body is something that touches what is most essential to her and is the most excellent character in the soul."[103]

The stigmata thus makes this substantial unity of soul and body appear—albeit as a carnal lived experience more than a metaphysical composition. It can even serve as tangible proof of such a unity, if necessary. Neither "accidental" nor "shameful," their connection is for Bonaventure more noble than each alone, and counted among "the most noble things" (*nobilissima*), which includes the necessary complex "body" itself that welcomes and reveals this very spiritual activity of the soul—the ardent love of Francis for the Crucified. Said otherwise, because this Bonaventurian mysticism philosophically interrogated has no other end than to convert our own sensible manner of being in the world, an activity of the soul or a lover not wholly given over to being made visible in the lived experience of our flesh would remain for Bonaventure unworthy of our state as creatures. Our bodies, made to manifest God like the incarnate Word, have no other end than to reveal this other visibility. Therefore, Bonaventure highlights in the *Breviloquium* that there appears here a certain "demand [*exigente*] for the future resurrection of the body": "Our soul will only be fully blessed [*plene beatua*] at the instant that its body will be restored [*restituatur*] to it because it possesses a natural and innate tendency to be inserted within it."[104] Thus the chiasm of these two substances in our future state of resurrection depends on the interlacing, or here the insertion (*insertam*) of our soul in our body today. Here the carnal relation becomes temporal in the sense that our capacity physically to phenomenalize God here below underwrites belief, and makes credible its possible manifestation in our body in the beyond. Perhaps the role of the body in revealing the meaning [*sens*] of the relation of the believer with the Resurrected is too often forgotten. Christians have progressively failed to exhibit its visibility, "to write on their faces the glad tidings of the Bible," and to allow in themselves "a new Bible in continuous course of creation," as Nietzsche famously said.[105] We will never finish converting and being converted in our own flesh, if we now accept (according to the initial guideline of this work) to see God by means of our senses and to touch him today. If not its very efficacy Francis has at least demonstrated its ultimate possibility: "The *impressio* of the stigmata is the mark of God in the sensible world."[106]

✦

The Blessedness of the Flesh. "Flesh in the flesh" (*caro secundum carnem*) in order to be truly a man—Bonaventure announces in a remarkable sermon on the nativity ("Sermon 2")—the Word is also made "flesh apart from the flesh" (*caro praeter carnem*) in order to avoid corruption, "flesh above the flesh" (*caro supra carnem*) for a marvelous operation, "flesh against the flesh" (*caro contra carnem*) for its own purification, and "flesh for the flesh" (*caro propter carnem*) in view of final salvation.[107] Far from denigrating the flesh, the Franciscan doctor establishes it as the guiding thread of the economy of salvation—from the Incarnation (flesh in the flesh) to the Resurrection (flesh for the flesh). In the act of "conversion" that avoids corruption (flesh apart from the flesh) and awaits its perfection (flesh against the flesh), the flesh becomes for man, by the mediation of God, a sort of "spectacle that renders our nature blessed" (*spectaculum ut naturam beatificaret*): "Behold," concludes the Seraphic Doctor, "why he was made flesh: to *render blessed* the soul and the flesh [*ut animam et carnem beatificaret*], which merits for him praise and glory."[108] The glorification of the flesh is therefore not solely reserved for a beyond, which is as distant as it is impenetrable, even though it finds its perfect realization in this very "beyond." There is, for Bonaventure, a blessedness of *being in the flesh* and *living in the flesh* from here below that all the deceptions of the sensible realm will not be able to lead astray if it is the case that our senses are not left to mislead us. "In my flesh I will see my God" says the Book of Job (Job 19:26) which, in Bonaventure, takes on an original meaning: no vision of God will be complete if, on the one hand, "we do not penetrate into the Word [*ingredietur ad Verbum*] by contemplation of his divinity," and, on the other hand, "we do not go out to the flesh [*et egredietur ad carnem*] by the consideration of his humanity."[109]

The "conversion of the flesh" in Bonaventure (chap. 6) not only indicates the optional term to the "solidity of the flesh" in Tertullian (chap. 5) and the "visibility of the flesh" in Irenaeus (chap. 4). On the contrary, it marks the accomplishment of an economy of salvation, which has no other end than that of making an address *to us* and *to our very corporeity* in "the pattern of the one who lives in the flesh" (*exemplum viventum in carne*).[110] That which was revealed in the "formation" of Adam (Irenaeus) and totally assumed by Christ in the betrothal of our "sister the flesh" (Tertullian) now appears as "transformed" in order to give to the disciple in his own bodily experience the capacity to read something of the carnal experience of God (Bonaventure): "The manner is obvious [*patet etiam*] by which God is hidden [*lateat*] in the interior of all the objects of sensation and knowledge," concludes Bonaventure at the terminus of the vast movement of leading all things back [*reconduction*] in the *De reductione artium ad theologiam*.[111]

✦

Neither the manifestation of God preparing his reception either as "relation" (Augustine) or "phenomenon" (Erigena), or as "detachment" (Eckhart) [part I], nor his incorporation as flesh in its "visibility" (Irenaeus), its "solidity" (Tertullian), and by its "conversion" (Bonaventure) [part II], is sufficient to speak the *whole* of Christian experience. One does not pass all alone to God, even by his own body transfigured and converted by "the very ardent love of the crucified" (Saint Francis). The experience of the "other" [part III] brings to completion the "manifest God" [part I] as well as his "incorporated flesh" [part II]. The three—God, the flesh, and the other—only deliver, so to speak, a single and same reality, forming the different facets of a unique act of donation of God to man and of reception of God by man. At the end of the road only the path taken will be measured, thus to render us inexcusable "with the other" [part III] for *not always seeing* him, yet only when all has been done to enlighten us, both on the part of our vision of God [part I] as on our sensation of the divine [part II]: "The one who is not illumined by created things, is a blind man [*caecus est*]. The one who is not woken up by so many cries is deaf [*surdus est*]. The one who is not pressed to praise God by all his works is a mute [*mutus est*]. The one who is not forced to recognize the First Principle by all the signs is an idiot [*stultus est*]. Open your eyes [*aperi oculos*], listen with your soul [*aures spirituals admove*], loosen your lips [*labia tu solve*], apply your heart [*et cor tuum appone*]: every creature will show you how to understand, praise, love, serve, glorify and adore your God."[112]

Part Three

The Other

Alterity Thematized

The notion that intersubjectivity and alterity were not thematized as such until the dawn of the twentieth century is a scholarly commonplace. At best medieval thought would exhibit a certain "sensibility for relation to the other" but nothing more.[1] This "platitude" certainly has its reasons and even its justification in the history of philosophy. The thought of the other is marked by its origin: the constitution of subjectivity in Descartes, of which the danger of closing in on itself in the famous solipsism leads to a fresh thinking of intersubjectivity in Husserl. Yet the following observation is still pertinent and is, in fact, all the more massive as it cuts to the heart of a history of thought that is nuanced to say the least. Patristic and medieval thought contain many "hidden treasures" to be discovered, which a certain love affair with novelty tends to forget. And I have already shown it in relation to God as source of the ego (part I) and to the flesh as full manifestation of the divine in the density of our humanity (part II). Precisely because the divine acquires true status as engendering subject (part I) and the flesh reveals its visibility as well as its solidity (part II), we can no longer speak in the same old way about alterity (part III). At least since Saint Augustine, such an observation is well known. The metaphysical return to the ego (Descartes) finds its roots and its initial motif in the mysticism of interiority: "Lo you were within [*intus*] but I outside [*foris*] searching there for you . . . You were with me [*mecum eras*] and I was not with you [*et tecum non eram*]."[2] Thus read the famous lines from the *Confessions*. The philosophical question of alterity finds in the corpus of theology a conceptuality that, if not the strongest, is at least the most original.

But there is much more to this philosophical reflection with theological roots. For if the reflexive act of return to the self is rooted in the theological conviction of a God present within ("it is no longer I who live," says Saint Paul, "but Christ lives within me" [Gal. 2:20]), the irruption of the other at the heart of the self no longer escapes from the rule of an engendering of the other with me at the heart of the Trinity itself. Whether it is a matter of "community" (Origen, chap. 7), "alterity" (Aquinas, chap. 8) or "singularity" (Duns Scotus, chap. 9), these different traits essential to contemporary philosophy find their first outlines in patristic and medieval thought. If it is of course permissible to treat the question of otherness independently of all inquiry into the divine, then alterity as such nevertheless finds a true foundation in the *Divine Third*. This has already been shown. "*Condilectio*" or the devout love of the "third" reaches its height in the Trinitarian divine love that no human reciprocity could ever match: "When a being gives its love to another," says Richard of Saint Victor in his *De Trinitate*, "and when it loves the other alone, there is a *dilectio*, but not *condilectio* [*sed condilectio non est*] . . . There is *condilectio* properly speaking [*condilectio autem jure dicitur*] when two friends [the Father and Son] together love a third [the Holy Spirit] in a harmony of *dilectio* [*concorditer diligitur*], a sociality of love [*socialiter amatur*] where the affections of the two are unified in the fire of love that they have for the third."[3] Things are utterly clear here. The thought of the other, at least in the general context of our reasoning from reduction (part I: God), and then from constitution (part II: the flesh), is not born independently of the love of God in myself (part III: the other).

In this sense, but this sense alone, the "way" of the fifth *Cartesian Meditation* of Husserl will inspire everything that follows, at least insofar as it founds the question of intersubjectivity in phenomenology, and brings to light for a new day patristic and medieval philosophy: first with Origen and the thematic of the communion of saints as possible mode of community (chap. 7), then Thomas Aquinas and the relation of one angel to another as a harbinger of the relation of the *ego* to the *alter ego* (chap. 8), and finally Duns Scotus and the haecceity of otherness—so well studied today—in order to detect an identified mode of its singularity (chap. 9). Let us recall here the Augustinian closing to this capital text of the *Cartesian Meditations*. In this way we will pass straight to the evidence of this indispensable exchange between medieval philosophy and phenomenology, especially insofar as the question of alterity is concerned: *noli foras ire, in te redi, in interiore homine habitat veritas*—"do not go far from yourself but rather enter within, for there dwells the truth."[4]

Chapter 7

✦

Community and Intersubjectivity (Origen)

Communio Sanctorum

As I have already said, one could certainly find much to reproach in a conception which finds everything new about phenomenology to be rooted in certain historical modalities such as patristic and medieval philosophy by hiding every innovation. The objection, if founded, does not see that it is a result of a misinterpretation, taking as second that which is first (phenomenology) and first that which is second (medieval philosophy). Let me explain. Patristic and medieval philosophy are not only the *occasion* for a phenomenology already constituted which would require of its modes of implication only an ultimate verification. As I noted above, the "sealed source" of medieval philosophy awaits its *aggiorniamento*, not by being phenomenology's flavor of the week but by virtue of its exemplarity for contemporary styles of thought sometimes poorly founded in a veritable tradition. But we are interrogating and discovering the tradition anew because we have *eyes to see* that such is a much too facile approach to the tradition. In other words, far from being satisfied with an application of phenomenology to medieval philosophy, it should be first recognized that medieval philosophy itself is fat with phenomenology already, even though only the phenomenological attitude as such would make its birth and establishment possible. Concerning the question of the "other" in particular (part III) and perhaps even more than the questions of "God" (part I) or the "flesh" (part II), phenomenology at least as a method appears with such a fructifying potentiality that it is apt to renew virtually everything, and if not the reading of texts themselves, then at least the interpretation of the authors under the urgent condition that they find some *meaning for us*.

In this chapter what we indicate here will be seen in an exemplary way through the guidance of Origen (especially his *Homilies on Leviticus* and *Homilies on Ezekiel*), but with Bernard of Clairvaux as a necessary fulcrum (especially his *Commentary on the Canticle* and treatise on the *Love of God*). If community is a mode of intersubjectivity as Husserl says, or better, if "being with" is a fundamental mode of "being self" as Heidegger says, then the theological expectation of a final being together in the communion of saints will have something to say to the philosophical search for a concept of community that is not the simple aggregate of individuals. So Henry Creuzel asks: "Before the moment of final resurrection comes, are the saints *interested* in their brothers still on earth?"[1]

The question is not only theological. It is first and foremost philosophical in the sense that our own egoity depends on intersubjectivity with the other man. It is not at all here a simple question of the "self," whether incorporated in God or thought starting from God (part I); nor is it a question of the flesh, however apt it is to be converted to God (part II). Rather it is a question of the possibility for a community of humans to be rooted in the divine in order to constitute in him and with him a new mode of unprecedented intersubjectivity (part III). Said otherwise, the theological dogma of the communion of saints is also a phenomenological hypothesis for the constitution of otherness—if it is indeed the case that community, here with phenomenology, as well as over there with theology—originally precedes all declaration of egoity. "The originality of Husserl resides in this methodological progression from solipsism [*solus ipse*] to community [*Vergemeinschaft*]," says Paul Ricoeur in relation to the father of phenomenology.[2] And Origen says, "The Apostles expect me also [*et ego*] to take part in their joy . . . For there is not *for them* some perfect joy by which *they* would not be afflicted by *our* errors [*pro erroribus nostris dolen*] and cry over *our* sins [*et lugent nostra peccata*]."[3] Passion in God as a capacity to "suffer with," and intersubjectivity as a mode of our "being with" thus make *empathy* and *community* the two privileged modes of an alterity that is philosophically (and definitively) founded. Even more, the theological and existential inquiry into a possible empathy between the living and the departed becomes here all the more important because the doctrine of the *communio sanctorum* is not definitively fixed with Origen in the third century; it does not yet appear in the Apostles Creed ("I believe in the community of saints"), nor even, for that matter, in the Nicene-Constantinopolitan Creed.[4] Unaware of its formulation, perhaps Origen had unwittingly laid the foundation for a possible *communio sanctorum* at the time when the proximity of the Parousia no longer seemed as clear as it did in earlier times. This will be a gain for theology inasmuch as it makes more precise its own conceptuality, and for philosophy as well, for there it can discover the premises of an idea of community.

Suffering with: A Mode of Empathy

Passion

Intercorporeity, not only carnal but even spiritually converted in the apprehension of the Word made flesh (chap. 6: Bonaventure), is not sufficient in itself to constitute a true intersubjectivity—even though, as we will see, it does found community. Man is not only a body; he is also a multiplicity of affects by which he experiences his body (*Körper*) as his own flesh (*Leib*). "A totally foreign being can only be originally given by the medium of empathy (*Einfühlung*)."[5] In order to constitute a community (*Vergemeinschaft*), or better, a communion of saints (*communio sanctorum*) more than a simple apprehension of bodies is therefore necessary. Considering oneself as another ought to make us capable of seeing the lived experience of the other, in relation to whom we are able to live "as if" (*als ob*) we were experiencing what he himself experiences. In this condition alone (that is, the possible "apperceptive transposition of otherness"), the dead take care of the living, the living take care of the dead, and the divine takes care of the human. It would therefore seem to be necessary that God is capable of experiencing what man experiences—assuming all of human experience except sin, though taking on himself its weight.

Passion in Man. In phenomenology, no proper experience is originally given outside of the act of constitution: "One's own experience is the essence of experience."[6] In order to understand God, nothing is given to man except precisely his own experience as man. Thus Origen rightly says, in his sixth *Homily on Ezekiel*, interpreting the compassion of the Lord for Jerusalem starting from human experience (Ez. 16:5): "I will borrow an example from men [*exemplum ab hominibus accipiam*], and if the Holy Spirit helps me, I will pass [*transmigrabo*] to Jesus Christ and God the Father."[7] The experience of man as described in this homily paradoxically deploys the modes of an "empathy" (*Einfühlung*), the power of which has nothing to envy from the long analyses of the modes of apprehension of the other from Dilthey or Husserl: "When *I* address myself *to a man* and implore him to take pity on me, if he is without mercy, he *does not suffer* [*nihil patitur*] from what I have to say; but if he is a sensitive soul, if his heart is not severe or hardened, he hears me, takes pity on me and he *suffers viscerally* [*mollintur viscera eius*] by my prayers."[8]

Beyond the "pathos of the self by God" (chap. 3: Eckhart) rendered visible in a "soteriological flesh" (chap. 4: Tertullian), a "pathos of man *tout court*" therefore constitutes in Origen every relation of one man to another: to suffer or not to suffer, or to endure or not to endure (*patior*), that which the other lives. Without necessarily designating some kind of alteration, which is evidently not fitting for God, the word "passion" in Origen (*passio*) designates in this case "a sentiment or an affection"[9]—or to say it in Heideggerian terms, a "fundamental affective tonality."[10] The question here is not simply, to suffer or not to suffer, if we understand by pathos nothing more than the original impression to which the other makes me subject. We must understand the *particular mode* of suffering involved: "suffering nothing" (*nihil patitur*)—which is of course not the same as suffering the nothing (*nihil*)—or suffering that involves "visceral emotion" (*mollintur viscera eius*). For Origen then, the *originality of suffering* precedes the *modes of suffering*. For man as for God it is not a matter of not suffering (*apatheia*) as has been so often decreed by theology hiding a latent Stoicism. Rather it is a matter of suffering or passively enduring as God himself suffers or endures—in the same way (following Saint Bonaventure above) that we can come to see as God sees, understand as God understands, feel as God feels, and so on.

This entire matter concerns the possibility of an "apperceptive transposition" of oneself to the other. Does the other suffer "from me," not in my place since it is always *mine* alone, but rather in his "visceral emotion"? Or does he always experience this suffering only in the mode of an alleged impassibility which is imagined to be dissolved by suffering all the more as it asserts suffering's unbearable presence by its very refusal of it? The hypothesis of a communion of saints is suspended precisely here in this crucial alternative between not partaking of suffering or a possible suffering of the other *as* I suffer myself. If it is true that the other is not able to suffer in my place, but only *like* me suffering or *with* me suffering, then nothing, neither man nor God, will catch up with my inherent affects and my most profound lived experience. Thus the transfer of the *passion of man* to the *passion of God* put in operation by the Alexandrian Father: "understand," he says, "something *similar* concerning the Savior [*tale mihi quiddam intellige super Salvatorem*]."[11]

Passion of God. Origen's originality in the treatment of the question of the other starting from the thematic of the communion of saints is not only, as is often overemphasized (as in Moltmann or Varillon), found in his having transposed the suffering of the Son into the passivity of the Father: "The Father himself is not impassible" (*ipse Pater non est impassibilis*).[12] For all its just celebrity and originality, it must not be forgotten that in this formula of Origen the "suffering of God" *also precedes his passion*. The divine pathos is not merely the cause of his incarnation, but its origin—and even its very being: "The Savior descended to the earth by pity for humankind. He patiently endured our passions before [*antequam*] suffering the cross and deigning to take on flesh. For if he did not suffer [*si enim non fuisset passus*], he did not come to partake of human life."[13] Thus the "Incarnation not only preceded the Passion, but in a certain sense the Passion preceded the Incarnation!"[14] Suffering *in* God—that which the Father shares with the Son on the cross—ought not to obscure the original suffering *of* God: the unity of the Father, Son, and Spirit in the pathos for man from before the foundation of the world. Thus Levinas said: "Suffering—extreme passivity."[15] Such likely constitutes the very being of God in his relation with the other: he is the *pathos of joy* or the *suffering of desolation*.[16] This perspective does not entail, of course, that the divine being is altered in its essence and ceases to remain God by falling into some kind of powerlessness, but rather that he takes on himself our *pathos* in order to make of it his own *passion*: "God takes on *our manners of being* [*mores nostros supportat Deus*]," insists Origen, "as the Son of God takes on our passions [*sicut portat passions nostras Filius Dei*]."[17]

The "apperceptive transposition" of man to God—in his double assumption of our manners of carnal being by the Son and our original affects by the Father—reaches its height precisely here. As we will see in the following chapter on Thomas Aquinas's reflections on angelic alterity, even though I am "here" (*hic*) and he is "there" (*illic*),[18] God does not merely act *as if* (*als ob*) he is with me in my "here," but he even is made fit by his resurrection to dwell *there* where I am, *with* me and not *without* me, in this that I suffer or undergo at the heart of my most original affects. The horizontal significations of the "here" of our earth (*hic*) and of the "there" of the Kingdom (*illic*) is sometimes easily replaced by misleading theological categories that are too vertical, namely of the "below" (as terrestrial world) and the "above" (as the celestial world). The "overhanging transcendence [*transcendance de surplomb*]" already finds its full term in Christianity, especially with Origen and the original empathy of God. We will soon see that the resurrection of the Son does not separate two worlds as two discordant entities, but unifies them in the communion of saints, in the complementarity of two different visions of the same world. The path that leads from God to man, but not from man to God, permits the full realization of that which only remains programmatic in Husserl: "The intrinsically first other (the first 'not-Ego') is the other Ego."[19] God who is always "other than myself" (*ego alter*) is uniquely revealed at the same time as an "other myself" (*alter ego*) inasmuch as he espouses fully the affects which are originally my own.

"What," then, "is this passion [*quae est ista passio*]," asks Origen, "that the Savior has suffered for us [*quam pro nobis passus est*]"—and which, we could add, founds any possible communion of saints? *Caritas est passio*: "It is the passion of charity."[20]

Passion of Charity. To speak of "charity" (*caritas*) as a type of relation to the other in God and as a passion (*caritas est passio*) is not to oppose it to an action (*actio*) of which human desires would be the archetypes. On the contrary, it constitutes the very being of God insofar as "passion" in him (*passio*) is always immediately translated into "com-passion" (*com-passio*): "Incapable of suffering [*ô apathes*], he suffers because of his love for men [*ôs philanthropos peponthen*]," insists Origen in his *Commentary on Matthew*.[21] God is indifferent to nothing in the life of man. Passion as "com-passion," ordinarily called "charity" (*caritas*), determines the meaning of the divine pathos. Not only a possible mode of passibility, charity totally determines the divine and constitutes its very being: *Deus caritas est* (1 Jn. 4:8).[22] There is passion in the divine because there is compassion and thus charity in him—and not the inverse. The Father does not first suffer himself in an autarkic self-contemplation. He suffers man in his Son, through whom he accepts suffering and undergoes all that we suffer. The divine suffering (*pathos*) comes from the passion of charity or compassion (*passio caritatis*)—which is not the compassion of a passion still more original. In phenomenological terms, the Father discovers the Son—and man in him—as an "intrinsically first other" who constitutes his "other Ego."[23] For both God and man the other (*alter ego*) is always already there at the heart of oneself (*ego*). One does not leave oneself in order to find the other or encounter him. God thus experiences what man experiences, not because he experiences everything in his very being and is transformed in his essence, but because it belongs to his divine decision to have "sympathy" with all that man undergoes: "And the Father himself, God of the universe, full of indulgence, mercy and pity: is it not true that he suffers in some way [*nonne quodammodo patitur*]? . . . The Father himself is not impassable [*ipse Pater non est impassibilis*]. If we pray, he has pity and compassion [*miseretur et condolet*]; he experiences a passion of charity [*patitur aliquid caritas*] . . . , and takes on himself human passions for us [*et propter nos humanas sustinet passions*]."[24]

The experience of God through man does not subsist therefore only at the level of an intercorporeity with the Son by the exercise of the senses (spiritual) converted in the crucible of faith (chap. 6: Bonaventure). It occurs also at the heart of a foundational empathy with the Father by which God makes the decision to experience and undergo all that humanity experiences and undergoes and of sympathizing with all that humanity lives (chap. 7: Origen). "Intercorporeity with the Son" and "compassion of the Father" are thus the two modes by which a communion of saints in the Holy Spirit becomes possible, since, on the one hand, my Savior "still weeps over my sins" (*luget etiam nunc peccata mea*) and "awaits our conversion" (*expectat ut convertamur*), and, on the other hand, *the saints themselves* "await my taking part, even me [*et ego*], in their wisdom."[25]

Compassion

Bernard of Clairvaux, in his *Commentary on the Song of Songs*, directly inherits from Origen's *Homilies on Ezekiel* (and *on Leviticus*) this double suspension of the Savior and of the saints themselves as constitutive components of all alterity for the sake of engendering a true community (the communion of saints). There is a long detour from one to the other, though Origen will come to benefit a posteriori from Bernard. It is likely, as is well known, that Origen's *Commentary on the Song* was probably in Bernard's hands when he was laid up in the infirmary of Clairvaux (in 1124) with William of Saint-Thierry. His sickness did not stop him from commenting, at William's request, on the spiritual meaning of the Song of Songs. Thus William confesses in his *Vita prima* of Saint Bernard: "Being sick in our residence I myself felt extremely tired and totally exhausted by the illness which had so long affected me. On hearing this, Bernard sent me his brother Gerard, of blessed memory, in order to urge me to come to Clairvaux, promising me that, on my arrival, I would not tarry either to be healed or die . . . Two sick men passed the time taking care of ourselves by exploring the *spiritual physics* of the soul and the remedies of the virtues against the sickness of the vices."[26] The *passion of God* in Origen (*ipse Pater non est impassibilis*) is in Bernard made the *compassion of God* (*Deus est impassibilis sed non est incompassibilis*). The second corrects the first and inoculates it against its possible anthropomorphic tendencies.[27]

Deification and Transformation. The first warning of the Cistercian abbot concerns this question of alterity when it attempts to constitute a community—with the Lord, but also with the saints: we do not become *one* with the other by *forgetting our own personality.* A hasty reading of the fourth and last degree of the love of God in the *De diligendo Deo* could lead to such a false view: "Man loves himself for the sake of God alone" (*ne seipsum diligat homo nisi propter Deum*).[28] The psychological and spiritual realism first requires that we recognize that such an experience is not or perhaps barely produced "in this mortal life" (*in hac mortali vita*) except in "rare moments" (*raro interdum*) and perhaps "only once" (*vel semel*) and "in passing" (*raptim*) in the "space of an instant" (*unius vix momenti spatio*).[29] In other words, that which serves as the summit of love is likely not one of the conquests realizable here below (*in via*). But the non-accessibility of the experience *in actuality* does not prohibit us from describing it *by right*, at least as a possibility.

The Cistercian quest, inherited from Origen, for the meaning of community by means of the intersubjectivity of man and God seems to announce the Eckhartian way that we studied above. "Loving the creature for God's sake alone" harkens back to "disappearing *somehow as if* one did not exist" (*perdre tamquam qui non sis*), to "no longer having any awareness of oneself" (*et omnino non sentire teipsum*), and even to "being almost reduced to nothing" (*et paene annullari*).[30] Briefly, at least at first glance, there is no difference between the *exclusive love of God* as "forsaking oneself" in Bernard developing Origen, and *detachment* as "quest for nothing" in Eckhart.[31]

The text cited imposes a nuance that definitively separates the Cistercian élan and Rhineland *nihilité* on this question of alterity. Never does Bernard require that his brothers exist no longer in their personalities, or to forget themselves to the point of detachment from all, including themselves and God. He recommends to them only that they act "somehow as if" (*tamquam*), emphasizing that in this supreme state man will be "almost" (*paene*) reduced to nothing and thus not totally dissolved into the divinity: "To eliminate from oneself everything that prevents one from truly being oneself—such is not to *lose oneself* but to *rediscover oneself*" (Étienne Gilson).[32] The observation is important, as I have already indicated, because it distinguishes Christianity from any mysticism of "emptiness" (Buddhism, Zen, etc.), including certain ambiguous formulas of Rhineland detachment that are falsely interpreted.

All anachronism aside, the warning of the abbot of Clairvaux rises up here in an exemplary fashion and ought to be understood as not dissolving all alterity in pure detachment from the self: *the resurrection is not annihilation but transformation.*[33] It is certainly true that the deification (*deificari*) of man will resemble the "little drop of water poured into much wine," but only insofar as it "seems to be totally lost [*deficere a se tota*] by taking on its taste and color."[34] What is expected in this fourth degree of love is not detachment or the forgetting of the self in the sea of deity, but a metamorphosis or transformation of the self in the Trinity. In the terms of alterity of the phenomenological tradition, the fourth degree of love does not come to be lost in a kind of "affective fusion" in God (the *Einsfühlung* of Lipps), but rather enters into a true "empathy" (the *Einfühlung* of Scheler) in which man remains himself by letting himself be transformed or by "becoming other [*alia*]" in God and through God:[35] "Of course, human nature will persist [*manebit quidem substantia*]," says Bernard, "but under another form [*sed in alia forma*], in another glory [*alia gloria*] and another power [*alia potentia*]."[36]

Such a "divine-human empathy," with its surprising modernity at the heart of an ancient discourse (the fourth degree of love), is fully realized in terms of an "apperceptive transfer" of which Bernard of Clairvaux and William of Saint-Thierry seemed to share the premises: "It will surely come to pass one day that the work is conformed to [*conformet*] and accords with [*concordet*] its author. It is therefore necessary that one day we will enter into his sentiment [*in eumdem nos affectum transire*]."[37] This is a remarkable phrase worthy of elaboration. "Affective participation" as intentional mode of empathy ("a directing of feeling toward the other's joy or suffering")[38] finds here its most exemplary illustration in a "transfer of affects" (*nos affectum transire*). Bernard reveals the lineaments of such in his *De Diligendo* and Saint Paul the foundation in the hymn at the heart of his Letter to the Philippians: *hoc enim sentite in vobis, quod et in Christo Jesu*, "Let that sense [*ressenti*] be in you that is also in Christ Jesus" (Phil. 2:5). Stressed by Saint Paul, then grounded in Origen and developed by Bernard, there occurs, if not a transfer of properties between man and God, at least an affective transport which ideally makes the experience of man the experience of God, the second "making other" the first (*in alia forma*), though always maintaining it in its original form (*manebit quidem substantiam*). The "conforming" (*conformatio*) and "concord of hearts" (*concordet*) is accomplished only as a result of a "transfer" (*transire*) by which the sentiments (*affectus*) that are in man (*nos*) become progressively God's own (*in eumdem*), in that he transforms them, not to dissolve them but to purify them. Deification (*deificari*), for Bernard, is not a dissolution of the human into the divine, but on the contrary an "affection" (*affici*) or even "liquefaction" (*liquiscere*) of the human affect—like the "transfer of fluxes" in Husserl—flowing into the divine affect without being suppressed or annihilated: "To be thus affected is to be deified [*sic affici, deificari est*] . . . It will thus necessarily be that in the saints all human attachment is liquefied in an unspeakable fashion [*ineffabili liquescere*], and is completely poured into the will of God [*atque in Dei penitus transfundi voluntatem*]."[39]

Compassionate God. "To be affected" (*affici*) is "to be deified" (*deificari*). Does this mean that God himself is affected when we are transformed in him? The question has some merit since a God without affect would be, at least biblically speaking, contrary to his nature and condescension: "I have seen the misery of my people" (Ex. 3:7). The imaginary dialogue of Bernard with the possible "pathetic" derivatives of Eckhart is displaced for the sake of a dialogue with Origen: *ipse pater non est impassibilis*—"the Father himself is not impassable." Though a direct dialogue with Origen's *Homilies on Ezekiel* is impossible to prove, Bernard seems in fact to correct Origen's formula in his *Commentary on the Canticle*.[40] The funeral elegy ("Sermon 26") given by Bernard sometime after the death of Gerard, his brother in the flesh (1138) is likely the most moving and beautiful of the *Sermons on the Canticle*: "The one who is attached to God is 'one spirit with him' (1 Cor. 6:17). He is transformed [*mutatur*], as it were, whole and entire [*quemdam totus*], in the sentiments of God [*in divinum affectum*] . . . And *though God is impassable* [*porro impassibilis est Deus*], he is *not incapable of compassion* [*sed non incompassibilis*]. It is always fitting for him to have pity and to pardon."[41]

It is certainly true that man is transformed by God (*patitur*) in a transfer of affects (*affectum transire*), by which his deification is produced (*deificari*) without dissolution (*manebit quidem substantia*). But it is not the same for God. Positing such would risk the accusation of the anthropological reduction, submitting him to our proper affects and reducing him to our humanity. Bernard takes care to emphasize, against Origen, the thesis of the *divine impassability* according to the canon of medieval philosophy and theology in general—hence avoiding the condemnation of theopaschism. God is impassable—*impassibilis est Deus*—at least in the sense that he does not suffer necessarily *that which* we suffer and *as* we suffer. Here at least it is right to correct Origen. But such a conception of impassability does not prohibit a certain form of "*compassibility*" or "*compassion*": *non est incompassibilis*—"he is not incapable of compassion." Briefly then, the thesis of the impassability of God is not contrary to his "compassibility." Having made this distinction is certainly all to the Cistercian abbot's merit. The impassability of the Father, necessarily maintained because he is not man and does not suffer like us, however requires in its place a form of "compassion" which renders him so evidently close to man that one is no longer able to accuse him of some sort of *indifference* to the spectacle of human misery.[42]

Let me mention the exemplary definition of God that Bernard gives in the *De Consideratione*: *non est affectus Deus, affectio est*—"God is not affected, he is affection." God is "not affected" because the affect of man (*affectus*) is almost always exterior or received from outside: we receive our affects without choosing, nor deciding to undergo them. He is nevertheless "affection" because the active love that he shows (*affectio*) is always interior and intentional: he makes the choice of compassion to that which we suffer.[43] The rejection of affect in God (*affectus*) maintains his impassability, and the necessity of his love or affection (*affectio*) makes possible his "compassibility" or "compassion." The God who is, in Bernard, "impassable but not incapable of compassion" is a valid development of Origen's "Father who is not impassable." Not that Bernard needs at all costs to maintain the impassability of the Father, but Bernard realized that his passability ought not to be identified with our human sensibility, though God is not unfeeling, theologically speaking: "On the one hand, in order to deny the anthropomorphic representation of a God submitted to his passions, it is necessary to recognize the impassability of God. On the other hand, this impassability ought not to be understood as insensitivity, for in God as well suffering is characteristic of love" (E. Housset).[44]

Compassionate Man. The abbot of Clairvaux, in the context of this pathic alterity (Origen) corrected by the active compassion of God, comes to welcome this affection (*affectio*) and compassion of the divine (*non est incompassibilis*). He admits himself to be justly affected (*affectus*) by the death of his brother Gerard in the midst of his *Sermons on the Canticle* ("Sermon 26"). The virtues of the *compassionate God*, precisely in the context of the communion of saints, are transferred and assigned to [*affectée à*] the *compassionate man*, necessary for him also in order to constitute a new mode of community. The songs of joy of the *Canticle* seem of little significance, for Bernard, when sadness and grief strike: "What can this canticle say to me [*quid mihi et cantico huic*]," he confides to his religious brothers, "who resides in the depths of bitterness [*qui in amertudine sum*]?"[45] Contradicting any suspicion of a Bernardine flight into the intelligible, the abbot of Clairvaux reveals in a new way how he lives and, through his own experience, inhabits *for himself* the *affectus* that he has always proclaimed, in many other times and places, as the "compassionate" seat of God himself. For it is not enough to speak about experience, even in the most beautiful sermons (*dicere*); it is necessary to traverse experience (*ex-perire*) in order to attain true wisdom (*sapientia*). Bernard himself is not exempt from this: sometime after mourning for his brother, there ceased the illusion of all mastery of the self in suffering ("I am overcome"). He could no longer smother within his conscience that which can only be expressed externally ("this needs to come out"): "I was able to master the tears [on the day of the funeral] but not my sadness . . . [But now] I confess I am overcome [*fateor, victus sum*]. Let that which I suffer within come out [*exeat*]; it is necessary [*foras quod intus patior*]. Yes, let it be seen by the eyes of my brothers, so that, knowing my sadness, they will judge my laments with more indulgence and console me with more tenderness."[46]

We see here with great force—as is always the case with great men, or at least with great saints—that in the confession of weakness great power is articulated. This is not merely a spiritual matter, but more basically it concerns the human. One does not conquer his passions simply by taking control of them, but rather by expressing them and offering them to another who is capable of welcoming them (whether human brothers or God).[47] In the midst of the passion of torment the Christian speaks more—or at least otherwise. Despite his tears, Bernard's bitterness does not have the last word, as if he were writing a *Treatise on Despair*. Rather, rooted in the conviction of the communion of saints, Bernard pleads with his own dead brother who has become *himself* also "*impassable* but *not incapable of compassion*" by virtue of his union with the "Merciful God" (*qui inhaeres misecordi*). What is true of God becomes true of man once he becomes fully held within God. The "transport of sentiments" between man and God (through Jesus Christ; see Phil. 2:5) is transposed into a "transfer of affects" between men—both of whom are caught in God. Hence Bernard implores *in via* the compassion of the deceased *in patria*. The *divine-human empathy* of an "impassable God not without compassion" forms and transforms the *human-human empathy* of those who are recognized to be "capable of compassion as well" through him and in him. The *properly human affection* of the deceased Gerard (*affectus*) is not in this sense "weak" for Bernard (*imminutus*), as if those held in the divine glory are supposedly indifferent to human misery. It is on the contrary "metamorphosized" or "transformed" (*immutatus*), made capable of giving in the beyond—through compassion (*compassio*) and love (*affectio*)—what his passion (*passio*) or affection (*affectus*) is able to offer to affection here below, unable to surrender itself without immediately suffering for it: "You also must be merciful [*esse misericordem*], you who are united to the Merciful [*qui inhaeres misericordi*] and henceforth delivered from misery. You who are no longer able to suffer [*qui non pateris*], you are capable of compassion [*compateris tamen*]. Your affection [*affectus*] is not diminished [*non est imminutus*] but is transformed [*sed immutatus*]."[48]

With Bernard of Clairvaux, developing Origen, the "suffering with" of the divine-human empathy seems perfectly accomplished. What had begun with Origen ("The Father himself is not impassable") is completed by Bernard ("God is impassable but not incapable of compassion"). The basic characteristic of the genesis of the other is not its dissolution into some kind of annihilation or vacuity (a possible result of a bad reading of Eckhart), but rather its individuated recognition in a community capable of welcoming it: the communion of saints in the Word himself. At the end of this work we will return to this specific path of alterity: only *haecceitas* will confer on the other his true singularity, making of charity the proper name of all community, as Christianity understands it (chap. 9: Duns Scotus). With Origen, therefore, the path is not finished. For the "suffering with" of divine-human empathy still waits to be constituted for all as a true *communio sanctorum*. Said otherwise, the transfer of affects is not sufficient to make the communion because the relation is not grounded in a certain carnal experience at the root of all community, either human or divine. Rediscovering and even preceding the experience of the conversion of the senses described by Saint Bonaventure, Origen establishes the episode of the hemorrhaging woman in the Gospel of Mark (5:25–34) as the source of a renewal of feeling [*la sensation*] at the very heart of the communion (of saints). In a similar way as the reading of Martha and Mary served as Eckhart's framework for understanding the meaning [*le sense*] of "detachment," so also the passage about the hemorrhaging woman serves as Origen's support for expressing the virtue of the "carnal being with" as the ultimate and privileged mode of community. From "common sense" to "common world" a perfect complicity will be established between man and God, so that between the divine and human there will no longer be, as it were, two separated spheres, but rather an intercorporeity that will be revealed to be capable of enduring, even in the beyond.

Being with: A Mode of Community

Common Sense

Once the Bernardian detour is accomplished—in order to correct Origen's pathos of the Father before him and Eckhart's deification as dissolution after him—we can return to the Alexandrian in order to accomplish properly the leap from empathy to community. In passing from the *Homilies on Ezekiel* ("suffering with" or divine-human empathy) to the *Homilies on Leviticus* ("being with" as mode of community), Origen traverses the ford that marks the boundary between pathos and the kinesthesia in which the passions always remain enrooted: the hemorrhaging woman's "approach [*idcirco accessit*] signifies having truly understood [*et quia vere intellexit*] the holy flesh [*quae esset caro sancta sanctorum*]."[49]

Understanding the Flesh. "To understand the flesh" (*intellegere carnem*) and "to approach it" (*accedere*): such is, for Origen, what the hemorrhaging woman accomplishes in a twofold sense: comprehension as grasping a phenomenon and as the filling of an intention. Only an *intentionality of the body*, as we have already discussed in regard to Bonaventure above though without yet envisaging it in the context of a constitutive community of saints, simultaneously orients and innervates, as it were, the recognition of the woman who touches the "flesh of Christ." Instead of purely and simply requesting salvation, the woman much more profoundly attempts *incorporation into the Son* by touching his garment: "Through this contact full of faith [*et fideli tactu*] she draws from the flesh [*elicuit ex carne*] a force that purifies her from impurity and heals her of the evil that she suffered."[50]

In this divine-human *corps à corps*, as a prefiguration of the communion of saints (being incorporated into the Son), it is not sufficient for the woman "to grasp" the body of Jesus just as one takes hold of an object in order to appropriate it. The *filling of the bodily intention* is such that "touching the flesh of Jesus" (*tagat quis carnem Iesu*) can only be understood "after the manner described above" (*quo supra exposimus*): *tota fide*—"with complete faith."[51] The "comprehension of the flesh" (*intellegere carnem*) is therefore not, to speak in Husserl's terms, a simple apprehension of a bodily substance (*Körperlichkeit*). On the contrary, it gives and is given in the modality of touch—for *faith* is the place of the conversion of the senses—which precisely renders it carnal (*Leiblichkeit*): by her faith that saves her ("daughter, your faith has saved you," Mk. 5:34), the woman deciphered or recognized in the flesh of the other (namely Jesus's and the modes of being of his body) "the same power to espouse the things that I have touched in my own" (Merleau-Ponty).[52] Said otherwise, since the Word of God dwells in his own flesh in the same way that I experience my own flesh, I can and ought to understand that only the "comportment of *his* flesh" suffices for me to render myself both other *and* carnal: "Only a similarity connecting, within my primordial sphere, that body over there with my body can serve as the motivational basis for the 'analogizing' apprehension of that body as another animate organism."[53]

Because the woman "approaches Jesus" in faith (*accedat ad Iesum*) by realizing that she approaches "the Word made flesh" (*tamquam ad Verbum carnem factum*), her "touching the flesh of sacrifice" reciprocally sanctifies her as by a recoil: "touching the flesh of the sacrifice in order to be sanctified" (Lev. 6:15).[54] What saves this woman is therefore not her *admission of fault* ("she told him everything," Mk. 5:33)—for the communion of saints is not satisfied by the sole ambition of salvation. It is rather her *faith in the flesh of the Word* and her possible incorporation in him ("if I only touch the hem of his garment . . . ," Mk. 5:28). The "apperception by analogy" is such here that what this woman experienced in herself of God (that power that "came forth from the flesh of Jesus"—*elicuit ex carne*) made her recognize the other—the incarnate Word—both as an "other me" (touching me as I can touch him) and "an other *than* me" (I can never, in touching him, truly feel in the same way that he feels when he touches me): "Who touched me?" (Mk. 5:30).[55] The other *of* man (*alter ego*), the incarnate Word, is no less the other *than* man (*ego alter*) since everyone recognizes both for him and the other the irreducible opacity that separates him from all flesh—and even more so for the flesh of God since he explicitly espouses the flesh of man all the while veiling his divinity.

In Origen's perspective the divine-human "touching-touched" is somehow so present here that it becomes the principal—and probably original—intentional aim in the communion of saints: that by which an *intersubjectivity* is forged starting from a communion of *intercorporeity*. A few gradual steps, from the simple "search for Jesus" to "contact with the Savior," mark the carnal apprehension of the incarnate Word. Contrary to what typically passes for a beatific "vision," for Origen as much as for Bonaventure later (as also, finally, in a completely different order in Merleau-Ponty), *touching* the lover rather than *seeing* him, constitutes the highest degree of certitude that one has been grasped by him: "We can explain in order and expound with convenient distinctions the levels of progress (*qui sit profectus*) moving from the act of *touching* the garment of Christ (Mt. 9:20; hemorrhaging woman), *washing* his feet with tears and *drying* them with the hair on her head, and how it is preferable to *anoint* his head with myrrh (Lk. 7:44–6; Mary of Bethany), and finally of the superiority of *resting* on his breast (Jn. 13:24, 21:20; the disciple whom Jesus loved)."[56]

Origen's spiritual reading of an episode of scripture does not remain a simple touching-touched event for a woman "enfleshed" via the incarnate Word (Péguy),[57] in a relation that we could no longer share: "Perhaps we could also say that *we also* [*et de nobis*] have touched the holy flesh of the Word of God and that *we* are sanctified." What was for the hemorrhaging woman both carnal and spiritual (by the intentionality of her body) remains always accessible to us by means of the exercise of our own interior senses. Such a *sensory ascesis*, already deciphered in the light of the conversion of the senses in Bonaventure, becomes in Origen the condition of the experience of a common mode shared by men and God within the sphere of the communion of saints. Let us now investigate: (a) the manner in which man has "sensed" God, and (b) the proper way that God "perceives" man, thereby constituting their common intercorporeity.

Sense of Man and Sense of God. (a) It is fitting first to show how the believer, *in via* during the terrestrial life, finds some ways to clear a path toward the incarnate Word, thereby participating in those who form *in patria* his resurrected body (the communion of saints). Origen comments extensively on a number of the "sacrifices of reparation" for which the Book of Leviticus states that it is necessary to "pay back five times as much" when one errs by holding back some offering to God (Lev. 5:16). Because the number five "almost always designates our five senses [*pro quinque sensibus accipitur*]," to sacrifice to God means to offer *our bodily senses themselves* in order to convert them in the crucible of faith and thus to render them spiritual: "Thanks to the senses of the interior man (*interioris hominis sensus*) who has become pure of heart, we *see* God (Mt. 5:8); we have ears to *understand* Jesus' teaching (Mt. 11:15); we perceive this *odor* about which the Apostle speaks when he says that we are the pleasing aroma of Christ (2 Cor. 2:15); we obtain this *taste* about which the prophet says 'taste and see the goodness of the Lord' (Ps. 33:9); and we obtain this *touching* that John mentions when he speaks of 'what we have looked upon, and touched with our hands concerning the Word of life' (1 Jn. 1:1)."[58]

Like the "spiritual senses" in Bonaventure, the "interior senses" in Origen do not designate any *other senses* than the bodily ones, but these *same senses* converted in the service of the apprehension of the Word as body of the church. The *restitution* and *sanctification* of the senses—"we now *restore* [*restituamus nunc*] these five senses to holy activities"—makes man newly capable of espousing the *modes of being* of the Word: in the body of the church, for now, as the place of his "flesh" and of the manifestation of the "communion of saints."

Seeing *like him*, hearing *like him*, feeling *like him*, tasting *like him* and touching *like him*: we await these things in our sojourn on earth (*in via*), which we will receive tomorrow in the Kingdom (*in patria*). Between those in heaven and those on earth, the difference is not of nature but of degree. The act of the resurrection is already fully realized from the morning of Easter—an event that the Parousia itself will only announce the full realization. Origen's famous doctrine of the "preexistence of souls"—the only idea of Origen's justly condemned as heresy—contradicts the premises of the communion of saints in the carnal apprehension of God by the interior senses.[59] The *continuity* between the beyond and the here-below requires the conservation of that which properly constitutes the lived experience of Christian faith as apprehension of the incarnate Word: a mode of flesh (*Leib*), not in the sense of "body and spirit," but as a "concrete emblem of a general manner of being" by which what is lived in the body (*Körper*) is at the same time the sign and symbol of the flesh that experiences it (*Leib*).[60]

(b) What is true of man (the hemorrhaging woman), for Origen, is also true of God (in the form of the incarnate Word). The same thing goes, in *Against Celsus* (I, 48), for Jesus himself, who "touching the leper" (Mt. 8:3) is understood not only to deliver him from "physical leprosy by a *sensible touch*" as comprehended by the crowd, but also to deliver him from "the *other leprosy* by his *truly divine touch*."[61] For Christ, leprosy of the body is only the physiological support of a more profound leprosy, which indicates a mode of being of the flesh: the disgrace of a corporeity struck by sin (Gen. 3:7), in relation to which his flesh is incorporated to ours by his resurrection, thereby effecting our deliverance. Far from pushing us to flee our bodies, the Christian experience of the "conversion of the senses," as Origen sees it here, invites us to indwell them otherwise, namely, *like* Christ and *in* Christ. Paradoxically touch is all the more divinized (in the spiritual senses) as it is humanized (in the incarnation), always passing through the experience of the Word made flesh.

Touching the Word who touches us, seeing him who sees us, feeling him who feels us, and so on: such is precisely the meaning of intercorporeity, or the divine-human "chiasm" through which we constitute a unity out of our senses. Said otherwise, the "spiritual senses" appear—precisely for the first time with Origen—as a properly Christian mode of their unification by the "*common sense*": "To all these actions of the interior senses, we add one, for the sake of relating them all to a single God [*ut ad unum Deum haec cuncta referamus*]."[62]

This unity of the senses in the apprehension of the Word made flesh announces the unity of those among the communion of saints who, by means of senses converted in him, apprehend him *in the same fashion* whether "in heaven" or "on the earth." The beatific vision itself does not suppress the senses in order to appear in the order of the soul alone. On the contrary, it demands the *whole and entire man* who has converted his own senses in the here below in order to consecrate them already as a lived experience of his flesh in the beyond (*Leib*), and which survive somehow the decline of his body here below (*Körper*). For the believer resurrection is not a Platonic survival of soul in eternity (*psychê*), but rather being "transformed" carnally (1 Cor. 15:51) in the encounter between oneself and the other in the lived experience of the flesh (*Leib*). What matters is the way that I live in the "body" in order to constitute it as "flesh": such is what is already hidden with the Father in the anticipation of the final resurrection or the total incorporation of carnal beings in the spiritual body of Christ or the church.[63]

Flesh of Scripture and Flesh of the Word. The Logos is not only "embodied in Scripture" as Henri de Lubac investigated in his profound study of the senses of scripture in Origen.[64] He is also "incarnated in a body" according to an original experience that only descriptive phenomenology can hope to elucidate: "In the last days," says Origen in the opening lines of his *Homilies on Leviticus*, "the Word of God assumed a flesh drawn from Mary [*ex Mariae carne*], thus making his entrance into this world. One thing was that which was seen in him [*aliud erat quod videbatur in eo*], and another thing was that which was understood [*aliud quod intelligebatur*], for the vision of the flesh was offered to all, though only to a few was given the knowledge of the divinity."[65] The act of "comprehending" the flesh of the Word (*intellegere carnem*) by the "interior senses" (*sensus interioris*) is therefore not identified with the exercise of intellection of the "senses of Scripture" (*sensus scripturae*). To say therefore of the letter of scripture, that it is "like the flesh of the Word of God and the skin covering his divinity" does not dispense us from placing all our attention *first on the flesh of the Word* (descriptive phenomenology) and then on the letter of the text (hermeneutics of scripture).[66] The Alexandrian does not negate the carnal experience of the Word made flesh in deciphering there at the same time a spiritual apprehension—no more than he suppresses the literal sense in traversing it completely.

Everything is a matter here of conversion (of the letter or the senses), and not of an overcoming or a flight (outside the text or beyond the body). The detour by way of the "common sense" of man and God requires that we no longer separate the worlds, nor divide time, nor tear apart the flesh. The "in common" of man and God constitutes their very being—as opposed to the conception according to which their being in common, adding one to the other, would then make their community. As far as Christianity is concerned, one is either "with God—'*Emmanuel*'" or one is not at all: "the *community of being*—as opposed to a being of community—behold what it must now be," in phenomenology (Heidegger, Nancy) as much as in theology (Origen).[67]

The carnal community of man and God realized here below (the hemorrhaging woman) expects in this sense to be conserved and metamorphosized in the beyond: "Truly I say to you, I will not drink of the fruit of the vine until the day that I drink it *anew* in the Kingdom of God" (Mk. 14:25). The exegetical commentary on the "new wine" develops the quasi-phenomenological description of the hemorrhaging woman (still in the *Homilies on Leviticus*), justifying this "community of being" that the Christian mode of intersubjectivity amplifies in the *communio sanctorum* rooted in the figure of the resurrected Christ.

The Community of Being

Origen's homilies on what will later be called the communion of saints in "anticipation of new wine" (Lev. 10:9) constitute, as their French translator in the celebrated *Sources chrétiennes* series would say, "les pages les plus émouvantes des *Homélies sur le Lévitique*."[68] Beyond the virtuosity of his prose, the originality of the Alexandrian is found as much in the "precession," as it were, of the Father's compassion over the single passion of the Son ("passion in God"), as in the possible apperception of the Word by the spiritual senses in the communion of saints ("the common sense"). Without falling into some heterodoxy, the *communio sanctorum*, as an exemplary mode of community in Origen, establishes the hypotheses of a potential solidarity of all men, both on "earth" as in "heaven." It is no longer enough to disunite the community constituted by those who live in the heavenly homeland with the Father (*in patria*), on the one hand, and those who, still in becoming, remain pilgrims on the earth (*in via*), on the other hand. The path always matters more than the results, and those who dwell "over there" (*illic*) are not indifferent to anything that is done "down here" (*hic*). The intercorporeity of man and God in God's deliberately chosen compassion, on the one hand (Origen-Bernard), and in the exercise of the spiritual senses, on the other (Origen-Bonaventure), are united together in order simultaneously to constitute a "common time," a "common world," and even a "common flesh" between God and men and among men themselves.

A Common Time. Concerning time as a mode of community, it is not fitting, according to Origen, to separate, on the one hand, a terrestrial temporality that we know and within which we are the sole actors, and, on the other hand, a celestial eternity in which the blessed rejoice in their well-being in a unilaterally a-temporal world. For both the phenomenologist (Husserl) and the theologian (Origen) there is no recognition of the other than by means of the constitution of a "common time": "*Private time*," says Paul Ricoeur regarding the father of phenomenology, "is ordered by relation to an objective *common time* of which it is a mode of appearing."[69] Said otherwise, and returning to the question of the communion of the living on earth and in heaven in Christ (*communio sanctorum*), the temporality of the blessed is neither able nor ought negatively to take position against those humans on earthly pilgrimage. Without both the celestial and terrestrial, no intersubjective relation is possible. That "my Savior even now [*etiam nunc*] weeps over my sins" in "anticipation of the new wine" (Lev. 10:9) signifies that the terrestrial temporality is not indifferent at all to the fulfillment of celestial temporality.[70] The first is not opposed to the second, no more than the second is necessarily a more enviable mode. Either of them and both together—as two divergent but complementary *perspectives* on the vision of God—are ordered *to* each other in order to constitute *together* a single and unified "incarnate temporality" in the common knowledge of the Eternal One himself: "*Eternal life* is *to know you* the one true God and the one you have sent, Jesus Christ" (Jn. 17:3).

The Pascalian formula of a "Jesus in agony until the end of the world" thus indicates, and retrospectively in Origen, less the act of agony itself in some kind of Dolorism that is resolutely absent from his theological perspective than the *dimension of expectation* [*l'attente*] by which the Word constitutes a "common texture" (Merleau-Ponty) of man and God and among men by means of his own Body, the church.[71] Far from attributing merely a carnal suffering to the divinized Christ in his own body, "it appears more likely," says Henri de Lubac, "that throughout this homily [of Origen's] we have to do with Christ contemplated *not as he is in himself alone* but as *mystically united to man*."[72] The Son's act of waiting [*attente*] for our own conversion is repeated by an "expectation of the saints" [*attente des saints*] which already constitutes his body. Perfection, for Christianity, is not realized in some philosophical eternal immutability, but rather in the progressive constitution of a "common temporality" among men in the single apperception (spiritual) of the Word made flesh: "In their departure from here below, the saints no longer obtain immediately the full recompense of their merits. They wait for us [*sed expectant etiam nos*] while we delay and drag on. There is not for them some perfect joy within which they are not afflicted by our erring [*pro erroribus nostris dolent*] and do not weep over our sins [*et lugent nostra peccata*]."[73]

The "passion of charity" that God has for men is transformed into *compassion among men* if it is the case that humans now live and experience themselves *and* others totally *in* God. Auto-affection and hetero-affection are reciprocally engaged with one another in order to constitute the communion of saints and a renewed mode of alterity. Because Christ "does not want *to be alone* [*non vult solus*] in the Kingdom to drink the wine, he waits for us [*nos expectat*]." And because the saints do not want to "proceed on to perfection *without us* [*sine nobis*]," they wait for us also.[74] In this shared expectation, both of God for men and among men in God, solipsism (*solus ipse*) is definitively shattered. The Son's not wanting to be alone means not only, in soteriological perspective, never to break his communion with the Father as at Gethsemane, but it is even more, in eschatological perspective, never to be unloosed of his relation to man until the end of time: "It is enough for a Christian [*christianos*] to be brought to trial," insists Origen in the Greek version of his *Homilies on Jeremiah*, "in order that the Christ [*o Christos*] be brought to trial."[75] Each sin of man "crucifies anew" the very One who died on the cross once and for all.[76] There is discovered in this pathos of the divine flesh the pathos of all the saints, by which we are introduced, in virtue of this "common time," to a "common world" between man and God.

A Common World. "The *communio sanctorum*," says Karl Barth, "can be achieved only in the distinctive *triangle* of God, a man and a fellow-man—the two latter being united in a definitely ordered relationship."[77] Nothing in fact is more foreign to Christianity than every form of spiritualism that pretends to justify some kind of direct communication with the dead, or with those who are with God. For both theology and phenomenology there is only a "common world" by means of an "enactment of community" (*Vergemeinschaft*) by which both are recognized to pertain identically to the same world.[78] Said otherwise, that is, in the perspective of the communion of saints, the *koinonia* formed by the collection of saints on earth as in heaven does not live first by way of an already constituted community, but only from the *shared intentional aim* of one and the same God: what matters for Husserl—as well as Origen—is not what they say "*about* community" but how the one and the other advance step by step "*toward* community."[79] For genetic phenomenology and Christian eschatology, egoity is not the root of community (*Vergemeinschaft* or *koinonia*) but rather stems from and is constituted by it: "We are the body of Christ [*corpus sumus Christi*] and his members in every part [*et membra ex parte*]," says Origen commenting on 1 Cor. 12:27.[80] The "part of the body of Christ" that we are only becomes complete to the degree that not our spirit alone but our body whole and entire comes along with the spirit to submit to God: "If I come to force my flesh and all my members to be in agreement with the spirit [*in consonantiam spiritus trahere*], then I will become perfectly submitted [*tunc perfecte videbor esse subiectus*]."[81]

The "community of the world," that is, among men in the incarnate Word therefore comes first from the capacity of each man "totally" (*ex integro*) to submit his own body to the body of Christ, the church. It is meaningless to point out the absence from the body (*Körper*) of those who are in heaven in order to prohibit intersubjectivity since it is founded on the lone modes of being common to the flesh (*Leib*). What perishes in death is the bodily senses only insofar as they remain "unsubmitted" to their spiritual conversion. To be resurrected with Christ and to commune with those who already constitute his body does not negate either my own flesh or theirs. On the contrary, it is only a matter of attempting to convert, in the unity of a "common world" (the incarnate Word), my bodily senses so that they finally become "spiritual" along with those who are already in heaven and contemplate God with their interior senses. In such a conversion of corporeity both mystical and intersubjective, perhaps I then come to sense *how* one senses God along *with* those who in the Son are with the Father; to understand *how* he must be heard; to see *how* he must be seen; and so on. The *communion of saints* does not make appeal to some "repayment," as is sometimes believed, as if God is engaged in a sort of ghastly bargaining as unworthy of the hope of men as it is of the grace of God. Likewise it does not seek to live a "mutual union" or an illusory "fusion" of the living and dead that a deceptive etymology lends to thought (*cum-unio*). Only the mystery of "participation" or "shared support" (*com-munis*) of the life of one by another in Christ accounts for it:[82] "*My* essential position consists in being able to respond to this essential misery of the other and finding resources to do so. The Other who dominates me in his transcendence is thus the stranger, the widow and orphan toward whom I am obligated."[83]

In the Christian conception of the communion of saints, however, the responsibility of *the one for the other* is not played out in the asymmetry of their direct encounter. This is its difference with the direct relation of Levinas and Judaism ("Am I my brother's keeper?" Gn. 4:9). Because the Word is incarnated just as I am in my flesh, Christ "stands *between* me and my neighbor."[84] For the Levinasian verticality of the face-to-face encounter [*face-à-face*] there is substituted the (Merleau-Pontian) *corps-à-corps*.[85] From the perspective of the end of time, that is, of the Parousia, this "common world" ever in genesis, in the progressive submission of my own body to the body of Christ (and to those who are held within it), finds its full realization in the goal of the church as "common flesh" in which "all will be in all" (1 Cor. 15:28).

A Common Flesh. By virtue of the possible "empathy" of God to man and the necessary "carnal apprehension" of the Resurrected that still shows its value for thought today, the Son himself awaits [*attend*] in his flesh (*Leib*) of which we are the members, the time to submit finally to the Father the entire creation still in process of being accomplished: "When the Son will have achieved his work and led all his creation to the supreme perfection, then he will submit himself [*ipse dicitur subiectus*] in those he has submitted to the Father."[86] What was often heretically interpreted here as the disobedience of the Son to the Father in the anticipation [*l'attente*] of the total "remuneration" or "reconciliation" of all things in him (*apocatastasis*) actually leads to the hypothesis of a real and effective communion of saints to its term: "When all things will have been submitted to him," says Saint Paul, "then the Son himself will submit [*upotagêstai*] to the One who has submitted all things to him, in order that God will be all in all" (1 Cor. 15:28).[87] It is not the Son himself who is disobedient before the final submission, but only the creation, which, in the Son, accomplishes the act of submission and being *brought to be with* the Father—in the threefold sense of "remission," "remuneration," and "recapitulation."[88] The flesh of the Son somehow carries the stigmata, not by some original incompleteness of his own body (by which he would then definitively leave the sphere of the divine), but of an incompleteness which is that of *creation* and of *man* himself whose gaze is still turned away from God because of sin: "What is lacking in the afflictions of Christ I fill up in my *flesh* [*sarxi mou*] for the sake of his *body* [*sômatos autou*] which is the Church [*ekklesia*]" (Col. 1:24). The "inhabitation" of the Son in *the body of the church* therefore expresses, even today, the lived experience of *his own flesh in ours*. His *body*, at once resurrected (in himself) and still on the way toward resurrection (in his link with the creation) is of such a kind that he awaits the incorporation of all humanity into his church and, through it, the realization of the "interpenetration" of all men among themselves: "The Savior does not want to receive his perfected glory *without you* [*sine te*], that is, without *his people* who are *his body* and *his members*. For he wants *to dwell* as the soul [*sui ipse velut anima habitare*] of this body of his Church in these members of his people . . . so that truly will be accomplished the word of the prophet: 'I *will dwell* among them and walk with them'" (Lev. 26:12).[89] In the intercorporeity that here creates the specific situation of alterity at the heart of the communion of saints, the unity of the flesh of man and of the flesh of God in the resurrected Christ is therefore not, in the last instance, a unity of fusion, but only of interpenetration, even of "coupling" or "combining" (*Parung*), to use the terminology of Husserl.[90] The "carnal similitude" of man and God do not suppress that which is *proper* to the flesh of God or to the flesh of man: a vivification and indwelling of the members of his body for the flesh of God and, for the flesh of man, a welcoming of such an inhabitation for the sake of participating in the complete submission of the creation to the sole resurrected flesh of the Son of man.

If there is in Origen a *hermeneutic of the text* (de Lubac's senses of scripture), it is founded on a *phenomenological description of the body* in general—the original empathy of God in the pathos of the Father and the pathos of the Son, the experience of intercorporeity in the conversion of the senses and the genesis of communion in the temporal, worldly, and carnal community. "The pure—and so to speak, still dumb—psychological experience, which now must utter its own sense with no adulteration" thus finds in the Alexandrian its greatest raison d'être.[91] The entire creation does not speak but by means of the body, and remains in the expectation of the carnal praise of all the saints, themselves unified in the resurrected Christ and built up in him, by, as it were, a living "ossificiation," the body of the church. The "community" of saints gives rise to thought here as *the* exemplary relation of "intersubjectivity" in Origen, not, in the first place however, as it is *articulated* in acts of praise, but rather as it is *made* by the movements of the flesh which "speak" themselves. The other creates me as the flesh speaks me and thus establishes the engendering egoity (Eckhart) as an engendered community (Origen): "All of these bones *speak* [*omnia ossa ista loquuntur*]," exclaims the Alexandrian at the end of his *Homilies on Leviticus*, "they *sing* a hymn [*hymnum dicunt*] and *give thanks* to God [*et gratias agunt Deo*] . . . Each bone among these bones was feeble, broken by the hand of a strong man. It had neither the joint of charity [*non habebat iuncturam caritatis*], nor the nerves of patience [*nos nervos patientiae*], nor the veins of the vivifying spirit [*non venas vitalis animi*] and the vigor of faith [*et fidei vigorem*]. But when the One came who was to collect [*colligeret*] that which was dispersed, and to unite [*coniungeret*] that which was disjointed, linking bones and joints, he began to construct [*aedificare coepit*] the holy body of the Church [*sanctum corpus Ecclesiae*]."[92]

✦

What is produced for man in his relation to God—community as mode of intersubjectivity—has not yet received its full justification with Origen, according to a structure of alterity fully identified. Said otherwise, it is not sufficient for the living or the deceased to be imagined in an incorporated whole, even if in the incarnate Word. It is necessary instead to show that living *for each with the other and in God* signifies further that one is not only with the other in a third, but one receives oneself from this Third who exceeds and totally overflows us all. After the homiletic detour by way of Origen concerning the communion of saints, there comes the Thomist way concerned with the question of the angels (*Summa theologiae* Ia. Q. 50–64). We never simply descend from heaven with Aquinas (the angels) in the sense that for the medievals heaven is never as "pure" as when it offers *for us* a structure of alterity that the "separated philosophy" cannot deliver. Corresponding to the phenomenological question posed at the beginning of the *Cartesian Meditations* (how is a man able to know another man, or "what about the *other ego*?")[93] is the answer given by the treatise on the angels of Saint Thomas's *Summa*: "Do angels know each other? [*utrum unus angelus alium cognoscat*]" (*Summa*, 1a, q. 56, a. 2). Of course, the rapprochement of angels and alterity would appear absurd if (a) Husserl himself had not suggested it, and if (b) so many *Treatises on the Angels* of the Middle Ages had not furnished precisely its highest degree of conceptuality.

(a) Just a passing note, then, on the "Prolegomena" to the *Logical Investigations* (1901), which ought to be sufficiently convincing: "*Mathematical angels* may no doubt use *other methods of calculus* than ours—does this mean that they may have *different axioms and theorems*?" Husserl's point is clear and seems to be confirmed later in *Ideas I* (1913). If the angels and even God could adopt other methods in order to know what we know, it would still be necessary that they take the *same perspectives* on the world that we also have: "It is proven true that everything that has the character of a spatial object is able to be perceived not only by men but even by God . . . as far as modes of appearances are concerned." Briefly, for angels, men, and God, a certain community is at least possible, even if in a purely fictive and non-confessional mode.[94]

(b) Concerning the Middle Ages: it is wrong to accuse medieval philosophy of not having "thematized" the question of alterity as such, at least as Thomas Aquinas (chap. 8) and Duns Scotus (chap. 9) are concerned. With the treatise on the angels of the *Summa* (1a, qq. 50–64), a reflection on a clearly differentiated alterity is undertaken, though Thomists have rarely indicated its striking pertinence for current discussions—though let an exception be made for the "language of the angels according to the Scholastics."[95] We will come to this in due course.

After seeing the other in the sphere of "community" (Origen) and before circumscribing him in his "singularity" (Scotus) it will be necessary to reveal him as such in his "constituted egoity"—a task loaded on the back of Aquinas. At the heart of the most confessional thought (the angels) is articulated something radically phenomenological (the structure of relation to the other). Of course, it is not necessary to believe in the existence of angels in order to think within their horizon. For in this case their existence matters even less than their appearance or mode of phenomenalization. We find in this new model of alterity given by angelology the roots for a newly constituted egoity (alterology). To say it differently, the treatise on the angels of Saint Thomas reread together with the *Cartesian Meditations* (especially the fifth) seems to build anew the entire phenomenological structure of alterity. We can at least recognize that this structure, if not fully based on God himself, has been researched so thoroughly in the twentieth century (e.g., by the *Cartesian Meditations*) but did not remain unthought until then (e.g., in the *Summa Theologiae*), albeit in a theological rather than phenomenological context and with a completely different goal in mind, one that was soteriological rather than gnoseological.

Chapter 8

Angelic Alterity (Thomas Aquinas)

With the treatise on the angels in the *Summa* of Thomas Aquinas (Ia, qq. 50–64) alterity is truly constituted, though now identified with a shared structure of "knowledge" and not merely affectivity (as in Origen). When an angel comes to "know [*cognoscit*] another angel" (q. 56, a. 2) an *ego* discovers an *alter ego*. The sky of theology serves in a new way as a model for the renewal of the earth of philosophy: angelic alterity for the sake of the formation of intersubjectivity (Thomas Aquinas), after the communion of saints for the sake of the genesis of community (Origen) but before the charitable union conceived as an invitation to singularity (Duns Scotus). In each case, as always, it is a matter of the same undertaking: we are capable of receiving ancient models in order to make fruitful the most advanced contemporary research. For we would certainly believe wrongly that we have discovered new frontiers on our own when our ancient predecessors have already done much of the imaginative work well before us. We will therefore not be offended to find, at the heart of theological reflection on the angels, a bold starting point from which to think the philosophical constitution of the other. For Aquinas what differentiates men from angels is not only the difference by species proper to the angelic nature, but also the substantial union with a body by which they are differentiated from men: "Not being composed of matter and form, but being composed of subsistent forms, the non-corporeal substances ought to be distinguished by species [*in specie*] . . . And the very fact that the soul of man has need of a body in some fashion in order to act shows that it is an intellectual nature at an inferior degree to that of the angel, which is never united to a body [*qui corpori non unitur*]."[1]

From this we could certainly conclude that the angels no longer have anything to say to us today. Their "disincarnation" would be the condition for their demythologization (I will return to this shortly) and even for their eradication from our reflection. Yet Thomas adds, surprisingly, that the angels take on a corporeity *in order to appear*. If they "are" not a body, they must still "assume" one: "It is not for themselves [*propter seipsos*] that the angels need to assume bodies [*indigent corpore assumpto*] but for us [*sed propter nos*]."[2] Not "being" bodies, the angels "have" or "assume" them, at least in their manner of appearing to man. Far from suppressing corporeity (part II) and especially the fundamental hypothesis of a possible conversion of the senses (chaps. 6 and 7), the carnal appearance of angels, on the contrary, confirms it (chap. 8). Christianity is forever and always the declension of a carnal mystery, which evidently includes the apparently most non-carnal beings themselves: the angels. The paradox is sound because the exception proves the rule, as in the Book of Tobit: "the angel which appeared to Tobit [*apparuit Tobiae*] was seen by all [*ab omnibus videbatur*]."[3]

What is appropriate to "angelic" knowledge (Thomas Aquinas), as for "saintly" communion (Origen) does not involve remaining in the heaven of its intellections, nor of being satisfied in a contemplation indifferent to everything human. On the contrary, the angel comes to man and is very precisely sent to him as a "messenger" (*angelos*), not for the sake of being incarnate—the difference between the angel and the Word made flesh is essential (contra, once again, the Gnostic *Christos angelos* thesis)—but primarily in order to protect him, even to take care of him or contemplate him: "Every man in the pilgrim state receives the protection of an angel [*custos angelos disputatur*]."[4] In this angelic custody or guardianship of man (just as a cleric carefully keeps the host in a pyx [*dans la "custode"*] in order to protect it) there is articulated inchoately at least a fully constituted alterity discovered by medieval philosophy in its treatment of the nature of the angels. The reasons for rooting alterity at the heart of reflection on the angels are not carried in this direction in the absence of the corporeity of the superior creatures, nor even in the purity of their actions which restrains them from sin. Such motifs move them away *from us* so much that they can do nothing *for us* in their radical strangeness. Only the *identified concern* that each angel takes in regard to the other, as well as for each man in particular, indicates also the *care for the other* that is found in contemporary research on alterity: "The fact of not evading the burden imposed by the suffering of others defines ipseity itself" (Levinas).[5]

Should the angel Damiel in Wim Wenders's *Wings of Desire* regret the fact of not being incarnate? Can he? Posing the question of the constitution of alterity in relation to the angels while reading Thomas Aquinas does not allow us to accept such a conclusion. On the contrary, the actions and gestures of the human world cannot remain without interest for those who live in the divine world. There are not—neither for them nor for us—two worlds, as our investigation of Origen already made plain. There are instead two *different manners* of living in the same world. Even if observed through the insurmountable transparency of a car window, the little things that fill our daily experience are not foreign to the angels who serve as guardians of humanity, if also in a different mode altogether than our own (apparent, not substantial flesh) and with a completely different purpose (the invocation of the message of God rather than the incarnation in humanity). What remains buried within the order of nostalgia for Wim Wenders is in Thomas Aquinas already realized in hope and specifically related to a newly constituted alterity.

Everything is shared between the angel and man, as I will now show, including the experiences of a "passer-by who, under the rain, shut her umbrella with a twitch of the hand and was left drenched . . . ; a schoolboy who described to his astonished teacher how a fern emerges from the earth . . . ; a blind woman fumbling around for her watch as she felt my presence."[6]

✦

Return of the Angels

According to a classical *theologoumenon*, the angel always falls by way of envy (*peccatium invidiae*) or pride (*peccatum superbiae*). According to Thomas Aquinas, the fallen angel sins by way of envy when he competes, not only with the divine glory (sin of pride), but also with a glory falsely believed to be complete in itself and given to men (sin of envy): "After the sin of pride, the angel experiences the sin of envy because he is saddened by the good of men."[7] Envy is not lacking in Wim Wenders's angel Damiel, whose volatile wings of Desire make him such a fickle personality. The antinomy between angelic spirituality and human corporeality leads him always to seek to retain the benefits of one all the while enjoying the privilege of the other. Thus Damiel reflects: "The wonder of a living spirit is to witness, day after day, for eternity, the spiritual, nothing but the spiritual in people—but sometimes I tire of my eternal spiritual existence. I wish I no longer hovered over everything eternally, I would like to feel in myself a weight that abolishes the limitless and drags me down to earth."[8] But does the angel here suffer from an "unendurable perfection" or "density that crushes it" as Rilke says in the *Duino Elegies*?[9]

Paradoxically, though as an understandable aftereffect, at the very moment of the celebrated return of the angels on the cultural and cinematic scene—with Rilke's *Duino Elegies* and Wenders's *Wings of Desire* and *Faraway, So Close!*, or Michel Serres's *La légende des anges*—the cohort of seraphim, cherubim, and other spiritual creatures seems to escape the clutches of Western theology. Protestant theologian Rudolph Bultmann, in his work to demythologize theology, did not hesitate to hold responsible the New Testament's belief in spirits for "making the message of the Christian faith incomprehensible for our time" (1955: the era of the "electric lightbulb," "photography," and "modern medicine").[10] Likewise Catholic theologian Christian Ducoq suggested that the biblical data on maleficent spirits was "relevant as an image of the world that provided the context of revelation, but is not guaranteed by it."[11] Is it that both the rapid development of modern technology and (worse yet) the revelation of the Word made flesh together should have extinguished all belief in angelic realities? This decline of angelology in Western theology was not lost on Henri Corbin who, precisely as a philosopher, placed it in the spotlight, but rediscovered it in a new place: Islam. He specifically blamed the doctrine of the two natures (*homoousios*) that develops across Christianity from Saint Paul to the Councils of the Fathers, in order to uncover behind it a supposedly primitive sense of Christianity as a "prophetology," thereby retrieving from the beginning an angelology starting from Islam.[12] The angels therefore no longer have citizenship within the Western church at least historically defined as such, *ad intra* by the contestations of contemporary theologians (Catholic and Protestant) and *ad extra* by the denial of a true Christian angelology by recourse to Islam. Our concern here is not reopening some polemic on the subject of the angels. Perhaps, anyway, they already have enough to worry about in their role as messengers (*angelos*) between God and men, which is more or less uniformly recognized in virtually every tradition. Yet the specific displacement of angelology put in operation by Henri Corbin, from theology (whether Christian or otherwise) to philosophy (starting from phenomenology in particular), authorizes a new philosophical interrogation that concerns the legitimacy of such a return of angelology.

In Light of the Cartesian Meditations

From the vantage of such a rapprochement between phenomenology and theology—the fecundity of which will only be measured a posteriori and not a priori—we will attempt to decode the treatise on the angels in Thomas's *Summa* (Ia., qq. 50–64) in light of the fifth *Cartesian Meditation* of Husserl. By a sort of automatic recoil, I will also be forced to show how in Husserl himself there is found a nostalgia for angelic knowledge, away from which much recent phenomenology has made it its task to swerve.

We will take then the fifth of the *Cartesian Meditations* as a guide for understanding Thomist angelology: on the one hand, as a guiding thread to be sure (we will therefore follow it step by step in the course of this confrontation), but also, on the other hand, as the boundary zone of our investigation (we will have to mark the boundary lines at each step in order not to fall into gross anachronism or an arbitrary comparison). Paradoxically, in guise of a beginning, the *quaestio* on the self-knowledge of the angels of the *Summa* begins in a strangely similar way as the fifth *Cartesian Meditation* opens: Thomas asks, "Does the angel know itself? (q. 56, a. 1)," and Husserl wonders what happens "when I reduce myself by the phenomenological *epochê* to my absolute transcendental ego" (§42).

The Broken Circle

Angelic Solipsism

Angelic Self-Knowledge. Descartes himself—along with Husserl as his inheritor and even Descartes's own objectors—acknowledged the connection between angelic knowledge and the innate ideas that emerge in the experience of the cogito. Such is the meaning of Burman's retort to Descartes in 1648: "Concerning the idea of the angel, it is certain that we form it starting from the idea of our mind and that we only have knowledge of it from the starting point of our own mind; even if angels do not exist at all, we can think about them only by observing ourselves."[13] Instead of following Burman here and responding directly to this objection, Descartes cuts short the interview and, blaming the clumsiness (*ineptus*) of the Angelic Doctor on this question of the angels, instead justifies their apparition from scripture alone: "It is preferable to follow Scripture on this point and confess that the angels were young men, that they appeared as such and as similar things."[14] Just the voluntary interruption of the interview by Descartes is enough to condemn any thesis of a common measure between Thomist angelology and Cartesian egology. But this would be based on a mistaken conception, as Jean-Luc Marion has said, of Descartes's "*théologie blanche*."

As the Angelic Doctor himself will soon show us, not only does Descartes substitute a phenomenology of the angels for any substantialization of their corporeity ("the angels were young men and appeared as such"), but even their cogito is nothing other already in Thomas Aquinas than the act of angelic self-knowledge. Such a move is essentially repeated by Husserl. The operation of methodological doubt aside: the angel is already reduced in advance. In fact, according to Saint Thomas, the angel always already knows itself by virtue of the proper and specific immanence of its mode of knowledge. Whereas in the transitive action of human knowledge the intellect "transitions" or passes from the knowing subject to the object known ("the object or matter on which the action is exercised is separated from the agent"), in the imminent action of the angelic intellect the object itself is seen directly and immediately united to the one who knows ("in order for the action to be produced, in the immanent action it is necessary for the object to be united to the agent").[15] Because that which is to be known (the intelligible forms) is identically and in act that which is known (the angel as subsistent intelligible form), the angel comes to an immediate and pure experience of itself. Man on the contrary, always only in potency relative to that which ought to be known and having access to it only by virtue of a composition of matter and form, knows himself (at least *in statu viae*) in a mediated fashion, starting from a process of knowing founded on the apprehension of the sensible.

Morning and Evening Knowledge. Where does this pure egological experience come from that the angel alone has of itself? Here we find the distinction in the angelic intellect between "morning knowledge" (*cognitio matutina*) and "evening knowledge" (*cognitio vespertina*). Morning knowledge, says Thomas citing Augustine, gives access to "the primordial being of things [*cognitio autem ipsius primordialis esse rerum*], knowledge pertaining to things as they are in the Word [*secundum quod res sunt in Verbo*]," such that evening knowledge, by contrast, is "the knowledge of created being as existing in its own nature [*cognitio autem ipsius esse rei creatae secundum quod in propria natura consistit*]."[16] And when the angel knows things in their own nature (evening knowledge)—in other words according to a natural, as opposed to supernatural, knowledge—he knows them, says Saint Thomas, either by means of the "reasons of things" (*rationes rerum*) which are in the Word, or by the "innate species" (*species innatus*) that he sees in the things but without drawing it out of them.[17] According to this latter mode of knowledge (of things by their innate species) the angel will know itself in perfect totality. Since the angel is pure form, for Thomas, to the exclusion of all matter, each angel is itself its own unique species or form, so that between angels there is no difference but that of species: "The angels are not composed of matter and form; there are no two angels therefore of the same species."[18] There are so many species of angels as there are angels. When the angel knows itself it knows perfectly and entirely the species that he is in himself, and as a creature starting from his own created nature.

In this difficult debate on the modes of angelic knowledge, Thomas has maintained a remarkable consistency regarding "evening knowledge" as natural knowledge by the selfhood of things and of oneself, outside of all supernatural illumination: in this act of knowledge, the angel apprehends things and himself starting from the ideas that the Word has impressed in him, but without direct relation to them. We will find by virtue of a surprisingly smooth transposition from the angelic intellect to the human intellect the Cartesian theory of "innate ideas" as "first seeds of truths that nature has deposited in the human spirit" and that the second meditation will leave at least implicitly to be worked out in the experience of the cogito.[19] From the immanence of the angelic intellect to itself in Thomas to the immanence of the cogito in Descartes, there is only a small step to be taken (every reserve aside about the act of suspension performed by the subject on itself). A trace of a pure idealism in Aquinas will therefore paradoxically be found in this mode of angelic knowledge. The angel in Thomas's reflection thus strangely opens a certain pre-Cartesian access to a pure egological experience, by means of a nature prohibited to man who is always submitted—at least during his terrestrial sojourn—to the mediation of the sensible. Separating such an experience of the cogito in Husserl and Descartes from the angelic knowledge in Thomas suffices already to crystallize the ideal of the transparency of consciousness to itself perpetuated through Husserlian phenomenology.[20]

The Source of the Ego. Even so, such a Cartesian-Thomist convergence does not suffice to bring to light the originality of the Husserlian enterprise, both the constitution of the ego starting from itself as source and horizon of an unsurpassable finitude, as well as the question of the exit from solipsism. Concerning the constitution of the ego: here does the boundary and guiding thread of a reading of Thomist angelology in light of the *Cartesian Meditations* come to light insomuch as, paradoxically, a greater proximity is simultaneously deciphered between the Thomist angelic ego and the Cartesian ego, on the one hand, and the Cartesian and Husserlian egos, on the other. In fact, whereas the innate ideas or *species innatus* arise for Thomas evidently from the Word—and Descartes does not deny at all this supernatural origin either—for Husserl on the contrary there is no other source for the pure ego but oneself and only oneself, constituting itself, reducing at once the world and oneself in all its natural modalities of apprehension (the double *epochê*). The sharp divide between Aquinas/Descartes and Husserl reveals to us with new clarity the unbridgeable distance that separates the infinite and finite and that many contemporary phenomenologies carry on in their turn as some sort of criterion of phenomenological orthodoxy. Once the impressions of the Word within the self (Aquinas) and the divine guarantee (Descartes) are refused, there rises up with force the famous objection of solipsism that inaugurates the fifth *Cartesian Meditation*: Husserl asks whether from the moment of the march toward the transcendental ego has one not "become a *solus ipse* . . ." all alone?[21] It is here that we can return with renewed vigor to the interrogation of angelology pursued by Aquinas when he asks: "Can an angel know another angel?" (Ia, q. 56, a. 2). Likewise, again, the father of phenomenology asks: "What about other egos?" (*Cart. Med.*, §42).

The Exit from Angelic Solipsism into an Alter-Angelology

Husserl announces early on the necessity of an exit from the egological solitude of the subject or the urgency of "breaking the circle" (*Cart. Med.* §42). Yet he accomplishes it only much later (*Cart. Med.* §50). Does this suggest that the angel in its natural immateriality is able to escape such a detour? With the goal of an exit from angelic solipsism starting from the constitution of an "alter-angelology" (angel/angel), the proximity of the angelic ego of Thomas and the transcendental ego of Husserl emerges anew: just as in fact Husserl distinguishes between the "march toward the transcendental ego" (first *Cartesian Meditation*) and "the determination of the transcendental domain as phenomenological intersubjectivity" (fifth *Cartesian Meditation*), so also does Thomas Aquinas distinguish between the self-knowledge of the angel (Ia, q. 56, a. 1) and the knowledge of one angel by another (Ia, q. 56, a. 2).

Immediacy and Mediation. At the heart of the quarrel between Thomas Aquinas and Arab philosophy—which immediately brings to mind Henri Corbin's fight waged against historic Christian theology by way of recourse to Islam, as we saw above—the Angelic Doctor adopts an original position that fights simultaneously on two fronts: against Averroes on the one hand, who makes the angel capable of knowing the essence of other angels without intermediary, and against Avicenna, on the other hand, legitimating a possible and total knowledge of one angel by another starting from its own essence. Hence immediate knowledge of the essence of the other and mediate knowledge by the essence of the self are the two boundaries not to be crossed according to Thomas Aquinas. Against Averroes, Thomas must challenge the impossible infringement of the intimate and immanent union of the act of knowledge and the object known in the angel: in its indivisible unity, the angel is only able to know itself in its own essence and not the essence of the other angel, otherwise the angel risks being divided against itself. Against Avicenna it is necessary to refute the idea of a common essence among the angels, which realizes—as if each angel was not already in itself its own species—only the common genre of the angels but not each angel in its specific individuality.

Let us retain only two essential points from this debate: against Averroes, *the angel alone knows itself integrally in its own essence* (and it is not known in this way by other angels), and against Avicenna, *knowledge of the other angel by an angelic subject—its alter ego—cannot be had starting from the knowledge of its own essence* (hence the necessary recourse to another mode of knowledge that Thomas will term knowledge by similitudes, as we will shortly see).[22] In phenomenological terms that will join us back up with Husserl, the first position sacrifices the ego in that it divides the angelic ego from itself (what Husserl calls the sphere of immanence), whereas the second cheaply loses alterity by dissolving into a genre which alters the specificity of the other (against which Husserl is also fighting when he prohibits the reduction of the monadic community of the ego to a pure identity of monads). For Thomas therefore, inter-angelology requires, as does Husserl in the constitution of intersubjectivity, that egoity and alterity are held together at the same time. In this way do their solutions principally appear, if not identical, at least parallel: in Thomas's use of similitudes (*similitudines*) in Ia, q. 56, a. 2, resp., and Husserl's use of the analogizing knowledge of the other in *Cart. Med.* §50.

Analogy and Similitude. "Do angels know each other? [*Utrum unus angelus alium cognoscat*]?"[23] In order to respond to this question, Thomas first recalls (in a way that evokes the transparency of the Husserlian ego) that only the angel knows himself perfectly in his own nature and its causes: "Each angel has received the reason of its own species [*ratio suae speciei*] according to both natural and intelligible being [*secundum esse naturale et intelligibile*]."[24] To say that each angel knows itself perfectly according to natural being (*secundum esse naturale*) implies that it has natural and immediate access to itself by means of its own substance (evening knowledge) and without the mediation of any species imprinted on it. For Thomas, the angel is for itself "a form subsisting in a natural being . . . like the color in the wall that possesses a natural being," as a necessary category of its own substance.[25]

Concerning angelic knowledge of another angel or any other creature: such is not operated according to natural being (by substance) but only according to intelligible being: "The reasons of other natures both corporeal and spiritual are impressed only according to intellectual being [*secundum esse intelligibile tantum*], so that by these impressed species [*per species impressas*] it is able to know spiritual and corporeal creatures."[26] By contrast to the Word, in whom the reasons of things preexist according to their nature, the substance (nature and cause) of an angel remains therefore, for another angel, always opaque or forbidden. Such is not a fault of its nature—since nothing that can be known remains unknown to it—but rather only conformity to its creaturely status and respect for the divine omnipotence. As a created being, the angel is certainly not the cause of any created thing. No more than the foreman is able to produce or modify the plan of the architect, even as he knows his designs, so the angel is not able to know another angel according to the reasons of its nature or the substance in which it receives from God, as an architect, the intelligible reasons. These reasons (*rationes*) that Thomas names the "*species impressae*" (impressed species) are therefore impressed on the angelic intellect by the divine Word so that by him an angel gains knowledge of another angel and of all creation. In terms that remain Thomist—of which the phenomenological accents ought not to be lost on us—the angel knows another angel not "according to its natural being" (*secundum esse naturale*), but "according to its intentional being" (*secundum esse intentionale*).[27] The intentionality of the other angel, in order to take up the Thomist example of color, does not make it known in its substance (like color which is substance only for the wall), but only according to its intentional being, as "in the medium that communicates color to the eye (light) and thus having only an intentional being."[28]

The paradigm of light as support of the intentionality of the other—whether *alter-angelus* of Thomas or *alter-ego* of Husserl—is understood here as that which authorizes a certain knowledge of the other without reducing it to the total transparence to itself enjoyed by the ego. God does not "give" one angel to another in order to be known in what they are and in the reasons for which they are, but only in what they have *in common* when they are: namely, the being of receptacles of the intelligible ideas that God inscribes in them. In a similar way to the communion of saints (supra), the community of the world shared by angels is enacted therefore not in their being or in their reasons for being, but only by reference to the divine Word who alone exists most fully. The intentionality of the other angel or of the *alter-angelus* in Thomas, like the intentionality of the other or of the *alter-ego* in Husserl, is therefore founded on a *third term*—the light of the Word in Thomas, the common world in Husserl—which alone opens access to alterity.

Toward a Common Term. In the context of inter-angelological knowledge, such a community, if not of nature at least of the world of divine light shared among the angels, renders null and void any scheme of causality and reserves the creationist model to God alone. The created spiritual natures are tied together in a relation, not of causality but of resemblance or similitude:

"Even if there is no causality [*absque causalitate*] among the angels, a shared similitude [*similitude*] is sufficient for them to be known."[29] This establishment of a double similitude or a "redoubled similitude" among the angels and then between the angels and God finally makes possible the constitution of an inter-angelology. The first similitude is the likeness of the angel to God inasmuch as it is the most perfect created image of the latter: "The knowledge of angels is closer to specular knowledge since the angelic nature is like a mirror [*quoddam speculum*] which presents the likeness of God [*divinam similitudinem repraesentans*]."[30]

Thus the second similitude, of angel to angel, arises by their common capacity to understand—not to produce—the first similitude between the uncreated and the created: "The relations of causality have nothing to do at all with the knowledge of one angel by another, except by reason of the similitude [*nisi ratione similitudinis*] that they establish between cause and effect."[31] One angel knows another not by penetrating its substance or producing its cause, but only by recognizing in it, by means of its impressed species applied by God (and which God alone knows perfectly), the same capacity to receive the divine creative power and to be its image. Only such a "redoubled similitude"—between the angels and God and then among the angels themselves—founds a community of world shared by the angels, which finally makes possible an inter-angelology through an escape from angelic solipsism. In phenomenological and Husserlian terms, the angelic ego escapes from the solitude of its *solus ipse* by the analogizing knowledge of the other angel as image of God and capacity to receive his image. The other angel or *alter-angelus*, however, remains in its nature an enigma to the angel who seeks to know it (rather like the insoluble enigma of the fourth term in the Husserlian experience of the flesh as touching-touched, as I described in chapter 6, above)—yet they nevertheless know each other, or better, recognize each other in that they both partake of the same relation to God the Creator. Here they become for each other an *alter-angelology*.

The typically Husserlian accents of the exit from angelic solipsism in Thomas Aquinas—not in the nature of the concepts per se but rather in the progressive unfolding of his thought—ought not to escape the awareness of those who have at least a cursory understanding of Husserl's solution. In §50 of the *Cartesian Meditations*, what makes possible the coupling or pairing (*Paarung*) together with the other is not a flight from the ego but, well to the contrary, a constitution of the alterity of the other starting from the very ego. The alter ego, always unfathomable in its own nature, is posed as an apodictic evidence starting from its resemblance (or similitude for Thomas) with my own sphere of belonging. "It is clear from the very beginning that only a similarity connecting, within my primordial sphere, that body over there with my body can serve as the motivational basis for the 'analogizing' apprehension of that body as another animate organism [another flesh]."[32] No more than the human ego of Husserl escapes from its ego to constitute the other by its analogizing apperception, so the angelic ego of Thomas ought not to discard its self-transparency in order to know by similitude the ego of the other angel (a knowledge thus of its functions more than its nature). Even further, while only the appearing of a "*common world*" can definitively found the intersubjectivity of the alter-ego (in §55 of the *Cartesian Meditations*), only a God shared as unsurpassable horizon of the angelic world makes possible an inter-angelology (in the second article of question 56 of the *Summa*, 1a pars).

Can we go any further in the comparative analysis of Thomist angelology and Husserlian egology? In the end, if these seem to be drawn together, as far as kinds and styles of solutions are posed, as exits from solipsism, it nevertheless appears as if their respective contents cannot be any farther apart: for Thomas, the constitution of the *alter-angelus* by immaterial species and innate ideas, and, for Husserl, the constitution of the *alter-ego* by flesh (*Leib*) and body (*Körper*).

The Debate about the Flesh of Angels

Reduction to the Sphere of Ownness

Pure Spirits? Contrary to Thomist angelology, the constitution of an "intersubjective sphere of belonging" in Husserl is created by the constitutive power of the flesh in correlation to the body. It does not start from the lone ideality of the ego. There is nothing more opposed, at least at the level of the second reduction (that is, to the flesh and not only to the ego), than Thomist *inter-angelology* and Husserlian *inter-subjectivity*. In order to carry this opposition to full term, and by virtue of the Husserlian reinvestment of corporeity, we would still have to show in a definitive and radical way that the angels have not adopted bodies. Setting aside the virtually obsolete debates on the "flesh of angels," the question of angelic corporeity remains no less a fundamental *theologoumenon*. However, from the dogmatic point of view, the ecumenical councils have not, properly speaking, settled the question. The decree of Lateran Council IV (1215), virtually contemporaneous with Thomas Aquinas, states that God is "the unique principle of all things, creator of all visible and invisible beings, spiritual and incorporeal . . . that is, the angelic creatures and those of this world." To be sure, this council was less interested in defining the corporeal or spiritual nature of the angels than in their properly creaturely state that they share with those substances ordinarily called corporeal.[33] The theological upshot (which we cannot take up in the context of this study) is that the spirituality of the angel cannot, I suggest, be threatened in its nature by any corporeity.

Nevertheless, considering only the apparitions of angels in the scriptures (and thus ignoring abstract theological quibbles), the solution to this question does not seem self-evident. Listen only to Thomas Aquinas: "Some claim that the angels never assume a body and that all the apparitions mentioned in Scripture take the form of prophetic visions, or in other words that they are only visions of the imagination . . . But repeatedly the Scriptures speak of angels who appear as if everyone saw them. This is the case for the angels that appeared to Abraham: they are seen by him, his whole family, by Lot and all the inhabitants of Sodom. Similarly, all see the angel who appears to Tobit. These demonstrate that such manifestations take place in bodily visions, of which the object, exterior to the subject, can be seen by everyone. The object of such a vision can therefore only be a real body [*tali autem visione non videtur nisi corpus*]."[34]

Barely has Aquinas admitted the reality of such an angelic corporeity (at least in order to appear to man) that he hastens to add: "Since the angels are not bodies and do not have bodies, sometimes they assume a body [*angeli corpora assumant*]."[35] Such an assumption of a body by the angels in order to appear to man is not self-evident, since precisely, and contrary to us humans, they are not a body and do not have a body. We must therefore ask if indeed a passage is necessary, at least theologically, from a *disincarnated inter-angelology* (angel/angel) to an *incorporated inter-angelo-anthropology* (angel/man).

Angelic Incorporation and Christic Incarnation. We will not broach here the famous debate about hylomorphism applied to the angel and which had divided the medieval West between Muslim thinkers (Averroes and Avicenna) and Christian thinkers (Bonaventure and Duns Scotus). Let us only take note that the original position adopted by Aquinas consists in understanding the angel less in terms of matter and form but rather in potency and act (which justifies our preceding analysis of angelic intuition in terms of the actuality of knowledge and of the known): "If in the angel there is not the composition of matter and form, there is however composition of act and potency" (Ia, q. 50, a. 2, ad. 3). Armed with such a solution in principle, we can approach anew the question of angelic corporeity in the history of theology in order finally to confront it with the Husserlian sense of corporeity.

As we have already emphasized in relation to the *solidity of the flesh* in Tertullian, it is fitting to distinguish the angelic incorporation from the Christological incarnation. In his *De carne Christi*, Tertullian opposes to the Gnostic Marcion a necessary distinction between the flesh of Christ and the flesh of angels. And in the face of the strong development of the Judeo-Christian theme of the *Christos Angelos*, for Tertullian Christ does not take on flesh in the same way as the angel does in its appearance to man: "Consequently I summon those who propose that the flesh of Christ, after the example of angels, is not born even as it was made flesh, to confront the reasons why Christ as well as the angels have appeared in the flesh [*in carne processerint*]. No angel has ever descended in order to be crucified, to know death, to be resurrected. Never have the angels had such a reason to take on a body [*corporandum*] and this is the reason why they have not been incarnated [*acceperint carnem*] by the passage of birth: not having come in order to die, they have not come either to be born. But the Christ, sent in order to die, necessarily had to be born in order to be able to die [*nasci quoque necessario habuit ut mor posset*]."[36] If I can be allowed here a Heideggerian interpretation that is a little rash, the flesh of Christ is first and principally a "*flesh for death*" (*ut mori*), and therefore also for resurrection. The flesh of angels, however, is at best a *flesh for appearing* (*in carne processerint*), but not for birth and death. Thus, very early on in the history of theology (and in order to counter the Gnostic heresies) the incorporation of angels (*ad corporandum*) and the incarnation of Christ (*acceperit carnem*) came to be distinguished.

We have not yet mentioned the relevance of Origen to the question of the angels, though in his *Peri Archôn* he follows Tertullian but further specifies the terms. If he attributes a corporeity to the angels—which he terms "subtle" or "ethereal"—such a corporeity has nothing to do with the Christic incarnation. When the resurrected Christ first appears to the Eleven, he shows himself to them precisely as an anti-angel, beyond and below the angelic state, namely that he did not assume (at least merely) an angelic corporeity: "Look at my hands and feet. It is I. Look, touch me: a spirit does not have flesh and bones as you see that I have" (Lk. 24:36). Even beyond the phenomenological accent of a resurrected Christ who appears "in flesh and bone" (*Cart. Med.*, §50), though protecting ourselves against an overly hasty interpretation, such words as these require a distinction between a Christic flesh or body and an angelic body. Origen concludes from this: "Christ does not have a body like those of the demons, for theirs is something subtle, like a light breath, which most think is incorporeal. But Christ has a solid and tangible body [*corpus solidum et palpabile*]."[37]

When Origen grants to the demons and spirits a certain kind of corporeity, but of a nature both ethereal and subtle, it is done less in order to confer on them a body than it is to conserve for the Trinity alone an exclusive and total incorporeality: "It is a privilege of the nature of God, Father, Son and Holy Spirit to understand their existence apart from any material substance [*sine materiali substantia*] and any association with bodily addition [*absque ulla corporeae adiectionis*]."[38] The definitive doctrine of the Fathers, confirmed by the ecumenical councils with the *homoousios* will be: on the one hand, the complete immateriality and non-corporeality of the Holy Trinity, and on the other hand, the solid and tangible corporeality of the Word made flesh. When Henri Corbin accuses this very doctrine of being the locus of the ruin of the theology of angels, let us observe in response only that the problem is in fact resolved from the moment that it is suppressed. Yet the entire task of Christian angelology consists precisely in attempting to give meaning and form to an appearance of angels that is always subaltern to both the Trinitarian non-corporeity and the Christic corporeity.

Bodies without Flesh? It is Augustine who confirms this distinction between angelic incorporation and Christic incarnation in a dazzling formula from *Sermon* 362: *cum essent angelic corpus, non caro*, "since the angels are bodies, they are not flesh."[39] Flesh and body—and let us recall the title of Didier Franck's famous book[40]—though truly "*caro et corpus*" and not "*Leib und Körper*." Here at least the distinction is critical (supra). Is the superposition possible? We ought to doubt it, as has already been suggested in relation to Tertullian. Nevertheless this remains minimally the index of a major difficulty yet to be resolved, theologically as much as philosophically. And perhaps this is the reason why Augustine (and we with him) hesitates about the status of angelic incorporation, particularly once distinguished from Trinitarian noncorporeity and Christic corporeity: "I must confess it is beyond my powers of penetration to settle one question I have just alluded to: do angels work through the constant and stable spiritual quality of their own bodies to take and fit to themselves some grosser matter from the lower elements which they can change and turn rather like clothes into any physical manifestation they please, even into true ones, as our Lord turned true water into true wine (Jn. 2:9)? Or do they transform their own proper bodies into whatever form they wish as it suits their purposes [*accommodate ad id quod agunt*]?"[41]

Does the angel truly have or simply borrow a body? The question is open. The task is Aquinas's to resolve. Yet every angelic body, to be sure—whether borrowed or true—has no other sense but to appear *accommodate ad id quod agunt* ("in relation to the work that they have to accomplish"). This new dimension of appearing for (whether something or someone) leads us, properly speaking, into a phenomenology of the angel, which attempts to escape from a purely ontic or reified conception of the body. Now tied to this line of ontic corporeity and phenomenological corporeity is the crucial and exemplary relation of Thomas Aquinas and Edmund Husserl.

A Phenomenology of the Angel

Definition of the Phenomenon. At phenomenology's very point of departure, in the *Logical Investigations*, the original concept of the *phenomenon* first designates the "concept of what appears or what can appear, of the intuitive as such."[42] The phenomenal object is therefore both the intuited object *hic et nunc* (this lamp along with the value it has for the perception that one comes to have of it) and the concrete, subjective lived experience of this intuition (for example, when we perceive the lamp sitting there in front of us).[43] On the one hand, the appearance is always addressed to a proper subject ready to receive it, and on the other hand, the appearance is necessarily tied to an object (ideal or concrete) capable of producing it. Therefore the phenomenon in no way designates an illusion but rather the thing itself appearing to consciousness, my consciousness, such as it appears. In this sense—as we have already made mention in relation to Eckhartian "detachment" as a mode of the "reduction"—phenomenology renounces and suspends all ontological questioning about the *quid* of the thing or its nature and is interested only in its *quomodo*, that is, its modes of appearing. Starting from this definition of the phenomenon, on which the fifth *Cartesian Meditation* takes root, a phenomenology of the angel becomes possible, yet only to the degree that the angel as such appears and insofar as such an appearance is necessarily accompanied in me by an intuitive, originary lived experience.

A Body for Appearing. The "transcendental reduction to the sphere of belonging" or to the "sphere of owness" (*Cart. Med.*, §44), for Husserl, consists precisely in suspending, in a redoubled reduction that is no longer merely eidetic (starting from the bodily ego), everything that is not me and therefore foreign, including intentionality itself. The point of departure of this new work of reduction—and which is of crucial significance to the question of the corporeity and alterity of angels—is, Husserl says, "first to abstract from that which confers on animals and humans their specific character as living and personal beings."[44] The perception of the body of the other will therefore not be that of its objective body (*Körper*) equipped with its specific traits as a biological "living being." If it is necessary to live and to have a body in order to appear (*Leib*), this life does not first designate the collection of traits constitutive of the living. Here the door opens to a possible phenomenology of the angel starting from Thomist angelology.

In the tradition that passes from Tertullian to Origen and Augustine, the angels do not appear as such to man, but rather "in relation to the work that they have to accomplish"—*accommodate ad id quod agunt* (Augustine).[45] The first proper determination of the angel consists therefore in being the envoy or messenger of God to men (*mal'ak* in Hebrew and *angelos* in Greek). If every angelic appearing is not necessarily tied to speech—as in Saint Francis's vision of the winged Seraph in the form of the cross, for example, where, precisely, the flesh itself became speech in the experience of the stigmata—it never remains gratuitous or arbitrary in the context of Christian theology for the simple reason that it always claims to be an expression of an Other. This is why, as we have already had occasion to emphasize, when Thomas Aquinas affirms that "the angels are not a body and do not have a body that is naturally united to them [but] they sometimes assume a body [*corpora assumant*]," he immediately hastens to add that the angelic assumption of a body is not "in itself" as nature or substance, but is only "for our sake" (*propter nos*) to whom the angel appears: "It is not for themselves [*propter seipsos*] that the angels have need to assume a body, but for our sake [*propter nos*]."[46] And Descartes, whom we have seen renouncing the debate on the nature of the angels in his interview with Burman, did not finally seem to answer anything in concluding that "it is best for us to follow Scripture and believe that they were young men, or *appeared* as such, and so forth."[47]

In phenomenological terms, the intercorporeity of the angelic body and human body (and thus no longer simply an intra-angelic intersubjectivity) is left to be elucidated in Thomas Aquinas, insofar as the intentionality of the body of one—albeit only assumed and not constitutive of its nature—has meaning and its raison d'être only in and through its manifestation to the other. The suspension of all ontic position of corporeity and reduction to its pure phenomenality: such is exactly the sense of the second reduction from *Körper* to *Leib* that Husserl puts in operation. "Thus there is included in my ownness . . . a sense, a 'mere Nature' that has lost precisely that 'by everyone' and therefore must not by any means be taken for an abstract stratum of the world . . . Among the bodies [*Körper*] belonging to this Nature and included in my particular ownness, I then find my animate organism [*Leib*] as uniquely singled out—namely as the only one of them that is not just a body but precisely an animate organism [or flesh]."[48]

An Aftereffect for Phenomenology. In a synchronic reading of the history of philosophy, by his distinction between *Körper* and *Leib*, Husserl extends in a certain conceptual manner—at least at the level of the sole modalities of the manifestation of the body and its flesh—the Thomist imperatives for angelic corporeity that assumes a body and appears as such (phenomenal body) without however being itself a body (objective body). In the same way that the angel alone knows itself perfectly and escapes from the solitude of its ego by virtue of the similitudes shared with the other angel, so also does the same angel uniquely seem capable of adopting for man this type of manifestation of a corporeity totally freed from all natural position in order to be *made visible* to others. The first reduction to the ego and the second reduction to corporeity both seem capable of being deciphered, at least in part, in a contemporary rereading of Thomist angelology guided by Husserl's *Cartesian Meditations.*

But in order to lead this process of intercorporeity between angels and men (*inter-angelo-anthropology*) to completion in its mode of appearing for the other, a last question with new Husserlian resonance remains unresolved: is the angel who assumes a body for my sake able to dwell in his body as I am incarnate in my flesh by the successive series of its kinestheses? This interrogation, crucial in the virtually insurmountable distance that it creates between Thomas and Husserl, could in fact render void the entirety of the enterprise that I have undertaken. For if the angel is not able to dwell in its own body as I am incarnate in my own, how could it then, in rigorous terms, address itself to me and accompany me toward a community of angels and the blessed? If there is indeed a mutual knowledge among the angels starting from the similitudes impressed on them by the Word, are they not then ever condemned to remain locked up in this angelic monadic community, no longer able to appear for the other since this other is no longer only the other himself (other angel, *alter ego*) but the other than himself (man, *ego alter*)?

Rilke's nostalgia in the *Duino Elegies* for the angel suffering from too much perfection is probably justified here. And the dream of the angel Damiel—"to have a fever, fingers blackened from the journal, feeling his frame when walking or finally feeling what it is like to remove his shoes under the table and stretch his toes"—vanishes here into the realms of an ever-unrealizable utopia.[49] And yet, against the temptation of holding the angel in check in its communication with man, should we still maintain with Pierre Boutang that "the article of Thomas Aquinas entitled 'Do angels know singulars' is a text which could without a doubt rescue Rilke from his most profound evil without sacrificing his poetic genius"? Here "the ninth *Elegy* would be totally different, without a doubt."[50]

Toward a Common World of Angels and Men

In response to the question "is the angel able to dwell in its body as I am incarnate in mine?" in relation to which Rainer-Maria Rilke and Wim Wenders are the prophets of our time, I should say—if I still dare here to use phenomenology—that it is not theologically speaking the nature of the angel to be able to experience my lived sensory experiences or *Erlebnis*, by reason of its substantial (as opposed to phenomenological) incorporeity, such that I always experience myself, that is to say, starting from the passive syntheses of my senses. In this sense, therefore, there is nothing in common between the angel and man and the enterprise collapses on itself. Aquinas himself formulates this objection of an unbridgeable gulf between purely spiritual creatures and those that are spiritual and corporeal—and thereby transposes the question of sensory lived experience to that of the apprehension of singulars: "Knowledge is a kind of assimilation of knower to the known. But it seems impossible that the angel is assimilated to the singular as singular, since it is immaterial and the singular has matter as a principle. The angel is therefore not able to know singulars."[51] A phenomenological response to the argument, which would make possible for the angel a knowledge of singulars for which access seems reserved to man, calls for the satisfaction of a twofold requirement: the angel ought to be able to be substituted for me and occupy my place which ordinarily befits me in my here (*hic*) (what Husserl calls the "apperceptive transposition starting from my own body"), and what is sensed (the sensed object) is effectively the object as I would sense it if its over there (*illic*) were my here (*hic*). Upon this twofold requirement will rest, as we will see later (in the following chapter on Duns Scotus), the knowledge of the other as a singular being.

The Angel in My Place

Responding to the first requirement for a possible "apperceptive transposition" of the angel and man demands that we make a return to the meaning of the constitution of alterity. The operation of the encounter of the other as other, starting from my flesh, is operated first according to Husserl by a fiction, namely that of a "liberation of my [own] perspective and a transfer into another perspective."[52] The other does not remain other to me to the degree that I accept to enter also into the analogical dimension of "as if I here were also over there" (*Cart. Med.*, §54). The Husserlian theme of the here and the there, starting from a here from which the world appears, seems to respond again, like an echo, to the question of the "local movement of angels" as elaborated by Thomas Aquinas (Ia, q. 53). Even more—and to highlight the implicit Husserlian ideal of angelic knowledge (which Jean-Louis Chrétien brought out in his article, "Le langage des anges selon la scolastique")[53]—the local movement of angels in their appearing for man may sometimes stretch to the accomplishment, in a paradigmatic fashion, of this which, in humanity, is always only an imaginative fiction. The impossible but ideal and necessary substitution of the here for the over there constitutive of human intersubjectivity for Husserl, seems paradoxically to be realized in the possible, real, and total—though under different modes—"apperceptive transposition" of the angel and man in Thomas.

Here and There. For man at least, the here and there are clearly distinguished for Thomas and Husserl in a kind of continuous movement, meaning the switch from one place to another that is common to the community of the living: "The continuity of local bodily movement results from the fact that the body leaves in a successive and not sudden manner the place in which it previously appeared." In this sense, the material body of man, like every material body, "is localized because it is contained and measured by place."[54] However, for the angel, the here and there is distinguished with difficulty to the degree that the spiritual creature alone, unique among all creatures in this way, is made capable of leaving or remaining in a place without continuity or contact with surrounding bodies: "The angel is able to leave instantaneously [*simul*] the place that it occupies, and can occupy instantaneously any other place. Thus its movement is not continuous." Thus the angel "far from being measured by place, rather contains it."[55] Among all the creatures, only the angel seems capable of passing from one place to another instantaneously (*simul*). Of course, this does not mean that the same angel is capable of occupying two places at the same time—the gift of ubiquity remains the singular privilege of God, and particularly of Christ in his post-paschal appearances—but only as it is able to occupy every perspective (the *Abschattungen* of Husserl) successively, in passing instantaneously from one perspective to another or one place to another. But the very notion of instantaneity (*instanti*), Aquinas specifies, is no longer a rigorous enough term adequate to the angel. Containing time more than it is contained by it, we are finally obliged "to say that there is no extreme moment during which the angel would be the starting point." When the angel is here I am assured that he is not there, but since he is no longer here I cannot know if he is already there or not. I grasp the angel—or better: the angel grasps me—when it is with me. But as soon as it is no longer here, I can no longer discern where it is. Further, knowing only its "here" (*hic*), if it is my own here at the same time, nothing prevents the possibility that its "over there" (*illic*) that I do not yet know is already also my "future here," that "hence" (*illinc*) I still only consider a distant "over there." The "over there" of the angel "from whence" the world already appears to it is already perhaps my "future over there" where the angel, awaiting me there, welcomes me from the moment that it gets to my "present here." By the yardstick of this Husserlian scheme of the here and there the entire peregrination of the angel Raphael with Tobit is able to be reinterpreted, the angel who both marches before and follows behind in the form of a dog, "accompanying Tobit and arranging felicitously everything that happens to him" (Tb. 5:27).

What is only an imaginative fiction in Husserl, transposing me to the over there of the other while I remain here, seems to be fully realized in the angelo-anthropological interaction as described by Thomas Aquinas in the question on the movement of the angels. This will make evident the meaning and mission of the guardian angel in the treatise on the divine government in the *Summa*, who could both accept to prepare my over there by its here ("every man," says Thomas, "in the pilgrim state receives a guardian angel"),[56] as well as temporarily to refuse straightforwardly such a welcome in order not to be substituted for the divine here that its command first designates as mine ("the guardian angel never fully abandons man, but sometimes it partially abandons him in the sense that it does not prevent him from being submitted to some test, or even from falling into sin, according to the orders of the divine judgment").[57]

Does the "apperceptive transposition" of the angel and man, once realized, and therefore released from the merely analogical modality of the "as if," allow the angel effectively to sense things such as I sense them (according to my *Erlebnis*), and such as they are when I sense them (in their *Erscheinungen*)?

The Guardian Angel. Responding to this second requirement of a common angelo-anthropological phenomenality—and thus achieving the constitution of a common world shared by angels and men, and not merely between angels alone—requires that we return once again to the nostalgia of Rainer-Maria Rilke and Wim Wenders: does the angel really suffer from the weight of too much perfection? Does the angel possess a perennial envy of the human condition, like Damiel who makes the irreversible decision for a human incarnation at the foot of the Berlin Wall? Falsely condemned, as the first part of Wenders's film suggests, to observe the world through a prism of only black and white shades, is the angel not rather in reality the one who from all eternity already partakes of the colors of the world—those that appear to us and those that we do not yet know—albeit *otherwise* than that which is appropriate for us humans?

Neither being a body nor having one, but only "assuming" one, the angel evidently cannot apprehend singulars such as we do, namely, starting from the passive syntheses of our senses. The critique of Wenders, Rilke, and even of some thinkers from the Middle Ages (Averroes, Avicenna, Bonaventure) begins precisely here, inasmuch as each, in his own way, does not hesitate to reject the possibility that angels, and even God (Averroes, for example), could know singulars.[58] By contrast, Thomas asserts that this negation of the knowledge of singulars for angels is both "contrary to the Catholic faith" as to divine providence: "If the angels do not know singulars, they cannot exercise any providence through activities in the world, since every action has for its principle a singular being."[59] The guardian angel in fact ought to reg(u)ard everything that I regard—in the double sense of that which concerns me, and that which I am focused on—in order, precisely, to guard me. If, however, by virtue of its incorporeal nature, the angel does not apprehend the singulars in the way that I do, how does it know them? Everything that goes under the name of my sensitive powers (sight, touch, hearing, taste, smell), the angel also knows, says Thomas, but not by means of these powers themselves, for its perception is definitively unified, but by means of a single faculty of knowledge—the intellect (*intellectum*)—which is alone capable of embracing every singular even to the smallest detail: "The order of things is such that the more elevated a being is, the more its power has unity and extension . . . The angel is by order of nature superior to man. It is unreasonable therefore to say that man knows by any one of his faculties something that the angel does not know by its unique faculty of knowledge [*per unam vim suam cognoscitivam*] which is the intellect [*scilicet intellectum*]."[60]

Knowledge of Sensibles. Nothing that I apprehend by my senses in a scattered and diverse fashion is prohibited to the angel who also attains to it, though not by sensation but rather starting from its unique faculty of intelligence. For an angel to know sensibles as sensibles does not mean that it knows only the universal causes (as Avicenna proposed). Here the angel is like an "astronomer who knows the eclipse only in its general conditions and not in the particular circumstances of its time and place, which only sensible knowledge is able to reach."[61] Such a knowledge of the eclipse through causes, as we have already seen above, is essentially reserved to God alone, the architect of the world. As for knowledge in its singularity and its particular circumstances of time and place, the angel receives these through the power of God by *infused species* (morning knowledge in the supernatural light of the Word) like the master communicating to one of his disciples an idea that the disciple could not produce himself: "The angels, by the species that God infuses in them, know things in their universal nature as well as in their singularity, as these species are multiple representations of the simple and unique essence of God" (Ia, q. 57, a. 2, resp.). To return to the example of the eclipse, while God alone possesses the power to produce it, as a creature the angel, along with man, partakes of the power to admire it, but the angel by his intellect in the divine light and man by his senses in the world. In this way both together see a *single and same* eclipse though in different *ways*. The hierarchy of the angels and the logic of the return to God are inverted here in a paradoxical *chassé-croisé* movement: the more the angel is elevated in knowledge of intelligibles and thus approaches God, the more in fact it is abased—as an accompaniment, it seems, to the kenosis of the Word—in the knowledge of sensibles.[62]

Faraway, so close!—the farther away the angel is from the sensibles in order to contemplate God, at the same time he is drawn nearer to that which is given to be seen by man. Knowing from all eternity the sensibles as sensibles but not through sensation, there is hardly any need for the angel Damiel of *Wings of Desire* to be surprised by the colors of the Berlin Wall after his fall into a body. It has already been given to him from time immemorial to see them in the infused light of the Word. Yet in order to do this it is necessary for him to exercise the eye of his intelligence by turning it to this infused light that contains the whole of man and the world.

A Community of Worlds

An Analogon of Singulars. Like the communion of saints (chap. 7), but now through a common knowledge of singulars, even under their respective modalities, there emerges a common world between angels and men: seeing things by way of different organs (sensations for men and intelligence for angels) does not prevent them from seeing the same thing. Here a new kind of similitude or *analogon* is deciphered, similar to the identity of relations discovered among angels, but now this *analogon* is no longer simply knowledge of universals (sufficient for the knowledge of another angel by infusion of divine light), but knowledge of universals as they make known at the same time singularity as it is simultaneously inscribed in the world and God: "The angels know singulars through universal forms regarding both their universal principles as similitudes of things [*similitudines rerum*] and their principles of individuation."[63] Such a community of worlds between angels and men does not imply, however, that it is necessary to reduce the angel to man, no more than in Husserl the community of monads sharing the same world reduces alterity but rather reinforces it.[64]

In fact, if there is an *analogy* between angels and men concerning what is known (singulars), this similitude is not reiterated in the mode according to which the thing is known (intelligence/sensation). As Husserl emphasized, if there is an analogy between the body of the other and my own body ("It is clear from the very beginning that only a similarity connecting, within my primordial sphere, that body over there with my body can serve as the motivational basis for the 'analogizing' apprehension of that body as another animate organism [another flesh]"),[65] this analogy does not make of the body of the other a pure *analogon* or image of what is appropriate for me ("what I actually see is not a sign and not a mere analogue, a depiction in any natural sense of the word; on the contrary, it is someone else").[66] The fact that the angel knows what I know, though under a different mode, does not turn me into an angel or the angel into a man. To the contrary, precisely because we know the same things without knowing them in the same way, we can indeed appear to each other as other (*ego alter*) on the ground of the identity not of our natures but of the world that we share together: "It is implicit in the sense of my successful apperception of others that their world, the world belonging to their appearance systems, must be experienced forthwith as the same as the world belonging to my appearance-systems; and this involves an *identity* of our appearance-systems."[67]

An Irreducible Alterity. In the context of a Thomist angelology read in light of the *Cartesian Meditations*, the angel and man seem therefore first called to appear to each other. In order to respect, of course, the necessary distance and alterity of the orders of creation, the angel is not reduced to man, and vice versa. Although the one power takes the place of the other in an apperceptive transposition of angel and man, knowing what the other knows in an analogy of the world perceived in the apprehension of singulars, both nevertheless remain irreducible to each other in their modalities of the apprehension of this common world (whether intellect or sensation). In the last instance, therefore, the angel is not the *alter ego* of man but his *ego alter* that ultimately shares with him, if not the same intentional aim in the world, at least the same experience—irreducible to a psychological or moral meaning—of the same world.

Swan Dive [Le Saut de L'ange]. Here in the appearing of the angel for another there remains an insoluble enigma which is at the same time the same as the ordinary experience of the other described by Husserl: "actually the sensuously seen body is experienced forthwith as the body of someone else and not as merely an indication of someone else. Is not this fact an enigma?"[68] When the angel appears to me, if I am made capable of seeing it, in its appearing to me it does not remain only the index of its presence since *its* body is not properly speaking its body, but only what has been assumed in order to be seen by my gaze. The angel, whether a subtle and ethereal body, as for Origen, or a soul without a body but assuming one, as in Aquinas, the problem of the angel fades before the One—the only one—who has already resolved the enigma of the other in being given integrally as *flesh* and *body* for the other: the incarnate Christ. Starting from this unique divine incarnation, what must be thought or rethought theologically, and even phenomenologically, are all the modalities of various incarnations, whether of man or of angels. In the unique measure that it pleases God, as Saint Paul puts it, "to reconcile all things through him and for him, whether on earth or in heaven" (Col. 1:20), the angels, as "actors" [*personnes de jeu*] in the drama that rejoins man and God, ought then to be reintegrated as "*persons in Christ*." The angelic *swan dive* [*saut de l'ange*] is performed *in the incarnate and resurrected* Word—here courting, perhaps, the opposite risk of no longer existing. If the destiny of the angels "is not contemporary with our drama," says Hans Urs von Balthasar, "yet it is not without relation to them."[69]

✦

Fortsetzung folgt. In a penultimate image, the angelic saga from *Wings of Desire* is accomplished: "we have embarked." At the last moment a ray of sunlight comes finally to tear the sad sky of Berlin. In this way also does the prologue of Saint John begin: "In the beginning was the Word . . . And the Word became flesh and tabernacled among us. And we have beheld his glory" (Jn. 1:1–14). The last image is that of a message (sent by an angel?) inscribed on the screen: "To be continued." Whether proclaimed by Rilke or Wenders or as revealed in Thomist angelology properly understood, it is because it all begins paradoxically when the wings of a nostalgic desire are clipped, when the dove, as in the famous passage from Kant, stops "cleaving in free flight the thin air, whose resistance it feels, [and] might imagine that its flight would be still easier in empty space."[70] In an exemplary way with Duns Scotus, and with the question of the angels always in mind, alterity will thus increase progressively with singularity, by definitively obviating any neutrality. The "haecceity of the other," accomplishes full alterity (Duns Scotus) and thus confers on the "community," both logically and chronologically, its true foundation in charity (Origen), and on intersubjectivity its authentic identity (Aquinas).

Chapter 9

✦

The Singular Other (John Duns Scotus)

From the Neutral to the Other

Angels "know singulars"—*angeli singularia cognoscunt* (*Summa theologiae*, Ia, q. 57, a. 2)—albeit in a unique mode, by a successful "apperceptive transposition." Following Thomas Aquinas we have shown that by means of this shared knowledge a structure of alterity is truly constituted. At this point the revelation of the other is not yet fully disclosed. It is only with Duns Scotus that it emerges completely. For it is not sufficient *to know the collection of singular things* in order *to recognize them as singular*. Haecceity stems from actuality in that it identifies what is still lacking in being: "At the heart of the real in Thomas Aquinas," says Etienne Gilson, "the act of being is found; in Duns Scotus haecceity is found."[1] This unique formula of the celebrated medievalist is enough to justify my purpose, at least historically: the *tode ti* or the *hoc aliquid*—the fact of being "this thing"—of the Subtle Doctor rises to the level of the Angelic Doctor's *esse* or act of being.

But for contemporary reflection the question of haecceity seems more pertinent than actuality. Behind, or rather coming through the question of individuation is the recent accusation of "neutrality" in contemporary philosophy. Levinas's charge against Heidegger, namely, that his ontology is defined as a "philosophy of the neuter," is well known: "To place the Neuter dimension of being above the existent that which unbeknown to it this Being would determine in some way . . . is to profess materialism. Heidegger's late philosophy becomes this faint materialism."[2] More recently Jean-Luc Marion has turned the argument against Levinas himself and the irreducible vis-à-vis of the face: "The injunction of obligation toward the other leads, in reality, to the neutralization of the other *as such*." In the substitution of the other for every other by the face the other is not individualized to the point of becoming "irreplaceable by any other." Respect and responsibility, be they for me or the other, establish in fact the other in the Kantian manner as *an* abstract universal to which I am obliged, but not as *this* concrete singular who has no other particularity then of being made, precisely, "other of every other." *Haecceitas*—a word if not directly from Scotus at least from the Scotist tradition—will therefore designate the other "as *such*" because it provokes me to make myself "a *such*." We will therefore not be content with *the* face, but will require of some *such* face that it envisage me in order to give me my "form" singularly disentangled from every other.[3]

A second reason, also relevant to modern philosophy, invites a renewed interrogation of haecceity, no longer as the *singularization of the other*, but the *individuation of the thing*. On the forgetfulness of being is superimposed, according to Heidegger, another forgetting, all the more forgotten as it is left uninterrogated: "the thing." Phenomenology, however, claims haecceity only to forget it immediately. One ought only to remember Heidegger's remarks to his students in his 1936 course, *What Is a Thing?*, the little maid Thrace laughing at Thales with his head lost in the stars: "The story is that Thales, while occupied in studying the heavens above and looking up, fell into a well. A good-looking and whimsical maid from Thrace laughed at him and told him that while he might passionately want to know all things in the universe, the *things* in front of his very nose and feet were unseen by him" (Plato, *Theatetus*, 174a).[4] And so goes, for Heidegger, the very drama of philosophy since Plato: interrogating beings, the philosopher has lost the "meaning of things" [*sens des choses*]—not in the sense of knowable objects but the things [*des affaires*] that concern us (*Sache* in German or *thing* in English).[5] But what "concerns us" [*fait notre affaire*], according to the philosopher, is paradoxically much less the granite, flint, limestone, or sandstone—so many specific determinations of the thing—but rather "the rock as thing," "the thingness of the thing." As the famous example of the "luncheon on the grass" explains: "we pose this question in order to know what a rock is, and a lizard taking a sunbath on it, a blade of grass that grows beside it, and a knife which perhaps we hold in our hands while we lie in the meadow."[6]

The strangest thing is that Heidegger himself lacked that which he nevertheless sought after so ardently: (a) first because he missed haecceity; (b) second because he always attached the thing to its being an entity. (a) We could have believed that his habilitation on Duns Scotus—actually Thomas of Erfurt (*Treatise on the Categories of Duns Scotus*)—would have led him to *haecceitas*, that is toward "this singular other" common to the species, provided that it itself possesses the principle of individuation that singularizes it. This is not the case. This text, already in the tradition of Husserl's *Logical Investigations*, on the contrary, turns to the treatment of logic. Here the promising notion that "what really exists is the individual" is left undeveloped.[7] (b) Regarding the thingness of the thing then—he could have caught that which logic had lost. But from the 1936 course on *What Is a Thing?* which is essentially concerned with objectivity in Kant, to the 1950 lecture on *The Thing*, which is in quest of a new "proximity" between man and beings, Heidegger never treats *this* thing that is *this* rock, *this* lizard, or *this* blade of grass. Instead he is concerned with the thing in the neutrality of being or the light of the neutral Fourfold in which it is given: the sky, earth, divinities, and mortals. The lingering of the source in the pouring of the jug says nothing about *this* jug or *this* water or *this* source, or even of *this* delay in the act of pouring—except precisely that the jug (or source) contains everything that it is not, that is, being or its light.[8]

Moving to Duns Scotus after Thomas Aquinas requires a double interrogation: (a) first, in *haecceitas*, in the determination of "this thing" (*haec*), is there something that escapes from the neutrality of otherness even to the point of defining it in its singularity as un-substitutable by all alterity (in the encounter with Levinas)?; (b) and then, can there be found in such a principle of individuation that which is separated from such an attachment to the thingness of the being, which in reality reveals nothing of itself except the very being that it protects in the ontological difference (in the encounter with Heidegger)? There will be something to say about the *actuality* of medieval philosophy (in the double sense of the actuation of its potentiality and the actualization of its positions) only at this price. And it is a safe bet that in the following we will have to make some subtle Scotist distinctions in order to express simultaneously man—*this* Franciscan—who is held a recluse in his own relation to the world, and *my* singular humanity which is sought also in the hermeneutic of a text of which nothing remains if it is not clarified in my context.

A framework ought to be established in order to speak of haecceity, of "this" (*hoc*), which makes it the other of every other: such is the task of contemporary philosophy inasmuch as it tells us something of our relation to the world. But it turns out that Scotus more than any other was the initiator of the framework of modernity. For the first time, perhaps, in the history of philosophy, he opened toward finitude or the "self-enclosed horizon of our existence." Disparaged as the destroyer of being (Gilson), or honored for delimiting the "only possible ontology" (Deleuze), he remains no less the one through whom either tragedy or salvation comes. He is therefore the frontier of and for our world, even more than a Descartes or a Kant, both of whom depended on him more than they were aware. This finitude becomes the common place of modern philosophy (from Heidegger to Sartre, Merleau-Ponty to Camus). Here Scotus is the father and we are all his children. Our task is first to give this "framework of finitude" all the pregnant fullness and consistency that it already has in Scotus himself, then to inscribe there the haecceity of man and, finally, of angels.

The Framework of Finitude

Saint Paul states it with precision, and we would do well to listen to him: "Do you not know that then you were without the Messiah . . . *without God in the world*" (Eph. 2:12). Without requiring Scotus to make the absurd profession of atheism (which was meaningless, at any rate, in the Middle Ages), it may nevertheless be the case that times past have returned: "Atheism is neither simply nor in the first place a theoretical problem: it is first what is a priori to existence."[9] So says Jean-Yves Lacoste with precision. The Subtle Doctor, at least, does not himself adhere to atheism, but nevertheless makes it conceptualizable precisely when he makes possible the thought, albeit impossible in his opinion, of doing without any theological sphere. It is in this case to philosophy's honor, as much as Christianity's, that they are willing to go there, not in order to confront an enemy but rather to penetrate to its depths. The way of univocity, the limitation of nature to our nature and the affirmation of the positivity of contingency thus mark the boundaries, both ancient and new, in which the haecceity of the "this" will establish itself, even to the point of overflowing, ultimately, into the new and other order of charity.[10]

The Way of Univocity

Univocity, and therefore Duns Scotus, inaugurates modernity. A single formula of Gilles Deleuze is enough to demonstrate this: "There has only ever been one ontological proposition: Being is univocal. There has only ever been one ontology, that of Duns Scotus, which gave being a single voice."[11] What does that mean? It is beyond the scope of this study to develop the general meaning of univocity in the Subtle Doctor. Many brilliant commentaries have shown it. It is sufficient here only to retrace its paths, the very ones that establish univocity for us today as a result—and at the heart of which haecceity is inscribed.[12]

The Univocal Concept. The topic of the formulation of the univocity of the concept of being, the third distinction of the first book of the *Ordinatio*, is a warning for us: "I say that God is not only conceived by an analogical concept [*in conceptu analogo*] to the concept of the creature, that is, [a concept] which is entirely other [*omnino sit alius*] than the one that is said of the creature, but in a certain univocal concept [*in conceptu aliquo univoco*] to him and the creature."[13] To say it simply, and because simplicity often has the merit of clarity despite the inevitability of simplification, to say that God is both "good" and "not good" or "wise" and "not wise" in the sense that goodness and wisdom proper to the Creator is excluded from creatures, is not suitable (analogy). Not that God is not supremely wise, nor that creatures do not participate in it from a real point of view, but only that he also is logically submitted to a common concept of being that pertains to him as to the angel, man, and the rock (univocity).

The argument is clear and is announced in the following paragraph of the *Ordinatio*: Even when I doubt whether God is infinite or not, whether there is one God or many, whether he is created or uncreated, never do I doubt that I possess a "concept" of this that I doubt: "Every intellect that is certain of a concept and dubious of man possesses a concept of which it is certain [*habet conceptum de quo est certus*] besides the concepts that it doubts."[14] Its proximity with the Cartesian cogito ought not deceive us, even though it certainly conditions access to it. Scotus is not affirming here that I am certain of the *I* who doubts beings, but rather that I possess a definite and univocal *concept* of being [*étantité*] in order to be able to doubt beings [*des étants*] or their conceptual determinations. All seems as if—and we consider that this is always the case for the Subtle Doctor, even including the principle of individuation—a certain logical anteriority must erect itself before all differentiation: a common and univocal concept of God and creatures makes possible their differentiation, without which, in reality, they would be identical.

The Stages of Univocity. For the sake of full understanding, I will now retrace this path of univocity in order then to extract haecceity which stands out against this community.[15] First, the initial and perhaps the most fundamental proposition of the *Ordinatio*, which is found in its prologue: "The first natural *object* of our intellect is being as being [*l'étant en tant qu'étant*]."[16] Being as being thus becomes an "object of our intellect"—*obiectum intellectus nostri*—and precisely as an object, can be represented and become representable. The metaphysical (but not theological) concept of God and creatures will henceforth become accessible to our understanding, now without any negativity. Likewise it will become useless and false to distinguish within the *ens* (like Thomas Aquinas some decades earlier) the essence (*essentia*) and the act of existence (*esse*). What was true of God alone, namely, the identification of essence and existence, here becomes true of the creature as well: "It is simply totally false to say that *esse* is something other than *essentia*."[17]

Whence comes the second thesis: "Being, *according to its most common reason*, is the first object of the intellect."[18] A further step is taken here: an object of the intellect, being is now "under its most common reason"—*secundum suam rationem communissimam*. The point made here is critical because it maintains the univocity on which will be implanted not the equivocity of beings, but the differentiation of their forms as well as their material in a unique principle of individuation or singularization (*haecceitas*). Said otherwise, Scotus emphasizes that there is no "this" that is not identically a "that" but to the degree that "there is a common element in the being [*est in re 'commune'*] which is not from itself this one [*quod non est de se hoc*], and which by consequence is not reluctant not to be this one [*et per consequens ei de se non repugnant non-hoc*]."[19] In a more trivial fashion, when I do not even know things in their proper essences (rock, lizard, grass), I still do not cease to consider that there is something of the thing, or rather, of the being in its concept, which appears to me and remains irreducible. Hence it is appropriate to link the common being to the contemporary concept of the "phenomenon," at least insofar as it is considered to be the irreducible appearing of something that appears.[20]

The third step finally opens the way that leads us to the limitation of nature and then its contingency as such: this common being, states the *Reportata parisiensa*, is "common in itself to *perfect* and *imperfect things* [*commune enim est secundum se perfectis et imperfectis*]."[21] One would have thought, indeed wrongly if one consults the Thomist analogy alone, that such a community of nature is given by participation in the divine being, and that created things, even imperfect, receive a lesser measure of their perfection that resides in the Creator. But this is not the case. This common concept of being that precedes all its distinctions and differentiations extends to all, both to God, understood metaphysically, and to creatures.

Horizontality and Verticality. If we stick only to philosophy, in relation to which, as we will see later, theology carves out a totally distinct space, *horizontality* prevails over verticality, or, to say it in the most contemporary terms, the *immanence of concepts and of their significations* takes precedence over the transcendence of their existing content and their perfections. Paradoxically, common being becomes somehow almost nothing "at all"—and I say nothing here of that which ordinarily makes the primacy and particularity of Being. In fact, once *esse* is identified with *essentia* every being or every essence should be able to become *this* being or *this* essence (*this* humanity of Peter which is distinguished from *this* humanity of Paul and that of every other singular). To say it in phenomenological terms—if also according to a thematic of alterity which becomes Duns Scotus's only by the act of "pure love" in theology—there is no "other me" (*ego alter*) without posing first an "other myself" (*alter ego*). The uniqueness of the genus is here drawn to the extreme, and nothing first descends to the intellect if not genus itself, which loses its name to the point of becoming *common* to the creator and creature. Being made capable of articulating everything in a common way (*ens commune*), the perfect as the imperfect, the better as the worse, being or the originary essence undifferentiated as object of the intellect does not get lost in the whole since, starting from this community it succeeds at expressing or formulating that which is—almost—nothing of this whole that it names (*haecceitas*).

We ought to see here that it is necessary to go farther (to the common essence of all beings) in order to get through to that which is closer (to what makes the singularity of "this being here" distinct from every other being). Here arises the exigency in Scotus for a necessary limitation of nature to my own nature if it is the (finally unprovable) case that the singular beings that I experience are those same ones that constitute my most ordinary being [*étantité*].

The Limitation of Nature to My Nature

The Hypothesis of a Rupture. The original relation that Scotus establishes between the natural and supernatural justifies, I suggest, the relevance of his quest for haecceity. The research into the singular will be revealed in fact to be all the more grounded as it will be capable of saying something about our humanity. The prologue of the *Ordinatio* is clear, and authorizes no detour: "It is impossible to show by the light of natural reason that something of the supernatural is present in the wayfarer [*nullum supernaturale potest ratione naturali ostendi inesse viatori*], nor is it necessarily required for the perfection of the latter [*nec necessario requiri ad perfectionem eius*], nor even does the one who possesses it know that it is present in him [*nec etiam habens potest cognoscere illud sibi inesse*]."[22]

Let it be clearly understood: Duns Scotus is not denying here that there is some kind of inscription of the supernatural in the natural; far from it. A simple repetition of his theory of the *imago Dei* is enough to make the point.[23] He only indicates—but it is indeed much in regard to the future of philosophy—that pilgrim man, in the state here below, does not succeed, starting from his natural reason alone, in showing that the supernatural is both required (*requiri*) and present (*inesse*). Nothing can be built on the old precept that "all men desire happiness," says Hannah Arendt—basing herself on Duns Scotus and carrying out his thought—except, at best, that they have the "will to suffer."[24] The rupture of metaphysics and the theological therefore requires neither the rejection of a natural desire for God in man nor the exclusion of God as his most natural end, but only the refusal of every access to him starting from our nature alone: "I admit that God is the natural end of man [*concedo Deum esse finem naturalem hominis*]," says Scotus in the *Ordinatio*, "but this end is not attained naturally, but rather supernaturally [*sed non naturaliter adipiscendum sed supernaturaliter*]."[25] The interdict made by philosophy only reinforces the theological. Since the way of nature is not sufficient to discover or attain the supernatural, "only *theology* is able to justify the need for theology"—but not philosophy.[26]

The Finite as Such. The separation of metaphysics (no access to the supernatural by means of natural reason) on the one side, and theology (the revelation of the supernatural by the supernatural and it alone) on the other—far from only excluding him, gives them the gift of their own proper integrity. The world is all the more the world insofar as it is refused to be allowed to transcend [itself], and revelation is all the more itself as it is self-nourishing. Here arises the new question proposed by Duns Scotus in relation to the ways of access to God (*Ord.* d. 2, q. 1), which is all the more radical as it maintains nature in its necessary limitation to my own nature in this world: "Why does not the intellect, the object of which is being [*quare intellectus cujus objectum est ens*], find repulsive the idea of something infinite [*nullam invenit repugnantiam intelligo aliquod infinitum*]?"[27]

The interrogation is here incisive and patent: even if the natural ought not to be content *by right* with the natural, if it is the case that it also holds the finitude of its sinful failure, why would it not be by the fact of this very finitude its own and unique good? Independently of the envisaged solution by the resistance of the will before the limits of our finitude (sin), the breach is open by the very posing of the question. For the first time in the history of philosophy—and it is not any less established from the moment that one considers the anteriority of Scotus to Kant and of course to Heidegger—the finite is not left to be thought here by opposition to and delimitation of the infinite. Nothing else is given to man but such a limitation of nature to his own present state—somehow always plugged up by the horizon of its finitude. And "if one were to argue starting from these things which are objects of faith [*ex creditis*]," adds Scotus in the prologue, "reasoning does not strike against the Philosopher [*non est ratio contra philosophum*] since he does not admit as a premise the object of faith."[28] It is therefore not an understatement to see in Duns Scotus the figure of a Scholastic philosopher "so strangely contemporary to our most urgent questionings."[29]

The Horizon of Finitude. This limitation of nature to my nature, at least in my radical incapacity to transcend it by my intelligence alone, in no way moves us away from haecceity. On the contrary, it leads us to it, here not by means of the community of being (univocity) but by reduction to our own humanity (finitude). Our impossible access to the supernatural will require that we consult only our own nature. Not yet blessed, let alone God himself, the proper "this" which makes the thing as though other to every other will designate *for us* first the nearest "this" (*haec*) of *this* rock or *this* man made in our finitude, rather than the "that," farther away, of *this* angel or *this* God given only in his self-revelation. The obscurity of the apprehension of the singular, as we can experience it today, will be measured by the density of *our* singularity taken here below in the positivity of our contingency.

The Positivity of Contingency

A repetition of the *entire* Scotist theory of creation, fall, and redemption is necessary in order to gauge our experience of such a limitation of our intellection, which is in reality all the more powerful as we ignore it. Such will not however be our task here, since it would bypass for the most part the fixed boundaries of this final chapter. However, (a) an ontological reason, (b) a metaphysical motif, and (c) a theological argument together allow the thinking of a real *positivity of contingency* in Scotus, a thinking of the sort that what will be the most appropriate or singular will not necessarily at the same time break the seal of failure or sin.

The Mode of Contingency. (a) First from the ontological point of view, that is, of the structure of the world, Duns Scotus sometimes formulates statements of a surprising modernity: "I say that contingency is not merely a privation or a defect of Being like the deformity . . . which is sin. Rather, contingency is a *positive mode of Being*, just as necessity is another mode."[30] Everything depends on what we understand contingency to be: either the possibility of the choice of contraries in liberty, or the structure of the world as such. But one does not go without the other—and, in a word, it is to be faithful to the principle of prudence in Aristotle to indicate that there is never either deliberation or decision without the positivity of a world itself capable of mutability and change.[31] What is conformed to Aristotelianism—the pure respect of a contingency not first derived from some kind of human failure—is nonetheless highly original in the context of Christianity in regard to sin.

The Expansion of Man to God. (b) From here comes the second innovation: metaphysics, at least in its collision with revealed theology, and which now breaks definitively with the Greek context. The sphere of contingency extends now from man to God. Precisely where human contingency is typically opposed to divine necessity—whether, for example, the superlunary world (Aristotle), "reasons of fittingness" (Augustine), or "necessary reasons" (Anselm)—Duns Scotus surprisingly states in the prologue to the *Lectura*: "The main part of theology is concerned with *contingent* truths [*de contingentibus*]: the incarnation, the creation of the world by three persons, that man will be beatified by the divine essence—these are all truly *contingent* truths, whereas the engendering of the Son by God the Father is an *eternal* truth."[32]

The incarnation, the creation, and beatification are therefore of the order of divine contingency in the sense of a free decision of God *ad extra* (deciding, that is, on their being or non-being), while the engendering of the Son by the Father pertains to the order of necessary truths since it is directly demanded by his nature *ad intra* (it must be). The *extension of contingency to God* all the more enlarges the sphere of his freedom as it also seems to articulate, through univocity, beings in their pure haecceity. The fact that "I love God" (*me diligere Deum*) or that "God loves me," says Scotus in the prologue to the *Lectura*, is of the same kind of contingency as the "falling rock" (*lapidem descendere*). Even as it is always identically repeated, the rock that continually falls again and again remains in fact no less an ever new event (*novum*), at least in view of all the circumstances that could prevent its fall (the presence of another object or a cement that holds it fast). Such is the case, then, by analogy, of the love of God for me as of my love for him. Given to each other in pure "gratuity," what is true of the rock (its fall) is even truer of man and God (their reciprocal love), since the freedom of the latter overflows significantly the apparent necessity of the first. The seal of freedom thus marks everything of the order of haecceity (*this* rock that is falling or *this* man who is loving) to the point of making the contingency of each being (being capable of falling or not, or loving or not) the very principle of its singularization.[33] We can find there the most contemporary requisites, which once again show that Duns Scotus opens the path of our own modernity: "Individual existence of every sort is, quite universally speaking, 'contingent' [*zufallig*]," Husserl emphasizes in *Ideas I*, whereas Jean-Luc Marion will define contingency etymologically in *Being Given* as "that which touches me," or which "affects me" (*contingit*) in the sense, precisely, that nothing that is singular could be considered unable to come to me or "fall on me."[34]

Incarnation by Glorification. (c) The last reason is a purely theological motif in the economy of redemption. It gives to the world all of its positivity and therefore to haecceity all the density of its singularity. The formula of Duns Scotus in the *Reportata parisiensa* is known but no less remarkable: "if no angel or man had fallen [*si nec fuisset Angelus lapsus nec homo*], Christ would still have been predestined [to be incarnate] [*adhuc fuisset Christus sic praedestinatus*], even if no other being but Christ had been created."[35] We rediscover here the phenomenological motif of the incarnation that first came to light in our study of Irenaeus. Here, as in Irenaeus, the incarnation does not bear a direct relation to sin, but instead, for Scotus, God becomes man, not primarily for the sake of reparation or satisfaction, but through the pure *glorification and manifestation* of the Father in the Son, and of man, then, in his beatitude. Finitude is therefore not first marked by a failure, since that is not first the cause of its assumption by the Word. The sin of Adam marks, to be sure, a delay in glorification, but it is not the sole cause of reparation: "If Adam had not sinned [*nisi aliquis prius peccasset*]," adds Scotus, "Christ whole and entire would have been immediately glorified [*statim fuisset totus Christus glorificatus*]."[36]

A conclusion therefore imposes itself, inherited from Avicenna but articulated by Scotus himself: "Let those who deny contingency be tortured until they admit that it is possible not to be tortured."[37] The usual primacy of necessity over contingency is here suddenly reversed, counteracting virtually every trace of Hellenism in revelation: *contingency* (a) first as a structure of the world having a real positivity in order to justify its consistency and an absolute freedom for man; (b) then extended to God, making of his works *ad extra* (incarnation, creation, beatification) acts of an absolute freedom over-against any "necessary reason;" (c) and finally, related to Christ, unfolding all of his density in a salvation primarily operated for the sake of glorification, rather than satisfaction or reparation. At this point virtually everything is said about haecceity, even if it was always ever only an implicit question. If there is singularity—of essence and existence since these are identified with one another for Scotus—it only has meaning for me if it concerns *me* and therefore transforms *me*. In this case then the "quid" or "what-ness of the thing [*Ding*]" can be transmuted into a "haec" or "this" of the thing [*de l'affaire*] (*Sache*) in order that the haecceity of singularity is drawn from the univocity of the entity.

Singular Man

I have already emphasized that for Duns Scotus it is necessary to reach the farthest (the univocity of the concept of being) in order to rejoin the closest (the haecceity of the singular). What is true of the passage from univocity to haecceity is even truer of the haecceity of beings themselves—for the angels in particular, who again make their appearance here. In his treatise on the angels (*Ord.*, II, d. 3, p. 1) the Subtle Doctor resolves the question of the "distinction of angels into persons" by suggesting that it is necessary "to begin by inquiring about the distinction of material substances into individuals [*de distinctione individuali in substantiis materialibus*]."[38] Existentially closer to the more concrete (the rock or the man) in order to reflect on the most abstract (the angel), Scotus privileges (at least in the order of the text) the haecceity of the contingency that is closest to us in its determinations (the haecceity of the rock for me) in relation to the brilliance of its shining in the most distant (the direct intuition of singulars for the angels). A new reversal of the field of metaphysics is enacted here, for the primacy of the singular over the universal is established (on top of the reversal enacted by the primacy of contingency over necessity): "The individual bears a certain perfection that the common does not [*individuum includit aliquem perfectionem quam non includit commune*]."[39]

Before Scotus everyone thought that the epistemological primacy of the universal over the singular, or the common over the individual, was self-evident. It was therefore left completely uninterrogated. Whether Plato's "exemplary forms" or Aristotle's "universal concepts" drawn by induction from the particular, there was never a "science but of the universal."[40] But the primacy established by Scotus is not first ontological, like the superiority of the first substance maintained by the Stagirite ("the individual man" or "the individual horse") over the second substance ("man and animal").[41] To the contrary, the individual (*individuum*) defeats "in perfection" the common (*commune*), not simply in its being, but in its epistemological principle or concept: "The *concept* of this essence under the reason of being [*conceptus illius essentiae sub ratione entis*] is more imperfect than the *concept* of this essence as it is this essence here [*ut haec essentia est*]."[42]

The question is therefore not only *ontological*, residing in the Scotist refusal of the distinction between essence and existence. On the contrary, it is in the first place *epistemological*, in the sense that it challenges the primacy of the universal over the singular left previously unquestioned in the order of knowledge. So the Subtle Doctor asks in essence if it could be the case that man has knowledge of singulars, or at least that knowledge of singulars is better than the apprehension of the universal, which is still inaccessible to him in his state as wayfarer. The case of the rock, the man, and the angel will thus serve as the main thread woven through an investigation that has no other end than of delimiting, on the one hand, haecceity in relation to univocity (the paradigm of the rock) and of extracting, on the other hand, the kind of singularity proper to man (found in between the modes of haecceity of the rock and the angel).

The Case of the Rock or the Cause of Singularity

A Sufficient Reason. Is univocity consequently necessary for differentiation, and even for singularity in order to assure its haecceity? "Positing community in nature itself" (*posita communitate in ipsa natura*), responds the *Ordinatio*, "it is necessary to find a cause of singularity [*causam singularitatis*] that adds [*superaddit*] something to the nature of the singular being."[43]

The impossible individuations of singular being either through matter (Aristotle, Thomas Aquinas), quantity (Gilles of Rome and Godfrey of Fontaines), or double negation (Henry of Ghent), are too well known to repeat.[44] The key point is that even for Scotus one must "add" (*superaddit*) something (a cause) to the nature of the singular being in order to make it truly singular. Not that nature is the singular being, since every empirical view is sufficient to show it (some such rock is not some other rock), but in the sense that a cause (*causa*) ought to justify it, much like the future idea of "sufficient reason (Leibniz), though the principle is reserved here to haecceity alone (why is this rock some *such* rock and not another one or otherwise?). Here I point out again the role of a treatise on the angels (*Ord.*, II, d. 3, p. 1)—"again" since already the angelology of Thomas has already done the work of convincing us of the pertinence of Scholastic angelology for clarifying the contemporary question of alterity. Here it is made a formal rule: "In things, independently of every operation of the intellect, there is a certain unity [*aliqua unitas*] which is *inferior to numerical unity* [*minor unitate numerali*], in other words the *unity proper to singularity* [*sive unitate propria singularis*], and which is nevertheless *real* [*realis*]."[45]

Almost everything is contained in this unique statement: "the cause of singularity" (*causa singularitatis*) is found in an autonomous principle of unity, anterior to every numerical, material, quantitative, qualitative, or existential determination, and which makes this being to be precisely *this* nature. This is called the "unity proper to singularity" (*unitate propria singularis*). In the next section, we will examine this first negatively, then positively.

The Unity Proper to the Singular. Negatively, and picking up again a famous paradigm inherited from the Stagirite, what makes "Socrates himself" is neither his material (size, morphology, weight, etc.), nor his form (his membership in humanity in general), nor even his difference with the man Plato: "Not being something does not explain what something is."[46] Accusing Dionysian apophatic theology of getting lost in the haze of an all too neutral conception of the universality of God—"I intensely hate negations [*negationes etiam non summe amamus*]"[47]—Scotus will demand that haecceity designate a *positive* principle, a "cause of singularity," by which it determines the essence to exist particularly, not in the sense of mattering to any other in general, and always replaceable by a new other, albeit irreducible to the sphere of the same (Levinas), but rather as *such* a particular other all the more un-substitutable as it is named *positively such*, and not by comparison with other beings that inhabit the same space: "Material substance," says the Subtle Doctor, "is individuated [*sit individua*] by a positive entity [*per aliquam entitatem postitivam*] that through itself determines the nature to singularity [*per se determinantem naturam ad singularitatem*]."[48]

Positively, a common form (the human soul) and a common material (the human body) are sufficient to compose a human *quiddity* (a being corresponding to this definition). But in order for there to be a human individuality (Socrates), the composition, itself individual, of an individual form ("this human soul" of Socrates) and an individual material ("this human body" of Socrates) is required. Here lies Scotus's originality. Socrates is not Socrates merely by means of the composition of a human soul and body, but by his individual manner of making up *his* soul and *his* body. Haecceity first attains neither the soul (form), nor the body (matter), nor the unity of the two (the composite), but the collection of what is given (form, matter, composite) as it originally holds the principle of this entire essence produced by God: "inferior to numerical unity" (*minor unitate numerali*), as indicated above, within the meaning of the most original anteriority.[49] What makes "Socrates Socrates" does not come in the first place from his difference with another, or from his components or his composite (matter-form), but rather, as has been rather poorly formulated though not without pedagogical value, from his "Socratesness"—that is, from his own particular way of expressing his essence or his humanity as body and soul, both singularized in their respective essences and in the composite itself.[50] Said in a more contemporary idiom, though far removed from Scotus, at least in terminology: the person of Socrates (his way of uniting his body and his own soul) performs his humanity (being the *particular* man Socrates) and his humanity (participating in the genre or the species of humanity in general) does not make his person (being Socrates). Against the Stagirite, there is for Socrates some kind of *definition*: not in his universality (humanity) but precisely as he alone defines a type of universal individuated by itself and through itself alone, and by which his essence appears—his "Socratesness." Gilson translates this idea judiciously with the following formula: "It is a matter here of an individuation of the quiddity, but not by the quiddity" (at least the premises of this were already discovered in Aristotle; see *Metaphysics*, Book Lambda, 5).[51]

The Homogenization of Individuation. From the philosophical point of view, though in anticipation of a theological guardianship of the distinction of persons, that which is true of the haecceity of Socrates is true of every being for Scotus. What is true of man, because at first glance more obvious for us, is also and in the first place true of this rock as this most ordinary being, which is also singularized in its form: "I hold that if this rock [*huic lapidi*] is not left to be divided into subjective parts, it must necessarily be by reason of something *positive* intrinsic to it [*per aliquid positivum intrinsecum*]. I term this something positive self-caused individuation [*per se causa individuationis*]."[52]

It would be wrong to complain here about some kind of homogenization of the individuation of man with the haecceity of the rock. On the contrary, by pure respect for contingency, as we have seen above (and in order to remain at the level of what is given by nature to my nature), the principle of individuation first touches the collection of beings—and *for me* the priority is those who are *the closest* to me, including myself. From a didactic point of view (that is, God's), even haecceity would be true first of the divine essence and then of angels, men, and rocks; from a heuristic point of view (my own), it is first about *this* rock or *this* lizard rather than *this* angel or *this* God.

A question still remains and catches back up with our second interrogation: once the haecceity of this rock is determined starting from its "internal cause" by which its essence itself is singularized, how then do we pass from the simple *singularity* of singular beings to the *unicity* of this singular being that is *this man* Socrates, standing between the thingness of the rock and the immateriality of the angel?

The Case of Man or the Call of the Name

Two reasons, one philosophical, the other theological, suggest that we should not consider the humanity of *this* man Socrates in the same way that we approach *this* stone by the wayside or *this* blade of grass in the meadow. In his treatise on the angels, which examines the principle of individuation, Scotus says: "Not only faith [*secundum fidem*] but also philosophy [*secundum philosophiam*] obliges us to consider that each man has his own intellective soul [*aliam et aliam animam intellectivam*]."[53] Faith and philosophy are therefore the two points of view from which to envisage the singularity proper to man, that is, of "every man."

Against the Common Intellect (Averroes). (a) First, the philosophical point of view: the argument is carried out against that "accursed Averroes [*illus maledicti Averrois*] who imagined that there exists a single intellect for all men [*de unitate intellectus in omnibus*]."[54] For the Subtle Doctor—whose subtlety is in danger of being reduced to scorn here—it is certainly not essential to conform to the Aristotelian program for which man is distinguished, according to his species, from animals and vegetative life by means of his intellective soul. The famous and complex debate about the common intellect finds in haecceity its most profound objection. What makes humanity human in fact is not the intellective soul as such, according to a purely formal division, but the act of considering "*each* man" as having "his own intellective soul" (*aliam et aliam animam intellectivam*). Men neither share nor divide up a single intellect, no more than the rock is individuated by its quantity or extension. But each man, on the contrary, "enacts his intellectuality or humanity"—in the same way that he once "enacted his humanity" by realizing *through himself* human tasks—since he differentiates it and singularizes it in its own beingness. Socrates and Plato do not share a common intellect, but *each* are, by *their own* intellect, beings or essences capable of singularizing their own humanity.

Singularization through Being (Moses). (b) The theological point of view: here haecceity finds *in God* and *for man* its true motive. (i) In the name of God revealed to Moses; (ii) in the determination of the singular other through love in Saint John.

(i) The address of Yahweh to Moses first marks for Scotus in the *Treatise on First Principles* an attempt to reach God through the concepts that man knows are accessible to his humanity here below—namely, univocal being: "Lord our God, to Moses your servant who sought to know from you, the most true master, by which name he ought to call you before the children of Israel, *seeking thereby what the intelligence of mortals could conceive of you*, you have responded by revealing your true and blessed name: I am the one who is [*ego sum qui sum*]. You are the true being [*verum esse*], you are being whole and entire . . . Help me, Lord, to know what our natural reason can attain in taking as a point of departure the being [*ens*] that you have attributed to yourself."[55]

The "metaphysics of exodus" (Gilson) or "project of ontotheology" (Vignaux) seems to be totally contained here in the context of this demonstration of the "First Principle" for a metaphysical determination of God starting from God himself, who somehow condescends to man, not necessarily in order to reveal to him his own name, but rather what is comprehensible to humanity: *esse* is reduced to *ens commune*.[56] But against every metaphysics or ontotheology, there is, it seems to me, more to this name than the simple declaration by God of that which man can comprehend. "He who is," for Scotus, only tells us positively that he "is" in his universality (*esse*) only if he remains negatively inaccessible to us in his singularity: *Ego sum qui sum*—"I am This One [*hic*] who I am."[57] The name of being ascribed to God by virtue of his accessibility to man shows therefore a defect of metaphysics (as opposed to establishing it). The proper name of God, following the Jewish tradition (YHWH), remains completely unsayable—not because of its grandeur or universality, but by its *singularity* and *haecceity*: "In God," states the prologue to the *Ordinatio*, "the first subject of all theology in itself is the divine essence insofar as it is 'this one here' [*essentia ut haec*]."[58]

At least in the "theology that God knows" (*theologia divina*)—but not man, as we will see below—the "*essentia ut haec*" also denotes the nature and *proper name* of God as singularity, inaccessible to us here below but making up his true being in the beyond. Aristotle already affirmed that the "state of joy that we possess only fleetingly but that God possesses constantly" does not come from his immateriality but his singularity.[59] What accounts for the response of God to Moses, according to Scotus, is therefore not, except by default, the univocity of his being with every being—"I *am* the one who *is*"—but, on the contrary the singular appellation of himself through himself as the self-existent [*innascible*] source of every possible singularity: "*I* am *the One* who is." Far from being and close to the Name—such is the novelty of the Scotist interpretation of the formula addressed to Moses (Ex. 3:14), by the singularity of "the One [*Celui*]" rather than the requisite of Being, by the call of the name rather than by the metaphysics of Exodus.[60]

Singularization through Charity (Saint John). (ii) The determination of the singular other by charity is also sustained completely in the Scotist call, man directly addressed by God, making him exist in his singularity at the same time as God conceives man starting from his own singularity: *Amo, volo ut sis*—"I love you, I will that you be."[61]

The first meaning to attribute to the formula is that "love gives being" (I love you/you are).[62] But there is more to this in the thought of Scotus, who escapes precisely from the double neutrality of alterity (Levinas) and ontology (Heidegger). Only the singularity of the one who gives or rather "is given" since he is love itself ("*I* love you"), conferring being to *this* singular being that he desires even in his essence (". . . *you* are")—Socrates rather than Plato, or better, Peter, builder of his church (Mt. 16:18) rather than Judas the betrayer (Jn. 13:30). To be and to be individuated by love (*I* love you/*you* are) is, for Scotus, not to exist or to be actualized, but to respond to the call of one's own essence, ever determined by the One who "is charity [*agapê estin*]" (1 Jn. 4:8), and who wants me for me (Jer. 1:5).[63] The singularization by love will thus extend, as I will now show, from the *love of the other by God* to the *love of God by the other* and from the *love of God by the other* to the *love of the other by me*, who is also in the image of God.

Pure Love

God's Love of the Other. Contrary to a stereotype widespread even among the best exegetes of Scotus, the "love of the other by God" principally aims for the *other* and not, in some kind of divine quasi-self-sufficiency, for God *himself*. The pure love (*amor purus*) by which God loves man is not a reflexive love turned on itself in a sort of auto-contemplation of the Aristotelian type. He loves man only in a free and gratuitous fashion without expectation of return. The "love of justice" (*amor justitiae*) excludes any love of profit. God does not love in the mode of possession—whether loving himself (*sibi*) or me (*mihi*). No reciprocity can explain his love for me, since he never ceased loving me, even when I stopped loving him: "God is not the object of his own charity [*Deus non est objectum caritatis suae*]," says Scotus in the *Reportata parisiensia*, "since he understands the good as my good [*ut incluendo quod est bonum mihi*] or he understands it as his own good [*nec incluendo ut bonum sibi*]."[64]

So God does not love man in order for man to render him glory, but on the contrary, he loves man *for the sake of man* and in order first that man himself loves from the glory by which God loves him and thus loves himself: "I regret having to say," says Camille Bérubé, remarking on Léon Veuthey and some of the other best interpreters of Scotus, "that this metaphysics of the love of God as the final cause of itself is neither Scotist nor Thomist, for nothing is the final cause of its being . . . By creating them God wants *other creatures than himself* to have a pure, disinterested love in themselves, like God has of himself, so that they will finally arrive at the goodness of the beatific vision. It is *not in order to satisfy a need to be loved*, but by a *pure liberality*."[65]

The Other's Love of God

The counterpart on the side of the other is thus imposed: the "love of God by the other"—and not uniquely the "love of the other by God"—is not built on any kind of reciprocity. The other loves God, not so that God will love him—trapped in an exchange, but first in order to learn from him how to love oneself, as well as the other and God, in the same purely disinterested way that God loves: "The principal reason of what is lovable in relation to the will is not that it is good for me [*mihi*], for you [*tibi*] or even for him [*nec etiam sibi*] . . . This is why the first and most perfect reason which makes God lovable is his absolute goodness [*absoluta bonitas sua*], as he is good in himself, for he loves and is loved in a love of justice [*amor justitiae*]."[66]

A triple reduction or "bracketing" (resuming, here, the development of the phenomenological *epochê* by Eckhart—of myself (*mihi*), the other (*tibi*), and God (*sibi*) leads us to consider disinterested love, or the "love of justice," that which is loved by God and which ought to be loved by my loving God. The absolute goodness of God merits my love because by it I resemble him in this purely liberal way of loving.

My Love of the Other. The "love of the other by me" will thus pass in an ultimate way through God in order to receive from him the gratuity of love. I will myself love the other only in a unique way when I desire myself also, in a purely disinterested way as the image of the disinterested God, as he himself loves, loving God and myself in a disinterested way: "Thus loving God I love myself [*diligo me*] and I love my neighbor [*et proximum*], desiring for myself and him the love of God [*ex caritate volendo mihi et sibi velle*] and by this love the possession of God in himself [*et per dilectionem habere Deum in se*]."[67] I can therefore desire for you your own desire for God in the sense that I desire that you also can live by participating in the pure love by which God loves and also calls me to love myself: "I desire God [*volo Deum*] and I want you to desire God [*volo te velle Deum*], and in this way I love you out of charity [*ex caritate*] because I want for you [*tibi*] the good of justice [*bonum justitiae*]."[68]

The *love of the other by God*, *love of God by the other*, and *love of the other by me* (in the image of God) are together fed by the same disinterestedness.

"Paradoxically" I love the other all the more as I do not love that he loves me, or rather I only love him for what he is—as a possible and probable future lover of God, independently of all of my personal interests, even against them: "To love God by a love of charity," we find subtly expressed in the *Ordinatio*, "means to desire the object in itself [*secundum se*] even if, impossibly [*etiamsi per impossibile*] he did not respond to the good of the one who loves [*circumscriberetur ab eo commoditas ejus ad amantem*]."[69]

In some sense God is looking for "friends to love" or some others to love with him—"*vult alios habere condilentes*"—not for himself, for liberal love is his very nature (which has been termed "love donation"), even to the point of giving the donation of the gift itself.[70] Co-loving with us, the Subtle Doctor extends *condilectio* to man (that is, the "love of a third"), which, in Richard of Saint Victor, is reserved to the Spirit alone. In the same way that in Richard the Spirit does not loathe, but even desires that the Son be loved much, even more by the Father than himself, so also ought I not be reluctant to desire that my neighbor be much and even more loved by God than myself. In other words, man is integrated in his heart to the *perichoresis* of the Trinity, and the glory of God is full not of the praise of the self for the self, but of the glory of the other for the other by which man himself loves in this same (pure) love by which God loves.[71]

Singular Angel

The Theological Motif

The Intention of God. Passing from the singularity of man to the singularity of the angel, the true reason of haecceity—mine and the other's, if it is true that there was something learned from the nature of angels—seemed to be more directly theological than philosophical, of the order of faith rather than of reason. In Christianity intentions (*intentiones*) can certainly be ascribed to God, but these intend first the *singularization* of the individual (angels and men) and not the *obeisance* to a law in community (a people). God understood as Trinity does not desire merely such or such act, or even such or such disposition of the heart, albeit operated for love of him. He first wants *me* in my pure ipseity: "Peter, James, and John," thus recounting the specific disciples Christ took aside (Mt. 14:33). The ego engendered by the community (Origen) and constituted by subjectivity (Aquinas) is now articulated in a haecceity required by the context of faith (Scotus). The *case of the angel* thus serves in a new way as the paradigm of alterity, but here, specifically, in the quest for an identified singularity: "Of all the most principal entities [*in principalissimis entibus*]," Scotus says circumspectly in his *Treatise on the Angels*, "the individual [*individuum*] corresponds the most to the intention of God [*est a Deo principaliter intentum*]."[72]

From the Singular to Singulars. The distinction of the philosophical and theological orders still does not justify treating of one (metaphysics) and dispensing with the other (charity). We can only regret the numerous analyses of Scotus that think they can treat of haecceity in a unilaterally philosophical fashion.[73] Not that there is no singularity outside of the theological and the vision of God—far from it in fact—but only that the pursuit of a "cause of singularity" (*causam singularitatis*) finds its full accomplishment only in God who contains singularly the essence of every singular being as well as their most proper names: from *some particular* rock on the wayside (passed without even being seen), to *some particular* angel (Gabriel) sent to the Mother of God to announce her blessed mission (Lk. 1:26). The movement is not from the universal to the singular in the Subtle Doctor's highly theological perspective, but rather from the *Singular* to *singulars*, so that individuality becomes the ultimate *realitas entis*—"the ultimate reality of being"—and so that the universal becomes, as if by excess, relegated to the realm of pure abstraction in the nominalism of William of Ockham.[74]

The Act of Love. The rational creature loves God not only for himself and for its own creaturely sake, but it loves *this neighbor for God's sake*—"wanting for itself and the neighbor the love of God"—for such a love alone singularizes both of them in a call to be *their* own essence, as it does even for me in *my* own essence: "The entire theology of Scotus," says Gilson, "is marked by this truly capital thesis, that the first free act encountered in the collection of being is an *act of love*."[75] Theologically I receive my haecceity from God who is Haecceity itself, as well as the desire for the other to receive his own haecceity from God. In its spiritual and Franciscan roots, haecceity, from the point of view of love, is "the philosophical expression of what St. Francis wanted to say when he said 'Brother' ":[76] not only because philosophically every man is distinguished from every other being by his own intellect, but first theologically because he receives, for himself and for the other, this haecceity of God himself as pure singularity who singularizes him and confers on him his *unique* beauty. Thus it is "the implacable logic of Scotism to stress more than any other system the *unique* and *singular* character of the *beauty of the individual*. The Scotist aesthetic is one of 'this' and 'that,' in other words an *aesthetic of haecceity*: it is therefore parallel to the increasing individualization of art."[77]

The Case of the Angel or the Irreducible Obscurity

The Privilege of the Blessed. A double call—God to me and me to the other for God—therefore constitutes the theological singularity of man, entirely turned by his free will toward this Singularity that summons him. But is it fitting for us, in our present state (*pro statu isto*) to claim the angelic condition for which this haecceity seems explicitly established? Should we forget our starting point in the unsurpassable context of finitude in which the haecceity of "this" is inscribed for us? The essential, in Scotus, is not in fact the evident and necessary singularization of angels into proper individualities (as opposed to unique species, contra Aquinas). Although implicit, the question of *our knowledge* of this Singularity that is God (thus divesting us of the knowledge of both the angels and the blessed) is of no less critical importance: "In God and for the blessed, the first subject of all theology in itself [*theologia in se*] is the divine essence as just this one [*est essentia ut haec*]."[78]

Our Theology. Theology "in itself" (*in se*) or "enjoyed by God" (*divina*), as I have already, but only made mention, is distinguished from "our" theology (*theologia nostra*) or that "enjoyed by man" (*theologia tradita*). In fact, the first knows, in the beatific vision, the essence of God "as just this one" (*ut haec*), that is, in his proper nature and singularity. By contrast, our theology, attached to our finitude here below, attains through the mediation of scripture only "this essence" of God (*haec essentia Dei*), that is, as determined not properly and positively in his singularity, but in a derivative and negative fashion, such that I can conceive his essence starting from its distinction with other essences.[79] Said otherwise (and in spite of the subtlety of the argument here), the impossible apprehension, in my state as wayfarer, of the singularity of *the One* who is singularity itself means that such a haecceity remains at least invisible and *invisable* starting from my own finitude:[80] "Not the sun, but the eye of the owl explains why it does not see the sun."[81] Against a strange defect of our nature here below which always prefers universality to singularity, paradoxically my human being-there will sometimes be satisfied with the universal, less because of a lack of amazement at the "*essentia ut haec*" than because of my incapacity to receive it: "The intellect . . . has recourse to universal concepts precisely because it is incapable of knowing haecceity."[82]

A Certain Happiness in Misery. However, there is a certain happiness at the heart of this misery. In my state of peregrination, having no direct access (a) to the singularity of God, (b) to myself, (c) or to the other, will in fact be the most certain proof of their unfathomable mystery here below. (a) Regarding God, the human intellect differs from the angelic intellect in that it does not have an immediate apprehension of singularity: "The *angelic intellect*," notes Scotus, "*directly* knows the singular. *Our intellect* does not know it in that way."[83] The impossible transgression of our finitude, at least in the present state (*hic et nunc*) demands that we remain human—even though we are entitled to aspire to our own beatification. (b) From here comes the fact that "our soul does not know itself by means of its essence."[84] We will know "singulars in their own reasons in the fatherland [*in patria*] . . . but in the present state [*sed pro statu ipso*] our intellect knows nothing but what can be produced by an image."[85] In a word, therefore, we only have access to ourselves by means of "representations." And what we apprehend of ourselves here below is not our own haecceity, but only the accidents, or at least images of our most proper being. (c) This is why, from the point of view of the other, according to a felicitous isomorphism that appeared in the later works of Ricoeur, "the soul knows itself as others" (*anima intelligit se sicut alia)*—"soi-même comme un autre" [oneself as another]—as Aristotle argues "that it thinks only moved by phantasms [*mota a phantasmatibus*]."[86] The singular other—an appropriate name for every being but especially of the other man—is given to me like myself, appearing first and most often in his *accidentality* rather than in his *haecceity*: the face, nose, or color of the other's eyes (accidents) tell me nothing about his proper humanity as he singularizes it as a "this" (*haec*). Therefore in the present state, in fact if not by right, "the soul cannot think itself before having thought what is other to it" (Boulnois).[87]

Desiring the Singular

Enjoying the Singularity. But the Subtle Doctor does not despair as he remains in the philosophical sphere of contingency. To know the singular *indirectly* is not to pass it by completely. On the contrary—and here we have perhaps reached the fine point of Scotist haecceity—what I do not know of singularity *intellectually*, I experience by a pure motion of my *will*. The primacy of the will over the intellect, though subsuming it more than negating it, makes singularity for us here below the place of an *experience* or a *pleasure*, rather than a knowledge and a vision of essence: "It is not necessary to conclude that singularity, as condition of the object, is not known because the mode of expression of the singular is indirect," notes Camille Bérubé. "It is expressed in a universal concept but the intellect no less knows that *this object enjoys singularity*, that it is endowed with unity and incommensurability."[88] Without fully grasping the haecceity of the other, I understand, without truly arriving there, at least that it lives and experiences like me its own haecceity. The exception of course is God's grasp of himself. And such another will envisage me as some *such* particular other, though not in the sense that along with him I would ever renounce being *such*—but only *to know me and him* as such, that is, in the fullness of haecceity, by way of God who alone (creatively) knows us as *such*.

Contingency at All Costs. Against William of Ockham, Scotus refuses in advance to affirm, on the one hand, that "the *first known* in the order of time is the singular," and, on the other hand, that "the first *clearly* known can be the singular."[89] Certainly Ockham does not fulfill the work of Scotus (as is sometimes thought) by handing over to man what the latter refused to give him: the immediate knowledge of singulars. On the contrary, Ockham transforms him, at the cost of surpassing the horizon of finitude. The consequence of this move remains to be assessed. For in order, with William of Ockham, "to combat the old idea that the singular is ineffable" (P. Alféri), it would be necessary beforehand either to provide man with such an access to the ineffable world, or to hold that such an ineffability belongs to the mundane and that we possess the key to it. The transparency of singulars in the Venerable Doctor pays the price, therefore, of the disappearance of the weight of their contingency that the Subtle Doctor maintained.[90]

A Blessed Opacity. A (blessed?) opacity remains between me and myself, the other and God in Scotus and thus makes of this haecceity, however impenetrable, the *ultima realitas entis*, "the ultimate reality of being." Never reduced to pure transparency and yet constitutive of all reality, Scotist haecceity in its impenetrable obscurity—at least for us here below—joins up together with a number of the most contemporary approaches, especially, for example, in Maurice Merleau-Ponty: "If we succeed in describing the access *to the things themselves*," we find in his posthumous *The Visible and the Invisible* (1964), "it will only be through this *opacity* and this *depth*, which never cease: there is no thing fully observable, no inspection of the thing that would be *without gaps* and that would be *total*; we do not wait until we observe it in order to say that the thing is there; on the contrary, it is the appearance it has of being a thing that convinces us immediately that it is possible to observe it. In the *grain of the sensible* we find the assurance for a series of cross-checkings, which *do not constitute the ecceity* [*sic*] *of the thing*, but are derived from it."[91]

The singular other—myself, some such particular being, the other, and God—always remains impenetrable by the very fact of its singularization. That which ought to be the failure of man (the impenetrability of singularity, but his pleasure nevertheless) actually signals his greatest success: *to be and remain man*, and not completely in the light of God beyond or totally capable of him in his state here below. As Pascal said: "Man is neither angel nor beast, and the misfortune is that he who would act the angel acts the beast."[92]

✦

In his quasi-Franciscan love for the *singularity of the sensible*, Gerard Manley Hopkins also understood the importance of haecceity, as necessary in its variety as it is multilayered and strange. If not the cause, his reading of Scotus was at least the sign: "At this time I had first begun to get hold of the copy of Scotus on the Sentences in the Baddely library and was flush with a new stroke of enthusiasm. It may come to nothing or it may be a mercy from God. But just then when I took in any *inscape* of the sky or sea I thought of Scotus."[93] This "inscape" or "haecceity" which at this point for Hopkins may have come to nothing, in reality leads *to everything*, at least according to the course that we have taken in this book: (I) it leads wholly to *God*, precisely where the "tension of metaphysics and theology" (Augustine) leads to the

"God phenomenon" (Erigena) and then to the "suspension" of everything including oneself (Eckhart); (II) it leads wholly to the *flesh* when its "visibility" (Irenaeus) also produces its "solidity" (Tertullian) and "conversion" (Bonaventure); (III) it leads, finally, wholly to the *other*, when the alterity engendered starting from "community" (Origen) is constituted by true intersubjectivity (Aquinas) and simultaneously specifies its authentic singularity (Scotus). The path appears here to suggest itself as a summa for our time, as our conclusion will show in the following pages. But the "way" matters more than the results, which with Hopkins and in a tradition of thought at once poetical and mystical, opens onto the *contemplation of the Father*, source of every "dappled thing," and in whom the singularities are truly worthy of being praised in their "pied beauty": "Glory be to God for dappled things / For skies of couple-colour as a brinded cow / For rose-moles in all stipple upon trout that swim . . . Whatever is fickle, freckled (who knows how?) / With swift, slow; sweet, sour; adazzle, dim / He fathers-forth whose beauty is past change: Praise him."[94]

By Way of Conclusion

Toward an Act of Return

"We want to return to the things themselves [*auf die 'Sachen selbst' zurückgehen*]."[1] If the return to the "things" (*Sachen*) is the attempt to get back to "acts of consciousness" rather than to "beings" (*Ding*), the demonstration is again that the phenomena do not relate only to phenomenology. In other words, the bracketing of the world (reduction) and the return to its modes of apprehension (constitution) allow the revelation of the lived experiences of those things that fundamentally make us what we are: our proper relation to God, to the body, and to others. The mystical dimension also serves here as a crucible for phenomenology, and vice versa—much like art, poetry, literature, and other similar disciplines. Better, it discloses some *acts* where concepts would otherwise be expected, and describes *some manners of being* where one searches in vain for beings or a complete juxtaposition of beings. I am convinced therefore that in this work the following has been demonstrated: the choice of fields in which to work was in no way arbitrary, (a) neither from the point of view of concepts, (b) nor from the point of view of authors.

The Unity of Concepts

(a) Concerning first the concepts—and to begin a new synthesis—*God, the flesh and the other* are, today and yesterday, the ground for a history in which "we live, move and have our being" (Acts 17:28). (I) God first. It has been shown that his transcendence is not a simple position of existence, but is first an egoity as engendered in him from self to self. From "relation" and not simply "substance" (Augustine), the divine is revealed then as "phenomena" (Erigena) and delivers to us an access to him simply as an "ego" pure and detached from everything (Eckhart). (II) The *flesh* second. The "visibility" of the body is given to view in the formation of Adam (Irenaeus), its "solidity" in the incarnation of Christ (Tertullian), and its "conversion" in the transformation of the senses (Bonaventure). (III) The other, finally. From the human to the divine and among men themselves there is constituted a single and same "intersubjective community" received from God (Origen), in a "model of alterity" forged long ago with the question of the angels (Thomas Aquinas), and according to a "mode of singularity" which makes of otherness the most elevated mode of all haecceity (Duns Scotus).

A common world is thus constituted between men and God, the world "*tout court*." What is appropriate to Christianity as it espouses the mode of incarnation at once phenomenological (*Leiblichung*) and theological (*Menschwerdung*) is to make the totality of the world a "lifeworld" (*Lebenswelt*) common to all humanity and all divinity. There is not, then, *God* on the one side, and then the *flesh* separately, and finally the *other*. In reality, the flesh (part II) receives its density only from the God who is manifest in it (part I), while the other (part III) reveals a new mode of fraternity inasmuch as it derives from a unique paternity (part I) never separated from its incarnate Son (part II). The *totality of man* can certainly be articulated in terms of "recapitulation" (Irenaeus), "assumption" (Thomas Aquinas), or "integration" (Balthasar). But for our time man is understood above all in the mode and capacity of his own "*manifestation*" or "*phenomenalization*" at the heart of the incarnate Word (Col. 1:15–18). The equivalence of being and appearing—"*soviel Schein, soviel Sein*" (so much appearing, so much being)—is associated with the return to the things themselves as a return to acts of consciousness: "*Zur Sache selbst!*," "return *to* the thing itself" as Heidegger glossed it.[2] Like the phenomenon, "God" thus has no other reason for being than *being manifest* (part I), the "flesh," no other reason than *being incarnate* (part II) and the "other," no other reason than *uniting* us with the One who is thus revealed (part III).

The three terms—God, the flesh, and the other—do not only make *one*, in the community of an experience that this spiritual and intellectual approach would not be able to share. After the example of the great *summas of theology* and of the *exitus-reditus* movement initiated by John Scotus Erigena (*Periphyseon*), one will climb back up a posteriori from the other to the flesh and from the flesh to God, only after having described a priori the manifestation of God, and having analyzed the density of the flesh and finally having constituted alterity according to the mode of an intersubjectivity received from a Third. In the hypothesis of an *act of return*, no longer here "to the things themselves" (phenomenology) but "to God himself" (theology), the ascending movement *a parte creaturae* receives therefore its raison d'être from the descending movement *a parte Dei* which founds it completely. Like the *Breviloquium* of Bonaventure it was fitting in this sense to follow the didactic way, even though we have additionally taken the heuristic approach.[3]

The Necessity of Authors

(b) From the point of view of authors, the detour through both the fathers of the church (Irenaeus, Tertullian, Augustine) and the medievals (Erigena, Bonaventure, Thomas Aquinas, Eckhart, Duns Scotus) wanted to show in each case that medieval philosophy did not merely begin with Boethius and that there was not, for them, some pure philosophy independent of a specific theological intention. The false ambition to "de-theologize medieval philosophy," in the sense that the theological concepts treated in each chapter would only bear a philosophical significance, is meaningless, both by the yardstick of the medieval horizon and that of our own time. Trinity, theophany, the birth of God in the self, the visibility of Adam's body, the solidity of the flesh of Christ, conversion of the senses, community of saints, alterity of angels, and the singularity of the other are so many ways, today as much as yesterday, to unfold that which belongs to our common humanity and to God himself. The *théologies d'occasion* are not such in the sense that the "*theologoumena*" would only be the pretext for the deployment of "*philosophemes*" which would have comprised the very substance of what is to be believed.[4] In our opinion, there is nothing more absurd than making good use of a Trinitarian reflection for the sake of a purely logical conceptualization of the nature of the "three and one," or of calling on the Eucharist in order to debate metaphysically about substance and accident independently of what the author confesses and of what is subjectively experienced in the very act of incorporation. The medievals themselves believed and practiced what is here in question, being themselves students of the highest spheres of logic (Abelard, Duns Scotus, William of Ockham), or alternatively remaining always anchored in a mysticism which sometimes criticized the abstract use of theology (Bernard, Eckhart, Suso). In both cases—as much as in every case—faith is an attitude and an act of adhesion, not a collection of dogmas or an occasion for philosophical reflection.

As has been emphasized from the very beginning with the support of Etienne Gilson, no one has to share this belief in order to make it the place of his work in all good conscience. The medievalist will legitimately study the fathers and the medievals independently of any conviction of faith. But, as we have also said, it must never be forgotten that the medievals themselves never read, thought, spoke, or wrote *independently* of this light of faith in which they always lived. Medieval philosophy is unique in the sense that it is at the same time the place where philosophy appears impossible to distinguish from theology *and* the fulcrum by which these two disciplines are separated. In order better to study medieval thought we must therefore take note: the pluralism of medieval thought is no longer sufficient to justify research that is ever more sophisticated. The dissolution into historicism sometimes gets broken up into pluralism. I am certainly not advocating the reassertion of a teleological vision of the history of philosophy (Hegel). But the "community of thinkers" also establishes a "community of thought" with even the most ancient of our forebears. This ought not to be forgotten—even under the pompous title of the philosopher as "functionary of mankind."[5]

Toward a Liberation

In contrast to the "liberation of philosophy by theology" (Balthasar), a "liberation of theology by philosophy" will take place today.[6] It is evident that this does not mean that it is necessary to enslave philosophy to theology as in the past, but rather that the task is set today for philosophy, and phenomenology in particular, to place itself at the service of that which it is not—with the knowledge that the excess of its technical nature *ad intra* too often leads us to forget its fecundity *ad extra*.[7] The relation therefore of *potentia absoluta* to *potentia ordinata* does not only apply to the relation of God to the world, but also determines the relation of theology to phenomenology, at least as far as the contribution of phenomenology to medieval philosophy is concerned: "To give *to another* the power of doing something, rather than of doing it *by oneself* alone" (William of Auxerre).[8] It is true, some will say, that theology in its grandeur is sufficient in itself, which, in a word, liberates philosophy and justifies its autonomy. *By right*, it is fitting to leave philosophy to itself and theology to itself—unless one accepts, as we tend to do in relation to medieval philosophy today, the encroachment of philosophy onto the terrain of theology in order to extract that which would *only* allegedly lie within the jurisdiction of philosophy. But, in fact, the true grandeur of theology is totally different. In the act of his kenosis, God becomes the proper object of theology and makes the choice not to be satisfied in himself. He who could demonstrate anything by himself (the absolute power of theology) nevertheless leaves to be shown and revealed by another that which it does not and ought not to exhibit all alone (the conditional power of phenomenology). Far from some kind of serfdom or a petty service, phenomenology and theology respond to each other in a mutual way, similar to the incessant dialogue between God and man. There is nothing here of some new method, a flavor of the day or the blusterings of the spirit of the age. It is first and above all a matter of *experience*.

The Book of Experience

Hodie legimus in libro experientae—"Today we read from the book of experience." This formula of Bernard of Clairvaux, cited in the "Introduction," ought now to serve as the spearhead for a new path of research, one even more *fundamental*.[9] The *ontic* diversity of the fields of study—"God, the flesh, and the other"—still in fact awaits its *ontological grounding*. Said otherwise, and in the terms of Martin Heidegger, the regional ontologies require a fundamental ontology by which they are fully justified.[10] Experience, at least in the medieval epoch, furnishes us with the key. In the germination of the Middle Ages, and in particular the monastic renaissance (eleventh to twelfth centuries), life takes precedence again over work, and the community over the emergence of individualities. Here emerge the attitudes from which concepts derive and are tied together the lived experiences where discourse is rooted. The act of a return to the things themselves opens therefore onto the act of an ascent to experience itself, which includes the reading and production of texts themselves: "Experiences are understood," warns

Martin Heidegger in a preparatory note from his course on the *Philosophical Foundations of Medieval Mysticism* (1918–1919), "and indeed, genuinely so, and as such, they are themselves . . . Above all: understandability *does not mean* 'rationalization,' *dissolution of experience* into its 'logical components.' "[11]This is precisely "understood." If medieval mysticism is not opposed to the burgeoning dialectic, nor affective theology to Scholastic philosophy, then that is because every élan toward God requires a certain formalization (intuition with concept) and all rigor in argumentation finds its end in contemplation (concept with intuition).[12] Philosophical experience joins up with monastic experience in a new way—of which the ancient secrets of Anselm of Canterbury, Bernard of Clairvaux, Hugh and Richard of Saint Victor along with others, mark the steps of a path yet to be taken.[13]

NOTES

Translator's Foreword

1. See, for example, John van Buren, *The Young Heidegger: Rumor of the Hidden King* (Indiana University Press, 1994), esp. 157–202; and Ted Kisiel, *The Genesis of Heidegger's Being and Time* (Berkeley: University of California Press, 1993).

2. Falque's first monograph, on Saint Bonaventure, was explicitly "theological" (though we already know enough to be wary of assuming then that there is no philosophy within it, or worse, that it has no import for philosophy); Emmanuel Falque, *Saint Bonaventure et l'entrée de Dieu en théologie* (Paris: Vrin, 2001).

3. The specifically phenomenological path of this process is emphasized by the subtitle of the recent Spanish translation: "*reflexiones fenomenológicas*." See *Dios, la carne y el otro: De Ireneo a Duns Escoto: Reflexiones fenomenológicas* (Bogotá, Colombia: Siglio del Hombre, 2012).

4. See Hans-Dieter Gondek and Laszlo Tengyeli, *Neue Phänomenologie in Frankreich* (Berlin: Suhrkamp, 2011), a powerful study that seeks to characterize the distinctive elements of the numerous instantiations of the French tradition of phenomenology today, and which devotes significant chapters to a number of his contemporaries, but unfortunately no space to Falque's work.

5. Recently translated into English: Emmanuel Falque, *The Metamorphosis of Finitude: An Essay on Birth and Resurrection*, trans. George Hughes (New York: Fordham University Press, 2012).

6. Ibid., x.

7. In Nietzsche, as Didier Franck has shown, the dogma is the "eternal recurrence," and in Heidegger the dogma is similar to Kant, or rather a development of it: the a priori, and dogmatic, refusal of the pertinence of the Christian God for the philosophical understanding of the human, for the intelligibility of the human as such. The question in the latter case especially is whether or not this refusal itself implies a theology, what we would have to call the "blank" theology of Heidegger's philosophy. For the former argument see Franck's *Nietzsche et l'ombre de Dieu* (Paris: Presses Universitaires de France, 2010). For Michel Henry's little-known discussion of the resurrection, see his conclusion to *Philosophy and Phenomenology of the Body*, trans. Gerard Eitzkorn (The Hague: Martinus Nijhoff, 1975), 183–222, esp. 208–10.

8. Emmanuel Falque, *Les noces de l'Agneau* (Paris: Cerf, 2011).

9. Hans Urs von Balthasar, *The Glory of the Lord*, vol. 5: *The Realm of Metaphysics in the Modern Age*, trans. John Riches et al. (San Francisco: Ignatius, 1991), 656.

10. Ibid., 646.

11. This is made explicit, and in an extended manner, vis-a-vis the analysis of Christ's anxiety in his own human being-before-death in *Le passeur de*

Gethsémani (Paris: Cerf, 1999). In this case, Christ's cry of dereliction from the cross, for example, is paradigmatically human, according to faith the most human of human words to have ever been uttered. Thus their very theological character bears within it the possibility of deepening the philosophical inquiry concerning our humanity as finite and as mortal.

12. It is worth recalling here Jean-François Courtine's brief comments in *Phenomenology and the "Theological Turn": The French Debate*, by Dominique Janicaud et al. (New York: Fordham University Press, 2000), 121–26.

13. This does not mean "uninfluenced" by phenomenology: Xavier Tilliette, of course, has written volumes on Merleau-Ponty, for example. See Tilliette, *Maurice Merleau-Ponty ou la mesure de l'homme* (Paris: Seghers, 1970).

14. See, in the first place, Jean-Luc Marion, "On the Foundation of the Distinction between Theology and Philosophy," in *Philosophy, Religions and Transcendence*, ed. Philippe Capelle-Dumont (Manila: Ataneo University Press, 2010), 47–76; and Jean-Luc Marion, "Remarques sur l'utilité en théologie de la phénoménologie," *Archivio di Filosofia* 79, no. 2 (2011): 11–22.

15. See *Certitudes négatives* (Paris: Grasset & Fasquelle, 2010).

16. Emmanuel Falque, "The Phenomenological Act of *Perscrutatio* in the *Proemium* of St. Bonaventure's *Commentary on the Sentences*," *Medieval Philosophy and Theology*, 10, no. 1 (2001): 1–22; Emmanuel Falque, "Metaphysics and Theology in Tension: A Reading of Augustine's *De Trinitate*," in *Augustine and Postmodern Thought: A New Alliance Against Modernity?* ed. Lieven Boeve (Leuven, 2009), 21–55; and Emmanuel Falque, "*Lavartus pro Deo*: Jean-Luc Marion's Phenomenology and Theology," in *Counter-Experiences: Reading Jean-Luc Marion*, ed. Kevin Hart (South Bend, Ind.: Notre Dame University Press, 2007), 181–99.

17. Which includes a brief introduction to his thought and a working bibliography: Tarek Dika and Chris Hackett, eds., *Quiet Powers of the Possible: Interviews in Contemporary French Phenomenology* (New York: Fordham University Press, 2015).

18. Christina M. Gschwandtner, *Postmodern Apologetics? Arguments for God in Contemporary Philosophy* (New York: Fordham University Press, 2013), 184–208.

19. Christina M. Gschwandtner, "Corporeality, Animality, Bestiality: Emmanuel Falque on Incarnate Flesh," *Analecta Hermeneutica* 4 (2012): 1–16.

20. This appeared as the second chapter of Boeve, *Augustine and Postmodern Thought: A New Alliance Against Modernity?* See n. 16, supra.

Preface to the English-Language Edition

1. See the *Metamorphosis of Finitude: An Essay on Birth and Resurrection* (New York: Fordham University Press, 2012) and *Passer le Rubicon, philosophie et théologie: Essai sur les frontières* (Brussels: Lessius, 2013), currently being translated. I also add *Saint Bonaventure et l'entrée de Dieu en théologie* (Paris: Vrin, 2000), which will soon appear in English as well.

***Fons Signatus*: The Sealed Source**

1. Max Scheler, *Vom Ewigen im Menschen* (1922), in *Gesammelte Werke* (Bonn: 1970), vol. 5, p. 13. Compare the English translation, *On the Eternal in*

Man, trans. Bernard Noble (Hamden, Conn.: Archon Books, 1972), 18: "As the method used in the descriptive study of Weltanschauungen, [it] is in fact a 'common whore' [*Mädchen fur alles*]. It is in the very fact that it *is* a 'common whore' [*Mädchen fur alles*] that its outstanding, positive value lies."

2. Ibid.

3. Maurice Merleau-Ponty, *Phenomenology of Perception*, trans. Colin Smith (New York: Routledge, 2002), viii.

4. Alain de Libera, *Penser au Moyen Âge* (Paris: Seuil, 1991), 25.

5. Pierre Alferi, *Guillaume d'Ockham: Le singulier* (Paris: Minuit, 1989), 7.

6. Olivier Boulnois, in St. Bonaventure, *Les six jours de la création* (Paris: Desclée/Cerf, 1991), preface, p. 10.

7. Jean-François Courtine, *Suarez et le système de la métaphysique* (Paris: Presses Universitaires de France, 1990), 91–98.

8. Rémi Brague, "L'anthropologie de l'humilité," in *St. Bernard et la philosophie* (Paris: Presses Universitaires de France, 1993), 152.

9. Emmanuel Martineau, *Malevitch et la philosophie* (Lausanne: L'Âge d'Homme, 1977), 13.

10. Falque, *Saint Bonaventure et l'entrée de Dieu en théologie*, 22.

11. See, respectively, Bonaventure, *Sententiae sententiarum*, prooemium, I, 1 (Quarrachi); Martin Heidegger, *Identity and Difference*, trans. Joan Stambaugh (Chicago: University of Chicago Press, 2002), 57 (English translation modified). To sound (*ergründen*) and to found (*begründen*) are also in Heidegger's *Being and Time*, §7. For all of this I refer you to my article, "Le *proemium* de *Commentaire des Sentences* ou l'acte phenomenologique de la *perscrutatio* chez saint Bonaventure," in *Archivum Fransiscanum Historicum* (Rome: Grottaferrata, 2004), 275–300.

12. Hans-Georg Gadamer, "Heidegger et l'histoire de la philosophie," in Martin Heidegger, *Cahiers de l'Hern* (1983; Paris: Grasset, 1989), 124.

13. These are, of course, the stages of the present work.

14. See Alain de Libera, *La philosophie médiévale* (Paris: Presses Universitaires de France, 1989), 72–73.

15. Claude Romano, *Le chant de la vie: Phénoménologie de Faulkner* (Paris: Gallimard, 2005), 18–19 (emphasis in original).

16. See A. de Muralt, *La métaphysique du phénomène: Les origines médiévales et l'élaboration de la pensée phénoménologique* (Paris: Vrin, 1985); and D. Perler, *Théories de l'intentionnalité au Moyen Âge* (Paris: Vrin, 2004).

17. See Martin Heidegger, *Being and Time*, trans. Joan Stambaugh (New York: SUNY Press, 1996), §7, p. 24.

18. John Scotus Erigena, *On the Division of Nature*, bk. 1 (452B).

19. Tertullian, *De Resurrectione carnis*, IX, 2–3.

20. Thomas Aquinas, *Summa Theologiae*, respectively Ia, q. 56, a. 2, ad. 3 (on intentionality) and Ia, q. 51, a. 2, ad. 1 (on the angelic assumption of body in order to appear to us).

21. Edmund Husserl, *Logical Investigations*, vol. 2, "Introduction," §2 (volume 1 in the 2001 Routledge edition, ed. Dermot Moran, p. 168). See also Jean-Luc Marion's commentary on this text that is decisive for the birth of phenomenology: *Reduction and Givenness*, trans. Thomas A. Carlson, §1.1, "Two Interpretations and a Broadening" (Evanston, Ill.: Northwestern University Press, 1998), 4–11.

22. Edmund Husserl, *The Idea of Phenomenology*, trans. Lee Hardy (Dordrecht, Neth.: Springer, 1999), 19.

23. Edmund Husserl, *The Crisis of European Sciences and Transcendental Phenomenology*, trans. David Carr (Evanston, Ill.: Northwestern University Press, 1970), 394–95.

24. Heidegger, *Being and Time*, 17.

25. Rémi Brague, *St. Bernard et la philosophie*, 151–52 (emphasis added). This conviction is developed by the apposite finale of another article of Brague's, "Un modèle médiéval de la subjectivité: La chair," in *Ibn Rochd, Maimonide, Saint Thomas d'Aquin, Colloque de Cordoue, 8–10 mai 1992* (Paris: Climat, 1992), 62: "I have emphasized some points of contact with certain contemporary problems which could make this concept pertinent to our concerns today. In doing this, however, I do not intend to enroll the history of philosophy in the service of such or such of our intellectual modes. Yet I think that *contemporary reflections ought not to be limited to dialogue with either ancient or modern authors*, and that the medieval authors in particular ought to be considered *fully valuable partners and worth listening to*" (emphasis added).

26. Scheler, *Vom Ewigen im Menschen*, in *Gesammelte Werke*, vol. 5, p. 13, cited by Jean Greisch, *Le buisson ardent et les lumières de la raison*, vol. 2, p. 367 (emphasis added). Compare, again, the English translation, *On the Eternal in Man*, 18: "The descriptive method, *not* aiming at essential philosophical insights, of reducing given religious and metaphysical systems . . . to their *original empirical contents*, i.e. of *reconstructing* and re-intuiting the basis of what appears in them . . . thereby revitalizing its *original meaning* and restoring its perceptual validity for today—this, as the descriptive study . . ."

27. Henri Bergson, *Matter and Memory*, trans. Nancy Margaret Paul and W. Scott Palmer (New York: Humanities, 1970), 240–41: "But there is a last enterprise that might be undertaken. It would be to seek *experience at its source*, or rather, above this decisive turn where, taking a bias in the direction of our utility, it becomes properly *human* experience." See Maurice Merleau-Ponty's comments in *L'union de l'âme et du corps chez Malebranche, Biran et Bergson* (1968; Paris: Vrin, 2002), 111–17.

28. Bernard of Clairvaux, *Sermons on the Canticle*, vol. 1, *Sources chrétiennes* 414, Serm. 3, 1 (Paris: Cerf, 1996), 101.

29. See Martin Heidegger, *Gesamtausgabe* 60, letter to Fr. Von Hermann dated from March 27, 1919, cited by Rémi Brague, *Saint Bernard et la philosophie*, 186: "In the posthumous papers of Heidegger, there is found a single page that has relation to Bernard of Clairvaux. It bears the title: 'On the *Sermones Bernardi in canticum canticorum*.' It contains the manuscript copied by Heidegger (written in lowercase letters) of *Serm.* 3."

30. Heidegger, *Being and Time* §6, p. 20 (Eng. translation modified).

31. Martin Heidegger, *Traité des catégories et de la signification chez Duns Scot* [*Treatise on the Categories and Signification in Duns Scotus*] (Paris: Gallimard, 1970), 32 and 35.

32. Max Scheler, *The Nature of Sympathy*, trans. Peter Heath (New Brunswick, N.J.: Transaction, 2008); Edith Stein, "The Phenomenology of Husserl and the Philosophy of St. Thomas Aquinas," in *Knowledge and Faith*, trans. Walter Redmond (Washington, D.C.: Institute of Carmelite Studies, 2000); and

Hannah Arendt, *Love and St. Augustine* (Chicago: University of Chicago Press, 1996).

33. Edmund Husserl, *Ideas I*, trans. F. Kersten (Boston: Martinus Nijhoff, 1982), respectively §59, p. 136 and §24, p. 44.

34. Martin Heidegger, "Letter to Krebs" (January 9, 1919), in *Supplements: From the Earliest Essays to "Being and Time" and Beyond*, ed. John van Buren (Albany, N.Y.: SUNY Press, 2002), 69–70. "Epistemological insights, extending to a theory of historical knowledge, have made the *system* of Catholicism problematic and unacceptable to me, but not Christianity and metaphysics, these, though, in a new sense . . . I firmly believe that I—perhaps more than your colleagues who officially work in this field—have experienced what the Catholic Middle Ages bears within itself regarding values and that we are still a long way off from appreciating them."

35. See Immanuel Kant, "Architectonic of Pure Reason," in *The Critique of Pure Reason*, trans. Norman Kemp Smith (Boston: Bedford St. Martins, 1965), 653–65.

36. See I. Bochet's book *Augustin dans la pensée de Paul Ricoeur* (Paris: Editions de la faculté jésuite de Paris, 2004), as well as my review in *Transversalités: Revue de l'Institut catholique de Paris* 92 (October-December 2004). For the triple *epochê* in the act of reading (of the author, reader, and the referent), see Paul Ricoeur, "The Hermeneutical Function of Distantiation," in *Hermeneutics and the Human Sciences*, trans. John Brookshire Thompson (New York: Cambridge University Press, 1998), 131–44.

37. Jean Decorte, "L'art de lire au Moyen Âge," in *Le vaste monde à livre ouvert: Manuscrits médiévaux en dialogue ave l'art contemporain* (Lannoo, 2004), 95–106, citation from p. 96.

38. Hugh of Saint Victor, *De Verbo Dei*, in *Six opuscules spirituels*, *Sources chrétiennes* 155, V, 1 (Paris: Cerf, 1969), 77.

39. See Saint Bonaventure, *The Soul's Journey into God*, I, 7 (Mahwah, N.J.: Paulist, 1978): "He has taught the knowledge of truth according to the threefold mode of theology: symbolic, literal and mystical, so that through the symbolic we may rightly use sensible things" (62–63).

40. Edmund Husserl, *Cartesian Meditations*, trans. Dorian Cairns (Boston: Kluwer Academic, 1995), §16, pp. 38–39.

41. Bonaventure, *Hexaemeron* [*The Six Days of Creation*], XIII, 12. See my commentary *Saint Bonaventure et l'entrée de Dieu en théologie* (Paris: Vrin, 2000), §12, esp. pp. 178–80. On the exposition of the status of the book and hermeneutics, see below, chap. 6.

42. I take the opposite stance from Paul Ricoeur, not because mediation has no value, far from it in fact, but only in the sense that too much for him centers on the modalities of the text and its act of reception by the reader, and he forgets the immediate lived experience which is also a key question and takes primacy. See his *Conflict of Interpretations* (London: Continuum, 2004), 10: "substituting, for the short route of the Analytic of *Dasein* [which I attempt to rediscover in medieval philosophy], the long route which begins by analysis of language [the mediation of texts]" (text in brackets added by Falque. –Trans.).

43. Martin Heidegger, *Phenomenological Interpretations of Aristotle*, trans. Richard Rojcewicz (Bloomington: Indiana University Press, 2001), 149.

44. See C. Sommer's definitive demonstration in *Heidegger, Aristote, Luther: les sources aristotéliciennes et néotestamentaires de Être et temps* (Paris: Presses Universitaires de France, 2005).

45. I will not engage here in a debate from the past that has been exhausted now for decades. I will retain only an agreement with Gilson that one does not need to have Christian faith as a *conditio sine qua non* for the study of medieval philosophy. Yet it ought to be recognized, nevertheless, that the medievals themselves did not think outside of the light of faith, which prohibited them from choosing between philosophy and theology and thereby amputating one or the other part of their body. See R. Imbach's fine-tuned discussion in "La philosophie médiévale et l'histoire," in Christian Trottmann and Anca Vasiliu, actes du colloque du samedi 23 octobre 2004 (Collège International de Philosophie), *La philosophie médiévale : Historiographie d'hier et de demain*, forthcoming.

46. Etienne Gilson (under the Latin name Stephanus), "Les recherches historico-critiques et l'avenir de la scolastique," in *Scholastica ratione historico-ristauranda* (Rome: 1951), 133–42 (citation 139).

47. Ibid.

48. Ibid., 137.

49. Ibid., 142. Let me add that this realization that the philosopher as necessarily attached to theology and made fruitful by it in all of its convictions of faith, becomes more and more present as Gilson's work develops. Thus, in 1974, only a few years before his death (1978) and exactly fifty years after writing *The Philosophy of St. Bonaventure* (1924), he will avow that "this attempt to define Bonaventure as a philosopher has no less gravely deformed his figure" (in *S. Bonaventura, 1274–1974* [Rome: Grotafferata, 1974], 2).

50. Henry Dumery, *Critique et religion: Problèmes des méthodes en philosophie de la religion* (Paris: Sedes, 1957), 18 (emphasis added).

51. For this distinction see Jean Greisch, *Le buisson ardent et les lumières de la raison* (Paris: Cerf, 2002), vol. 1, p. 34.

52. Bonaventure, *The Soul's Journey into God*, I, 7, p. 63 (English translation modified).

53. Jean Baruzi, "De l'emploi légitime et de l'emploi abusif du mot mystique," in *L'intelligence mystique* (Paris: Berg International, 1985), 67.

54. For exegesis of this verse (*Sententiae sententiarum*, Prooemium, I, 1), see my article on the *Proemium* of Bonaventure, *supra*. Concerning the different meanings of "worldview" (*Weltanschauung*), see Edith Stein, "La signification de la phénoménologie comme conception du monde," in *Phénoménologie et philosophie chrétienne* (Paris: Cerf, 1987), 1–4.

Introduction to Part One

1. Martin Heidegger, "The Onto-theo-logical Constitution of Metaphysics" (1957), in *Identity and Difference*, 55 (English translation modified).

2. Falque, *Saint Bonaventure ou l'entrée de Dieu en théologie*, "Introduction," 19–27: "l'hypothèse phénoménologique et le *Breviloquium*."

3. Respectively, Immanuel Kant, *Critique of Pure Reason* (1781), "Transcendental Dialectic," chap. 3, "The Ideal of Pure Reason," p. 525: "Transcendental theology . . . believes that it can know the existence of such a being through mere concepts, without the help of any experience whatsoever, and is then entitled

onto-theology"; and Martin Heidegger, "The Onto-theo-logical Constitution of Metaphysics" (1957), in *Identity and Difference*, 42–73.

4. See Frederic Nef, *Qu'est-ce que la métaphysique?* (Paris: Gallimard, "Folio-Essais," 2004); in particular 231–412 (4th part): "l'onto-theo-logie introuvable." I will note however, and in contrast to the allegations of the author, that this attestation of an "onto-theo-logie introuvable" in the history of thought does not stand up against the works of the phenomenologists themselves—to the contrary. It is precisely in the searching that one recognizes that they haven't found it. This does not make vain the enterprise itself but rather justifies it at least negatively. As for him wanting to draw the conclusion that it is necessary to take the "exact contre-pied" of the overcoming of metaphysics (23), this is an affirmation that, I think, leaves the debate in the triviality of a fight. The "vulgate du depassement" (217) ought itself certainly be overcome. This does not qualify, if we approach it properly, the quest for *another discourse*—but orients it this time less toward the incrimination of categories of the past (the negative side of onto-theo-logie) and more toward the opening of new concepts or new fields for thought (the positive side of the exit of metaphysics).

5. Alain de Libera, *La philosophie médiévale* (Paris: Presses Universitaires de France, 1992, 2nd ed. corr.), "Que sais-je," n. 1044, pp. 72–73 (emphasis mine). Demonstration established definitively by J.-F. Courtine, *Inventio analogiae: Métaphysiques et ontothéologie* (Paris: Vrin, 2005), 1st part, pp. 11–99: "Métaphysique et pensée de l'être."

6. Martin Heidegger, *Traité des catégories et de la signification chez Duns Scot* (1915; Paris: Gallimard, 1970). (I say "without knowing it," because in 1915, Heidegger thought, like everyone else then, the work was by Duns Scotus himself.)

7. See Nef, *Qu'est-ce que la métaphysique?*, 5th part, pp. 740 and 746 ("La metaphysique—le retour"): "The themes of the end, of overcoming, of the accomplishment and death of metaphysics does not truly contain an argument. . . . Throughout this book we have defended the possibility of a metaphysic which preserves the theoretical ideal, or better, the theoretics of the Greeks, and it is in this perspective that we have highlighted the importance of speculative metaphysics, the insufficiency of descriptions and conceptual analyses, intriguing in themselves."

8. See Jean-Luc Marion, *On Descartes' Metaphysical Prism: The Constitution and Limits of Onto-theo-logy in Cartesian Thought*, trans. Jeffrey L. Kosky (Chicago: University of Chicago Press, 1999), 6–7.

9. Boethius, *De Trinitate*, in *Courts traits de théologie* (*oposcula sacra*) (Paris: Le Cerf, 1991), chap. 4, pp. 135–36, translation modified: "If one turns these categories toward God in order to attribute them to him, all these attributes undergo a transformation [*at haec cum quis in divinum vertit praedicationem, cuncta mutantur quae praedicari possunt*]" (trans. Alain de Libera, *Métaphysique et noétique, Albert le Grand* [Paris: Vrin, 2005], 145).

Chapter 1

1. See respectively, Justin, *Dialogue with Trypho*, VIII, 1–2 (in E. Robillard, *Justin, L'itinéraire philosophique* [Paris: Cerf, 1989], 143); and B. Sesboüé, *Jésus-Christ dans la tradition de l'Eglise* (Paris: Le Cerf, 1990), 97–98 ("un 'c'est-a-dire' ou un redoublement"): *Nous croyons . . . en un seul Seigneur Jésus-Christ,*

le Fils de Dieu, ne Monogène du Père, c'est–à-dire de la substance du Père, *Dieu de Dieu, Lumière de Lumière, vrai Dieu de vrai Dieu*, engendré non pas créé, consubstantiel au Père ["We believe . . . in one Lord Jesus Christ, the Son of God, only-begotten of the Father, *that is, of the substance of the Father*, God from God, Light from Light, true God from true God, *begotten not made, one in being with the Father*"] (Council of Nicaea 325 A.D.).

2. See respectively, Hans Küng, *Être chrétien* (Paris: Le Seuil, 1978), 141; and A. Grillmeier, "Jésus de Nazareth, dans l'ombre du Fils de Dieu au Christ image de Dieu," in *Comment être chrétien? La réponse de H. Küng* (collective) (Paris: Desclée de Brouwer, 1978), 128.

3. See Michel Henry, *I Am the Truth*, trans. Susan Emanuel (Stanford, Calif.: Stanford University Press, 2003), 10–11. See my contribution made in the presence of the author (Collège International de Philosophie): "Michel Henry théologien: A propos de *C'est moi la vérité*," *Laval théologique et philosophique* 57, no. 3 (October 2001): 525–36.

4. See Jean-Luc Marion, *The Idol and Distance*, trans. Thomas A. Carlson. (1977; New York: Fordham University Press, 2001), xxxvii.

5. Martin Heidegger, "Introduction to 'What Is Metaphysics?'" (1949), in *Pathmarks*, trans. William McNeil (Cambridge, Eng.: Cambridge University Press, 1998), 279.

6. Heidegger, *Identity and Difference*, n. 3 p. 57.

7. The inscription of *Holzwege* (Heidegger) and its reference to "the path in the forest encumbered with undergrowth" and to "the lumberjacks and foresters who know these paths" seems in fact to indicate—despite the German expression "*auf dem Holzweg sein*" (to take a wrong path)—first the opening of a *new way*, or of a *side road* that opens along the impasse.

8. I take the hypothesis of a "discovery-concealment" from the work of Edmund Husserl, *The Crisis of European Sciences and Transcendental Phenomenology*, in which the author designates Galileo as "a genius who at the same time discovered and concealed" (52): "Discovering" in the sense that he discovered "mathematical nature, the methodical idea . . . the law of causality" (52–53); and "concealing" in the sense that he "*represents* the life-world, *dressing it up* as 'objectively and actual true' nature" (51) (trans. modified).

9. St. Augustine, *De Trinitate* (Bibliotheque Augustinienne, Paris: Desclee de Brouwer, 1955), V, 4, p. 429 (vol. 15): "We begin therefore by responding to the adversaries of our faith concerning those questions for which the expression does not equal the thought, nor the thought the reality." [Note: Falque uses this bilingual Bibliotheque Augustinienne edition of the *De Trinitate*, and he often freely modifies the translation for his own purposes. In this chapter, therefore, I stick to close renderings of Falque's French, especially where he departs from the Bibliotheque Aug. Finally, our references will be to the page numbers of the Bibliotheque Aug. edition, along with the universal book and division numbers of the *De Trinitate*. –Trans.]

10. Augustine, *De Trinitate*, V, 4, p. 429.

11. Aristotle, *Organon*, *Categories* 4, 1b, 25 (in *The Complete Works of Aristotle*, ed. Jonathan Barnes [Princeton, N.J.: Princeton University Press, 1984], 1:4); and Augustine, *De Trinitate*, V, 6, p. 433. Double inversion of *ubi* and *quando* and *situs* and *habitus* (also occurring in the *Confessions*, IV, 16, 28); referred to

by Irénée Chevalier in *La théorie augustinienne des relations trinitaires, analyse explicative des textes* (reprinted *Divus Thomas* [Librairie de l'Université, Fribourg, 1940]), n. 1, p. 12. Whatever one considers this double transfer to be (the Stagirite himself does not respect a fixed order of enumeration when he studies each category in particular), the reference to Aristotle remains no less explicit.

12. Augustine, *De Trinitate*, V, 6, p. 433.

13. Ibid., V, 4, p. 429.

14. Profession of faith of Arius in Saint Athanasius, *De Synodis*, in *Nicene and Post-Nicene Fathers*, 4.2, §22. In the context of this work I am not able to develop any further the Arian argumentation, particularly as it concerns the relation of the unbegotten (*agennêtos*) to the begotten (*gennêtos*) which separates the Father and the Son into two distinct substances. These debates are probably well enough known to the reader. For more of the details of Arianism we offer to the reader the entire "profession of faith of Arius" which comes down to us from St. Athanasius (*De Synodis*), as well as to the simple summary of the argumentation by P. Gallay in the introduction to Gregory Nazianzen, *Discours théologiques: Sources chrétiennes*, vol. 250 (Paris: Cerf, 1979), 25–28.

15. Augustine, *De Trinitate*, V, 6, p. 435: "But note that the Father is called Father only because he has a son, and that the Son is called son only because he has a Father. These are not qualifications pertaining to the order of substance" (*non secundum substantiam haec dicuntur*).

16. B. Sesboüé, *Jésus-Christ dans la tradition de l'Eglise* (Paris: Desclée, 1982), 102.

17. Aristotle, *Metaphysics*, bk. Lambda.

18. Augustine, *De Trinitate*, V. 5, p. 433.

19. Aristotle, *Metaphysics*, bk. Lambda.

20. J. Moltmann, *The Crucified God*, trans. R. A. Wilson and John Bowden (London: Society of Christian Missionaries, 1974), 235 : "What happened on the cross was an event between God and God. There was a profound division in God inasmuch as God abandons God and is contradicted."

21. Augustine, *De Trinitate*, V, 6, p. 435: "The Son is ever-begotten [*semper natus est*], and has never begun to be Son [*nec coepit unquam esse Filius*]."

22. Ibid., V, 6, p. 435. We can complete this reference by quoting the following passage (*DT*, V, 6, p. 433): "In God there is no accidental attribution at all because in him there is nothing changing."

23. Ibid., V, 6, p. 433.

24. Ibid., VII, 7, p. 531.

25. See Falque, *St. Bonaventure et l'entrée de Dieu en théologie*, §4, pp. 55–63: "la fin de l'empire du *ti esti*."

26. Augustine, *De Trinitate*, V, 6, p. 433 (translation modified).

27. I recall here, of course, the work of Stanislas Breton, *L'esse in et l'esse ad dans la métaphysique de la relation* (Rome, 1951).

28. Aristotle, *Categories*, 1b 25–26, p. 4.

29. Augustine, *De Trinitate*, V, 6, p. 435.

30. Ibid., V, 6, p. 435. "These appellations do not pertain to the order of substance but to relation [*sed secundum relativum*], relation which is not an accident [*quod tamen relativum non est accidens*] because it is foreign to change."

31. Ibid., VII, 2, p. 511. See also *DT*, VII, 2, p. 513: "It is not truly according to this model, but . . . [*non ergo ita, sed* . . .]."

32. Aristotle, *Categories*, 5, 2a, 25, p. 4.

33. Augustine, *De Trinitate*, VII, 2, p. 511. "ad aliquid coloratum referetur color" (color refers to the something that is colored). See Aristotle, *Categories*, 5, 2a, 25, p. 4.

34. Augustine, *De Trinitate*, VII, 2, p. 511.

35. Ibid., VII, 2, pp. 513–15. Without developing any further this argument that is at once scriptural and theological directed against the Arian interpretation of Christ exclusively as "power and wisdom of God" (1 Cor. 1:24) I note only here that the question of the meaning of this verse—standing at the beginning of both book VI, I (p. 469) and book VII, I (p. 503) of *De Trinitate*—suffices to indicate the nicely polemical character of the present discussion.

36. I will return later to the question of the possible validity of this structure by means of introducing a distinction between "relative qualification" and "absolute qualification."

37. Augustine, *De Trinitate*, VII, 4, p. 519.

38. Ibid., VII, 4, p 519.

39. As in the Nicene-Constantinopolitan Creed.

40. It is to Balthasar's merit that he emphasized this scheme of "aesthetic expression" as a solution to the aporias of Trinitarian theology (which the bishop of Hippo neither could nor should have used in his personal reappropriation of the Greek-Latin tradition): "The Father is the ground, the Son is the manifestation; the Father is content, the Son form . . . Here, too, there is no ground without manifestation, no content without form. In the beautiful these two things are but one; and they rest in one another." Hans Urs von Balthasar, *The Glory of the Lord*, vol. I: *Seeing the Form*, trans. Erasmo Leiva-Merikakis (San Francisco: Ignatius, 1982), 611.

41. Though not explicit in these books of *De Trinitate*, this distinction is made manifest in *De Diversis quaestionibus VII ad Simplicianum*, 83, q. 51 (Bibliothèque augustinienne, vol. 10, p. 132; see also the complementary note n. 51, p. 730).

42. Augustine, *De Trinitate*, VI, 11, p. 497.

43. Etienne Gilson, *Introduction à l'étude de Saint Augustin* (Paris: Vrin, 1943), 277.

44. Augustine, *De Trinitate*, VII, 5, p. 523.

45. Ibid., VII, 5. P. 523.

46. Ibid., VII, 7, p. 527.

47. Eberhad Jüngel, "Silencing God through the Exaggeration of Language," in *God as the Mystery of the World*, trans. J. C. B. Mohr (Grand Rapids, Mich.: Eerdmans, 1983), 255–60.

48. Heidegger, *Identity and Difference*, 54–55: "Someone who has experienced theology in his own roots, both the theology of the Christian faith and that of philosophy, would today rather remain silent about God when he is speaking in the realm of thinking."

49. Marion, *On Descartes' Metaphysical Prism*, 336: "By destitution, one must understand a disqualification which does not criticize metaphysics in its own order, but takes precautions against its unjust crossing into 'the order of charity' by reducing it from the point of view of this very same charity."

50. Augustine, *De Trinitate*, V, 1 (prologue), p. 425.
51. Ibid., 7, p. 527.
52. Ibid., V, 1, p. 425.
53. Ibid., V, 1, p. 425.
54. See Jean-François Courtine, *Suarez et le système de la métaphysique* (Paris: Presses Universitaires de France, 1990), 98. The author himself emphasizes here the occurrences of the term "other" (italicized in the text) indicating in this way—and paradoxically starting from Thomas Aquinas—the break which separates philosophy (*prima philosophia*) from theology (*scientia divina*).
55. Augustine, *De Trinitate*, VII, 11, p. 543 (translation modified).
56. See Immanuel Kant, "On the Failure of All Attempted Theodicies" (1793), trans. M. Despland, in *Kant on History and Religion* (Montreal: McGill-Queen's University Press, 1973), 283–97. "That this time of testing ought to be, to the eyes of the supreme wisdom, the absolute condition of joy that we will taste one day . . . is a position that can be stated, but not one that can be understood . . . ; the knot can *be cut*, but not *untied*" (concerning the justification of "evils" in the context of theodicy).
57. Blaise Pascal, *Pensées*, ed. L. Lafuma (Paris: Seuil, 1962), n. 308, and ed. L. Bruschvicg (Paris: Flammarion, 1993), n. 793.
58. I. Chevalier, *Saint Augustin et la pensée grecque* (Université de Fribourg, Librairie de l'Université, 1940), 75 (emphasis mine).
59. Augustine, *De Trinitate*, V, 6, p. 434.
60. Ibid., V, 7, p. 438.
61. Ibid., V, 9, pp. 442–45.
62. Ibid., VII, 2, pp. 508–9.
63. Ibid., VII, 2, pp. 508–11.
64. Ibid., VII, 7, p. 511.
65. Ibid., VII, 7, p. 527.
66. See respectively: (1) for Descartes, *Rules for the Direction of the Mind* (*Regulae ad directionem in genii)*, Rule VI, in *Descartes: Philosophical Essays*, trans. Laurence J. Lafleur (Indianapolis, Ind.: Bobbs-Merrill, 1964), 165: "In this respect, the secret of the entire method consists in the fact that in all things we diligently note that which is most absolute. For *from certain points of view* certain things are more absolute than others, while *from another point of view* they are more relative." See in support, Jean-Luc Marion, *Sur l'ontologie grise de Descartes*, §13 (Paris: Vrin, 2002), pp. 78–85, esp. n. 22, pp. 80–81; for Husserl, *Cartesian Meditations* (1929), "1st Meditation," § 10, pp. 23–25: "Digression: Descartes' Failure to Make the Transcendental Turn." The hypothesis of a "missed turn" in Descartes returns in Husserl's *The Crisis of the European Sciences*, 82–83.
67. Augustine, *De Trinitate*, VII, 2, pp. 508–11.
68. Ibid., VII, 2, p. 511. In this entire passage, Augustine reproduces explicitly the same examples as the Stagirite himself in order to designate the "correlation" in play in every relative qualification (master/slave . . .). See Aristotle, *Categories*, VII, 6b25, p. 12.
69. Augustine, *De Trinitate*, VII, 2, p. 511.
70. Aristotle, *Categories*, VII, 8b12, p. 14.
71. Augustine, *De Trinitate*, VII, 9, p. 537.

72. Ibid., V, 7, p. 439. "Father and Son are not called such in relation to each other in the same way as "friends" or "neighbors" are. One speaks of a friend relative to a friend and if the two friends love in the same way, the friendship is identical [*aequaliter*] in both of them. One speaks of 'neighbor' in relation to a neighbor, and since the neighbors are equally neighbors to each other . . . , the neighborship is identical [*aequaliter*] in both of them. Yet 'son' is not relative to a son but to a father."

73. Aristotle, *Categories*, VII 6b25, p. 11.

74. Augustine, *De Trinitate*, V, 7, p. 439. "It is therefore not in the sense of his relation to the Father that the Son is equal to the Father, and it remains the case that he is in a sense absolute [*ad se dicitur*]. But all absolute qualification has a substantial value [*quidquid autem ad se dicitur, secundum substantiam dicitur*]. It remains the case therefore that the equality of Son pertains to the substantial order [*restat ergo ut secundum substantiam sit aequalis*]."

75. Ibid., VI, 4–6, pp. 477–83.

76. Ibid., VI, 1, p. 469.

77. Chevalier, *Saint Augustine et la pensée grecque*, 83.

78. Augustine, *De Trinitate*, V, 9, p. 445.

79. Ibid., V, 6, p. 433.

80. Ibid., VII, 2, p. 511.

81. Ibid., V, 10, p. 449.

82. Ibid., V, 10, p. 449.

83. See Falque, *Saint Bonaventure et l'entrée de Dieu en théologie*, §4, pp. 55–63.

84. Thomas Aquinas, *Summa Theologiae, Prima pars*, q. 29 a. 4. resp.

85. Martin Heidegger, *The End of Philosophy*, trans. Joan Stambaugh (Chicago: University of Chicago Press, 2003), 15: "For this reason, metaphysically thought, God is called the *summum ens*. The apex of his being consists in his being the *summum bonum* . . . The summum bonum is rather the purest expression of causality which is appropriate to the purely real, in accordance with its effectuating the persistence of everything that can persist."

86. Thomas Aquinas, *Summa Theologiae*, Ia, q. 3 a. 4 ad. 2.

87. Jean-Luc Marion, "Thomas Aquinas and Ontotheology," in *Mystics: Presence and Aporia*, ed. Michael Kessler and Christian Sheppard (Chicago: University of Chicago Press, 2003), 38–73: "The *esse* that Thomas Aquinas recognizes for God *does not open any metaphysical horizon*, *does not belong to any onto-theo-logy*, and remains such a distant analogy with what we once conceived through the concept of *being*, that God proves *not to take any part in it*, or *to belong to it*, or even—as paradoxical as it may seem—*to be*. *Esse* refers to God only insofar as God may appear as *without being*" (64, emphasis added). For the noble confession of a "retraction" see the original French text, "Saint Thomas d'Aquin et l'onto-théo-logie," *Revue thomiste* (January-March 1995): n. 2, p. 33: "On these two points (onto-theology and a confusion of Being and beings) I ought to nuance my position in *God without Being* by the following *partial retractions*" (emphasis added).

88. Heidegger, *The End of Philosophy*, p. 6 (emphasis added).

89. One will find some refinements of this key distinction, although never formulated in these terms, in J.-B. Lotz, *Martin Heidegger et Thomas d'Aquin* (Paris: Presses Universitaires de France, 1988), 29–46.

90. Grimm's tale of "The Hedgehog and the Hare" is already used by Heidegger in order to state the "Conciliation" (*Austrag*) of being and beings. See Heidegger, *Identity and Difference*, 62–63.

91. See *supra*.

92. Thomas Aquinas, *Summa Theologiae*, Ia q. 45 a. 3 resp.

93. Thomas Aquinas, *Summa Contra Gentiles*, book II ("The Creation"), ch. 18, n. 2. "For creation is not a changing thing, but is *the mere dependence of created being on the principle by which it is*, and therefore comes under the category of *relation*."

94. Infra, chap. 4 (Irenaeus): "Creation and Fabrication."

95. Emmanuel Levinas, *Totality and Infinity: An Essay on Exteriority*, trans. Alfonso Lingis (Pittsburgh: Duquesne University Press, 2002), 47, 48 (italics added).

96. Ibid., 42 (emphasis added).

97. Marion, *The Idol and Distance*, 219.

98. See John Scotus Erigena, *De la division de la nature* (*Periphyseon*), bk. I, 465A.

99. John Scotus Erigena, *Commentary on the Gospel of John* (Paris: Cerf), *Sources Chrétiennes*, vol. 180, ch. XXI, 298 A, p. 101.

Chapter 2

1. John Scotus Erigena, *On the Division of Nature* (*Periphyseon*). For the Latin text used in this work, see the *Patrologia Latina* (*PL*, vol. 122) and for the *Expositiones in Ierarchiam Calestem*, see the *Corpus christianorum continuatio medievalis* (*CCCM*, 31) (Turhnolti: Brepols, 1975).

2. Thomas S. Kuhn, *The Structure of Scientific Revolutions*, 3rd ed. (Chicago: University of Chicago Press, 1996).

3. Erigena, *On the Division of Nature*, I, 446D.

4. This way is developed by Jean-Luc Marion in *The Idol and Distance*, 143: "The name [in Denys] comes to us as unthinkable within the thinkable, because the unthinkable in person delivers it to us, just as a perfect, unknown, and anonymous poem reveals all of the poet and conceals him infinitely. It is up to distance to use the language that identifies it."

5. See especially on this point and concerning this debate: Jacques Derrida, "Sauf le nom: (Post-Scriptum)," in *On the Name*, trans. Thomas Dutoit (Stanford, Calif.: Stanford University Press, 1995), 35–87 (completed by "How to Avoid Speaking: Denials," trans. Ken Frieden, in *Languages of the Unsayable: The Play of Negativity in Literature and Literary Theory*, ed. Sanford Budick and Wofgang Iser [Stanford, Calif.: Stanford University Press, 1987], 3–70); and Jean-Luc Marion, "In the Name: How to Avoid Speaking of It," in *In Excess: Studies of Saturated Phenomena*, trans. Robyn Horner and Vincent Berraud (New York: Fordham University Press, 2002), 128–61.

6. Erigena, *Expositiones in Ierarchiam caelestem*, IV, 17.

7. Heidegger, *Being and Time*, § 7, pp. 24–25: "The Greek expression *phainomenon*, from which the term 'phenomenon' derives, comes from the verb *phainesthai*, meaning 'to show itself.' Thus *phainomenon* means what shows itself, the self-showing, the manifest. *Phainesthai* itself is a 'middle voice' construction of *phainô*, to bring into daylight, to place in brightness. . . . Thus the

meaning of the expression 'phenomenon' is *established as what shows itself in itself*, what is manifest."

8. Etienne Gilson, *La philosophie au Moyen Âge* (Paris: Payot, 1947), 222.

9. Respectively, René Roques "Traduction ou interprétation ? Brèves remarques sur Jean Scot traducteur de Denys," in *Libres sentiers ver l'erigenisme* (Rome: Edizioni dell'Ateneo, 1975), 126; and Albert le Grand, *In Phys*., lib. I, tr. 1, c.1: "nostra intentio est omnes dictas partes (physicam, metaphysicam, mathematicam) facere Latinis intelligibiles." Cited in Marie-Dominique Chenu, *Introduction à l'étude de saint Thomas d'Aquin*, 5th ed. (Paris: Vrin, 1993), 36.

10. John Scotus Erigena, *Areopagitica*, *Praef* (preface to the translation of the works of Denys), *PL*, 122, 1032 B-C.

11. Roques, "Traduction ou interpretation?" 99–130 (cit. 104). Concerning the deviation between Erigena and Hilduin in the work of translating Denys, see G. Théry's very thorough study "Scot Érigène traducteur de Denys," in *Bulletin de Cange* 6 (1931): 1–94.

12. F. Bertin, in Erigena, *De la division de la nature*, bks. I and II (Paris: Presses Universitaires de France, 1995), n. 17, p. 201.

13. I do not agree, in this sense, with Jean-Luc Marion: neither in postulating that the work of the Greek fathers, and Denys in particular, "consists in *liberating* Christian theological concepts from their Greek horizon," since the influence of Neoplatonism appears evident in the return of the *epeikena tês ousias* in Denys (see "In the Name: How to Avoid Speaking of It," *In Excess*), nor in holding *distance* as the unique and final word of negative theology insofar as it would accept at the same time a certain proximity (cf. *The Idol and Distance*, §15, "Immediate Mediation," 162–79). However, the fact remains that the interpretation of Denys in either case could not have led us anywhere but here. Only the negation of the way of eminence by Erigena, substituting in its place the idea of a divine Nothingness, will on the contrary be (as I will show) the unique way, on the one hand, to render negative theology its Christian specificity (the manifestation of God and the incarnation of the Word) and to give it, on the other hand, a reversal of trajectory (no more toward the transcendence of God but into the immanence of man and the world by theophany).

14. See chap. 2 (infra): "The Nihilation of Eminence."

15. Roques, "Traduction ou interpretation?" 127.

16. John Scotus Erigena, *Versio operum S. Dionysii*, in *PL* 122, 1035A–1036A. The expression of "negative theology" is in reality not found in Denys himself, and, much like the word "proof" in Aquinas, he never speaks of negative theology but only of a "negative (or apophatic) way." The application of the terms *negative* and *affirmative way* to the "theological discipline" explicitly enacted here by Erigena prejudges nothing of the content of these doctrines. It marks nevertheless a decisive advance toward the exemplifications of a "negative theology" formula—which "is nothing but very modern" (see Jean-Luc Marion, *In Excess*, 129–30).

17. Denys the Areopagite, *Mystical Theology*, V, 1048 A (in *Pseudo-Dionysius: The Complete Works*, trans. Colm Luibheid and Paul Rorem [Mahwah, N.J.: Paulist, 1987], 141): "Again, we climb even higher than this. It is not soul or mind, nor does it possess imagination, conviction, speech or understanding . . . It cannot be grasped by the understanding since it is neither knowledge or truth . . .

It falls neither within the predicate of nonbeing nor of being . . . There is no speaking of it, nor name nor knowledge of it."

18. See Boethius, *Contre Eutychès et Nestorius*, in *Courts traits de théologie* (Paris : Le Cerf, 1991), chap. 1, pp. 53–54; see F. Bertin in Erigena, *Periphyseon*, bk. I, n. 1, p. 190.

19. John Scotus Erigena, *Periphysion*, I, 441 A.

20. Bertin, in Erigena, *De la division de la nature*, bk. III, vol. 2, back cover.

21. A rigorous analysis of this imperious necessity of an exit from "the metaphysics of presence" both in Husserl as in Heidegger can be found in Jean-Luc Marion, *Reduction and Givenness*: trans. Thomas A. Carlson (Evanston, Ill.: Northwestern University Press, 1998). On Husserl, see 49–56 ("The 'Phenomenon Reduced' to Present Objectivity"), and on Heidegger see 56–61 ("From the Unapparent Phenomenon to the 'Phenomenon of Being' "). The author has moreover drawn out of himself all the implications for negative theology in a heated debate with J. Derrida, in *In Excess*, chapter 6 ("In the Name: How to Avoid Speaking of It"), and in particular, p. 128, which fixes the perspective: "That the two questions of the 'metaphysics of presence' and 'negative theology'—questions which to all appearances come from such dissimilar provenances—should today end up encountering one another, indeed, end up being by and large superimposed, could be surprising."

22. Denys the Areopagite, *Mystical Theology*, 1000 B, p. 136.

23. J.-C. Foussard, "*Non apparentis apparitio*: Le théophanies de Jean Scot Érigène," in *Face de Dieu et théophanies*: *Cahiers de l'Université Saint-Jean de Jérusalem* 12 (1986): 120–48; citation p. 123. Jean-Claude Foussard, along with Francis Bertin, are among the more important interpreters of Erigena in French, neither of them wallowing in pure historicism. They heroically continue with an important work, giving to Erigena the place which rightly belongs to him in medieval philosophy.

24. Erigena, *Periphyseon* I, 482 A-B.

25. See Jean-Luc Marion, *God without Being* (1982), trans. Thomas A. Carlson (Chicago: University of Chicago Press, 1991), 138.

26. Erigena, *Periphyseon* III, 680 D–681 A.

27. F. Bertin in Erigena, *De la division de la nature*, vol. 1, n. 62, p. 216 (rightly cited in Jean-Luc Marion, *In Excess*, n. 3, p. 129). We should be grateful to René Roques for having, since his earliest works, noted this slippage in the meaning of the negative in Erigena. See "Jean Scot Érigène" in *Dictionnaire de spiritualité* (Paris: Beauschesne, 1973), col. 741: "Jean Scot précise qu'on doit entendre *aussi de manière négative* tous les superlatifs in 'uper' auxquels Denys recourt après la double démarche de l'affirmation et de la négation, et que les interprètes des *Noms divins* ont souvent expliques dans un sens positif" (italics mine).

28. Erigena, *Periphyseon* I, 462 C.

29. Roques, "Jean Scot Érigène." For a more developed thematization of this *radicalization of Denys in the meaning of the negative*, see also Roques's "Traduction ou interprétation?" 127; as well as, in the same work (*Libres sentiers ver l'erigenisme*): "Tératologie et théologie in Jean Scot Érigène," 13–43, a thesis on the excess of dissemblance over resemblance.

30. I recall here of course the title of the project of Emmanuel Levinas, *Otherwise Than Being or Beyond Essence*.

31. John Scotus Erigena, *Expositiones in Ierarchiam caelestem* (*CCCM* 37), IV, 1, lines 72–78. Cited and translated by F. Bertin in Erigena, *De la division de la nature*, I–II, n. 1, p. 94.

32. F. Bertin in Erigena, *De la division de la nature*, bk. I and bk. II, introduction, p. 39.

33. Marion, *Reduction and Givenness*, 2.

34. Respectively, Anselm of Canterbury, *Proslogion*, II, 2; and Thomas Aquinas, *Summa Theologiae*, Ia q. 1 a. 8 ad. 2.

35. Erigena, *Periphyseon*, II, 589 B. The French here is borrowed from the translation of J. Jolivet's monograph on Erigena, *Histoire de la philosophie: La philosophie médiévale* (Paris: Gallimard, 1969), vol. 1, p. 1255. I offer my thanks to this interpreter, specifically for putting me on the trail of Erigenism by virtue of this very formula that I have borrowed from him. Bertin's French translation runs thus: *Dieu ne se connaît donc pas dans sa quiddité, car Dieu n'est pas un quid objectivé* ("God does not know himself in his quiddity, for he is not an objective *quid*"; Erigena, *De la divisione de la nature*, 375). Despite the immense merit of his work, on this point it seems too far removed from the letter of the text to draw out adequately its specificity.

36. Jean-Claude Foussard, "*Non apparentis apparitio*: Le théophanisme de Jean Scot Érigène," 122 (italics added). Concerning the meaning and the necessity of such a "reduction" or *epochê* of the divine *quid*, see my work, *Saint Bonaventure et l'entrée de Dieu en théologie*, § 4, pp. 55–63: "La Fin de L'Empire du *ti esti*" (*quid, quis, quomodo*).

37. (*Apérité* is the French neologism to translate Heidegger's *Offenständigkeit*, which is translated into English as "openness," "being open," or "standing open," etc. –Trans.)

38. Heidegger, *Being and Time*, §9, p. 40 and §2, p. 5, respectively.

39. See Marion, *Reduction and Givenness*, "The Hermeneutics of Nothing as Being," 176–81.

40. Erigena, *Periphyseon*, II, 589 B. Note that the term "quiddity" is not yet fixed in the Carolingian epoch and so its employment to translate "that which is" (*quid sit*) is misguided. One cannot therefore reduce the question of the beingness (*étantité*) of God to his essentiality (*essentialité*) without anachronism. See J. Jolivet, *Histoire de la philosophie*, vol. 1, p. 1255.

41. See Meister Eckhart, "Sermon 71": "'When Paul is raised from the earth, his eyes are opened and he sees *nothing*' (Ac. 9:8). Nothing (*das Nichts*): this was God." We will return to this in the following chapter.

42. Erigena, *Periphyseon*, II, 589 B-C.

43. Ibid., II, 589 B.

44. Erigena, *Versio Maximi, praef.*, 1196 A–B. Cited and translated by M. Cappuyns, *Jean Scotus Érigène: Sa vie, son oeuvre, sa pensée* (Louvain, Belg.: Abbaye de Mont César, 1933), 323.

45. Erigena, *Periphyseon*, II, 585 B.

46. Heidegger, *Being and Time*, § 2, p. 25.

47. For the definition of *Dasein* as "being-there" distinct from that which is both "subsistent" (*vorhanden*) and "available" (*zuhanden*) see Heidegger, *Being and Time*, § 12. Concerning the meaning of Erigenian apophaticism, both as "negative theology" (humanity unable to know God) and "negative anthropology"

(humanity unable to know humanity), see Bernard McGinn's profitable article "The Negative Element in the Anthropology of John the Scot," in *Jean Scot Érigène et l'histoire de la philosophie*, ed. R. Roques (Paris: Centre national de la recherche scientifique, 1977), 315–25.

48. F. Bertin, "Les origines de l'homme chez Jean Scot," in Roques, *Jean Scot Érigène et l'histoire de la philosophie*, 307–14 (citation 308–9).

49. Erigena, *Periphyseon*, I, 446 D.

50. Heidegger, *Being and Time*, § 7: "The Concept of the Logos," p. 28. See Aristotle, *De Interpretatione*, 4, 17 a 3–7 (*Complete Works*, vol. 1, p. 26): "Every sentence is significant (not as a tool but, as we said, by convention), but not every sentence is a statement-making sentence, but only those in which there is truth or falsity. *There is not truth or falsity in all sentences*: prayer is a sentence but it is neither true nor false."

51. Denys the Areopagite, *Mystical Theology*, 1025 B, p. 138. "For this would be really to see and to know: to praise the Transcendent One in a transcending way, namely through the denial of all beings. We would be like sculptors who set out to carve a statue. They remove every obstacle to the pure view of the hidden image, and simply by this act of clearing aside they show up the beauty which is hidden."

52. Erigena, *Periphyseon*, III, 665 D. "The original nature of creatures has always existed in an inalterable way in the Wisdom of God . . . ; but since their original nature is knowable only by God . . . , and since no created understanding has ever been able to know it in its own essence until now, the original nature of creatures began to exist by means of a generation in time, acquiring some quantitative and qualitative properties, in which it is thus able, under a sort of vestment [*veluti quibusdam vestimentis*], to *reveal* implicitly its existence [*operta postest manifestare quia est*], but not at all its essence [*non autem quid sit*]." J.-C. Foussard rightly indicates this notion of the vestment as paradigm of the hidden and revealed in Erigena: "*Non apparentis apparitio* . . . ," 128. I will return to this exemplary confirmation of this Erigenian model of *unveiling* rather than of *stripping bare* in the constant passage from the hidden to the "secrets of nature" (*arcanum, mysterium, secretum*), when I discuss (infra) the *manifest* or *revealed* in the intelligible and sensible realms of created beings (theophany). See E. Jeauneau, "Le cache et l'obscur (quatre thèmes érigéniens)," in *Etudes érigéniennes* (Paris: Etudes Augustiniennes, 1987), 221–42.

53. Heideggerian definition of "the preliminary concept of phenomenology," *Being and Time*, § 7, p. 30.

54. Heidegger, *Being and Time*. See the passage from § 6 ("the task of a destruction of the history of ontology") to § 7 ("the phenomenological method of research").

55. See Heidegger, *Being and Time*, § 6, p. 21: "If the question of being is to achieve clarity regarding its own history, a loosening of the sclerotic tradition and a dissolving of the concealments produced by it is necessary. We understand this task as the *destructuring* of the traditional content of ancient ontology." The French translation of "Destruction" (Martineau), translated also by "déconstruction" (Granel) or "désobstruction" (Vezin) thus takes leave of the false idea of the annihilation of the history of philosophy where it would be first a matter of its appropriation. See Jean Greisch, *Ontologie et temporalité* (Paris: Presses Universitaires de France, 1994), 98.

56. John Scotus Erigena, *Expositiones en Ierarchiam caelestem*, II, 3, lines 526–27.

57. Erigena, *Periphyseon*, I, 464 A.

58. Ibid., I, 482 A-B.

59. René Roques, "Traduction ou interprétation ? Brèves remarques sur Jean Scot traducteur de Denys," in *Libres sentiers vers l'érigénisme*, 127.

60. Erigena, *Periphyseon*, I, 465 A.

61. Ibid., I, 504 B.

62. Ibid., I, 508 B.

63. See Jean-Luc Marion, *God without Being*, 106. See on this point the just retractions the author himself made concerning the possibility of the attribution of the Thomist *esse* to a "God without Being" who is not, for all that, a "God with being." Jean-Luc Marion, "Saint Thomas Aquinas and Onto-theology" in *Mystics*, 38–73. Marion's famous "retraction" is edited out of the revised English text. See "Saint Thomas d'Aquin et l'ontotheologie," *Revue thomiste* (January-March 1995): 31–66, n. 82, p. 65: "Such was my position, notably in *God without Being*. It is now clear that I ought today to present a *retraction* on this point, and I happily do so: for Thomas Aquinas himself, another view should be envisaged—that of thinking being starting from the unknowability of God, directly and without intermediary of any other name (even the Good) but even so no less radically."

64. Heidegger, *Being and Time*, § 12, p. 50.

65. Erigena, *Periphyseon*, respectively I, 463 B and III, 687 A.

66. Husserl, *Logical Investigations*, vol. 2, "Fifth Investigation," § 8, p. 550: "If the peculiar character of intentional experience is contested, if one refuses to admit, what for us is most certain, that being-an-object consists phenomenologically in certain acts in which something appears, or is thought of as our object, it will not be intelligible how being-an-object can itself be objective for us."

67. Erigena, *Periphyseon*, I, 452 B-C.

68. Ibid., I, 452.

69. For this famous division of nature that structures the entire *Periphyseon* and upon which we will not comment any further since it is amply explicated by a number of Erigenian exegetes, we refer only to the opening of the text, I, 441. See also the introduction to F. Bertin's French translation which traces this structure, 37–39.

70. Erigena, *Periphyseon*, I 445, D.

71. Ibid., III, 678 C.

72. Foussard, "*Non apparentis apparitio . . .* ," *Cahiers de l'Université Saint-Jean de Jérusalem* 12: 124.

73. Erigena, *Periphyseon*, I, 454 A–454 B.

74. Ibid., I 454 C.

75. Ibid., I, 455 B. On the meaning of this "divine auto-creation" as "auto-manifestation" and its impossible reduction to a facile pantheism, see the very good article of J.-C. Foussard, "Non apparentis apparitio . . . ," 120–48, and especially 123–28.

76. Ibid., III, 678 B.

77. Henri Bergson, *Introduction to Metaphysics*, trans. T. E. Hulme (Indianapolis, Ind.: Hackett, 1999): "To philosophize, therefore, is to invert *the habitual direction of the work of thought* . . . Modern mathematics is precisely an effort

to substitute *the being made for the ready-made*, to follow the generation of magnitudes, to grasp motion, no longer from without and in its displayed result, but from within and in its tendency to change; in short to adopt the mobile continuity of the outlines of things."

78. It is probably with Bonaventure that all the Trinitarian consequences of such a view were drawn out before its usage in the metaphysics of Leibniz. On this point see my work *Saint Bonaventure et l'entrée de Dieu en théologie*, 75–78: "L'hypothèse monadologique."

79. Erigena, *Periphyseon*, III, 677 B.

80. Ibid., I, 459 D—460 A.

81. Roques, "Scot Érigène," *Dictionnaire de spiritualité*, 741–42.

82. Ibid., I, 452, C.

83. Ibid., III, 643 B.

84. Ibid., I, 442 B.

85. Ibid., III, 642 D.

86. On this point, see my work *Saint Bonaventure et l'entrée de Dieu en théologie*, § 6, pp. 83–90: "De la sortie de la métaphysique à la Trinite créatrice."

87. Erigena, *Periphyseon*, I, 452 D.

88. Ibid., I, 453 A.

89. Ibid., I, 453 B. This theme will be taken up again by Bonaventure in relation to the angels in *Breviloquium*, II, 8, 2 (V, 226 a). See *Saint Bonaventure et l'entrée de Dieu en théologie*, 88.

90. Erigena, *Periphyseon*, I, 460 A. "But if you have recourse to the other etymological origin of this name, which would conceive *theos*, God, as not at all deriving from the verb *theôrô*, I see, but from the verb *theô*, I run, you will be confronted by the same rule. Because the one who runs is opposed to the one who does not run, as slowness is opposed to swiftness. God will therefore be *upertheos* [*sic*], more than runs [*plusquam currens*]."

91. I refer here to the work of J. Miernowski, *Le Dieu néant: Théologies négatives à l'aube des temps modernes* (Leiden, Neth.: Editions Brill, 1998), chap. II, pp. 22–38 ("Vaincre la dissimiliarité par l'analogie" [Aquinas]), and chap. III, pp. 39–53 ("Vaincre la dissimilarité par l'amour" [Ficino]).

92. Erigena, *Expositiones in Ierarchiam caelestem*, IV, 17.

93. Even though it could be discerned already in § 7 of *Being and Time*, the expression "phenomenology of the inapparent" is a very late formulation in Heidegger, from the "Zähringen Seminar" [1973], in Heidegger, *Four Seminars*, trans. Andrew Mitchell and François Raffoul (Bloomington Indiana: Indiana University Press, 2003), pp. 64–83.

94. Martin Heidegger, *Being and Time*, § 7, pp. 25 and 31, respectively.

95. Erigena, *Periphyseon*, I, 446 D p.: "It is *not only the divine essence* [*non enim essentia divina*] which the word God connotes; but this mode [*modus ille*] under which *God* shows himself [*ostendit*] to the intellectual and rational creature . . . which is frequently also called God by holy Scripture. The Greeks used to call this mode a *theophany* [*theophania*], that is to say an *appearance of God* [*hoc est Dei apparitio*]. Here is an example of this theophany: 'I saw the Lord seated' (Is. 6:1), and other analogous formulae, since it is *not the Essence* of God [*non ipsius essentiam*] that the prophet saw, but *a theophany* created by Him [*sed aliquid ab eo factum*]."

96. Ibid., III, 633 A–633 B. We should be grateful, first to Hans Urs von Balthasar, and then to Jean-Claude Foussard for having brought to light this structure of phenomenalization proper to Erigena, even though neither of them explicitly drew out the consequences for phenomenology itself. See, respectively, Hans Urs von Balthasar, *The Glory of the Lord*, vol. 4: *The Realm of Metaphysics in Antiquity*, trans. Oliver Davies et al. (Edinburgh: T&T Clark, 1989), 343–55; and Jean-Claude Foussard, "*Non apparentis apparitio*: Le théophanisme de Jean Scot Érigène," (*Cahiers de l'Université Saint-Jean de Jérusalem* 12), 120–48. The translation of *non apparentis apparitio* as "appearance of the one who does not appear (or "is inapparent")" is borrowed from Foussard. The translation by "appearance of what is non apparent" (F. Bertin) leaves too neutral, it seems to me, the very One (God) who is called to appear.

97. Erigena, *Periphyseon*, I, 449 C. On the famous tri-partition of the phenomenon mentioned here (*Offenbarung/Schein/Ershceinung*), see Heidegger, *Being and Time*, § 7 ("The Concept of the Phenomenon"), pp. 23–8. See also the commentary of Jean Greisch, *Ontologie et temporalité: Esquisse d'une interprétation intégrale de Sein und Zeit* (Paris: Presses Universitaires de France), 102–4: "Qu'est-ce qu'un phénomène?"

98. Erigena, *Commentarius in evangelium Iohannis*, I, XXV, 301 D–302 B. See the complementary note of F. Bertin in Erigena, *De la division de la nature*, vol. 1, n. 17, pp. 201–2.

99. Erigena, *Commentarius in evangelium Iohannis*, 302 B: "Similarly, perfectly purified souls or the intelligences (angelic) *are theophanies* [*thophaniae sunt*]; in them, God manifests himself to those who seek him and love him."

100. Heidegger, *Being and Time*, § 7, p. 29.

101. Erigena, *Periphyseon* IV, 760 A. "In its totality human nature subsists in the totality of all created natures, because in it all creatures have been constituted (under a synthetic mode) . . . , and by it all creatures will be saved." It is appropriate to retain the Latin vocabulary of "constitution" (*constituta*) instead of translating it as "création" (F. Bertin), in order not to lose the properly phenomenological vision of Erigena here.

102. Erigena, *Omelia Iohannis* . . . , ch. XIX, 294 A–294 B.

103. Erigena, *Periphyseon*, II, 536 B. On this central theme of the human mediator as fully involved in the manifestation of God, see the very profitable article of F. Bertin, "Les origines de l'homme chez Jean Scot," in *Jean Scot Érigène et l'histoire de la philosophie* (Centre national de la recherche scientique, 1977), 307–14, particularly 308: "L'homme theophanique."

104. Erigena, *Periphyseon*, III, 733 B.

105. The theme of the creation of "primordial man," even before Adam is named, was inherited from Gregory of Nyssa (*De imagine*, 185 B). See F. Bertin, "Les origines de l'homme chez Jean Scot" (in *Jean Scot Érigène et l'histoire de la philosophie*), 307–14 (theme of the "Manence de l'homme," 307); as well as J. Trouillard, "La notion de théophanie chez Érigène," in *Manifestation et révélation*, Revue de l'Institut Catholique de Paris (Paris: Beauschesne, 1976), 15–39 and "L'unité humaine selon Jean Scot Érigène," in *L'homme et son prochain* (Paris: Presses Universitaires de France, 1956), 298–301.

106. Erigena, *Periphyseon*, V, 1021 B. For this Erigenian if also phenomenological design of eschatology, see respectively, Jean-Claude Foussard, "Apparence

et apparitio: La notion de 'phantasia' chez Jean Scot Érigène" (in *Jean Scot Érigène et l'histoire de la philosophie*, 337–48) and T. Gregory, "L'eschatologie de Jean Scot," 377–92.

107. Heidegger, *Being and Time*, § 7, p. 31: "The phenomenological concept of the phenomenon, as self-showing, means the being of beings."

108. Erigena, *Periphyseon*, I, 450 C.

109. Ibid., V, 905 B–905 C.

110. See E. Jeauneau, "Le symbolisme de la mer chez Jean Scot Érigène," in *Études érigéniennes*, 289–96: "The sea is not here that perfidious element that Augustine was often describing. It evokes the mystery of the immensity of God" (389).

111. Quoted in X. Lacroix, *Le corps de chair* (Paris: Le Cerf, 1994), 236.

112. Erigena, *Periphyseon*, I, 445 C–445 D. The phenomenological establishment of the structure of the call as a "third reduction" after Husserl and Heidegger can be found in Jean-Luc Marion, *Reduction and Givenness*, chap. IV, § 6, pp. 167–202.

113. Erigena, *Commentary on the Gospel of John*, XXI, 298 A.

114. Ibid., XXV 300 D.

115. Erigena, *Periphyseon*, V, 926 C–926 D. On the face-to-face divine-human irreducibility of the visage, see Jean-Claude Foussard, "La notion de *phantasia* chez Jean Scot" (in *Jean Scot Érigène et l'histoire de la philosophie*, 346–48).

116. Erigena, *Commentary on the Gospel of John*, chap. XXVII, 304 D–305 A. On the meaning of such a "phenomenology of the cry" in Christianity, as a "cry of the flesh"—supremely from the cross, see my work *Le passeur de Gethsémani, Angoisse, souffrance et mort: Lecture existentielle et phénoménologique* (Paris: Le Cerf, 1999), 157–60: "L'excès du corps souffrant."

117. Hans Urs von Balthasar, *The Glory of the Lord: Seeing the Form*, 464.

Chapter 3

1. On this distinction, see my essay "Tuilage et conversion de la philosophie par la théologie," in *Philosophie et théologie, 1996–2006*, ed. Falque and Lielinski (Paris: L'Harmattan, 2005), 45–56. See also my remarks on the Wojtylian usage of the word "phenomenology" in "Ecce Homo: Voici l'homme," in *Jean-Paul II et la culture contemporaine* (Paris: Le Cerf, 2005), 157–86. The point is clear: the use of the term "phenomenology" in the context of theology is principally and exclusively referred to as a collection of descriptive phenomena—in a tradition running from the *Phenomenology of Spirit* of Hegel to the *Truth of the World* of Hans Urs von Balthasar (the French title, *Phénoménologie de la vérité*, will be discussed). By contrast, phenomenology, when it is a matter of the mode of thought founded by Husserl, is always based on the method called "reduction." In this sense, as far as I can see, there is no phenomenology independent of such an *epochê*, however the term is elsewhere used.

2. Meister Eckhart, "Sermon 52," in *Du Détachement et autres textes*, trans. G. Jarczyk and P.-J. Labarrière (Paris: Rivages, 1995), 56. [Falque takes quotations from, and often subtly revises, various French translations of Eckhart's works. His selection is based on the translation's "availability" and especially its "philosophical conceptuality" (see fn. 1, p. 138, of original text). I continue the practice from previous chapters of translating Falque's French quotation of the chapter's primary sources directly, and without reference to equivalent, contemporary

English editions (unless otherwise noted). *Usually*, Falque utilizes *Du Détachement et autres textes*, trans. G. Jarczyk et P.-J. Labarrière (Paris: Rivages, 1995) for Sermons 52 and 71 (henceforth, *Dét.*), and *Le château de l'âme*, trans. Jarczyk and Labarrière (Paris: Carnets Desclée de Brouwer, 1995), for Sermons 2 and 86 (henceforth, *Chât.*) –Trans.] For key texts of reference in French, see Meister Eckhart, *Sermons*, trans. J. Ancelet-Hustache (Paris: Seuil, 1974 [vol. 1], 1978 [vol. 2], 1979 [vol. 3]); *Oeuvres de Meister Eckhart: Sermons-traités*, trans. P. Petit (Paris: Gallimard, 1942) (henceforth, Gal.); Meister Eckhart, *Traités et sermons*, trans. Alain de Libera (Paris: Garnier-Flammarion, 1995) (henceforth, GF); and *La mystique rhénane d'Albert le Grand à Maitre Eckhart* (Paris: OEIL, 1983), chap. 4, pp. 231–316 (this is probably the best introduction to the work of Eckhart available in French).

3. See respectively, Martin Heidegger, "Philosophical Foundations for Medieval Mysticism," in *The Phenomenology of Religious Life*, trans. Matthias Fritsch and Jennifer Anna Gosetti-Ferencei (Bloomington: Indiana University Press, 2004), 231–54; and Michel Henry, *The Essence of Manifestation*, trans. Girard Etzkorn (The Hague: Martinus Nijhoff, 1973), § 49, pp. 424–37 (quotation p. 427).

4. Concerning this, one should read the luminous work of S. Bongiovanni, "Phénoménologie et mystique spéculative: Edmond Husserl et Maitre Eckhart: De la réduction *au* 'je' a la réduction *du* 'je,'" in *L'anneau immobile: Regards croises sur Maitre Eckhart: Husserl, Hegel, Laozi*, ed. S. Bongiovanni, G. Jarczuk, P.-J. Labarriere, and B. Vermander (Paris: Ed. des Facultés Jésuites de Paris, 2005), 18–58. This volume appeared unfortunately after the redaction of the present chapter. It confirms the pertinence of the link established here (Husserl-Eckhart) though I regret not being able to further dialogue with this text. If the perspectives are the same (reduction and conversion), the means of establishing the position are radically different. I focus principally on a reading of the sermons on Martha and Mary (Sermons 2 and 86). Bongiovanni, on the other hand, focuses on Sermon 52: "Blessed are the poor in spirit." (However, I do comment on this sermon briefly below.)

5. See Edmund Husserl, *Nachwort* (1930), "Afterword to My Ideas Pertaining to a Pure Phenomenology and to a Phenomenological Philosophy," in *Ideas Pertaining to a Pure Phenomenology and to a Phenomenological Philosophy, First Book*, trans. R. Rojcewicz and A. Schuwer (The Hague: Springer, 1990). This call for a new *phenomenological praxis* begins with Husserl and despite a relation to theology needing redefinition, appears in Natalie Depraz, *Husserl* (Paris: Armand Colin, 1999), 86–88. See also H. Spielberg, *Doing Phenomenology: Essays on and in Phenomenology* (The Hague: Nijhoff, 1975).

6. Edmund Husserl, *The Crisis of European Sciences and Transcendental Phenomenology*, 37.

7. Dorion Cairns, *Conversations with Husserl and Fink* (The Hague: Martinus Nijhoff, 1976), 91. Cited with commentary in Natalie Depraz, "Seeking Phenomenological Metaphysics: Henry's Reference to Eckhart," trans. Gregory B. Sadler, *Continental Philosophy Review* 32 (1999): 303.

8. E. de Miribel, *Comme l'or purifie par le feu, Edith Stein (1891–1942)* (Paris: Plon, 1984), 119: "The life of man is nothing other than a *path toward God.* I have attempted to get through to the end without the help of theology, its proofs and methods; in other words, I have wanted *to attain God without God.* It was

necessary for me to eliminate God from my scientific thought in order to open the way to those who do not know, as you do, the sure route of faith that passes by the Church . . . I am aware of the danger that accompanies such a process and of the risk that I have myself incurred, if I did not *feel so profoundly tied to God* and *a Christian at the root of my heart*" (emphasis added).

9. Edmund Husserl, "Manuscript of 1933," in *Husserliana* 7, p. 9. Discussed in Jocelyn Benoist, "Husserl: Au-delà de l'ontologie," *Études philosophiques* (October-December 1991): 433.

10. Husserl, *The Crisis*, 297; Eckhart, "*Du Dét.*," Gal., p. 20. The parallelism between Husserl and Eckhart is established in Depraz's presentation on the text of the *Crisis* (309).

11. Husserl, respectively, *Ideas I*, §32, p. 61; Husserl, *Cartesian Meditations*, § 12, p. 27; "Afterword to My Ideas . . . ," 216.

12. Husserl, *Ideas I*, § 57, p. 133, and § 58, p. 134.

13. Emmanuel Levinas, *Discovering Existence with Husserl*, trans. Richard A. Cohen and Michael B. Smith (Evanston, Ill.: Northwestern University Press, 1998), 83: "It is very difficult to take seriously the brief indications Husserl gives about God in the *Ideas*, seeking, in the marvelous success of the play of intentions constituting a coherent world, a teleological proof for the existence of God."

14. See Jean-Luc Marion, *Being Given: Essay on the Phenomenology of Givenness*, trans. Jeffrey L. Kosky (Stanford, Calif.: Stanford University Press, 2002), 23–27.

15. Husserl, *Ideas I*, § 57, p. 133.

16. Husserl, *Cartesian Meditations*, §11, p. 26: "This '*transcendence*' is part of the intrinsic sense of anything worldly, *despite* the fact that anything worldly necessarily acquires all the sense determining it, along with its existential status, exclusively from my experiencing, my objectivating, thinking valuing, or doing, at particular times."

17. Edith Stein, "Husserl and Aquinas: A Comparison" (1929), in *Knowledge and Faith*, ed. Walter Redmond (Washington, D.C.: Institute of Carmelite Studies, 2000), 32.

18. Husserl, *Cartesian Meditations*, §16, p. 38.

19. A. Löwith, "L'*epochê* de Husserl et le doute de Descartes," in *Revue de métaphysique et de morale* (October-December 1957): note 4, p. 407.

20. John XXIII, Opening of Vatican Council II (Oct. 1, 1962), S. Oec. Conc. Vat. II, *Constitutiones Decreta Declarationes* (1974), 863–65.

21. Eckhart, *Sermon 4*, GF, n. 703. See Gal. 243.

22. It is hardly necessary here to recall the following point, except for neophytes: egocentric philosophy as a return toward the I or the ego (Descartes, but also Eckhart and Augustine before him) has nothing to do with the egoism which refuses all alterity, and so on.

23. Eckhart, *Entretiens spirituels* (*Talks of Instruction*), GF, p. 80.

24. Henry, *The Essence of Manifestation*, § 39, p. 310: "The existential union of man and God is only possible on the ground of their ontological unity . . . The radical independence of man with regard to the whole of divine creation and to God himself signifies his identity with him."

25. P.-J. Labarrière (and G. Jarczyk), in Meister Eckhart, *Le château de l'âme*, p. 37: "Meister Eckhart reveals here the profundity and intransigence of what

one could call his articulated monism . . . : 'one becomes two; the two are one, light and spirit; the two are enveloped in eternal light' " (citing Eckhart, "Sermon 86").

26. Eckhart, *Commentaire sur le prologue de Jean* (*Commentary on the Prologue of St. John)*, in *L'oeuvre latine de Maître Eckhart* (Paris: Cerf, 1988), vol. 6, n. 2, p. 27: "By explaining these words and the others that follow, the author's purpose [Eckhart is speaking of himself], as in all of his writings, is to explain the affirmations of the holy Christian faith and of Scripture in the two testaments by means of the natural reason of the philosophers."

27. Taken up again in Labarrière and Jarczyk's collection. On this point, even though it does not make mention of this possible phenomenological interpretation of the episode, see the instructive article of M. de Gandillac, "Deux figures eckhartiennes de Marthe," in *Métaphysique: Histoire de la philosophie: Recueil d'études offert à Fernand Brunner* (Neuchâtel, 1981), 119–34.

28. Eckhart, "Sermon 86," *Chât.* 69.

29. Husserl, *Ideas I*, § 30, p. 56.

30. Eckhart, *Instructional Talks*, GF 78.

31. Eckhart, "Sermon 86," *Chât.* 73.

32. Eckhart, "Sermon 86," Gal., 246. I prefer here the French translation of P. Petit over that of P.-J. Labarrière (*Chât.* 71), insofar as the metaphor of "being stuck in the mud" [*embourbement*] makes clearer this danger of pure absorption in God without detachment.

33. Husserl, *Cartesian Meditations*, § 15, p. 35.

34. Respectively, Eckhart, "Sermon 86," *Chât.* 69; and Paul Ricoeur, "Introduction," *Ideas I*, trans. Paul Ricoeur (Paris: Gallimard, 1950), xx.

35. Ricœur, "Introduction," *Ideas I*.

36. Eckhart, "Sermon 86," *Chât.* 71.

37. Husserl, *Cartesian Meditations*, § 10, pp. 24–25.

38. Eckhart, "Sermon 5b," GF 256.

39. Eckhart, "Sermon 86," *Chât.* 73: "This is why he says: you concern yourself (Lk. 10:41), and he means: you stand *along with things* and the things are not *in you*; and they remain *within worry* who stand without being unfettered in all their enterprises. They remain without fetters who orient all their work in the ordained way after the image of the eternal light. These people stand *with things*, not *in things*."

40. Heidegger, *Being and Time*, § 41, pp. 178–83.

41. See J. Ancelet-Hustache's French translation, "*tu es vigilante* (*sorcsam*)" (you are watchful) in Eckhart, *Sermons* (Seuil), vol. 3, p. 174.

42. This is not the place to indicate some personal perspectives, independent of Eckhart, which could well illustrate the point. For these see my work, *Metamorphosis of Finitude: An Essay on Birth and Resurrection*, trans. George Hughes (New York: Fordham University Press, 2012), §17, pp. 67–76.

43. For this notion of "dwelling" (*bauen*) and its proximity to Eckhartian vigilance "beside the world" rather than "worldly care" (*besorgen*), see Heidegger, *Being and Time*, § 12, pp. 49– 55. See also his "Building, Dwelling, Thinking," in *Basic Writings*, ed. David Farrell Krell (New York: Harper Collins, 1993), 319–39.

44. Eckhart, "Sermon 86," *Chât.* 79.

45. Eckhart, "Sermon 5b," GF 255.
46. Eckhart, "Sermon 86," *Chât.* 78.
47. On the questions Henry poses to theology see my two contributions: "Michel Henry théologien: A propos de *C'est moi la vérité*," *Laval théologique et philosophique* 57, no. 3 (October 2001): 525–36; as well as "Y-a-t-il une chair sans corps? (autour de l'ouvrage de M. Henry, Incarnation, Paris, Seuil, 2000)," in *Phénoménologie et christianisme chez Michel Henry*, ed. P. Capelle (2004), 95–133 (with response by Henry, 168–82).
48. P.-J. Labarrière, *Le château d l'âme* (*Chât.*), 39: "Only a *third way*—which is called way and is nevertheless a home (Eckhart)—situates man at the heart of the ultimate . . . All is *drawn together* in the temporal-eternal instant . . . Marvelous is its *bringing together* of all interiority and exteriority, all active and passive comprehension" (emphasis added).
49. Henry, *The Essence of Manifestation*, 282: "The very speech wherein all things are contained, name and appellation, that which *designates* and that which *shows*, these must also be renounced in this poverty which is made of silence" (emphasis added).
50. Husserl, *Ideas I*, § 57, p. 132.
51. Eckhart, "Sermon 2." In this sermon Eckhart clearly distinguishes this "something elevated beyond here or there" (the spark of the soul in "Sermon 48") from the intellect as well as from the will (which he treats respectively). On this point see the instructive notes of Alain de Libera on this sermon, in *Traites et sermons*, GF, n. 26, p. 420, and n. 29, p. 421; as well as "Sermon allemand 77" in *Philosophes médiévaux des XIIIe et XIVe siècles*, ed. R. Imbach and M.-H. Meleard (Paris, 1986), 271–79.
52. Husserl, *Cartesian Meditations*, § 11, p. 25–26.
53. Ibid.
54. Eckhart, "Sermon 17," in *Sermons*, Seuil vol. 1, p. 156.
55. Ibid, p. 155 (implicitly citing Avicenne).
56. One should consult on this point the instructive article of B. Mojsisch, "Ce moi: La conception de moi de maître Eckhart: Une contribution aux lumières du Moyen Age," in *Revue des sciences religieuses* 70, no. 1 (January 1996): 18–30. See in particular p. 22 for the opposition of Eckhart to Aquinas and p. 23 for the original birth of self-consciousness in Eckhart.
57. Eckhart, *On Detachment*, *Dét.* 50.
58. Eckhart, "Sermon 86," *Chât.* 81.
59. See Thomas Aquinas, *Summa Theologiae*, IIa, IIae, q. 182, a. 1, resp.: "The contemplative life is concerned with the divine; the active life is concerned with the human: 'In the beginning was the Word' writes St. Augustine, 'behold that which Mary heard. The Word made flesh: behold that which Martha served.' "
60. Eckhart, *On Detachment*, *Dét.* 51.
61. Eckhart, "Sermon 86," *Chât.* 55.
62. Ibid., p. 85.
63. Eckhart, *On Detachment*, *Dét.* 56.
64. Infra, chap. 4 (Irenaeus), "The Visibility of the Flesh."
65. Eckhart, "Sermon 52," *Dét.* 56.
66. Eckhart, "Sermon 29," GF 328. And, respectively, Alain de Libera, "L'un ou la trinité ?" in *Les mystiques rhénans*: *Revue des sciences religieuses* (January

1996): 31–47; J. Lerfert, "Les cieux changent et le étoiles filent: Poétique trinitaire de Maitre Eckhart," *Nouvelle revue théologique* (January-March 2004): 86–105 (quotation p. 90).

67. Eckhart, "Sermon 2," *Chât.* 53.

68. Angelus Silesius, *Le pèlerine chérubinique* [*The Cherubinic Wanderer*] (Paris: Aubier, 1946), vol. 1, pp. 61–62.

69. Eckhart, "Sermon 86," *Chât.* 75.

70. Eckhart, "Sermon 2, " *Chât.* 59.

71. See Husserl, *Cartesian Meditations*, § 15, p. 35: "Above the I naively interested in the world will be established a *disinterested onlooker*, the phenomenological I."

72. Eckhart, "Sermon 86," *Chât.* 74.

73. Ibid., p. 73.

74. Ibid.

75. Ibid., p. 74.

76. Eckhart, *On Detachment*, *Dét.* 49–50.

77. Eckhart, "Sermon 86," *Chât.* 75.

78. See Etienne Gilson, *Le thomisme* (Paris: Vrin, 1983): "Thomist philosophy . . . is constituted in opposition to every doctrine which would not confer to *secondary causes* the complete measure of being and the efficacy to which they have the right."

79. Eckhart, "Sermon 86," *Chât.* 75.

80. Eckhart, respectively, "Sermon 5b" and "Sermon 6," GF 255 and 262.

81. Henry, *The Essence of Manifestation*, § 49, p. 432.

82. Eckhart, "Sermon 29," GF 330.

83. F. Bruner, *Maître Eckhart: Approche de l'oeuvre* (Geneva: Ad Solem, 1999), 74–75 (emphasis added).

84. Bull of John XXII, *In agro dominico* (March 27, 1329). Condemnations 10 and 22, respectively; reproduced in GF 410 and 412.

85. See my *Saint Bonaventure et l'entrée de Dieu en théologie*, § 10, pp. 137–49.

86. Eckhart, "Sermon 2," *Chât.* 56.

87. Bull of John XXII, GF, condemnation 13, pp. 410–11.

88. In this sense, we should wonder whether certain revivals of Eckhart today do not take the path of the "de-theologization" of medieval philosophy that I have interrogated in the introduction, above.

89. Eckhart, "Sermon 29," GF 326.

90. See Eckhart, "Sermon 12," GF 297; as well as the commentary of B. Mojsisch, "Ce Moi: La conception du Moi de Maître Eckhart," 18–30: "Each man possesses in himself a unique *something in the soul* which is not the soul itself but its *ground* or *origin*. It is toward this something that the possible intellect ought to be turned in order to be surpassed *as an I* in this something" (p. 22, emphasis in original).

91. Eckhart, "Sermon 12," GF 299.

92. Eckhart, "Sermon 2," *Chât.* 56.

93. Eckhart, "Sermon 6," GF 262.

94. Ibid.

95. Eckhart, "Sermon 2," *Chât.* 56.

96. Eckhart, "Sermon 14," GF 310.

97. Paul Ricoeur, *Oneself as Another*, trans. Kathleen Blamey (Chicago: University of Chicago Press, 1992), 3 (emphasis added).

98. *Ibid.*, "Sermon 14," GF 310.

99. Husserl, *Cartesian Meditations*, § 37, pp. 76–77: "The phenomenology developed at first is merely *static*; its descriptions are analogous to those of natural history, which concern particular types and, at best, arrange them in their systematic order. Questions of *universal genesis* and the *genetic structure* of the ego in his universality, so far as that structure is more than temporal formation, are still far away" (emphasis added).

100. Husserl, *Cartesian Meditations*, § 38, p. 77.

101. Eckhart, "Sermon 2," *Chât.* 51.

102. Ibid., 51–52.

103. Ibid., 53.

104. Eckhart, "Sermon 43," Seuil, vol. 2, p. 85.

105. Eckhart, "Sermon 2," *Chât.* 56.

106. See Plato, *Theaetetus*, 150b, in *Complete Works*, p. 167: "Now my art of midwifery [*maieutikê*] is just like theirs in most respects. The difference is that I attend men and not women, and that I watch over the labor of their souls and not of their bodies."

107. Bull of John XXII, condemnation 13, GF 411.

108. Eckhart, "Sermon 83," Seuil, vol. 3, p. 153. Concerning the status of the subject in Eckhart and the meaning accorded to this identification of egos, see the very instructive chapter of Alain de Libera in *La mystique rhénane, D'Albert le Grand à Maître Eckhart* (Paris: Seuil, 1994), 231–316, and especially 238–50.

109. Husserl, *Cartesian Meditations*, §38, p. 78.

110. Eckhart, quoted by Emilie Zum Brunn, "Un homme qui pâtit Dieu," in *Voici Maître Eckhart* (Grenoble: Jérome Millon, 1994), 269 (referring to F. Pfeifer, *Deutsch Mystiker des vierzehnten Jahrunderts*, vol. 2, *Meister Eckhart*, 337).

111. Eckhart, "Sermon 2," *Chât.* 60–61: "Jesus went to a little fortress and was received by a virgin who was a woman. Why? (1) It was necessary for her to be a virgin and a woman. (2) Now I told you that Jesus was received. (3) But I have not yet spoken about the little fortress, about which I am about to speak." Only the second point remains to be studied here.

112. Eckhart, "Sermon 2," *Chât.* 60.

113. Eckhart, *Book of Divine Comfort*, in *The Complete Mystical Works of Meister Eckhart*, trans. Maurice Walshe and Bernard McGinn (New York: Crossroads, 2010), 547. In this sense we could be tempted to see a quasi-precursor to Moltmann's theology of the cross (outside of his Trinitarian scheme, however), distinguishing, on the one hand, the "suffering of the Son," and on the other hand, "the suffering of the Father undergoing the suffering of the Son." See Jurgen Moltmann, *The Crucified God*, 243: "The suffering and the dying of the Son, forsaken by the Father, is another kind of suffering than the suffering of the Father in the death of the Son. . . . The Son suffers dying, the Father suffers the death of the Son."

114. Three positive aspects of suffering in Eckhart, summarized by J.-F. Malherbe in *Souffrir Dieu: La prédication de Maître Eckhart* (Paris: Le Cerf, 1992), 37.

115. Emmanuel Levinas, *Time and the Other*, trans. Richard A. Cohen (Pittsburgh: Duquesne University Press, 1990). For a Christological and phenomenological interpretation of suffering as "the impossibility of retreat" in the

relation of the Son to the Father, see my work *Le passeur de Gethsémani: Angoisse, souffrance et mort, lecture existentielle et phénoménologique* (Paris: Le Cerf, 1999), 119–74.

116. Eckhart, "Sermon 2," *Chât.* 60.

117. Eckhart, "Sermon 29," GF 330.

118. Eckhart, *Le grain de sénevé*, trans. A. de Libera (Paris: Arfuyen, 1996), distich VII, p. 29.

119. Eckhart, "Sermon 86," *Chât.* 84.

120. Eckhart, "Sermon 71," *Dét.* 89.

121. Eckhart, "Sermon 86," *Chât.* 77.

122. Alain de Libera, *Penser au Moyen Age* (Paris: Le Seuil, 1991), 330.

123. To trace this relationship in its concrete steps, see Philippe Capelle's instructive article, "Heidegger et Maître Eckhart," in *Les mystiques rhénans: Revue des sciences religieuses* (January 1996): 113–24. See also John Caputo, *The Mystical Element in Heidegger's Thought* (New York: Fordham University Press, 1986), chap. 4, pp. 140–217.

124. Martin Heidegger, *Country Path Conversations*, trans. Bret W. Davis (Bloomington, Ind.: Indiana University Press, 2010), 70 [translation of *Gelassenheit* modified from "releasement," utilized by this English translation, to "serenity." –Trans.].

125. Jean Greisch, "La contrée de la sérénité et l'horizon de l'espérance," in *Heidegger et la question de Dieu*, ed. Richard Kearney and Joseph O'Leary (Paris: Grasset, 1982), 181. See also Alain de Libera, in M. Eckhart, *Traites et sermons*, n. 12, p. 189: "We cannot exclude the possibility that Heidegger has underestimated the second dimension of *gelâzenheit* [as abandonment of the will itself]."

126. Greisch, "La contrée de la sérénité," 183.

127. Eckhart, "Sermon 71," *Dét.* 96.

128. Ibid., p. 96.

129. Ibid., p. 93.

130. Heidegger, *What Is Metaphysics?* 100 and 103, respectively.

131. See Libera, *La mystique rhénane, d'Albert le Grand à Maître Eckhart*, 285.

132. Eckhart, "Sermon 71," *Dét.* 89.

133. Ibid., p. 96.

134. Ibid., p. 96. See Heidegger, *Being and Time*, §18, p. 82: "The first two concepts of being (*zuhanden* and *vorhanden*) are *categories* and concern beings unlike *Dasein*."

135. Eckhart, "Sermon 71," *Det.* 96.

136. Ibid., p. 93.

137. Ibid., p. 96.

138. Ibid., pp. 97–98.

139. See P.-J. Labarrière's introduction to Eckhart's *Du détachement et autres textes*, 38.

140. See Heidegger, *What Is Metaphysics*? 101. Cf. also Marion's triple commentary, each time from a different perspective: *God without Being*, chap. 4, pp. 108–38; *Reduction and Givenness*, chap. 6, pp. 167–202 ; *Being Given*, §20, pp. 189–98.

141. Eckhart, "Sermon 71," *Dét.* 98.

142. Eckhart, "Sermon 23," Seuil, vol. 1, p. 201.
143. See Libera's translation, in *La mystique rhénane*, 285: "n'être de rien de rien."
144. Heidegger, *What Is Metaphysics?* 101.
145. Eckhart, "Sermon 71," *Dét.* 94 and 98–99, respectively.
146. Eckhart, *Treatise on Detachment*, *Dét.* 51.
147. Eckhart, "Sermon 71," *Dét.* 100.
148. Ibid., pp. 100–101.
149. Ibid., p. 101.
150. Ibid.
151. Ibid. Let me point the reader toward the famous definition of the love of God by Bernard of Clairvaux, *Le traite de l'amour de Dieu (De diligendo Deo)* (Paris: Le Cerf, 1984), *Sources chrétiennes*, 393, p. 61: "modus diligendi Deum, sine modo diligere." See my interpretative hypothesis (without however this reference in Eckhart as an explicit source): "Expérience et empathie chez Bernard de Clairvaux," in *Revue des sciences philosophiques et théologiques* (October-December 2005): 655–96.
152. Eckhart, "Sermon 52," *Dét.* 79.
153. Ibid., p. 75.
154. Ibid., p. 76.
155. Ibid., p. 75.
156. Ibid., p. 76.
157. Ibid.
158. Ibid., p. 75.
159. Ibid., p. 74.
160. Eckhart, "Sermon 29," GF 326.
161. Eckhart, "Sermon 52," *Dét.*, 79.
162. Ibid., p. 78.
163. Ibid.
164. Hadewijch Antwerp, Letter XIX, in *Complete Works* (Mahwah, N.J.: Paulist, 1980), 89.
165. Eckhart, "Sermon 52," *Dét.* 79.
166. Ibid.
167. Ibid., p. 80.
168. Husserl, *On the Phenomenology of Consciousness of Internal Time* (1893–1917), trans. John Barnett Brough (Dordrecht, Neth.: Kluwer Academic, 1991), §36, p. 79.
169. Eckhart, "Sermon 52," *Dét.* 81.
170. Ibid.
171. [This phrase is in English in the original. –Trans.]
172. Eckhart, "Sermon 52," *Det.* 82.
173. Ibid., pp. 82–83.
174. Ibid., p. 77. See my *Metamorphosis of Finitude: An Essay on Birth and Resurrection.*
175. Eckhart, "Sermon 52," *Det.* 84. Completed by "Sermon 29," GF 328: "Insofar as God *breaks through in me*, I *break through in him.*"
176. See my two contributions already cited above: "Michel Henry théologien: A propos de *C'est moi la vérité*," *Laval théologique et philosophique* 57, no. 3

(October 2001): 525–36; "Y a-t-il un chair sans corps?" in Philippe Capelle, *Phénoménologie et christianisme chez Michel Henry* (2004), 95–133, with responses from Michel Henry, 168–82.

177. Eckhart, *Commentary on the Gospel of John, Prologue*, in *Meister Eckhart: The Essential Sermons, Commentaries, Treatises and Defense*, trans. Edmund Colledge and Bernard McGinn (Mahwah, N.J.: Paulist, 1981), 167.

Introduction to Part Two

1. See, respectively, Emmanuel Levinas, "A Man God," in *Entre Nous: Essays on Thinking-of-the-Other*," trans. Michael B. Smith (London: Continuum, 2006), 50: "To solicit a thought thinking more than it thinks, the Infinite cannot incarnate itself in a Desirable, cannot, being infinite, enclose itself in an end [in this context Levinas mentions the "transubstantiation of the Creator into the creature"]"; and Emmanuel Levinas, "Meaning and Sense," in *Collected Philosophical Papers*, ed. Alphonso Lingis (Dordrecht, Neth.: Martinus Nijhoff, 1987), 106–7: "To be in the image of God *does not mean to be an icon of God*, but to find oneself *in his trace*" (emphasis added). And for Merleau-Ponty, *Signs* (Evanston, Ill.: Northwestern University Press, 1964): "And it is a little too much to forget that Christianity is, among other things, the recognition of a mystery in the relations of man and God, which stems precisely from the fact that the Christian God *wants nothing to do with a vertical relation of subordination*" (70–71; emphasis added).

2. Friedrich Nietzsche, *The Gay Science*, foreword to the 2nd ed. (1886). See *The Gay Science*, ed. Bernard Williams (Cambridge, Eng.: Cambridge University Press, 2001), 5. The translation by "flesh" and not "body" attested by Didier Franck, *Heidegger et le problème de l'espace* (Paris: Minuit, 1986), 127.

3. [*Cela même qui pense chez les homes est épanouissement de la chair (meleôn phusis) en tous et en chacun*], Parmenides, "Fragment 16," trans. Didier Franck, in *Chair et corps: Sur la phénoménologie de Husserl* (Paris: Minuit, 1981), 137, n. 17. The fragment serves as the epigram of the entire work, p. 8.

4. See Martin Heidegger, "Plato's Doctrine of the Truth," trans. Thomas Sheehan, in *Pathmarks*, ed. William McNeil (Cambridge, Eng.: Cambridge University Press, 1998), 155–82; Martin Heidegger, *What Is Called Thinking*, trans. J. Glenn Gray (New York: Harper and Row, 1968), 113–244; "Logos: Heraclitus B 50" in *Early Greek Thinking*, trans. David Farrel Krell (New York: Harper and Row, 1984), 61ff.; "Anaximander's Sayings," in *Off the Beaten Track*, ed. Julian Young and Kenneth Haynes (Cambridge, Eng.: Cambridge University Press, 2002), 242–81. See also Jean Greisch, "Le phénomène de la chair: Un ratage de *Sein und Zeit*," in G. Florival, ed. *Dimension de l'exister*, ed. G. Florival (Louvain-la-Neuve: Etudes d'Anthropologie Philosophique, 1994), 157–74.

5. See Plato, *Phaedrus*, 250 d: "Only beauty has had this prerogative of being capable of being manifest with the most force and which most attracts love." See the commentary of Jean-Louis Chrétien, *L'effroi du Beau* (Paris: Cerf, 1997), 60: "Love is not a god, but the appearance of the divine in changeable beauty; in the idea of the body, the same word designates the sensible and intelligible forms."

6. See E. von Ivanka, *Plato christanus: La réception critique de platonisme chez le Peres de l'Eglise* (1964; Paris: Presses Universitaires de France, 1990), 8: "The utilization of the schemas of Platonic thought in a Christian context

harbors, for the elements that Christianity holds in a fundamental way, dangers of caricature and deforming that a theological method formed by Aristotelianism did not know."

7. See on this point Heidegger's critique (however unjustified) of Nietzsche: "From the beginning, Nietzsche defined all his philosophy as the inversion of Platonism," in Martin Heidegger, *Nietzsche* vols 1–2, trans. David Farrell Krell (NewYork: Harper Collins, 1991), 205.

Chapter 4

1. Porphyry, attested by Saint Augustine, *City of God*, XXII, 26, p. 1167. "But, they reply, Porphyry says that in order to be happy the soul must flee the body [*ut beata sit anima, corpus esse omne fugiendum*]." See also "Sermon 241," §7: "Porphyry has said and written in these latter days: everything bodily must be fled. Everything bodily, he said, as if every body was for the soul simply dolorous chains." See also Thomas Aquinas, *De potentia*, Q. 5, 10, resp.: "As St. Augustine said, Porphyry thinks that, for the perfect beatitude of the human soul, it would be necessary to flee from everything bodily [*omne corpus fugiendum esse*]."

2. See E. von Ivanka, *Plato christianus*, 62–80.

3. Hans Urs von Balthasar, *The Glory of the Lord: A Theological Aesthetics*, respectively, vol. 2, *Clerical Styles*, 79; and vol. 1: *Seeing the Form*, 401 (citing Paul Claudel, *Sensation du divin*).

4. Balthasar, *The Glory of the Lord*, vol. 1, p. 410.

5. Michel Henry, *Incarnation* (Paris: Seuil, 2000), 15. The single mention of these two authors in the work (§24) is symptomatic of such a realization. Regarding the limitations of the interpretation of these two Fathers, which, I suggest, loses corporeity in an unbridled auto-affectivity, see my contribution already cited, "Y a-t-il une chair sans corps? Autour de l'ouvrage de M. Henry, *Incarnation*."

6. Irenaeus, *Against Heresies*, IV, 20, 7, p. 649: "gloria enim Dei vivens homo, vita autem hominis visio Dei." For the Latin, I refer to the edited volumes of *Sources chrétiennes*: book 1 (vols. 263 and 264), book 2 (vols. 293–94), book 3 (vols. 210–11), book 4 (vol. 100), book 5 (vols. 152–53). Page numbers in parentheses are to these editions. For the *Demonstration of the Apostolic Preaching* (henceforth *DA*), I utilize vol. 406 of the *Sources chrétiennes*.

7. Irenaeus, *Against Heresies*, III, 22, 3 (385).

8. See, respectively, Irenaeus, *Against Heresies*, IV, 20, 7 (474); *Against Heresies*, IV, 6, 5–6 (421); *Against Heresies*, III, 21, 10 (382).

9. Irenaeus, *Against Heresies*, III, 22, 4 (385–86).

10. Irenaeus, *Against Heresies*, III, 32, 2 (387).

11. I cannot further develop this conception of immanence as a "byproduct" of transcendence, but see my work *Metamorphosis of Finitude*, §5, pp. 16–19.

12. Irenaeus, *DA* §11 (99).

13. I borrow these terms from Jean-Louis Chrétien, *Lueur du secret* (Paris: L'Herne, 1985), 92–104.

14. Irenaeus, *Against Heresies*, V, 1, 1 (570).

15. Jean-Louis Chrétien, *The Ark of Speech*, trans. Andrew Brown (London: Routledge, 2004), 2.

16. Husserl, *Cartesian Meditations*, §16, pp. 38–39.

17. Mark the Ascetic, cited by X. Lacroix, *Le corps de chair* (Paris: Cerf, 1994), 236.

18. Jean-Louis Chrétien, *Saint Augustine ou les actes de parole* (Paris: Presses Universitaires de France, 2002).

19. Irenaeus, *Against Heresies*, V, 15, 3 (615). For the image of the "potter" and "surgeon" see *Against Heresies*, IV, 39, 2 (556). On the meaning of this "amorous *plasmatio*" see B. Sesboüé, *Tout récapituler dans le Christ: Christologie et sotériologie d'Irénée de Lyon* (Paris: Desclée, 2000), 146–48.

20. Irenaeus, *DA* §32 (129).

21. Ibid.

22. Charles Péguy, *Victor-Marie, Comte Hugo*, in *Oeuvres en prose complètes* (Paris: La Pléiade, 1992), 235. See my article, "Charles Péguy: Incarnation philosophique et incarnation théologique: Une histoire arrivée à la chair et à la terre," *L'amitié Charles Péguy* 102 (April-June 2003): 164–78. The proximity between Irenaeus and Péguy remains to be investigated, as if the second had drawn almost everything from the first, although it hardly needs mentioning that the texts of Irenaeus were rediscovered at the cusp of the twentieth century.

23. Irenaeus, *Against Heresies*, III 16, 6 (352). I invert the formula "according to the Father's good pleasure" in order to make the "*plasmatio*" of the Word to Adam more apparent, an act which performs his very incarnation. On this point, see Ysabel de Andia, *Homo vivens: Incorruptibilité et divinisation de l'homme selon Irénée de Lyon* (Paris: Etudes Augustiniennes, 1986), 154–58. See also G. Ruiz, "L'enfance d'Adam selon saint Irénée de Lyon," *Bulletin de littérature ecclésiastique* 89/2 (1988): 97–115.

24. I borrow this expression from Jean-Luc Marion, *In Excess*, 96: "the taking of flesh is where I am taken."

25. Irenaeus, *DA* §32 (129).

26. Irenaeus, *Against Heresies*, III, 22, 3 (385). Noteworthy is Irenaeus's insistence on the prefiguration of Adam in this sense rather than the fall. Such does not negate the second to the profit of the first, but rather, as we will see below, the fall is only properly understood by virtue of the prefiguration. There are thus two possible readings of the parallel between the two Adams in Romans 5:12–21, either with emphasis on the fall (Augustine) or the prefiguration of the Incarnation in the creation of Adam (Irenaeus).

27. Irenaeus, *DA* 11 (99).

28. Henri Bergson, "The Two Sources of Morality and Religion," in *Key Writings*, ed. John Mullarkey (London: Continuum, 2002), 307.

29. Irenaeus, *Against Heresies*, IV, 20, 1 (469). See the parallel in IV, 7, 4 (425).

30. See J. Mambrino, "Les deux mains de Dieu dans l'oeuvre de saint Irénée," *Nouvelle revue théologique* 59 (1957): 355–70. See also B. Sesboüé, *Tout récapituler dans le Christ*, ch. 8, pp. 183–99.

31. Irenaeus, *DA* 5 (91).

32. See Ysabel de Andia, *Homo vivens*, p. 67. She notes further the attribution to the Father of the "will" or "decision" to create, to the Son, the "execution" or "formation" of created things, and to the Spirit the "perfection" or "ordination" of creatures to God.

33. Irenaeus, *Against Heresies*, V, 16, 1 (617).

34. Ibid., V, 1, 3 (572).

35. Ibid., IV, 39, 2 (556). For the interpretation of Irenaeus in the context of "theological aesthetics," as distinguished from the simple "aesthetic theology," cf. Hans Urs von Balthasar, *The Glory of the Lord*, vol. 1: *Seeing the Form*, 79–117. See also my article "Hans Urs von Balthasar, lecteur d'Irénée ou la chair retrouvée," in *Nouvelle revue théologique* 115 (September-October 1993): note 5, 683–98.

36. Martin Heidegger, "The Origin of the Work of Art," in *Basic Writings*, 159.

37. Ibid. "The philosophy of this faith can of course assure us that all of God's creative activity is to be thought of as different from the action of a craftsman [*Handwerker*]."

38. See Thomas Aquinas, *Summa Contra Gentiles*, bk. 2, chap. 18, 2.

39. See Thomas Aquinas, *Summa Contra Gentiles*, Bk. 2, chap. 3, 2 and chap. 16, 7: "The divine power is the very substance of God . . . God is the act itself [*Deus autem est actus ipse*], not a being in act [*non ens actu*] by means of an act that is other than him . . . God's act is not an action which necessitates its reception in a patient: his action is his substance [*sua actio est sua substantia*]. In order to produce an effect, he does not therefore require subjacent material."

40. Heidegger, "The Origin of the Work of Art," 170–72. This perspective on creation as "work" is developed in my *Saint Bonaventure et l'entrée de Dieu en theologie*, 81–104.

41. [Reversing the order to fit with the reference above. The French has: "l'Esprit 'gouverne' . . . et que le Fils 'fait voir' en guise des deux mains du Pere." –Trans.]

42. Irenaeus, *Against Heresies*, V, 16, 1 (617). There are of course multiple references to the work of Heidegger here, attempting to reverse his philosophy against himself. What is true of the work of art is first true of the creation, establishing the Creator or artist (*artifex*) as the paradigm of all aesthetic work. For the "hand" see Didier Franck, *Heidegger et le problème de l'espace* (Paris: Minuit, 1986), ch. 8, pp. 91–103. See also Jean-François Courtine, *Heidegger et la phénoménologie* (Paris: Vrin, 1990), pp. 283–303. For the different modalities of being-in-the-world (*zuhanden, vorhanden, Da-sein*) cf. *Being and Time*, §12. For the distinction between "knowing or understanding" (*verstehen*) and "welcoming or receiving" (*lesen*) see Heidegger's "Lectures on Parmenides," in *What is Called Thinking?*, Lecture VIII, pp. 194–207. Finally, for man (or God?) as the "shepherd of being" see the famous passage in the "Letter on a Humanism," in *Basic Writings*, p. 221: "The essential grandeur of man assuredly does not rest in the fact that he is the substance of being . . . Man is the *shepherd of Being*."

43. Irenaeus, *Against Heresies*, V, 1, 1 (570).

44. Ibid., V, 15, 4 (616).

45. Ibid., V, 15, 3 (615).

46. Ibid., V, 15, 4 (616–17).

47. Respectively, ibid., II, 13, 3 (174); IV, pref. 4 (405); V, 8, 2 (588).

48. See A. Rousseau referring to Irenaeus in the first appendix to his translation of *Démonstration de la prédication apostolique*, *Sources chrétiennes*, vol. 406, pp. 358–59.

49. The formulation of "man as such" of Irenaeus can be further explored by my "man *tout court*" in both *Le passeur de Gethsémani* (Paris: Cerf, 199), 12, and *Metamorphosis of Finitude*, 55.

50. Retrieved and commented on by Irenaeus, *Against Heresies*, V, 7, 2 (586–87).

51. Saint Augustine, *The Literal Meaning of Genesis*, trans. Edmund Hill (New York: New City, 2002), L. III, 20, 30, p. 234: "after saying *to our image*, he immediately added, *and let him have authority over the fishes of the sea and the flying things of heaven* and of the other animals which lack reason, giving us to understand, evidently, that it was in the very factor in which he surpasses non-rational animate beings that man was made to God's image. That, of course, is reason itself, or mind or intelligence or whatever other word it may more suitably be named by."

52. Irenaeus, *Against Heresies*, V, 6, 1 (582).

53. Ibid., V, 9, 2 (592)—on the two component parts of a "living man" in order thereby to ground the famous *Against Heresies*, IV, 20.

54. Ibid., V, pref. (568).

55. I follow here the reading of A. Rousseau (*DA*, app. 1) explicitly taking position against Henri de Lubac, who insists too strongly on the Pauline trichotomy, thereby losing the weight of the body/soul couple yet given to the book of Genesis of body and breath: "We say bluntly on this point [of the Pauline trichotomy], the thought of Irenaeus does not appear to me to have been presented correctly by the eminent author [Henri de Lubac]" (357). See Henri de Lubac, *Theology in History* (San Francisco: Ignatius, 1996), 117–200. Should we thus say that "the gifts Christ carried to Adam" were not necessarily "in germ" in order only to take on the "work of restoration," but that they are "brought in a better way in Christ, comparatively to the original situation of Adam and then taking on a new step in the completion of man" (Fantino, *L'homme image de Dieu chez saint Irénée de Lyon* [Paris: Cerf, 1986], 165)? This is not so sure. It is certainly fitting to think a "transfiguration" (*transfiguratio*) or a "metamorphosis" of the Word and of all creation in him by the resurrection. But this more of the Spirit is not "superadded" purely and simply to the human composite. In Péguy, for example, the "insertion" of the eternal in the temporal is for the sake of a mutual taking part of the eternal and temporal. See Charles Péguy, *Victor-Marie, Comte Hugo*, in *Oeuvres en proses complètes*, 236 : "Seen from this side, the incarnation, this cardinal insertion, appears as a reception, a welcoming, even as a contemplation of the Eternal in the flesh." The rejection of the hypothesis of the "*plus ajoute*" of the Holy Spirit by virtue of the sole "profound unity that Irenaeus finds between creation and salvation" appears at the very least insufficient (Sesboüë, *Tout récapituler dans le Christ*, *op. cit.*, n. 18, p. 88). One's fidelity to de Lubac is not enough to maintain his projection of the supernatural into the Irenaean corpus, no more than the resurrection as "restoration of the lost likeness" is self-evident in the hermeneutic of the texts of the bishop of Lyon.

56. Irenaeus, *Against Heresies*, V, 8, 2 (588).

57. Ibid., V 18, 2 (623). Concerning the Spirit (*pneuma*), not as an original element of the tripartite nature of man, but as the Holy Spirit given by God, see A. Rousseau, *DA*, app. 1, p. 360: "Irenaeus understand the verse of St. Paul (1 Thess. 5:23) as relating to the gift of the Spirit to man and not an element of man as such. It would be necessary to wait until Origen (*Entretien avec Héraclide*, *Sources chrétiennes*, vol. 67, pp. 68–71) for the Spirit (*pneuma*) to be understood as an element of the human as such."

58. Irenaeus, *Against Heresies*, III, 22, 1 (383).
59. Ibid., IV, 20, 4 (471).
60. Charles Péguy, *L'argent suite*, in *Oeuvres en prose complètes*, 955.
61. Irenaeus, *Against Heresies*, V, 6, 1 (582).
62. Rousseau, *DA*, app. I, pp. 357–58.
63. Irenaeus, *Against Heresies*, V, 6, 1 (583).
64. For this doublet of icon-idol and its necessary deployment in a Dionysian (rather than Irenaean) perspective, see Jean-Luc Marion, *The Idol and Distance*, 1–8, as well as *God without Being*, 7–24.
65. Irenaeus, *Against Heresies*, IV, 6, 6 (421).
66. Ibid., IV, 6, 6 (421) and IV 6, 5 (421).
67. Sesboüé, *Tout récapituler dans le Christ*, 115.
68. Beyond this invocation of Balthasar, and such is the meaning I intend here, the French phenomenologists of our day who have worked in aesthetics have most often elected the invisibility of abstraction over the visibility of the figural: Malevich for Emmanuel Martineau, Kandinsky for Michel Henry, Rothko for Jean-Luc Marion, and so on. The properly "figural" meaning of the Incarnation of Christ in Irenaeus will thus serve to nourish the debate, less, perhaps, in order to overcome it than in order to assume a distinct position within it.
69. C. Grenier, "La revanche de l'image," *Communio* 25, no. 4 (July-August 2003): 37–53. For further illustration of this revenge of the image over the icon in contemporary art, as well as an assessment of its meaning, see Grenier's *L'art contemporain: Est-il chrétien?* (Paris: Jacqueline Chambon, 1999), 107–15. A similar reaction is found from the side of aesthetic philosophy rather than from art criticism, in G. Hébert, "Expérience picturale et phénoménologie française: La déhiscence du visible," in *Subjectivité et transcendance: Hommage à Pierre Colin*, ed. Philippe Capelle (Paris: Cerf, 2001), 189: "Does non-figurative painting bear the exorbitant privilege of being the sole place where the dehiscence of the visible can be enacted? Allow me to think that the price to pay is too steep."
70. Gilles Deleuze, *Francis Bacon: Logique de la sensation* (Paris: Seuil, 2002), 12 and 19 (see Francis Bacon's interview, *L'art de l'impossible: Entretiens avec David Sylvester*).
71. See Rousseau, *DA*, app. II, p. 365: "Image and likeness are correlative terms, to the point of being interchangeable." There is one exception: Irenaeus, *Against Heresies*, V, 6, 1.
72. I quickly draw out here the consequences of the double observation rapidly unfolded by A.-G. Hamman, *L'homme image de Dieu* (Paris: Desclée, 1987), 66–69: "For Irenaeus the image always involves the fashioned flesh, the plasma. It receives the image (*imago*) once and for all because it constitutes its very being . . . The word never designates the soul . . . The progressive assimilation to the likeness (*similitudo*) is the work of the Spirit (*pneuma*), the other hand which forms [the soul] of man (*psychê*)."
73. Irenaeus, *Against Heresies*, II, 23, 1 (220).
74. See Jean-Paul Sartre, *L'imagination* (Paris: Presses Universitaires de France, 1983), 1–4. I borrow the example of the statue in order to represent the thought of Irenaeus from Rousseau, *DA*, app. II, p. 367.
75. Irenaeus, *DA* 22 (115).

76. Irenaeus, *Against Heresies*, IV, 6, 4 (420). The formula of course approximates Heidegger's definition of the phenomenon in *Being and Time* §7: "Phenomenology means *apophainesthia ta phainomena*: disclosing starting from itself what is shown such that it is shown starting from itself."

77. Irenaeus, *Against Heresies*, IV, 17, 6 (460). For a fine analysis of this "literal" status of the image as "figurative" see J. Fantino, *L'homme image de Dieu chez saint Irénée de Lyon*, 94–95.

78. Irenaeus, *Against Heresies*, IV, 34, 1 (526).

79. Plato, *Republic*, 515b, Plato: *Complete Works*, ed. John M. Cooper and D. S. Hutchinson (Indianapolis, Ind.: Hackett, 1997), 1133: "Don't you think they'd suppose that the names they used applied to the things they see passing before them?"

80. Irenaeus, *Against Heresies*, IV, 39, 2 (556). Again, for the interpretation of Irenaeus in the context of a "theological aesthetics" in contrast to an "aesthetic theology," see Balthasar's monograph on Irenaeus in his *The Glory of the Lord*, vol. 2: *Clerical Styles*, 31–94.

81. Irenaeus, *Against Heresies*, III, 22, 3 (385).

82. I warn the visitor to Chartres, for I speak from experience: nothing that I describe here can be seen without the aid of an experienced guide, pointing it out to everyone who still cannot see it in broad daylight. In order to see it without displacing the reader from here to the cathedral, I recommend the beautiful book of A. Prache, *Chartres: Le portail de la sagesse* (Paris: Mame, 1994).

83. In contrast to Saint Irenaeus, Saint Augustine considers the sin of Adam and Eve to be found in taking "figuratively" the word of the serpent ("if you eat of it, you will surely not die"), which it was necessary to take "literally." Here sin is not only an act but also an intention, or better a manner of reading or a mode of interpretation—which is not without consequences in the context of a possible hermeneutical rereading of the meaning of the fall. See St. Augustine, *The Literal Meaning of Genesis*, bk. XI, 30, 39, pp. 451–52: "Finally not content with the serpent's words she inspected the tree herself, and saw that it was good for eating and fine to look at (Gen. 3:6), and not believing that she could die from it, she assumed, in my opinion, that God's words, *if you take a bite of it you shall die the death*, were not to be taken literally, but had some other meaning. And that is why she took some of its fruit and had a bite, and also gave it to her husband with her, maybe with a word of encouragement which Scripture does not mention, leaving it understood."

84. Irenaeus, *Against Heresies*, III, 22, 3 (385).

85. Ibid., IV, 14, 1 (446). The impossibility of comparison with Thomist and Scotist soteriology by virtue of the gap between "necessary reasons" and "the reason of fittingness" has been particularly well noted by B. Sesboüé, *Tout récapituler dans le Christ*, 146–47.

86. Ibid., IV, 14, 2 (447). I refer here of course to the phenomenological categories of Jean-Luc Marion, in order to make the figure of Adam in his flesh the "*adonné*" on which is "projected" the donation of the father. See Jean-Luc Marion, *Being Given*, §26.

87. Irenaeus, *Against Heresies*, V, 3, 2 (577).

88. Ibid., V, 14, 1 (608).

89. Ibid., IV, Praef., 4 (405).

90. Ibid., V, 16, 2 (618).

91. Saint Augustine, *Confessions*, book VIII, 12, 29, trans. Maria Boulding (Hyde Park, N.Y.: New City, 1997), 206–7: "Suddenly I heard a voice from a house nearby—perhaps a voice of a boy or girl, I do not know—singing over and over again, 'Pick it up and read, pick it up and read.' . . . Stung into action, I returned to the place where Alypius was sitting, for on leaving it I had put down there the book of the apostle's letters. I snatched it up, opened it and read in silence the passage on which my eyes first alighted: *Not in dissipation and drunkenness, nor in debauchery or lewdness, nor in arguing or jealousy; but put on the Lord Jesus Christ, and make no provision for the flesh or the gratification of your desires.*"

92. Irenaeus, *Against Heresies*, V, 6, 1 (583).

93. Ibid., III, 37, 4 (548).

94. The implicit reference to Levinas ought to be obvious where ethics defined as "metaphysics" makes the ontological structure of alterity the most basic place of its constitution. See Emmanuel Levinas, *Totality and Infinity*, 79: "The establishing of this primacy of the ethical, that is, of the relation of man to man . . . is one of the objectives of the present work. . . . *Metaphysics is enacted in ethical relations*" (emphasis added).

95. Irenaeus, *Against Heresies*, IV 37, 7 (550) and IV, 38, 1 (551), respectively.

96. See my work, *Le passeur de Gethsémani*, 47–54.

97. Irenaeus, *Against Heresies*, V, 7, 1 (586).

98. See Heidegger, *Being and Time*, §50, p. 232: "Angst about death must not be confused with fear of one's demise."

99. Irenaeus, *Against Heresies*, III, 23, 6 (391).

100. Ibid.

101. Ibid., V, 3, 2 (576–7).

102. Ibid., V, 6, 2 (585) continues: "Our bodies ought to be resurrected, not by virtue of their substance, but by the power of God."

103. Ibid.

104. Ibid., IV, 20, 2 (470). This text is heavily commented on by Balthasar and arguably constitutes the ultimate source of his "theological aesthetics." See *The Glory of the Lord*, vol. 2, *Clerical Styles*, 55–70.

105. Irenaeus, *Against Heresies*, IV, 19, 2 (476).

106. Ibid., V, 36, 3 (679).

107. See ibid., III, 19, 6 (370), for the "sign of Emmanuel," and III, 20, 1 (370–2) for the "sign of Jonah." See A. Antoine, "Le signe de Jonas: Comment dire la résurrection? Réflexion sur L'*Adversus Haereses* d'Irénée de Lyon," *Communio* 22, nos. 2–3 (March-June 1997): 165–83.

108. Saint Augustine, *Confessions*, bk. II, 4, 9, pp. 67–68. "We took enormous quantities, not to feast on ourselves but perhaps to throw to the pigs; we did eat a few, but that was not our motive: we derived pleasure from the deed simply because it was forbidden. . . . Enable my heart to tell you now what it was seeking in this action which made me bad for no reason, in which there was no motive for my malice except malice."

109. Irenaeus, *Against Heresies*, IV, 40, 3 (559).

110. Saint Augustine, *Confessions*, bk. III, 11, 20, p. 90.

Chapter 5

1. Tertullian, *La résurrection des morts* [*On the Resurrection of the Dead* (*De resurrectione carnis*)] (Paris DDB, 1980), II, 5, p. 43. [Unless otherwise specified, references are to the French editions utilized—and often modified—by the author. –Trans.] For *De resurrectione carnis* and *De carne Christi* I use the *Sources chrétiennes* edition, vol. 216 (and 217 for the notes) (Paris: Cerf, 1975).

2. J. Alexandre, *Une chair pour la gloire: L'anthropologie réaliste et mystique de Tertullien* (Paris: Beauchesne, 2001), n. 1, p. 165.

3. See respectively, Tertullian, *De resurrectione carnis*, IX, 2–3, p. 55; and Irenaeus, *Adv. Haer.* V, 6, 1 (582).

4. Tertullian, *De carne Christi*, I, p. 211.

5. Heidegger, *Being and Time*, §7, p. 24; Husserl, *Ideas I*, §132, p. 316.

6. Quintillian, *De institutione oratoria*, III, 6, 1–6; and Tertullian, *Adversus Marcionem*, bk. 1, XVII, 1; Tertullian, *Adversus Praxean* V, 1 (cited in note 12 of § 2 of *De carne Christi*, *Sources chrétiennes*, vol. II, p. 321).

7. Tertullian, *De carne Christi*, I, 2, p. 211.

8. Tertullian, *De resurrectione carnis*, II, 3, p. 43.

9. For example, see B. Sesboüé, *Jésus-Christ dans la tradition de l'Eglise* (Paris: Desclée, 1990), 73: "The arguments (of Irenaeus, Tertullian and later, of Origen) surprise us by their realism."

10. Tertullian, *Adversus Marcionem*, I, 24, 5, cited in R. Braun, *Deus christianorum: Recherches sur le vocabulaire doctrinal de Tertullien* (Paris: Etudes Augustiniennes, 1977), 301.

11. Tertullian, *De carne Christi*, XXII, 6, p. 301.

12. Ibid., XV, 2, p. 275.

13. See J.-P. Mahé's introduction to *De resurrectione carnis* (*La resurrection des morts*), trans. Madeleine Moreau (Paris: Desclée de Brouwer, 1980), 15; F.-M. Sagnard, *La gnose valentinienne et le témoignage de saint Irénée* (Paris: Vrin, 1947), II, 1, chap. 7, pp. 295–333.

14. Tertullian, *De carne Christi*, XIX, 5, p. 291.

15. Charles Péguy, *Dialogue de l'histoire et l'âme charnelle*, in *Gethsémani* (Paris: Desclée de Brouwer, 1992), 55.

16. Tertullian, *De carne Christi*, XX, 1, p. 291.

17. Ibid., XXII, 6, p. 301.

18. Ibid., XIII, 4, p. 267.

19. Ibid., X, 1, pp. 255–57.

20. Ibid., XI, 1, p. 259.

21. Ibid.

22. Maurice Merleau-Ponty, *The Visible and the Invisible* (Evanston, Ill.: Northwestern University Press, 1968), 147.

23. Tertullian, *De carne Christi*, XII, 2, p. 263.

24. Ibid., I, 3, p. 213.

25. Ibid., VI, 3, p. 235.

26. Ibid.

27. Ibid., I, 1, p. 211.

28. Ibid., V, 9, p. 231.

29. Ibid., XVIII, 7, p. 287.

30. Ibid., X, 3, p. 257.

31. Heidegger, *Being and Time*, § 53, p. 243.

32. Paul Claudel, *Sensation du divin*, in *Présence et prophétie* (Fribourg: Egloff, 1942), 55, 58.

33. Tertullian, *Adversus Praxeas* (Tertullian's *Treatise Against Praxeas*) (London: Society for Promoting Christian Knowledge, 1948), XXIX, 3, pp. 128/178. Compare with the double affirmation and distinction of the suffering of the Father and that of the Son, in Jorgen Moltmann, *The Crucified God*, 243.

34. Tertullian, *De carne Christi*, IV, 2, p. 223.

35. Ibid., IV, 3, p. 223.

36. Husserl, *Cartesian Meditations*, §44, pp. 92–99.

37. Tertullian, *De carne Christi*, IV, 3, p. 225.

38. For the conception of the "access to the world through the flesh of another" and "the interlacing of flesh" see, respectively, Franck, *Chair et corps*, 150–51; and Didier Franck, *Heidegger et le problème de l'espace* (Paris: Minuit, 1986), 97.

39. Tertullian, *De carne Christi*, VIII, 5–6, p. 251.

40. Ibid., VI, 3, p. 235.

41. Ibid., IX, 7–8, p. 255.

42. See Merleau-Ponty, *Phenomenology of Perception*, 112–70.

43. Husserl, *Cartesian Meditations*, §§44–47, pp. 92–105.

44. Charles Péguy, *Victor-Marie, Comte Hugo*, 236. For the neologism of "*encharnement*" (enfleshment), see Péguy, *Le porche du mystère de la deuxième vertu* (Paris: Gallimard, 1986), 74.

45. Tertullian, *De carne Christi*, IX, 3, p. 253.

46. Ibid., IX, 4, p. 253.

47. Husserl, *Crisis*, §28, p. 108. For the ultimate reduction to the flesh in the *Cartesian Meditations*, see the famous §44 of the fifth meditation, pp. 92–99.

48. Tertullian, *De carne Christi*, IX, 4, p. 253.

49. Tertullian, *De resurrectione carnis*, IX, 2–3, p. 55.

50. Husserl, *Ideas II*, § 36, p. 152.

51. Tertullian, *De carne Christi*, XII, 7, p. 265.

52. See B. Sesboüé, *Le Dieu du salut* (Paris: Desclée, 1994), 201.

53. Tertullian, *De carne Christi*, XIII, 4, p. 267.

54. Ibid., XII, 1, p. 261.

55. Ibid., XII, 6, p. 265.

56. See supra.

57. Tertullian, *De carne Christi*, XII, 6, p. 265.

58. Ibid.

59. It is probably in this sense that we can best understand the meaning of Jean-Luc Marion's remark where, before providing an egological interpretation of the Pauline formula, he first emphasizes that "it is appropriate to thematize . . . the life of Christ as a spiritual fact." See "A propos de *Réduction et donation*, Réponses à quelques questions," in *Revue de métaphysique et de morale* (January-March, 1991): 75.

60. Tertullian, *De carne Christi*, XII, 7, p. 265.

61. Ibid.

62. Ibid.

63. Ibid., XII, 2, p. 263.

64. Ibid., XII, 6, p. 265.
65. Ibid., XII, 3, p. 263.
66. Michel Henry, *Incarnation: Une philosophie de la chair*, §24, pp. 180–88.
67. Tertullian, *De carne Christi*, XII, 7, p. 265.
68. Ibid. It should be understood that I agree with the interpretation of Tertullian that Henry gives in *Incarnation*. If we can certainly hold that "the flesh is life auto-affected in the Son by the Father" (and here we would depend more on Irenaeus than Tertullian), the density and solidity of the flesh is such in Tertullian that it is related also to the "body" and not only to the lived experience of the flesh. One would be surprised to find Gnostic leanings in an author who relies on the most virulent of anti-Gnostic thinkers to develop his theses (see §24)! On this very point see my text, with Henry's response, "Y a-t-il une chair sans corps? Autour de l'ouvrage de M. Henry, *Incarnation*."
69. Tertullian, *De carne Christi*, XX, 1, p. 291.
70. Ibid., XX, 5, p. 293.
71. Ibid.
72. Ibid., XX, 6, p. 295. The reader would have taken note here of a Merleau-Pontian interpretation of Tertullian's description of the interlacing of flesh in the act of birth. On such intercorporeity, interlacing of flesh or the chiasm, see Maurice Merleau-Ponty, *The Visible and the Invisible*, 130–55.
73. Heidegger, *Being and Time*, § 48, p. 228.
74. Tertullian, *De carne Christi*, VI, 6, p. 237.
75. Ibid., VI, 6–7, p. 237. On the highest degree of Heideggerian certitude of the "*sum moribundus*" relative to the Cartesian "*cogito ergo sum*," see Martin Heidegger, *History of the Concept of Time: Prolegomena*, trans. Theodore Kisiel (Bloomington: Indiana University Press, 1985), §34, pp. 312–13.
76. Tertullian, *De carne Christi*, VI, 5, p. 237.
77. Edmund Husserl, *Husserliana*, vol. 14, p. 77 (quoted in Franck, *Chair et corps*, 98, n. 25). On the usage of this collection of concepts in Husserl, see Natalie Depraz's establishment of a terminological development in *Transcendance et incarnation: Le statut de l'intersubjectivité comme altérité à soi chez Husserl* (Paris: Vrin, 1995), 344–45.
78. Tertullian, *De carne Christi*, VI, 6, p. 237.
79. On the "disincarnated" meaning, at least in part, of the anguish of death in Heidegger (especially in *Being and Time*), see Didier Franck, *Heidegger et le problème de l'espace*, chap. V, pp. 65–80, esp. 76–78.
80. Tertullian, *De carne Christi*, XII, 5, p. 263.
81. Tertullian, *De resurrectione carnis*, XVIII, 9 and 11, pp. 69–70.
82. Tertullian, *De carne Christi*, V, 1, p. 227.
83. Ibid., V, 5, p. 229.
84. Ibid.
85. On the meaning and deformation of the "*credo quia ineptum*" into the "*credo quia absurdum*," see J.-P. Mahé, *De carne Christi*, vol. 2, *Sources chrétiennes*, vol. 217, p. 339.
86. On this point, particularly the distinction between anguish of sin and anguish of finitude, see my work, *Le passeur de Gethsémani, Angoisse, souffrance et mort*, 23–46 and 47–54.
87. Tertullian, *De carne Christi*, V, 1, p. 227.

88. Hans Urs von Balthasar, *The Glory of the Lord*, vol. 7: *The New Testament*, trans. Brian McNeil (San Francisco: Ignatius, 1989), 142.

89. Husserl, *Cartesian Meditations*, §16, pp. 38–39. This statement is the leitmotif of this second part of the present volume, concerned with the flesh, announced above, at the opening of the chapter on Irenaeus.

90. See Martin Heidegger, "Letter on Humanism," in *Basic Writings*, 230.

91. Tertullian, *De resurrectione carnis*, VIII, 2, p. 54.

92. Karl Barth, *Evangelical Theology: An Introduction* (Grand Rapids, Mich: Eerdmans, 1979).

93. Merleau-Ponty, *The Visible and the Invisible*, 147.

Chapter 6

1. On this point see my work, *Saint Bonaventure et l'entrée de Dieu en théologie: La Somme théologique de Breviloquium (prologue et première partie)* (Paris: Vrin, 2000). The present study, centered on the question of the flesh (*Breviloquium* IV, on the incarnation, and V, on grace) will therefore bring to completion my first essay, based principally on God's entrance into theology as Trinity (*Breviloquium* I). The doctrine of the conversion of the senses, following upon the Trinitarian a priori, constitute, as I see it, the second part of Bonaventure's great originality beyond his contemporaries (and Aquinas in particular!). Concerning the purely thematic filiation of Bonaventure from the first church fathers and Irenaeus in particular, see J. Plagnieux, "Aux sources de la doctrine bonaventurienne sur l'état originel de l'homme: Influence de saint Augustin ou de saint Irénée," in *S. Bonaventura, 1274–1974* (Rome: Collegio S. Bonaventura, 1974), vol. 4, pp. 311–28.

2. Hans Urs von Balthasar, *The Glory of the Lord*, vol. 1: *Seeing the Form*, 367–68.

3. Paul Claudel, *Sensation du divin*, in *Présence et prophétie*.

4. Bonaventure, *Sermon on the Nativity* 2, in *Opera Omnia* (Quaracchi, 1882–1902), vol. 9, p. 106.

5. Kant, *Critique of Pure Reason* (1781), p. 93 (B75, A51).

6. Rupert of Deutz, *De vita vere apostolica*, IV, 4, and IV, 6 (cited in M.-D. Chenu, *Introduction a l'étude de saint Thomas d'Aquin* [Paris: Vrin, 1950], 39).

7. Saint Francis of Assisi, *Sacrum commercium*, in T. Desbonnets and D. Vorreux, *Documents, écrits et premières biographies* (Éd. franciscaines, 1968), 1309.

8. Bonaventure, *Life of Saint Francis* (*Legenda maior*) III, 1 (Paris: Éd. franciscaines, 1968), 38.

9. Ibid.

10. Merleau-Ponty, *The Visible and Invisible*, 147.

11. Bonaventure, *Life of Saint Francis* III, 3, p. 39.

12. Ibid., II, 4, pp. 32–3.

13. Levinas, *Totality and Infinity*, p. 78.

14. Bonaventure, *Life of St. Francis* II, 4, p. 33.

15. See A. Lacau St. Guily, *Grünewald: Le retable d'Issenheim* (Tournai: Mame, 1996), 119: "This outrageous brutality by which torture and death are represented, this fascination with the decomposition of the body, tied to the dread of sin and the drama of fear, *antagonizes sensibility*, electrifies ordinary devotion

which gives pleasure to this *"physical" approach to the final drama of the Incarnation*, for which the *Crucifixion* of Issenheim is an intolerable and distressing vision" (emphasis added).

16. Scheler, *The Nature of Sympathy*, 89.

17. Saint Francis, *Canticle of Brother Son*, *Francis and Clare: The Complete Works* (Mahwah, N.J.: Paulist, 1982), 37.

18. Bonaventure, *Life of St. Francis* VIII, 6, p. 92.

19. Plato, *Timaeus*, 51a, *Plato: Complete Works*, 1255.

20. Gilbert Keith Chesterton, *Saint Francis of Assisi* (Peabody, Mass.: Hendrickson, 2008), 68.

21. Bonaventure, I *Sent.*, d. 34, a. 1, q. 4, concl. (I 594 a). Regarding this passage, see my work, *Saint Bonaventure et l'entrée de Dieu en théologie*, 71–75 (for the break with Denys), and 165–84 (for the usage of metaphor).

22. Saint Francis, *Canticle*, 37.

23. Bonaventure, *Les six jours de la creation* [*The Six Days of Creation*] (Paris: Cerf, 1991), XIII, 12, pp. 307–8. See my *Saint Bonaventure et l'entrée de Dieu en théologie*, 179.

24. Respectively, Saint Bonaventure, *Breviloquium* II, 4 (Paris: Éd. franciscaines, 1968), 75; and Edmund Husserl, "The Original Ark, the Earth, Does Not Move (Manuscript D 17)," in *Husserl: Shorter Works*, ed. Peter McCormick and Frederick A. Elliston (South Bend, Ind.: Notre Dame University Press, 1981), 222–23. See in particular 230: "Every being in general only has being-sense by virtue of my constitutive genesis and this has an 'earthly' precedence."

25. Maurice Merleau-Ponty, *L'oeil et l'esprit* (Paris: Gallimard, 1964), respectively, 9 (on science's renunciation of dwelling in things), 16 (on the "transubstantiation" of painting and painter), and 31 (on the inversion of vision).

26. Paul Ricoeur, "The Hermeneutical Function of Distanciation," in *Hermeneutics and the Human Sciences*, trans. John B. Thompson (Cambridge, Eng.: Cambridge University Press, 1981), 112.

27. Jean-René Bouchet, *Saint Dominique* (Paris: Cerf, 1988), 78–79.

28. G. Bedouelle, *Saint Dominique ou la grâce de la parole* (Paris: Fayard-Mame, 1982), 117–25 and 264, from the liturgy of Saint Dominic: "Light of the Church, Doctor of truth, model of patience and purity, give us in abundance this wisdom that you have so generously distributed—you, the Preacher of grace."

29. Letter of approval of the order in 1215 by Bishop Folques of Toulouse, in M. H. Vicaire, *Saint Dominique: La vie apostolique* (Paris: Cerf, 1965), 151–52.

30. Jordan of Saxony, *Libellus de principiis ordinis praedicatorum*, translated into French by M. H. Vicaire, in *Saint Dominique et ses frères: Évangile ou croisade?* (Paris: Cerf, 1967), §10, pp. 53–54.

31. Bedouelle, *Saint Dominique ou la grâce de la parole*, 170.

32. Jordan of Saxony, *Libellus*, §15, p. 56.

33. Thomas Aquinas, *Summa Theologiae*, IIa–IIae, q. 188, art. 4, resp.

34. Paul Ricoeur, "Philosophical and Biblical Hermeneutics," in *From Text to Action: Essays in Hermeneutics II*, trans. Kathleen Blamey and John B. Thompson (Evanston, Ill.: Northwestern University Press, 1991), 95.

35. Thomas Aquinas, *Summa Theologiae* IIa–IIae q. 187, a. 3 resp.

36. Ibid., IIa–IIae q. 181, a. 3, resp.

37. Ibid., IIa–IIae q. 188, a. 6, resp.

38. Paul Ricoeur, "Preface to Bultmann," in *Essays on Biblical Interpretation*, ed. Lewis Seymour Mudge (Minneapolis, Minn.: Fortress, 1980), 68.

39. These well-known categories of *énoncé* and *énonciation* inherited from Ferdinand Saussure can be found in Émile Benveniste, *Problèmes de linguistique générale* (Paris: Gallimard, 1974), vol. 2, pp. 215–29.

40. Bonaventure, *Breviloquium*, II, 11, p. 118. The references to the books of scripture and the world are drawn from Hugh of Saint Victor, *De sacramentis* I, 6, 5, and will be completed in his sermon *Unus est magister noster Christus*, translated into French as *Le Christ maître* (Paris: Vrin, 1990), §14, p. 45: "These two modes of contemplation and intelligence (the interior sense in the contemplation of divinity and the exterior sense in the contemplation of humanity) are also signified by the interior and exterior readings of the book which is written inside and outside [*per lectionem interiorem et exteriorem libri scripti intus et foris*] and about which it is said in the Apocalypse: 'I see in the right hand of the one seated on the throne a book written inside and outside [*librum scriptum intus et foris*] and sealed with seven seals' (Rev. 5:1)."

41. Hans Urs von Balthasar, *The Glory of the Lord*, vol. 2: *Clerical Styles*, 263.

42. Maurice Merleau-Ponty, *Signes* (Paris: Gallimard, 1960), 88.

43. Bonaventure, *Itinerarium mentis in Deum* [*Journey of the Mind to God*] I, 7, p. 35. Page numbers of the *Itinerarium* are to the Vrin French edition, *Itinéraire de l'esprit vers Dieu* (Paris: Vrin, 1960).

44. E. Ortigues, *Le discours et le symbole* (Paris: Aubier, 1962), 65.

45. Bonaventure, *Itenerarium*, I, 9, p. 35 (V, 298).

46. Trophime Mouiren, in Saint Bonaventure, *Breviloquium* II, *Le monde créature de Dieu* (Paris: Éd. franciscaines), "Introduction," p. 26.

47. Denys the Areopagite, *Mystical Theology* III, 1033B, in Pseudo-Dionysius, *The Complete Works*, 139.

48. Bonaventure, *Itinerarium*, I, 5, p. 31.

49. Ibid., I, 13–14, p. 39: "The sensible world elevates us to the consideration of God in his power, wisdom and goodness . . . This consideration can also extend to the (seven) modes of being of creatures [*conditionem creaturarum*] which thus render a (sevenfold) testimony [*testimonium*] to the power of God, his wisdom and goodness."

50. See, respectively, Saint Augustine, *De Trinitate* XI, I, 1; and Saint Bonaventure, II *Sententiae* 16, 1, 2, fund. 4 (Quaracchi, vol. II, p. 397). On this break between Augustine and Bonaventure, see Etienne Gilson, *The Philosophy of St. Bonaventure*, trans. Dom Illtyd Trethowan and Frank J. Sheed (New York: St. Anthony's Guild, 1965), chap. 7, pp. 184–85.

51. Augustine, *Confessions* VII, IX, 14, p. 170.

52. Hans Urs von Balthasar, *The Glory of the Lord*, vol. 2, *Clerical Styles*, p. 261. For the Trinitarian view of the world and the creative Trinity, see my work, *Saint Bonaventure et l'entrée de Dieu en théologie*, §11, pp. 150–64.

53. Maurice Blanchot, "The Secret of the Golem," in *The Book to Come*, trans. Charlotte Mandell (Stanford, Calif.: Stanford University Press, 2003), 86–91. Without citing Maurice Blanchot, one can find a *philosophical* critique of the reduction of the symbol to the sole "sign of recognition" in A. Séguy-Duclot, "Qu'est-ce qu'un symbole," *Philosophie* 57 (1998): 79–92, as well as a *theological* critique in R. Scholtus, "Sacrement, symbole, événement," *Études* 3774 (1992): 389–96. As

for the development, however classical, of sacramental theology, under the single auspice of "recognition," see L.-M. Chauvet, *Symbol and Sacrament*, trans. Patrick Madigan and Madeleine Beaumont (Collegeville, Minn.: Pueblo, 1995), 111–28.

54. Bonaventure, *Itinerarium*, I, 4, p. 31. For Duméry, see n. 1, p. 33.

55. Hugh of Saint Victor, *De diebus triebus*, *Patrologia Latina*, 176, 814 B.

56. Bonaventure, *Hexaemeron* XIII, 12 (Quarrachi V, 390), pp. 307–8 [page numbers are to the French edition, *Les six jours de la création* (Paris: Desclée, 1991)]. The link between hermeneutics and descriptive phenomenology needs to be deepened in a study (presently in course) centered on the status of the book in Hugh of Saint-Victor.

57. Falque, *Saint Bonaventure et l'entrée de Dieu en théologie*, §12, pp. 163–83.

58. Bonaventure, *Unus est magister noster Christus*, *Le Christ maître* (Paris: Vrin, 1990), §14, p. 45.

59. Bonaventure, *Breviloquium* V (Paris: Éd. franciscaines, 1968), V, 6 (Quarrachi V, 260), pp. 74–75.

60. Ibid.: "This contemplation exists in the prophets by a triple revelation, corporeal, imaginative and intellectual; in other righteous people it begins in speculation which commences in the senses and comes to the imagination, passing from the imagination to reason, reason to the understanding, and the understanding to the intellect, intellect to wisdom or knowledge by excess [*ad sapientiam sive notitiam excessivam*] which commences in this life and is realized in eternal glory."

61. Bonaventure, *Life of Saint Francis*, p. 30 (Quaracchi VIII, 508).

62. Bonaventure, *Breviloquium* V, 6, pp. 74–75.

63. Balthasar, *The Glory of the Lord*, vol. 2, *Clerical Styles*, 323.

64. Bonaventure, *De reductione artium ad theologiam*, II, 10 (Quaracchi V, 322); *Les six lumières de la connaissance humaine* (Paris: Éd. franciscaines, 1971), 68–69.

65. Bonaventure, *Itinerarium*, IV, 3, p. 75.

66. Bonaventure, *De reductione*, II, 9, p. 67: "Each sense, in fact, exercises its activity on a proper object, and avoids what is harmful and does not appropriate what is foreign; thus [*per hoc modum*] the sense of the heart leads a well-regulated life when it acts in relation to its proper object in such a way as to avoid negligence, etc."

67. Ibid.

68. Bonaventure, referring to Aristotle, *Breviloquium* II, 11, p. 117: "There has been given to man a twofold sense [*duplex sensus*], interior and exterior, pertaining to spirit [*mentis*] and flesh [*carnis*]." See Aristotle, *De anima*, III, 3, 429 a: "We define imagination [*phantasia*] as a movement engendered by sensation in act."

69. Bonaventure, resp. *Itinerarium*, II, 2, and II, 1, p. 45.

70. Balthasar, *The Glory of the Lord*, vol. 2: *Clerical Styles*, 321.

71. Balthasar, *The Glory of the Lord*, vol. 1: *Seeing the Form*, 423.

72. Bonaventure, *Breviloquium* V, VI, 6, pp. 73–75.

73. Karl Rahner, "The Doctrine of the Spiritual Senses in the Middle Ages," in *Theological Investigations*, vol. 16, trans. David Morland (New York: Seabury, 1979), 104–34.

74. Balthasar, *The Glory of the Lord*, vol. 1: *Seeing the Form*, 424 (emphasis added).

75. For the use of these concepts, see, of course, Emmanuel Levinas, *Totality and Infinity*, 33–35.

76. Bonaventure, *Soliliquium* VIII, 33–35, in Valentin-Marie Breton, *Saint Bonaventure* (Paris: Aubier, 1943), §3, 12–18, 288–92.

77. Bonaventure, *Breviloquium* V, I, 3, p. 31.

78. Balthasar, *The Glory of the Lord*, vol. 2: *Clerical Styles*, 325.

79. Ibid., vol. 1: *Seeing the Form*, 425.

80. I evoke here Stanislas Breton, *Deux mystiques de l'excès: J.-J. Surin et Maître Eckhart* (Paris: Cerf, 1985), chap. 3, pp. 167–91. On this point see my contribution, "De la préposition à la proposition: Mystique et philosophie chez Stanislas Breton," *Transversalites* 99 (2006): 17–36.

81. Bonaventure, *Itinerarium*, I, 3, p. 29, and I, 9, p. 35. On the meaning of this passage in Bonaventure, see A. Menard, "Le *transitus* dans l'oeuvre de saint Bonaventure, un itinéraire de conversion biblique et de conformation progressive au Christ pascal," *Laurentianum* 41, no. 3 (2000): 379–412.

82. Bonaventure, *Itinerarium*, p. 47.

83. See Plato, *Theatetus*, 194 b-195 b; Aristotle, *De Anima* II, 12, 424 a, 17–25.

84. Bonaventure, *De perfectione vitae ad sorores*, in Valentin Marie Breton, *Saint Bonaventure* (Paris: Aubier, 1943), 196–97.

85. Bonaventure, *De Hexaemeron*, I, 19, p. 112: "The center of the macrocosm is the sun; the center of the microcosm is the heart."

86. Ibid., I, 11, p. 106.

87. Bonaventure, *Vitis mystica*, III, 5 (Quaracchi VIII, 164). Translated in Balthasar, *The Glory of the Lord*, vol. 2: *Clerical Styles*, 333.

88. Merleau-Ponty, *The Visible and the Invisible*, 140.

89. Marc Richier, "Communauté, société et histoire," in Maurice Merleau-Ponty, *Phénoménologie et expérience*, ed. Marc Richier and Etienne Tassin (Grenoble, Fr.: Millon, 1992), 8.

90. Merleau-Ponty, *The Visible and the Invisible*, 144. Concerning the imperative of description in order to return to the "things themselves," see Merleau-Ponty's *Phenomenology of Perception*, ix: Phenomenology "is a matter of *describing*, not of explaining or analyzing. Husserl's first directive to phenomenology, in its early stages, to be a '*descriptive psychology*' or to '*return to the things themselves*,' is from the start a forswear of science."

91. On this complex enigma of the fourth term that I cannot develop here, see Maurice Merleau-Ponty, "The Philosopher and His Shadow," in *Signs*, 168; Merleau-Ponty, *The Visible and the Invisible*, 79.

92. Bonaventure, *Vitis mystica*, III, 5 (Quaracchi, VIII, 164).

93. Bonaventure, *Breviloquium* V, 6, p. 75.

94. Balthasar, *The Glory of the Lord*, vol. 2: *Clerical Styles*, 317.

95. Bonaventure, "De Triplica Via," III, 3 (Quaracchi, VIII, 14), trans. in Breton, *Saint Bonaventure*, 139.

96. Balthasar, *The Glory of the Lord*, vol. 1: *Seeing the Form*, 319.

97. See L. Belos, *Giotto à Assise* (Assise: Casa Editrice Francescana, 1989), 6: "The twenty-eight histories (painted by Giotto around 1270) are drawn from the *Legenda maior* of St. Bonaventure as the sole 'orthodox' narration of the life of the saint." For the stigmata scene see pp. 66–67.

98. Bonaventure, *Itinerarium mentis in Deum*, prologue, 2–3, pp. 21–23.

99. See Rémi Brague, "Un modèle médiéval de la subjectivité: La chair," in *Ibn Rochd, Maïmonide, Saint Thomas d'Aquin, Colloque de Cordoue, 8–10 mai 1992*, 36–62, esp. 42–45.
100. Balthasar, *The Glory of the Lord*, vol. 2: *Clerical Styles*, 273 (emphasis added).
101. Bonaventure, "De perfectione vitae ad sorores," VI, 11, trans. in Breton, *Saint Bonaventure*, 203.
102. Bonaventure, *Hexaemeron*, XXII, 23, p. 479.
103. Bonaventure, II *Sententiae* 1, II, 3, 2; translated in Balthasar, *The Glory of the Lord*, vol. 2: *Clerical Styles*, 315–16.
104. Bonaventure, *Breviloquium* VII, p. 93 and p. 113.
105. Friedrich Nietzsche, *Human, All Too Human: A Book for Free Spirits*, trans. R. J. Hollingdale (Cambridge, Eng.: Cambridge University Press, 1998), §98, p. 334.
106. Balthasar, *The Glory of the Lord*, vol. 2: *Clerical Styles*, 315.
107. Bonaventure, *Sermones de tempore*, Serm. II, pars 2, p. 107 (Quaracchi, IX, 106–10). An exemplary French translation of this sermon, moreover, for the question of the flesh that preoccupies us here, can be found in *Études franciscaines* 27 (1977): 84–90 (quotation from 86).
108. Bonaventure, *Sermones de tempore* 2, p. 88.
109. Ibid.
110. Ibid., p. 87.
111. Bonaventure, *De reductione*, §26, p. 85.
112. Bonaventure, *Itinerarium*, I, 15, p. 43.

Introduction to Part Three

1. F. Laupies, *Leçon philosophique sur autrui* (Paris: Presses Universitaires de France, 1999), 3: "Reflection on the other is late: *ancient and medieval thought ignore this question*." Yet the author exhibits some appropriate reserve: "In this context, patristic and medieval authors can be of great assistance: the fact of not having thought the question of otherness as such does not prevent, despite everything, *a real sensibility for relation to the other*" (7; emphasis added).
2. Saint Augustine, *Confessions* X, 27, 38, p. 262.
3. Richard of Saint Victor, *La Trinité* (*De Trinitate*), in *Sources chrétiennes*, vol. 63 (Paris: Cerf, 1958), Bk. III, c. 19, 927b, p. 209. On this see my "La condilection ou le Tiers de l'amour [Richard de Saint-Victor]" in *Archivo de Filosofia*, Actes du colloque Enrico Castelli, January, 2006.
4. Husserl, *Cartesian Meditations*, 147 (citation from Augustine, *De vera religione* 39, 72).

Chapter 7

1. Henri Crouzel, *Origène* (Paris: Lethielleux, 1984), 318.
2. Paul Ricoeur, *À l'école de la phénoménologie* (Paris: Vrin, 1993), 217; and Husserl, *Cartesian Meditations*, §56, pp. 128–31.
3. Origen, *Homélies sur le Lévitique* VII, 2, in *Sources chrétiennes* vol. 286, (Paris: Cerf, 1981), 317.
4. We in fact have to wait until the end of the fourth century for the insertion of the formula, "*credo in communionem sanctorum*" to be attested to in the

Apostles Creed (though never in the Nicene-Constantinopolitan Creed). Such a formula is in any case cited by Nicetas of Remesiana in his *Commentary on the Symbol* at the dawn of the fifth century, and repeated by Faustus of Riez (d. 485) and Caesarius of Arles (d. 542). For a historical investigation of this question see E. Lamirande, *La communion des saints* (Paris: Fayard, 1962), 11–20. For its theological meaning see Karl Barth, *Church Dogmatics* IV/2 (London: Continuum, 2004), 614–726, as well as P.-Y. Emery, *L'unite des croyants au ciel et sur la terre* (Taizé: Presses de Taizé, 1962), especially chap. 4, pp. 73–84.

5. Edmund Husserl, *Philosophie première* (1923–1924) (Paris: Presses Universitaires de France, 1972), vol. 2, lesson 53, p. 175.

6. "L'expérience du propre est le propre de l'expérience." A formula of Didier Franck, commenting on §44 of the *Cartesian Meditations*. See his *Chair et corps*, 92–93.

7. Origen, *Homélies sur Ézéchiel*, VI, 6, in *Sources chrétiennes* vol. 352 (Paris: Cerf, 1989), 229.

8. Ibid.

9. M. Fédou, *La sagesse et le monde: Christologie d'Origène* (Paris: Desclée, 1995), 325.

10. Heidegger, *Being and Time*, §29, pp. 126–31.

11. Origen, *Homélies sur Ézéchiel* VI, 6, p. 229.

12. Ibid., p. 231. See in particular Moltmann's interpretation of this formula in *The Crucified God*, 228. See also F. Varillon, *La souffrance de Dieu* (Paris: Centurion, 1975), 46–50.

13. Origen, *Homélies sur Ézéchiel*, VI, 6, p. 229.

14. M. Fédou, *La sagesse et le monde*, 327.

15. Emmanuel Levinas, "Useless Suffering," in *Entre Nous* (London: Continuum, 2006), 80. I have attempted to push to its limits the hypothesis of divine passivity in my *Le passeur de Gethsémani, Angoisse, souffrance et mort*, chap. 9, pp. 123–39.

16. The insistence on the pathos of the cross in the Origenist perspective ought not to lead us to forget the pathos of joy that is common to the Father and Son: "Imagine God's joy when the impure becomes chaste, when the unjust practices justice, when the impious becomes religious! The conversion of every man is cause for great feasting in God" (Origen, *Homélie sur les nombres*, XXIII, 2, in *Sources chrétiennes*, vol. 29 [Paris: Cerf, 1953], 426).

17. Origen, *Homélies sur Ézéchiel*, VI, 6, p. 231.

18. See Husserl, *Cartesian Meditations*, §§50–55, pp. 108–28.

19. Ibid., §49, p. 107.

20. Origen, *Homélies sur Ézéchiel*, VI, 6, pp. 229–31.

21. Origen, *Commentaire sur l'évangile selon Mathieu*, X, 23, in *Sources chrétiennes* vol. 162, (Paris: Cerf, 1970), 259.

22. According to the translation of *agapê* (*o theos agapê estin*) by *caritas* (*Deus caritas est*) in the Vulgate.

23. Husserl, *Cartesian Meditations*, §49, p. 107.

24. Origen, *Homélies sur Ézéchiel*, VI, 6, p. 231.

25. Origen, *Homélies sur Lévitique*, VII, 2, pp. 309–23.

26. William of Saint-Thierry, *Première vie de saint Bernard*, in *Oeuvres complètes de saint Bernard* (Vivès, 1873), vol. 8, XII, 59, pp. 40–41.

27. Here I reproduce in modified form a passage from my article, "Expérience et empathie chez Bernard de Clairvaux," *Revue des sciences philosophiques et théologiques* (October-December 2005): 655–96.

28. Bernard of Clairvaux, *Traité de l'amour de Dieu* (*De Diligendo Deo*), in *Sources chrétiennes*, vol. 393 (Paris: Cerf, 1993), 129.

29. Ibid.

30. Ibid., p. 131.

31. See Meister Eckhart, *On Detachment*, 49–52: "Detachment [*Abgeschiedenheit*] is being deprived of all creatures . . . It is so close to nothing that between perfect detachment and nothing there is nothing between them."

32. Étienne Gilson, *La théologie mystique de saint Bernard* (Paris: Vrin, 1947), 151. The famous exegete adds, as if highlighting the break with Eckhart: "Every difficulty that one believes to be found in the texts of St. Bernard on this point are reduced to a *misinterpretation*, because the soul which is *loosened* and *detached* from itself, *even to the point of renouncing what it is*, on the contrary is established in its proper substance as the divine love *changes* it" (emphasis added).

33. See my work, *Metamorphosis of Finitude*, chap. 5, 62–80. The meaning of the resurrection as transformation is well articulated by G. de Stexhe in his exegesis of the same passage from Bernard, "Entre le piège et l'abime," in *Qu'est-ce que Dieu: Hommage à l'abbé Daniel Coppieters de Gibson (1929–1983)* (Brussels: Facultés Universitaires de Saint-Louis, 1985), 415–54, esp. 445–49: "Eschatology does not mean the abolition of the body, but its transfiguring resurrection . . . It is only by being fully assumed in its *finite* and therefore bodily condition that man can approach the glory that is promised him in the fourth degree of love. What is called glory here is the full integration of the body in the very dynamism of the will released from all possessive fixation on the self" (emphasis in original).

34. Bernard of Clairvaux, *De Diligendo Deo*, 133.

35. On the philosophical debate concerning "affective fusion" in T. Lipps, see Max Scheler, *The Nature of Sympathy*, 18–36. One can also read with profit on this topic Edith Stein's dissertation, *Zum Problem der Einfühlung*.

36. Bernard of Clairvaux, *De Diligendo Deo*, 133. By contrast to the *Sources chrétiennes* translation, I translate "*substantia*" as human nature (*nature humaine*) and not "substance" (*substance*) in order to avoid a too substantialist and metaphysical reading of Bernard.

37. Ibid., p. 131.

38. Scheler, *The Nature of Sympathy*, 15.

39. *De Diligendo Deo*, 133. On this play of "affection" and "deification" see the pertinent analyses of Jean Leclercq to which I am indebted here, *Maurice Blondel lecteur de Bernard de Clairvaux* (Brussels: Lessius, 2001), 83–93 and especially 84–85. For the theme of the "transfer of fluxes" in Husserl, a central aspect of human intersubjectivity, and—I suggest—mystical empathy, see Edmund Husserl, *Zür Phänomenologie de Intersubjektivität*, in *Husserliana* 15 (1929–35), § 43. This passage has been commented on by Natalie Depraz, *Transcendance et incarnation: Le statut de l'intersubjectivité comme altérité à soi chez Husserl* (Paris: Vrin, 1995), §20, pp. 251–59.

40. If Bernard had in his hands Origen's *Commentary on the Canticle* at least during his encounter with William of Saint-Thierry in the infirmary of Clairvaux,

there is no proof that he had access to the *Homilies on Ezekiel*, in any case less available in the medieval world. See J.-P. Bouhot, "La bibliothèque de Clairvaux," in *Oeuvres complètes de saint Bernard de Clairvaux*, in *Sources chrétiennes*, vol. 380 (Paris: Cerf, 1992), 141–53. See also P. Verdeyen's note, "Une théologie de l'expérience," in *Sources chrétiennes*, vol. 380, 564–72.

41. Bernard of Clairvaux, *Sermons sur le canticle*, in *Sources chrétiennes*, vol. 431 (Paris: Cerf, 1978), 289.

42. Such is a misguided objection often addressed to medieval philosophy. As an example, see Hans Jonas, *Le concept de Dieu après Auschwitz* (Paris: Rivages poche, 1994), 27–28: "We are not in a position to maintain the traditional (medieval) doctrine of an absolute divine power without limit." On this point see my response in *Le passeur de Gethsémani*, 87–95.

43. Bernard of Clairvaux, *De la considération* (*De consideratione*) (Paris: Louis Vivès, 1866), vol. 2, V, VII, 17, p. 179.

44. E. Housset, *L'intelligence de la pitié: Phénoménologie de la communauté* (Paris: Cerf, 2003), 153. Despite his compelling analysis, it is surprising that he makes no mention of Bernard of Clairvaux, who is probably even more apt to sustain this thesis than Origen or William of Saint-Thierry, both of whom he cites. See my work, *Metamorphosis of Finitude*, §17, pp. 67–75, where Bernard serves as a corrective to Origen on this point.

45. Bernard of Clairvaux, *Sermons sur le Canticle*, 281.

46. Ibid., 283.

47. I return to this theme in *Le passeur de Gethsémani*, part 3.

48. Bernard of Clairvaux, *Sermons sur le Canticle*, 289. On the conversion of the *affectus* in the *affectio* operated by the resurrection as "transformation," see *Metamorphosis of Finitude*, part 2.

49. Origen, *Homélies sur Lévitique*, 191. For further elucidation of this interpretation of the hemorrhaging woman, see my *Le passeur de Gethsémani*, 147–53. This interpretation of Origen himself was absent from that book, though its solely phenomenological reading of the story accords completely with and is confirmed by our study here of Origen.

50. Origen, *Homélies sur Lévitique*, 191.

51. Ibid.

52. Merleau-Ponty, *The Visible and the Invisible*, 141.

53. Husserl, *Cartesian Meditations*, §50, p. 111.

54. Origen, *Homélies sur Lévitique*, 191.

55. I make, of course, an implicit reference here to the famous "touching-touched" experience developed by Husserl in *Ideas II* § 36 and Merleau-Ponty in a number of places, for example, *Phenomenology of Perception*, 368, *Signs*, 168, and *The Visible and Invisible*, 133.

56. Origen, *Homélies sur Lévitique*, 81. A detailed analysis of these modes of "*toucher origenien*" can be found in F. Bertrand, *Mystique de Jesus chez Origene* (Paris: Aubier, 1951), 49–142: (1) searching for Jesus, (2) approaching Jesus, (3) welcoming Jesus, (4) following Jesus, (5) contact with the Savior. A phenomenological reading of these diverse modes of divine-human touching is yet to be done.

57. The French neologism forged by Péguy ("*encharnement*") has no English equivalent. See his *Le porche du mystère de la deuxième vertu*, 74.

58. Origen, *Homélies sur Lévitique*, 151.

59. Fedou, *La sagesse et la monde*, 416. "The doctrine of the 'preexistence of souls' ought to be understood as the 'unique exception' to all the false condemnations of Origen's teaching." Let me express my debt to this work. Renewing and structuring the interpretation of Origen, it has served as the "touchstone" for a localization and development of crucial points of his thought.

60. Merleau-Ponty, *The Visible and the Invisible*, 147. "We must not think the flesh starting from substances, from body and spirit—for then it would be the union of contradictories—but we must think it, as we said, as the concrete emblem of a general manner of being."

61. Origen, *Against Celsus*, in *Sources chrétiennes* vol. 138 (Paris: Cerf, 1967), 207.

62. Origen, *Homélies sur Lévitique*, 151.

63. On the impossible division of terrestrial and celestial worlds, drawn precisely from Origen himself, see again my *Metamorphosis of Finitude*, chap. 7, pp. 95–111.

64. Henri de Lubac, *History and Spirit* (San Francisco: Ignatius, 2007), 385–426.

65. Origen, *Homélies sur Lévitique*, 67.

66. Ibid.

67. Jean-Luc Nancy, *La communauté désœuvrée* (Paris: Christian Bourgeois Éditeurs, 1986), 202.

68. "The most touching pages in the *Homilies on Leviticus*." M. Borret, "Introduction aux homélies sur le Lévitique d'Origène," in Origen, *Homélies sur Lévitique*, 32.

69. Paul Ricoeur, *A l'école de la phénoménologie*, 216–17.

70. Origen, *Homélies sur Lévitique*, 309.

71. Blaise Pascal, *Pensées*, n. 266 [B. 553/L. 919], ed. Léon Brunschvicg (Paris: Garnier-Flammarion, 1976), 198: "Jésus sera en agonie jusqu'à la fin du monde: il ne faut pas dormir pendant ce temps-là." For the meaning of "common texture" in the constitution of a visible unity of bodies and the world, see Merleau-Ponty, *The Visible and Invisible*, 142.

72. Henri de Lubac, *Catholicism: Christ and the Common Destiny of Man* (1938; San Francisco: Ignatius, 1988), 127.

73. Origen, *Homélies sur Lévitique*, 317.

74. Ibid., resp. pp. 313 and 317.

75. Origen, *Homilies on Jeremiah*, XIV, 7, in *Sources chrétiennes*, vol. 238 (Paris: Cerf, 1977), 81.

76. Fedou, *La sagesse et le monde*, 354.

77. Barth, *Church Dogmatics* IV/2: *The Doctrine of Reconciliation* (London: Continuum, 2004), 17–18.

78. See respectively Husserl, *Cartesian Mediations*, §56, pp. 128–31; and Ricoeur, *À l'école de la phénoménologie*, 217.

79. Ricoeur, *À l'école de la phénomenologie*, 217.

80. Origen, *Homélies sur Lévitique*, 315.

81. Ibid.

82. For the etymology of *communio sanctorum* as *com-munis* and not *cum-unio*, see J.-M. R. Tillard, "Communion," in *Dictionnaire critique de théologie*, ed. Jean-Yves Lacoste (Paris: Presses Universitaires de France, 1998), 236.

83. Levinas, *Totality and Infinity*, 215.

84. Dietrich Bonhoeffer, *Life Together* (New York: HarperCollins, 1954), 35. "In the spiritual community there exists no direct relation among those who share in it . . . Christ stands between me and others."

85. Maurice Merleau-Ponty, "Dialogue and the Perception of the Other," in *The Prose of the World*, trans. John O'Neil (Evanston, Ill.: Northwestern University Press, 1973), chap. 5, pp. 131–145. See esp. 185–86. On the impossibility of the repetition of the Levinasian perspective in Christianity, see my *Le passeur de Gethsémani*, 167–69, as well as the accurate remarks of Jean-Luc Marion's essay in homage to Levinas, "The Intentionality of Love," in *Prolegomena to Charity*, trans. Stephen E. Lewis (New York: Fordham University Press, 2002), 91–120, esp. 113–20.

86. Origen, *Homélies sur Hom. Lev.*, p. 315. An interpretation of 1 Cor. 15:23–8.

87. Cited by Origen, *ibid.*

88. On this point see the illuminating reflections of H. Crouzel, *Origène*, pp. 331–41, esp. 332.

89. Origen, *Homélies sur Lévitique*, 321.

90. Husserl, *Cartesian Meditations*, §51, pp. 112–13.

91. Ibid., §16, pp. 38–39.

92. Origen, *Homélies sur Lévitique*, 321–23.

93. Husserl, *Cartesian Meditations*, §42, pp. 89–90.

94. Husserl, *Logical Investigations*, 111; and Husserl, *Ideas I*, 362.

95. See Jean-Louis Chrétien, "Le langage des anges selon la scholastique," in *La voix nue* (Paris: Minuit, 1990), 81–98.

Chapter 8

1. Thomas Aquinas, *Summa theologiae*, Ia, q. 75, a. 7, resp. and ad. 2.

2. Ibid., Ia., q. 51, a. 2, ad. 1.

3. Ibid., resp.

4. Ibid., Ia., q. 113, a. 4, resp.

5. Emmanuel Levinas, *Difficult Freedom*, trans. Sean Hand (Baltimore, Md.: Johns Hopkins University Press, 1990), 89.

6. Wim Wenders, *Les ailes du désir* (*Wings of Desire*) (Paris: Flammarion, 1987), 23.

7. Thomas Aquinas, *Summa theologiae*, Ia, q. 63, a. 2, resp.

8. Wenders, *Wings of Desire*, 23.

9. Rainer-Maria Rilke, *Duino Elegies*, second and fifth elegy (passages cited and commented on by J.-F. Angelloz, *Rilke* [Paris: Mercure, 1952], 314).

10. Rudolph Bultmann, *New Testament and Mythology and Other Basic Writings*, trans. Schubert M. Ogden (Minneapolis, Minn.: Fortress, 1984), 4.

11. Christian Ducoq, "Satan, symbole ou réalité?" *Lumière et vie* 78 (May-August 1966): 105.

12. Henri Corbin, "L'evangile de Barnabe," *La foi prophétique et le sacre*: *Cahiers de l'Universite Saint-Jean de Jerusalem* 3 (1977). See 170–72 in particular for the accusations waged against Saint Paul and the doctrine of consubsantiality. See also Corbin's "Necessite de l'angelologie," *L'ange et l'homme*: *Cahiers de l'hermetisme* 3 (Paris: Albin Michel, 1978), 44: "Perhaps there is a correlation between the fact

that Islamic theosophy has always refused the idea of *homoousios* of Nicaean Christology, and the fact that [Islamic theosophy] has so well assured, both ontologically and gnoseologically, the world of the Angel and of angelophanies."

13. See René Descartes, *Conversation with Burman*, trans. John Cottingham (New York: Clarendon, 1976), 18.

14. Ibid.

15. Thomas Aquinas, *Summa theologiae*, Ia, q. 56, a. 1, resp.

16. Ibid., Ia, q. 58, a. 6, resp. See Augustine, *The Literal Meaning of Genesis*, IV, 29, 46, *On Genesis*, trans. Edmund Hill, O. P. and John Rotelle (Hyde Park, N.Y.: New City, 2002), 268–69.

17. Thomas Aquinas, *Summa theologiae*, Ia, q. 58, a. 7, resp.

18. Ibid., Ia, q. 50, a. 4.

19. René Descartes, *Rules for the Direction of Our Native Intelligence* (*Regulae ad directionem ingenii*), in *Descartes: Selected Philosophical Writings*, trans. John Cottingham et al. (Cambridge, Eng.: Cambridge University Press, 1988), 4. This is repeated in the second *Meditation* (*Meditations on First Philosophy*, trans. Donald A. Cress [Indianapolis, Ind.: Hackett, 1993], 64): "I know with evidence that there is nothing easier for me to know than my mind."

20. The perpetuation of such an ideal of the transparency of angelology in phenomenology is moreover also noted by Jean-Louis Chrétien, for whom the decline of angelic language remains the vanishing point and the criterion that "human language does not cease to have as a horizon." See Chrétien, *La voix nue*, 98.

21. Husserl, *Cartesian Meditations*, §42, p. 89.

22. For this debate see Thomas Aquinas, *De veritate*, q. 8, a. 7 (as well as the explanatory note on the opuscule on the angels of the *Somme théologique*, Éditions des jeunes [Paris: Cerf, 1963], n. 48, p. 399).

23. Thomas Aquinas, *Summa theologiae*, Ia, q. 56, a. 2.

24. Ibid., Ia, q. 56, a. 2, resp.

25. Ibid., Ia, q. 56, a. 2, ad. 3.

26. Ibid., Ia, q. 56, a. 2, resp.

27. Ibid., Ia, q. 56, a. 2, ad. 3.

28. Ibid.

29. Ibid., Ia, q. 56, a. 2, ad. 2.

30. Ibid., Ia, q. 56, a. 2, a. 3, resp.

31. Ibid., Ia, q. 56, a. 2, ad. 2.

32. Husserl, *Cartesian Meditations*, §50, p. 111. It is Paul Ricoeur who first exchanges "la chair autre" (other flesh) for "autre organisme" (other organism) in his *À l'école de la phenomenology*, 207.

33. Henry Denzinger, *The Sources of Catholic Dogma* (Fitzwilliam, N.H.: Loreto, 2002), Lateran IV, number 428.

34. Thomas Aquinas, *Summa theologiae*, Ia, q. 51, a. 2, resp.

35. Ibid.

36. Tertullian, *De carne Christi*, VI, 5, in *Sources chrétiennes*, vol. 216, pp. 235–36.

37. Origen, *Peri Archôn*, Praef. 8, in *Sources chrétiennes*, vol. 252, p. 87.

38. Ibid., I, 6, 4, p. 207.

39. Saint Augustine, Sermon 362, para. 17, in *Patrologia Latina*, vol. 39, ed. J.-P. Migne (Paris: Apud Garnier fratres, 1865), 1622.

40. Franck, *Chair et corps*.

41. Saint Augustine, *De Trinitate*, III, 1, 5, pp. 129–30.

42. Husserl, *Logical Investigations*, vol. 2, Inv. 6, app. §5, p. 341: "One will call 'phenomena' all the lived experiences in the unity of the lived experience of an I: *phenomenology* signifies then the theory of lived experiences in general."

43. Ibid.

44. Husserl, *Cartesian Meditations*, §44, p. 93.

45. Supra.

46. Thomas Aquinas, *Summa theologiae*, Ia, q. 51, a. 2, ad. 1.

47. Descartes, *Conversation with Burman*, 19.

48. Husserl, *Cartesian Meditations*, §44, pp. 96–97.

49. Wenders, *Les ailes du désir*, 25.

50. Pierre Boutang, preface to J.-M. Vernier, *Les anges chez Thomas d'Aquin*, vol. 3 (Paris: Nouvelles Éditions Latines, 1986), 14.

51. Thomas Aquinas, *Summa theologiae*, Ia, q. 57, a. 2, obj. 2.

52. Husserl, *Cartesian Meditations*, §§53–55, pp. 116–28.

53. See Jean-Louis Chrétien, "Le langage des anges selon la scolastique," in *La voix nue*, 81–98: "Before being considered to be something much more perfect in the angel than in man, language is like a perfection that it would be necessary also to attribute to the angel" (87).

54. Thomas Aquinas, *Summa theologiae*, Ia, q. 53, a. 1, resp.

55. Ibid.

56. Ibid., Ia, q. 113, a. 4, resp.

57. Ibid., Ia, q. 113, a. 6, resp.

58. See Thomas Aquinas, *De Veritate*, q. 8, a. 2.

59. Thomas Aquinas, *Summa theologiae*, Ia, q. 57, a. 2, resp.

60. Ibid.

61. Ibid.

62. This hypothesis of an angelic accompaniment to the kenotic movement of the Word, though not Thomist, is developed by Hans Urs von Balthasar, *Theo-Drama*, vol. 3: *Persons in Christ*, trans. Graham Harrison (San Francisco: Ignatius, 1992), chap. 4, pp. 465–504.

63. Thomas Aquinas, *Summa theologiae*, Ia, q. 57, a. 2, ad. 3.

64. Husserl, *Cartesian Meditations*, §50, pp. 108–12.

65. Ibid., §50, p. 111.

66. Ibid., §55, p. 124.

67. Ibid., §55, p. 125.

68. Ibid., §55, p. 121.

69. Balthasar, *Theo-Drama*, vol. 3: *Persons in Christ*, 490.

70. Kant, *Critique of Pure Reason*, 47.

Chapter 9

1. Etienne Gilson, *Jean Duns Scot: Introduction à ses positions fondamentales* (Paris: Vrin, 1952), 446.

2. Levinas, *Totality and Infinity*, 298–99.

3. Marion, *Prolegomena to Charity*, 93 (emphasis in original). Marion returns to this theme of haecceity developed in the context of alterity in *Being Given*, 258 and 324. See also Emmanuel Levinas, *Positivité et transcendence, suivi de "Levinas et la phenomenologie,"* ed. Jean-Luc Marion (Paris: Presses Universitaires de France, 2000), 301–4.

4. Text of Plato commented on by Heidegger in *What Is a Thing?* trans. W. B. Barton Jr. and Vera Detsch (South Bend, Ind.: Gateway Editions, 1967), 3.

5. Ibid., 1–5.

6. Ibid., 9.

7. Martin Heidegger, *Traité des catégories et de la signification chez Duns Scot* (1916; Paris: Gallimard, 1970), 78–79.

8. Martin Heidegger, "The Thing," in *Poetry, Language, Thought*, trans. Albert Hofstadter (New York: Harper Collins, 1971), 169.

9. Jean-Yves Lacoste, *Experience and the Absolute*, trans. Mark Raftery-Skehan (New York: Fordham University Press, 2004), 105.

10. Independently of every suspicion of atheism in Duns Scotus, we can note that the Subtle Doctor was probably the first to promote in the history of philosophy, if not the nonexistence of God, at least a God who is not first lovable by virtue of his existence. See Olivier Boulnois, "Si Dieu n'existait pas, faudrait-il l'inventer? Situation métaphysique de l'éthique scotiste," *Philosophie* 61 (March 1999): 50–74. He quotes Scotus on 56: "If, impossibly, another God was posed, who had not created us, and who ought not to be glorified by us, he would still be, in an absolute manner, sovereignly lovable by us" (Duns Scotus, *Reportata pariensa*, III, d. 27, q. un., n. 6). It should be noted, however, that it is less a question of the "nonexistence of God," whom it would be necessary to invent—despite the force of the hypothesis, pp. 55–56—than it is of the existence "of another God" (*alius Deus*), neither creator, nor glorifier, nor lovable by us. Perhaps it is therefore too much to affirm that "the hypothesis of a nonexistent God can be found rooted in Duns Scotus at the beginning of the fourteenth century." At best he is posed as "another existent" or rather another essence—these are always identified in Scotus.

11. Gilles Deleuze, *Difference and Repetition*, trans. Paul Patton (London: Athlone), 35.

12. For the translation and explication of univocity as "destruction" or rather "superposition" of Thomist analogy, let the reader consult Olivier Boulnois's introduction to, translation of, and commentary on Duns Scotus, *Sur la connaissance de Dieu et l'univocité de l'étant* (Paris: Presses Universitaires de France, 1988).

13. Duns Scotus, *Ordinatio*, I, d. 3, q. 2, §26. For the works of Duns Scotus, I use both the *Ordinatio* (vols. I–VII) and *Lectura* (vols. XVI–XIX) of the Vatican Balic edition (1950). For the *Reportata pariensa*, I use the Éditions Vivès, vols. XXIII–XXIV (as well as vol. XV for Book III of the *Ordinatio*). I have also referenced the *Tractatus de Primo Principio*, ed. E. Roche (New York: Louvain, 1949).

14. Duns Scotus, *Ordinatio*, I, d. 3, q. 2, §27, p. 94 [unless otherwise noted, page numbers are to the French edition of Scotus's *Ordinatio* in Boulnois, *Sur la connaissance de Dieu et l'univocité d'étant*–Trans.].

15. Here I resume, with some modification and accommodation, the suggestive but very precise exposé of Jean-Luc Marion, "Une époque de la métaphysique," in *Jean Duns Scot ou la révolution subtile*, ed. Ch. Goémé (Paris: FAC Éditions,

1982), 87–95. See also Olivier Boulnois's introduction to Scotus's *Sur la connaissance* for a thorough examination.

16. Duns Scotus, *Ordinatio*, prol., part 1, §1. I modify here G. Sondag's French translation of the prologue of the *Ordinatio* (*Jean Duns Scot, prologue de l'Ordinatio* [Paris: Presses Universitaires de France, 1999], 35), for his translation of *ens inquantum ens* as "being as being" [*être en tant qu'être*] completely loses Scotus's break of usage with Aristotle and Aquinas.

17. Duns Scotus, *Ordinatio*, IV, d. 13, q. 1 (cited and commented on by Marion, *Révolution subtile*, 89).

18. Ibid., I, d. 3, p. 1, q. 3, §185, p. 160.

19. Ibid., II, d. 3, q. 1, §38. I follow here Gilson's translation in *Jean Duns Scot*, 449, rather than Sondag's in *Le principe d'individuation* (Paris: Vrin, 1992), 103, inasmuch as the former shows more clearly haecceity's act of standing out from the community that founds it.

20. On this point see J.-M. Counet, "L'univocité d l'étant et la problématique de l'infini chez Jean Duns Scotus," in *Actualité de la pensée médiévale*, ed. J. Follon and J. McEvoy (Louvain: Ed. Peeters, 1994), 287–328—a judicious rapprochement between Scotus and the meaning of appearing in Sartre.

21. Duns Scotus, *Reportatus pariensa*, IV, d. 1, q. 1, n. 7 (Vivès, vol. XXIII, p. 535).

22. Duns Scotus, *Ordinatio*, prologue, n. 12, Sondag, *Prologue*, p. 43.

23. See Duns Scotus, *Ordinatio*, I, d. 3, p. 3, q. 4. Here he comments on Saint Augustine: "The mind is the image in the most perfect way, and completely when these acts of knowledge bring about in him the knowledge of God taken as object, for then the soul is an expressive similitude of the Trinity."

24. Hannah Arendt, *The Life of the Mind* (San Diego, Calif.: Harcourt, 1978), 134. See in particular her chapter on "Duns Scotus and the Primacy of the Will," which elucidates in a new, or rather modern way, the difficult arguments of the Subtle Doctor.

25. Duns Scotus, *Ordinatio*, prologue n. 32, p. 59.

26. Olivier Boulnois, *Duns Scot: La rigueur de la charité* (Paris: Cerf, 1998), 39.

27. Duns Scotus, *Ordinatio*, I, d. 2, q. 1, p. II (ed. Vivès, vol. VIII, 393b–486a).

28. Duns Scotus, *Ordinatio*, prologue, n. 12, p. 43. For the determination of finitude as such, independently of the linking of finite and infinite, see Martin Heidegger, *Kant and the Problem of Metaphysics*, trans. Richard Taft, 5th ed. (Bloomington: Indiana University Press, 1997), § 39, pp. 146–50. For the possible theological opening starting precisely from this conception of finitude, see my *Le passeur de Gethsémani*, 17–64.

29. Marion, "Une époque de la métaphysique," 95.

30. Duns Scotus, cited and commented on by Hannah Arendt, *The Life of the Mind*, 134–35.

31. See P. Aubenque, *La prudence chez Aristote* (Paris: Presses Universitaires de France, 1963), 65: "The theory of prudence is therefore attached to a cosmology, and more profoundly, to an ontology of contingency."

32. Duns Scotus, *Lectura*, prologue, n. 111, p. 187. [Unless otherwise specified, page numbers of the *Lectura* are to Sondag's French translation, *La théologie comme science pratique* (Paris: Vrin, 1996), p. 187. –Trans.]

33. Duns Scotus, *Lectura*, prologue, n. 172, p. 209: "It is contingent that a rock falls, and yet there exist some necessary truths in regard to its act of falling, for example, that it tends toward the center of the earth and makes a straight line. In a parallel way, the love of God is contingent, and yet there are necessary truths involved, for example, I ought to love God above all things."

34. Husserl, *Ideas I*, §2, p. 7; Marion, *Being Given*, 132–34. It is regrettable that Marion has not made profit of Husserl's mention of "individual being" in relation to contingency in order to tie them together in haecceity. This Duns Scotus does magnificently here.

35. Duns Scotus, *Reportata pariensa*, 3, d. 7, q. 4, n. 4 (L. Veuthey, *Jean Duns Scot: Pensée théologique* [Paris: Éd. Franciscaines, 1967], 83).

36. Duns Scotus, *Reportata pariensa*, 3, d. 7, q. 4, n. 5.

37. Duns Scotus, quoted by Hannah Arendt, *The Life of the Mind*, 134.

38. Duns Scotus, *Ordinatio*, II, d. 3, p. 1, n. 1, translated by Sondag, *Le principe d'individuation*, 87. In this third distinction, two parts are distinguished: the *De principio individuationis* (*pars prima*) and the *De cognitione angelorum* (*pars secunda*). The problem of individuation is posed within a theological context for Scotus, despite its pertinence to philosophy as such. One must not forget this as we proceed, for in doing so one would risk reducing individuation to a purely logical principle.

39. Duns Scotus, *Ordinatio*, I, d. 3, n. 50, p. 258.

40. Aristotle, *Metaphysics*, 1040a 1–2, in *The Complete Works of Aristotle*, vol. 2, ed. Jonathan Barnes (Princeton, N.J.: Princeton University Press, 1984), 1641. "Clearly there can neither be definition or demonstration of sensible individuals." On the relation of Aristotle to individuation, I refer the reader to the profitable article of B. Pinchard, "Le principe d'individuation dans la tradition aristotélicienne," in *Le problème de l'individuation*., ed. P.-N. Mayaud (Paris: Vrin, 1991), 27–50, and esp. 37–45 for the Scholastic repetition of Aristotelian questions.

41. Aristotle, *Categories*, chap. 5, 2a 10–18, in *The Complete Works of Aristotle*, vol. 1, ed. Jonathan Barnes (Princeton, N.J.: Princeton University Press, 1984), 4: "A *substance*—that which is called a substance most strictly, primarily and most of all—is that which is neither said of a subject nor in a subject, e.g., the individual man or the individual horse. The species in which the things primarily called substances are, are called *secondary substances* . . . both man and animal."

42. Duns Scotus, *Ordinatio*, I, d. 3, n. 66, p. 115.

43. Ibid., II, d. 3, q. 1, n. 42. Here I follow Gilson's exceptional translation of this passage in *Jean Duns Scot*, 452.

44. Beyond the famous chapter of Gilson on haecceity in *Jean Duns Scot*, 444–46, I direct the reader to Olivier Boulnois's profitable article, which, depending on Gilson, elaborates more precisely the historical positions: "Genèse de la théorie scotiste de l'individuation," in Mayaud, *Le problème de l'individuation*, 51–77, esp. 55–66.

45. Duns Scotus, *Ordinatio*, II, d. 3, p. 1, n. 30. I follow here Sondag's translation in *Le principe d'individuation*, p. 98. See also his brilliant introduction which leads instructively into some difficult questions.

46. Gilson, *Jean Duns Scot*, 453.

47. Duns Scotus, *Ordinatio* I, 3, n. 10, p. 85.

48. Ibid., II, d. 3, p. 1, q. 6, n. 142. See the pertinent comments in Gilson, *Jean Duns Scot*, 460; and Boulnois, "Genèse de la théorie scotiste de l'individuation," 66.

49. For a pedagogical application of the principle of individuation to the determination and distinction of Socrates and Plato, see G. Sondag, *Le principe d'individuation*, 71–72 and n. 2, p. 99.

50. J. Tricot in a note to his French translation of the *Metaphysics* of Aristotle (Paris: Vrin, 1981), bk. Zeta, 8, n. 2, p. 393: "The doctrine of individuation by form . . . will come to rejoin, in the history of thought, the theory of haecceity (*haecceitas*) by which Duns Scotus, in reaction to Thomism, sought to recognize in the individual an intelligibility analogous to that of the species. To him *Socratesness* appeared to contain as much reality as *Humanity*, inasmuch as it is the ultimate actuality of the form."

51. Gilson, *Jean Duns Scot*, 464. One will move Scotist haecceity closer to what is found in Aristotle, book Lambda of the *Metaphysics*, if, changing the question of the constitution of individuation (matter-form), one accepts the deictic—"your" matter, "your" form—the very principle of singularization: "And those of things in the same species are different, not species, but in the sense that the causes of different individuals are different, your matter and form and moving cause being different from mine, while in their universal formula they are the same" (Aristotle, *Metaphysics*, bk. Lambda, 5, 1071a 27–9, p. 1692).

52. Duns Scotus, *Ordinatio*, II, 3, p. 1, q. 2, n. 57, p. 112. Regarding the case of the rock, not only as paradigm of haecceity (*hic*) but of the production and comprehension of essences by God, the reader should consult the two famous exposés of the Subtle Doctor: *Ordinatio*, I, d. 35, q. un., n. 32, and *Lectura*, I, d. 26, q. un., n. 23–7.

53. Duns Scotus, *Ordinatio* II, d. 3, q. 6, n. 164, p. 164.

54. Ibid.

55. Duns Scotus, *Treatise on First Principles*, I, 1, trans. R. Imbach et al.; *Traité de premier principe*, in *Cahiers de la revue de philosophie et théologie* 10 (Paris: Vrin, 1983): 43.

56. For the interpretation of Scotus in light of the Thomist "metaphysics of Exodus," see Etienne Gilson, *The Spirit of Medieval Philosophy*, trans. A. H. C. Downs (Notre Dame, Ind.: University of Notre Dame Press, 1991), 52–54 for the definition of Christian philosophy as the "metaphysics of exodus." For the interpretation of the name of God revealed to Moses as ontotheology, see P. Vignaux, "Mystique, scolastique et exégèse," *Dieu et l'être: Exégèses d'Exode 3, 14 et de Coran 20, 11–24* (Paris: Centre d'Études de Religions du Livre, Études Augustiniennes, 1978), 208: "it does not appear possible to formulate any better the project of an ontotheology starting from revelation." See also Vignaux's study further centered on a reading of the *Ordinatio*, "Métaphysique de l'Exode et univocité de l'être chez Jean Duns Scot," *Celui qui est: Interprétations juives et chrétiennes d'Exode 3, 14.*, ed. Alain de Libera and E. Zum Brunn (Paris: Cerf, 1986), 103–26.

57. The "hic" of the haecceity of God is of course absent from the Latin, but at least contained conceptually in the "*qui*" of the formula *ego sum qui sum*.

58. Duns Scotus, *Ordinatio*, prologue, n. 170, p. 225.

59. Aristotle, *Metaphysics*, bk. Lambda, 7, 1072b 24–5. See p. 1695 "If therefore this state of joy that we possess only fleetingly, God possesses constantly, it is

admirable, and if he has it to a greater degree, this is even more admirable." See B. Pinchard's commentary, "Le principe d'individuation dans la tradition aristotélicienne," in Mayaud, *Le problème de l'individuation*, 34: "This does not mean that God has this joy because he is *less composite* and *less material* than we are, but because he is *more individual*" (emphasis added).

60. One can find a sketch of this new Scotist interpretation of Exodus 3:14 by the motif of singularity, as opposed to the community of being, in J.-M. Counet, "L'univocité de l'étant et la problématique de l'infini chez Jean Duns Scot," in Follon and McEvoy, *Actualité de la pensée médiévale*, 323: "As a response Moses receives the manifestation of God as *absolute singularity*, as the *pure singularity* of which the redundant, and thereby virtually superfluous, side is rightly the very condition of the gratuity of presence and therefore equally the condition of the possibility of the freedom of those who are called to be situated in relation to it."

61. The formula is attributed to Duns Scotus and developed by Hannah Arendt, *The Life of the Mind*, 104 and 144.

62. Marion, *God without Being*, 102.

63. Jer. 1:5: "Before I fashioned *you* in the womb I knew you; before *you* were born I set you apart; I am making *you* a prophet to the nations."

64. Duns Scotus, *Reportatus pariensa*, III, d. 27, q. un; ed. Vivès, XXIII, 481. Cited and commented on by Camille Bérubé, *L'amour de Dieu selon Jean Duns Scot, Porète, Eckhart, Benoît de Candfield et les capucins* (Rome: Instituto storico dei cappuccini, 2001), 194.

65. Bérubé, *L'amour de Dieu selon Jean Duns Scot*, 161 and 195 (emphasis added). See also from the same text the profitable studies consecrated to "L'amour de Dieu selon Jean Duns Scot," 145–203, and particularly the debate with Veuthey, "Amour métaphysique et infini selon Léon Veuthey," 195–98.

66. Duns Scotus, *Reportatus pariensa*, III, d. 27, q. un. Cited and commented on by Bérubé, *L'amour de Dieu selon Duns Scot*, 194.

67. Duns Scotus, *Ordinatio*, III, d. 28, q. un, n. 2. Ed. Vivès, XV, 379a. Cited and translated by Veuthey, *Duns Scot: Pensée théologique*, 147.

68. Duns Scotus, *Ordinatio*, III, d. 27, q. un. Ed. Vivès XV 379b. Compare Veuthey, *Duns Scot: Pensée theologique*, 147.

69. Duns Scotus, *Ordinatio*, III, d. 27, q. un, n. 2. Ed. Vivès XV 356a ; Veuthey, *Duns Scot: Pensée theologique*, 146.

70. Duns Scotus, *Ordinatio*, III, d. 32, q. un, n. 6. See C. Balic's article "Duns Scotus," *Dictionnaire de spiritualité* (Paris: Beauchesne, 1957), vol. 3, col. 1801–18 (citation found col. 1806). For the expression "love-donation" when speaking of charity, see Veuthey, *Duns Scot: Pensée theologique*, 146. For the Franciscan determination of God as self-donation to the point of complete abandonment (the gift of the gift), see my *Saint Bonaventure et l'entrée de Dieu en théologie*, 141–45.

71. On the meaning of *condilectio*, see Richard of Saint Victor, *De Trinitate*: *Sources chrétiennes* 63 (Paris: Cerf, 1958), book 3, c. 19, 927b, p. 209; as well as my article "Dieu charité," *Communio* (September-December 2005): 75–87.

72. Duns Scotus, *Ordinatio*, II, d. 3, p. 1, q. 7, n. 251, p. 204.

73. This line is opened by Etienne Gilson and repeated by the majority of commentators after him. His brilliant chapter on haecceity in *Jean Duns Scot* (444–66) remains centered on the question of individuation by matter or form,

without establishing any link with the problem of the intellection of angels that he previously examined (422–31).

74. Duns Scotus, *Ordination*, II, d. 3, q. 6, n. 15. See on this point Gilson's commentary in *Jean Duns Scot*, 464.

75. Gilson, *Jean Duns Scot*, 577. Such a love does not seem to be rooted explicitly in its theological topos for Gilson, as I just mentioned in a preceding note.

76. P. Doyles, "Scot et la tradition franciscaine," in Goémé, *Duns Scot ou la révolution subtile*, 44.

77. Edgard de Bruyne, *Etudes d'esthétique médiévale* (Bruges: De Tempel, 1946), vol. 3, pp. 347–70.

78. Duns Scotus, *Ordinatio*, prologue, n. 170, p. 225.

79. For the distinction between *theologia tradita* and *theologa divina*, see the prologue of the *Ordinatio*, n. 151 and n. 168 (and commentary, p. 178). For the difference between "the essence as this one [*ut haec*]" and "this essence" (*haec essentia*), see n. 170 (and accompanying commentary, pp. 177–81).

80. [Falque uses Marion's neologism *invisable* here, which comes from the French verb *viser*, "to aim at" and which signifies "that which cannot be aimed at or taken within the scope of vision." See Marion, *God without Being*, 13–14. –Trans.]

81. Gilson, commenting on Scotus repeating Aristotle: *Jean Duns Scot*, 466.

82. E. Bettoni, *Duns Scoto filosofo* (Milan: Vita e Penserio, 1966), 122. See also the rigorous discussion of the author with L. Veuthey in E. Bettoni, "The Originality of the Scotistic Synthesis," in *John Duns Scotus, 1265–1965*, ed. J.-K. Ryan and B.-M. Bonansea, Studies in Philosophy and the History of Philosophy, vol. 3 (1965), 28–44.

83. Duns Scotus, *Quaest. Subt.*, q. 15, n. 6, p. 438. Cited by Camille Bérubé, *La connaissance de l'individuel au Moyen Age* (Montreal, 1964), 158.

84. Duns Scotus, *Reportatus pariensa*, II, d. 3, §14 (XXII, 595a).

85. Duns Scotus, *Ordinatio*, III, d. 14, n. 5, p. 529.

86. Duns Scotus, *Reportatus pariensa*, II, d. 3, §15 (XXII, 595b). See Ricoeur, *Oneself as Another*, esp. the second study, on the interpretation of the Aristotelian phantasm (*De anima*, III, 3, 428a) in terms of alterity or "apperceptive transposition" (*sicut alia*), which is appropriate for Duns Scotus here.

87. Olivier Boulnois, *Être et representation: Une généalogie de la métaphysique moderne à l'époque de Duns Scot* (Paris: Presses Universitaires de France, 1999), 177. On this triple distinction of the knowledge of God, self, and the other in Scotus, see the illuminating pages of this work (174–88).

88. Bérubé, *L'amour de Dieu*, 173–74.

89. William of Ockham, *I Sententiae*, d. 3, q. 1 and q. 5. Cited by Bérubé, *L'amour de Dieu*, 268. On this break, specifically as it concerns the status of singulars and the genealogy of the problematic itself, see the suggestive essay by P. Vignaux, "Jean Duns Scot, Guillaume d'Occam," *Philosophie au Moyen Âge: Lire Duns Scot aujourd'hui* (Albeuve, Switz.: Castella, 1987), 180–209.

90. On the break between Scotus and Ockham, see the magisterial pages in P. Alféri, *Guillaume d'Ockham: Le singulier* (Paris: Minuit, 1989), §9, pp. 74–88 (citation 82).

91. Merleau-Ponty, *The Visible and the Invisible*, 77 (emphasis added).

92. Pascal, *Pensées*, L. 678/B. 358.

93. Gerard Manley Hopkins, *Journal* (entry for August 3, 1872), in *Poems and Prose*, ed. W. H. Gardner (New York: Penguin Classics, 1985), 126 (emphasis added). See the introduction to the French version of Hopkins, *De l'origine de la beauté suivi de Poèmes et d'Écrits*, trans. René Gallet and J.-P. Augier (Seyssel: Éd. Comp'Act, 1989), 8: "'Inscape' or 'nature' leads 'to the heart of the metaphysics of the singular.'" The commentator, Rene Gallot, says, a couple of pages later: "In Hopkins's work on beauty, the lights come to us, the vibration or the clashes of this encounter between *human finitude* and an *infinite singular*" (10). The encounter between Scotus, as we have portrayed him, and his poetic quasi-translation as it is given in Hopkins, cannot be said any better, perhaps, than that.

94. Hopkins, "Pied Beauty" (1877), in *Poems and Prose*, 30–31. There is of course the poem "Duns Scotus' Oxford" (1879), but there is nothing that speaks better this *haecceitas* that this experience of praise to the Father for "pied beauty" and "dappled things." Another vantage, no less magisterial, is found with Christ as the center (and no longer the Father considered as source) in the poem, "As kingfishers catch fire, dragonflies draw flame": "As kingfishers catch fire, dragonflies draw flame / As tumbled over rim in roundy wells / Stones ring; like each tucked string tells, each hung bell's / Bow swung finds tongue to fling out broad its name . . . for Christ plays in ten thousand places / Lovely in limbs, and lovely in eyes not his / To the Father through the features of men's faces" (in *Poems and Prose*, 51). See the beautiful commentary on these poems of René Gallet, *G.-M. Hopkins ou l'excès de la présence* (Paris: Fac. Editions, 1984), 82–85 (on "Pied Beauty") and 100–101 (for "As kingfishers . . ."). On the relation to the singular as such in Hopkins, see also Gallet's "G.-M. Hopkins: L'intensité singulière" in *Po&sie* 32 (1984): 99–109, and esp. 99–100, for the distinction between "inscape" and "instress" which I cannot address here. Finally, because the rapprochement with Hopkins is imposed by the subject of the haecceity of the other, see the superb article by Jérôme de Gramont, "Nature, monde, création," *Cahiers Diderot* 4 (1991): 99–122, esp. 116–19, for a commentary on the poems cited above. I thank these two interpreters of Hopkins, not only for their friendship, but also for their works, which lead me progressively from the haecceity of Scotus to the *inscape* and *instress* of Hopkins.

Conclusion

1. Husserl, *Logical Investigations*, vol. 1 [II/1], p. 168: "We absolutely do not want to be content with 'simple words,' a symbolic comprehension of words . . . We must go back to the things themselves. We desire to render self-evident in fully fledged intuitions that what is given here in a present abstraction is truly and really what the significations of words mean in the expression of the law."

2. See respectively Heidegger, *Being and Time*, §7, p. 30, and Heidegger, *History of the Concept of Time: Prolegomena*, §8, pp. 75–79. Concerning the relation of these two formulas, see Jean-Luc Marion, *Reduction and Givenness*, 7–49. Concerning the sliding from Husserl to Heidegger, see Jean-François Courtine, "Phénoménologie et science de l'être," in *Heidegger et la phénoménologie* (Paris: Vrin, 1990), 189; and Jerome de Gramont, *L'entrée en philosophie: Les premiers mots* (Paris: L'Harmattan, 1999), 114.

3. On the meaning of this descending movement of the *Breviloquium* in relation to the ascending climb of the *Itinerarium*, see my work *Saint Bonaventure et*

l'entrée de Dieu en théologie, 24–27. Concerning the preference for the heuristic path, at least for the finitude of modern man, see my justification in *Metamorphosis of Finitude*, §3, pp. 6–9.

4. I make implicit reference here to Henri de Lubac's *Théologies d'occasion* (*Theological Fragments*, trans. Rebecca Howell Balinski [San Francisco: Ignatius, 1989]), although in a completely different sense because for him the "*théologies d'occasion*" do not involve at all a servitude of theology to some philosophy.

5. Husserl, *The Crisis of European Sciences and Transcendental Phenomenology*, §7, p. 17: "We have also become aware in the most general way that human philosophizing and its results in the whole of man's existence mean anything but merely private or otherwise limited cultural goals. Therefore—how can we avoid it?—we are *functionaries of mankind*. The quite personal responsibility of our own true being as philosophers, our inner personal vocation, bears within itself at the same time the responsibility for the true being of mankind."

6. See my essay "Tuilage et conversion de la philosophie par la théologie," in E. Falque and A. Zielinski, *Philosophie et théologie en dialogue, 1996–2006* (Paris: L'Harmattan), 45–56, esp. 55; as well as my article "Philosophie et théologie: Nouvelles frontières," *Etudes* (February 2006): 201–10.

7. See Didier Franck, *Dramatique des phénomènes* (Paris: Presses Universitaires de France, 2001), 5: "Phenomenology, which was yesterday a conversion, an adventure, a new freedom of the gaze, is nothing today but a constituted object simply transmitted, and is henceforth only the amnesiac tradition of an object. Barely have we come to grasp the audacity of the reduction, and there conceals a phenomenology become document and monument, a phenomenology deserted or merely visited."

8. William of Auxerre, *Summa aurea*, vol. 4, chap. 4. See O. Boulnois, ed., *La puissance et son ombre: De Pierre Lombard à Luther* (Paris: Aubier, 1994), 131–39.

9. Bernard of Clairvaux, *Sermons sur le Cantique*, vol. I, in *Sources chrétiennes*, vol. 414 (Paris: Cerf, 1996), Serm. 3, 1, p. 101.

10. See Heidegger, *Being and Time*, §§3–4, pp. 7–12.

11. Heidegger, "The Philosophical Foundations of Medieval Mysticism," 232.

12. Supra.

13. And hence a new work on medieval philosophy will be undertaken under the title *Expérience philosophique et expérience monastique, XIe–XIIe siècles.*